International Conference on Computer Graphics, Visualization, Computer Vision and Image Processing 2017 and International Conference on Big Data Analytics, Data Mining and Computational Intelligence 2017

Held at the Multi-Conference on Computer Science and Information Systems (MCCSIS 2017)

Lisbon, Portugal
20 – 23 July 2017

Editors:

Yingcai Xiao
Ajith P. Abraham
Piet Kommers
Pedro Isaias
Luis Rodrigues

ISBN: 978-1-5108-6528-0

Printed from e-media with permission by:

Curran Associates, Inc.
57 Morehouse Lane
Red Hook, NY 12571

Some format issues inherent in the e-media version may also appear in this print version.

Printed by Curran Associates, Inc. (2018)

For permission requests, please contact International Association for Development of the Information Society (IADIS) at the address below.

International Association for Development of the Information Society (IADIS)
Rua Sao Sebastiao Da Pedreira
No. 100, 30, 1050-209
Lisbon, Portugal

Phone: 351 21 3151373
Fax: 351 21 3151244

secretariat@iadis.org

Additional copies of this publication are available from:

Curran Associates, Inc.
57 Morehouse Lane
Red Hook, NY 12571 USA
Phone: 845-758-0400
Fax: 845-758-2633
Email: curran@proceedings.com
Web: www.proceedings.com

INTERNATIONAL CONFERENCES ON

COMPUTER GRAPHICS, VISUALIZATION, COMPUTER VISION AND IMAGE PROCESSING 2017

and

BIG DATA ANALYTICS, DATA MINING AND COMPUTATIONAL INTELLIGENCE 2017

part of the

MULTI CONFERENCE ON COMPUTER SCIENCE AND INFORMATION SYSTEMS 2017

PROCEEDINGS OF THE INTERNATIONAL CONFERENCES

COMPUTER GRAPHICS, VISUALIZATION, COMPUTER VISION AND IMAGE PROCESSING 2017

and

BIG DATA ANALYTICS, DATA MINING AND COMPUTATIONAL INTELLIGENCE 2017

Lisbon, Portugal
JULY 21 - 23, 2017

Organised by
IADIS
International Association for Development of the Information Society

Volume Editors:
Yingcai Xiao
Ajith P. Abraham

Computer Science and Information Systems Series Editors:
Piet Kommers and Pedro Isaías

Associate Editor: Luís Rodrigues

TABLE OF CONTENTS

SHORT PAPERS

COMPUTER GRAPHICS, VISUALIZATION, COMPUTER VISION AND IMAGE PROCESSING

BIG DATA ANALYTICS, DATA MINING AND COMPUTATIONAL INTELLIGENCE

FOREWORD

These proceedings contain the papers of the 11th International Conference on Computer Graphics, Visualization, Computer Vision and Image Processing 2017 and of the International Conference on Big Data Analytics, Data Mining and Computational Intelligence 2017, which were organised by the International Association for Development of the Information Society, from 21 - 23 July, 2017. These conferences are part of the Multi Conference on Computer Science and Information Systems 2017, 20 - 23 July, which had a total of 652 submissions.

The Computer Graphics, Visualization, Computer Vision and Image Processing (CGVCVIP) 2017 conference intends to address the research issues in the closely related areas of Computer Graphics, Visualization, Computer Vision and Image Processing. The conference encourages the interdisciplinary research and applications of these areas.

Submissions were accepted under the following 5 main topics:

- Computer Graphics
- Visualization
- Computer Vision
- Image Processing
- Other Related Topics

The aim of the Big Data Analytics, Data Mining and Computational Intelligence (BigDaCI) 2017 is to serve as a forum to present current and future work as well as to exchange research ideas in this field.

BigDaCI'17 invites authors to submit their original and unpublished work that demonstrate current research using big data analytics, computational intelligence and other intelligent computing techniques and their applications in science, technology, business and commerce.
Submissions were accepted under the following areas and topics:
- Big Data Algorithms and Architectures
- Computational Intelligent Frameworks for Big Data Processing
- Data Mining Topics and Applications
- Big Data Applications
- Multi-Agent Systems: Models, Architectures and Applications

These conferences received 213 submissions from more than 38 countries. The Theory and Practice in Modern Computing conference has been integrated into BigDaCI'17. Its committees are listed as part of this proceedings book. Each submission has been anonymously reviewed by an average of five independent reviewers, to ensure that accepted submissions were of a high standard. Consequently only 33 full papers were approved which means an acceptance rate of 16%. A few more papers were accepted as short papers, reflection papers and posters. An extended version of the best papers will be published in the IADIS International Journal on Computer Science and Information Systems (ISSN: 1646-3692) and also in other selected journals, including journals from Inderscience.

Besides the presentation of full papers, short papers, reflection papers and posters, the conferences also included two keynote presentations from internationally distinguished researchers. We would therefore like to express our gratitude to Professor Nir Shavit, MIT (Massachusetts Institute of Technology, USA) and Dr. Dr. Norbert Streitz (Scientific Director, Smart Future Initiative, Germany) for accepting our invitation to be keynote speakers.

This volume has taken shape as a result of the contributions from a number of individuals. We are grateful to all authors who have submitted their papers to enrich the conference proceedings. We wish to thank all members of the organizing committee, delegates, invitees and guests whose contribution and involvement are crucial for the success of the conference.

Last but not the least, we hope that everybody had a good time in Lisbon, and we invite all participants for the next edition of this conference.

Yingcai Xiao, The University of Akron, USA
Computer Graphics, Visualization, Computer Vision and Image Processing 2017 Program Chair

Ajith P. Abraham, Machine Intelligence Research Labs (MIR Labs), USA
Big Data Analytics, Data Mining and Computational Intelligence 2017 Program Chair

Piet Kommers, University of Twente, The Netherlands
Pedro Isaías, The University of Queensland, Australia
MCCSIS 2017 General Conference Co-Chairs

Lisbon, Portugal
July 2017

PROGRAM COMMITTEE

COMPUTER GRAPHICS, VISUALIZATION, COMPUTER VISION AND IMAGE PROCESSING

PROGRAM CHAIR

Yingcai Xiao, The University of Akron, USA

BIG DATA ANALYTICS, DATA MINING AND COMPUTATIONAL INTELLIGENCE

PROGRAM CHAIR

Ajith P. Abraham, Machine Intelligence Research Labs (MIR Labs), USA

MCCSIS GENERAL CONFERENCE CO-CHAIRS

Piet Kommers, University of Twente, The Netherlands
Pedro Isaías, The University of Queensland, Australia

COMPUTER GRAPHICS, VISUALIZATION, COMPUTER VISION AND IMAGE PROCESSING

COMMITTEE MEMBERS

Adrian Jarabo, Universidad de Zaragoza, Spain
Aiert Amundarain, CEIT, Spain
Alessandro Rizzi, Università Degli Studi di Milano, Italy
Anna Tomaszewska, Technical University of Szczecin, Poland
Arcadio Reyes Lecuona, Universidad de Málaga, Spain
Arturo S. Garcia, University of Salford, United Kingdom
Bruce Campbell, Rhode Island School of Design, USA
C. C. Lu, Kent State University, USA
Carlo Nati, Working Group for the Development of Tecnoscientific Knowledge, Italy
Celmar Guimarães da Silva, University of Campinas, Brazil
Chang Ha Lee, Chung-Ang University, South Korea
Charalambos Poullis, Concordia University, Canada
Charalampos Georgiadis, The Aristotle University, Greece
Chien-hsing Chou, Tamkang University, Taiwan
Christos Gatzidis, Bournemouth University, United Kingdom
Creto Vidal, Federal University of Ceará, Brazil
Daniel Steffen, University of Kaiserslautern, Germany
Dmitriy Vatolin, Moscow State University, Russia
Fatima Nunes, University of São Paulo, Brazil
Galina Pasko, Uformia, Norway
Gilles Gesquiere, Liris, France
Giuseppe Patanè, CNR-IMATI, Italy
Hans-Jörg Schulz, University of Rostock, Germany

BIG DATA ANALYTICS, DATA MINING AND COMPUTATIONAL INTELLIGENCE

COMMITTEE MEMBERS

THEORY AND PRACTICE IN MODERN COMPUTING

COMMITTEE MEMBERS

KEYNOTE LECTURES

RE-DEFINING THE "SMART EVERYTHING" PARADIGM TOWARDS RECONCILING HUMANS AND TECHNOLOGY

Dr. Dr. Norbert Streitz, Scientific Director, Smart Future Initiative, Germany

ABSTRACT

My keynote presentation will address multiple issues in the intersection of the following three conferences at MCCSIS 2017: 1) Connected Smart Cities 2) ICT, Society, and Human Beings 3) Interfaces and Human-Computer Interaction.

Starting out with the context of living in the Urban Age, I will discuss different notions of "smart cities", being propagated as the blueprint for our cities in the future, and complement them with the concept of "hybrid" cities, i.e., integrating the virtual, digital world with the real, physical world of our urban environments. One can currently observe a big hype about the opportunities of smart cities based on an Internet of Things (IoT) infrastructure monitoring states and dynamics of urban objects and their combination with data about citizens obtained in urban contexts for providing smart services.

With the increasing penetration of IoT and the proliferation of smart services, one can actually speak of a "smart everything" paradigm permeating very diverse spheres of our society and determining our personal and public life in many ways. Thus, it is necessary to investigate the implications for individuals as well as for society. Exploring the challenges, but also the venues towards a human-/citizen- centered design approach, I will take a critical look at smart services based on matching people's profiles and interests with service options available at specific locations. A major focus will be on the risks resulting from these smart city installations, especially the serious infringements of privacy rights, i.e., usage of personal data without consent of the people concerned.

Besides the issues of privacy, designing interfaces and human-computer interaction or more general human-technology, resp. citizen-urban environment interaction is of major importance. A prominent challenge is the property that "traditional" affordances are often hidden in these kinds of environments. (=> invisible or disappearing computer). How can people know how to interact, when they are not aware of the options? How can people protect their privacy, when they don't "see" the sensors, the hidden devices? Another aspect is the shift from information design to experience design.

A critical reflection of different manifestations of the "smart everything and everywhere" paradigm is needed in order to meet the overall goal of reconciling humans and technology. A central aspect of this goal is to keep the human in the loop and in control. Therefore, a citizen-centered design approach for future cities is needed for helping us to go "beyond smart cities" and transform them into Humane, Sociable and Cooperative Hybrid Cities.

HIGH THROUGHPUT CONNECTOMICS: THE BUILDING OF A BRAINSCOPE

Professor Nir Shavit, MIT (Massachusetts Institute of Technology, USA

ABSTRACT

Connectomics is an emerging area of neurobiology that uses cutting edge machine learning and image processing techniques to extract brain connectivity graphs from electron microscopy images. This talk will describe how a team of researchers from MIT and Harvard plan to extract the complete connectivity graph of a cubic millimeter of brain tissue. Though it is the size of a grain of salt, the dataset is 2 Petabytes in size, and will contain about a hundred thousand neuron bodies and a billion synapses.

It has long been assumed that the processing of such large connectomics datasets will require mass storage and farms of CPUs and GPUs and will take years. I will discuss the feasibility of designing a high-throughput connectomics-on-demand system that runs on a multicore machine with less than 100 cores and extracts connectomes at the terabyte per hour pace of modern electron microscopes.

Full Papers

AN INTUITIVE INTERFACE FOR HUMAN PERFORMANCE TRACKING WITH SIMULATED CHARACTERS

Gökçen Çimen[1], Martin Guay[2], Stelian Coros[3] and Robert W. Sumner[2]
[1]*ETH Zurich, Switzerland*
[2]*Disney Research, Switzerland*
[3]*Carnegie Mellon University, USA*

ABSTRACT

One of the main challenges with tracking a live actor with a simulated character is modeling or specifying the character's mechanical system, together with the control parameters required to compute the torques. This process is so intricate, that it is mainly done by researchers and engineers—leaving this technology out of reach for casual users and digital artists. In this paper, we introduce a user-friendly interface that allows casual users to quickly model the character's mechanical system, together with the control parameters for tracking a live actor. A side effect of tracking with a simulated character is that free limbs such as tails are automatically activated into the full body control, instead of remaining static or movin g in a predetermined fashion. We show various motion examples with two biped characters: a raptor dinosaur, as well as an alien.

KEYWORDS

Performance tracking, simulated character, intuitive animation interface

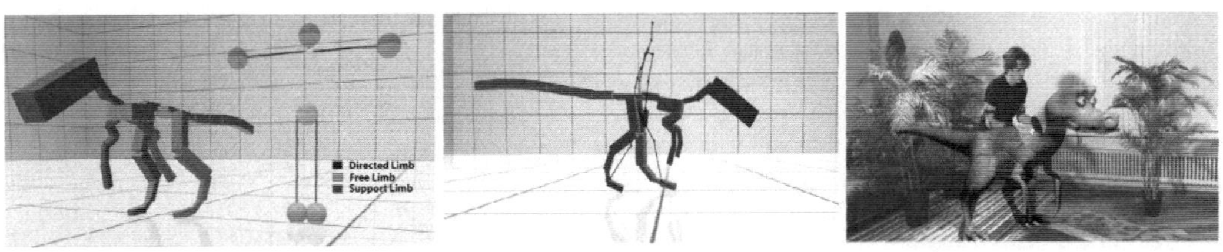

Figure 1. We present an interface (Abstract humanoid on the left) for tracking a human actor with a simulated character. Our interface simplifies to simply clicking and dragging, the process of creating an articulated rigid body system for a biped digital character, together with the control parameters used to compute torques for tracking the human actor in real-time. A side effect of our simulated character is that free limbs—such as tails—are automatically activated during tracking

1. INTRODUCTION

Motion capture is heavily used by the visual effects industry to allow a professional actor to craft the performance of a virtual creature. However, because the creature's shape and morphology often differs significantly from the actor's, a motion retargeting step is inevitable. A leading approach to retarget a human actor's motion onto a virtual character is to track shared features such as the feet and the hips using inverse kinematics. The problem with this approach is that it leaves free limbs, such as tails, static and without motion.

To address this issue, we embed the character into a physics-based simulation framework and track the actor's motion using optimal control. As a result, free limbs, such as a virtual creature's tail, are automatically animated to move in unique ways that are consistent with the character's overall performance.

While this simulation control concept is a promising approach to synthesize unique movements, its biggest drawback is its complex nature. Physics-based simulation unfortunately requires intricate knowledge of mechanics and control mechanisms, leaving it out of reach for most visual effects artists that lack scientific training.

This complexity comes from two main sources. First, the character must be provided with an articulated mechanical system including corresponding rigid body and joint properties. And second, a controller general enough to track various human motions in real-time must be set up and tuned so that its parameters are appropriate for the new character. In our work we use model-based inverse dynamics [Abe et al. (2007)].

In our research, we make physics-based retargeting more accessible with an intuitive user interface, designed around a general control framework, that allows both quickly designing the character's mechanical system as well as setting the controller parameters for optimal tracking. Our work relies on the core observation that, while *limbs* may be different, they often share a common function. For example, legs interact with the ground, and free limbs, such as tails, are used for balancing and controlling the character's overall orientation. Hence, we devised a bipedal limb-based abstraction where the user simply drags-and-drops from the abstract limbs to the simulated character's limbs to automatically fill the controller's parameters for tracking.

Our method comes with additional benefits. First of all, we can automatically clean-up contacts from the often noisy captured motion. This is possible thanks to the notion that certain limbs are used for support and interact with the ground. Secondly, our controller penalizes deviations from a natural pose, which can be used to control the style of the motion, simply by specifying a new default pose. And finally, the tracking can be performed in real-time. We show results of a raptor and alien tracking different motions.

2. RELATED WORK

In practice, tracking a human actor with a digital character is done as a feature-based optimization problem (inverse kinematics, or IK), where the distance between a set of features —such as the feet and hands positions—are minimized at each frame of the animation [Choi & Ko (1999)], [Shin et al. (2001)], [Tak & Ko (2005)]. Several works address foot contacts and foot skating issues in the context of tracking by altering the actor's captured trajectories [Kovar et al. (2002)], [Ikemoto et al. (2006)]. When the characters have different topologies (i.e. different joints hierarchies) and/or do not move in the same way, the tracked motion is likely to be unrealistic. For example, the legs of a dinosaur do not bend the same way as the legs of human, and the free limbs humans do not possess—such as a tail—remain static.

Controlling a simulated character to perform different motions is a problem that has been researched for several decades now. Yet it remains a challenge to go from a kinematic—strictly positional—signal, to a controlled motion using a simulated articulated character.

One of the motion skills that has been well studied is locomotion, and there are now robust controllers specifically designed for this. Typically, a set of locomotion *poses* are tracked with Proportional Derivative (PD) control of target joint angles, and a balancing strategy based on the inverted pendulum (IP) model is used to adjust the target poses online [Yin et al. (2007)], [Tsai et al. (2010)], [Lee et al. (2010)]. While these controllers are very robust, they can only track locomotion, and do not extend easily to other types of motions.

As a general approach to track human motion with a simulated character, Liu and colleagues developed a sampling-based approach that can successfully learn a feedback function to track contact-rich motion capture sequences [Liu et al. (2010)], [Liu et al. (2015)]. They learn a constant feedback function over the motion clip by using stochastic optimization along a black box rigid body simulator. Their framework has only been demonstrated with human character with well-studied proportions, masses and PD stiffnesses. In other words, this cannot be used directly to track human motion with non-humanoid characters such as a dinosaur.

Another line of works—so-called online optimization controllers—consider the control at a single time step and recompute the torques each time via inverse dynamics; assuming knowledge of the equations of motion [Abe et al. (2007)], [Da Silva et al. (2008)], [Macchietto et al. (2009)], [Mordatch et al. (2012)], [de Lasa et al. (2010)], [Rabbani et al. (2014)], [Levine & Popovic (2012)]. When the equations of motion of an articulated rigid body system are expressed in generalized coordinates, a linear relation between joint torques and joint accelerations can be established for a single time step. As a consequence, it becomes possible to minimize a collection of quadratic objectives under the hard linear constraint that the equations of motion hold.

Abe et al. (2007) focused on motions that remained in balance (static contacts) and subsequent works focused on planning and engineering features for various motion skills [Da Silva et al. (2008)], [Macchietto et al. (2009)], [Mordatch et al. (2012)], [de Lasa et al. (2010)], [Rabbani et al. (2014)], or relaxing physical realism for robustness [Levine & Popovic (2012)]. While this type of controller has been well studied, it requires a scientist or engineer for each new character or motion. In contrast, our automates the process for bipedal characters and allows casual users to set up the character's rigid body system together with the parameters of the controller, simply by clicking on our abstract limb-based interface.

Closest to our are methods that combine dynamics to alter a kinematic motion model as to better cope with interactions in a simulated environment [Ishigaki et al. (2009)], [Nguyen et al. (2010)]. These methods rely on simplified models of dynamics (not the full body) and the dynamics are used to alter a motion model that relies on pre-exiting motion clips; in both cases human captured motion. In contrast, our method is based on adapting motion capture data to virtual characters which have different body structures than human. The only prior information required is the user's character design choice.

To our knowledge, only a few prior works placed the control of simulated characters into the hands of casual users. Coros et al. (2010) allowed the user to change the body proportions of the character, resulting in different motions. Unfortunately, their method is specific to human locomotion. Closer to our effort is the work of Levine et al. (2012), which also uses multi-objective control to track animations. They use the bone lengths to initialize the rigid bodies, but relax the physical accuracy by allowing root activation. With their method, the character can only track the same character, and there is no retargeting or free limbs activation. In contrast, we allow the user to track human actors with different characters as well as different body parts associations.

3. OVERVIEW

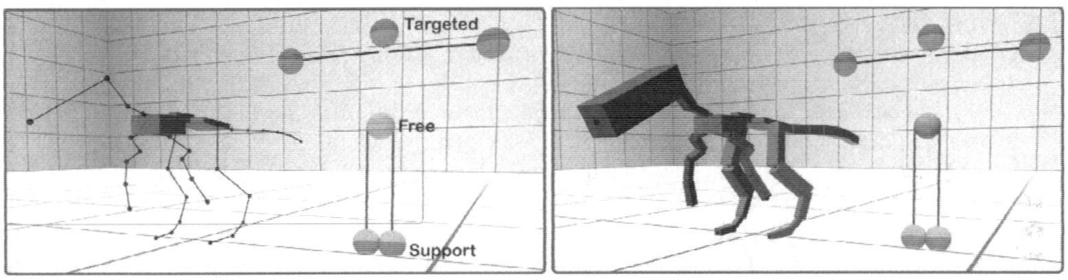

Figure 2. The user interface we use to create an articulated rigid body system and to quickly set control objectives based on a limb abstraction of the bipedal character. The user simply drags and drops a limb type from the abstract humanoid onto the limbs of the character to get it ready for simulated tracking

Our goal is to have a bipedal creature follow the motion of a human actor in real-time. While characters and the actor may be different morphologically, we observe that they often share a set of common features. In particular, most characters share a global position, global orientation, as well as a set of limbs whose end effector (EE) trajectories match, but at a different scale (see Figure 3).

While tracking only the re-targeted positions conveys the essence of the actor's motion, it leaves the free limbs of the character, such as the tail, without motion. To active the free limbs and provide the character with additional realism, we model the full body dynamics and regulate angular momentum with an additional control objective.

In order to mix different objectives while satisfying the equations of motion, we formulate our tracking as model-based multi-objective control [Abe et al. (2007)]:

$$\begin{aligned} \min_{\ddot{q},\tau,f} \quad & \sum w_i \; E_i \\ \text{s.t.} \quad & M(q)\ddot{q} - C(q,\dot{q}) = J_x^T f + [0 \; \tau]^T, \end{aligned} \tag{1}$$

which exploits the linear relation between joint accelerations $\ddot{q}$ and torques τ when the equations of motion are expressed in generalized coordinates, where the vector q is the root position, the root orientation and the set of joint relative orientations. The matrix $M(q)$ is the generalized mass matrix, $C(q,\dot{q})$ is the vector that combines gravitational forces, coriolis and centrifugal terms. The jacobian transpose J_x^T measures the change in position w.r.t. the generalized degrees of freedom and maps the cartesian ground reaction forces f into generalized forces, with the construction $[0\ \tau]^T$ avoiding root activation. Setting the weights w_i of the objectives is a cumbersome and time consuming task. To avoid setting all the weights manually, we introduce a limb abstraction—summarized in Table 1—that automatically sets the weights for each objective. Here we define a limb as a connected linear chain of bones attached to the body frame which is comprised of the pelvis and upper body (shown in grey in Figure 2).

Table 1. Our limb abstraction is comprised of three types. Support limbs, which drive the body to a desired location through ground reaction forces, and alternate between swing and stance states. Free limbs, which do not track a human body part, but help balance and control the character by regulating angular momentum. And finally, Targeted limbs which track a part of the human body such as the hands or head

Type	Role
Support	Carry the body through ground reaction forces and ensure contact constraints
Free	Does not track a human part, such as a tail, but participate in angular momentum control.
Targeted	Tracks a human part, but without contacts (e.g. head or hands).

The first step to realize our simulated tracker concept is to model the character's articulated rigid body system and to specify the type of limb, as well as target location on the human actor's skeleton. Hence, in the next section we describe our intuitive user interface to get the character simulation- and tracking-ready.

4. SIMULATED TRACKING INTERFACE

The input to our modeler is a bipedal character skeleton, and we provide the necessary widgets to track a human skeleton through our limb-based optimal control. We begin by modelling the character's mechanical system, i.e. the linked rigid bodies that approximate the mechanical properties of the character. The second step consists in attributing each of the character's limbs a type from one of our limbs (support, targeted or free). The user creates rigid bodies by clicking on the bones of the skeleton. We first initialize the rigid body shape with the orientation and size of the skeleton bone, and set the mass and friction to default values. In most cases, the user can use a facilitating function that fills a linear chain of bones with a linear chain of connected rigid bodies, starting from the root, as shown in our accompanying video.

Our limb-based abstraction implicitly encodes which human body part to track. Hence when setting the type of limb by drag-and-dropping a limb type from the limb-based abstraction (shown in Figure 2), the controller is automatically set ready for tracking the human actor. The ordering of the process does not matter, the user can set the type of limb during or after having modeled the articulated rigid body system.

5. ONLINE FEATURE RETARGETING

Generally, the features we track are human positions $x_r(t)$ and orientations $\theta_r(t)$, where r denotes reference motion. In particular, we track each of the human's end effector positions, together with the root position and orientation.

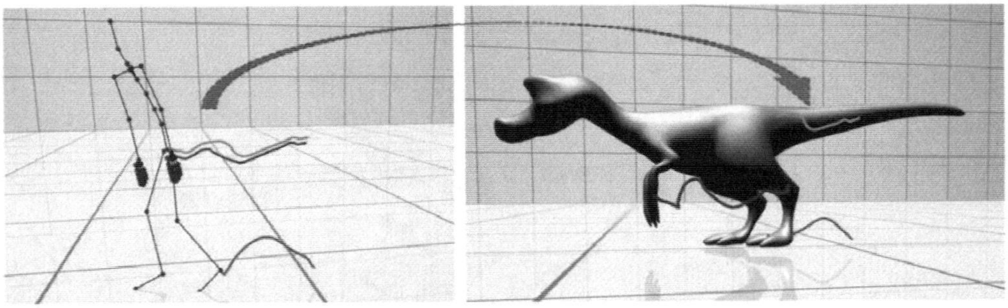

Figure 3. Some of the features in both the character and the human actor's match but at a different scale (e.g. the hand, feet and head, and pelvis positions). We retarget these trajectories to the position and scale of the simulated character for tracking

While the orientations can be tracked directly (i.e. $\theta_{des} = \theta_r$ where θ_{des} is the desired orientation), the positions need to be translated and scaled as to be reachable by a character with differently sized limbs. Secondly, because the captured motion can have noisy contact trajectories, we perform online cleaning-up of the end effectors at the extremity of support limbs.

Retargeting Human Position Trajectories. To ensure feasibility of tracked end effector positions, we first compute the differential coordinates of the actor's positions $\Delta x_r(t) = x_r(t + \Delta t) - x_r(t)$, and scale it down based on the proportions $\alpha = l_c \backslash l_r$, where l_* is the distance between a limb's end effector and root position for the rest pose, with c denoting character. This results in:

$$x_{des}(t) = \alpha\ \Delta x_r(t) + x(t), \tag{2}$$

where $x(t)$ is the end effector's position. This rescaling is illustrated in Figure 4.

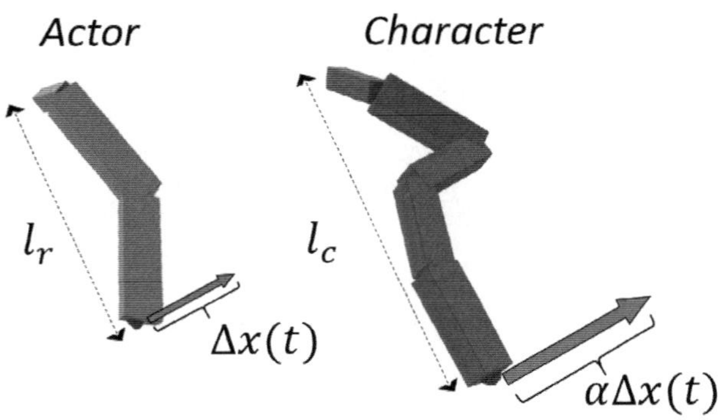

Figure 4. When retargeting the end effector positions to the character, we scale the relative displacements proportionally to each limb length, that we define as the distance between the end effector and the root of the limb

Online Contacts Clean-up. We process the end effectors (EEs) at the extremity of support limbs, as to clean the contacts in real-time. This is particularly challenging when the capture is being streamed in real-time, and we do not have the full trajectory to determine whether a position is supposed to be in contact and remain fixed, or it should be moving.

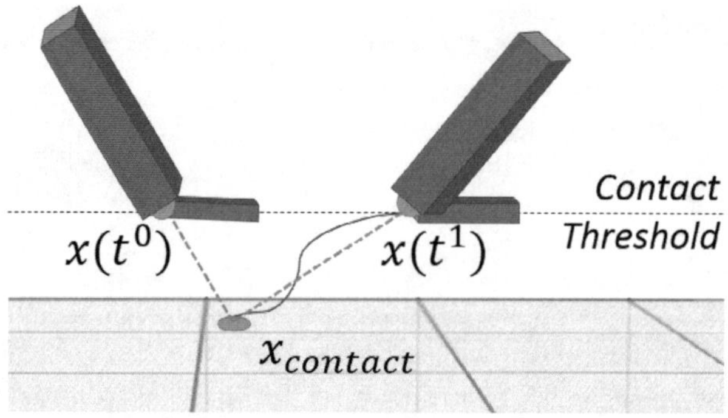

Figure 5. To clean contacts in real-time, we perform smooth-in and smooth-out transitions between the fixed (below the contact threshold) and the moving (above the contact threshold) end effector positions

Our solution to this problem is to keep the actor's end effector fixed when close to the ground (below a contact threshold), and to perform a smooth-in and a smooth-out to transition between the fixed contact position, and the moving position beyond the contact threshold. When the EE position gets below a threshold at time t^0, we project the position onto the ground using its velocity, and define this position as the contact position $x_{contact}$. We then perform a smooth transition between the EE position at the threshold position $x(t^0)$ and the contact position $x_{contact}$ using linear interpolation over a small time window. When the actor's EE position leaves beyond the contact threshold at time t^1, we perform a smooth out transition between the contact position $x_{contact}$ and $x(t^1)$ (see Figure 5).

6. CONTROL OBJECTIVES

We describe our objectives that include both tracking re-targeted positions to be reached by the character, as well as objectives for regulating angular momentum, and controlling style. Each type of limbs contributes to the overall sum of weighted objectives, and we describe at the end of the section how we automatically prioritize the weights based on the type of limb.

Our limb-based controller tracks the global root position, root orientation, the collection of end-effectors at the extremity of the limbs, as well as influences the tracking with additional full body angular momentum and pose regularization. We assemble this sum of weighted objectives (detailed below), and solve problem (1) for the optimal torques.

Target Position and Orientation. These objectives are used to track the retargeted positions x_{des} and orientations θ_{des}, by the character. We compute the desired acceleration for the concerned rigid body based on proportional-derivative (PD) control:

$$\begin{aligned} \ddot{x}_{des} &= k_p(x_{des} - x) + k_d(\dot{x}_r - J_x\dot{q}), \\ \ddot{\theta}_{des} &= k_p(\theta_{des} - \theta) + k_d(\dot{\theta}_r - J_\theta\dot{q}), \end{aligned} \tag{3}$$

where x and θ are the rigid position and orientation, k_p the proportional stiffness and k_d, the derivative value, which both remain constant for all motions. Here J_θ denotes the change in orientation for the rigid body, w.r.t. the all the joint orientations. From these desired accelerations, we measure the error to the character's current accelerations:

$$E_p = \| \ddot{x}_{des} - (J_x\ddot{q} + \dot{J}_x\dot{q}) \|^2, \tag{4}$$
$$E_o = \| \ddot{\theta}_{des} - (J_\theta\ddot{q} + \dot{J}_\theta\dot{q}) \|^2. \tag{5}$$

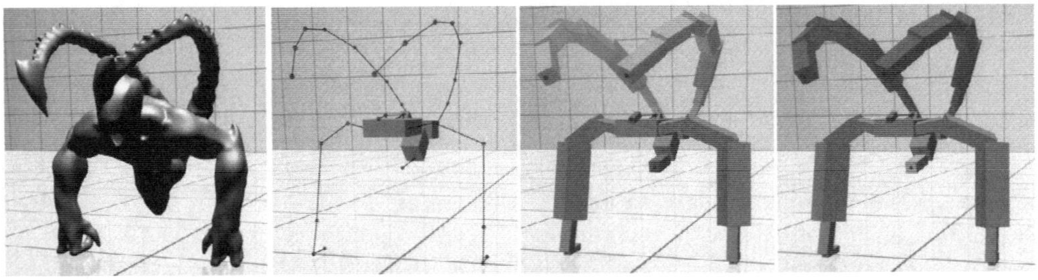

Figure 6. In this figure we see the result of setting two different types of limbs for the alien character. The limb association on the left sets the tails to free limbs, while the association on the right sets the tails to the targeted limbs, which allows the stingers at the tip to perform attacking motions

Angular Momentum (AM). The total angular momentum about a point (often the character's center-of-mass) gives a measure of the system's internal rotations. For example, when the actor's upper body bends forward, the total angular momentum changes, and we can minimize this change in AM w.r.t. to all the links (including the tail) to activate the tail's motion.

Hence we minimize the change in total angular momentum w.r.t. to the center of mass:

$$E_{AM} = |\dot{L}_{AM}|^2, \tag{6}$$

where

$$\begin{aligned} \dot{L}_{AM} &= R(q)\, M(q)\, (J_x^T \ddot{q} + \dot{q}_x^T \dot{q}), \\ R(q) &= [\,[\, r_1(q)\,]_x \dots [\, r_m(q)\,]_x\,], \end{aligned}$$

where $r_i(q)$ are the position vectors of the ith body links relative to the center-of-mass, $[\, r_i(q)\,]_x$ are the skew symmetric coefficients from the cross product, $J_x^T = [J_{x_1}^T \dots J_{x_m}^T]$ is the jacobian transpose mapping generalized coordinates to cartesian positions, and $M(q)$ is the mass matrix of the entire articulated rigid body system.

Pose Regularization. To control the style of the animation, as well as to prevent the character from entering unrealistic configurations, we penalize deviations from a rest pose. This regularization objective is the sum of errors between joint angle accelerations computed through PD control (similarly to equation (5)) with the desired pose defined as the rest pose in equation (3) resulting: E_j^{reg} for each joint j.

Total Sum of Objectives. Using equation (4) and (5), we define a root position and orientation objective E^{root}, as well as the set of end effector objectives $E_i^{EE}, i = 1,\dots,m$ with m limbs. With the angular momentum regulation and the pose regularization, the total sum of objectives we minimize is:

$$w^{root} E^{root} + \sum_i w_i^{EE} E_i^{EE} + w^{AM} E^{AM} + \sum_i w_j^{reg} E_j^{reg}, \tag{7}$$

which we set as the objectives in problem (1). But before solving the problem, we first need to set the weights of each objective.

Limb-based Prioritization. Solving the torques that minimize this sum of weighted objectives (7) is challenging in practice as the objectives may be conflicting and need to be prioritized. We observed that certain limbs play a more important role when it comes to performance tracking. For example, the support limbs need to provide clean contact positions and should be weighted higher. Hence, to accommodate the user in setting the weights, we use our limb-based abstraction to automatically set values.

To express the relative priorities of the objectives, we first define a maximum weight value w_{max}, and define each weight based on this maximum value, and on the type of limb. Hence, the global orientation and position being visually important are weighted with the maximum value $w_{root} = w_{max}$, the angular momentum playing a lesser role $w_{AM} = 0.5w_{max}$, and the objectives that depend on the type of limb (the end effectors, as well as the pose regularization) are summarized below:

Limb	w_i^{EE}	w_j^{reg}
Support	w_{max}	0.01 w_{max}
Targeted	0.5 w_{max}	0.02 w_{max}
Free	-	0.03 w_{max}

where $w_{max} = 4000$, and depends on the mass of the system.

7. RESULTS

Character setup. We created two characters using our interface described in Section 4. The first is a raptor dinosaur and the second an alien that walks on his hands and has two tails. In both cases, an artist created a mesh and a skeletal rig in Maya ([Autodesk (n.d.)]) without constraints regarding its skeleton. Our interface for the character set up allows quickly creating rigid bodies based off the skeleton, as well as setting different types of limbs for the tracking (see Figure 6 for different types of limb associations). All of the character set ups including the full articulated rigid body systems were created by the authors of this paper under three minutes each.

Capturing human motion. We captured all the actor's motions using an Axis Neuron ([Noitom (n.d.)) full body motion capturing system. The system as 13 captors and samples the motion at 120 frames per second. The character's motion is not always accurate and may include body interpenetrations, shakiness in the feet or hands, as well as unstable foot contacts.

Solver. We solve problem (1) at each time step $\Delta t = 0.01$, with linearly-constrained quadratic programming. We then integrate the generalized accelerations using the generalized equations of motion. Note that we do not send the torques to a cartesian rigid body simulator, but always perform the simulation in generalized coordinates. Our single threaded implementation runs in real-time on a 4.00 GHz Intel Core i7 machine. We used the same objectives and weights provided by our limb-based abstraction, to track human locomotion (forward and backward), as well as various expressions gestured with hands and upper body such as roaring, being scary and biting (shown in our accompanying video).

Using our limb-based controller across different characters. It is often the case that for each new character, the control objective weights must be adjusted to this new character's proportions. We tested using a similar limb attribution on both the raptor—which has a long and heavy tail with a long upper body—and an alien character—which has two long tails and no legs, but stands on his hands. We found our limb-based control framework to be quite robust in that regard, adapting quite well to changes in character morphology and producing motions that are characteristic to the character's intrinsic shape (shown in our accompanying video).

Controlling style through different rest poses. We experimented with our pose regularization to provide the motion with a different feel. For example, we changed the raptor's pose to have its head slightly tilting forward, which resulted in a sadder look for the motion (shown in our accompanying video).

8. LIMITATIONS AND FUTURE WORK

One of the main intricacies associated with multi-objective inverse dynamics [Abe et al. (2007)] are the conflicts between objectives and constraints, which may become unfeasible—causing the simulator to diverge and blow up. One of our remedies was to relax the hard position constraints and replace them with objectives (with a large weight value provided by the support-type of limb).

To alter the character's motion style, we simply changed a single pose regularization, to avoid becoming depending on large collections of data. However, the single pose regularization could easily be replaced with a data-driven pose function learned from a collection of example poses (using for example [Grochow et al. (2004)]. While our limb-based abstraction supports walking on hands and having multiple tails, it is designed specifically for bipedal characters. In the future, we could imagine extending our abstraction to the case of quadrupeds by introducing a coordinated stance-limb planner which transfers end-effector trajectories to the appropriate support limbs.

9. CONCLUSION

Setting the control parameters for a new simulated character is traditionally complex and requires engineering skills. In this paper, we introduced an intuitive interface for casual users to track human actors with a simulated character in real-time. Our limb-based abstraction simplifies the initial set up to clicking and dragging on a few nodes. A side effect of controlling the simulated character is the activation of free limbs such as the tails. While we greatly simplified the process of tracking human actors with bipedal characters, we left out tracking with quadrupeds and multi-legged creatures, which could address in the future by coordinating the stance limbs of the character.

REFERENCES

Abe, Y. et al, 2007. Multiobjective control with frictional contacts. *In 'Proceedings of the 2007 ACM SIGGRAPH/Eurographics Symposium on Computer Animation, SCA '07, Eurographics Association.* Aire-la-Ville, Switzerland, pp. 249–258.

Autodesk (n.d.), Maya. *Computer Animation and Modeling Software.*

Choi, K.-J. & Ko, H.-S, 1999. On-line motion retargeting. *In Proceedings of the 7th Pacific Conference on Computer Graphics and Applications, PG '99, IEEE Computer Society.*

Coros, S. et al, 2010. Generalized biped walking control. *ACM Trans. Graph.* Vol. 29, No. 4, pp. 130:1–130:9.

Da Silva, M. et al, 2008. Simulation of human motion data using short-horizon model-predictive control. *Computer Graphics Forum.* Vol. 27, No. 2, pp. 371–380.

de Lasa, M. et al, 2010. Feature-based locomotion controllers. *ACM Trans. Graph.* Vol. 29, No. 4, pp. 131:1–131:10.

Grochow, K. et al, 2004. Style-based inverse kinematics, *ACM Trans. Graph.* Vol. 23, No. 3, pp. 522–531.

Ikemoto, L. et al, 2006. Knowing when to put your foot down. *In Proceedings of the 2006 Symposium on Interactive 3D Graphics and Games, I3D '06, ACM*, pp. 49–53.

Ishigaki, S. et al, 2009. Performance-based control interface for character animation. *In ACM SIGGRAPH 2009 Papers, SIGGRAPH '09, ACM.* New York, NY, USA, pp. 61:1–61:8.

Kovar, L., Schreiner, J. & Gleicher, M, 2002. Footskate cleanup for motion capture editing. *In Proceedings of the 2002 ACM SIGGRAPH/Eurographics Symposium on Computer Animation, SCA '02, ACM.* pp. 97–104.

Lee, Y., et al, 2010, Data-driven biped control, *ACM Trans. Graph.* Vol. 29, No. 4, pp. 129:1–129:8.

Levine, S. & Popovic, J, 2012. Physically plausible simulation for character animation. *In* Proceedings of the ACM SIGGRAPH/Eurographics Symposium on Computer Animation, SCA '12. pp. 221–230.

Liu, L. et al, 2015. Improving sampling-based motion control. *Comput. Graph. Forum.* Vol. 34, No. 2, pp. 415–423.

Liu, L. et al, 2010. Sampling-based contact-rich motion control. *ACM Trans. Graph.* Vol. 29, No. 4, pp. 128:1–128:10.

Macchietto, A. et al, 2009. Momentum control for balance. *ACM Trans. Graph.* Vol. 28, No. 3, pp. 80:1–80:8.

Mordatch, I. et al, 2012. Discovery of complex behaviors through contact-invariant optimization. *ACM Trans. Graph.* Vol. 31, No. 4, pp. 43:1–43:8.

Nguyen, N. et al, 2010. Performance capture with physical interaction. *In Proceedings of the 2010 ACM SIGGRAPH/Eurographics Symposium on Computer Animation, SCA '10, Eurographics Association.* Aire-la-Ville, Switzerland, Switzerland, pp. 189–195.

Noitom (n.d.), Perception Neuron. *https://neuronmocap.com/content/axis-neuron-software*

Rabbani, A. H. et al, 2014. Anticipatory balance control. *In Proceedings of the Seventh International Conference on Motion in Games', MIG '14.* pp. 71–76.

Shin, H. J. et al, 2001. Computer puppetry: An importance-based approach. *ACM Trans. Graph.* Vol. 20, No. 2, pp. 67–94.

Tak, S. & Ko, H.-S, 2005. A physically-based motion retargeting filter. *ACM Trans. Graph.* Vol. 24, No. 1, pp. 98–117.

Tsai, Y. Y. et al, 2010, Real-time physics-based 3d biped character animation using an inverted pendulum model. *IEEE Transactions on Visualization and Computer Graphics.* Vol. 16, No. 2, pp. 325–337.

Yin, K., et al, 2007, Simbicon: Simple biped locomotion control. *ACM Trans. Graph.* Vol. 26, No. 3.

DOWNSAMPLING METHODS FOR MEDICAL DATASETS

Jesús Díaz-García, Pere Brunet, Isabel Navazo and Pere-Pau Vázquez
ViRVIG Group - Universitat Politècnica de Catalunya, C/ Jordi Girona, 1-3, Barcelona, Spain

ABSTRACT

Volume visualization software usually has to deal with datasets that are larger than the GPUs may hold. This is especially true in one of the most popular application scenarios: medical visualization. Typically, medical datasets are available for different personnel, but only radiologists have high-end systems that are able to cope with large data. For the rest of physicians, usually low-end systems are only available. As a result, most volume rendering packages downsample the data prior to uploading to the GPU. The most common approach consists in performing iterative subsampling along the longest axis, until the model fits inside the GPU memory. This causes important information loss that affects the final rendering. Some cleverer techniques may be developed to preserve the volumetric information. In this paper we explore the quality of different downsampling methods and present a new approach that produces smooth lower-resolution representations, yet still preserves small features that are prone to disappear with other approaches.

KEYWORDS

Medical visualization, volume rendering, downsampling, Gaussian filtering

1. INTRODUCTION

Medical datasets are continuously increasing in size. Although larger models may be available for certain research purposes, in the common clinical practice the models are usually of up to $512 \times 512 \times 2000$ voxels. These resolutions exceed the capabilities of conventional GPUs, the ones usually found in the medical doctors' desktop PCs. As a result, commercial solutions typically reduce the data by downsampling the dataset iteratively until it fits the available target specifications. The data loss reduces the visualization quality and this is not commonly compensated with other actions that might alleviate its effects.

Medical datasets are commonly stored as scalar fields, where each scalar represents the properties from the human anatomy (such as density values in Computational Tomography, CT). Downsampling scalar data implies an inevitable loss of information that provokes the loss of fine details and the modification of the original topology. Furthermore, since these scalar values are then used by means of Transfer Functions (TF, functions that map density values to opacity and color), downsampling a set of density values (e.g. by averaging) leads to inconsistencies when the transfer function is applied on coarser representations.

The downsampling process appears in many rendering techniques, such as the approaches that render large datasets by building a multiresolution structure (Boada et al., 2001). In these cases, intermediate nodes are also generated by subsampling the high resolution dataset. Again, using a simple downsampling scheme will produce important artifacts, such as the disappearance of small features. Some attempts have been developed to preserve the data, but they are commonly quite costly in terms of processing or data storage (Younesy et al., 2006, Sicat et al., 2014), or not suitable for medical datasets, such as when downsampling color data (Kraus and Brüger, 2008).

In this paper we analyze several downsampling methods and present a new approach that preserves small features for medical models, while keeping a low computation cost. Our contributions are twofold:

- An analysis of the effect of the most popular downsampling methods for medical datasets.
- A new low-cost downsampling filter tailored to preserve small features that can be combined with other methods such as multiresolution or bricking approaches.

The rest of the paper is organized as follows: Section 2 presents the previous work, Section 3 provides visual comparisons of previous techniques, and analyzes the factors that influence the quality of the final downsampled model. Section 4 presents our feature-preserving technique and discuss its advantages and shortcomings. Finally, Section 5 concludes this work by discussing the results and presenting some lines of future research.

2. PREVIOUS WORK

Medical imaging is challenged by the continuous increase in size of the datasets produced by capture devices (such as CT scanners). Even though GPUs also evolve, their horsepower lies behind the size of the data. This is especially true for physicians that receive the data from radiologists, since their workplaces are also commonly shared with other physicians, and, not being their main task the visualization of such data, they are not usually equipped with powerful GPUs. Thus, the data must be reduced in order to make it fit into their commodity GPUs and enable interactive inspection. Note that, this problem appears frequently in the clinical practice, since the datasets being captured continuously increase in size, and the GPUs cannot keep track with the growing size of the datasets.

As a result, a common approach is to compress the data and render from it. Since we want a solution that is applicable to modest PCs, this is often not a possibility since it implies large computation costs, and modern GPUs to perform the rendering. The interested reader can refer to the recent State of the Art by Balsa et al. (Balsa et al, 2014) for an introduction on compression for volume models.

Wang et al. (Wang et al., 2011) concentrate on the preservation of features in data reduction. This is done by assigning importance to the voxels according to the current transfer function. However, this requires an analysis of the dataset, and it is transfer function (TF) dependent. Therefore, if the TF changes, this computed data becomes invalid and has to be recomputed.

Younesy et al. (Younesy et al., 2006) improve the quality of the renderings in a multiresolution scheme by storing extra information for each node. Their initial analysis states that the ideal condition would be to store local histograms per coarse voxel, but in their implementation, these are substituted by an average density and its standard deviation. This multiplies the size of the dataset by three or four (depending on the precision of both values), and thus is impractical again for our case.

Sicat et al. (Sicat et al., 2014) present a technique for the storage of large datasets in a compressed way. They improve the consistent visualization of multiresolution volume datasets in comparison with the method of Younesy et al. by means of sparse *pdf volumes*. Again, this method does not suit our needs because it requires a higher amount of precomputation to generate their sparse structure, and uses important GPU resources for the decompression and rendering.

Díaz-García et al., (Díaz-García et al., 2016) perform a good work at *improving* the compressed dataset by applying what they call *adaptive transfer functions*, an algorithm that consists in using a small auxiliary structure that allows computing fitted TFs for the inner nodes in a multiresolution dataset. Their method succeeds at improving the final quality, but it is somewhat orthogonal to the analysis performed here. In any case, their approach can be combined with the filtering we present here, that can be used on the computation of the initial internal nodes dataset.

Kraus and Bürger (Kraus and Bürger, 2008) improve the reduction of the models, but using RGBA data. Since the medical models store the information as density values, and render them through the Transfer Functions, using colors has several shortcomings. First, using direct colors would multiply the model sizes by 4. Second, as already said, the interpolation in color space may produce larger artifacts than in density space, and therefore this plain interpolation is not suitable for medical models.

Kraus and Ertl. (Kraus and Ertl, 2001) also presented a method (named *topology-guided downsampling*) for downsampling volumetric datasets that tries to preserve the topology of the models. However, when applied to medical datasets, the results are limited, since, although the small features are preserved, the appearance of the subsampled models presents strong staircase artifacts and distort the position of the features (as shown later in this paper).

There is another family of methods tailored to improve the quality of the volumetric datasets by reducing noise. These are more suitable for datasets with high amount of noise and low resolution, such as the ones from ultrasound imaging. In general, such techniques are more focused on noise reduction, but sometimes they also combine the noise reduction with downsampling. Kwon et al. (Kwon et al., 2016), for instance, filter and denoise ultrasound images using a fast bilateral filter. As we will see in the next section, bilateral filter usually produces undesirable results for downsampling medical datasets such as the ones obtained from CTs. Another technique, more focused on noise reduction, is the method by Wang et al. (Wang et al., 2012). In our analysis, using noise reduction previous to subsampling does not improve the quality of the downsampled volumes.

There is also related bibliography about feature preserving downsampling methods for 2D images. Although these methods have not been designed specifically for volumetric datasets, their idea could be easily adapted to such case. For instance, Kopf et al. (Kopf et al. 2013) implement a content-adaptive downscaling method that uses a bilateral combination of two Gaussian kernels defined over space and color, calculated by means of an iterative process that can take long to finish. Öztireli and Gross (Öztireli and Gross 2015), on the other hand, formulate image downscaling as an optimization problem that maximizes a perceptual image quality metric based on the difference between the input and the output images. Also, more recently, Weber et al. (Weber et al. 2016) present an algorithm based on convolutional filters where input pixels contribute more to the output image the more their color deviates from their local neighborhood. They use a guidance image based on a preliminary downscaled image to be able to define pixel contributions, and a parameter λ that has to be manually adjusted, depending on the image, to provide the best results.

Besides these improved approaches, other typical filtering methods, such as averaging or Gaussian filtering will also be analyzed in the following section together with some of the aforementioned algorithms.

3. DOWNSAMPLING METHODS FOR MEDICAL DATASETS

We have analyzed several downsampling methods with volumetric datasets that range from the typical pure subsampling (e.g. taking one of the samples of the original dataset) to more elaborate approaches such as the topology-guided downsampling by Kraus and Ertl (Kraus and Ertl, 2001). The most important problem with most of the techniques is the lack of preservation of fine details. The analyzed techniques are:

- Subsampling
- Averaging
- Gaussian filtering
- Bilateral filtering
- Topology-guided downsampling (Kraus and Ertl, 2001)

For completeness, we have also experimented with other possibilities such as combining any of the previous downsampling methods with an extra previous noise reduction stage. Unfortunately, no significant gains are obtained. So, for the sake of clarity, we only comment the tested methods that exhibit noteworthy behavior and analyze the reasons behind their results. The results shown in the Figures of this paper have been obtained by ray-casting the volume models with appropriate transfer functions (TF). The density of samples along rays has been set to 1 sample per voxel of the original model, more than enough for the downsampled models. It should be observed that we are not performing an intrinsic analysis of these downsampling techniques, but an analysis of the resulting visual quality when they are used in the context of TF's and ray-casting volume rendering.

Subsampling refers to the method that, when downsampling a volume, for each subvolume of 8 voxels (2x2x2), chooses as the representative for the downsampled subvolume just one of the original values. In our case, we select one of the corners, although we did experiments with other samples with equivalent results.

The **averaging** filter simply consists in creating a new value by averaging all the values from the original volume. In our case, for one-level downsampling, this would consist in averaging the 8 values (2x2x2 subvolumes) of the upper level.

Besides those two simple methods, more elaborated techniques include Gaussian filtering and bilateral filtering. Both techniques have been extensively used in image processing algorithms. The core feature of Gaussian filtering is the noise reduction, at the cost of blurring edges. On the contrary, the bilateral filter is intended to preserve edges. In the following, we introduce both filters using the notation by Paris et al. (2007).

Gaussian filtering is a typical operation in image processing that consists in applying a low-pass filter over the image samples. Given an image I, the filtered version is computed as a weighted average of the neighboring pixels. So pixel p will have a value that depends on the pixels around a neighborhood q of the original pixel. Typically, this is denoted as:

$$GB[I]_{\mathbf{p}} = \sum_{\mathbf{q}\in\mathcal{S}} G_{\sigma}(\|\mathbf{p}-\mathbf{q}\|)\, I_{\mathbf{q}},$$

where S is the kernel support and G is a two-dimensional filter kernel expressed as:

$$G_\sigma(x) = \frac{1}{2\pi\,\sigma^2}\,\exp\left(-\frac{x^2}{2\,\sigma^2}\right)$$

In our case, to downsample volumetric models, we apply this transformation in 3D, so the neighborhood, instead of consisting of a rectangular region, corresponds to a cube.

The **bilateral filter,** similarly to the Gaussian filter, is a weighted average of a neighborhood of pixels. The main difference is that the bilateral filter, besides using a spatial Gaussian kernel, takes into account the variation in the values of the pixels to preserve the edges. The rationale behind this is that two pixels should be weighted similarly, not only if their positions are similar, but also if their intensities are comparable too. This results in a formulation such as:

$$BF[I]_{\mathbf{p}} = \frac{1}{W_{\mathbf{p}}}\sum_{\mathbf{q}\in\mathcal{S}} G_{\sigma_s}(\|\mathbf{p}-\mathbf{q}\|)\,G_{\sigma_r}(I_{\mathbf{p}}-I_{\mathbf{q}})\,I_{\mathbf{q}}$$

where W is a normalization kernel defined as:

$$W_{\mathbf{p}} = \sum_{\mathbf{q}\in\mathcal{S}} G_{\sigma_s}(\|\mathbf{p}-\mathbf{q}\|)\,G_{\sigma_r}(I_{\mathbf{p}}-I_{\mathbf{q}})$$

The bilateral filter appeared in several independent publications (Aurich and Weule, 1995, Smith and Brady, 1997, Tomasi and Manduchi, 1998), and has since then further improved, especially for speed (Paris and Durand, 2009).

Topology-guided downsampling is a method by Kraus and Ertl (Kraus and Ertl, 2001) that better preserves the topology of the scalar field by preferably selecting the values of critical points. To do this, every voxel in the original dataset is classified as a regular, a saddle, or an extremum point. Then, during dowsampling, the most representative sample in the neighborhood of each voxel is taken.

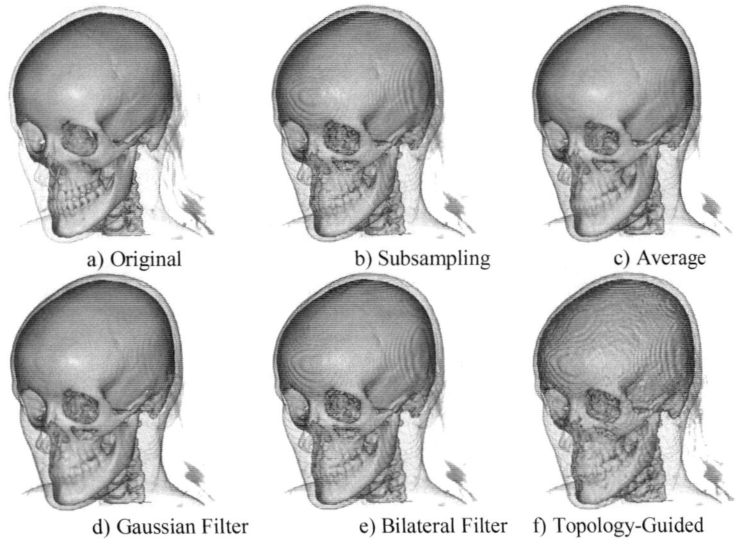

Figure 1. Effect of downsampling on the head model (5123) dataset to 1283. The algorithms applied are b) simple subsampling (taking one of the samples from the original model), c) averaging the 8 voxels from the higher resolution model, d) Gaussian filtering (σ=0.7 in voxel units), e) bilateral filtering (here we take σ=0.7 in voxel units, and σ=6 for the intensity-based Gaussians, in a range from 0 to 255), and f) topology-guided downsampling. The examples show that none of the most elaborate filters improve over the average or Gaussian filtering

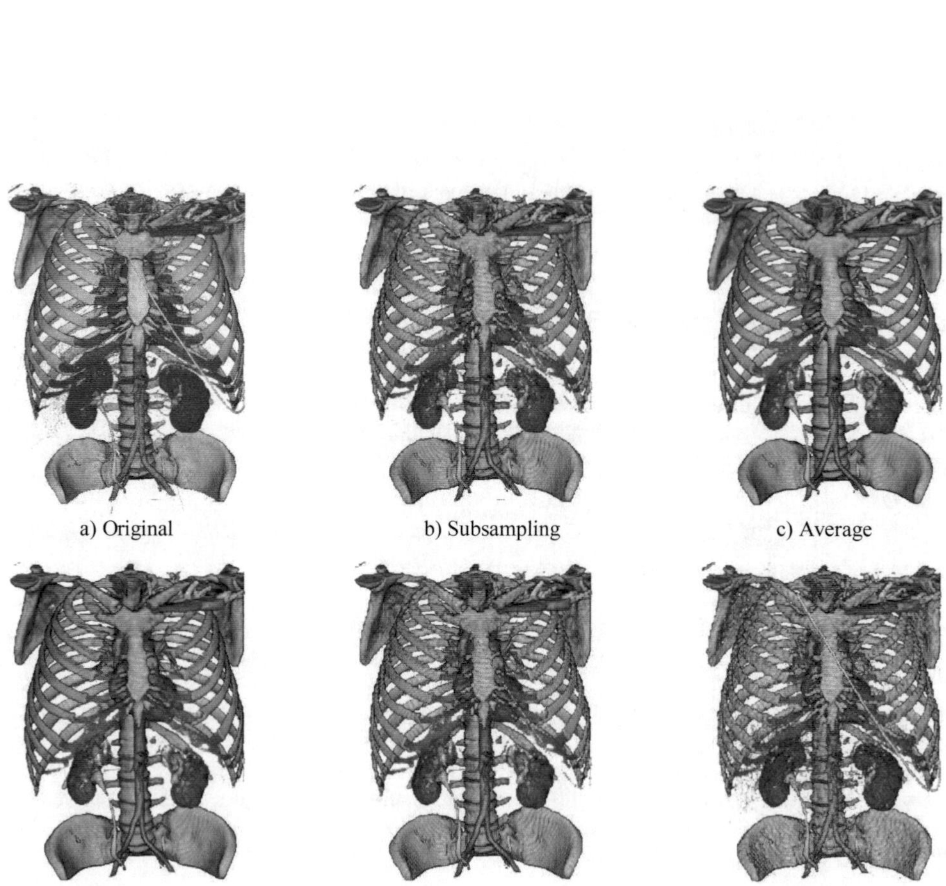

d) Gaussian Filter (σ=0.7) e) Bilateral Filter (σ's=0.7 & 6) f) Topology-Guided

Figure 2. Effect of downsampling on the body model (5123) dataset to 1283. Compared to the previous example, here the lack of preservation of small features is clearly visible: note how some tube-shaped elements disappear partially or even completely (in b-e). The results for the topology-guided downsampling are far from satisfactory. Even if the small features are in general preserved, the staircase artifacts make the result not usable for medical visualization

The effect of those algorithms onto medical data is illustrated in Figures 1 and 2. Note that the supposedly better choices, such as the bilateral filter and the topology-guided downsampling produce worse results than simpler approaches such as the Gaussian filter or the average filtering. Even just subsampling the model seems to produce comparable or even better results than those approaches. This is in part due to the fact that the relation between the filtered volume and the final rendered image is TF-dependent and highly non-linear, with the consequence that such successful image processing techniques show poor performance in terms of the quality of the final images. These artifacts are more visible for models that have small features such as the body model in Figure 2, where the loss of small features is evident. Furthermore, even though Topology-guided downsampling preserves some fine details, it produces undesirable, bumpy images, due to the fact that its sampling strategy modifies the location of the critical points.

Summarizing, the main disadvantages of the exposed methods for downsampling are the loss of details and the bumpiness of the produced results. The images shown in Figures 1 and 2 are just a subset of the experiments we carried out, but they are representative.

In order to overcome these problems, we have developed a new, Gaussian-based downsampling method that attempts to preserve small features and still produces smooth results at a low cost, and that requires no parameterization, so it runs completely unattended, without any need for user intervention. The implementation details of the proposed technique are presented in the next section.

4. FEATURE-PRESERVING VOLUME DOWNSAMPLING FILTER

4.1 Overview

The main objectives of our downsampling filter are:

- Preservation of details
- Fully automatic
- Low cost

In order to preserve details, our algorithm first simulates a downsampling step based on Gaussian filtering, and uses this information as a guidance image to give more importance to those regions that would previously suffer from excessive degradation so that features are preserved. Then, the real downsampling is performed. Another important factor is that the process should run unattended, that is, it should not require manual tweaking of parameters for good results. The rationale behind this is that the filter is intended for use with medical models, to rapidly downsample larger models that would not fit into the GPU. This downsampling should be done automatically, since no expert supervision can be carried out. As a result, the process must be robust to different models, and automatic.

4.2 Implementation

Given a volumetric scalar field V_n of resolution 2^n, to compute a coarser representation V_{n-k}; $k > 0$, our downsampling technique proceeds in three steps:

- First, a simulated coarser volume S_{n-k} is computed by means of Gaussian-filtering and subsampling.
- Secondly, the distance between V_n and S_{n-k} provides hints about the loss of features in the simulated downsampling step. Using this information we generate a filtered output F_n using Local Feature Kernels, which better preserve features that would otherwise disappear with standard filtering and subsampling.
- Finally, F_n is subsampled to obtain V_{n-k}.

At a more detailed level, to compute the filtered value F_n at each discrete sample position x we perform the following convolution:

$$F_n(x) = \sum_{i \in B_r} V_n(x+i) \cdot f_x(i)$$

where f_x is the normalized Local Feature Kernel at the position x with support B_r, a ball of radius r centered at the origin. f_x is in turn a product of a normalized global Gaussian kernel g and a distance kernel d_x:

$$f_x(i) = \frac{1}{\alpha} \cdot g(i) \cdot d_x(i), \quad \forall i \in B_r$$

The denominator is computed as:

$$\alpha = \sum_{i \in B_r} g(j) \cdot d_x(j)$$

and it ensures the sum of weights in f_x equals one. The distance kernel d_x is defined as the normalized absolute distance of values in the neighborhood of x between the original scalar field V_n and the simulated Gaussian-downsampled scalar field S_{n-k}:

$$d_x(i) = \frac{1}{\beta} |V_n(x+i) - S_{n-k}(x+i)|, \quad \forall i \in B_r$$

Again, the denominator ß ensures the normalization of weights in d_x. Note that V_n and S_{n-k} have different resolutions; sample positions in the kernel domain happen to be aligned with the center of V_n's voxels, but density values from S_{n-k} must be computed by tri-linear interpolation. The distance kernel assigns larger weights to those samples in V_n that are prone to disappear (those which most differ with S_{n-k}). As both g and d_x are combined into f_x, smoothing or sharpening is done depending on their weights, which are local to the filtered sample position x. Homogeneous regions will provoke homogeneous distance kernels, thus letting g_x filter the most part, whereas feature regions will provide more characteristic distance kernels for the feature selection task. Figure 3 shows a visual overview of the algorithm.

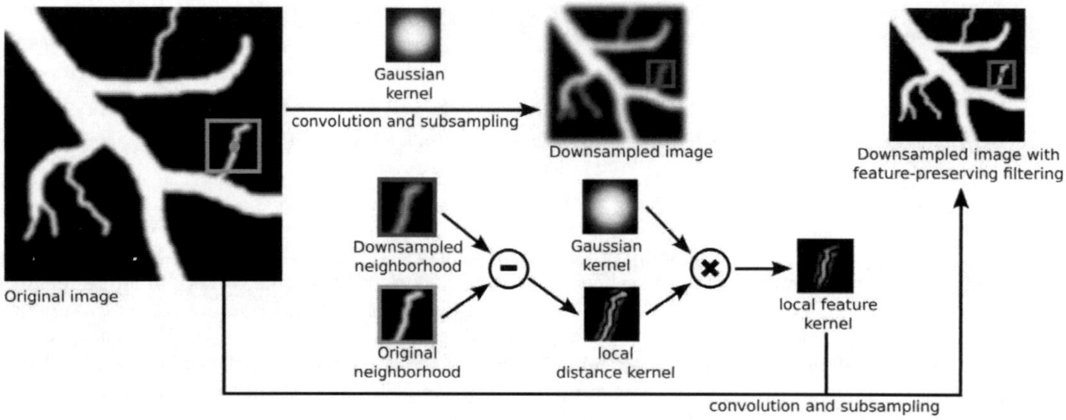

Figure 3. Overview diagram of our feature-preserving downsampling filter using Local Feature Kernels. As seen in the image, the technique first needs to perform a Gaussian-based downsampling to generate a guidance downsampled dataset. Then, the original dataset can be filtered with Local Feature Kernels, which are made of a combination of a Gaussian kernel and a distance kernel computed from the sample-by-sample neighbourhood differences between the original and the guidance datasets

4.3 Results

Without any optimization, running on a commodity PC (Intel Core i7 CPU, 8GB RAM) our algorithm takes up to 4 minutes in order to compute the downsampling for the thorax model from 512^3 to 128^3 voxels. Although it is a few times more costly than standard Gaussian-downsampling, it's affordable for a preprocess and scales linearly with the input dataset resolution, plus it clearly achieves higher quality results.

In all the comparisons, we reduce the models a ratio of 64:1, going from 512^3 to 128^3 in Figures 1, 2 and 5, and from 256^3 to 64^3 in Figure 4, for an aneurysm model with a lot of small features. Note how our method improves over all the others.

a) Original b) Average c) Bilateral filter d) Gaussian e) Topology-guided f) Our approach

Figure 4. Performance of our downsampling filter for an aneurysm, a model with a lot of small features. Most methods lose a lot of details, or result in overly exaggerated features, leading to undesirable visual artefact effects. Our system (shown in f) is the one that performs best

Figure 5 shows the effect of our downsampling filter compared to the averaging and Gaussian filtering methods for the previous shown models. We can see that for large models with small features, such as the thorax model on top, many of those details are preserved. Note how the ribs have softer shape, and the kidneys are not so transparent as in Figures 5b and 5c. The catheter going from the left shoulder to the hip is also quite preserved, such as the ureter.

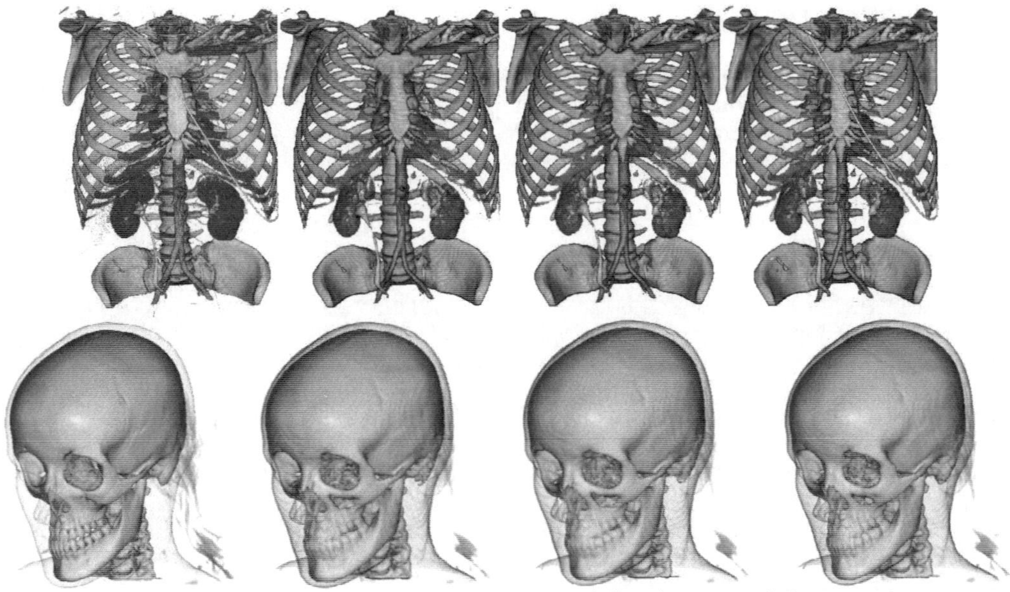

a) Original b) Average c) Gaussian d) Our approach

Figure 5. Our improved feature-preserving filter (d) improves the downsampling of the other approaches by preserving more small details and avoiding the ugly staircase effect that may appear using other techniques. The original dataset (a) has 5123 resolution, while the downsampled models have 1283. The Gaussian filter uses again the σ=0.7 as compared to voxel size. Notice how in the thorax model (top) some of the small features such as the catheter and some of the vessels are better preserved than with the other filters. The head model again preserves smaller features such as the creases of the bones better, while partially avoiding the staircase effects that are more noticeable in (b) both in the skin and the skull

5. CONCLUSIONS AND FUTURE WORK

Since medical models are now commonly available (you can get the data of your CT or MRI in a DVD after a medical test), the need of rendering such models in commodity PCs has grown. So downsampling is a key step in several scenarios, such as when the data must fit a small GPU, and when the models are huge enough that even the best GPU in the market cannot hold it. In these last cases, building a multiresolution scheme also involves downsampling the models to build the intermediate nodes.

In this paper we have analyzed several techniques for downsampling volumetric models and we have developed a new filtering method that adaptively smooths or preserves features depending on the topology of the surrounding region of the voxel being filtered. We do this by generating Local Feature Kernels. These are the product of a smoothing Gaussian kernel and a local distance kernel derived from the absolute distance between the full resolution dataset and a previous downsampling simulation. Our proposed heuristic identifies zones which are potentially likely to disappear, and gives them more importance when filtering. As a result, they are preserved after subsampling. We have shown that the technique improves the quality of several models with respect to other downsampling techniques, and it is especially suited for models with small features, such as the aneurysm. In our experiments we also found that the improvement over some models was more limited, but in any case, the quality was at least analogous to Gaussian filtering. Thus, our filter can be safely used in a vast majority of models.

Since the key of this filtering method resides in suitably adjusted Local Feature Kernels, we believe that our process can still be improved. In this line, we plan to further explore additional ways to determine their weights, variance, and radius.

ACKNOWLEDGEMENT

The material in this paper is based upon work supported by the Spanish Ministerio de Economia y Competitividad and by FEDER (EU) funds under Grant No. TIN2014-52211-C2-1-R. We would also like to thank the annonymous reviewers for their contributions and useful comments to improve the contents of this paper.

REFERENCES

Aurich and Weule, 1995. Non-Linear Gaussian Filters Performing Edge Preserving Diffusion. *Proceedings of the DAGM Symposium (DAGM'95)*, pp. 538-545. Springer Berlin Heidelberg.

Balsa-Rodríguez, M. et al., 2014. State-of-the-art in compressed GPU-based direct volume rendering. *Computer Graphics Forum*, 33(6), pp. 77–100.

Boada, I. et al., 2001. Multiresolution volume visualization with a texture-based octree. *The Visual Computer* 17, 3 (2001), pp. 185–197.

Díaz-García, J. et al., 2016. Adaptive Transfer Functions. *The Visual Computer.* 32, 6-8 (June 2016), pp. 835-845.

Hadwiger, M. et al., 2006. *Real-Time Volume Graphics*. A. K. Peters Ltd, Natick.

Kopf, J. et al., 2013. Content-adaptive image downscaling. *ACM Trans. Graph.* 32, 6, Article 173 (November 2013), 8 pages.

Kraus, M. and Ertl, T., 2001. Topology-Guided Downsampling. *Volume Graphics 2001*, pp. 223-234.

Kraus and Bürger, 2008. Interpolating and downsampling RGBA volume data. *Proceedings of Vision, Modeling, and Visualization' 08*, pp. 323–332.

Kwon et al., 2016. A fast 3D adaptive bilateral filter for ultrasound volume visualization, *Computational Methods Programs Biomedecine*, 2016 Sep;133:25-34. doi: 10.1016/j.cmpb.2016.05.008.

Levoy and Whitaker, 1990. Gaze-directed volume rendering. *SIGGRAPH Comput. Graph.* 24, 2, pp. 217–223.

Öztireli, A. C. and Gross, M., 2015. Perceptually based downscaling of images. *ACM Trans. Graph.* 34, 4, Article 77 (July 2015), 10 pages.

Paris et al., 2007. A Gentle Introduction to Bilateral Filtering and its Applications, *ACM SIGGRAPH 2007 course notes*, https://people.csail.mit.edu/sparis/bf_course/.

Paris and Durand, 2009. A fast approximation of the bilateral filter using a signal processing approach. *International journal of computer vision* 81.1 (2009): pp. 24-52.

Smith and Brady, 1997. SUSAN -- A New Approach to Low Level Image Processing. *International Journal of Computer Vision*, Vol. 23, number 1, pp. 45-78.

Sicat et al., 2014. Sparse PDF volumes for consistent multi-resolution volume rendering. *IEEE Transactions on Visualization and Computer Graphics*. (Proc. IEEE Vis.) 20(12), pp. 2417–2426.

Tomasi and Manduchi, 1998. Bilateral Filtering for Gray and Color Images. *Proceedings of the International Conference on Computer Vision* (ICCV'98), pp. 839-846.

Weber, N. et al., 2016. Rapid, detail-preserving image downscaling. *ACM Trans. Graph.* 35, 6, Article 205 (November 2016), 6 pages.

Wang et al., 2011. Feature-preserving volume data reduction and focus + context visualization. *IEEE Transactions on Visualization and Computer Graphics*. 17(2), pp. 171–181.

Wang et al., 2012. Adaptive Speckle Reduction in OCT Volume Data Based on Block-Matching and 3-D Filtering, *IEEE Photonics Technology Letters*. Volume: 24, Issue: 20, pp. 1802-1804.

Younesy et al., 2006. Improving the quality of multiresolution volume rendering. *Proceedings of Joint Eurographics/IEEE VGTC Conference on Visualization*, pp. 251–258. Eurographics Association, Lisboa, Portugal.

AUTOMATICALLY LEARNING AN INTUITIVE ANIMATION INTERFACE FROM A COLLECTION OF HUMAN MOTION CLIPS

Marcel Lüdi[1], Martin Guay[2], Brian McWilliams[2] and Robert W. Sumner[2]
[1]*ETH Zürich, Switzerland*
[2]*Disney Research, Switzerland*

ABSTRACT

In this paper, we automatically learn interpretable low dimensional generative representations of human walking motions using a variational autoencoder. By modeling the latent space of an autoencoder as a low dimensional multi-variate gaussian distribution, we can optimize for an encoding that produces disentangled, independent components which explain most of the variation in the data. The latent variables our model learns are intuitive to humans and can be directly manipulated in a graphical user interface (GUI) via sliders, to generate new walking motions in real time.

KEYWORDS

Intuitive interface, character animation, motion manifold

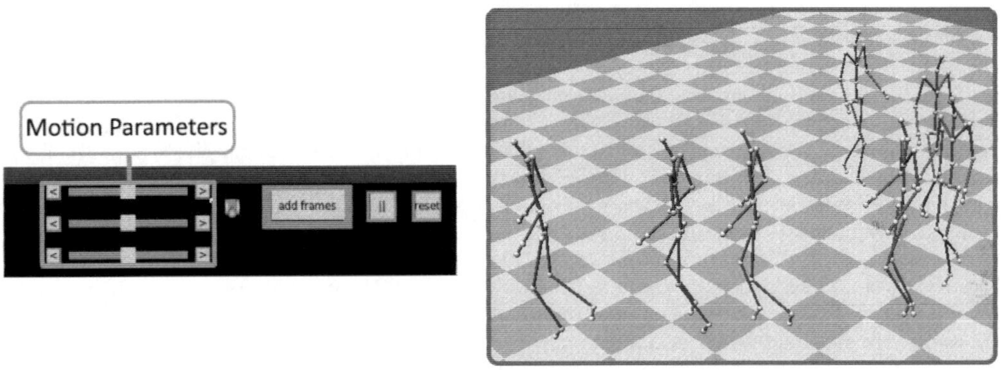

Figure 1. From a disorganized set of human walking motions, we automatically learn an intuitive animation interface with 3 sliders for synthesizing new human walking motions, similar to the ones in the data set. Our algorithm works without any alignment or pre-processing of the data set, and outputs parameters that make sense to humans. By modeling the space of motion as a deep neural network, and constraining the latent variables (our 3 controllers) to be as mutually independent as possible to each other, as well as to cover as wide variations as possible, we obtain parameters that are sensible to human interpretation. The first two dimensions control the left and right step length respectively, while the 3rd parameter controls turning left to right. The user presses "add frames" to generate and append a 1 second motion, to then manipulate the sliders again in a back-and-forth manner to generate longer walking motion sequences

1. INTRODUCTION

Controlling the motion of a digital character is a challenging task as the dimensionality of the character's digital representation is generally high. A long lasting goal of computer animation is to provide intuitive high-level controls for character's shape and motion (e.g. low dimensional parameterizations such as rigs). Data-driven techniques allow generating various new motions similar to the examples in the data-set.

However, the learned parameters are either too many, or not interpretable by humans for direct manipulation. For example, applying linear dimensionality reduction on human motion data does not lead to interpretable components, and is not fully automatic as it requires aligning the motion clips.

Deep neural networks, and more specifically convolutional autoencoders, have been recently used to automatically learn low dimensional representations of human motion from disorganized motion clips [Holden et al. (2016)]. However, the learned latent space could not be manipulated directly by humans, mainly due to three reasons. Firstly, the dimensionality required for successful reconstruction remains too high for human manipulation (256 dimensions). Secondly, the granularity of the latent variables can cause small changes in latent space to map to large changes in full space. And thirdly, entanglement in the network can cause the effect of individual latent variables to change when manipulating other variables. For example, a slider may control a foot position, while moving another slider changes the effect of the initial controller from moving the foot to moving a hand; as the network mixes the latent variables to reconstruct the motion.

In this work, we automatically learn a disentangled latent space with low granularity that is interpretable by humans and that can be manipulated directly via GUI sliders to generate new motions in real time. We draw upon the concept of variational autoencoders (VAEs) [Kingma & Welling (2014)], and represent the latent space as a multi-variate gaussian distribution, allowing us to seek a large coverage for each dimension, as well as independence between the dimensions during the training process. This is achieved by not only minimizing the traditional reconstruction cost w.r.t. network parameters, but also by penalizing deviations from a canonical multi-variate normal distribution, i.e. $H \sim N(0,I)$ in latent space, where each dimension should have standard deviation as close as possible to one. This prevents from learning a latent variable representation with extremely fine granularity, and also provides more independence between dimensions—thereby favoring disentanglement. As a result, each latent variable encodes a consistent portion of the motion space and the network preserves this consistency when changing the values of the other latent variables.

While optimizing for independence in the VAE latent space has been successful with various data-sets before, such as 2D face images and digits [Kingma & Welling (2014)], its application to 3D human motion is new and leads to challenges of its own. There is a tradeoff between the quality of the encoding and the meaningfulness provided by the disentanglement. Training directly for 3 dimensions that could be manipulated by a user leads to failures in the training process: the latent space is too small to successfully reconstruct the motion. By training a larger intermediate space of 20 dimensions, we obtain similar reconstruction quality, while at the same time obtaining independent latent variables that are interpretable by humans. However, 20 dimensions still remains too many for intuitive use, and the latent variables are not ordered according to importance. Hence we further reduce the dimensionality to 3 using linear dimensionality reduction, which leads to a compact set of variables the user can manipulate directly to generate new motions—as shown in Figure 1.

In short, we reduce the space of one second motion clips (61 frames) for a 66 d.o.f. skeleton (i.e. 4026 dimensions) to 20 dimensions with the VAE, and then reduce furthermore to 3 using a PCA. The first two components control the left and right step length respectively, and the third dimension controls turning left to right motions. Note that the effect of each slider remains consistent when modifying the other sliders. In our accompanying video, we show various examples of walking motions synthesized by sequentially appending one second motion clips generated by controlling our three sliders alone.

2. RELATED WORK

Learning generative models of motion. A large body of work utilizes statistical dimensionality reduction, both at the individual pose and animation clip levels, as an integral part of animation tools. In contrast to our work, the parameters of the learned models are not used by humans directly, but instead used to represent or constrain the character in various optimization-based tasks such as inverse kinematics [Grochow et al. (2004)], [Wei & Chai (2011)], [Holden et al. (2016)] or space-time optimization [Safonova et al. (2004)], [Chai & Hodgins (2007)], [Min et al. (2009)]. Additionally, training the model is not always fully automatic, or does not always succeed. For example, linear dimensionality reduction applied to motion clips—such as in [Safonova et al. (2004)], [Chai & Hodgins (2007)], [Min et al. (2009)]—requires first aligning the motion clips. Also, non-linear dimensionality reduction methods that can use fewer latent variables as the Gaussian Process Latent Variable Model (GPLVM) used in [Grochow et al. (2004)], does not scale to large data-sets.

In contrast, our learning process is fully automatic, successful when trained over large data-sets, and produces model parameters that are intuitive enough for human users to manipulate directly.

Similar to our work, Holden et. al [Holden et al. (2015)], [Holden et al. (2016)] use an autoencoder to automatically reduce a large disorganized data-set. In their work, they reduced down to 256 dimensions and the user cannot manipulate the latent variables directly as the granularity is high and the dimensions are entangled. In contrast, we reduce the latent space down to 3, and the effect of our latent variables on the motion remain consistent during editing—regardless of the configuration of the other dimensions.

Manually parameterizing motion data-sets. Another line of work lets the user parameterize motions w.r.t. to meaningful dimensions. Rose et al. [Rose et al. (1998)], in their paper *Verbs and Adverbs*, allow the user to label motion clips of a given category (e.g. walks, referred to as *verbs*) along stylistic dimensions (referred to as *adverbs*), and interpolate between them using radial basis functions. State machines with blend trees are often used in games and interactive applications to parameterize the character's motion w.r.t. a direction. While there has been works on automatically building motion parameterizations (e.g. [Kovar et al. (2002)] [Heck & Gleicher (2007)]), in practice they are built manually by taking perfectly aligned motion clips.

Deep Learning has proven very successful at finding intricate structures in high-dimensional data across various domains [LeCun et al. (2015)]. Deep learning algorithms are state-of-the art in object recognition [Krizhevsky et al. (2012)] [Ciregan et al. (2012)] and have been successful in video classification [Karpathy et al. (2014)], [Ji et al. (2013)] and speech recognition [Graves et al. (2013)]. Recently, there has been an interest in using deep convolutional network architectures as generative models to produce novel data from the network [Goodfellow et al. (2014)], [Vincent et al. (2010)]. The strength of deep conv. nets lies in their ability to automatically learn appropriate features in data-sets. For example, in image recognition, the first layers often produce filters similar to edge detection filters while deeper layers hold more complex filters corresponding to different objects [Zeiler & Fergus (2014)]. Our work applies deep conv. nets to learning a motion manifold of human motion.

Du et al. use a hierarchical recurrent neural network trained on a large motion capture data-set to classify different motions [Du et al. (2015)] and achieve state-of-the-art action recognition performance. Taylor et al. [Taylor & Hinton (2009)], [Taylor et al. (2011)] use conditional Restricted Boltzmann Machines (RBMs) to learn a time-series predictor which can predict the next pose of a motion given several previous frames; with improvements made using the spike-and-slab version of the recurrent temporal RBM [Mittelman et al. (2014)]. Holden et al. [Holden et al. (2015)], [Holden et al. (2016)] use a convolutional autoencoder to automatically compute a low-dimensional latent representation of human motion, which is then used inside a path-based motion synthesis interface. It is worth noting that deep conv. nets have been used in other areas of computer animation such as for the control of simulated characters. The network typically represents both a value function and a state-action feedback function within a deep reinforcement learning framework. Levine et al. [Levine & Koltun (2014)] use a neural network to learn optimal control policies for bipedal locomotion and [Peng et al. (2016)] for learning terrain-adaptive locomotion skills.

Variational Autoencoders. Variational autoencoders (VAEs) [Kingma & Welling (2014)], [Rezende et al. (2014)] have emerged as a successful way to efficiently learn probabilistic *generative* models of complex data distributions. VAEs compress the data by representing it as a distribution over a low-dimensional latent space whose parameters are learned by an encoding network. The VAE objective aims to simultaneously minimize both the reconstruction error of the decoder network and the *Kullback-Leibler* (KL) divergence between the distribution over the latent space and a standard normal distribution. New data examples can then be obtained by decoding samples taken from the latent distribution.

One well known problem with VAEs is that the latent variables are often uninterpretable. Recently, Higgins et al. [Rezende et al. (2014)] showed that with a minor modification – scaling the KL divergence by a factor, β – encourages the independence between the latent variables, resulting in *disentangled* representations which allows the latent variable to be directly interpretable.

In this work, we apply the idea of optimizing for independence in latent space to the case of human walking motion. As a result, the disentangled latent variables are interpretable by humans and the user can directly manipulate them to generate new motion sequences.

3. DATA ACQUISITION AND PRE-PROCESSING

Motion capture data often have different skeleton sizes (bone lengths) and dimensionality (number of joints). We first describe how we convert different skeletons into a uniform skeleton. The motion representation fed into the network can impact the learning performance. We wish an encoding that is invariant to global translations and rotations. Hence we convert the motions into a local body frame coordinate system, with the origin located on the ground where the root position is projected onto. By representing each joint position relative to this body frame, we can also easily measure the dissimilarity between poses by measuring the Euclidian distance between joint positions.

Animation Data

The data-set we used is mainly composed of walking motions over flat terrain with various left and right turns. It holds a few backward walks, runs, and uneven terrain, but holds no side stepping. The captured motion clips are sampled at 120 frames per second and the final data-set contains approximately 1.5 million frames of walking motion. We gathered motion clips both from the *CMU* data-set [CMU (n.d.)], as well as our in-house produced motions—performed using a *Perception Neuron* system [Ltd (n.d.)].

Data Formatting

We now convert the motion clips into a format suitable for training. First we reduce the temporal dimension by sub-sampling the clips at 60 frames per second by interpolating the joint angles for any missing poses. Then we convert the different skeletons into a common skeleton featuring 21 joints. We manually assign the correspondence between joints for the common skeleton. Given a joint correspondence, we transfer the joint angles and then scale the bone lengths to the target skeleton bone length. The final motion may still hold discrepancies, and thus we adjust the joint angles as to match the target skeleton as much as possible; using a full body inverse kinematics solve.

To convert the skeleton into a *body-local* coordinate system invariant to global translation and rotation, we start by computing the global 3D joint positions of the character. Then we compute the forward direction of the character using the vectors between left and right shoulders, as well as left and right hips, averaging them and taking the cross product with the vertical up axis **y**. We compute the relative positional and rotational velocity of each frame w.r.t. its body frame (origin on the ground where the root is projected onto) and store the values. We emphasize that the relative positions of the joints are relative to the body frame and not to a world origin.

Hence, the final global position of the animation is recovered by integrating the velocities of each frame over time. Finally, we compute the mean pose and standard deviation of the whole data set and normalize the each frame by removing the mean and dividing by the standard deviation—same is applied to the horizontal and rotational velocities.

4. VARIATIONAL AUTOENCODER

We model and train both an encoder Φ and decoder $\Phi^{\dagger}$, but note that only the decoder is used for motion synthesis. The encoder $\Phi(X)$ takes an input motion clip $X \in R^{k \times d}$ of d joints by k frames, and encodes it into a c-dimensional latent variable $H \in R^{c}$. From the latent space, a decoder $\Phi^{\dagger}(H)$ is used to compute a motion clip$\hat{X}$ of k frames. The full autoencoder architecture is shown in Figure 2, and we start by describing the encoder and then the decoder.

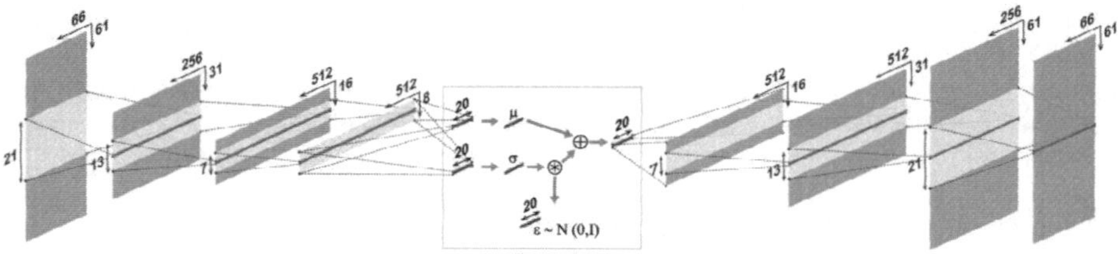

Figure 2. The structure of our variational autoencoder. The encoder represents the latent space as a multivariate gaussian distribution. During training, the mean and standard deviations are combined with a random sample to generate the latent sample corresponding to the input motion clip. See Training section for more details

Encoder

The encoder takes an input animation X and processes it through a traditional convolutional network, with the difference that its last layer outputs a *mean* $\Phi_\mu(X)$ and standard deviation $\Phi_{\log(\sigma)}(X)$ to represent the final latent space (as a multi-variate gaussian distribution).

Hence, the input animation first goes through three convolutional layers each followed by a max pooling layer to reduce the temporal resolution:

$$\Phi(X) = ReLU(\Psi(ReLU(\Psi(ReLU(\Psi(X * W_1 + b_1)) * W_2 + b_2)) * W_3 + b_3)) \quad (1)$$

where Ψ is a max pooling layer in the temporal axis with a reduction factor of 2 and $ReLU(x)$ is the nonlinear rectifying operation defined as $ReLU(x) = max(x, 0)$. The operator * denotes a convolution using weight matrices $W_i \in R\wedge(m_{i-1} \times m_i \times w_i)$ (m_{i-1} is the number of units in the previous layer), w_i the convolution filter width, and $b_i \in R^{m_i}$ are the biases.

After the three convolution layers, the sample goes through two separate fully connected layers resulting in the final the *predicted mean* and *predicted standard deviation*:

$$\Phi_\mu(X) = flat(\Phi(X)) \cdot W_\mu + b_\mu,$$
$$\Phi_\sigma(X) = flat(\Phi(X)) \cdot W_\sigma + b_\sigma,$$

where here $\cdot$ denotes a matrix multiplication, with weights $W_\mu \in R^{(s \cdot m_3) \times c}$ and $W_{log(\sigma)} \in R^{(s \cdot m_3) \times c}$ (given s dimensions for each neuron at layer 3) and the $flat()$ function reshapes the output to be one dimensional. In this case s is the number of units after convolutions (the before-last layer). The dimensionality of each layer of the encoder can be found in Figure 2.

Decoder

The decoder $\Phi^\dagger$ is similar to the encoder but in reverse order. It takes as input a latent space sample $H \in R^c$, processes it in a fully connected layer and then gives the result to a convolutional network which increases the temporal resolution with inverse pooling operations; each by a different margin. The inverse max pooling operation chooses the value of the closest hidden unit on the temporal axis. Hence after the inverse pooling, each neuron chooses its value based on the previous neuron that is closest temporally. The factor by witch the temporal dimension is up-sampled is chosen such that the original poses are still present in the new layer. This means that we actually gradually fill the holes in the animation by generating the missing frames. Finally the neurons are activated using a rectified linear operation, resulting in the decoder function:

$$\Phi^\dagger(H) = \Psi^\dagger(ReLU(\Psi^\dagger(ReLU(\Psi^\dagger(flat^\dagger(H \cdot W_0 + b_0)) * W_1 + b_1)) * W_2 + b_2)) * W_3 + b_3 \quad (2)$$

where $flat^\dagger$ reshapes the flat output of the fully connected layer for further processing into the convolutional layers. In this case, the output of the $flat^\dagger$ function is a matrix $H' \in R^{s \times m_0}$ where s is the number of frames after down sampling the original input and m_0 is the number of hidden units in the first layer. $\Psi^\dagger$ denotes an inverse pooling operation. However, for decoding, the expansion factor is fixed to 2 for all layers to reflect the max pooling from the encoder. The output of this network is an animation clip $\hat{X} \in R^{n \times d}$ with n frames.

5. TRAINING

Given a collection of motion clips X, the autoencoder is trained to encode the motion clips into latent space and then decode them back into full space. We minimize the error between each initial clip and the reconstructed clip. The difference with traditional autoencoders is that we represent the latent variables as a multi-variate gaussian distribution and we maximize for independence (disentanglement) between components by penalizing each standard deviation from a value of one, which also provides large coverage for each dimension and prevents from high granularity. This is realized through a KL-divergence term that penalizes the distance of the gaussian distribution generated by the network $H(\Phi_\mu(X), \Phi_\sigma(X))$to a canonical multi-variate gaussian distribution $N(0, I)$ [Kingma & Welling (2014)]. Both terms together with additional sparsity $\gamma||\theta||_1$ encouraging fewer network parameters θ, results in total cost:

$$Cost(X, \theta) = \alpha||X - \Phi^{\dagger}(H(\Phi_{\mu}(X), \Phi_{\sigma}(X)))||_2^2 + \beta KL(\Phi_{\mu}(X), \Phi_{\sigma}(X)) + \gamma||\theta||_1, \quad (3)$$

where

$$KL(\mu, \sigma) = \frac{1}{2}\sum_{i=0}^{c}(\mu_i^2 + \exp(\log\sigma_i)^2 - 1 - 2\log(\sigma)_i) \quad (4)$$

During training, the sample given to the decoder is computed using the generated mean and standard deviation from the encoder: $H(\Phi_{\mu}(X), \Phi_{\sigma}(X)) = \Phi_{\mu}(X) + \epsilon * \exp(\log\Phi_{\sigma}(X))$, where ϵ is a random sample generated from a standard normal distribution $\epsilon \sim N(0,1)$.

At the start of training the β is set to zero such that the network first learns a stable reconstruction before optimizing the distribution. Over the course of the session β gets increased using a sigmoid function which lets the network adapt to the additional cost term.

The training of the network is similar to training a traditional autoencoder. The weights are initialized using the "fan-in" and "fan-out" criteria, while the biases are initialized to zero. The motion clips are randomly drawn from the database and the cost function is minimized using stochastic gradient descent with derivatives computed via Tensorflow [Abadi et al. (2015)], internally using the adaptive gradient descent algorithm Adam. To avoid over fitting to the training data, we used a dropout of 0.2. The variational autoencoder is trained over 200 epochs on two NVIDIA Titan X GPUs.

Figure 3 shows the evolution of the error during training. The autoencoder first learns a hidden representation of the input before being exposed to the KL-divergence term, i.e. before increasing β. Once it reaches a certain value, the reconstruction error increases to minimize the additional KL-divergence cost.

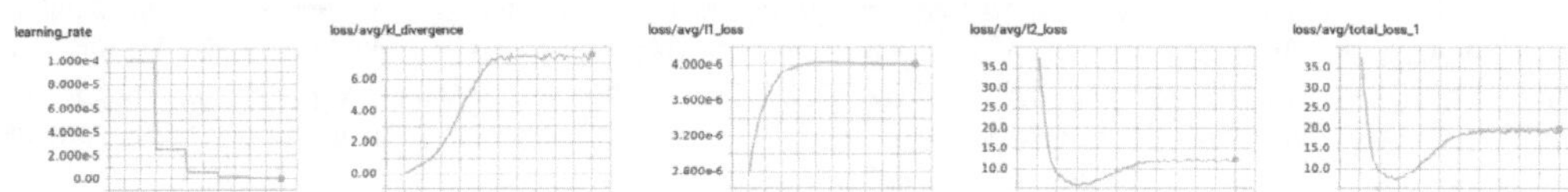

Figure 3. Value of the loss function during the training of our variational autoencoder. The l2-loss is the reconstruction error and the l1-loss is the regularization term

Linear Reduction

We reduced the full space of one second walking motion clips to 20 latent variable spaces. To further reduce the hidden space dimensions, we apply linear dimensionality reduction (principal component analysis) on a subset of the motion clips, and extract the 3 most significant components for the user to manipulate. We first encode the subset of motion clips using the encoder. We compute a linear projection matrix from the encoded motion clips, which allow us to map a 3 dimensional space to the 20 dimensional latent space. As a result, the user can manipulate the 3 sliders shown in Figure 1 to generate believable motions.

6. RESULTS

Our variational autoencoder was trained on the walking motion data-set described in Section 3. We implemented an interactive interface to visualize the reconstructed motions, which is shown both in Figure 1 and the accompanying video. The user can change either the hidden units (1 of the 20 values), or the final reduced 3 which map to the 20 dimensions. Evaluating the network is fast: from the hidden values, we can synthesize a one second motion clip and render the animation instantly—in real-time.

The initial 20 dimensions are disentangled and some of the variables play a clear role such as turning or stepping length, while others have a smaller influence on the resulting motion. To reduce the number of redundant dimensions, we performed principle component analysis (PCA) on the latent values computed with a subset of the training data (in Section 5). This way, we can retain only the three most important components, leaving out those that had little influence on the motion.

The first two components are associated with the left and right legs. Their magnitudes control the step length: a large value for the first component control step length of the left leg, and the second for the right leg. The sign of the components control the phase of the walk: a negative value for the left leg takes a first step with the left leg, while a positive value shifts the step later in time. In Figure 4 we show the first pose generated by manipulating these two components.

The third dimension controls the direction in which the character turns. A negative value creates a rotation to the left while a positive value turns in the other direction. Given only these three components, we were able to generate a variety of motions, as shown in the accompanying video. Naturally, further customization and refinement is possible by manipulating some of the individual hidden components (one of the 20 sliders). While the effects on the motions can be subtle, they can provide additional leaning to the right or to the left, or hunching/straightening of the back.

Finally, to generate a longer motion, the user appends several motion clips generated from the three controls sequentially. We blend the synthesized motions over a small temporal window. To facilitate the generation of the next sequence the starting point of the character is set such that the beginning matches the end of the previous animation as closely as possible. To this end the first two dimensions are reversed to change the starting leg of the animation.

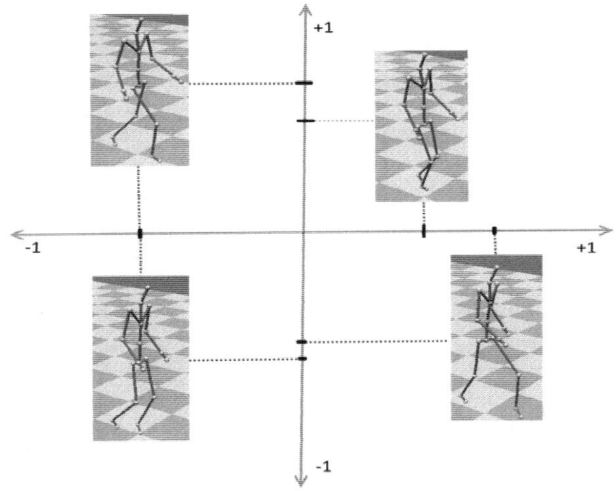

Figure 4. The first two components of the low-dimensional space and their effect on the first pose of the motion. The first dimension (x axis in pink) controls the left leg. Its magnitude controls the length of the step while the sign controls the phase of the step, where a positive value causes the left leg to take a first step. The second dimension (y axis in blue) is analogous to the first but for the right leg

Comparing with PCA on Full Space

In practice non-linear dimensionality reduction techniques such as the GPLVM do not scale well to large data sets. Hence in practice, principal component analysis is used in animation, but this requires aligning the motion clips. We demonstrate here that a PCA cannot be applied directly to the full space to automatically extract meaningful parameters.

We take the normalized training set and subtract the per clip mean. Each motion clip corresponds to a 4026 dimensional point and we reduced it to 5. Unlike with the VAE, none of the first 5 components could capture body movement and they could only capture full body positioning. In other words, the PCA directly applied to the full space cannot compute useful dimensions interpretable by humans. In contrast, we automatically compute roughly disentangled latent dimensions. That is, the effect of a latent variable on the motion remains same—regardless of the values of the other dimensions.

7. LIMITATIONS AND FUTURE WORK

Because we optimize for large standard deviations (close to 1), and because our model hold few latent variables—the reconstruction error can be larger than with a traditional autoencoder. On the other hand, each dimension is more independent and better suited for human interpretation.

An important parameter in our model is the latent space dimensionality. In practice there is a trade-off between having few dimensions and the quality of the reconstruction. Our goal is to obtain few dimensions, but in our experience less than 20 resulted in substantially low reconstruction errors. With too few latent components, the model cannot capture enough variation to generate believable results. We were successful by training an intermediate disentangled latent space and then further reducing to 3 using linear dimensionality reduction. In the future we will investigate ways of ordering the dimensions with respect to their importance during the optimization process directly.

Related to the number of latent variables is the length of the input motion sequence. Longer clips require the model to be more expressive meaning the number of latent variables required is higher for accurate reconstruction. After experimentation, we chose 61 frames covering a range of 1 second motions. In this time, a normal walking motion takes about two steps which lends itself well as a cutting point. The filter widths are chosen such that they cover the whole clip. Increasing this value too much results in smoothed out reconstructed motions, or sometimes even failure to converge. Setting too small a width will produce noisy outputs, as the system is not designed to learn the smoothness from the data alone.

Finally, we trained our VAE mainly on forward walking motions with turns, which means we cannot generate backward or side stepping motions. This could be addressed by augmenting the data-set and giving equal importance to all the different types of motions. Learning transitions between different motion types, e.g. between walking and running remains an open question. We believe this may be possible to achieve in the future by interpolating in the appropriate latent space.

8. CONCLUSION

We applied the concept of a variational autoencoder to learn a low dimensional, generative representation of human walking motion. Within a fully automated process, we were able to reduce the space of one second human walking motions, down to 3 dimensions, that the user can directly use to generate novel walking sequences (as shown in Figure 1). The main benefit of our approach is that the learning process automatically identifies disentangled latent variables, whose effect remains consistent throughout the editing process. Hence, the variation induced by each dimension on the generated motion is consistent and interpretable by a human. As a consequence, the latent variables can be directly manipulated via sliders to create believable animations; including walking around corners as well as taking long or short steps, as shown in our accompanying video. In the future, we plan on extending this approach to other types of motions such as running, as well as for automatically learning stylistic attributes.

REFERENCES

Abadi, M. et al, 2015. *TensorFlow: Large-scale machine learning on heterogeneous systems*. http://tensorflow.org/

Chai, J. & Hodgins, J. K, 2007. Constraint-based motion optimization using a statistical dynamic model. *ACM Transactions on Graphics (TOG)* Vol. 26.

Ciregan, D. et al, 2012. Multi-column deep neural networks for image classification. *In Computer Vision and Pattern Recognition (CVPR), 2012 IEEE Conference on, IEEE*. pp. 3642–3649.

CMU (n.d.). *Carnegie Mellon University Mocap Database*. http://mocap.cs.cmu.edu/

Du, Y. et al, 2015. Hierarchical recurrent neural network for skeleton based action recognition. *In Proceedings of the IEEE Conference on Computer Vision and Pattern Recognition*. pp. 1110–1118.

Goodfellow, I. et al, 2014. Generative adversarial nets. *In Advances in Neural Information Processing Systems*. pp. 2672–2680.

Graves, A. et al, 2013. Speech recognition with deep recurrent neural networks. *In 2013 IEEE international conference on acoustics, speech and signal processing, IEEE*. pp. 6645–6649.

Grochow, K. et al, 2004. Style-based inverse kinematics. *ÁCM Trans. Graph.* Vol. 23, No. 3, pp. 522–531.

Heck, R. & Gleicher, M, 2007. Parametric motion graphs. *In Proceedings of the 2007 Symposium on Interactive 3D Graphics and Games, I3D '07, ACM.* New York, NY, USA, pp. 129–136.

Holden, D. et al, 2016. A deep learning framework for character motion synthesis and editing. *ACM Trans. Graph.* Vol. 35, No. 4, pp. 138:1–138:11.

Holden, D. et al, 2015. Learning motion manifolds with convolutional autoencoders. *In SIGGRAPH Asia 2015 Technical Briefs, SA '15, ACM.* New York, NY, USA, pp. 18:1–18:4.

Ji, S. et al, 2013. 3d convolutional neural networks for human action recognition. *IEEE transactions on pattern analysis and machine intelligence.* Vol. 35, No. 1, pp. 221–231.

Karpathy, A. et al, 2014. Large-scale video classification with convolutional neural networks. *In Proceedings of the IEEE conference on Computer Vision and Pattern Recognition.* pp. 1725–1732.

Kingma, D. P. & Welling, M, 2014. Auto-encoding variational bayes. *International Conference on Learning Representations, ICLR* .

Kovar, L. et al, 2002. Motion graphs. *In Proceedings of the 29th Annual Conference on Computer Graphics and Interactive Techniques, SIGGRAPH '02, ACM.* New York, NY, USA, pp. 473–482.

Krizhevsky, A. et al, 2012. Imagenet classification with deep convolutional neural networks. *In Advances in neural information processing systems.* pp. 1097–1105.

LeCun, Y. et al, 2015. Deep learning. *Nature.* Vol. 521, No. 7553, pp. 436–444.

Levine, S. & Koltun, V, 2014. Learning complex neural network policies with trajectory optimization. *In ICML.* pp. 829–837.

Ltd, N. (n.d.). *Perception Neuron.* https://neuronmocap.com/content/axis-neuron-software

Min, J. et al, 2009. Interactive generation of human animation with deformable motion models. *ACM Transactions on Graphics (TOG).* Vol. 29.

Mittelman, R. et al, 2014. Structured recurrent temporal restricted boltzmann machines. *In Proceedings of the 31st International Conference on Machine Learning (ICML-14).* pp. 1647–1655.

Peng, X. B., 2016. Terrain-adaptive locomotion skills using deep reinforcement learning. *ACM Transactions on Graphics (Proc. SIGGRAPH 2016).* Vol. 35, No. 4.

Rezende, D. J. et al, 2014. Stochastic backpropagation and approximate inference in deep generative models. *In Proceedings of the 31st International Conference on Machine Learning (ICML-14).* pp. 1278–1286.

Rose, C. et al, 1998. Verbs and adverbs: Multidimensional motion interpolation using radial basis functions. *IEEE Computer Graphics and Applications.* Vol. 18, pp. 32–40.

Safonova, A. et al, 2004. Synthesizing physically realistic human motion in low-dimensional, behavior-specific spaces. *In ACM SIGGRAPH 2004 Papers, SIGGRAPH '04, ACM.* New York, NY, USA. pp. 514–521.

Taylor, G. W. & Hinton, G. E, 2009. Factored conditional restricted boltzmann machines for modeling motion style. *In Proceedings of the 26th annual international conference on machine learning, ACM.* pp. 1025–1032.

Taylor, G. W. et al, 2011. Two distributed-state models for generating high-dimensional time series. *Journal of Machine Learning Research.* pp. 1025–1068.

Vincent, P. et al, 2010. Stacked denoising autoencoders: Learning useful representations in a deep network with a local denoising criterion. *Journal of Machine Learning Research.* pp. 3371–3408.

Wei, X. & Chai, J, 2011. Intuitive interactive human-character posing with millions of example poses. *IEEE Comput. Graph. Appl.* Vol. 31, No. 4, pp. 78–88.

Zeiler, M. D. & Fergus, R, 2014. Visualizing and understanding convolutional networks. *In European Conference on Computer Vision.* pp. 818–833.

A METHOD OF VOLUME CALCULATION FOR 3D MODELS DESCRIBED BY BÉZIER SURFACES USING EXAMPLE OBJECTS OF BIOMEDICAL ORIGIN

Aleksandrs Sisojevs[1], Katrina Boločko[2] and Olga Krutikova[2]
[1]*Ventspils University College*
101 Inženieru Str., Ventspils, LV-3601, Latvia
[2]*Riga Technical University, Faculty of Computer Science and Information Technology,*
2 Daugavgrīvas Str., Riga, LV-1048, Latvia

ABSTRACT

This paper describes a method of computing volume for 3D objects bounded by Bézier surfaces using example models of biomedical origin. The authors present three different theorems for volume calculation, based, based on different properties of researched models, acquired by projection of surface vertices on coordinate system origin point, axis and plane. The proposed approach is based on using methods of differential geometry: surface integrals of scalar fields, Euler integral of the first kind and Beta functions. Experimental results prove the accuracy of presented theorems. The proposed method can be successfully used to calculate the volume of different 3D models, including objects of biomedical origin.

KEYWORDS

Beta Function, Bézier Surfaces, Integral, Volume

1. INTRODUCTION

Determining the volume of three-dimensional surface can be a very complex task, depending on the object's construction method. There are different ways a 3D model of an object can be described. Most commonly used approaches are approximation by primitives, polygonal mesh approximation or use of parametrical surfaces [Sun13a, Wro06a]. work [Sis09a] a method of volume estimation for objects bounded by Bézier surfaces.

While different methods exist for model construction, it should be noted that parametric surfaces have a significant role in 3D modeling of complex objects, because they can describe curved models with high precision. At the same time, the problem of precise volume calculation can be very critical in many areas. For example, precise volume calculation of biomedical objects can significantly increase the accuracy and reliability of medical diagnosis. Therefore, the use of a precise model and its volume estimation can have a significant impact on biomedical engineering. Authors previous work [Sis09a] describes a volume estimation method for models of biomedical objects bounded by Bézier surfaces. The method was based on surface integrals of scalar fields.

In this paper, an approach for calculating the volume of three-dimensional objects described by Bézier surfaces is proposed. 3D models of biomedical origin are considered as the object of study, but the proposed method can be used on any model that is described by Bézier surfaces.

2. OBJECT OF STUDY

The data for the research is acquired from Computer Tomography (CT) scans of a human head. The scans were processed and a pathological zone or Region of Interest (ROI) was found on each slice. Then this information was used to construct a 3D model of a pathological zone in brain tissue (Figure 1).

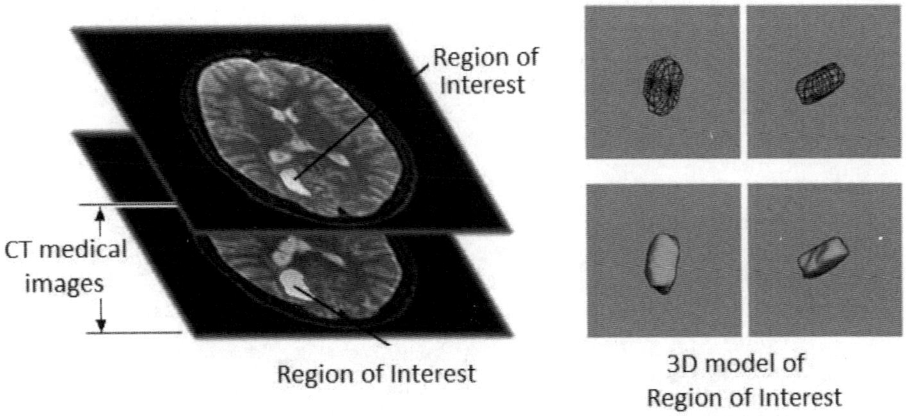

Figure 1. Research Object – a 3D Model of a Pathological Zone (ROI) in Brain Tissue

The acquired 3D model was described using Bézier surface. The approach for constructing the 3D model can be found in [Sis09a].

2.1 Definition

Bézier surfaces can be described in mathematical form as a tensor multiplication [Rog90b]:

$$S(u,v)=\sum_{i=0}^{n}\sum_{j=0}^{m} p_{i,j}\cdot b_{i,n}(u)\cdot b_{j,m}(v) \tag{1}$$

where: $p_{i,j}=(x_{ij};\ \ y_{ij};\ \ z_{ij})$ – array of control points.

Bernstein polynomials (1) can be acquired from the following binomial equations:

$$b_{i,n}(u)=\binom{n}{i}\cdot u^{i}\cdot(1-u)^{n-i}=\frac{n!}{i!\cdot(n-i)!}\cdot u^{i}\cdot(1-u)^{n-i} \tag{2}$$

Bernstein polynomial derivative can be calculated as follows:

$$\frac{db_{i,n}(u)}{du}=\begin{cases} -n\cdot(1-u)^{n-1}; & i=0 \\ \dfrac{i-n\cdot u}{u\cdot(1-u)}\cdot b_{i,n}(u); & i\in[1;3n-1] \\ n\cdot u^{n-1}; & i=3n \end{cases} \tag{3}$$

A normal vector to the vertex of Bézier surface and module (length) of the vector can be found using the following equations:

$$\vec{n}=(A\quad B\quad C)\text{ and }|\vec{n}|=\sqrt{A^{2}+B^{2}+C^{2}} \tag{4}$$

where:

$$A=\begin{vmatrix} \dfrac{\partial S_Y(u,v)}{\partial u} & \dfrac{\partial S_Z(u,v)}{\partial u} \\ \dfrac{\partial S_Y(u,v)}{\partial v} & \dfrac{\partial S_Z(u,v)}{\partial v} \end{vmatrix};\ B=\begin{vmatrix} \dfrac{\partial S_Z(u,v)}{\partial u} & \dfrac{\partial S_X(u,v)}{\partial u} \\ \dfrac{\partial S_Z(u,v)}{\partial v} & \dfrac{\partial S_X(u,v)}{\partial v} \end{vmatrix};\ C=\begin{vmatrix} \dfrac{\partial S_X(u,v)}{\partial u} & \dfrac{\partial S_Y(u,v)}{\partial u} \\ \dfrac{\partial S_X(u,v)}{\partial v} & \dfrac{\partial S_Y(u,v)}{\partial v} \end{vmatrix}. \tag{5}$$

3. PROPOSED METHOD OF VOLUME CALCULATION

One of the most actual problems in object analysis is the calculation of object's volume. In this work, a method is proposed that allows to calculate the volume of the object using integral calculations. Input data for the method is a 3D object that is described with a set of Bézier surfaces. This set can be described as an array of surfaces $S(u,v)$. Assuming, that the object's volume is the sum of curved objects volume:

$$V_{obj} = \sum V_{element} \quad (6)$$

where: V_{obj} – object's volume;

$V_{element}$ – curved object's volume.

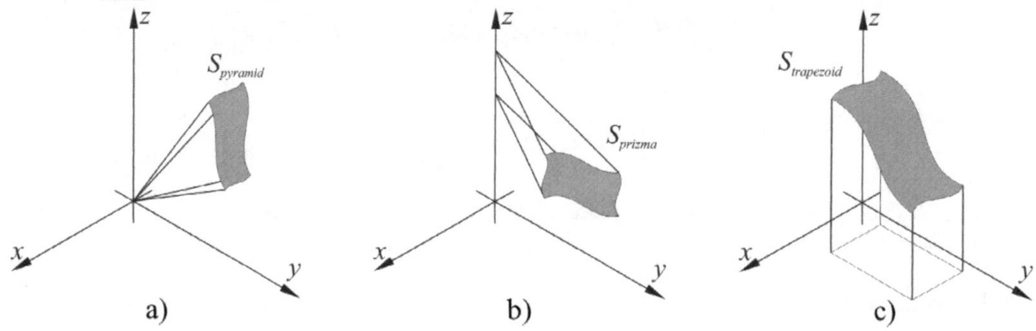

Figure 2. Examples of Curved Objects

3.1 Limitations of the Proposed Method

The proposed method has limitations in practical application that are connected to the form of the object's surface. Let's observe several examples, shown on figure 3. Figure 3 shows examples of surfaces (the side view), normal vectors at random points, and a set of the object's points projected on coordinate system axis. In the case shown on Figure 3a, the computed volume V_1 has a positive value. If the normal vectors would point to opposite directions, the volume V_1 will be negative. In the case shown on Figure 3b the surface has a self-crossing point (loop). In this case, part of the object's volume, computed by using a set of surface points has an opposite sign (V_1<0 and V_2>0). As seen from Figure 3c, when self-crossing is involved, this problem always appears despite the chosen projection method. Thus, the proposed method of volume estimation gives an incorrect result, because the final volume is the algebraic sum of partial volumes V_1, V_2, …, etc. This problem could be solved by dividing the surface into an equivalent set of surfaces without loops. In this case, some of these new surfaces should be investigated in terms of changing the normal vector directions, so the new model would correspond to the modelled object.

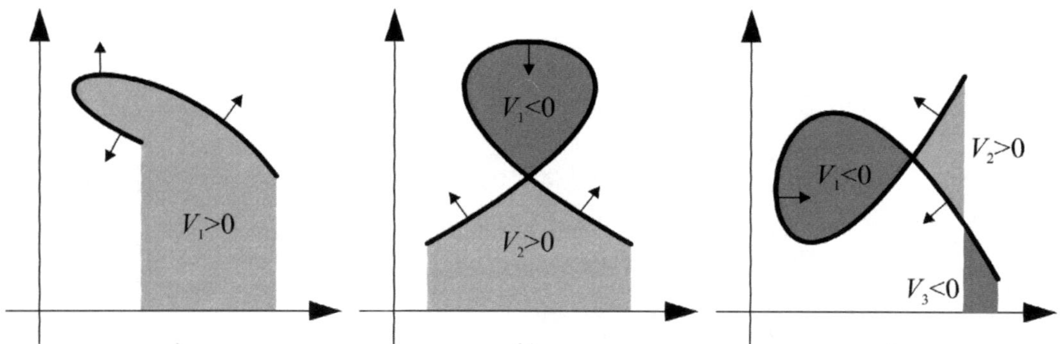

Figure 3. Examples of Surfaces

3.2 Theorem 1

The volume of curved pyramid that is constructed by projecting rays from the set of Bézier surface vertices to the coordinate system's origin may be calculated as follows:

$$V_{pyramid} = \frac{1}{3} \cdot \sum_{i1=0}^{n} \sum_{j1=0}^{m} \sum_{i2=0}^{n} \sum_{j2=0}^{m} \sum_{i3=0}^{n} \sum_{j3=0}^{m} T(i1, i2, i3, u) \cdot T(j1, j2, j3, v) \cdot \det(M), \tag{7}$$

where:

$$T(i1, i2, i3, u) = \begin{cases} -\frac{1}{3}, & i4 = 0 \\ f(i1.i2.i3, n) & i4 \in [1;\ \ 3 \cdot n - 1], \\ \frac{1}{3} & i4 = 3 \cdot n \end{cases} \tag{8}$$

where: $i4 = i1 + i2 + i3$;

$$f(i1.i2.i3, n) = \binom{n}{i1} \cdot \binom{n}{i2} \cdot \binom{n}{i3} \cdot \frac{(i4-1)! \cdot (3n - i4 - 1)!}{(3n-1)!} \cdot \left[i2 - \frac{i4}{3} \right], \tag{9}$$

and:

$$M = \begin{pmatrix} x_{i1,j1} & y_{i1,j1} & z_{i1,j1} \\ x_{i2,j2} & y_{i2,j2} & z_{i2,j2} \\ x_{i3,j3} & y_{i3,j3} & z_{i3,j3} \end{pmatrix} \tag{10}$$

An example of the curved pyramid is shown on Figure 2a.

3.3 Theorem 2

The volume of curved prism, that is constructed by projecting rays from the set of Bézier surface vertices on the coordinate system's axis may be calculated as follows [Sis2013a]:

$$V_{prizma} = \frac{1}{2} \cdot \sum_{i1=0}^{n} \sum_{j1=0}^{m} \sum_{i2=0}^{n} \sum_{j2=0}^{m} \sum_{i3=0}^{n} \sum_{j3=0}^{m} T(i1, i2, i3, u) \cdot T(j1, j2, j3, v) \cdot \det(M), \tag{11}$$

The value of matrix M depends on the axis that is used for projecting and constructing the curved prism. When using axis *Ox* matrix M takes the following form:

$$M = M_{OX} = \begin{pmatrix} 0 & y_{i1,j1} & z_{i1,j1} \\ x_{i2,j2} & y_{i2,j2} & z_{i2,j2} \\ x_{i3,j3} & y_{i3,j3} & z_{i3,j3} \end{pmatrix}. \tag{12}$$

Analogically, when projecting on axis *Oy* matrix M takes the following form:

$$M = M_{OY} = \begin{pmatrix} x_{i1,j1} & 0 & z_{i1,j1} \\ x_{i2,j2} & y_{i2,j2} & z_{i2,j2} \\ x_{i3,j3} & y_{i3,j3} & z_{i3,j3} \end{pmatrix}, \tag{13}$$

Finally, when projecting on axis *Oz*:

$$M = M_{OZ} = \begin{pmatrix} x_{i1,j1} & y_{i1,j1} & 0 \\ x_{i2,j2} & y_{i2,j2} & z_{i2,j2} \\ x_{i3,j3} & y_{i3,j3} & z_{i3,j3} \end{pmatrix}. \tag{14}$$

An example of the curved prism is shown on Figure 2b.

3.4 Theorem 3

The volume of curved trapezoidal prism, constructed by projecting rays from the set of Bézier surface vertices on the coordinate system plane can be calculated as follows:

$$V_{trapezoid} = \sum_{i1=0}^{n}\sum_{j1=0}^{m}\sum_{i2=0}^{n}\sum_{j2=0}^{m}\sum_{i3=0}^{n}\sum_{j3=0}^{m} T(i1,i2,i3,u)\cdot T(j1,j2,j3,v)\cdot \det(M), \qquad (15)$$

The value of matrix M depends on the plane that is used for projecting and constructing the trapezoidal prism. When projecting on plane *xOy* matrix M takes the following form:

$$M = M_{XOY} = \begin{pmatrix} 0 & 0 & z_{i1,j1} \\ x_{i2,j2} & y_{i2,j2} & z_{i2,j2} \\ x_{i3,j3} & y_{i3,j3} & z_{i3,j3} \end{pmatrix}, \qquad (16)$$

Analogically, when projecting on plane *xOz* matrix M takes the following form:

$$M = M_{XOZ} = \begin{pmatrix} 0 & y_{i1,j1} & 0 \\ x_{i2,j2} & y_{i2,j2} & z_{i2,j2} \\ x_{i3,j3} & y_{i3,j3} & z_{i3,j3} \end{pmatrix}, \qquad (17)$$

Finally, when projecting on plane *yOz*:

$$M = M_{YOZ} = \begin{pmatrix} x_{i1,j1} & 0 & 0 \\ x_{i2,j2} & y_{i2,j2} & z_{i2,j2} \\ x_{i3,j3} & y_{i3,j3} & z_{i3,j3} \end{pmatrix}. \qquad (18)$$

An example of curved trapezoidal prism is shown on Figure 2c.

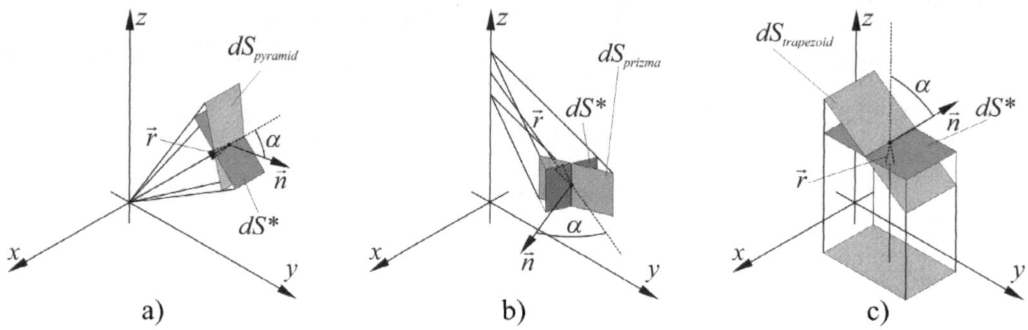

Figure 4. Differential Volume Estimation

3.5 Proof 1

In order to calculate the curved pyramid's volume the example from Figure 2a is considered. First, the differential volume $dV_{pyramid}$ must be found. Figure 4.a. illustrates this task. It is evident, that if the vector $\vec{r}$ is perpendicular to dS^* the differential volume can be calculated as follows:

$$dV_{pyramid} = \frac{1}{3}\cdot|\vec{r}|\cdot dS^* \qquad (19)$$

where: $\vec{r}$ – radius-vector from point (0; 0; 0) to surface vertex.

Taking into account that infinitely small values are used in calculations, it may be assumed that the following equation may be used:

$$dS^* = \cos\alpha \cdot dS_{pyramid} \qquad (20)$$

where: α – angle between vector $\vec{r}$ and normal $\vec{n}$ to $dS_{pyramid}$.

By substituting values from (20) and (19) and by integrating the equation the following can be acquired:

$$V_{pyramid} = \frac{1}{3} \cdot \iint_{(S_{pyramid})} |\vec{r}| \cdot \cos\alpha \cdot dS_{pyramid} \tag{21}$$

By converting (21) to double integral using the properties of surface integrals of scalar fields:

$$V_{pyramid} = \frac{1}{3} \cdot \int_0^1 \int_0^1 |\vec{r}| \cdot \cos\alpha \cdot \sqrt{A^2 + B^2 + C^2}\, du dv \tag{22}$$

Now, the value of $\cos\alpha$ can be calculated as follows:

$$\cos\alpha = \frac{\vec{r} \cdot \vec{n}}{|\vec{r}| \cdot |\vec{n}|} = \frac{r_X \cdot n_X + r_Y \cdot n_Y + r_Z \cdot n_Z}{|\vec{r}| \cdot |\vec{n}|} \tag{23}$$

By inserting expressions (4) and (23) into (22), after transformations the following equation is acquired:

$$V_{pyramid} = \frac{1}{3} \cdot \int_0^1 \int_0^1 (r_X \cdot n_X + r_Y \cdot n_Y + r_Z \cdot n_Z) du dv \tag{24}$$

Vector $\vec{r}$ in case of pyramid can be described as follows:

$$\vec{r} = (S_X(u,v) \quad S_Y(u,v) \quad S_Z(u,v)) \tag{25}$$

By inserting expressions (4) and (25) into (24), after transformations the following equation is acquired:

$$V_{pyramid} = \frac{1}{3} \cdot \int_0^1 \int_0^1 (A \cdot S_X(u,v) + B \cdot S_Y(u,v) + C \cdot S_Z(u,v)) du dv \tag{26}$$

By inserting (1) and (3) into (5) and (26), after transformations the following equation is acquired:

$$\begin{aligned} V_{pyramid} = \frac{1}{3} \cdot \int_0^1 \int_0^1 \Bigg[& \left(\sum_{i1=0}^{n} \sum_{j1=0}^{m} \sum_{i2=0}^{n} \sum_{j2=0}^{m} \sum_{i3=0}^{n} \sum_{j3=0}^{m} x_{i1,j1} \cdot y_{i2,j2} \cdot z_{i3,j3} \cdot f(u,v) \right) - \\ & - \left(\sum_{i1=0}^{n} \sum_{j1=0}^{m} \sum_{i2=0}^{n} \sum_{j2=0}^{m} \sum_{i3=0}^{n} \sum_{j3=0}^{m} x_{i1,j1} \cdot z_{i2,j2} \cdot y_{i3,j3} \cdot f(u,v) \right) + \\ & + \left(\sum_{i1=0}^{n} \sum_{j1=0}^{m} \sum_{i2=0}^{n} \sum_{j2=0}^{m} \sum_{i3=0}^{n} \sum_{j3=0}^{m} y_{i1,j1} \cdot z_{i2,j2} \cdot x_{i3,j3} \cdot f(u,v) \right) - \\ & - \left(\sum_{i1=0}^{n} \sum_{j1=0}^{m} \sum_{i2=0}^{n} \sum_{j2=0}^{m} \sum_{i3=0}^{n} \sum_{j3=0}^{m} y_{i1,j1} \cdot x_{i2,j2} \cdot x_{i3,j3} \cdot f(u,v) \right) + \\ & + \left(\sum_{i1=0}^{n} \sum_{j1=0}^{m} \sum_{i2=0}^{n} \sum_{j2=0}^{m} \sum_{i3=0}^{n} \sum_{j3=0}^{m} z_{i1,j1} \cdot x_{i2,j2} \cdot y_{i3,j3} \cdot f(u,v) \right) - \\ & - \left(\sum_{i1=0}^{n} \sum_{j1=0}^{m} \sum_{i2=0}^{n} \sum_{j2=0}^{m} \sum_{i3=0}^{n} \sum_{j3=0}^{m} z_{i1,j1} \cdot y_{i2,j2} \cdot x_{i3,j3} \cdot f(u,v) \right) \Bigg] du dv \end{aligned} \tag{27}$$

where:

$$f(u,v) = b_{i1,n}(u) \cdot \frac{db_{i2,n}(u)}{du} \cdot b_{i3,n}(u) \cdot b_{j1,m}(v) \cdot b_{j2,m}(v) \cdot \frac{db_{j3,m}(v)}{dv}; \tag{28}$$

By summing the series (27) after transformations the volume integral value, given in (5) can be obtained. Wherein:

$$T(i1,i2,i3,u)=\int_0^1 b_{i1,n}(u)\cdot\frac{db_{i2,n}(u)}{du}\cdot b_{i3,n}(u)du \quad (29)$$

$$T(j1,j2,j3,v)=\int_0^1 b_{j1,m}(v)\cdot b_{j2,m}(v)\cdot\frac{db_{j3,m}(v)}{dv}dv \quad (30)$$

Value of matrix M is given in (8). Values of equations (29) and (30) are considered in section Proof 4.

3.6 Proof 2

In order to calculate the curved prism volume, the example in Figure 2b is considered. First, the curved prism differential volume dV_{prizma} must be found. Figure 4.b. illustrates this task. It is evident, that if the vector $\vec{r}$ is perpendicular to dS^* the differential volume can be calculated as follows:

$$dV_{prizma}=\frac{1}{2}\cdot|\vec{r}|\cdot dS^* \quad (31)$$

where: $\vec{r}$ – perpendicular vector from axis Oz to surface vertex.

Analogically to Proof 1, equations (19) – (24), it is necessary to assume the value of vector $\vec{r}$ for the considered case:

$$\vec{r}=(S_X(u,v) \quad S_Y(u,v) \quad 0) \quad (32)$$

In this case, the volume integral takes the following form:

$$V_{prizma}=\frac{1}{2}\cdot\int_0^1\int_0^1(A\cdot S_X(u,v)+B\cdot S_Y(u,v))dudv \quad (33)$$

By inserting formulas (1) and (3) into (5) and (33), after the transformations the volume integral, given in (11) may be acquired. The value of matrix M for this case is described in (14). Wherein the formulas (29) and (30) remain unaffected in case of curved prism.

It is evident, that analogically, by projecting to axis Oy or Oz the truth of (12) and (13) can be proven.

3.7 Proof 3

In order to calculate the volume of trapezoidal prism, the example shown on Figure 2c is considered. First, the curved trapezoidal prism differential volume $dV_{trpezoid}$ must be found. Figure 4.c. illustrates this task. It is evident, that if the vector $\vec{r}$ is perpendicular to dS^* the differential volume can be calculated as follows:

$$dV_{trapezoid}=|\vec{r}|\cdot dS^* \quad (34)$$

where: $\vec{r}$ – perpendicular vector from plane xOy to surface vertex.

Analogically to Proof 1, equations (19) – (24), it is necessary to assume the value of vector $\vec{r}$ for the considered case:

$$\vec{r}=(0 \quad 0 \quad S_Z(u,v)) \quad (35)$$

In this case, the volume integral takes the following form:

$$V_{trapezoid}=\int_0^1\int_0^1 C\cdot S_Z(u,v)dudv \quad (36)$$

By inserting formulas (1) and (3) into (22) and (36), after the transformations the volume integral, given in (15) may be acquired. The value of matrix M for this case is described in (16). Wherein the formulas (29) and (30) remain unaffected in case of curved trapezoidal prism.

It is evident, that analogically, by projecting to planes xOz or yOz the truth of (17) and (18) can be proven.

3.8 Proof 4

Taking (3) into accound, the volume integral (29) is considered for three different cases. In case of $i4\in[1;\ \ 3n-1]$ the following equation can be acquired:

$$\begin{aligned}
&\int_0^1 b_{i1,n}(u)\cdot\frac{db_{i2,n}(u)}{du}\cdot b_{i3,n}(u)du = \\
&=\binom{n}{i1}\cdot\binom{n}{i2}\cdot\binom{n}{i3}\cdot\left[i2\cdot\int_0^1 u^{i4-1}\cdot(1-u)^{3\cdot n-i4-1}du - n\cdot\int_0^1 u^{i4}\cdot(1-u)^{3\cdot n-i4-1}du\right]= \\
&=\binom{n}{i1}\cdot\binom{n}{i2}\cdot\binom{n}{i3}\cdot\left[i2\cdot B(i4;3\cdot n-i4)-n\cdot B(i4+1;3\cdot n-i4)\right]= \\
&=\binom{n}{i1}\cdot\binom{n}{i2}\cdot\binom{n}{i3}\cdot\frac{(i4-1)!\cdot(3n-i4-1)!}{(3n-1)!}\cdot\left[i2-\frac{i4}{3}\right]
\end{aligned} \tag{37}$$

$\int_0^1 u^{i4-1}\cdot(1-u)^{3\cdot n-i4-1}du$ – Euler integral of the first kind. The solution for this integral is the Beta function $B(i4;3\cdot n-i4)$.

When $i4=0$, it means that $i1=i2=i3=0$. In this case, the integral (29) takes the following form:

$$\int_0^1 b_{i1,n}(u)\cdot\frac{db_{i2,n}(u)}{du}\cdot b_{i3,n}(u)du=\left\{\frac{1}{3}\cdot(1-u)^{3\cdot n}\right\}\Bigg|_0^1=-\frac{1}{3} \tag{38}$$

When $i4=3\cdot n$, it means that $i1=i2=i3=n$. In this case, the integral (29) takes the following form:

$$\int_0^1 b_{i1,n}(u)\cdot\frac{db_{i2,n}(u)}{du}\cdot b_{i3,n}(u)du=\left\{\frac{1}{3}\cdot u^{3\cdot n}\right\}\Bigg|_0^1=\frac{1}{3} \tag{39}$$

Taking into account the results of equations (37) – (39) the integral (29) can be described as (8).

4. EXPERIMENTAL TESTS

Experiments were conducted using three examples of 3D geometric objects that were bounded by multiple Bézier surface sets: free-form cylinder (with a priori known approximate volume), a model of human head fragment and a model of a pathological zone in brain tissue. The models are shown on Figure 5. The models shown on Figure 5b and Figure 5c are acquired by using a set of images obtained by Computer Tomography and Magnetic Resonance Imaging.

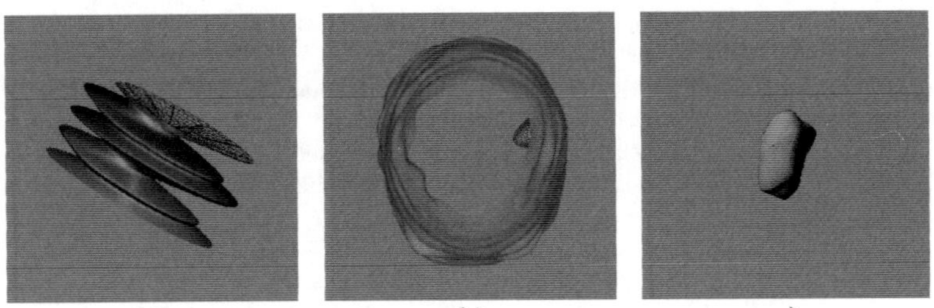

a) b) c)

Figure 5. Experimental Models

The volumes of experimental models were calculated using different volume estimation methods: the proposed method, graphic integration and Trapezoidal and Cavalieri methods [Smi06a]. The results are shown in Table 1.

Table 1. Experimental Results

Method of calculation	"Free-form cylinder"	"Human head model"	"Pathological zone model"
Calculation in analytic form	904.216,05	2.802.491,60	9.157,55
Graphic integration 10×10	904.234,59	2.802.798,76	9161,02
Graphic integration 100×100	904.216,24	2.802.494,68	9.157,58
Trapezoidal and Cavalieri method	917.364,31	2.825.806,26	9.420,89

As can be seen from the experimental results, the proposed method correctly estimates volume of all example models.

5. CONCLUSION

In this work, a method for calculating the volume of a 3D object bounded by multiple Bézier surface sets is proposed. Three different cases of volume calculations are described, based on different properties of researched models: projection of surface vertices on coordinate system origin point, axis and plane. The method is based on using method of differential geometry: surface integrals of scalar fields, Euler integral of the first kind and Beta functions. The conducted experiments prove the correctness of presented theorems. The proposed method can be successfully used to calculate the volume of different 3D models, including objects of biomedical origin.

ACKNOWLEDGEMENT

The research was supported by the National Research Programme "The next generation of information and communication technologies" (NexIT, Project 2).

REFERENCES

[Juh00a] Juhász, I. Computing Volume of Solids Bounded by Bézier Surfaces. Mathematical Notes, Miskolc, Vol. 1., No. 2., 2000, pp. 127—133.

[Lu07a] Lu, L., Choi, Y.-K., Wang, W., Kim, M.-S. Variational 3D Shape Segmentation for Bounding Volume Computation. Journal Computer Graphics Forum, Volume 26, Issue 3, 2007, pp. 329–338.

[Ras05a] Rasmussen, A.F. and Floater M.S A point-based method for estimating surface area. Electronic Proceedings of the SIAM conference on Geometric Design, Phoenix, 2005.°

[Rog90b] Rogers D.F., Adams J.A. Mathematical Elements for Computer Graphic, 2nd Ed. – Boston: McGraw-Hill, 1990. – 611 p.

[Sis09a] Sisojevs, A., Boločko, K. and Glazs, A. 3D Modeling of Free-Form Object (Interpolation, Visualization and Volume Estimation). The 17th International Conference WSCG'2009: Communication Papers Proceedings, 2009, pp. 125.-128.

[Sis13a] Sisojevs, A. An Approach of Semi-numerical Computing Volume of Solids Bounded by Rational Bézier Surfaces. Scientific Journal of RTU: Technologies of Computer Control, Nr.14, 2013, pp. 25.-31.

[Smi06a] Smitha S., Revathy K., Kesavadas C. Segmentation and Volume Estimation of Brain Tissues from MR Images. IMECS, 2006, pp 543-547

[Sun13a] Sun, F., Choi, Y.-K., Yu, Y., Wang, W. Medial meshes for volume approximation. http://dblp.uni-trier.de/db/journals/corr/corr1308.html#SunCYW13

[Wan06a] Wang, R., Zhou, K., Snyder, J., Liu, X., Bao, H., Peng, Q., Guo, B. Variational Sphere Set Approximation for Solid Objects. Journal Visual Computer, 2006, Vol. 22, Issue 9, pp. 612-621.

[Wro06a] Wronecki, J., Concept Modeling with NURBS, Polygon and Subdivision Surfaces. Proceedings of the 2006 American Society for Engineering Education Annual Conference & Exposition

A CAD MODELING METHOD FOR CAR FORM DESIGN BASED ON CE-BÉZIER

Fan Liu[1], Xiaomin Ji[2] and Lunqing Gong[1]
[1]*School of Mechanical and Precision Instrument Engineering, Xi'an University of Technology. NO.5 South Jinhua Road, Xi'an, Shaanxi, China*
[2]*School of Art and Design, Xi'an University of Technology, NO.5 South Jinhua Road, Xi'an, Shaanxi, China*

ABSTRACT

As the early stage of automobile production, the form design plays an important part for the product's success in the future market. However, the form design of a car is difficult and time-consuming because it is related to the considerations not only on aesthetics but also on engineering technology. This study proposes a parameterized CAD model used for the car form design and discusses the method to modify the model by changing some parameters. By analyzing the relationship between the sub-surfaces on the car surface, a geometry model is established for the half-car surface by 16 quadrilateral sub-surfaces. Each sub-surface is described by CE-Bézier surface. In this way, a parameterized CAD model for the half-car surface is established by taking the control points, shape parameters and trimming parameters of CE-Bézier surface as the parameters. Furthermore, the modifying methods for the CAD model are proposed by changing different kind of parameters.

KEYWORDS

Car form design, Parameterized CAD model, CE-Bézier surface, Modifying method

1. INTRODUCTION

Car's form design is related to the aesthetics and engineering technology. Usually, the aesthetics of a car's form is reflected in its visual features such as its sizes, proportions of each part and some characteristic lines in the car's appearance. While in the field of engineering technology, the study would be on the base of a physical or CAD model established only after aesthetic design stage. If the result of engineering technology study (manufacture, aerodynamics, e.g., a car with excellent modeling which have poor aerodynamic characteristics) is not so satisfied, some modifications of the model should be carried out by returning to the stage of aesthetic design. This process will probably be repeated and crossed many times. For the car's form design, a method to combine the aesthetic design with engineering technology together would be necessary and helpful. Fortunately, it is found that the CAD model of a car surface would play the connecting role to these two fields.

A car's surface is composed of several surfaces to fulfill the requirements from function, manufacture and aesthetics. As a result, the establishment and modification of a CAD model for the car surface would be difficult and time-consuming. In this paper, a parameterized CAD model used for the car's form design is proposed and the method to modify the model is presented by changing some parameters in the CAD model.

Computer Aided Geometric Design (CAGD) is the foundational technology for establishing the CAD model of automobile in industrial design (Bodein Y. et al, 2013; Liu Y. J. et al, 2011). McCormack J. et al, (2004) presented shape grammars as a method to design the front view of vehicles in the given brand language, in which dozens of rules were made to define the car face features. Fu L. T. et al, (2014) defined the characteristics of streamline styling and presented a novel approach for designing streamline-based surface features in automotive design, in which a base shape was established, and various parameters were set by users to control the outline of car body. Vieira M. and Shimada K. (2005) divided the car design into three dimensions of stylist, CAD and interpretation-emotional, to identify and extract characteristic lines, and the relationship between the characteristic lines in different automobile styles and CAD parameters was emphasized. Sußner G. et al, (2004) tried to evaluate surface quality of car body by presenting a new technique for the tessellation of trimmed surfaces. However, in recent years, the advantages of traditional parameterized surfaces such as Bézier or NURBS are difficult to reflect in design or engineering field, for the reason that the weight factor and the continuity increase the complexity of calculation (Les P. and Wayne T., 1997). In order to meet the practical requirements, a series of new modeling methods have been proposed in these years, including a few new parametric curves and surfaces, such as C-Bézier (Zhang J. W., 1996), λ-Bézier (Yan L. L. and Liang J. E., 2011), Quasi-Bézier (Chen J., 2013), H-Bézier (Qin X. Q. et al, 2014), triangular Q-Bézier (Oruc H., and Phillips G. H., 2003) and CE-Bézier (Qin X. Q. et al, 2010). However, the shape of Bézier patch can only be controlled by the control points, whose controllability is worse than CE-Bézier; and the modification for the weight of each control point of NURBS surfaces can only affect the local shape around the point, while in a CE-Bézier surface, the parameter can adjust the shape of the whole direction of u or v, which is more suitable for automotive design. After comparison, among all the methods for curves and surfaces, CE-Bézier method has the characteristics of better adjustability for curves and surface by the shape parameters, which makes the modification of the CAD model more flexible and convenient.

This study proposes a modeling and modifying method to establish parameterized CAD model for half-car surface by CE-Bézier surface. An initial parameterized CAD model is established and could be modified conveniently by adjusting some control points, shape parameters and trimming parameters of the CE-Bézier surfaces. A software plug-in is written to help the modification of the CAD model. As a result, the new designed car in the example shows that different models can be generated by different shape parameters. It would be possibly to improve the aerodynamic performance during the car's form design stage by optimizing the shape parameters according to the feedbacks from CFD simulation in the future study.

2. GEOMETRICAL AND CAD MODEL OF A HALF-CAR SURFACE

2.1 Geometrical Model

(a) Half-car surface (b) Sub-surfaces (c) Unfolded outline of sub-surfaces

Figure 1. Geometrical model for half-car surface

The entire surface of a car is symmetric. To simplify this research, half-car surface is studied in this paper. By neglecting some details such as door handle, lights, rearview mirror, grille, etc., the half-car surface would be shown as Figure 1(a) visually. It could be divided into 16 sub-surfaces mainly along the style lines and the edges of parts, shown as Figure 1(b). And with more detailed division, the amount of divided surfaces is increased, and the parts neglected can be generated, which use the same approach in this paper. Let all the adjacent surfaces be with same adjacent edges, the unfolded outline of 16 sub-surfaces is shown as Figure 1(c). This is an initial geometry model (template for short) to qualitatively describe the spatial orientations and positions of 16 sub-surfaces. In the following sections, the CAD model for half-car surface will be established by CE-Bézier and its modifying method will be described.

2.2 CAD Model

By introducing 4 additional shape parameters, CE-Bézier (cubic extension Bézier) surface provides additional controllability besides adjusting the control points. In this paper, CE-Bézier surface is used to describe the 16 sub-surfaces respectively.

For given 4×4 control points $P_{i,j}$ and shape parameters $-2\leq\alpha_u, \alpha_v, \gamma_u, \gamma_v\leq 1$, the CE-Bézier surface would be

$$Q(u,v)=\sum_{i=0}^{3}\sum_{j=0}^{3}P_{i,j}b_{i,3}(u;\alpha_u,\gamma_u)b_{j,3}(v;\alpha_v,\gamma_v) \tag{1}$$

where

$$\begin{cases} b_{0,3}(u)=(1-\alpha_u u)(1-u)^2 \\ b_{1,3}(u)=(2+\alpha_u)(1-u)^2 u \\ b_{2,3}(u)=(2+\gamma_u)u^2(1-u) \\ b_{3,3}(u)=(1-\gamma_u+\gamma_u u)u^2 \end{cases} \tag{2a}$$

$$\begin{cases} b_{0,3}(v)=(1-\alpha_v v)(1-v)^2 \\ b_{1,3}(v)=(2+\alpha_v)(1-v)^2 v \\ b_{2,3}(v)=(2+\gamma_v)v^2(1-v) \\ b_{3,3}(v)=(1-\gamma_v+\gamma_v v)v^2 \end{cases} \tag{2b}$$

are the basic functions, α_u, α_v, γ_u and γ_v are the shape parameters.

Changing 16 control points will result in the modification of CE-Bézier surface, which is same to other kinds of bi-cubic free-form surfaces. In addition, adjusting of the shape parameters α_u, γ_u, α_v, γ_v can also influence the shape of surface. Generally speaking, the surface will be far away from the control points with the shape parameters decreasing while the control points remain unchanged. That means the adjustment of surface is more flexible.

Mathematically, the geometrical model of hale-car surface in Figure 1(c) can be described by

$$S=\bigcup_{k=1}^{16}Q_k \tag{3}$$

here Q_k is the sub-surface No. k in Figure 1(c) expressed by Equation (1).

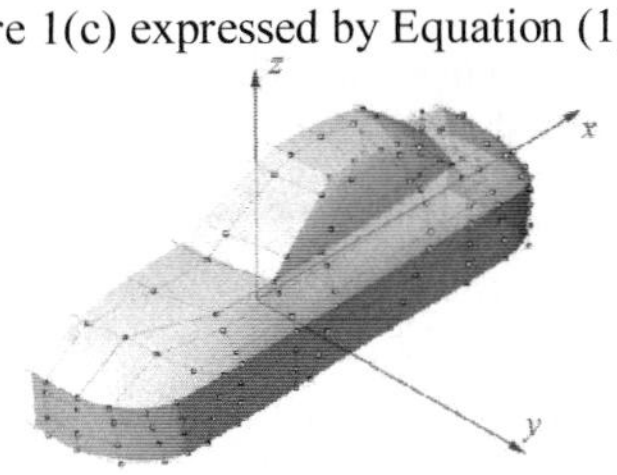

Figure 2. Parameterized CAD model for half-car surface

Let the adjacent sub-surfaces have same edge and set all the shape parameters α_u, γ_u, α_v, γ_v to be 1.0, S would be a sets of CE-Bézier sub-surfaces with G^0 continuity. In this case, S is called the initial model. In any CAD system, the initial CAD model of the half-car surface could be established easily. With different control points, the shape of the initial CAD model would be different. This is same to other kinds of bi-cubic free-form surfaces. However, when the control points remain unchanged, the surface cannot be modified according to the requirements from the viewpoints of aesthetics and engineering technology. The advantage of CE-Bézier surface lies in its modification flexibility. The total number of the control points would be 148 and the shape parameters would be 64 for the half-car surface CAD model. Figure 2 is a parameterized CAD model for the half-car surface established in Rhinoceros.

3. MODIFICATION OF CAD MODEL

Before the form design, the car's main dimensions (length, width, height) is determined according to the company's development plan and market feedback. In order to carry out the form design, a CAD model should be established. In this paper, a method to establish the model is proposed based on modifying the initial parameterized CAD model shown as Figure 1. The initial model is taken as a template and new CAD model is established by changing some parameters in the initial model. It would be much easier than modeling from beginning. The method could be described as following steps:

1. Adjusting the positions of the control points in some sub-surfaces to change the car's form style and main dimensions;
2. Adjusting the shape parameters to modify the local curvature variation for some sub-surfaces. This often might occurs in the case to improve the aerodynamic performance of the car during the early design stage;
3. Generating the transition surface and modifying the style lines (the junction lines of adjacent sub-surfaces) for the requirements of aesthetics.

The modification is carried out in a coordinate system shown as in Figure 2.

After finishing the modifications, a mirror operation is carried out to generate an entire car surface.

3.1 Changing the Main Dimensions and Form Style

3.1.1 Changing Main Dimensions

In the initial parameterized CAD model, the main dimensions of a car is defined as L_0, W_0 and H_0, respectively. From the desired dimensions (L, W and H) of a new car, the scale coefficients S_x, S_y, S_z in the directions X, Y, Z could be calculated by

$$\begin{cases} S_x = L / L_0 \\ S_y = W / W_0 \\ S_z = H / H_0 \end{cases} \tag{4}$$

By multiplying the scale coefficients with the coordinates of the control points in the initial model, the new control points could be determined. Rebuilding the model with the new control points, a new CAD model could be obtained only with the length, width, height changed. The comparison before and after changed is shown as in Table 1. Of course, the change among the sub-surfaces is uniform in this step. That might be not the desired result. In the next steps, further modification would be done.

Table 1. Comparison of changing main dimensions

Item	Length(mm)	Width(mm)	Height(mm)	CAD Model
Initial	4600	1900	1300	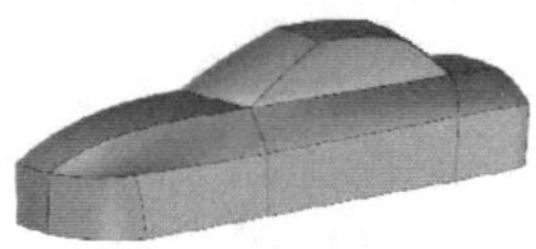
New1	4173	1883	1267	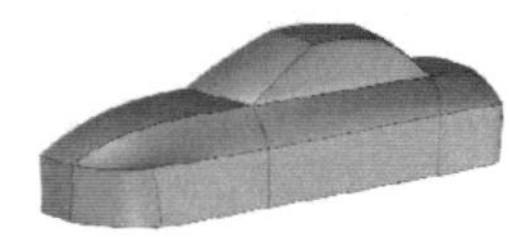

3.1.2 Changing Form Style

The car's form style is a visual and psychological experience. It can be influenced by the many factors such as the main dimensions, shape and orientation of each sub-surface, proportions between sub-surfaces, etc. In the parameterized CAD model, changing the control points could result in the modification of such factors so that the form style would be changed.

This study considers only two cases of control point. One is the coincident control points occurred in the corner point where several sub-surfaces intersected. Another is the control points for the two adjacent surfaces (edge control points). In the latter case, all the 4 control points would be changed simultaneously. It is a move operation to the 4 control points practically. As for the control points inner a single sub-surface, it is easy and not to be considered in this paper.

Table 2. Comparison of changing control points

Item	$p^{(2)}_{0,0}$	$p^{(2)}_{0,1}$	$p^{(2)}_{1,0}$	$p^{(2)}_{2,0}$	$p^{(2)}_{3,0}$	$p^{(2)}_{3,1}$	CAD Model
Initial	23,348,481	7,117,481	455,348,762	1010,588,829	1564,588,829	1364,231,882	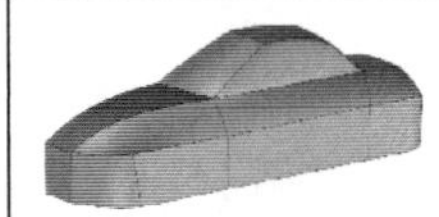
New2	23,527,297	1,176,290	161,611,650	681,784,691	1266,818,756	1157,280,760	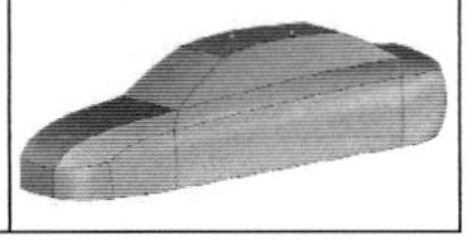

Table 2 shows an example of this case, in which the modification of the control points of the bonnet changes the styling of the bonnet, and then alters the whole car style. The number in parentheses represents the serial number of the sub-surface in Figure 1 (c).

3.2 Changing the Local Shape of Single Sub-Surface

Table 3. Comparison of changing shape parameters

Item	$\alpha^{(2)}_u$	$\gamma^{(2)}_u$	$\alpha^{(2)}_v$	$\gamma^{(2)}_v$	CAD Model
Initial	1.00	1.00	0.90	0.90	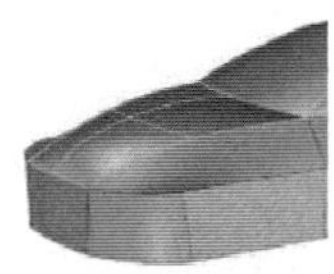
New3	0.10	0.10	-0.10	-0.10	

The local shape of any single sub-surface could be modified by adjusting its shape parameters. Usually this kind of modification is slight and mainly used to adjust the local curvature of the surface. Table 3 shows the shape adjusting for the area of bonnet. By modifying the shape parameters α_u, γ_u, α_v, and γ_v, the surface of bonnet becomes flatter and be far away from the control points.

3.3 Changing the Junction Line of Surfaces

The initial parameterized CAD model is of G^0 continuity. After the modifications described above, the continuity is not changed. In the practice, G^1 continuity might be expected for some adjacent sub-surfaces from the viewpoints of aesthetics or aerodynamics. In this case, further modification should be carried out. Mathematically, it is to modify adjacent sub-surfaces from G^0 to G^1 continuity. While in visual, the junction line of two adjacent sub-surfaces usually gives the impression of car's style line. Therefore, this kind of modification can be viewed as changing the junction line of two adjacent sub-surfaces. Comparing with the modifications described above, this is some little complex. The algorithm is described as follows:

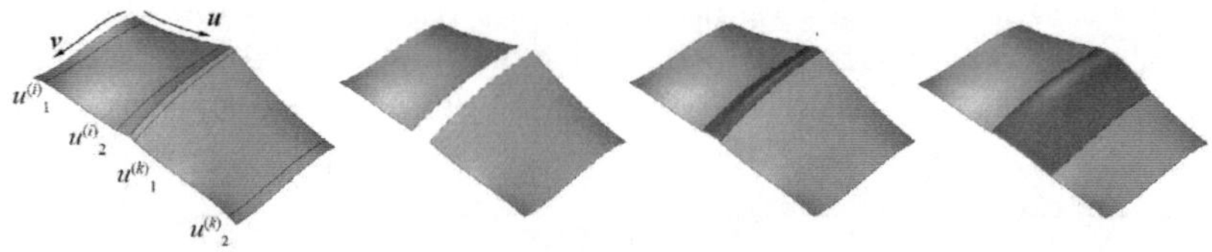

(a) G0 adjacent sub-surfaces (b) Trimming (c) Transition surface (d) Adjusting trimming parameter

Figure 3. Generating transition surface

1. Trimming two adjacent sub-surfaces along the direction of adjacent line, see Figure 3(a). Here u(i)1, u(i)2, u(k)1 and u(k)2 are called trimming parameters, i and k are the different serial number of the sub-surface in Figure 1 (c). Then a blank space is left, see Figure 3(b). This area would be filled by an additional 4×4 CE-Bézier surface (called transition surface in this paper) and the transition surface is required G1 continuous with the two trimmed sub-surfaces simultaneously.
2. By setting 4 shape parameters for the transition surface, the 16 control points could be calculated based on G1 continuity constraint.
3. Generating the transition surface according to the 16 control points and 4 shape parameters, see Figure 5(c).
4. Adjusting the trimming parameter to modify the according to the 16 control points and 4 shape parameters, see Figure 3(d).

Table 3. Comparison of changing trimming parameters

Item	$u^{(2)}_1$	$u^{(2)}_2$	$v^{(2)}_1$	$u^{(2)}_2$	$u^{(11)}_1$	$u^{(11)}_2$	$v^{(11)}_1$	$u^{(11)}_2$	CAD Model
Initial	0.05	0.95	0.05	0.95	0.05	0.95	0.05	0.95	
New4	0.05	0.80	0.05	0.05	0.20	0.95	0.05	0.05	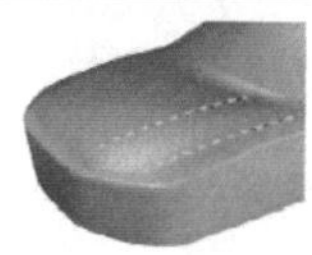

Table 3 gives an example for the junction line modification. The junction line between bonnet (No.2 in Figure 1(c)) and front fender (No.11 in Figure 1(c)) is modified by adjusting the trimming parameter $u^{(2)}_2$ of bonnet from 0.95 to 0.80 and $u^{(11)}_1$ of front fender from 0.05 to 0.20. Curvature radius of the transition surface is increased and the junction line became rounder. On the contrary, the junction line of these two surfaces would be sharper and obvious in visual. And when the parameters in same direction of the 2 surfaces are set as 0 and 1 respectively, the 2 surfaces are G^0 continuous.

4. SOFTWARE TOOL FOR CAR FORM DESIGN

A software plug-in is written by using Grasshopper (a plug-in program to generate 3D model by program algorithm running in Rhinoceros environment) in this paper to help the modification of the CAD model. It runs as a plug-in for the software Rhinoceros 5.0 and the user interface is designed by Rhinoscript. All the parameters adjusting in the form of slider for the convenience and intuition in operation. All of the control points and additional parameters are in their default values in the beginning, and the user can determine which should be adjusted according to the design goal. With the help of this software, an expected CAD model for a new car could be generated by modifying the initial parameterized CAD model step by step. The process and corresponding interfaces are shown as Figure 4.

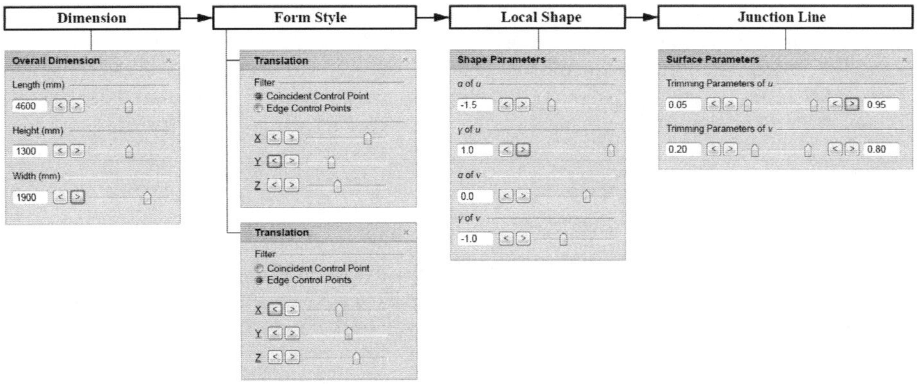

Figure 4. Software process and interfaces

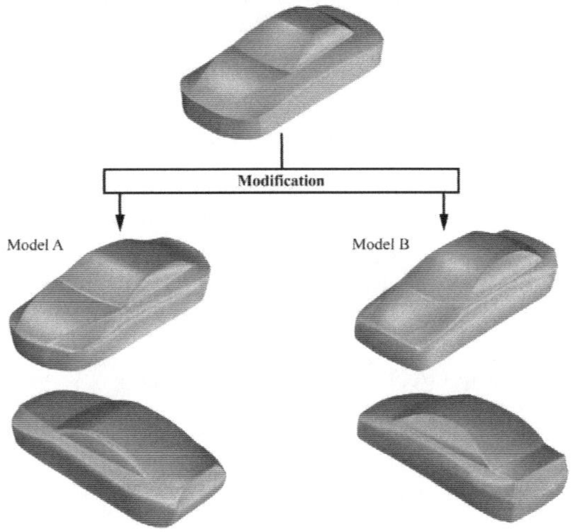

Figure 5. Examples

Two examples are given in Figure 5, in which the initial template evolves into various final styling, model A and model B. The streamline modeling of model A is more modern, while the model B is more traditional and discreet, however, they all have the same surface distribution structure in geometry view and the same data structure in CAD view. Besides, in the future study the parameters can be modified automatically according to the feedback from CFD system, to pursuit excellent aerodynamic characteristics.

5. CONCLUSIONS AND FUTURE WORK

Some conclusions could be summarized as follows:

1) The initial parameterized CAD model of the car surface is feasible and effective to generate different appearance of car during the early form design stage.
2) CE-Bézier surfaces is ideal for describing the car's surface due to its flexibility for surface modification. A CE-Bézier surface is the fundamental composing element for the entire car surface model. By adjusting the 16 control points, 4 shape parameters or 4 trimming parameters for related surface, the car surface can be modified as required.
3) The software plug-in based on the proposed method is a helpful tool for the modification of the car's CAD model in Rhinoceros. In the software, the parameters are adjusted in the form of sliders. The operation is convenient and intuitive.

In the future studies, the method proposed in this paper will be compared with CFD. Some relationships between the parameters in the CAD model and aerodynamic resistance would possibly be established by simulating the aerodynamic performance of the car's CAD model. Furthermore, the car's appearance with optimal aerodynamic performance could be obtained. Of course, some factors in aesthetics should be taken into account at the same time.

ACKNOWLEDGEMENT

The authors are grateful to the reference for their helpful suggestions and comments which have improved the paper. This work is supported by the Nation Natural Science Foundation of China (nos.51305344) and Postgraduate Training Project (2016) of Xi'an University of Technology.

REFERENCES

Book

Les P. and Wayne T., 1997. *The NURBS Book (the second edition)*. Springer, New York, USA.

Journal

Bodein Y. et al, 2013. A Roadmap for Parametric CAD Efficiency in the Automotive Industry. *Computer-Aided Design*, Vol. 45, No. 10, pp. 1198-1214.

Liu Y. J. et al, 2011. Industrial Design Using Interpolatory Discrete Developable Surfaces. *Computer-Aided Design*, Vol. 43, No. 9, pp. 1089-1098.

McCormack J. et al, 2004. Speaking the Buick Language: Capturing, Understanding, and Exploring Brand Identity with Shape Grammars. *Design Studies*, Vol. 25, No. 1. pp. 1-29.

Fu L. T. et al, 2014. Modeling Flow Features with User-guided Streamline Parameterization. *Computer-Aided Design*, Vol. 46, pp. 263–268.

Vieira M. and Shimada K., 2005. Surface Mesh Segmentation and Smooth Surface Extraction Through Region Growing. *Computer Aided Geometric Design,* Vol. 22, No. 8, pp. 771-792.

Sußner G. et al, 2004. Interactive Examination of Surface Quality on Car Bodies. *Computer-Aided Design*, Vol. 36, No. 5, pp. 425-436.

Zhang J. W., 1996. C-curves: an Extension of Cubic Curves. *Computer Aided Geometric Design*, Vol. 13, No. 3, pp. 199-217.

Yan L. L. and Liang J. E., 2011. An Extension of the Bézier Model. *Applied Mathematics and Computation*, Vol. 218, No. 6, pp. 2863-2879.

Hu G. et al, 2015. Shape Modification for λ-Bézier Curves Based on Constrained Optimization of Position and Tangent Vector. *Mathematical Problems in Engineering*, Vol. 2015.

Hu G. et al, 2016. Approximate Multidegree Reduction of λ-Bézier Curves. *Mathematical Problems in Engineering*, Vol. 2016.

Chen J., 2013. Quasi-Bézier Curves with Shape Parameters. *Journal of Applied Mathematics*, Vol. 2013.

Qin X. Q. et al, 2014. Construction of PH Splines Based on H-Bézier Curves. *Applied Mathematics and Computation*, Vol. 238, pp. 460–467.

Oruc H., and Phillips G. H., 2003. q-Bernstein Polynomials and Bézier Curves. *Journal of Computational and Applied Mathematics*, Vol. 151, No. 1, pp. 1-12.

Qin X. Q. et al, 2010. Geometric Design and Adjustment of Shape for Developable CE-Bézier Surfaces. *Journal of Xi'an Jiaotong University (in Chinese)*, Vol. 44, No. 3, pp. 47-51.

EVOLUTIONARY GENERATION OF 3D SHAPE MODELS

Satoshi Yonemoto and Masaya Sugawa
Graduate School of Information Science, Kyushu Sangyo University, Japan

ABSTRACT

We introduce a method for generating evolutionary 3D shape models. Given several initial models and the initial model's content ratio, our method generates novel and plausible 3D shapes. Our method is based on evolutionary computation (genetic algorithm). Our model consists of several parts defined by a structure graph. In the evolutionary operations, two-step crossover and mutation are executed. In part crossover, type of parts may be exchanged. Properties such as scale or detailed shape are usually inherited from the parents. In mutation, a new type of part which does not exist in the initial models can be appeared. We demonstrate the effectiveness of our evolutionary generation of 3D shapes, which reflects a user's intention and takes diversity of 3D shapes into account simultaneously.

KEYWORDS

Evolutionary computation, 3D shape modeling, part crossover and genetic algorithm

1. INTRODUCTION

Automatic 3D model generation remains challenging. Recently, many procedural generation techniques such as terrain texture synthesis or 3D character modeling are proposed (Sims, 1991) (Smelik, 2009) (Merrell, 2011) (Guo, 2014). This approach is expected to grow from now on. On the other hand, as a semi-automatic way, evolutionary design systems based on interactive evolutionary computation (IEC) have been developed (Bentley, 1999). The IEC is a generic approach, so it is used for various contents creation tasks. For example, in related work (Nishino, 2001), IEC is introduced to efficiently support a process of users' new 3D geometric shape creation in early design stage. However, in the IEC, the fitness function must be provided by a user his/herself. Therefore, this approach takes much time to input user preferences.

Our goal is to develop an evolutionary 3D shape model generation method, which reflects a user's intention and takes diversity of shape models into account simultaneously. Xu et al. (Xu, 2012) propose mixing model parts using a genetic algorithm to evolve original shape variations. According to advance research by Xu et al., mixing different shape models is usually seen as evolution of shape. The generated models do not necessarily reflect a user's intention but, various interesting models can be generated. It is notable that part crossover algorithm is proposed. Part crossover in our work refers to this idea. Kalogerakis et al. (Kalogerakis, 2012) also propose a new shape synthesis method by mixing existing shapes. Unlike evolutionary approach, probabilistic model is designed to represent the structure class of shapes. Given 100 training models, this method can synthesis roughly 100 new shape models. It is interesting to note that the generation rules are automatically acquired from initial models.

Figure 1 shows our framework with evolutionary 3D shape model generation. First, user prepares several initial models. The initial models are equivalent to shape resources. User expects mixing the initial models and creating mashup models. In initial set generation stage, their initial models are assigned as a member of the individuals, and the rest individuals are randomly selected from model database. Selection process is based on the initial model's content ratio user defined. In crossover, first, part crossover between two individuals selected as parents is executed. Next, property crossover is executed, where their properties such as scale or shape may be exchanged. That is, this exchange is applied at the genetic code level. Part evolution (or degeneration) is gradually executed. In mutation, type of parts or some of the properties may be exchanged at the genetic code level. The generated models are picked up by user, and then they are displayed in a model gallery.

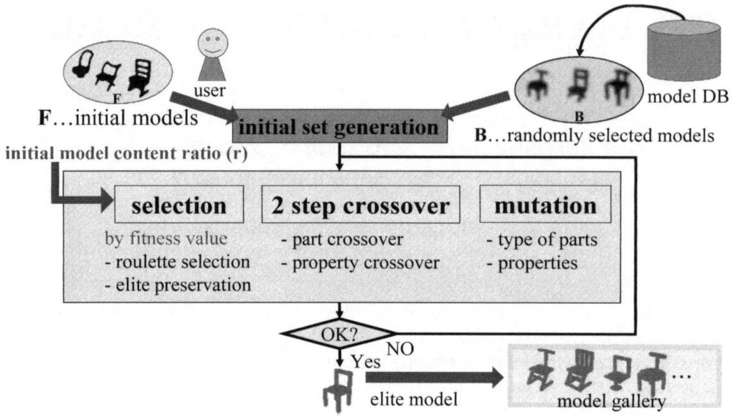

Figure 1. Our framework for evolutionary 3D shape model generation

2. 3D SHAPE MODEL

2.1 Structure Graph

In our work, 3D shape model consists of one or more parts. The parts configuration is defined as a structure graph (Zheng, 2013) (Huang, 2016) (Liu, 2015). Their parts are strongly connected. Each part is represented by grouping several shape primitives (i.e., a sub graph). Figure 2 illustrates an example of a structure graph 'chair'. In this case, the graph consists of three nodes, and it has two edges. This means that the seat surface (p_1) and the leg part (p_2) are securely connected and similarly, the seat surface and the backrest (p_3) are securely connected. However, each part (the sub graph) can be replaced by evolutionary operations such as crossover or mutation.

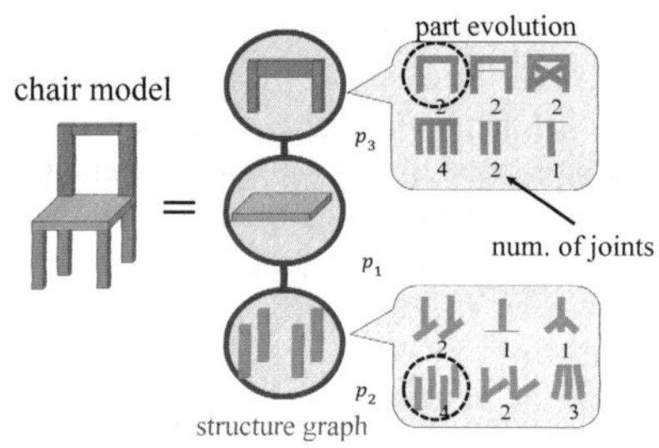

Figure 2. An example of structure graph. Each part can be replaced with the different type of parts

2.2 Shape Primitive

Shape primitive is used to construct a part. Shape primitive is represented by generalized cylinder. This model enables bending or side surface shape deformation (as necessary). The side surface shape can be represented by several curve segments. Figure 3 illustrates typical shape variations of shape primitive (bending) and parts connection. The part model is represented by grouping several shape primitives. The shape primitive has several joints (pins) to connect with the other primitive. That is, shape complexity with part model is characterized by such joint properties.

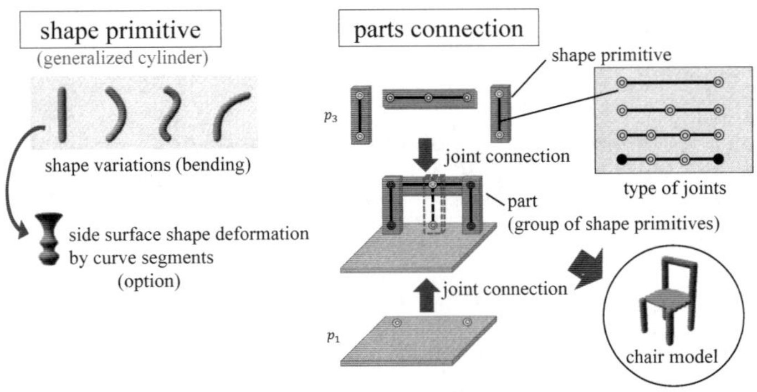

Figure 3. Shape primitive and parts connection. The part model consists of several shape primitives

3. EVOLUTIONARY GENERATION

3.1 Initial Set Generation

Initial set consists of initial models F and the other models B randomly selected from model database. Initial models are prepared by user. Adding to the initial set, new models reflecting a user's intention can be generated. Figure 4 shows an example of initial set which consists of five individuals. This set includes three initial models (user defined) and two unrelated models (randomly selected). Based on the initial models and the initial model's content ratio r, new models are generated by subsequent evolutionary operations.

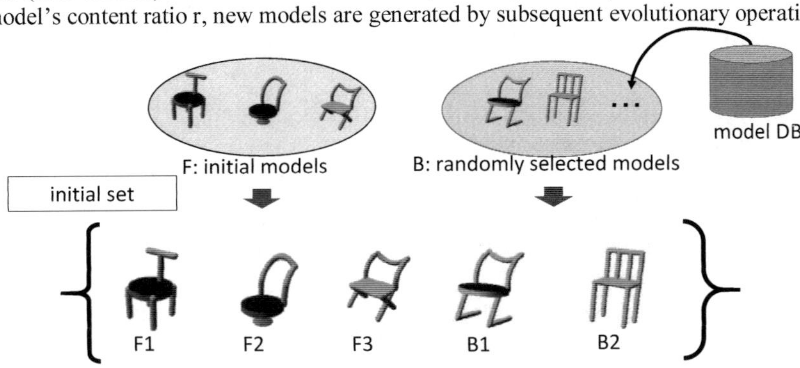

Figure 4. An example of initial set. The initial models $\{F_1, F_2, F_3\}$ are included

3.2 Two-step Crossover

Our approach adopts two-step crossover: part crossover and property crossover. First, part crossover is executed, and next, property crossover is executed. Figure 5 illustrates our crossover for a chair model. In part crossover, from parent *A* and *B*, child *C* and *D* are created (that is, *A* and *B* are replaced by *C* and *D*). The child *C* has *B*'s seat backrest, *A*'s leg part and *A*'s seat surface. The child *D* has *A*'s seat backrest, *B*'s leg part and *B*'s seat surface. In property crossover, their properties such as scale or shape may be exchanged (finally child *C'* and *D'* are generated). Changing parts connection results in another primitive addition. This exchange is applied at the genetic code level. Of course, the sub graph constituting the part is modified at the timing.

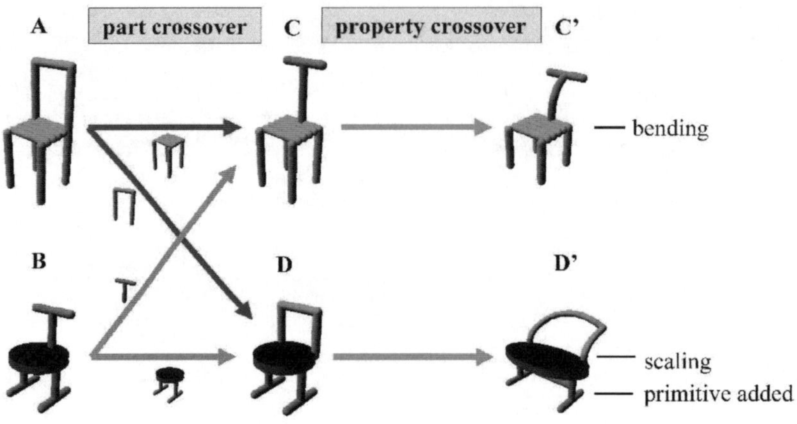

Figure 5. Two-step crossover. Part crossover and property crossover are executed

3.3 Fitness

To succeed the nature of initial models, the content ratio r is used as fitness value. This means that advanced models can be generated in accordance with the user's intention. The fitness value for individual *j* is given by the following equation 1:

$$fit(j) = Ke^{-\frac{(error(j)-(1-r))^2}{2\sigma^2}}, \ldots (1)$$

where K and σ are coefficients, and $error(j) = \frac{\sum_{k=1}^{n} min_{i\in F} d_{p_k}(i,j) + min_{i\in F}\, d_s(i,j)}{n+1}$.

The fitness calculation process is as follows (see equation 1).

1. Calculate $d_{p_k}(i,j)$, that is, *including-part dissimilarity* between initial model i and individual j.
2. Calculate scale dissimilarity $d_s(i,j)$ in the same way.
3. For each *j*, calculate $min_{i\in F} d_{p_k}(i,j)$ and $min_{i\in F}\, d_s(i,j)$.

Distance between the normalized $error(j)$ for the number of the parts and the ratio *r* indicates the fitness value. For example, if the ratio *r* is set to 0.8, individual *j* including about 80% of the parts with the same properties such as shape or scale corresponds to the elite model. Figure 6 illustrates an example of fitness calculation process. In this example, the models consist of two parts p_1 and p_2. *Including-part dissimilarity* between three initial models $\{F_1, F_2, F_3\}$ and individual *j* is calculated for each part p_k. In this example, the normalized $error(j)$ was 0.2 (three minimum values $d_{p_1} = 0.0$, $d_{p_2} = 0.5$ and $d_s = 0.1$ were used). If the ratio r is set to 0.8, then $fit(j)$ is about 1.0. The results show that the individual j includes about 80% of the similar parts with the initial models.

We think the other fitness functions can be introduced into our framework. For example, the following evolution rules can be given: more complex shape evolution, more squared shape evolution and so on.

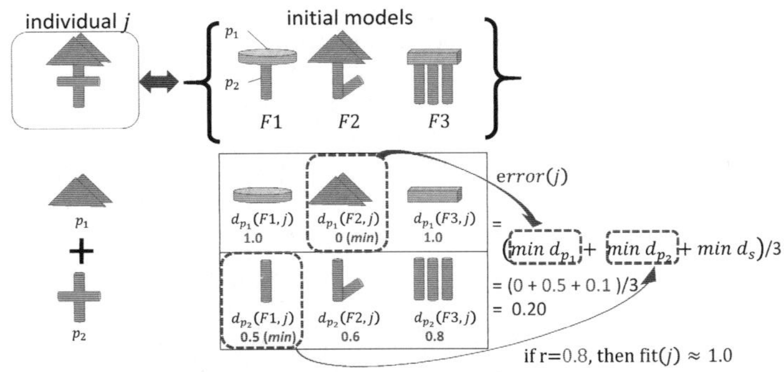

Figure 6. Fitness calculation process. Fitness calculation procedure for individual j is illustrated

4. RESULTS

4.1 Evolutionary Generation Results

We tested our framework with evolutionary 3D shape model generation. The main goal of our approach is to demonstrate the effectiveness of evolutionary generation method which can make the individual inherits the properties from parts of the initial models that user defined.

Figure 7 shows the result of part crossover without property crossover. In this experiments, the initial set is set to five individuals. In 2nd generation, part crossover is applied for both the parents (0, 2) and the parents (1, 4). The new individual 0 consists of the exchanged parts, i.e., 0's seat surface, 2's leg part and 2's seat backrest (0-2-2). However, the individuals inherit the properties such as detailed shape or scale from the parent with the same id.

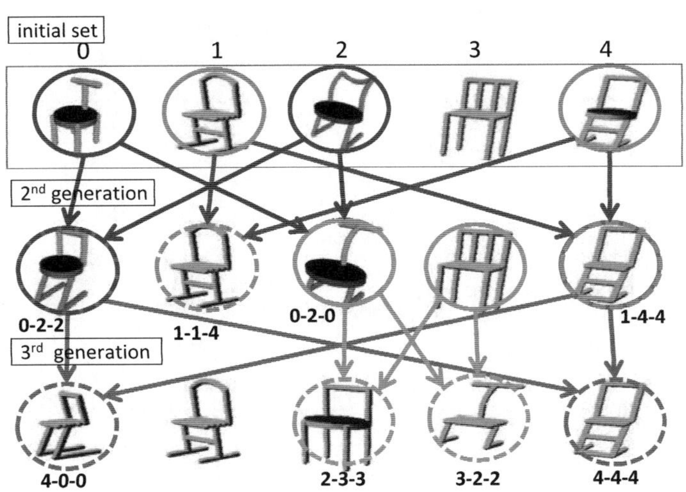

Figure 7. Part crossover results. Properties with the same id are taken over

Next, we tested the evolutionary generation. Figure 8 shows the result of evolutionary generation with crossover and mutation. In this experiments, shape primitives have just bending and scaling properties. The crossover indicates two-step crossover. In this experiments, the initial set is set to five individuals including three initial models that user defined. In 2nd generation, two-step crossover is applied for the parents (0, 3). The new individual 2 consists of the exchanged parts, 0's seat surface, 3's leg part and 3's seat backrest

(0-3-3). The new individual 4 consists of the exchanged parts, 3's seat surface, a new leg part and 3's seat backrest (3-M-0). The new leg part has been created by mutation.

We conducted an experiment to verify the initial model content ratio *r*. We made a comparison of the elite models generated under the different ratio *r*: 0.2, 0.8 and 1.0. Figure 9 shows the comparison results. When *r* is set to 1.0, it is considered whether every part of the elite model was contained in the initial models or not. When *r* is set to 0.8, the elite model is partially like the initial models. When *r* is set to 0.2, the elite model is certainly dissimilar.

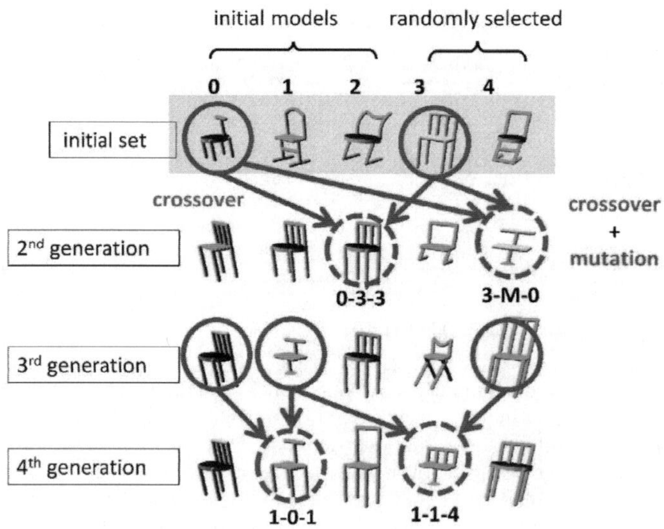

Figure 8. Evolutionary generation results. Five individuals are set (including three initial models)

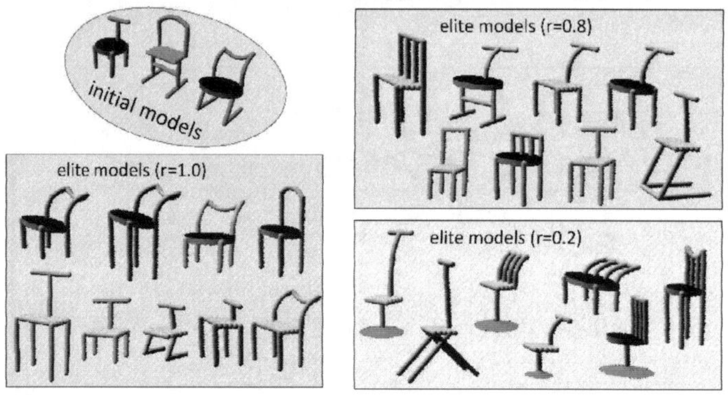

Figure 9. Comparison of the elite models. They are generated under the different ratio *r*

4.2 Fitness Evaluation

We conducted verification of validity of our fitness value. Figure 10 shows a graph which includes several individuals generated in a certain generation. In this evolutionary generation, fifty individuals are set, and three initial models are prepared. The ratio *r* is set to 0.8. Each individual is classified across the fitness value. So-called elite model indicates the fitness value is more than 0.9. The elite model certainly includes 80% of the parts with the same properties as the initial models. On the other hand, the model is exactly equivalent to the initial model is situated in less than 0.9. As expected, the model situated in near 0 is still far from the initial models.

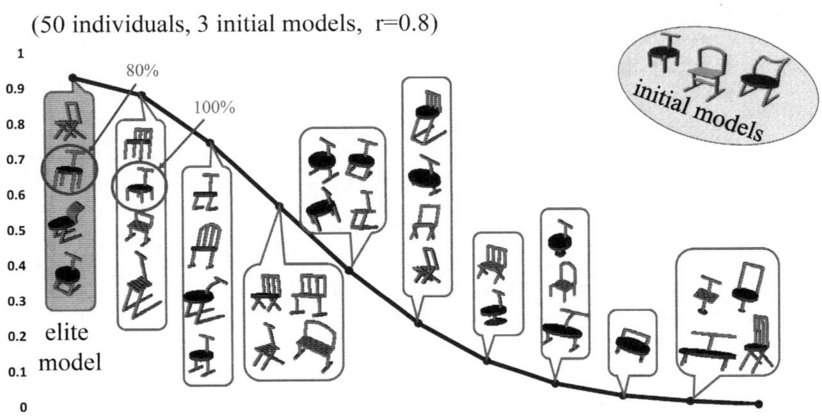

Figure 10. Fitness and individuals. For r=0.8, plausible individuals are generated

4.3 Part evolution

Figure 11 shows an example of a family tree generated by part evolution process. The target part is chair's part p_2 discussed in the previous experiments. This investigation focused on the family tree with four legs. The other family trees can be generated in the same way. They are gradually evolved by adding a single primitive ("1") or one pair of primitives ("2"), starting from the root. During the generation, degeneration by backtrack has also happened. Actually, this evolution or degeneration proceeds in property crossover. In the figure, scale parameters are not reflected, but they may be changed into an easy-to-view state. In order to acquire plausible shape models, it is important to develop diversity of shapes. Although they makes complex shape by adding more shape primitives, our approach saves the evolution level by setting the upper limit number of primitives.

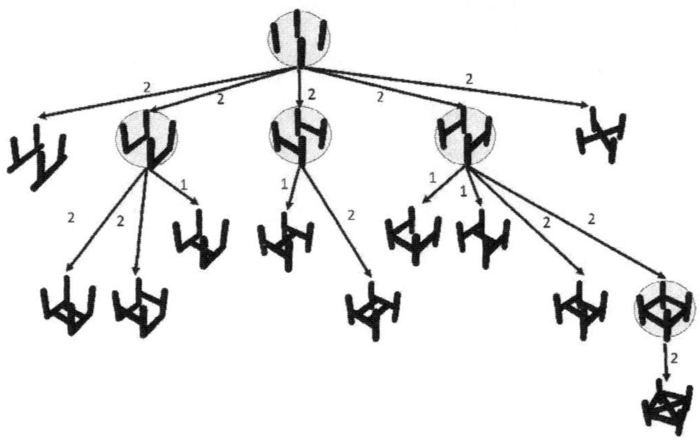

Figure 11. Part evolution in property crossover. A family tree of four legs are generateD

5. CONCLUSION

We have presented a method for generating evolutionary 3D shape models, which reflects a user's intention and takes diversity of 3D shapes into account simultaneously. From the initial models prepared in advance, plausible models can be generated. In our approach, it is supposed that user expects mixing the initial models and creating mashup models. The mixing is controllable by initial model's content ratio the user defined. The mashup models can be created by evolutionary scheme. As evolutionary operations, two-step crossover and mutation are executed. In part crossover, type of parts may be exchanged. The properties such as scale or shape are usually inherited from the parents. The change of the shape properties depends on the increase or decrease of shape primitives for each part. The part evolution from the parent individuals proceeds gradually in the property crossover. In mutation, new type of part which does not exist in the initial models can be appeared.

We have developed the prototype system for generating the evolutionary 3D shape models. As a fitness value, the initial model's content ratio is used. Our implementation has several limitations. Although our goal is to realize various 3D shape model generation, we have just applied for simple shape models such as chair or container. We would also like to look into expansion of the evolutionary generation through developing more complex part generator. Alhashim, I., et al. (Alhashim, 2014) proposed a method for novel 3D model creation by topology-varying shape blending. This interesting method enables generation of multiple sequences of blended 3D shapes. We plan to improve our evolution scheme further into a similar shape blending algorithm as future work.

REFERENCES

Alhashim, I., et al. 2014. Topology-varying 3d shape creation via structural blending, *in ACM Transactions on Graphics*, vol.33, no.4.

Bentley, P., 1999. *Evolutionary design by computers*. Morgan Kaufmann, San Francisco, USA.

Guo, X., et al. 2014. Creature grammar for creative modeling of 3D monsters. *Graphical Models*, vol.76, no.5, pp.376-389.

Huang, S., et al., 2016. Support substructures: support-induced part-level structural representation, *in IEEE transactions on visualization and computer graphics*, vol.22, no.8, pp. 2024-2036.

Kalogerakis, E., et al., 2012. A probabilistic model for component-based shape synthesis. *in ACM Transactions on Graphics*, vol.31, no.4, p.55.

Liu, H., et al., 2015. Replaceable Substructures for Efficient Part - Based Modeling. *in Computer Graphics Forum*. vol. 34., no. 2, pp.503-513.

Merrell, P., 2011. Model synthesis: a general procedural modeling algorithm. IEEE transactions on visualization and computer graphics, vol.17, no.6, pp.715-728.

Nishino, H. et al., 2001. A 3D modeling system for creative design. *in Proceedings of 15th International Conference on Information Networking*, pp. 479-486.

Sims, K., 1991. Artificial evolution for computer graphics. *in Proceedings of SIGGRAPH*, pp.319-328.

Smelik, RM., et al., 2009. A survey of procedural methods for terrain modelling, in Proceedings of the CASA Workshop on 3D Advanced Media In Gaming And Simulation.

Xu, K. et al., 2012. Fit and diverse: set evolution for inspiring 3D shape galleries, *in ACM Transactions on Graphics*, vol.31, no.4.

Zheng, Y., et al., 2013. Smart variations: Functional substructures for part compatibility. *in proceedings of Computer Graphics Forum*, pp.195-204.

IRIDESCENT SHADING MODEL FOR BIOLOGICAL STRUCTURES

Fukun Wu[1,2], Li Xiao[1] and Yi Cao[1]
[1]*Institute Of Applied Physics and Computational Mathematics, Beijing, China*
[2]*Software Center for High Performance Numerical Simulation, China Academy Of Engineering Physics, Beijing, China*

ABSTRACT

Rendering biological iridescences due to subwavelength structures has been a challenge in ray tracers. The colors are joint actions of interference, diffraction, absorption and scattering of light on microscopic structures. This paper proposes a general iridescent shading model that allows to render the complex backscattering and anisotropic iridescent colors of Morpho butterflies photo-realistically. The presented model builds on the optical interactions of light and scales of butterfly wings with a quasi-periodic arrangement of tree-like ridges. Multilayer film interference equation is first introduced to analyze the multiple reflection, refraction and absorption of light inside ridges. It is extended to incorporate the microfacet scattering coefficient to account for the anisotropic wave characteristics. We demonstrate the validity of the proposed method by visualizing butterfly examples which match the experimental description of iridescence properties.

KEYWORDS

Biological iridescences, iridescence shading model, backscattering and anisotropic, multilayer film interference equation, microfacet scattering coefficient, irregular arrangement

1. INTRODUCTION

When light interacts with objects coated with the multilayer film structures such as soap bubble, Newton's rings and pearlescent materials, it can undergo multiple reflection and refraction inside the films, leading to the superimposing on each other and interference.

As a representative of structural colors, butterfly iridescence is determined by the interaction of light and tree-like periodic ridge structures on wings. This type of mechanism widely exists in many creatures such as insects, birds and fishes. In biology, a lots of investigations and studies have been paid to the microstructure of butterfly wings and the cause of structural iridescences (Vukusic et al. 1999, Gralak et al. 2001), which reported accurate measurements of optical properties on butterfly surfaces. However, due to lacking the ability to describe phase information of light, it is not sufficient to rendering real-world butterfly iridescent colors in current raytracers. Multiple works have been proposed to solve that problem. For example, Kinoshita and Yoshioka (Kinoshita and Yoshioka 2005) constructed the separate lamellae model to model the interference effects of butterflies. Sun (Sun 2006) also proposed an iridescent shading process to render biological iridescences in RGB-based renderers using analytical calculation and numerical simulation. However, these simplified models cannot describe the anisotropy and scattering phenomena generated by rough microstructures on butterfly surfaces.

This paper presents a generalized wave bidirectional scattering distribution function models in order to accurately simulate the iridescent effects of ridge structures. Firstly, this model analyzes the biological structure of butterfly, then constructs the rendering model. Multi- beam interference equations are used to explain the multiple reflection and refraction of light inside films, where Fresnel coefficient for dielectric and metallic are introduced respectively to visualize complex refraction and photon absorption.

2. RELATED WORK

The research on the structural colors such as diffraction from wavelength-scale periodic structures (Stam 1999, Cuypers 2012, Wu 2013), interference from multilayer film structures (Smits and Meyer 1990, Dias 1991, Gondek 1994, Ďurikovič and Kimura 2005, Jakob 2014) and biological iridescences (Kinoshita et al. 2002, Lee and Smith 2009, Wu 2015) is paid to the increasing attention in computer graphics, physical optics and biology. So far, researchers have proposed multiple methods associated with structural colors. In biology, for example, Michelson (Michelson 1911) studied the specific butterfly and explained the generation mechanism, where the reflected light in a specific wavelength range has the much high reflectance. Later, scientists investigated the structural colors of insects, and indicated that the colors were caused by the superposition of light. When the insect is immersed into liquid with different refractive indexes, the observed iridescence shows the obvious hue variation. With the development of electric microscope, it is demonstrated that structural colors has the similar optical mechanism with the multilayer film interference, where butterfly ridges are regarded as multilayer films with a finite width. A series of interference models such as separate lamellae model (Kinoshita et al. 2002) and multilayer film model (Hirayama et al. 1999, Hirayama et al. 2000) have been developed to analyze the color mechanism.

In computer graphics, multiple classical ray-based techniques have been developed where the bidirectional scattering distribution function is used to model the reflection behavior of light on surfaces (Smith and Meyer 1990, Dias 1991, Pharr and Humphreys 2010). Icart and Arqu` es (Icart and Arqu` es 2000), for example, constructed physics-based BRDF model for multilayer systems consisting of homogeneous and isotropic thin films with rough boundaries, which can account for interference, diffraction and polarization effects. Weidlich and Wilkie (Weidlich and Wilkie 2009) provided a particular reflectance model for rendering labradorescence based on the physical characteristics of such materials. Hirayama et al. (Hirayama et al. 2000) constructed a comprehensive multilayer film interference model to model scattering characteristics of rough multilayer surfaces. Sun (Sun 2006) proposed an iridescent shading process for rendering the biological iridescences of butterflies and beetles due to multilayer interference based on analytical calculation and numerical simulation. Few of the previous models, however, takes into account specific geometric properties of Morpho butterfly wings or other sub-wavelength microstructures.

3. RIDGE GEOMETRY OF MORPHO BUTTERFLY

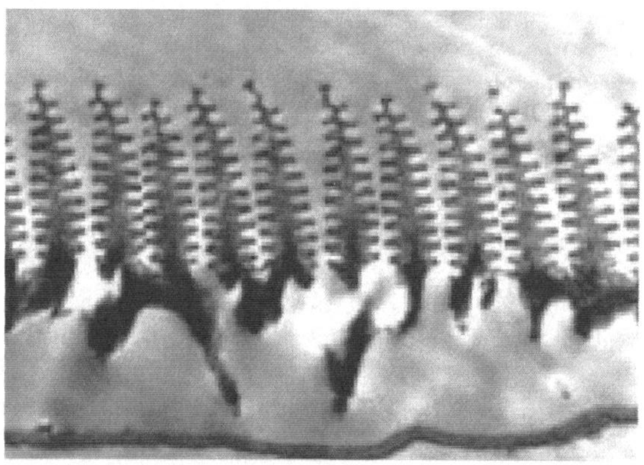

Figure 1. The geometric model of ridge microstructures on Morpho butterfly scale [2]

In biology, the researchers have made significant investigations on the microstructure of butterfly wings by means of optical microscope and electron microscope (Vukusic et al. 1999, Kinoshita et al. 2005). In this article, we focus on a male Morpho rhetenor with brilliant structural colors. This species of butterfly wings are covered with a layer of scales with the approximated size of 100 μm which are regularly arranged in the form of roof tiles. Meanwhile, a group of ridges with tree-like arranged structures are similar to a diffraction grating from the viewpoint of the horizontal direction. These ridge structures on scales consist of alternate layers of cuticle and air, their thicknesses are set to 50nm~150nm, and the degree of refraction of the cuticle is approximated as 1.56. There may be certain pigments or dyes below each scale which are replaced by the scattering spectrum in the experiment. When light interacts with the tree-like ridges, it undergoes multiple reflection and refraction inside the multilayer structures. These beams are superimposed on each other to produce interference. When incident light is monochromatic, light reaching viewpoint is coherent and the result will show a group of bright and dark streaks on imaging plane. Contrarily, one will see a set of colored stripes which change along with the viewing angle in case that the light source is white.

This paper presents a geometry of cross-section of ridge structure as shown in Figure 1. Ridges have tree-like multilayer films consisting of staggered arrangement of cuticle and air. It has been demonstrated that iridescent colors from butterfly biological structures can be explained using multilayer film theory.

4. IRIDESCENT ILLUMINATION MODEL

4.1 Multi-beam Interference

Based on the electron microscope investigations and biological experiments (Vukusic et al. 1999), the striking structural colors from Morpho butterfly are produced by multiple layers of cuticle and air inside ridges on wing surfaces. The multilayer structure provides us with a solid basis for analytically and numerically solving the wave equation for iridescences.

When light interacts with multilayer films, it undergoes multiple reflection, transmission and absorption inside films. It is desired to develop a more general model that take complex interactions into consideration. In this work, we analytically compute multilayer film interference based on the recursive composition method to visualize optical properties of butterfly wings.

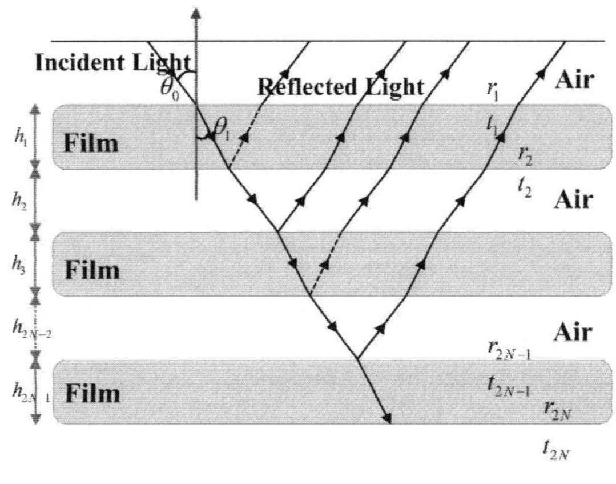

Figure 2. Interference modeling from the multilayer film structures of ridges

As an example, consider a pair of cuticle and air layers as shown in Figure 2. Given a thickness H and a refractive index n_j, j = 0,1,2. The r_1, r_2, t_1 and t_2 denote the reflection and transmission coefficients of light propagating from air to film, and the r_1 and t_1 denote the reflection and transmission coefficients of light propagating from film to air, which are derived using the Fresnel equations. The refractive angle complies with Snell's law. The indices of refraction of the air and the cuticle are denoted as n_0 and n_1 respectively where $n_0= n_2$.

Hence the reflectivity of light from a pair of cuticle and air layers in Figure 2 are formulated as

$$\begin{aligned} E_1^{(r)} &= rE_0^{(r)} \\ E_2^{(r)} &= t_1 r_2 t_1' E_0^{(r)} e^{i\delta} \\ E_3^{(r)} &= t_1 r_2 (r_1' r_2) t_1' E_0^{(r)} e^{i2\delta} \\ E_3^{(r)} &= t_1 r_2 (r_1' r_2)^2 t_1' E_0^{(r)} e^{i3\delta} \end{aligned} \quad (1)$$

where δ $=4\pi/\lambda\ n_1 H cos\theta_1$ denotes the phase difference of two adjacent reflected or transmitted light propagating through the film. According to the interference theory of multilayer films, the composite reflectance $\bar{r}$ and transmittance $\bar{t}$ of this single layer film can be further formulated as

$$\bar{r} = \frac{E_1^{(r)} + E_2^{(r)} + \ldots}{E_0^{(r)}} \approx \frac{r_1 + r_2 e^{i\delta}}{1 + r_1 r_2 e^{i\delta}} \quad (2)$$

Similarly, the transmitted coefficient is given by

$$\bar{t} \approx \frac{t_1 + t_2}{1 + r_1 r_2 e^{i\delta}} \quad (3)$$

For two or more M-layer thin film system, we can iterative the calculation of the reflection and transmission coefficients from the last layer adjacent to the substrate to the first layer. For the Mth layer, for instance,

$$\bar{r}_M = \frac{r_M + r_{M+1} e^{i\delta_M}}{1 + r_M r_{M+1} e^{i\delta_M}} \quad (4)$$

$$\bar{t}_M = \frac{t_M t_{M+1}}{1 + r_M r_{M+1} e^{i\delta_M}} \quad (5)$$

where δ is defined as

$$\delta_M = \frac{4\pi}{\lambda} n_M H_M \cos\theta_M \quad (6)$$

Assume the Mth layer and the substrate as a whole, then add the (M-1)th layer and calculate the scattering coefficients, namely

$$\bar{r}_{M-1} = \frac{r_{M-1} + \bar{r}_M e^{i\delta_{M-1}}}{1 + r_{M-1} \bar{r}_M e^{i\delta_{M-1}}} \quad (7)$$

$$\bar{t}_{M-1} = \frac{t_{M-1} \bar{t}_M e^{i\delta_{M-1}}}{1 + r_{M-1} \bar{r}_M e^{i\delta_{M-1}}} \quad (8)$$

where $\delta_{M-1}=4\pi/\lambda\ n_{M-1} h_{M-1} \cos\theta_{M-1}$. The calculation process is repeated until the first layer adjacent to air. Finally, we can obtain the composite reflectance and transmittance coefficients of the multilayer film system. In the ray tracer, the bidirectional reflectance distribution function (BRDF) is defined as the ratio of output energy to input energy, namely

$$R = \frac{I_o}{I_i} = \frac{E_o^2}{E_i^2} = \frac{(E_i \bar{r}_1)^2}{E_i^2} = \bar{r}_1^{2} \quad (9)$$

where E_o and E_i denote the radiant energy of the incident and reflected light respectively. Based on the energy conservation law, the corresponding bidirectional transmittance distribution function BTDF = $1-R$.

4.2 Reflection and Transmission Coefficients

According to the above section, the reflection and transmission coefficients on film surfaces play a key role in producing iridescent colors of butterflies It affects them spatial distribution of radiant energy by changing the amplitude variation of light, which are determined by Fresnel Equation 10. In experiments, light is assumed to be unpolarized and randomly oriented. Hence, the reflectance of multilayer film structure is approximated as the average of squares of the parallel and perpendicular polarization terms, namely BRDF = 0.5 • ($R^{\parallel}$+ $R^{\perp}$).

$$
\begin{aligned}
r_j^{\parallel} &= \frac{n_j \cos\theta_{j-1} - n_{j-1}\cos\theta_j}{n_j \cos\theta_{j-1} + n_{j-1}\cos\theta_j} \\
t_j^{\parallel} &= \frac{2n_{j-1}\cos\theta_{j-1}}{n_{j-1}\cos\theta_j + n_j \cos\theta_{j-1}} \\
r_j^{\parallel} &= \frac{n_{j-1}\cos\theta_{j-1} - n_j \cos\theta_j}{n_j \cos\theta_j + n_{j-1}\cos\theta_{j-1}} \\
r_j^{\parallel} &= \frac{2n_{j-1}\cos\theta_{j-1}}{n_j \cos\theta_j + n_{j-1}\cos\theta_{j-1}}
\end{aligned}
\qquad (10)
$$

where $r^{\parallel}$ and $r^{\perp}$ denote the Fresnel coefficients for parallel polarized light, $t^{\parallel}$ and $r^{\perp}$ denote the coefficients for perpendicular polarized light, and n_{j-1} and n_j denote the refractive indexes of incident and transmitted medium respectively. The transmitted angle complies with Snell's law.

In physical optics, refractive index is wavelength- dependent which describes the speed ratio of light with certain wavelength between media and air. It reflects in multiple directions and generates chromatic dispersion effects when the incident light is not monochromatic. In this paper, the refractive index is replaced by the average for the visible spectrum to simplify the calculation process of the interaction of light and material. Specially, the refractive index of the cuticle of Morpho butterfly is set to 1.56.

5. SIMULATION

We implemented our wave model for rendering iridescent colors of objects coated with multilayer thin films by creating a new material plugin for the PBRT system (Pharr and Humphreys 2010). All of the images in this work were produced using Maya software on a Dell T7600 workstation with a 2.40 GHz Intel Xeon CPU E5-2609 and a NVIDIA Quadro 6000.

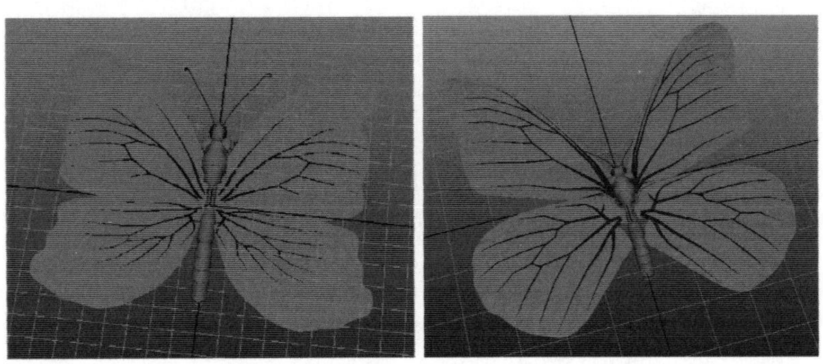

Figure 3. Visualization results of volume dataset clipped by a plane

The male Morpho rhetenor with a large number of small scales is a typical butterfly that exhibits structural color. The scales, in turn, are covered with a series of quasi-periodic ridges with subwavelength structures as shown in Figure 1. Specifically, each ridge is a tree-like structure with the separation of 675 nm, which consists of alternate layers of cuticle and air with the same thickness of 90 nm. The index of refraction of the cuticle is approximated as 1.56.

Using our generic knowledge of the structures found on Morpho butterflies, two geometric models of Morpho butterfly are set up using Maya software as showed in Figure 3. The perceptibly iridescent material is attached to the wings of Morpho butterfly, while materials of the head, body and legs are selected from the material library in Maya.

Figure 4. Rendered butterfly wings with the added bump and texture mappings

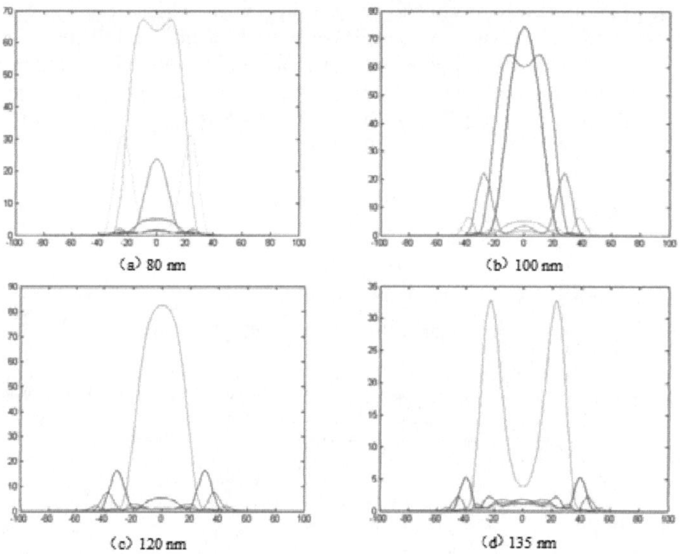

Figure 5. Angular dependence of reflected light intensity in a plane perpendicular to ridges with different film thicknesses for various wavelengths

The approximated Morpho butterfly wing with several air-cuticle layers was rendered at different camera positions using our optics model as illustrated in Figure 4 where the light source position is fixed. The color of the butterfly wings is a very intense blue that quickly fades to a violet when viewed near grazing and there exists some gloss due to the bump and texture mappings. Figure 5 describes the angular dependence of reflected light intensity from ridges with different film thicknesses (from left to right and top to bottom, 80nm, 100nm,120nm,135nm). These results demonstrate that the film thickness determines which wavelength plays a key role in some direction. The color variation is in agreement with the Sun's previous work (Sun 2006).

(*a*) 80 nm (*b*) 100 nm (*c*) 120 nm (*d*) 135 nm

Figure 6. Iridescent renderings of Morpho butterflies consisting of tree-like ridge structures with cuticle films of different thicknesses

In Figure 6, our rendering technique can generate iridescent effects of butterflies that differ greatly in appearance by adjusting the thickness of cuticle layer in ridges. The majority of the scattered power is found at wavelengths shorter than 550 nm when thickness is less than 90 nm, while the longer wavelengths is highly reflected by the ridge structure with the increase of the thickness. The four butterflies are rendered with different structural parameter values, where the thickness of cuticle layer is set to 80 nm, 100 nm, 120 nm, and 135 nm respectively. From left to right, they rendered colors of wings are violet, green, yellow and red. Comparing these cases, a color shift from the violet to the red happens. These renderings also agree with the observed iridescences and experimental measurements of Morpho butterflies.

(*a*) photograph (*b*) 102nm

Figure 7. Comparison of real photograph (left) and iridescent rendering of Morpho butterfly using our model (right)

The approach proposed in this article is applicable to other cases of iridescence rendering. The iridescent objects can be biological or nonbiological. For example, a ground-truth verification of the proposed model is also presented in Figure 7.

6. CONCLUSION

In this paper, we construct a novel illumination model to visualize the iridescent colors caused by the interaction of light and layered structures of Morpho butterfly where the indices of refraction, thicknesses and the irregular geometry of ridges play an important role. This model can produce provably high-quality renderings with high reflectivity in a specific wavelength range and the diffusive light in a wide angular range in the PBRT framework by creating a new material plugin. Based on the measurements of optical and electron microscopes, the multi-beam interference equation is applied to solve wave characteristics of ridges consisting of alternate layers of cuticle and air. The regularity and irregularity of geometry of ridges on butterfly surfaces are taken into account together to accurately exhibit backscattering and anisotropic optical characteristics. Compared with the current real photo, we have shown that this model suffices to describe the natural optical effects, and have facilitated its practical application in Maya software.

REFERENCES

Cuypers, T. et al., 2012. Reflectance model for diffraction, *ACM Transactions on Graphics,* Vol.31,No.5 .

Dias M., 1991. Ray tracing interference color. *IEEE Computer Graphics and Applications,* Vol.11, No.2, pp. 54–60.

Ďurikovič R. and Kimura R., 2005. Spectrum-based rendering using programmable graphics hardware. *Proceedings of the 21st Spring Conference on Computer Graphics*. pp. 233-236.

Gondek J. et al., 1994. Wavelength dependent reflectance functions. *Proceedings of SIGGRAPH '94*. pp. 213–219.

Gralak B. et al., 2001. Morpho butterflies wings color modeled with lamellar grating theory. *Optics Express*, Vol. 9, No.11, pp. 567–578.

Hirayama H. et al., 1999. Visualization of optical phenomena caused by multilayer films with complex refractive indices. *Proceedings of the 7th Pacific Conference on Computer Graphics and Application*. pp. 128–137.

Hirayama H. et al., 2000. Rendering iridescent colors appearing on natural objects. *Proceedings of the 8th Pacific Conference on Computer Graphics and Application*. pp. 15–22.

Icart I. and Arqu` es D., 2000. A physically-based brdf model for multilayer systems with uncorrelated rough boundaries. *Rendering Techniques*, pp. 353–364.

Jakob W., 2014. A comprehensive framework for rendering layered materials. *ACM Transactions on Graphics*, Vol.33, No.33, pp:1-14

Kinoshita S. et al., 2002. Photo- physics of structural color in the morpho butterflies. *Forma*, Vol. 17, pp. 103–121.

Kinoshita S. and Yoshioka S., 2005. Structural colors in nature:the role of regularity and irregularity in the structure. *ChemPhysChem*, Vol. 6, pp. 1442–1459.

Lee R. and Smith G., 2009. Detailed electromagnetic simulation for the structural color of butterfly wings. *Appl. Opt.*, Vol.48,No.21, pp.4177–4190.

Lee R., 2009. *A novel method for incorporating periodic boundaries into the FDTD method and the application to the study of structural color of insects*. PhD thesis, Georgia Institute of Technology.

Michelson A., 1911. Lxi.on metallic colouring in birds and insects. *Philosphical Magazine,* Vol.21,pp. 554–567.

Pharr M. and Humphreys G., 2010. *Physically based rendering:from theory to implementation*. Morgan Kaufmann Publishers, San Francisco, USA.

Smits B. and Meyer G., 1990. Newton's colors:simulating interference phenomena in realistic image synthesis. *Proceedings of Eurographics Workshop on Photosimulation, Realism and Physics in Computer Graphics*. pp.185–194.

Stam J., 1999. Diffraction shaders. *Proceedings of SIGGRAPH '99*. pp. 101–110.

Sun Y., 2006. Rendering biological iridescences with rgb-based renderers, *ACM Transactions on Graphics,* Vol.25, No.1, pp.100–129.

Vukusic P. et al., 1999. Quantified interference and diffraction in single morpho butterfly scales. *Proceedings of the Royal Society B:Biological Sciences*, Vol. 266, No. 1427, pp. 1403–1411.

Weidlich A. andWilkie A., 2009. Rendering the effect of labradoescence. *Proceedings of Graphics Interface*. pp. 79–85.

Wu F.-K. and Zheng C.-W., 2013. A comprehensive geometrical optics application for wave rendering. *Graphical Models*, Vol.75,No.6, pp. 318–327.

Wu F.-K. and Zheng C.-W., 2015. Microfacet-based interference simulation for multilayer films. *Graphical Models* ,Vol.78, pp. 26–35.

NEW ALGORITHMS FOR ANTI-ALIASED DISTANCE TRANSFORMATIONS

Ingemar Ragnemalm
Information Coding Group, Dept of EE, Linköping University, 581 83 LINKÖPING, Sweden

ABSTRACT

The anti-aliased Euclidean distance transform is a recent development that redefines the distance transform concept, in particular the concept of precision and correctness, and has been shown to benefit certain applications. This paper presents and evaluates new versions of the anti-aliased distance transform. Our vector-based version simplifies the algorithm while providing a richer output in the form of vector data, with no measurable degradation in quality compared to the algorithm it is based on. Finally, we use a new method for measuring errors based on generating exact ground truth images.

KEYWORDS

Distance function, Distance transform, Euclidean, Anti-aliased

1. INTRODUCTION

A distance transformation (DT) is defined as a transformation taking a binary image as input, generating a distance map as output, which is an image where each pixel holds the distance to the closest object pixel. An alternate name for the distance map is distance field, a term mostly used in the computer graphics field.

The distance transform was originally presented by Rosenfeld and Pfalz (1966), extended to weighted DTs by Montanari (1968), and the more efficient integer-weighted DTs by Barrow et al (1977), extensively researched by Borgefors (1986). Danielsson (1980) and Fischler and Barrett (1980) simultaneously and independently presented the Euclidean Distance Transform (EDT), also called Vector Distance transform. Since sequential implementations of these algorithms were initially not error-free, much attention has been given the task of making error-free algorithms, the first by Rutowitz (1989) and Ragnemalm (1989). An overview over such algorithms was made by Fabbri et. al. (2008)

However, these algorithms were made for binary images, and therefore subject to distortion by thresholding of the input signal. This distortion is up to one pixel distance, which makes the error of the original EDT, 0.09 pixel distances according to Danielsson (1980), insignificant in comparison.

A variation of the algorithm, taking this into account, is the Anti-Aliased EDT (AAEDT), by Gustavson and Strand (2011). This algorithm has gotten attention from the industry, but so far there has been limited further development on the subject published. Linnér & Strand (2014a) made an implementation of AAEDT using a propagation front/contour processing/ordered propagation algorithm. Linnér and Strand (2014b) have also investigated a 3D implementation. Finally, Illic et al (2015) applied the method to voxelized 3D scenes.

In the following, we present two new variants of the AAEDT, and analyze the result.

2. THE ANTI-ALIASED EUCLIDEAN DISTANCE TRANSFORM AND RELATED EFFORTS

The Anti-Aliased Distance Transform (AAEDT) is a distance transform which is defined for binary images with anti-aliased edges, that is grayscale images with grayscale values only in edges. This is in contrast to traditional DTs, which are defined for strictly binary images. We assume that the images represent underlying continuous shapes as the input signals. The grayscale values are used for adjusting the distance values in order to approximate actual edge positions of the underlying shapes.

The original application of the AAEDT by Gustavson and Strand (2011) was for shape representation purposes. Earlier, Valve (Green 2007) presented a related method which was used for shape representation, for example of text. The AAEDT can be considered a preprocessing for this application. More recently, Adamsson (2015) presented a master thesis applying the AAEDT to scalable font representation, showing that an anti-aliased pixel representation is a possible alternative to classic spline representations.

However, the EDT has many other applications, for example those proposed by Ye (1988), which suggests that there are applications where AAEDT may give improvements due to its higher precision.

3. EXISTING ALGORITHMS FOR AAEDT

In this section, we will briefly summarize the current AAEDT algorithms, on which we base our new algorithms. The principle for AAEDT is to use anti-aliasing grayscale information along edges to estimate a precise location for the true edge.

The core of the algorithms is an edge distance estimate presented by Gustavson & Strand (2011), where the grey value of a pixel is interpreted as coverage, from which an edge estimate can be computed as a scalar value. In order to calculate distance values beyond the edge estimate, the original AAEDT algorithm uses a vector-based EDT, with multiple scans over the image. Thus, the algorithm, apart from the edge offsets, is similar to Danielsson's original EDT (1980), using multiple scans over the image.

Thus, we define AAEDT based on Linnér and Strand (2014a) as the Euclidean distance d_E from a point p to a feature (edge) point p_w plus an offset d_f based on the grayscale of the pixel p_w, as in formula 1:

$$d_{AAEDT}(p) = \min(d_E(p, p_w) + d_f(p_w)) \tag{1}$$

The most basic version of the edge estimate, as stated by Gustavson & Strand (2011) is a simple linear ramp, as in formula 2. We call this AAEDT type 1:

$$d_f(p_w) = 0.5 - \alpha(p_w) \tag{2}$$

The term $d_f(p_w)$ is the distance adjustment and $\alpha(p_w)$ the grayscale value of the edge pixel p_w, defined from 0 to 1. This is a rather rough measure, and a better measure can be obtained based on the gradient direction of the edge. The gradient is measured with a pair of 3x3 operators, shown in Figure 1.

-1	$-\sqrt{2}$	-1
0	0	0
1	$\sqrt{2}$	1

-1	0	1
$-\sqrt{2}$	0	$\sqrt{2}$
-1	0	1

Figure 1. Pair of operators for gradient measurement

Given the direction of the gradient, it is now possible to estimate the edge adjustment $d_f(p_w)$ with higher precision. Now, the question is where the edge must be located to split a square (the pixel) in two parts whose areas will be proportional to the gray level of the pixel. One part will have an area proportional to α and the other to $1-\alpha$. The solution is described by Gustavson & Strand and available in their implementation on-line. We call this AAEDT type 2.

Gustavson & Strand (2011) describe one more variant, where the offset is recalculated based on the direction to the edge pixel. We call this AAEDT type 3.

Linnér and Strand (2014a)(2014b) base their algorithms on the type 2 AAEDT. It is simpler than type 3 and still shows considerable improvement. In this work, we have followed their example and base our results on AAEDT type 2.

4. ERRORS AND PROBLEM CASES FOR AAEDT

Since the edge estimate is an approximation of the true edge, the AAEDT can not be error-free. However, the magnitude of that error should be compared to the maximum sampling error as well as the maximum error in case a non-error-free EDT is used. Furthermore, we will here analyze special cases where the error may be larger than in the typical cases. We will not solve the problem of reducing these errors, only clarify the source of the errors.

According to Gustavson & Strand (2011) as well as our investigations below, the biggest errors occur around sharp corners, like the convex points of the fins on the dolphin test image used by Gustavson & Strand (2011), in Figure 2. Gustavson (2012) also presented an example where an error occurs in a concavity. In either case, the problems occur in high curvature areas, where the assumption of a smooth edge is no longer valid, and the sampled data can not represent the detail.

To the right in Figure 2 is an extreme close-up of the anti-aliased tip of the fin, with curves illustrating the actual edge (dashed line) and the estimated edge in that pixel (solid line). The fin has too high curvature for the AAEDT to get a good description of the edge.

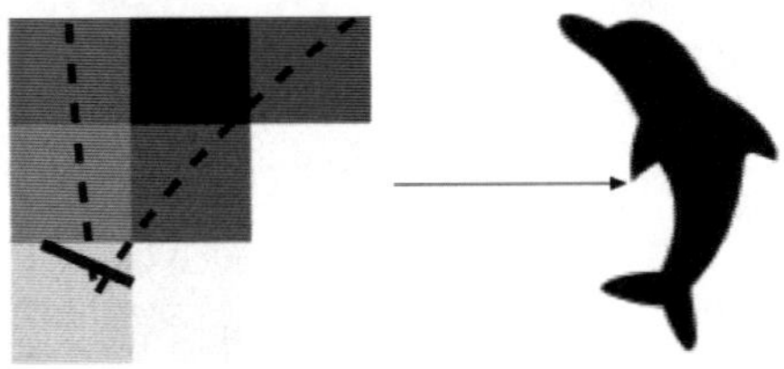

Figure 2. Right: The dolphin image. Left: Tip of fin, with edge (dashed) and estimated edge (solid)

In this context, it should be stressed that distance transforms, even "error-free" Euclidean distance transforms, do not produce the exact distance to the object, that is the edge. Rather, most algorithms are guaranteed not to do that because they generally over-estimate the distance. By measuring the distance to the closest object pixel, they overshoot the edge in all cases except for extreme cases.

5. ANTI-ALIASED EUCLIDEAN DISTANCE TRANSFORM USING ONLY VECTORS

This section introduces a new variant of the AAEDT, with the goal of providing a vector field rather than a scalar distance map, with the intention of broadening the scope of applications for the algorithm. There are numerous applications that can take advantage of the vector information, for example computing Dirichlet tessellations and Convex hulls from sampled data (Ye, 1988). Thus, we conclude that the modification is an interesting extension. The previously described algorithms use scalar offsets based on grayscale values and gradients of the edges, while this variant skips the scalar offsets and uses vectors throughout. For short, we call it "Vector AAEDT" or VAAEDT".

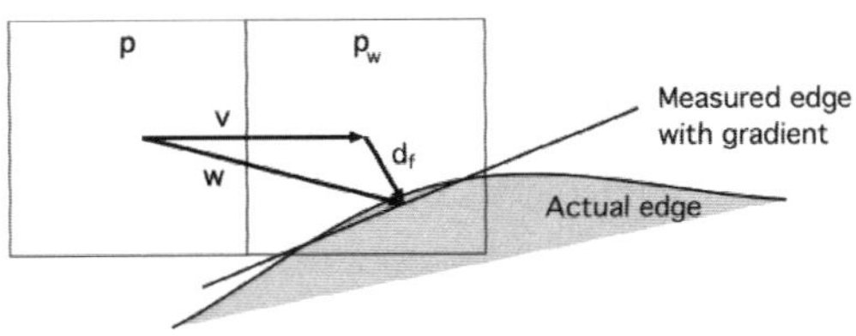

Figure 3. The VAAEDT vector w is the sum of the initialization step and the EDT vector v

The initialization and a first distance measurement step of the algorithm are illustrated by Figure 3. The grayscale value and the gradient are used to estimate a distance value, but the gradient also gives a direction, so we can just as well store the result as a vector, which is what the following EDT uses anyway.

In Figure 3, a distance propagation step is illustrated by the vector v used by AAEDT, to the center of the pixel, and the VAAEDT vector w, which goes directly to the edge, by adding a vector equal to d_f times a unit vector along the gradient. The resulting distance for either case can now be used when comparing to other neighbors.

Finding the vector instead of a scalar is truly straight-forward. For the original AAEDT, the data may be initialized as follows:

```
gx := gradientimage[y][x].r;
gy := gradientimage[y][x].g;
a := (im[y][x].r + 1) / 2; // Get alpha from signed image
df := -edgedf(gx, gy, a); // Calculate df with Stefan's procedure.
im[y][x] := pixel(0, 0, df, 1); // Zero vector plus offset
```

For VAAEDT, the initialization is changed to this:

```
gx := gradientimage[y][x].r;
gy := gradientimage[y][x].g;
a := (im[y][x].r + 1) / 2; // Get alpha from signed image
df := -edgedf(gx, gy, a); // Calculate df with Stefan's procedure.
im[y][x] := pixel(-df*gx, -df*gy, 0, 1); // Vector only
```

It should be noted that the gradient must be normalized in order for this to work, but that is also needed for the edgedf() function that finds the distance.

This simple change produces a variant of the algorithm which has a few advantages. It should be noted that the result is not exactly the same, but extremely close, as we will see later in the evaluation. Thus, the precision is not an issue, so the major question should be whether it has some other advantage. We can identify the following ones:

- Simpler computations. While the AAEDT has to transport three pieces of information from pixel to pixel, a 2-component vector (x, y) and a scalar offset value, VAAEDT will only need the vector, which gives us the opportunity to reduce memory accesses as well as memory demand. Furthermore, all distance computations are simplified by not adding an offset value for each component in a distance comparison. It is also possible to skip the square root and use only multiplications when making comparisons.
- Algorithms using VAAEDT data as input may take advantage of the vectors, and if they do, they get vectors pointing directly to the (estimated) edge. We expect this to have an impact on certain applications.
- The modification makes it easier to apply any existing EDT algorithm. Instead of having the offset built into the entire computation, it only changes the initialization and the computation will be the same, as long as the algorithm can handle floating-point (or fixed-point) vector components.

There are, of course, also drawbacks. Since the classic algorithms are bound to the pixel grid, the vector components of the EDT will always be integer, which can be an advantage in making highly optimized implementations on hardware where integer arithmetics have advantages.

Still, the simpler computations has potential to result in faster computations. Since neither our implementation of the official one were made for performance, it is meaningless to compare them by timing them. Rather, we choose to compare the performance in number of computations and memory accesses. With modern computers, the main concern is (as commonly known) memory accesses, so we should primarily consider them.

For AAEDT, a distance value is calculated (using color channels of an image) like this:

```
d := sqrt(p.r*p.r + p.g*p.g) + p.b;
```

For VAAEDT it can be computed like this:

```
d := sqrt(p.r*p.r + p.g*p.g);
```

For distance comparisons, it can also be simplified by removing the square root, using the squared distance:

```
d := p.r*p.r + p.g*p.g;
```

Thus, AAEDT must access R, G and B, perform two multiplications and two additions, while VAAEDT can reduce this to only accessing R and G, potentially leading to less memory access (we may optionally remove the B channel altogether), and then performing only two multiplications and one addition.

We summarize the computational differences in Table 1.

Table 1. Analysis of AAEDT vs VAAEDT in terms of memory access and operations

Algorithm	Data items to read	Square root	Multiplications	Additions
AAEDT	3	1	2	2
VAAEDT	2	0	2	1

We conclude that the new algorithm does not only have a richer output, but also has less memory demand as well as fewer computations, and therefore has potential to perform better.

6. ANTI-ALIASED WEIGHTED DISTANCE TRANSFORM

The original AAEDT uses the Euclidean distance transform. However, the calculations for computing the offset calculated on the edge can also be applied to a weighted, scalar distance transform, a.k.a. Chamfer DT (Montanari 1968), resulting in the Anti-Aliased Weighted Distance Transform (AAWDT). Considering that the AAEDT is not exact, combining it with another approximative distance is worth evaluating.

Two implementations were made with different precision, both using pseudo-Euclidean floating-point masks. There are many other options, but we consider this enough to investigate the alternative. The lower precision version uses a 3x3 neighborhood with distance 1 for 4-neighbors and sqrt(2) for 8-neighbors, while the higher precision version adds “knight’s move” neighbors with distance sqrt(5) to give the precision of a 5x5 neighborhood. To this, the edge offset described by Gustavson and Strand (2011) was added, that is the gradient based improved version.

Although the result is likely to be better than a conventional weighted DT, it shows noticeable errors on a significantly higher magnitude than all versions using Euclidean distances and we conclude that the AAWDT is a marginal side result. See the evaluation below. Still, it has hereby been given some examination to verify this, and we conclude that the original algorithm’s use of EDT was a sound choice.

7. EVALUATION

In order to evaluate the algorithms described above, we have implemented the VAAEDT, AAWDT as well as, in order to guarantee a fair comparison, our own AAEDT type 1 and 2, and interface to the official implementation of AAEDT type 3. We also created a ground truth image generator for polygons. We wish to note that this is the first time we try this approach, and to our knowledge it has not been used by other researchers, so its relevance and measurement methods are still up for scrutiny.

Earlier evaluations of the AAEDT (Gustavson and Strand 2011 and Linnér and Strand (2014a) used vector shapes rendered in higher resolution binary images, using a conventional EDT to create a reference. This provides a reasonable approximation of a ground truth, but it also means that no exact ground truth image was used.

Our ground truth images are based on shapes for which exact distances can conveniently be calculated. As test image, an image of a procedurally generated polygon was used. The choice of this image was made in order to include sharp corners of varying angles and edges of varying angles, while at the same time being a shape for which it is straightforward to generate distances procedurally. Thus, this test image is deliberately created to cause problems for AAEDT, by including corners so sharp that they can not be well represented after sampling. Indeed, our experiments reveal several kinds of errors.

The shape is an 8-cornered star-like shape, where each part of the star has different width. Each of the eight parts i □ [1..8] cover the angle $i*2\pi/36$. This image was generated in one binary version, one anti-aliased version, and one with the exact distance to the closest edge - the exact ground truth distance map for this shape. Vertices are placed on either an inner or outer circle, with radii 100 and 200 pixels, respectively.

Figure 4. From left to right: Binary test image, zoomed detail, anti-aliased test image, zoomed detail, exact distance to edge (ground truth)

The test images are shown in Figure 4, together with zoomed details (triangles) and the resulting ground truth. The difference images are amplified so that the differences are emphasized and visible. To begin with, we look at the difference between the ground truth and what the algorithms produce.

First of all, let us see how EDT performs. The difference to ground truth is shown in Figure 5.

Figure 5. Difference to ground truth for EDT (left) and AAEDT type 1 (right)

Since these images are signed, zero is 50% gray, so a totally error-free result in a flat gray image. As the figure shows, EDT is in no way exact. Now only do we get errors near sharp edges, but we also get noticable errors in other areas, with false gradients stemming from aliasing along edges.

Figure 6. The difference from ground truth for AAEDT, VAAEDT and AAWDT

Also in Figure 5, we see the errors of AAEDT type 1, which is a great improvement over EDT. Let us continue with the type 2 algorithms in Figure 6.

From Figure 6, it is clear that AAWDT is quite unimpressive compared to its Euclidean counterparts. It makes some improvements near the edge, but the errors of WDT grow with distance and quickly dominate.

Finally, in Figure 7 we show the difference between ground truth and the official implementation of AAEDT, from the publicly available source file edtaa3func.c (Gustavson and Strand 2011), which is the AAEDT type 3.

Figure 7. Difference between ground truth and type 3 AAEDT using the official implementation vs ground truth

The actual differences from ground truth is illustrated by Table 2. The values are pixel distances. RMS refers to all pixels that are not object pixels, that is non-zero pixels.

It is clear from the table that the precision of all AAEDTs are except AAWDT come out very close with these measurements. As shown in Figure 6 and 7, the errors vs ground truth is largest near sharp convex corners. However, it is also visible in Figure 7 that the official implementation (type 3) has the best precision near the edges.

Table 2. Error measurements vs ground truth

Algorithm	Max and min difference	RMS
Ground truth	0.00, 0.00	0.00
AAEDT type 2	0.8778, -0.6181	0.2701
VAAEDT	0.8283, -0.2341	0.2541
AAEDT type 3	0.8658, -0.1463	0.2644
AAWDT	4.0513, -1.2943	0.7962
EDT	1.9674, 0.0000	0.6531

The error level for EDT outperforms AAWDT in these measurements. Most notably, we confirm that the AAEDTs (all three variants investigated except the AAWDT) are significantly more exact than EDT.

As noted above, we consider this investigation a kind of first try on assessing DTs this way, using a true ground truth rather than resizing images, and we find the question open to variations of the measures that can describe the precision in the most relevant way. At this time, however, we wish to leave that for future work.

8. DISCUSSION AND FUTURE WORK

We feel that the arrival of the AAEDT fundamentally changes the whole EDT concept. Many past questions are resolved and new ones arrive. In particular, the focus on computing error-free Euclidean DTs to the edge of a shape has been a chase after errors smaller than the sampling errors, but since the AAEDT is based on information that takes sampling into account, with the anti-aliasing, we can now talk about another level of precision.

Clearly, AAEDT makes no claims about being error-free, with the distance to the edge being an approximation, but the approximation is better than an error-free EDT with up to one pixel distance sampling error.

Being rid of the sampling error, many applications benefit. So far, we have seen results in shape representation (Adamsson 2015, Gustavson and Strand 2011) and graphics effects (Green 2007). Many other applications remain to be investigated.

Apart from applications, future work includes adapting the more advanced AAEDT type 3 to output vector data, and further studies on how to work with exact ground truth images.

9. CONCLUSIONS

We have presented two new variations of the anti-aliased distance transform. The first, and most significant, is a version that uses only vectors, which may have advantages in computation speed but also in application flexibility, by being able to produce a vector field instead of a scalar field. Second, we also investigate the use of weighted distance transforms for this purpose, but conclude that the approach does not show any advantages.

We have also introduced a more exact evaluation method, based on shapes for which exact ground truth images are calculated, as opposed to comparing to higher resolutions as was done in earlier work.

Finally, we have used this evaluation method to perform a precision measurement agains a ground truth image based on a polygonal shape, which confirms that the vector-based algorithm is at least as good as the corresponding AAEDT, and also confirms that all examined AAEDT algorithms are considerably more exact that earlier distance transforms including Euclidean ones.

REFERENCES

Adamsson, G. (2015), Fast and approximate text rendering using distance fields, Master Thesis, Linköping University, LiTH-ISY-EX--15/4868--SE.

Barrow, H.G. et. al., 1977, "Parametric correspondence and chamfer matching: two new techniques for image matching", Proc. IJCAI'77 vol 2, pp 659-663

Borgefors, G., "Distance Transformations in Digital Images", 1986, Computer Vision, Graphics and Image Processing 34, pp 344-371.

Danielsson, P.E., 1980, "Euclidean Distance Mapping", Computer Graphics and Image Processing 14, pp 227-248.

Fabbri, R., Luciano Da F. Costa, Julio C. Torelli and Odemir M. Bruno, 2008, "2D Euclidean Distance Transform Algorithms: A Comparative Survey", ACM Computing Surveys, Vol 40, No 1, Article 2.

Fischler, M.A., Barrett, P. , "An iconic transform for sketch completion and shape abstraction", 1980, Computer Graphics and Image Processing 13, pp 334-360.

Green, C., 2007, "Improved Alpha-Tested Magnification for Vector Textures and Special Effects", SIGGRAPH 2007

Gustavson, S., 2012, "2D Shape Rendering by Distance Fields" in OpenGL Insights: OpenGL, OpenGL ES, and WebGL community experiences, ed. Patrick Cozzi, Christophe Riccio, 2012: 978-1-4398-9376-0

Gustavson, S., Strand, R., 2011, "Anti-aliased Euclidean distance transform", Pattern Recognition Letters 32, pp252-257.

Ilic, V., Lindblad, J. and Sladoje, N., 2015, "Precise Euclidean Distance Transform in 3D from voxel coverage representation", Pattern Recognition Letters 65, pp184-191.

Linnér, E., Strand, R., 2014a, "A Graph-Based Implementation of the Anti-Aliased Euclidean Distance Transform", 22nd International Conference on Pattern Recognition.

Linnér, E., Strand, R., 2014b, "Anti-Aliased Euclidean Distance Transform on 3D Sampling Lattices", DCGI 2014, pp 88-98.

Montanari, U., 1968, "A Method for Obtaining Skeletons Using a Quasi-Euclidean Distance", Journal of the ACM, vol 15 (4), pp 600-624

Ragnemalm, I., "Contour Processing Distance Transforms", 1989, Proc. 5th Int Conf on Image Analysis and Processing.

Rutowitz, D., "Efficient processing of 2-D images", 1989, Proc. 5th Int Conf on Image Analysis and Processing.

Rosenfeld, A., Pfaltz, J.L., 1966. Sequential operations in digital picture processing. Journal of the ACM 13 (4), 471–494.

Ye, Q.-Z, 1988, "The signed Euclidean distance transform and its applications", 9th Int. Conf. on Pattern Recognition.

OPENMV: A PYTHON POWERED, EXTENSIBLE MACHINE VISION CAMERA

Ibrahim Abdelkader[1], Yasser El-Sonbaty[1] and Mohamed El-Habrouk[2]
[1]*Dept. of Computer Science, Arab Academy for Science & Technology, Alexandria, Egypt*
[2]*Dept. of Electrical Engineering, Faculty of Engineering, Alexandria, Egypt*

ABSTRACT

Advances in semiconductor manufacturing processes and large scale integration keep pushing demanding applications further away from centralized processing, and closer to the edges of the network (i.e. Edge Computing). It has become possible to perform complex in-network image processing using low-power embedded smart cameras, enabling a multitude of new collaborative image processing applications. This paper introduces OpenMV, a new low-power smart camera that lends itself naturally to wireless sensor networks and machine vision applications. The uniqueness of this platform lies in running an embedded Python3 interpreter, allowing its peripherals and machine vision library to be scripted in Python. In addition, its hardware is extensible via modules that augment the platform with new capabilities, such as thermal imaging and networking modules.

KEYWORDS

WSNs, Embedded, Image Processing, Machine Vision, Smart Camera, Python

1. INTRODUCTION

Embedded smart cameras have a wide range of applications from automation and robotics to complex in-network image processing such as distributed object tracking and localization (Ercan et al, 2007) and distributed surveillance (Bramberger et al, 2006). This paper presents OpenMV—a new low-cost, low-power embedded smart camera platform for machine vision and wireless sensor networks applications. OpenMV is designed with low-cost and usability in mind. It can be scripted in Python 3 and comes with an extensive machine vision library, an IDE and example scripts. The IDE allows viewing the frame-buffer and uploading and executing scripts via serial over USB or sockets, enabling remote development and deployment.

The remainder of this paper is organized as follows: Section 2 presents a survey of related low-power smart camera platforms. Section 3 and 4 introduce the proposed smart camera hardware and software architectures. Finally, the conclusions and future work are presented in Section 5 as well as a comparison between existing platforms and the proposed platform.

2. RELATED WORK

This chapter presents a survey of existing low-power embedded smart camera platforms. Their design specifications, main features and limitations are reviewed. In addition, a comparison between the following platforms and the proposed platform is presented in Table 1 at the end Section 5.

2.1 eCam

eCam (Park & Chou, 2006) is an ultra compact (1.1x0.7 inches) wireless image sensor node that consumes about 230mW of power. eCam combines a single package VGA sensor/lens with an Eco (Park & Chou, 2006) wireless sensor platform and a 170mAh Lithium-Polymer battery. See Figure 1. eCam supports JPEG compression via an external JPEG codec, which also serializes the image data to the host controller (located on the Eco node) due to the lack of a hardware camera interface. The Eco node's MCU (nRF24E1) is a VLSI chip integrating a radio transceiver and an 8051 core that runs at a few MHz with a few KiBs of RAM. The radio transceiver has a maximum data-rate of 1Mbps which can only support 1.5FPS streaming.

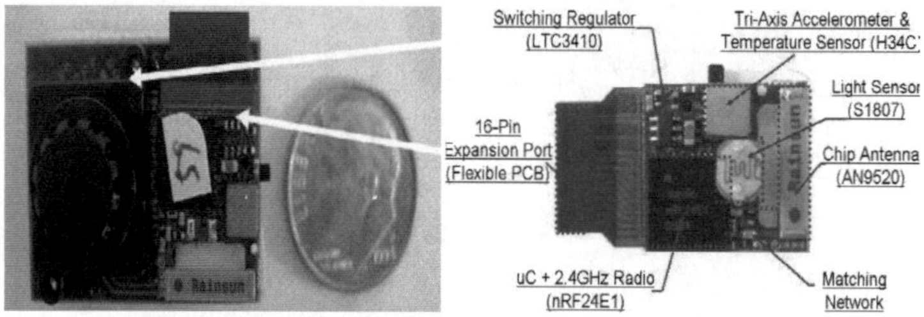

Figure 1. (a) eCam: Ultra compact camera node. (b) Echo Node

2.2 CMUCam3

CMUCam3 (Rowe et al, 2007) is an embedded camera based on NXP's LPC2106 MCU (a 32-bit 60MHz ARM7 MCU with on-chip 64KiB of RAM and 128KiB of flash) and an OV6620 image sensor, see Figure 2.

Figure 2. CMUcam3: Main board, sensor and an MMC memory card for mass storage

Due to its limited memory, the CMUCam3 stores frames in a 1MiBs FIFO chip (AL4V8M440). This approach increases cost and power requirements. Additionally, it does not allow the image to be accessed randomly without copying parts of the frame to the SRAM first, which slows down the frame-rate. The CMUCam3 implements a set of optimized image processing algorithms in C, in addition to image compression libraries and a scripting engine. CMUCam3 consumes about 500mW of power.

2.3 Pixy (CMUCam5)

Pixy (CMUcam5, 2015) is the new version of CMUCAM3, featuring a 200MHz dual core (ARM Cortex-M4/M0) LPC4330 MCU with 264KiBs of RAM 1MiB of Flash, see Figure 3.

Figure 3. Pixy (CMUCam5)

Unlike its predecessor, Pixy is designed specifically to recognize colored objects. Pixy does not provide a scripting language, nor does it provide any other image processing features. However, the default firmware image can be replaced with a custom one. For extensions, the Pixy camera uses an I/O header on the back side to breakout the UART, SPI and I2C peripherals, possibly to be used for interfacing radio and/or hardware modules.

2.4 Mesheye

MeshEye (Hengstler et al, 2007) is a smart stereo-camera targeted at intelligent surveillance applications. MeshEye is based on a 50MHz ARM7 (AT91SAM7S) processor, with 64KiB of RAM and 256 KiB of flash, see Figure 4. MeshEye has a unique stereo-vision system that continuously tracks the position, range, and size of moving objects. This information is used to trigger a higher resolution color camera to capture an image of the object for further processing.

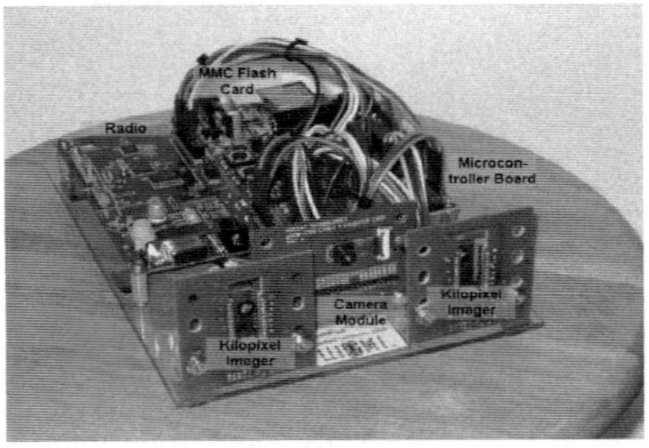

Figure 4. MeshEye Prototype

2.5 MicrelEye

MicrelEye (Kerhet et al, 2007) is a fully integrated wireless camera, designed for cooperative distributed image processing applications. MicrelEye consists of an Atmel MCU+FPGA system-on-chip (SoC), an OV7620 VGA image sensor and an LMX9820A Bluetooth transceiver, see Figure 5.

Figure 5. MicrelEye node

MicrelEye nodeThe MicrelEye architecture is unique in that it uses a SoC with configurable logic blocks. Using FPGAs allows exploiting parallelism to optimize some image processing algorithms. For example, optical flow performance can be optimized using FPGAs (Nagy et al, 2006). In addition, an optimized support vector machine-like (SVM-like) algorithm is implemented on MicrelEye for people detection and counting. The algorithm is partially implemented on the FPGA. The first steps (image readout, background subtraction...) are implemented on FPGA, whereas feature extraction and SVM are implemented on the microcontroller. In addition to image processing, the FPGA is also used to implement the image sensor interface and to access an external 1MBs SRAM, which is used to store frames for later processing.

3. OPENMV SMART CAMERA

In this section, the OpenMV platform is introduced and discussed in detail, including the image sensor, microcontroller, networking, extensions, software and firmware.

3.1 Overview

The main board measures 1.4"x1.2" and consists of the image sensor, the MCU, power supply, a micro-SD card slot and extension headers, see Figure 6. In addition, built-in RGB and IR LEDs are provided on board, for status indication and night vision, respectively.

Figure 6. OpenMV's main board

3.2 Image Sensor

OpenMV uses OmniVision's OV7725 VGA CMOS sensor. The OV7725 supports cropping and windowing to output arbitrary frame sizes, as well as standard resolutions. The OV7725 was chosen mainly for its low-cost and its high sensitivity in low-light operation (enabled by its 6.0x6.0μm pixels). The OV7725 does support JPEG, however the MCU has a hardware JPEG encoder. JPEG compression is mainly used to transfer frames to the host for debugging, however it can enable advanced features such as medical images compression (El-Sonbaty et al, 2003).

3.3 Microcontroller

OpenMV is based on the STM32F7 ARM Cortex-M7 dual-issue MCU running at 216MHz. The MCU features 512KiBs SRAM, 2MiBs flash (part of which is used for lookup tables and internal flash filesystem) DMA and DMA2D, USB OTG, a single precision FPU, DSP instructions, a digital camera interface (DCMI), JPEG encoder, timers and multiple serial peripheral interfaces such as I2C, SPI and UART.

The MCU's SRAM is divided into two non-contiguous blocks; a main block and a core-coupled memory (CCM). The main block is used for the frame buffer, and for storing computed integral images (Crow, 1984) and other temporary images when needed, while the CCM is used exclusively for the stack, heap and data.

3.4 Networking

The main OpenMV board is decoupled from the networking modules using extension modules (or shields). This decoupling allows the camera to work with different networks (such as WiFi, BLE or Zigbee) using different radio transceivers to easily integrate the sensor into existing network infrastructures.

3.5 Power Consumption

To minimize idle power consumption, the CPU can enter low-power modes from which it can be awaken via interrupts. Additionally, in a few key places in the code, such as waiting for an image readout, the *WFI* (Wait For Interrupt) instruction is executed to force the processor to suspend execution until an IRQ is received. Furthermore, the MCU supports switching to lower frequencies (frequency scaling).

3.6 Extensions

The extension headers breakout the ADC/DAC, PWM, I2C, SPI and UART interfaces, allowing the camera to be interfaced to motors, network modules and other sensors such as thermal and distance sensors. A low-resolution thermal imaging shield was designed allowing the sensor to be used for presence detection. Other shields including WiFi, BLE and LCD shields were also designed, see Figure 7.

(a) (b)

Figure 7. OpenMV hardware extensions. (a) WiFi module. (b) BLE (Bluetooth Low-Energy) module

4. OPENMV SOFTWARE ARCHITECTURE

The software architecture consists of a number of hardware abstraction layers (HALs), middleware and userspace software, see Figure 8.

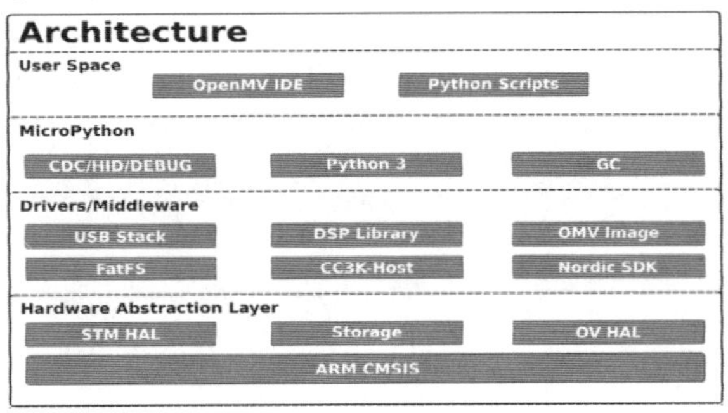

Figure 8. Software architecture shows the hardware abstraction layers, middleware and userspace software

The glueware/middleware layer includes the USB stack, FatFS (Cha, 2005) filesystem, DSP libraries, network drivers and optimized machine vision code. On top of those layers, the camera runs a lightweight implementation of Python3 called MicroPython (MicroPython, 2013) which allows user access to peripheral drivers and compiled machine vision code using Python scripts. The userspace level consists of a cross-platform IDE designed specifically for the camera, which can view the frame buffer, access sensor controls, upload scripts and run them on the camera via USB (or WiFi/BLE if available).

4.1 Machine Vision Support

The OpenMV image processing library implements a fairly comprehensive set of image processing algorithms and supports multiple image formats (PGM/PPM, BMP, JPEG for still images, and MJPEG and GIFs for videos). The image processing library is implemented in optimized C code while exporting a user-friendly API which can be called from Python scripts.

4.2 Basic Image Processing Functions

The image processing library includes basic image handling functions such as loading/saving images from the filesystem to memory (or the frame buffer), cropping, scaling and blending. In addition, basic drawing functions for visualizing results are also implemented, such as drawing lines, rectangles, circles and strings, and setting/getting image information and pixels. Furthermore, the library provides image filtering functions are implemented such as median, midpoint, Gaussian smoothing functions and histogram equalization.

4.4 Advanced Image Processing Functions

The OpenMV image processing library also provides several advanced image processing functions, such as QR Code detection and decoding, ApriTags (Olson, 2011) support, face and eyes detection using Viola-Jones Haar cascade (Viola & Jones, 2001) and iris estimation by analyzing the gradient vectors in an eye (Timm & Barth, 2011). See Figure 9.

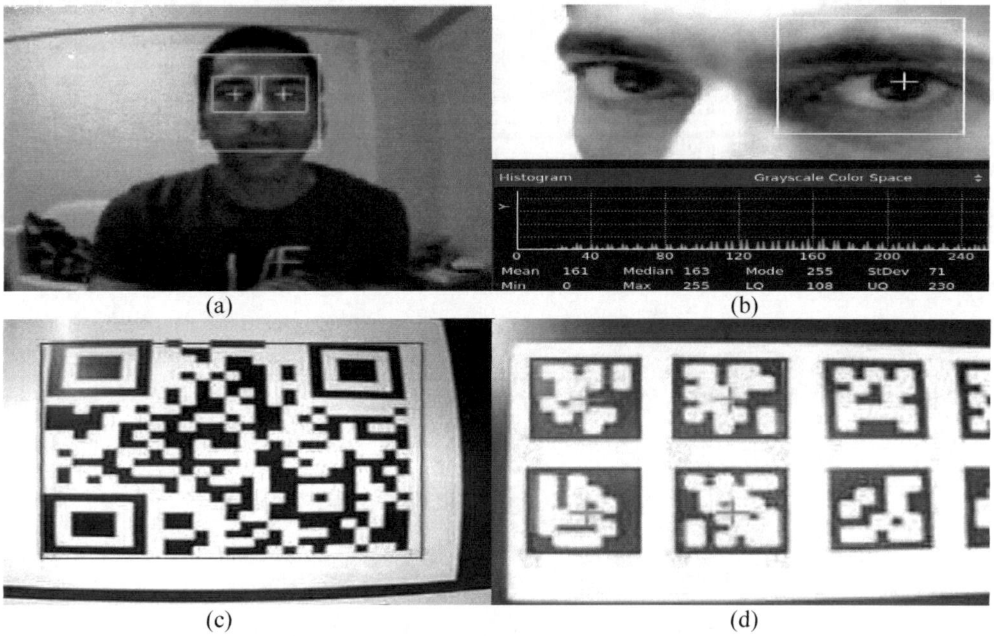

Figure 9. Advanced machine vision features: (a) Face and eyes detection running on OpenMV
(b) Iris localization

Many algorithms have been proposed for matching partially occluded objects, such as matching connected lines (El-Sonbaty & Ismail, 2003). To accomplish this, the image library includes FAST (Rosten & Drummond, 2006)-ORB (Rublee et al, 2011) detector for keypoint extraction and description respectively, in addition to Histogram of Oriented Gradients (HoG) (Dalal & Triggs, 2005; Bilinski et al, 2009). Additionally, the library implements fast template matching via Normalized Cross Correlation (NCC) (Lewis, 1995) with both extensive search and Diamond Search (DS) (Zhu & Ma, 2000), optical flow for estimating the direction of movement and finally, the Canny edge detector and Hough transform for detection of lines in an image.

5. CONCLUSION

This paper presented OpenMV, a machine vision platform, suitable for use in wireless sensor networks and the IoT. The platform runs an embedded Python3 interpreter and implements an optimized image processing library which can be called from Python user scripts. The OpenMV main board is decoupled from networking modules to allow interfacing to different networks. In addition to its commercial availability, OpenMV is open-source hardware and software, which means it can be built from source for use in research purposes. Future work includes hardware upgrade to the new STM32FH 1-1.5MiBs SRAM/400MHz, Cortex-M7 MCU.

Table 1. A comparison of image sensor platforms

Sensor	eCam	CMUCam3	Pixy (CMUCam5)	MeshEye	MicrelEye	OpenMV
Power	230mW	500mW	700mW	260mW	N/A	500mW
Networking	nRF24E1	N/A	N/A	Zigbee	BLE	WiFi/BLE/Zigbee/nRF24x
Processor Type	VLSI uC/2.4Radio	μC	μC	μC	μC+FPGA	μC
Clock Speed	20MHz	60MHz	204MHz	55MHz	14MHz	216/400MHz (Dual issue)
RAM	4KiB SRAM	64KiB SRAM	264KiB SRAM	64KiB SRAM	16KiB SRAM	512KiB/1.5MiBs SRAM
ROM	External EEPROM	128KiB	1MiB	256KiB	20KiB	1-2MiB
External Storage	No	SD Card	No	MMC	No	uSD/Flash
FPU/DSP Or Acceleration	No	No	FPU, DSP	No	FPGA	FPU, DSP
Image Buffer	N/A	FIFO	Internal SRAM	MMC	External SRAM	Internal SRAM
Programmable/Scriptable	No	Yes	No	No	No	MicroPython
Image Sensor	OV7640 (0.3MP)	OV6620 (0.1MP)	OV9715 (1MP)	ADNS-3060 ADCM-2700	OV7640 (0.3MP)	OV7725 (0.3MP)
Hardware JPEG Encoder	(External) Yes	No	No	No	No	Yes
Image Processing	No	Face detection, Convolutions, color tracking, Frame Differencing	Color Tracking	Object Detection and Tracking	Image Classification.	Face detection FAST/ORB Iris/Eye , Optical flow, Color tracking, QR-Code, AprilTags
Open Source	No	Yes	Yes	No	No	Yes
BOM Cost	N/A	N/A	N/A	N/A	N/A	$16@1000s
Commercially available	No	No	Yes	No	No	Yes
Dimensions	2.0x2.8 cm	5.5x5.7 cm	5.3x5.0 cm	N/A	5x5x3 cm^3	3.0x3.5 cm

REFERENCES

Bilinski, P. et al, 2009. Multiple object tracking with occlusions using HOG descriptors and multi resolution images. In Crime Detection and Prevention (ICDP 2009), 3rd International Conference on (pp. 1-6). IET.

Bramberger, M. et al, 2006. Distributed embedded smart cameras for surveillance applications. Computer, 39(2), 68-75.

Cha, N. 2005. FatFs generic FAT file system module. http://elm-chan. org/fsw/ff/00index_e. Html.

CMUcam5 (Pixy): http://www.cmucam.org/ (2013).

Crow, F. C. 1984. Summed-area tables for texture mapping. ACM SIGGRAPH computer graphics, 18(3), 207-212.

Dalal, N. & Triggs, B., 2005. Histograms of oriented gradients for human detection. In 2005 IEEE Computer Society Conference on Computer Vision and Pattern Recognition (CVPR'05) (Vol. 1, pp. 886-893). IEEE.

El-Sonbaty, Y. & Ismail, M. A., 2003. Matching occluded objects invariant to rotations, translations, reflections, and scale changes. In Scandinavian Conference on Image Analysis (pp. 836-843). Springer Berlin Heidelberg.

El-Sonbaty, Y. et al, 2003. Compressing sets of similar medical images using multilevel centroid technique. In Proceedings of Digital Image Computing: Techniques and Applications.

Ercan, A. O. et al, 2007. Object tracking in the presence of occlusions via a camera network. In Proceedings of the 6th international conference on Information processing in sensor networks (pp. 509-518). ACM.

Hengstler, S. et al, 2007. MeshEye: a hybrid-resolution smart camera mote for applications in distributed intelligent surveillance. In Proceedings of the 6th international conference on Information processing in sensor networks (pp. 360-369). ACM.

Kerhet, A. et al, 2007. A iow-power wireless video sensor node for distributed object detection. journal of real-time image processing, 2(4), 331-342.

Lewis, J. P., 1995. Fast normalized cross-correlation. In Vision interface (Vol. 10, No. 1, pp. 120-123).

MicroPython: http://micropython.org/ (2013).

Nagy, Y. et al., 2006. VHDL-based Simulation of a Parallel Implementation of a Phase-based Algorithm for Optical Flow. In 2006 IEEE International Conference on Video and Signal Based Surveillance (pp. 27-27). IEEE.

Olson, E., 2011. AprilTag: A robust and flexible visual fiducial system. In Robotics and Automation (ICRA), 2011 IEEE International Conference on (pp. 3400-3407). IEEE.

Park, C. & Chou, P. H., 2006. eCAM: ultra compact, high data-rate wireless sensor node with a miniature camera. In Proceedings of the 4th international conference on Embedded networked sensor systems (pp. 359-360). ACM.

Park, C. & Chou, P. H., 2006. Eco: Ultra-wearable and expandable wireless sensor platform. In International Workshop on Wearable and Implantable Body Sensor Networks (BSN'06) (pp. 4-pp). IEEE.

Rosten, E. & Drummond, T. (2006). Machine learning for high-speed corner detection. In European conference on computer vision (pp. 430-443). Springer Berlin Heidelberg.

Rowe, A. G. et al, 2007. CMUcam3: an open programmable embedded vision sensor.

Rublee, E. et al, 2011. ORB: An efficient alternative to SIFT or SURF. In Computer Vision (ICCV), 2011 IEEE International Conference on (pp. 2564-2571). IEEE.

Timm, F. & Barth, E., 2011. Accurate Eye Centre Localisation by Means of Gradients. VISAPP, 11, 125-130.

Viola, P. & Jones, M., 2001. Rapid object detection using a boosted cascade of simple features. In Computer Vision and Pattern Recognition, 2001. CVPR 2001. Proceedings of the 2001 IEEE Computer Society Conference on (Vol. 1, pp. I-511).

Zhu, S. & Ma, K. K., 2000. A new diamond search algorithm for fast block-matching motion estimation. IEEE transactions on Image Processing, 9(2), 287-290.

3D FACE RECONSTRUCTION FROM IMAGE(S) BASED ON GENDER AND ETHNICITY GENERIC MODELS

Zexi Liu[1] and Fernand Cohen[2]
[1]*Kepler Group LLC, New York, NY 10016, USA*
[2]*Drexel University, Electrical & Computer Engineering, Philadelphia, PA 19104, USA*

ABSTRACT

In this paper, we describe a novel approach for creating a 3D face model from an image or images of a human face taken at a priori unknown poses using gender and ethnicity specific 3D generic face models. This process starts with a generic face model, which is morphed as images of the person become available using pre-selected point landmarks that are tessellated to form a high resolution triangular mesh. The 3D face synthesis allows for accurate pose estimation as well as face identification in 3D. The estimation of the unknown pose is achieved through the use of a Levenberg-Marquardt optimization process. Encouraging experimental results are obtained in controlled environment with high resolution images under ideal illumination condition, as well as for images taken in uncontrolled environment under arbitrary illumination with low resolution cameras.

KEYWORDS

3D Reconstruction; Subdivision; Ray Tracing; Pose Estimation

1. INTRODUCTION

Face detection and recognition is an important component of a biometrics technology system and it has proven its usefulness in law enforcement by helping identifying or narrowing down possible suspects from surveillance cameras at crime scenes, or by finding suspect according to the description from witnesses. Since the advent of 9/11, it also became an important tool in securing homeland safety against potential terrorist attacks by tracking and identifying such individual(s). Face is a nearly convex three-dimensional (3D) object, and hence it will be natural to recognize faces in 3D with the added benefits of being independent of lighting conditions and appearance due to pose.

1.1 Related Work

There are different modalities that one can use for obtaining data from an individual's face, ranging from high resolution scanner to stereoscopic camera system (Beeler et al. 2010; Graham et al. 2016). A much cheaper and more user-friendly modality would be to use a photogrammetry tool chain (Snavely et al. 2006; Furukawa and Ponce 2008; Furukawa et al. 2010), which uses regular digital cameras or camcorders. However, the reconstructed 3D object or 3D scene is much coarser than the method proposed in (Beeler et al. 2010; Graham et al. 2016) and hence more suitable for reconstructing large objects such as buildings (Snavely et al. 2007). In previous works, efforts were concentrated in establishing point correspondences.

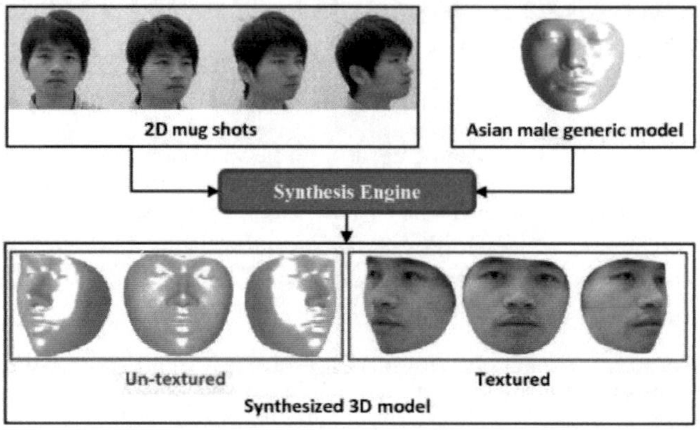

Figure 1. 2D-to-3D Synthesis

An alternative is to use morphable model methods, for example, the Active Appearance Model (Cootes et al. 2001), the Active Shape Model (Ginneken et al. 2002), and a series of derivative models (Zhang and Cohen 2002; Huber 2016), to locate landmark points on the face. With these points being located on both the images and the morphable model, the mode is morphed with an iterative optimization to produce a 3D model that best fits the landmarks in the images. The reconstruction methods in (Zhang and Cohen 2002; Park et al. 2010) follow this procedure.

1.2 System Overview

Our system consists of three parts: a surveillance system that captured images of a person; a 2D-to-3D synthesis part that construct a 3D face based images of the individual and a generic 3D face model; and a recognition part that recognizes the individual. 2D images are captured using cameras. The synthesis engine morphs a generic face model in accordance with a mug shot image (or images) of an individual, and reconstruct a 3D face model for that particular person (Figure 1). The recognition engine compares the reconstructed face individual model to 3D models of individuals stored in a database. This is based on a 3D surface global alignment algorithm that uses the average point-to-point distance between the two surfaces as the metric for alignment.

1.3 Generic Models

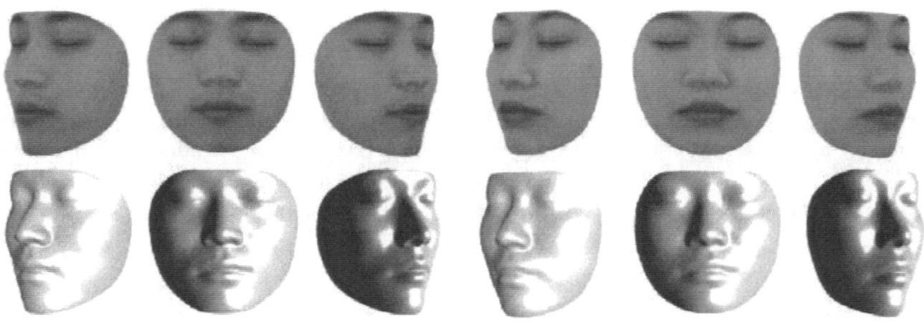

(a) Asian male (b) Asian female

Figure 2. Average face (with and without texture)

In this work, generic models are obtained using a 3D scanner and by averaging faces from the same gender and ethnic group. The method of calculating the average face is described in (Liu 2016). It uses 134 feature points based on an extended version of the MPEG-4 Face Definition Parameters (Pandzic 2003) along with the Loop subdivision algorithm (Loop 1987; Huang et al. 2014) to obtain high density 3D surface. The same set of feature points will also be used in 3D face synthesis. The average face is shown in Figure 2. We use the same method to establish dense point-to-point correspondences between the 2D images and the generic model for reconstruction/synthesis. This is described in the following section.

2. 3D HUMAN FACE SYNTHESIS

The traditional morphable model (Zhang 2002; Huber 2016) with Levenberg-Marquardt (LM) algorithm (Levenberg 1944) has its inherent drawbacks in reconstructing a 3D face model. It highly depends on the consistency of the extracted feature points as it seeks an average result between the inconsistent feature points. Since the morphing transformation used is an explicit polynomial transformation, averaging between inconsistent points globally impacts the overall morphed fit (Liu 2016). Our solution is to extend the feature points through loop subdivision of the triangle tessellation (see Figure 3) to generate new feature points upon which the individual 3D face is constructed. The inconsistency becomes now locally instead of globally confined. The accuracy of the synthesized model improves, as more images are acquired. Our reconstruction/synthesis process is capable of generating 3D face model based on a single image or multiple images.

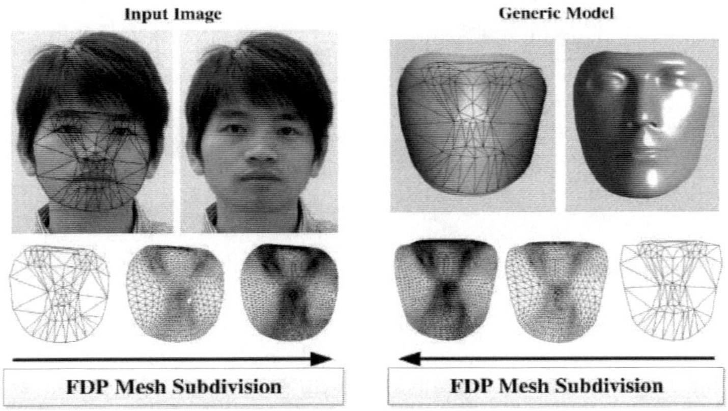

Figure 3. Loop Subdivision

2.1 Single Image

The overall procedure of obtaining a synthesized model from a frontal image and a generic model is shown in Figs. 4 and 5. Based on pre-selected feature points, both the image and the generic model are partitioned into triangular meshes based on Delaunay triangulation. Note that the feature points in the image and the generic model have an already established point-to-point and triangle-to-triangle correspondences. Next, the point density on both frontal image and generic model is increased using the loop subdivision algorithm (Loop 1987).

This process leads to a very dense correspondences between the input image mesh and the generic model mesh. The synthesized model is then formed by combining the (x_I, y_I) values from the image with the z values sampled from the generic model: $(x_I, y_I, z_p = z(x_g, y_g, -1))$ (see Figure 4). To explain the function $z(\cdot, \cdot, \cdot)$, we can trace an imaginary ray from point $V(x_g, y_g, -1)$ to the generic model and the intersection point P (see Figure 5). The synthesized model consists then of dense points (x_I, y_I, z_p), with the appearance (intensity) at the point $(x_I, y_I, z(x_g, y_g, -1))$ being $I(x_I, y_I)$. The method preserves some basic shape of the eyes, nose, mouth, and overall face. Note that the z values as expected are not accurate as they are sampled from the generic model and are not influenced by the frontal image. With only one frontal image available, having a gender/race generic model results in realistic z values. Improvement on z values will come about when more than one image of the person is obtained.

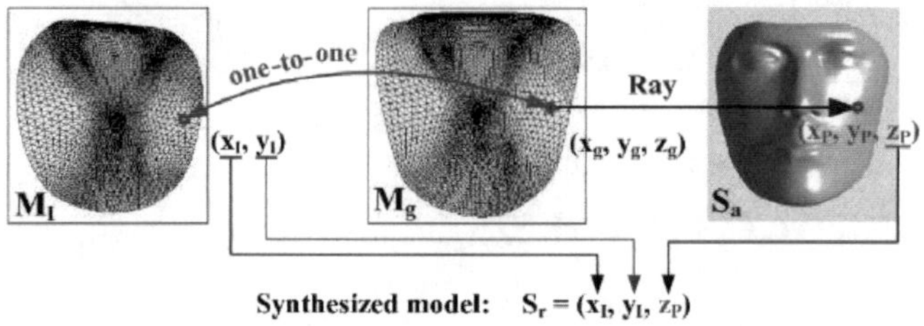

Figure 4. Synthesize 3D Face Model

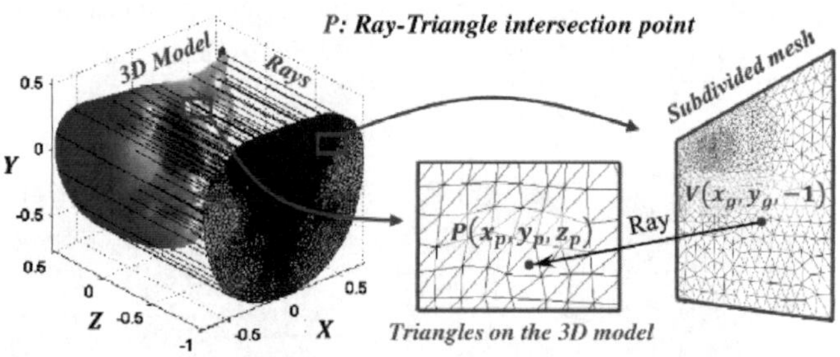

Figure 5. Ray tracing

2.2 Multiple Images

As mug shots of individual faces usually consist of both frontal image and profile image per standard police procedures, we improve on the face reconstruction by updating the z values that were limited to the z values of the generic model and hence did not really represent the z values of the actual person (see Figure 6). By making use of the profile image (90-degree mug shot), the z values are enhanced by replacing the z values on the synthesized model with the x values in the profile image (see Figure 7). Note that for recognition (see the experiment section) even if some z values are incorrect (see Figure 6(b) eye, nose, and mouth areas); the personalized model is still helpful in classifying the individual based on the frontal image only.

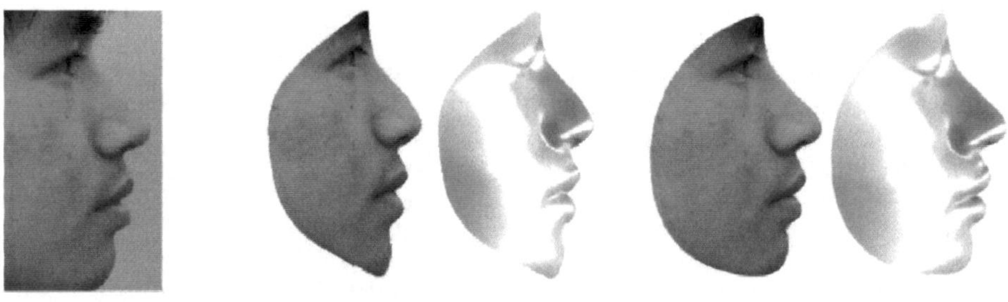

(a) Profile image (b) Frontal only (c) Frontal + profile

Figure 6. Enhanced Synthesis Result

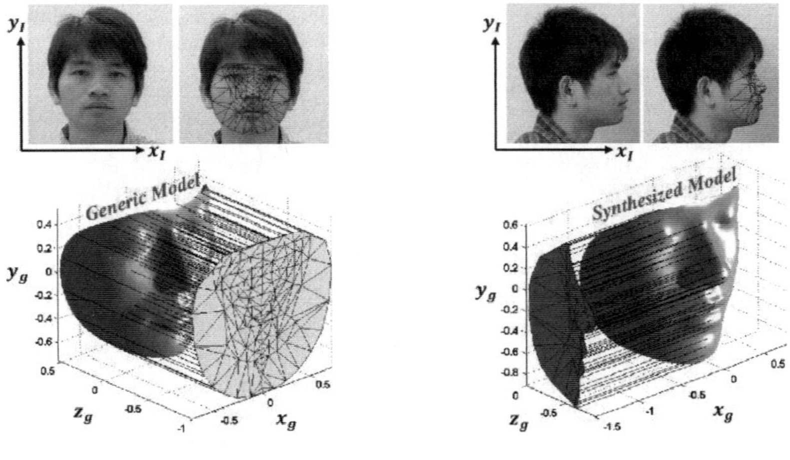

(a) (x_I, y_I) replace (x_g, y_g) (b) x_I replaces z_g

Figure 7. Synthesis with Ray-Tracing

Any additional image taken from an arbitrary angle can also be used in updating the personalization process. The update process is as follows: 1) Estimate the view point of the given image by running the LM algorithm (Yang and Zhang 2002); 2) then apply the pose parameters on the generic model so that the model is rotated and in sync with the same pose as in the image; 3) When side-view images are taken between 0~90 degrees, parts of the side of the face will be occluded, but since a face is roughly symmetric the personalization algorithm uses information from the visible side to stitch the missing side (see Figure 8b); 4) rotate the model back to the frontal position; 5) flip the model horizontally in order to augment the invisible/occluded half of the face; 6) register the left half and the right half of the face together using common feature points; 7) generate the symmetry plane in order to delete the overlapping half; 8) then merge the two halves into a single synthesized generic model. Steps 1 and 2 are demonstrated in Figure 8(a). Step 4~8 are shown in Figure 8(b).

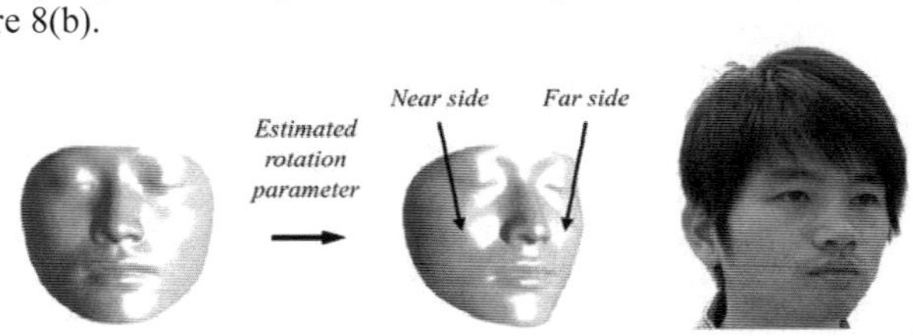

(a) Rotate the generic model as in the image

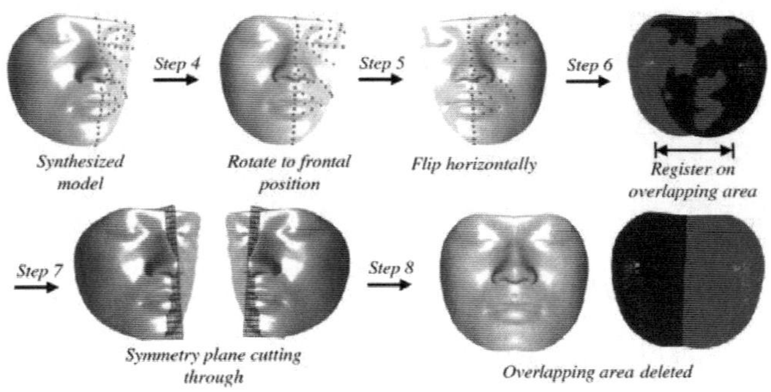

(b) Steps of reconstructing a complete face

Figure 8. Synthesis based on a non-frontal image

To refine the synthesized model using multiple images, we iteratively use the synthesis routine on all the acquired images one by one starting with the frontal image, where the output model of the previous iteration will be the input model for the next iteration. The iterative process refines the model by using more images leading to accurate reconstruction (see Table 1). The sub-resolution error indicates that the proposed method is as accurate as the 3D scanner itself.

3. 3D HUMAN FACE RECOGNITION

In 3D domain the recognition/identification of face model is reduced to the registration of 3D surfaces. We implemented a simple but effective classifier that accentuates the dissimilarity between different individuals resulting in large classification errors between model faces for different individuals, while resulting in sub-resolution errors when models are from the same individual. The classifier makes use of the correspondences between feature points on the face in computing these distance errors. The recognition process is shown in Figure 9. We construct the benchmark models using the high-res images; whereas we use the "arbitrarily acquired" low-res images to construct test models. After we obtain the 3D face models, the classifier is applied. The algorithm first registers two surfaces (benchmark and test) using the Iterative Closest Point (ICP) algorithm (Bouaziz 2013) and then evaluates the point-to-point distances. Each test model is compared with all benchmark models. Experiment results are reported in the next section.

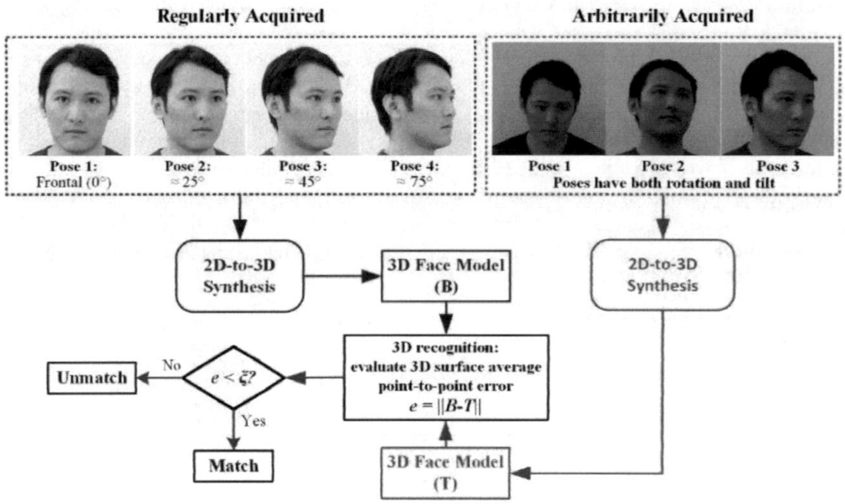

Figure 9. Recognition Process

4. EXPERIMENTS

We first test the effectiveness of the iterative synthesis by using 15 Asian male test subjects. Each of them has 4 images taken. The reconstruction error is the average point-to-point distance between the reconstructed model and the 3D scanned "true" face. The error decreases with more pose images (See Table 1). The time consumption of synthesizing one 3D face model is about 0.5 seconds. We also tested the method on Asian female and Caucasian male and obtained similar results. But due to the length constrain, only the Asian male results are reported here.

Table 1. Iterative Synthesis

	Scenario	Error*
1	Synthesize with pose [1]	1.731±1.357
2	Synthesize with pose [1+2]	1.423±1.287
3	Synthesize with pose [1+2+3]	1.273±0.932
4	Synthesize with pose [1+2+3+4]	0.894±0.736

* mean and standard deviation (unit: mm) * Scanner resolution=1.136 mm

We also test the reconstruction with different generic models (see Table 2). The following expected conclusions are drawn: 1) The combination of correct gender and ethnic average model results in the smallest errors (Cases 1, 5, and 9) in each group; 2) The combination of incorrect gender and incorrect ethnic model yields the largest errors (cases 6 and 8) justifying and warranting the usage of gender/ethnic based generic model; and 3) Ethnic models play a more important role than gender models in the reconstruction process.

Table 2. Synthesize Using Different Generic Models

	Scenario	Error
1	Synthesize AM using AM model	0.894±0.736
2	Synthesize AM using AF model	0.948±0.880
3	Synthesize AM using CM model	1.659±1.185
4	Synthesize AF using AM model	0.962±0.849
5	Synthesize AF using AF model	0.902±0.801
6	Synthesize AF using CM model	1.846±1.202
7	Synthesize CM using AM model	1.632±0.925
8	Synthesize CM using AF model	1.885±1.067
9	Synthesize CM using CM model	0.877±0.701

* AM = Asian males; * AF = Asian females;
* CM = Caucasian males; * Scanner resolution=1.136 mm

Finally we test the recognition process (see Figure 9) on 12 different scenarios as indicated in Table 3. Pose 1 is the frontal view. Pose 2 is the side-view approximately 25-degree horizontal rotation. Pose 3 is the side-view approximately 45-degree. Pose 4 is the side-view approximately 75-degree. The numbers in the [*] indicate which pose images are used to reconstruct the 3D model. For instance, [1+2+3+4] means all 4 pose images are used. [2+3] means only pose 2 and 3 are used. This recognition test is a process of discovering a matching test model (T models) for each given benchmark model (B models). The match rate in Table 3 is defined as the number of successful matches / the total number of benchmark models.

Table 3. Recognition Experiment Results

	Benchmark Models	Test Models	Match Rate
1	4 image, Pose [1+2+3+4]	4 image, Pose [1+2+3+4]	100%
2	4 image, Pose [1+2+3+4]	3 image, Pose [1+2+3+4]	100%
3	3 image, Pose [2+3+4]	2 image, Pose [2+3]	100%
4	3 image, Pose [2+3+4]	2 image, Pose [3+4]	98%
5	2 image, Pose [1+5]	2 image, Pose [1+5]	100%
6	2 image, Pose [2+3]	2 image, Pose [2+4]	100%
7	2 image, Pose [2+4]	2 image, Pose [3+4]	98%
8	1 image, Pose [1]	1 image, Pose [1]	98%
9	1 image, Pose [1]	1 image, Pose [1]	94%
10	1 image, Pose [1]	1 image, Pose [1]	92%
11	1 image, Pose [2]	1 image, Pose [1]	94%
12	1 image, Pose [2]	1 image, Pose [1]	94%

The following observations are based on Tables 3:

a) The frontal image with 2 or 3 side-view images in both benchmark models and test models produce better result.
b) The recognition results are getting worse with fewer images.

5. CONCLUSIONS

We presented a novel method to reconstruct 3D human faces using a 2D image and a gender/ethnic based 3D generic models. Our method uses pre-selected point landmarks on both the image and the generic model through a subdivision routine in order to establish dense correspondences between tessellated landmarks on the image and the generic model. The established correspondences allows for a unique 3D model to be created and personalized to the observed individual face using the x-y information from the 2D image and z information from the 3D generic model. With more mug shots of individual faces, we improve on the face reconstruction by updating the z values and personalize them to the individual face. The method is capable of using a single image or a mixed set of images taking at different angles with different lighting conditions (hence independence of lighting and pose). The method can also be extended to sketches created by a forensic artist, and it does not require high-end single-lens reflex (SLR) cameras or a professional studio as long as the images are not blurred.

REFERENCES

Beeler, T. et al, 2010. High-quality Single-shot Capture of Facial Geometry. *In ACM Transactions on Graphics*, Vol. 29, Issue 4, No. 40.

Bouaziz, S. et al, 2013. Sparse Iterative Closest Point. *In Computer Graphics Forum*, Vol. 32, No. 5, pp 113–123.

Cootes, T. et al, 2001. Active Appearance Models. *In IEEE Transactions on Pattern Analysis and Machine Intelligence*, Vol. 23, No. 6, pp 681–685.

Furukawa, Y. and Ponce, J., 2008. Accurate, Dense, and Robust Multi-view Stereopsis. *In IEEE Transactions on Pattern Analysis and Machine Intelligence*, Vol. 32, pp 1362–1376.

Furukawa, Y. et al, 2010. Towards Internet–scale Multi–view Stereo. *IEEE Conference on Computer Vision and Pattern Recognition*. San Francisco, USA, pp. 1434–1441.

Ginneken, B. et al, 2002. Active Shape Model Segmentation with Optimal Features. *In IEEE Transactions on Medical Imaging*, Vol. 21, No. 8, pp 924–933.

Graham, P. et al, 2016. Near-instant Capture of High-resolution Facial Geometry and Reflectance. *In Computer Graphics Forum*, Vol. 35, No. 2, pp 353–363.

Huang, Y. et al, 2014. Feature-adaptive Rendering of Loop Subdivision Surfaces on Modern GPUs. *In Journal of Computer Science and Technology*, Vol. 29, No. 6, pp 1014–1025.

Huber, P. et al, 2016. A Multiresolution 3D Morphable Face Model and Fitting Framework. *11th International Joint Conference on Computer Vision, Imaging and Computer Graphics Theory and Applications*, Rome, Italy.

Levenberg, K., 1944. A Method for the Solution of Certain Non–linear Problems in Least Squares. *In Quarterly of Applied Mathematics*, Vol. 2, pp 164–168.

Liu, Z., 2016. 3D Computational Archaeology and Face Synthesis using Novel Surface Modeling and Registration Techniques, Ph.D. Dissertation, Drexel University, Philadelphia, pp 60-63.

Loop, C., 1987. Smooth Subdivision Surfaces Based on Triangles, Master Thesis, University of Utah.

Pandzic, I. and Forchheimer, R., 2003. *MPEG-4 Facial Animation: The Standard, Implementation and Applications*. John Wiley & Sons, Inc, New York, NY, USA.

Park, U. et al, 2010. Age–invariant Face Recognition. *In IEEE Transactions on Pattern Analysis and Machine Intelligence*, Vol. 32, No. 5, pp 947–954.

Snavely, N. et al, 2006. Photo Tourism: Exploring Image Collections in 3D. *In ACM Transactions on Graphics*, Vol. 25, Issue 3, pp 835–846.

Snavely, N. et al, 2007. Modeling the World from Internet Photo Collections. *In International Journal of Computer Vision*, Vol. 80, No. 2, pp 189–210.

Yang, R. and Zhang, Z., 2002. Model-based Head Pose Tracking with Stereovision. *Proceedings of the Fifth IEEE International Conference on Automatic Face and Gesture Recognition*, Washington DC, USA, pp. 242–247.

Zhang, C. and Cohen, F., 2002. 3D Face Structure Extraction and Recognition from Images using 3D Morphing and Distance Mapping. *In IEEE Transactions on Image Processing*, Vol. 11, No. 11, pp 1249-1259.

TECHNIQUE OF INFORMATION HIDING FOR 3-D PRINTED OBJECTS WITH TRANSMISSION IMAGES OF NEAR-INFRARED RAYS

Kazutake Uehira[1], Masahiro Suzuki[2], Youichi Takashima[3] and Hideyuki Torii[1]
[1]Kanagawa Institute of Technology, 1030 Shimo-ogino, Atsugi, Kanagawa 243-0292, Japan
[2]Tokiwa University, 1-430-1 Miwa, Mito, Ibaraki 310-8585, Japan
[3]NTT Service Evolution Laboratories, 1-1 Hikari-no-oka, Yokosuka, Kanagawa 239-0847, Japan

ABSTRACT

This paper presents a technique of embedding information inside 3-D printed objects and reading the embedded information by utilizing transmission images of near-infrared rays. Conventional techniques of digital watermarking cannot embed information in real objects such as 3-D printed objects because they can only be applied to digital content. In this technique, information is first embedded in digital data for 3-D printing. Then, the information embedded in the digital data is also embedded inside the 3-D printed objects when they are fabricated with the data. The main bodies of the objects are fabricated from materials whose transmittance of near-infrared rays is high. The inside of the objects is structured with fine domains that are fabricated from materials whose transmittance of near-infrared rays is low. The dispositions of the domains express the embedded information. Because the dispositions of the domains can be detected in transmission images of near-infrared rays, the embedded information can be read from the detected dispositions. In the experiment, a test sample was fabricated with a fused deposition-modeling 3-D printer. The main body was fabricated from blue resin that had high transmittance of near-infrared rays. The fine domains were fabricated from white resin that had low transmittance of near-infrared rays. Transmission images were taken using a near-infrared flashlight, which had a 1550-nm wavelength, and an InGaSa camera. The results obtained from the experiment indicate that the dispositions of fine domains inside the test sample can be detected by the naked eye. These findings demonstrate the feasibility of the proposed technique.

KEYWORDS

Digital watermarking, information hiding, 3-D printer, 3-D printing, digital fabrication, additive manufacturing

1. INTRODUCTION

In recent years, researchers have actively studied digital fabrication, i.e., techniques for fabricating real objects with 3-D printers from digital 3-D models. For example, they have examined the feasibility of manufacturing final products with 3-D printers. In the near future, it is believed that consumers will be able to purchase 3-D printers for their homes and manufacture final products by themselves. Moreover, many people believe that digital fabrication will change the ways in which products will be manufactured and physically distributed in the near future (Berman, 2012; Garrett, 2014; Weller, Kleer, & Piller, 2015).

The value of a real object fabricated with a 3-D printer from a 3-D model would be enhanced if useful information about the object could be stored invisibly inside it so that the user can access it as needed. For example, information for accessing a particular website could be embedded inside a fabricated object, and the website could provide important documents, such as instruction manuals or written guarantees, which are often difficult to find when users need them. Because the information is embedded inside the object, the user cannot see it just by looking. That is, under most circumstances, he or she would use the fabricated object without being aware of the embedded information, but could access important documents by reading the information embedded in the object when necessary. This would be very convenient because user would not need to keep any documents or have to search for saved documents. Thus, embedding information inside fabricated objects will enhance the value of these objects.

Many techniques have been proposed for embedding information in digital content, often for the purpose of protecting copyright of digital content (Alface & Macq, 2007; Wang, Lavoue, Denis, and Baskurt, 2008). However, few techniques have been developed for embedding information inside a real object produced by a 3-D printer. One such technique involves first constructing some parts, one of which has a visible pattern, and then assembling these parts into one product that has the patterned part inside (Willis and Wilson, 2013).

We previously proposed and evaluated a technique in which information is embedded in 3-D printed objects while they are being fabricated (Okada, Silapasuphakornwong, Suzuki, Torii, Takashima, & Uehira, 2015; Silapasuphakornwong, Suzuki, Unno, Torii, Uehira, & Takashima, 2016; Suzuki, Silapasuphakornwong, Takashima, Torii, Unno, & Uehira, 2016; Suzuki, Silapasuphakornwong, Unno, Uehira, & Takashima, 2015). In this technique, information is first embedded in digital data for 3-D printing. It is then embedded in a 3-D printed object by structuring its interior with fine domains that are formed at the same time as its main body. The fine domains have different physical characteristics from the surrounding main body of the object. The embedded information is expressed in terms of the dispositions of the fine domains. For example, the existence or nonexistence of fine domains at designated positions can represent "0" or "1." The fine domains are detected by using nondestructive inspections such as X-ray photography or thermography to read out the embedded information from the object. In our previous studies, fine cavities were used as the fine domains, and we found that the embedded information could be read out from the objects.

Previous studies considered the conditions under which users fabricate 3-D printed objects from a single material because 3-D printers are now becoming popular among consumers. In fact, however, some 3-D printers that are in use now can fabricate real objects consisting of multiple materials; such printers will be widely used among consumers in the near future. Techniques for conditions under which users fabricate 3-D printed objects from multiple materials are required.

This paper presents a technique of embedding information in 3-D printed objects fabricated from multiple materials and reading the embedded information from the objects. The basic concept and principle of this technique are described in Section 2. An experiment that was conducted to evaluate the feasibility of the technique is described in Section 3. The feasibility of the technique is then discussed on the basis of the results obtained from the experiment.

2. TECHNIQUE OF INFORMATION HIDING WITH TRANSMISSION IMAGES OF NEAR-INFRARED RAYS FOR 3-D PRINTED OBJECTS

Figure 1 outlines the concept underlying the technique. Providers of models for 3-D printing first create their content on 3-D modeling software such as 3-D computer-aided design (CAD) software or 3-D computer-graphics (CG) software. The providers also construct digital data of the information to be embedded when the real object is produced. The embedded information is used, for example, to enhance the value of the fabricated real object. The value-enhancement information in Figure 1 is a URL of a website. They then integrate the data of the value-enhancement information into the content and finally provide the integrated content to their customers. The customers use 3-D printers to fabricate real objects from the integrated content. Note that the fine structures inside the objects are formed at the same time the objects are fabricated. The structures inside express the value-enhancement information and are detected by nondestructively testing the interiors of the fabricated objects; in so doing, the customers can access the value-enhancement information embedded inside the fabricated objects by detecting the structures inside and decoding them. For instance, a customer who bought the 3D model of the cat in Figure 1 could read the URL from the fabricated object and visit the website.

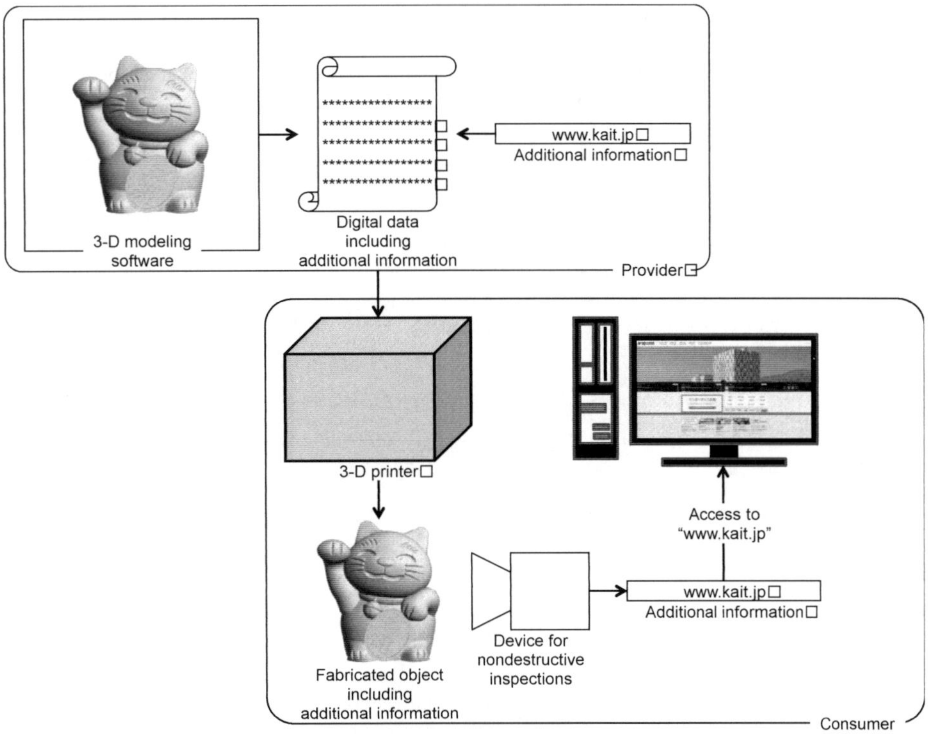

Figure 1. Basic concept underlying technique including our proposal in this study

Figure 2 shows an example of expressing information with fine structures inside 3-D printed objects. The structures inside consist of fine domains, and the dispositions of the fine domains express information. Although there are various ways of expressing information through the dispositions of fine domains, the example shown in Fig. 2 involves binary data: "0" or "1" is expressed based on the existence or nonexistence of a fine domain in a designated position. Each domain is fabricated from materials that have different physical characteristics, such as optical transparency, acoustic conduction, or heat conduction, from those of the materials making up the main bodies of the fabricated objects. Because the physical characteristics of the domains differ from those of the main bodies, the dispositions of fine domains can be detected by using nondestructive testing techniques, such as radioscopy, ultrasonography, and thermography, and the information expressed through the dispositions of the fine domains can be decoded.

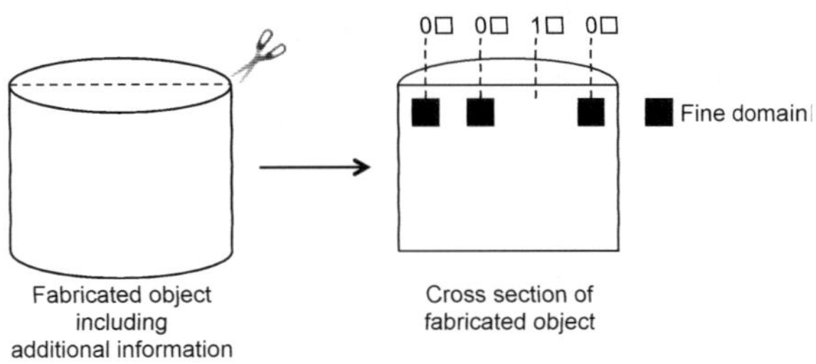

Figure 2. Example of expressing information with dispositions of fine domains inside 3-D printed objects

Figure 3 outlines the principles behind using transmission images of near-infrared rays to detect fine structures inside real objects fabricated with 3-D printers. Here, the main body of the object is fabricated from materials whose transmittance of near-infrared rays is high. The fine domains inside the object are fabricated from materials whose transmittance of near-infrared rays is low. A near-infrared light source is positioned behind the object and illuminates the object. A near-infrared camera is positioned in front of the object, and it records the transmission images of near infrared rays passing through the object. The luminance in the images is darker in the areas where the fine domains exist. Thus, the existence or nonexistence of the fine domains can be detected from the images, and the embedded information can be read from the detected dispositions of the fine domains.

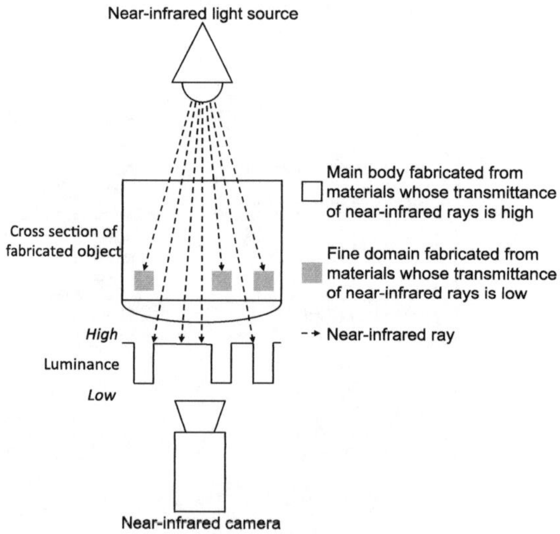

Figure 3. Principle behind using transmission images of near-infrared rays to detect dispositions of fine domains inside 3-D printed objects

3. EVALUATION

3.1 Methodology

A 3-D model of a test sample was generated with 3-D modeling software (Metasequoia 4, Tetraface, Tokyo, Japan). Figure 4 is a schematic diagram of the model. The model was designed as a cuboid 50 mm wide, 50 mm high, and 10 mm deep. The main body of the cuboid and the fine domains inside it were fully filled. There were four dispositions of the fine domains. Each disposition had 25 fine domains, and corresponded with one of four conditions that consisted of combinations of two fine-domain sizes and two spacing distances between fine domains. The two sizes of the fine domains were 1 × 1 mm and 2 × 2 mm, and the two spacing distances between the fine domains were 1 mm and 2 mm. When the sizes were 1 × 1 mm and the spaces were 1 mm, information volume expressed by the disposition was 30.86 bits per cm. When the sizes were 2 × 2 mm and the spaces were 1 mm, the information volume was 12.76 bits per cm. When the sizes were 1 × 1 mm and the spaces were 2 mm, the information volume was 14.79 bits per cm. When the sizes were 2 × 2 mm and the spaces were 2 mm, the information volume was 7.72 bits per cm. The distance from the top surface of the cuboid to each fine domain was 1 mm, and the depths of the fine domains themselves were 1 mm. Thus, the cuboid had a main body that was fully filled and inside it were four dispositions of fine cavities that were fully filled.

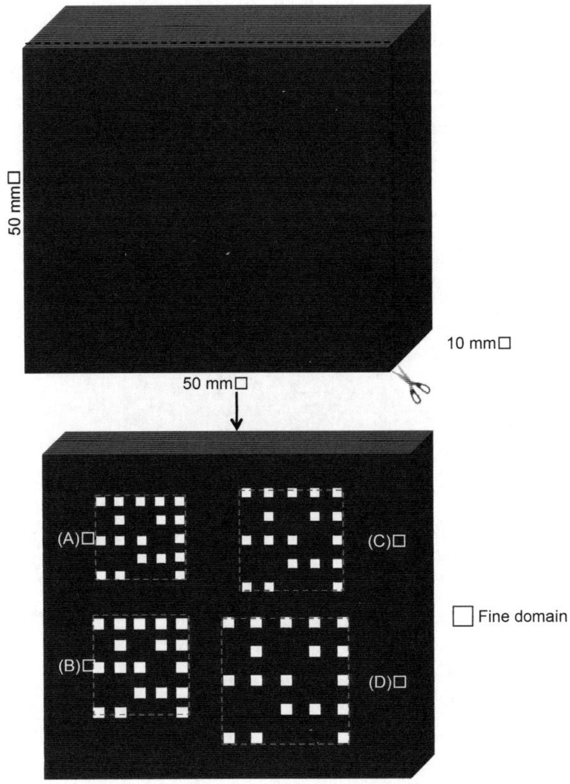

Figure 4. Schematic diagram of test sample:
(A) The sizes of the fine domains were 1 × 1 mm, and the spaces between the fine domains were 1 mm;
(B) The sizes of the fine domains were 2 × 2 mm, and the spaces between the fine domains were 1 mm;
(C) The sizes of the fine domains were 1 × 1 mm, and the spaces between the fine domains were 2 mm;
(D) The sizes of the fine domains were 2 × 2 mm, and the spaces between the fine domains were 2 mm

A real object was fabricated from the 3-D model by using a fused deposition-modeling 3-D printer (Value3D MagiX MF-2200D, Mutoh Industries, Tokyo, Japan). The material of the main body was opaque blue polylactic acid filament that had high transmittance of near-infrared rays. That is, the real object was an opaque blue cuboid that was 50 mm wide, 50 mm high, and 10 mm deep. The main body of the real object was fabricated with 100% infill density. The material of the fine domains was opaque white polylactic acid filament that had low transmittance of near-infrared rays. The four dispositions of fine domains inside the real object were formed on the same scale as that of the 3-D model. Specifically, the sizes of the fine domains were 1 × 1 or 2 × 2 mm, the spaces between fine domains were 1 or 2 mm, the depth from the top surface of the real object to each fine domain was 1 mm, and the depth of the fine domains themselves was 1 mm. The fine domains were fabricated with 100% infill density. Thus, the opaque blue real cuboid used as the test sample had a main body with a 100% infill density and four dispositions of fine domains inside it.

The transmission images of near-infrared rays were taken using a near-infrared flashlight and an InGaAs near-infrared camera. The flashlight had a 1550-nm wavelength, and it was positioned behind the test sample. The camera had a 128 × 128 pixel resolution, and it was positioned in front of the test sample. The images were examined to see if the dispositions of the fine domains could be detected by the naked eye.

3.2 Results and Discussion

Figure 5 shows the images taken in the experiment. The luminance in the images corresponds to the strength of the near-infrared rays. High luminance indicates that the near-infrared rays are strong, and low luminance indicates that the near-infrared rays are weak. The areas where the fine domains existed are darker than the other areas, and this was caused by the difference in transmittance of near-infrared rays between them. All the dispositions of the fine domains can be seen in the images. These results indicate that the dispositions of the fine domains can be detected if the sizes of the fine domains are 1 × 1 mm and the spaces between the fine domains are at least 1 mm. These findings indicate the feasibility of the proposed technique.

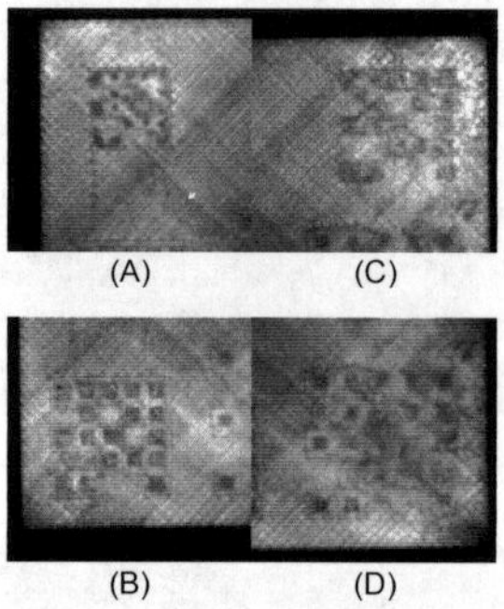

Figure 5. Transmission images of near-infrared rays:
(A) The sizes of the fine domains were 1 × 1 mm, and the spaces between the fine domains were 1 mm;
(B) The sizes of the fine domains were 2 × 2 mm, and the spaces between the fine domains were 1 mm;
(C) The sizes of the fine domains were 1 × 1 mm, and the spaces between the fine domains were 2 mm;
(D) The sizes of the fine domains were 2 × 2 mm, and the spaces between the fine domains were 2 mm

We intend to extend the results that we obtained for our techniques to different materials with many colors in the future. The characteristics of individual materials are different. Hence, we will explore suitable techniques to read hidden information from various types of materials.

4. CONCLUSION

We proposed and evaluated a technique of embedding information inside 3-D printed objects and reading the embedded information by utilizing near-infrared transmission images. In this technique, the main bodies of the objects are fabricated from materials whose transmittance of near-infrared rays is high. The inside of the objects has fine domains that are fabricated from materials whose transmittance of near-infrared rays is low. The dispositions of the domains express information. The information can be read out from the objects by detecting the dispositions of the internal domains from near-infrared transmission images. In an experiment, a test sample was fabricated with a fused deposition-modeling 3-D printer. The main body was fabricated from blue resin that had high transmittance of near-infrared rays. The fine domains were fabricated from white resin that had low transmittance of near-infrared rays. Transmission images were taken using a near-infrared flashlight with 1550-nm wavelength and an InGaSa camera. The results obtained from the experiment indicated that the dispositions of fine domains inside the test sample could be detected by the naked eye. These findings indicate the feasibility of the proposed technique.

ACKNOWLEDGEMENT

This work was supported by the Japan Society for the Promotion of Science (JSPS: KAKENHI Grant Number 15H02707).

REFERENCES

Alface, P. R., and Macq, B., 2007, From 3D mesh data hiding to 3D shape blind and robust watermarking: a survey. *Transactions on Data Hiding and Multimedia Security II*. pp. 91–115.

Berman, B., 2012, 3-D printing: The new industrial revolution. *Business Horizons*, vol. 55, no. 2, pp. 155–162.

Garrett, B., 2014, 3D printing: New economic paradigms and strategic shifts. *Global Policy*, vol. 5, no. 1, pp. 70–75.

Okada, A., Silapasuphakornwong, P., Suzuki, M., Torii, H., Takashima, Y., and Uehira, K., 2015, Non-destructively reading out information embedded inside real objects by using far-infrared light. *Proceedings of SPIE 9599: Applications of Digital Image Processing XXXVIII*. San Diego, CA, pp. 95992V-1–95992V-7.

Silapasuphakornwong, P., Suzuki, M., Unno, H., Torii, H., Uehira, K., and Takashima, Y., "Nondestructive readout of copyright information embedded in objects fabricated with 3-D printers". Digital-forensics and Watermarking: 14th International Workshop, IWDW 2015, Tokyo, Japan, October 7–10, 2015, Revised Selected Papers. Shi, Yun-Qing; Kim, H. J.; Pérez-González; F.; Echizen, I. eds. Cham, Switzerland, Springer International Publishing, 2016, pp. 232–238, (Lecture Notes in Computer Science, Volume 9569), ISBN 978-3-319-31959-9.

Suzuki, M., Silapasuphakornwong, P., Takashima, Y., Torii, H., Unno, H., and Uehira, K., "Technique for protecting copyrights of digital data for 3-D printing, and its application to low infill density objects". The Eighth International Conferences on Advances in Multimedia (MMEDIA 2016). Westphall, C. M.; Gersbeck-Schierholz, B. eds. Lisbon, Portugal, 2016-02-21/25, International Academy, Research, and Industry Association. p. 56–59, ISBN 978-1-61208-452-7.

Suzuki, M., Silapasuphakornwong, P., Unno, H., Uehira, K., and Takashima, Y., 2015, Copyright protection for 3D printing by embedding information inside real fabricated objects. *The International Conference on Computer Vision Theory and Application*. Berlin, Germany, pp. 180–185.

Wang, K., Lavoue, G., Denis, F., and Baskurt, A., 2008, A comprehensive survey on three-dimensional mesh watermarking. *IEEE Transactions on Multimedia*. vol. 10, no. 8, pp. 1513–1527.

Weller, C., Kleer, R., and Piller, F. T., 2015, Economic implications of 3D printing: Market structure models in light of additive manufacturing revisited. *International Journal of Production Economics*, vol. 164, pp. 43–56.

Willis, K. D. D., and Wilson, A. D., 2013, Infrastructs: Fabricating information inside physical objects for imaging in the terahertz region. *ACM Transactions on Graphics*. vol. 32, no. 4, pp. 138:1–138:10.

CONVNET FEATURES FOR AGE ESTIMATION

Ali Maina Bukar and Hassan Ugail
Centre for Visual Computing, University of Bradford,, Richmond Road, Bradford, BD7 1DP, UK

ABSTRACT

Research in facial age estimation has been active for over a decade. This is due to its numerous applications. Recently, convolutional neural networks (CNNs) have been used in an attempt to solve this age old problem. For this purpose, researchers have proposed various CNN architectures. Unfortunately, most of the proposed techniques have been based on relatively 'shallow' networks. In this work, we leverage the capability of an off-the-shelf deep CNN model, namely the VGG-Face model, which has been trained on millions of face images. Interestingly, despite being a simple approach, features extracted from the VGG-Face model, when reduced and fed into linear regressors, outperform most of the state-of-the-art CNNs. e.g. on both FGNET-AD and Morph II benchmark databases. Furthermore, contrary to using the last fully connected (FC) layer of the trained model, we evaluate the activations from different layers of the architecture. In fact, our experiments show that generic features learnt from intermediate layer activations carry more ageing information than the FC layers.

KEYWORDS

Age estimation, ConvNet, Deep learning, Pretrained ConvNet, Partial least squares regression

1. INTRODUCTION

The human face is an important biometric because it carries a vast amount of information about an individual. Advantageously, it is simple and easy to capture an image of the face, even when the subject of interest is uncooperative. Faces are used as cues for recognising identities (Parkhi *et al.* 2015), kinship (Xia *et al.* 2012), underlying emotions (Rahulamathavan *et al.* 2013) and even diseases (Cuendet *et al.* 2016). Most importantly, the structure of the human face is highly indicative of age (Fu *et al.* 2010).

Research in automatic facial age estimation (AFAE) has been active for over a decade. Being a demographic attribute of the human face, AFAE has several real life applications including demographic studies, multi-cue identification, access control, surveillance, targeted advertisements and human-computer interaction systems.

Similar to face detection and recognition, facial age estimation is obstructed by several factors such as head pose variation, occlusion, facial expressions, illumination variation and clutter background, to mention but a few. Yet, it is also challenged by other internal and external factors including gender, genes, health and lifestyle. Hence, several approaches have been documented in the literature to circumvent these problems (Fu *et al.* 2010).

Traditionally, age estimation has been achieved via a vital two-step procedure, consisting of feature extraction and pattern learning (Bukar *et al.* 2016; Huang 2009). As an initial mechanism, feature extraction is the process of parameterising the face with a view to defining an efficient descriptor. Several researchers focused on this concept, thereby devising numerous feature extraction methods including but not limited to, anthropometric models, statistical models, local binary patterns (LBP), and histograms of gradients (HOG). Biologically inspired features (BIF), which convolve images with Gabor filters followed by pooling, has been one of the most successful and widely used feature extraction technique (Huang 2009; El Dib & El-Saban 2010; Weng *et al.* 2013). To be precise, the best performing estimation result on the FGNET-AD (Lanitis *et al.* 2002) benchmark database, reported by El-dib *et al.* (2010), utilised BIF. For comprehensive reviews, the reader should refer to (Fernandez *et al.* 2014; Fu *et al.* 2010).

The second step to achieving age estimation is pattern learning, which is the automatic mapping of facial features to target ages. Generally, researchers approach age-learning either as a multi-class classification, regression task, or ranking problem. Support vector machines (SVM) and support vector regression (SVR) are the two most commonly used algorithms for classification and regression, respectively. Other forms of regression used in the literature include linear regression (Bukar *et al.* 2015), quadratic regression (Lanitis *et al.* 2002), partial least squares variants (Guo & Mu 2013) and canonical correlation analysis (CCA) based methods (Guo & Mu 2013).

Recent advances in convolutional neural networks (CNN), has resulted in a major shift in paradigm. Using CNNs, features are automatically learned, facilitating the building of systems that learn from end to end. Hence, researchers have attempted to solve the problem of age estimation using CNNs. One of the earliest works is that of Wang *et al.* (2015) where they used a 5 layered CNN to extract facial features. Their experiment on the two FGNET-AD (Lanitis *et al.* 2002) and Morph (Ricanek & Tesafaye 2006) databases yielded good results. However, they were unable to outperform state of the art algorithms. This could be due to the shallow nature of the architecture. Levi and Hassner (2015) proposed a six layered CNN for age group classification. Niu *et al.* (2016), used a four layered CNN to treat AFAE as an ordinal regression problem. Yi *et al.* (2014), segmented the face into patches that were fed into a multi-scale 3 layered sub-networks, afterwards the outputs of the sub-networks were aggregated using a final layer. A similar approach was used by (T. Liu *et al.* 2016), however, instead of using 23 patches, they downsampled it to 8 patches per face. Liu *et al.* (2015) fused regression and classification via a 22 layer deep CNN in order to perform apparent age estimation.

With the exception of (Wang *et al.* 2015), all other researchers we mentioned above that used CNNs for AFAE, failed to compare their results to the FGNET-AD database. Some compared their results using the Morph database but there are discrepancies in the methods deployed. Some used the protocol suggested by Guo and Mu (2013), while the rest randomly used 80% for training and 20% for testing.

To this end, we propose to bridge the gap by carrying out a number of contributions. Since there are very deep CNN models that have been trained on millions of face images, we have chosen to avoid the idea of retraining from scratch. Rather, we plan to use transfer learning to extract ageing features. A suitable dimensionality reduction algorithm will then be used to reduce the size of the extracted features prior to age-pattern learning. We will then conduct an extensive evaluation of our approach on the two benchmark databases; FGNET-AD and Morph II.

Thus, this work is aimed at investigating the need to train a new CNN from scratch. Will the pretrained architectures that were carefully modelled on millions of images suffice for the problem of age estimation, or do we need to label more training images for better age estimation? We also want to explore, analyse and evaluate which layer of the existing model is most suitable to use for feature extraction. Furthermore, the effect of alignment, as well as data augmentation will be rigorously investigated.

2. BACKGROUND AND RELATED WORK

In recent years, convolutional neural networks (ConvNets or CNNs) have had a great impact on computer vision and machine learning fields due to their ability to learn complex features using nonlinear multi-layered architectures (LeCun *et al.* 2015). Although originating in the early 1990s, ConvNets were forsaken by the research community due to the assumption that feature extraction using gradient descent will always over fit due to local minima (LeCun *et al.* 2015). However, its remarkable success in the ImageNet competition of 2012 altered the negativity associated with them. Today, state-of-the-art deep models are used in almost all computer vision applications including, but not limited to, detection (Russakovsky *et al.* 2015), recognition (He *et al.* 2015), classification (Huang *et al.* 2016), and information retrieval (Zhong *et al.* 2016).

Generally, there are three ways of deploying ConvNets; training a network from scratch, fine tuning an existing model, or using off the shelf CNN features. The latter two approaches are referred to as transfer learning (Oquab *et al.* 2014). Training ConvNet from scratch requires an enormous amount of data, often in millions (Vedaldi & Lenc 2015). Fine tuning involves transferring the weights of the first n layers learned from a base network to a target network. The target network is then trained using a new dataset for a specific task; usually different from that of the base network.

Research has shown that ConvNets efficiently learn generic image features (LeCun *et al*. 2015; Azizpour *et al*. 2015). Thus these features can be used directly with simple classifiers to solve computer vision problems. This involves removing the last output layer of a trained ConvNet and using the activations of the last fully connected layer as features. Hence the ConvNet is used as a feature extractor instead of being a classifier. This approach is known as off-the-shelf feature extraction and has been used by several researchers (Azizpour *et al*. 2015; Sharif Razavian *et al*. 2014; Zha *et al*. 2015) to achieve promising results. As a rule of thumb, researchers advise that this approach should be the first approach to solving a computer vision task (Azizpour *et al*. 2015). Interestingly, studies also show that for a dataset with a small number of images, the off-the-shelf feature extraction technique outperforms both fine-tuning as well as training a network from scratch (Athiwaratkun & Kang 2015).

Despite the numerous research conducted by using off the shelf features, focus has been concentrated only on object classification, detection, segmentation, and instance retrieval. This technique has not been exhaustively applied on the problem of age estimation. As stated earlier, recent works on age estimation have concentrated on training ConvNets from scratch (Wang *et al*. 2015; Levi & Hassner 2015; Niu *et al*. 2016; Yi *et al*. 2014) and fine tuning existing networks (Liu *et al*. 2015).

Furthermore, we have noticed that due to the nature of the problems studied in the past, all the reported work employed binary classifiers such as SVM and random forest after the feature extraction. Here we will investigate the performance of ConvNet features when used alongside linear regression techniques. We have also observed that in the literature (Azizpour *et al*. 2015; Sharif Razavian *et al*. 2014), activations of the last fully connected layer are used. In this paper, we will be investigating other layers of the ConvNet to thoroughly understand the effect of different activations along the hierarchy. Additionally, researchers almost always use models such as AlexNet (Krizhevsky *et al*. 2012) and OverFeat (Sermanet *et al*. 2013), which were trained on the ImageNet dataset. In this work, we have chosen to use VGG-Face descriptor, due to its depth and similarity of the base dataset (i.e. human face) to the data we are working with.

2.1 VGG-Face Model

VGG-Face (Parkhi *et al*. 2015), developed at Oxford University's Visual Geometry Group (VGG), is the application of the very deep ConvNet architecture VGG-16 (Simonyan & Zisserman 2014). Trained on a database of 2.6 million face images and comprised of 2622 unique identities, the database used is made of up to a thousand instances of each subject.

The model is configured to take a fixed sized 224 x 224 RGB image as an input; as a form of pre-processing, they initially center-normalise all the training images. The deep architecture is made of a stack of 13 convolutional layers with filters having uniform receptive field of size 3 × 3 and a fixed convolution stride of 1 pixel. As shown in Figure 1, groups of these convolution layers are followed by five max-pooling layers. The stack of convolution layers are then followed by three fully connected layers; FC6, FC7 and FC8. The first two have 4096 channels, while FC8 has 2622 channels which are used to classify the 2622 identities. The model's implementation also incorporates 2D alignment and triplet loss embedding. Parkhi *et al.* (2015) have shown that the model outperforms Google's FaceNet (Schroff *et al*. 2015) and DeepID (Sun *et al*. 2014) on YouTubeFaces (Wolf *et al*. 2011).

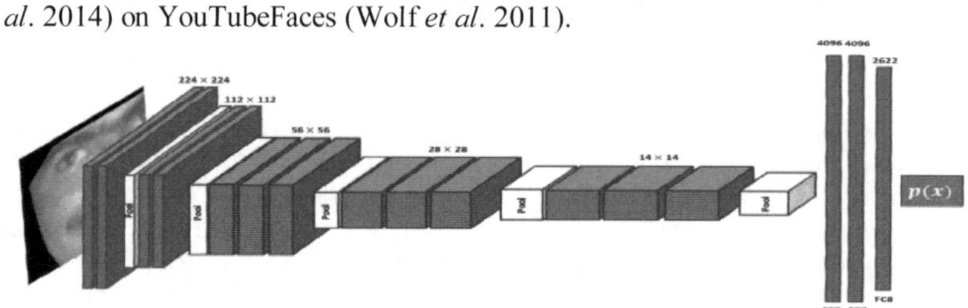

Figure 1. VGG-Face Model Architecture

3. METHOD

Our approach is to use weights from different layers of the VGG-Face model to extract deep features. Dimensions of the resulting features are then reduced before using regression for age estimation.

3.1 Feature Extraction

Given an input image $\boldsymbol{X}_0$ represented as a tensor $\boldsymbol{X}_0 \in \mathbb{R}^{H \times W \times D}$ where H is the image height, W is the width and D the colour channels, and a pre-trained L layered ConvNet expressed as a series of functions $g_L = f_1 \to f_2 \to \cdots f_L$, let $\boldsymbol{X}_1, \boldsymbol{X}_2 \dots \boldsymbol{X}_L$ be the outputs of each layer in the network. The output of the ith intermediate layer can be computed from the function f_i and the learned weights $\boldsymbol{w}_i$ via $\boldsymbol{X}_i = f_i(\boldsymbol{X}_{i-1}; \boldsymbol{w}_i)$.

In order to fully investigate and evaluate which layer yields optimum results, the activation of five layers; the last two convolution layers (conv5_2, conv5_3), the last max-pool layer (pool5) and first two fully connected layers FC6 and FC7 of the VGG-Face model, are used as separate feature channels.

3.2 Dimensionality Reduction and Regression

Due to large dimensions of the extracted features, ranging from 4096 in FC7 to 100352 in conv5_2, there is a need to reduce the feature dimensions thus removing redundant information. Moreover, it is a well-known fact that, for n observations and p features, the regression estimate is actually not well-defined in a situation whereby $p > n$.

In the past, researchers (Azizpour *et al.* 2015) used principal component analysis (PCA) for dimensionality reduction. However, PCA only explores the internal structure of the predictor variables (features) without considering their relationship to the response variables. Hence, PCA most likely discards important discriminatory features. As such, we are using partial least squares regression (PLS) (Wold 1975) in this work.

PLS reduces data dimensions by creating latent variables which capture directions of highest variance in the predictors (features), as well as the directions that best relate the response to the predictor variables. Thus, it conducts a simultaneous decomposition of data, thereby retaining the most discriminatory features. Moreover, the technique also performs linear regression using the computed latent variables.

Let $\boldsymbol{C} \in \mathbb{R}^p$ be a $n \times p$ matrix of extracted features, and $\boldsymbol{D}$ be a $n \times r$ matrix of response variables. PLS decomposes the two matrices into,

$$\begin{aligned} \boldsymbol{C} &= \boldsymbol{T}\boldsymbol{P}^T + \boldsymbol{E}, \\ \boldsymbol{D} &= \boldsymbol{T}\boldsymbol{Q}^T + \boldsymbol{F}. \end{aligned} \tag{1}$$

$\boldsymbol{T}$ is a $n \times k$ matrix of k linear latent variables $k \ll p$, $\boldsymbol{P}$ and $\boldsymbol{Q}$ are loadings, while $\boldsymbol{E}$ and $\boldsymbol{F}$ are matrices of residuals. By solving an optimisation problem, the scores $\boldsymbol{T}$ can be computed directly from the feature set $\boldsymbol{C}$,

$$\boldsymbol{T} = \boldsymbol{X}\boldsymbol{S}, \boldsymbol{S} = \{s_1, s_2, \dots s_k\}, \tag{2}$$

where, $\hat{\boldsymbol{s}}_k = argmax_s\, \boldsymbol{s}^T \boldsymbol{C}^T \boldsymbol{D}\boldsymbol{D}^T \boldsymbol{C}\boldsymbol{s}$ such that $\boldsymbol{s}^T \boldsymbol{s} = 1$ and $\boldsymbol{s}^T \boldsymbol{C}^T \boldsymbol{C}\boldsymbol{s}_i = 0$, for $i = 1 \dots k-1$. Furthermore, the PLS regression coefficient is defined as

$$\beta^{PLS} = \boldsymbol{S}\boldsymbol{Q}^T. \tag{3}$$

Hence, the relationship between the predictor $\boldsymbol{C}$ and response variable $\boldsymbol{D}$ is formulated as

$$\boldsymbol{D} = \boldsymbol{C}\beta^{PLS} + \boldsymbol{F}. \tag{4}$$

In this work, $\boldsymbol{D}$ is an $n \times 1$ vector representing ages.

4. EXPERIMENTS AND RESULTS

In this section, we will discuss the procedure we used for an extensive evaluation of the proposed method of age estimation. All images used in our experiments were cropped to a size of 224 x 224 and a data pre-processing step was deployed; this will be discussed shortly. Finally, features were extracted and fed into a PLS-age-learner, after which results were fully evaluated and compared to state-of-the-art algorithms.

4.1 Evaluation Datasets

Experiments were performed on two popular and publicly available benchmark databases, the FGNET-AD and Morph Album II datasets.

The FGNET-AD consists of 1002 colour and grayscale images of 82 unique subjects from different races. Although the age distribution ranges between 0-69 years, over 700 images are within the 0 - 20 age range and therefore, the distribution of the data is highly skewed. The subjects display varying facial expressions and head poses. Other photographic variations include resolution, illumination and sharpness. Furthermore, all the images have been annotated with 68 landmarks. The majority of documented works have used FGNET-AD for evaluation as it is one of the earliest databases used for age estimation.

Morph Album II is the largest publicly available longitudinal face database, consisting of 55,134 images of 13,000 individuals. The age distribution lies between 16 - 77 years, with a median age of 33 years. Each subject has up to 4 images which were collected within a period of 4 years. The database contains people from different ethnicities, with various head poses and facial expressions. The image quality has varying scale, rotation, and translation as well as illumination. Recently, most researchers have used this database for the evaluation and comparison of algorithms.

4.2 Data Splitting Protocol

FGNET-AD was evaluated using the leave one-person out (LOPO) cross-validation method (Geng *et al.* 2007). This iterative procedure involves training the age estimation algorithm with the images of 81 subjects and testing with the images of the individual that was left out. Thus, by the end of all 82 folds, each subject will have been used for testing once; results are calculated based on all the estimations. LOPO emulates a real life scenario where an estimation algorithm is tested on images that it didn't come across during training.

Morph II database was split using the protocol suggested by (Guo & Mu 2013). The database is divided into three 3 non-overlapping partitions; S1, S2, and S3 (Others). The algorithm was trained and tested twice. Firstly, S1 was used for training and then tested on a combination of S2 and S3. In a second run, S2 was used for training, while reserving S1 and S3 for testing. Finally, the results of the two tests were averaged.

4.3 Image Pre-Processing

The FGNET-AD images were aligned using the 68 landmark annotations provided with the dataset. Furthermore, the image backgrounds were removed to increase image purity (see Figure 2), we then conducted data augmentation, during the training phase, to compensate for the small dataset. Each image was responsible for the generation of 7 additional images; this was achieved through random cropping and warping to the mean shape, as shown in Figure 2.

For the Morph database, we used Zhu and Ramanan's (2012) algorithms to detect and annotate the faces with 68 landmarks, thereafter the images were aligned.

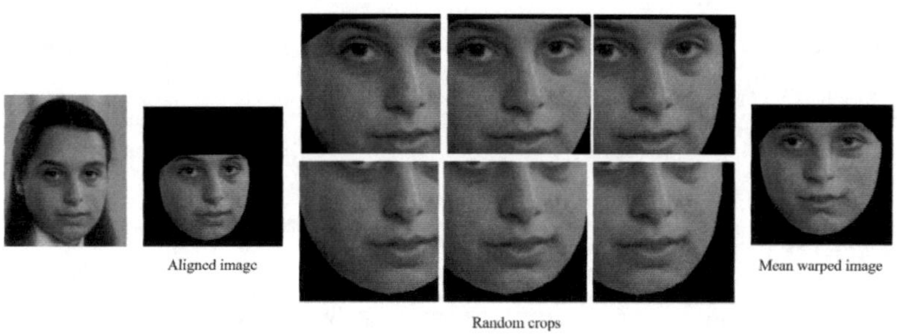

Figure 2. Pre-processing of FGNET-AD images

4.4 Implementation of Age Estimation

Utilising the procedure described in Section 3, five sets of estimations were conducted per experiment. Each estimation was performed by extracting features using one of the five layers of the VGG-Face model; conv5_2, conv5_3, pool5, FC6, or FC7 layers. Then, as proposed earlier, we deployed PLS for dimensionality reduction and afterwards, regression. In all the experiments, the numbers of PLS latent variables were chosen via cross-validation. In order to evaluate the effect of image alignment, we conducted two sets of experiments on the Morph database i.e. with and without alignment, denoted as *wAlg* and *woAlg* respectively.

4.5 Results Evaluation

To evaluate the performance of our algorithm and procedures, two metrics were used throughout our experiments, the Mean Absolute Error (MAE) and Cumulative Score (CS), given by

$$MAE = \sum_{i=1}^{N} | y - y' | / N, \quad (5)$$

$$CS(m) = N_{error \leq k} \; / \; N \times 100\%, \quad (6)$$

where y is the ground truth age, and y' is the estimated age, N the number of test images, and $N_{error \leq l}$ denotes the number of images on which the system makes absolute error not higher than l years.

Initially, the performance of our five features were compared, as can be seen in Tables 1,2, 3 and Figure 3, features extracted using conv5_2 activations outperform the rest on both databases. It is also obvious that the performance degrades as we move higher along the hierarchy towards the FC7 layer. This suggests that the generic features learnt from intermediate layer activations carry more ageing information than the latter layers that are more specific to the problem of face identification. Table 3 also shows that image alignment increases the performance of the off-the-shelf features extracted. We have also observed that PLS has a remarkable dimensionality reduction capability as it reduced thousands of features to few (between 17 and 24 latent variables).

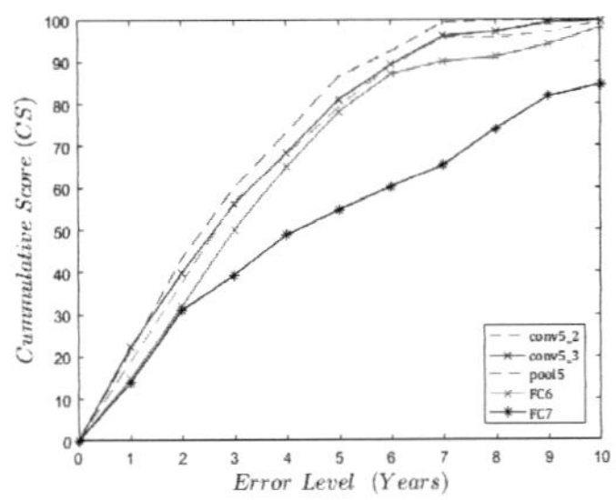

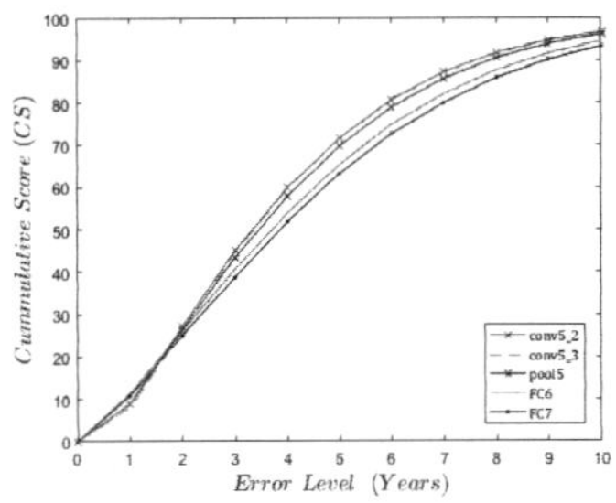

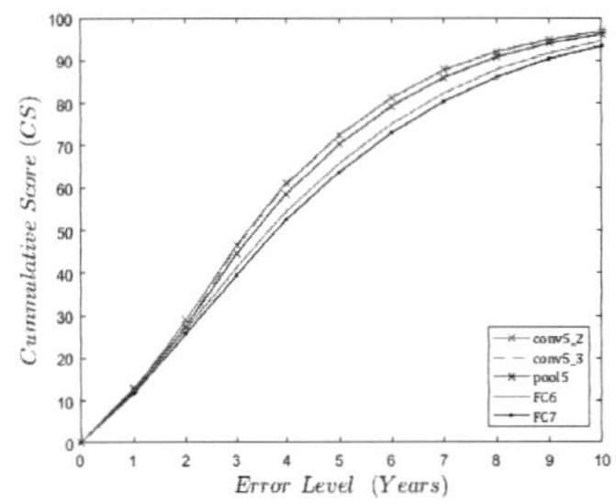

Figure 3. Comparison of CS (a) FGNET-AD (b) Morph *woAlg* (c) Morph *wAlg*

Table 1. Evaluation of our extracted features on FGNET-AD

Layer	Latent Vars	MAE
Conv5_2	18	2.70
Conv5_3	18	2.83
pool5	18	2.97
FC6	18	3.89
FC7	18	5.51

Table 2. Evaluation of our features on Morph II *woAlg*

Layer	Tr. Set	Latent Vars.	MAE	Avg. MAE	CS < 10 years
conv5_2	S1	17	3.93	3.92	96.71%
	S2	17	3.91		
conv5_3	S1	17	3.95	3.94	96.61%
	S2	17	3.93		
pool5	S1	17	4.06	4.05	96.06%
	S2	17	4.03		
FC6	S1	24	4.33	4.31	94.32%
	S2	24	4.29		
FC7	S1	24	4.50	4.51	93.26%
	S2	24	4.51		

Table 3. Evaluation of extracted features on Morph II wAlg

Layer	Tr. Set	Latent Vars.	MAE	Avg. MAE	CS < 10 years
conv5_2	S1	17	3.84	3.83	96.82%
	S2	17	3.82		
conv5_3	S1	17	3.87	3.87	96.75%
	S2	17	3.86		
pool5	S1	17	4.01	3.99	96.18%
	S2	17	3.97		
FC6	S1	24	4.27	4.26	94.43%
	S2	24	4.25		
FC7	S1	24	4.45	4.45	93.40%
	S2	24	4.45		

Next, we compared the performance of our best results with state-of-the-art algorithms. As can be seen in Table 4, our results on FGNET-AD using data augmentation supersedes what has been reported over the years.

Table 4. Comparison of our best MAE result to state-of-the-art algorithms on FGNET-AD

Method	MAE
BIF(Guo *et al.* 2009)	4.77
C & H BIF (Han *et al.* 2013)	4.60
OHR (Chang *et al.* 2011)	4.48
LSR (Chao *et al.* 2013)	4.38
CNN (Wang *et al.* 2015)	4.22
BI. AAM (Hong *et al.* 2013)	4.18
EBIF (El Dib & El-Saban 2010)	3.17
Proposed	**2.70**

This further proves the power of ConvNets and their efficiency, especially after conducting meticulous pre-processing steps such as alignment, background removal and augmentation. The performance of our approach on the Morph database is also superior to most of the state-of-the-art algorithms, as can be seen in Table 5.

Table 5. Comparison of our best MAE result to state-of-the-art algorithms on Morph II database

Layer	Tr. Set	MAE	Avg. MAE
FMBS (T.-J. Liu *et al.* 2016)	S1	3.96	3.99
	S2	4.01	
KCCA (Guo & Mu 2013)	S1	4.00	3.98
	S2	3.95	
KPLS (Guo & Mu 2011)	S1	4.21	4.18
	S2	4.15	
3-step (Guo & Mu 2010)	S1	4.44	4.45
	S2	4.46	
BIF (Guo *et al.* 2009)	S1	5.06	5.09
	S2	5.12	
Proposed	S1	3.80	**3.83**
	S2	3.76	

5. CONCLUSION

We have investigated the use of off-the-shelf ConvNet representations for the problem of age estimation. Using activations from different layers of the VGG-Face model, experiments were conducted on both FGNET-AD and Morph Album II databases. With the simultaneous dimensionality reduction capability of partial least squares regression, we have demonstrated that promising results can be achieved without having to train a ConvNet from scratch, specifically for age estimation. This is obviously an interesting finding especially due to the challenge of annotating face ages. The experiments conducted in this work have shown that in contrast to most researchers' assumptions, the activations of the last fully connected layer may not be the best solution for all problems. Furthermore, we have demonstrated that data augmentation and alignment affect the performance of the ConvNet features. While our result on the Morph database was comparable to state-of-the-art algorithms, background removal, as well as data augmentation, may yield even better results. We are optimistic that more off-the-shelf ConvNet models and powerful supervised dimensionality reduction algorithms (such as the PLS) can be applied to other computer vision problems.

REFERENCES

Athiwaratkun, B. & Kang, K., 2015. Feature Representation in Convolutional Neural Networks. *arXiv preprint arXiv:1507.02313.*

Azizpour, H. et al., 2015. From generic to specific deep representations for visual recognition. In *Proceedings of the IEEE Conference on Computer Vision and Pattern Recognition Workshops*. pp. 36–45.

Bukar, A.M., Ugail, H. & Connah, D., 2016. Automatic age and gender classification using supervised appearance model. *J. Electron. Imaging*, 25(6), pp.1–11.

Bukar, A.M., Ugail, H. & Connah, D., 2015. Individualised Model of Facial Age Synthesis Based on Constrained Regression. In *Image Processing Theory, Tools and Applications (IPTA), 2015 5th International Conference on*. IEEE, pp. 285–290.

Chang, K.Y., Chen, C.S. & Hung, Y.P., 2011. Ordinal hyperplanes ranker with cost sensitivities for age estimation. *Proceedings of the IEEE Computer Society Conference on Computer Vision and Pattern Recognition*, pp.585–592.

Chao, W., Liu, J. & Ding, J., 2013. Facial age estimation based on label-sensitive learning and age-oriented regression. *Pattern Recognition*, 46(3), pp.628–641.

Cuendet, G.L. et al., 2016. Facial Image Analysis for Fully Automatic Prediction of Difficult Endotracheal Intubation. *IEEE Transactions on Biomedical Engineering*, 63(2), pp.328–339.

El Dib, M.Y. & El-Saban, M., 2010. Human age estimation using enhanced bio-inspired features (EBIF). *2010 IEEE International Conference on Image Processing*, pp.1589–1592. Available at: http://ieeexplore.ieee.org/lpdocs/epic03/wrapper.htm?arnumber=5651440.

Fernandez, C., Huerta, I. & Prati, A., 2014. A Comparative Evaluation of Regression Learning Algorithms for Facial Age Estimation. *FFER in conjunction with ICPR, in press. IEEE.*

Fu, Y., Guo, G. & Huang, T., 2010. Age Synthesis and Estimation via Faces : A Survey. *IEEE Transactions on Pattern Analysis and Machine Intelligence*, 32(11), pp.1955–1976.

Geng, X. et al., 2007. Automatic Age Estimation Based on Facial Aging Patterns. , 29(12), pp.2234–2240.

Guo, G. et al., 2009. Human age estimation using bio-inspired features. In *Computer Vision and Pattern Recognition, 2009. CVPR 2009. IEEE Conference on*. IEEE, pp. 112–119.

Guo, G. & Mu, G., 2010. Human age estimation: What is the influence across race and gender? In *2010 IEEE Computer Society Conference on Computer Vision and Pattern Recognition-Workshops*. IEEE, pp. 71–78.

Guo, G. & Mu, G., 2013. Joint estimation of age, gender and ethnicity: CCA vs. PLS. In *Automatic Face and Gesture Recognition (FG), 2013 10th IEEE International Conference and Workshops on*. IEEE, pp. 1–6.

Guo, G. & Mu, G., 2011. Simultaneous dimensionality reduction and human age estimation via kernel partial least squares regression. *Proceedings of the IEEE Computer Society Conference on Computer Vision and Pattern Recognition*, pp.657–664.

Han, H. et al., 2013. Age Estimation from Face Images : Human vs . Machine Performance.

He, K. et al., 2015. Deep residual learning for image recognition. *arXiv preprint arXiv:1512.03385*.

Hong, L. et al., 2013. A new biologically inspired active appearance model for face age estimation by using local ordinal ranking. In *Proceedings of the Fifth International Conference on Internet Multimedia Computing and Service*. ACM, pp. 327–330.

Huang, G., Liu, Z. & Weinberger, K.Q., 2016. Densely connected convolutional networks. *arXiv preprint arXiv:1608.06993.*

Huang, T.S., 2009. Human age estimation using bio-inspired features. *2009 IEEE Conference on Computer Vision and Pattern Recognition*, pp.112–119. Available at: http://ieeexplore.ieee.org/lpdocs/epic03/wrapper.htm?arnumber=5206681.

Krizhevsky, A., Sutskever, I. & Hinton, G.E., 2012. Imagenet classification with deep convolutional neural networks. In *Advances in neural information processing systems*. pp. 1097–1105.

Lanitis, A., Taylor, C. & Cootes, T., 2002. Toward Automatic Simulation of Aging Effects on Face Images. *IEEE Transactions on Pattern Analysis and Machine Intelligence*, 24(4), pp.442–455.

LeCun, Y., Bengio, Y. & Hinton, G., 2015. Deep learning. *Nature*, 521(7553), pp.436–444.

Levi, G. & Hassner, T., 2015. Age and Gender Classification using Convolutional Neural Networks. , pp.34–42.

Liu, T. et al., 2016. Age Estimation Based on Multi-Region Convolutional Neural Network. In *Chinese Conference on Biometric Recognition*. Springer, pp. 186–194.

Liu, T.-J. et al., 2016. Age estimation via fusion of multiple binary age grouping systems. In *Image Processing (ICIP), 2016 IEEE International Conference on*. IEEE, pp. 609–613.

Liu, X. et al., 2015. Agenet: Deeply learned regressor and classifier for robust apparent age estimation. In *Proceedings of the IEEE International Conference on Computer Vision Workshops*. pp. 16–24.

Niu, Z. et al., 2016. Ordinal regression with multiple output cnn for age estimation. In *Proceedings of the IEEE Conference on Computer Vision and Pattern Recognition*. pp. 4920–4928.

Oquab, M. et al., 2014. Learning and transferring mid-level image representations using convolutional neural networks. In *Proceedings of the IEEE conference on computer vision and pattern recognition*. pp. 1717–1724.

Parkhi, O.M., Vedaldi, A. & Zisserman, A., 2015. Deep face recognition. In *British Machine Vision Conference*. p. 6.

Rahulamathavan, Y. et al., 2013. Facial expression recognition in the encrypted domain based on local fisher discriminant analysis. *IEEE Transactions on Affective Computing*, 4(1), pp.83–92.

Ricanek, K. & Tesafaye, T., 2006. Morph: A longitudinal image database of normal adult age-progression. In *7th International Conference on Automatic Face and Gesture Recognition (FGR06)*. IEEE, pp. 341–345.

Russakovsky, O. et al., 2015. Imagenet large scale visual recognition challenge. *International Journal of Computer Vision*, 115(3), pp.211–252.

Schroff, F., Kalenichenko, D. & Philbin, J., 2015. Facenet: A unified embedding for face recognition and clustering. In *Proceedings of the IEEE Conference on Computer Vision and Pattern Recognition*. pp. 815–823.

Sermanet, P. et al., 2013. Overfeat: Integrated recognition, localization and detection using convolutional networks. *arXiv preprint arXiv:1312.6229*.

Sharif Razavian, A. et al., 2014. CNN features off-the-shelf: an astounding baseline for recognition. In *Proceedings of the IEEE Conference on Computer Vision and Pattern Recognition Workshops*. pp. 806–813.

Simonyan, K. & Zisserman, A., 2014. Very deep convolutional networks for large-scale image recognition. *arXiv preprint arXiv:1409.1556*.

Sun, Y., Wang, X. & Tang, X., 2014. Deep learning face representation from predicting 10,000 classes. In *Proceedings of the IEEE Conference on Computer Vision and Pattern Recognition*. pp. 1891–1898.

Vedaldi, A. & Lenc, K., 2015. Matconvnet: Convolutional neural networks for matlab. In *Proceedings of the 23rd ACM international conference on Multimedia*. ACM, pp. 689–692.

Wang, X., Guo, R. & Kambhamettu, C., 2015. Deeply-learned feature for age estimation. In *2015 IEEE Winter Conference on Applications of Computer Vision*. IEEE, pp. 534–541.

Weng, R. et al., 2013. Multi-feature ordinal ranking for facial age estimation. In *Automatic Face and Gesture Recognition (FG), 2013 10th IEEE International Conference and Workshops on*. IEEE, pp. 1–6.

Wold, H., 1975. *Quantitative sociology: international perspectives on mathematical and statistical model building, chapter path models with latent variables: the NiPALS Approach.*, Academic, London.

Wolf, L., Hassner, T. & Maoz, I., 2011. Face recognition in unconstrained videos with matched background similarity. In *Computer Vision and Pattern Recognition (CVPR), 2011 IEEE Conference on*. IEEE, pp. 529–534.

Xia, S. et al., 2012. Understanding kin relationships in a photo. *IEEE Transactions on Multimedia*, 14(4), pp.1046–1056.

Yi, D., Lei, Z. & Li, S.Z., 2014. Age estimation by multi-scale convolutional network. In *Asian Conference on Computer Vision*. Springer, pp. 144–158.

Zha, S. et al., 2015. Exploiting image-trained CNN architectures for unconstrained video classification. *arXiv preprint arXiv:1503.04144*.

Zhong, Y., Arandjelović, R. & Zisserman, A., 2016. Faces in places: Compound query retrieval. In *BMVC-27th British Machine Vision Conference*.

Zhu, X. & Ramanan, D., 2012. Face detection, pose estimation, and landmark localization in the wild. In *Computer Vision and Pattern Recognition (CVPR), 2012 IEEE Conference on*. IEEE, pp. 2879–2886.

RECOGNITION OF DYNAMICAL SITUATIONS ON THE BASIS OF FUZZY FINITE STATE MACHINES

Vladimir V. Deviatkov and Igor I. Lychkov
Bauman Moscow State Technical University, Vtoraya Baumanskaya 5, Moscow, Russia

ABSTRACT

Automatic recognition of situations with moving objects in videos is crucial in various application fields. Trajectory-based methods for recognition of situations with moving objects in videos include finite state machines, hidden Markov models, dynamic time warping, etc. Methods based on dynamic programming like hidden Markov models and dynamic time warping are robust under noisy conditions but require preparation of training datasets that can be difficult in case of rare situations. Methods based on finite state machines make it possible to eliminate training stage at all but lack robustness under noisy conditions. This paper introduces a novel method of situation recognition that combines advantages of finite state machines and dynamic programming. The proposed method was benchmarked on recognition of situations with moving objects in road traffic scenarios. Experimental results confirmed efficiency of the proposed method on real videos.

KEYWORDS

Computer vision, moving objects, time series, recognition of situations, dynamic programming

1. INTRODUCTION

Recognition of situations with multiple moving objects in videos is critical in such fields as road traffic monitoring and control, prevention of terrorist attacks, multimedia information retrieval. In spite of the great attention paid to this problem by scientific community, it still remains unresolved in general case. According to the Google Scholar service thousands of papers relevant to recognition of situations in videos were published in scientific journals and conference proceedings in last two years.

Existing methods for recognition of situations in videos can be divided into three main groups (Turaga et al, 2008): non-parametric methods, volumetric methods and time series recognition methods. Non-parametric methods (Lin et al, 2016; Wang et al, 2016; Shatalin and Ovchinnikov, 2015; Tokarev and Abramov, 2015) extract essential features from video frames and apply template matching techniques. Volumetric methods (Seo and Milanfar, 2011; Everts et al, 2013; Soomro and Zamir, 2014) treat video as three-dimensional array of pixels, detect regions of interest using Harris3D, STIP algorithms, compute their descriptors using HOF, HOG3D, SURF3D algorithms and train classifier to make final decision. Time series recognition methods detect positions of moving objects on each video frame using background subtraction in case of a fixed-mounted camera or using appearance-based detection techniques in case of a moving camera, then compose moving object trajectories using Kalman filter, particle filter, finally apply time series recognition techniques. This paper concerns time series recognition methods as they can be easily extended to consider various types of sensors like radars, LIDAR sensors, GPS units beyond video cameras.

Hidden Markov models (HMM) (Ji et al, 2013), dynamic time warping (DTW) (Pham et al, 2014; Fang, 2009), finite state machines (FSM) (Noorit and Suvonvorn, 2014; Trinh et al, 2011; Kerr et al, 2011) are the most popular approaches to recognition of time series which show state of the art performance (Fang, 2009; Kumar, 2013; Bhuyan, 2012). HMM and DTW transform the recognition task into a variational problem of finding an optimal function that maximizes the integral over the given time series. These approaches are based on dynamic programming paradigm (Bertsekas, 2005). Integral calculation reduces noise and suppresses distinct outlier samples, thus eliminates recognition errors. However, such approaches require massive training datasets which can be rather difficult to prepare, especially in the case of rare situations. On the other hand FSM can be designed by experts without training datasets but they lack robustness in presence of noise. Even a single sample-outlier can cause a false state transition of FSM and force the recognition procedure to fail. Filtering techniques make it possible to suppress noisy samples, however in practice it is difficult to find good values for filter parameters. To do this one must know statistical characteristics of noise or evaluate them from training dataset analysis. This paper proposes a novel method of situation recognition that uses FSM as a template of situation and dynamic programming as an algorithm for situation template matching with time series data. Such a combination of approaches results in a training free method which is robust under noisy conditions.

The rest part of the paper is organized in the following way. Section 2.1 discusses the internal procedure of the proposed method for recognition of situations in videos. Section 2.2 provides an example of FSM design for a particular situation in the road traffic scenario, describes an experimental setup and its results. Section 3 concludes the paper.

2. BODY OF PAPER

2.1 Proposed Method for Situation Recognition

Time series $\{x_t\}_{t=0}^{N}$ is a finite sequence of feature samples $x_t = [x_{1t}, x_{2t}, \ldots, x_{mt}]^{\mathrm{T}}$ that characterizes a moving object over a certain time interval $T = \{0,1,2,\ldots,N\}$, $t \in T$. Moving object features are numerical characteristics of object motion and position such as co-ordinates, speed, orientation angle, etc. Situation is a particular pattern of time series to be recognized.

We use fuzzy finite state machines (FuFSM) formalism to represent situations. FuFSM has a set of states $S = \{1,2,\ldots,n\}$, input alphabet $U = \{1,2,\ldots,n\}$ and a transition function f such that $s_{t+1} = f(s_t, u_t)$, $s_t \in S$, $u_t \in U$, $t \in T$. Each FuFSM state $s \in S$ is described by a fuzzy set with a membership function $\mu_s : \mathrm{dom}(X) \rightarrow [0;1]$, where $\mathrm{dom}(X)$ is a range of values for X feature. Denote a set of membership functions $\{\mu_s\}$ for all FuFSM states $s \in S$ as μ. Thus, situation can be represented as a tuple $A = \{S, U, f, \mu\}$.

Consider a time series $\{x_t\}_{t=0}^{N}$ and a sequence of states $\{s_t\}_{t=0}^{N}$ provided by a FuFSM A such that $\forall t \in [0; N-1]\, \exists u_t \in U : s_{t+1} = f(s_t, u_t)$. For each sample x_t of a time series compute its membership $\mu_{s_t}(x_t)$ to a FuFSM state s_t. The membership function value $\mu_{s_t}(x_t)$ characterizes the degree of conformance of the sample x_t to the FuFSM state s_t. Let ξ_A be a similarity $\{x_t\}_{t=0}^{N}$ measure between time series $s \in S$ and a sequence of FuFSM states $\{s_t\}_{t=0}^{N}$:

$$\xi_A(\{s_t\}, \{x_t\}) = \sum_{t=0}^{N} \mu_{s_t}(x_t) \tag{1}$$

The best sequence of FuFSM states $\{s_t\}_{t=0}^{N}$ that maximizes the similarity measure ξ_A for the given time series $\{x_t\}_{t=0}^{N}$ can be used to compute an overall similarity measure between the time series $\{x_t\}_{t=0}^{N}$ and a FuFSM A:

$$\gamma_A(\{x_t\}) = \max_{\{s_t\}} \xi_A(\{s_t\}, \{x_t\}) \tag{2}$$

Let $A^{(1)}, A^{(2)}, \ldots, A^{(K)}$ be the FuFSMs that represent K distinct situations. Recognition of situation consists in determining the situation whose FuFSM maximizes the similarity measure (2) for a given time series.

Let $w_{ts} \in [0; +\infty]$ be the weight of the state $s \in S$ at time instance $t \in T = \{0,1,\ldots,N\}$. The weight of a particular state at N^{th} time instance is maximal cumulative sum of membership among all possible paths in a FuFSM state graph which start in any initial state at 0th time instance and finish in this particular state at N^{th} time instance. Weights of states are computed using the following procedure. Consider the stages of the procedure for a FuFSM with a particular state graph (figure 1).

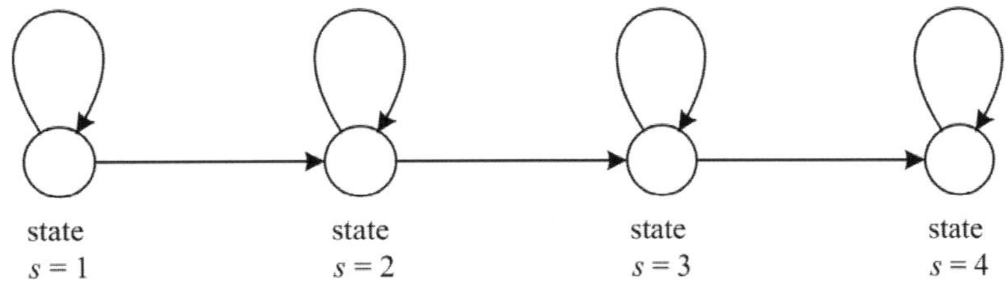

Figure 1. FuFSM state transition graph for discussed example

Stage 1. Membership $\mu_s(x_0)$ of 0th sample of time series is computed for all states $s \in S$ (figure 2, a).

Stage 2. Weights w_{0s} of all states at 0th time instance are assigned to the corresponding values of membership functions $\mu_s(x_0)$ (figure 2, b).

Stage 3. Weights of all graph edges starting from the vertex of state with previously computed weight are assigned to its weight (figure 2, c).

Stage 4. Compute membership $\mu_s(x_1)$ of 1st sample for the next time instance for all states $s \in S$ (figure 2, d).

Stage 5. For each state at the 1st time instance incoming edge with the maximum weight is selected. Weight w_{1s} of state $s \in S$ is computed as sum of its membership function and the weight of selected incoming edge (figure 2, e).

Then stages 3 – 5 are applied in a loop for other samples of time series at time instances $t = 2,3,\ldots,N$.

Finally, value of the maximal weight w_{Ns} among all states $s \in S$ for the last time instance N is a similarity measure γ_A between a time series $\{x_t\}_{t=0}^{N}$ and a situation represented by a finite state machine A.

Thus, at each time instance t weight w_{ts} of a distinct state $s \in S$ is a maximal possible sum of membership values of t vertices passed through on a path from any initial state to final state $s \in S$. The proposed procedure results in an optimal solution provided that membership function of each state can take non-negative values only (Bertsekas, 2005).

The discussed procedure can be expressed formally:

$$w_{0s} = \mu_s(x_0), \forall s \in S$$

$$w_{ts} = \mu_s(x_t) + \max_{\substack{s^* \in S: \\ \exists u \in U, f(s^*,u)=s}} w_{(t-1)s^*}, \forall s \in S, \forall t \in \{1,2,\ldots,N\}$$

$$\gamma_A(\{x_t\}) = \max_{s \in S} w_{Ns}$$

Similarity measure introduced as a sum of membership functions (1) has a serious drawback. The similarity measure can take considerable values even when there are no samples that belong to a certain state. In practice all states are valuable for recognition of situation. To consider this requirement we propose three modifications.

At first we modify the equation of the similarity measure as follows:

$$\xi_A(\{s_t\},\{x_t\}) = \sum_{t=0}^{N} C_{s_t} \cdot \mu_{s_t}(x_t)$$

where $C_s = N \Big/ \sum_{t=0}^{N} \mu_s(x_t)$ is a scale coefficient that assigns greater weights to states represented by a small amount of samples in a time series.

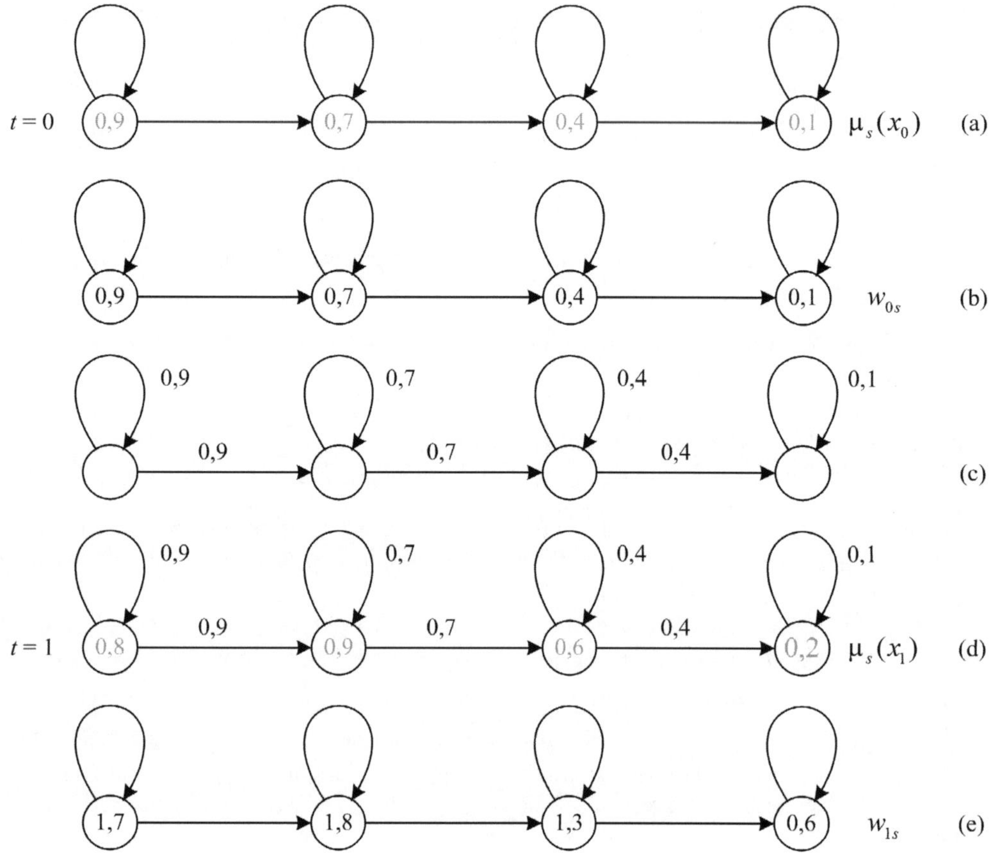

Figure 2. The procedure for state weight computation (membership function values are printed in grey color; weights of states and edges are printed in black color)

At second we propose to reconstruct the optimal path in graph that maximizes the sum of scaled membership functions:

$$s_N^{onm} = \arg\max_{s \in S} w_{Ns},$$

$$s_{t-1}^{onm} = \arg\max_{\substack{s \in S: \\ \exists u \in U\ f(s,u) = s_t^{onm}}} w_{(t-1)s}, \forall t = N, \dots, 2, 1$$

At third the final similarity measure in the form of product of membership sums over distinct states is computed:

$$\gamma_A^{umoz}(\{s_t^{onm}\}, \{x_t\}) = \prod_{s=1}^{n} \sum_{t=0}^{N} \begin{cases} \mu_s(x_t), & s = s_t^{onm} \\ 0,01, & s \neq s_t^{onm} \end{cases}, \tag{3}$$

where 0,01 is an operand that eliminates the zero value of a product.

Such a similarity measure is more sensitive to distinct states of FSM. Whenever a certain state is represented by a small number of samples in the time series, the similarity measure (3) takes low value and corresponding situation would not be recognized.

2.2 Experimental Setup and Results

The proposed method was applied to recognize conflict situations in road traffic intersection. Traffic conflict is a situation when a vehicle driver uses hard braking or evasion maneuver to avoid collision with another vehicle (Allen et al., 1978). Frequency of traffic conflicts is a measure of traffic safety on the intersection.

Consider a traffic conflict situation involves two moving objects A and B (cars). Each moving object is described with two features: position co-ordinate on trajectory and speed magnitude. Time series $\{x_t\}_{t=0}^{N}$ sample has the following structure: $x_t = [z_{At}, v_{At}, z_{Bt}, v_{Bt}]^{\mathrm{T}}$, where z_{At} is the object A co-ordinate, z_{Bt} is the object B co-ordinate, v_{At} is the object A speed, v_{Bt} is the object B speed. Object trajectories are divided into four segments depending on object position relative to the dangerous zone of trajectories overlapping. Dangerous zone is the trajectory segment; within this segment moving object may collide with another object. Each object may be located far, near, inside or after the dangerous zone (figure 3). These four object A trajectory segments correspond to fuzzy sets with membership functions $\mu_{Afar}(z_A)$, $\mu_{Anear}(z_A)$, $\mu_{Ainside}(z_A)$, $\mu_{Aafter}(z_A)$. Four segments of object B trajectory correspond to fuzzy sets with membership functions $\mu_{Bfar}(z_B)$, $\mu_{Bnear}(z_B)$, $\mu_{Binside}(z_B)$, $\mu_{Bafter}(z_B)$. Each object can move fast, slow or stand still. Thus, speed range is divided into three intervals corresponding to fuzzy sets with membership functions $\mu_{moves}(v)$, $\mu_{slowly\_moves}(v)$, $\mu_{still}(v)$.

Figure 3. Object trajectory segments on a road traffic intersection

Compose two FuFSMs: one for dangerous situations of traffic conflict, another for safe situations of passing intersection without conflicts. Both FuFSMs have a state transition graph, shown on figure 1. Tables 1 and 2 present descriptions of FuFSM states. For instance, description "B stays near" means that position co-ordinate z_{Bt} of object B must belong to a trajectory segment represented by a fuzzy set with a membership function $\mu_{Bnear}(z_B)$ and speed of object B must belong to a speed interval represented by a fuzzy state with a membership function $\mu_{still}(v)$.

Table 1. States of FuFSM representing traffic conflict

State 1	State 2	State 3	State 4
A moves near B moves near	A moves inside B moves near	A moves inside B stays near	A moves after

Table 2. States of FuFSM representing safe intersection pass

State 1	State 2	State 3	State 4
A stays near B moves near	A moves near B slowly moves near	A moves inside B stays near	A moves after

In order to compute membership function of FuFSM state for a time series sample we use math operation of minimum. For instance, state 1 membership function of FuFSM for dangerous situation can be calculated as follows:

$$\mu_{danger}([z_{At}, v_{At}, z_{Bt}, v_{Bt}]^{\mathrm{T}}) = \min\{\mu_{Anear}(z_{At}), \mu_{Amoves}(v_{At}), \mu_{Bnear}(z_{Bt}), \mu_{Bmoves}(v_{Bt})\}$$

Initial videos with moving cars were recorded using publicly accessible streaming video camera (http://www.abbeyroad.com/crossing) mounted on a road traffic intersection. To get time series of object features we processed the videos using object detection and tracking method proposed in (Lychkov, 2016). During experiments, we processed 60 videos including 27 videos of traffic conflicts and 33 videos of safe intersection passes. Experimental results are presented in table 3. The average recognition rate was 92 %. The experiments confirmed efficiency of the proposed method.

Table 3. Experimental results

	Number of conflict situations	Number of safe situations
Overall number	27	33
Successfully recognized	24	31
Not recognized	3	2

3. CONCLUSION

The main contribution of the paper consists in combining two approaches within a complete method for recognition of situations in videos. On the one hand, proposed method uses FSM to represent situation templates in a natural form understandable by humans. FSMs can be composed manually by experts without any training samples, which is critical in case of rare situations. On the other hand, proposed method uses dynamic programming to find the optimal solution for recognition problem under noisy conditions. Efficiency of the proposed method was confirmed by experimental results on recognition of situations in road traffic scenarios.

ACKNOWLEDGEMENT

This work was supported by the Ministry of Education and Science of the Russian Federation R & D State project №2.5048.2017 / BP.

REFERENCES

Allen, B.L. et al, 1978. Analysis of traffic conflicts and collision. *In Journal of the Transportation Research Board*. Vol. 667, pp. 67–74.

Bertsekas, D.P., 2005. *Dynamic Programming and Optimal Control*. Athena Scientific, Belmont, USA.

Bhuyan, M.K., 2012. FSM-based recognition of dynamic hand gestures via gesture summarization using key video object planes. *In International Journal of Computer and Communication Engineering*. Vol. 1, № 6, pp. 248-259.

Trinh, H. et al, 2011. Detecting human activities in retail surveillance using hierarchical finite state machine. *Proceedings of the IEEE International Conference on Acoustics, Speech and Signal Processing*. Prague, Czech Republic, pp. 1337-1340.

Everts, I. et al, 2013. Evaluation of color STIPs for human action recognition. *Proceedings of the IEEE Conference on Computer Vision and Pattern Recognition*. Portland, USA, pp. 2850-2857.

Fang, C., 2009. *From dynamic time warping (DTW) to hidden Markov model (HMM)*. Technical Report No. ECE742.

Ji, X. et al, 2013. Hidden Markov Model-based Human Action Recognition Using Mixed Features. *In Journal of Computational Information Systems*. Vol. 9, № 9, pp. 3659-3666.

Kumar, S.K. et al, 2013. HMM Based Enhanced Dynamic Time Warping Model for Efficient Hindi Language Speech Recognition System. *In Mobile Communication and Power Engineering*. Springer Berlin Heidelberg, pp. 200-206.

Lin, S.M. et al, 2016. Vision-Based Fall Detection through Shape Features. *Proceedings of the IEEE International Conference on Multimedia Big Data*. Taipei, Taiwan, pp. 237-240.

Lychkov, I.I., 2016. Optimalnoe otslezhivanie dvizhustchikhsya ob'ektov v videopotoke. *Innovatsionnye tekhnologii v oblasti tekhnicheskikh nauk: Sbornik trudov po itogam nauchno-prakticheskoi konferentsii*. Russian Federation, pp. 5–13.

Noorit, N. and Suvonvorn, N., 2014. Human Activity Recognition from Basic Actions Using Finite State Machine. *Proceedings of the International Conference on Advanced Data and Information Engineering*. Kuala Lumpur, Malaysia, pp. 379-386.

Pham, C.H. et al, 2014. Human action recognition using dynamic time warping and voting algorithm. *In VNU Journal of Science: Computer Science and Communication Engineering*. Vol. 30, № 3, pp. 22-30.

Seo, H.J. and Milanfar, P., 2011. Action recognition from one example. *In IEEE transactions on pattern analysis and machine intelligence*. Vol. 33, № 5, pp. 867-882.

Seto, S. et al, 2015. Multivariate Time Series Classification Using Dynamic Time Warping Template Selection for Human Activity Recognition. arXiv preprint. IEEE. arXiv:1512.06747.

Shatalin, R.A. and Ovchinnikov, P.E., 2015. Algoritm obnaruzheniya neshtatnykh situatsii v zadachakh videonablyudeniya na osnove metoda glavnykh component. *Perspektivnye informatsionnye tekhnologii: Sbornik trudov mezhdunarodnoi nauchno-prakticheskoi konferentsii*. Samara, Russian Federation, Vol. 1, pp. 240-244.

Soomro, K. and Zamir, A.R., 2014. Action recognition in realistic sports videos. *In Computer Vision in Sports*. Switzerland, Springer International Publishing, pp. 181-208.

Tokarev, V.L. and Abramov, D.A., 2015. Metody vydeleniya neshtatnykh situatsii v informatsionno-izmeritelnykh sistemakh videonablyudeniya. *In Izvestiya TulGU. Tekhnicheskie nauki*. Vol. 11, P. 1, pp. 258–265.

Turaga, P. et al, 2008. Machine recognition of human activities: A survey. *In IEEE Transactions on Circuits and Systems for Video Technology*. Vol. 18, № 11, pp. 1473-1488.

Wang, B. et al, 2016. Laplacian LRR on Product Grassmann Manifolds for Human Activity Clustering in Multi-Camera Video Surveillance. arXiv preprint. IEEE. arXiv:1606.03838.

USING TENSORFLOW TO DESIGN ASSISTIVE TECHNOLOGIES FOR PEOPLE WITH VISUAL IMPAIRMENTS

Davide Mulfari, Alessandro Palla and Luca Fanucci
Dept. of Information Engineering, University of Pisa, Italy

ABSTRACT

TensorFlow is an open source deep learning framework developed at Google that enables developers to conceive a wide variety of applications based on artificial intelligence principles. In this paper, we employ such software resources towards the development of a computer vision system for people with visual impairments. We propose a wearable assistive technology solution consisting of a single board computer connected to a camera mounted on the user's glasses. A TensorFlow based software runs on the board in order to real time classify the images captured by the camera, while a text to speech process vocalizes the still's content for the blind person. In this way, the system provides an audio description of the objects in the user's surrounding environment and it may help these people to better detect the things around them.

KEYWORDS

Wearable devices; Assistive Technology; Blind Users; Google TensorFlow; Embedded systems; Deep Learning

1. INTRODUCTION

Nowadays, deep learning allows computational models that are composed of multiple processing layers to learn representations of data with multiple levels of abstraction. These methods have dramatically improved the state-of-the-art in speech recognition, visual object recognition, object detection and many other domains.

In this paper, we focus on the object recognition task and we evaluate deep learning techniques in the field of Assistive Technology (AT) towards the development of a wearable computer vision (CV) system intended for visually impaired users. The CV system is designed to recognize the objects within the images and it currently supports TensorFlow: it is a deep learning software framework released by Google [Abadi et al. 2016] and it is especially designed for pattern recognition activities. In our work TensorFlow has been deployed on a single board computer, while a local software application computes the visual data from a wearable camera placed on the user's glasses. This is a critical feature allowing us to achieve a wearable tool aimed at exploring the user's surrounding environment. We propose to use low cost smart glasses acting as a standard wired web camera in order to provide end user with the ability of moving his head towards the chosen target, i.e., an object he wishes to explore. Our solution supports also an integrated, off-line, text to speech service to vocalize the detected objects' name for its user. In this way, the computer vision system provides an audio description of the objects in the user's surrounding environment and it may help people with visual impairments to better detect the things around them.

The major contribution of this paper is to present our design choices together with an initial implementation of the proposed solution. For these reasons, the rest of the paper is structured as follows. Related works are discussed in the next section. Section 3 describes the proposed CV solution, while a case study is given in Section 4. Finally, conclusions and future works are drawn in Section 5.

2. RELATED WORKS

In AT scenarios, computer vision is an evolving technology that enables the development of multiple systems, such as mobility aids [Fanucci et al. 2011]. Most closely related to our work are the systems discussed by M. Poggi: this author proposes the usage of deep learning for supporting users who are visually impaired [Poggi et al. 2016].

In the field of human computer interaction, CV technology enables you to achieve a wide range of specialized interfaces for people with disabilities. Eye tracking is a technique whereby an individual's eye movements are measured so that the researcher knows both where a person is looking at any given time and the sequence in which their eyes are shifting from one location to another [Poole et al. 2016]. In the last years, eye tracking systems have greatly improved, and play now a critical role in the AT field. Devices capable of eye tracking can detect and measure eye movements, identifying the user's gaze direction (typically on a screen). The acquired data are then recorded for subsequent use, or directly exploited to provide commands to the computer in active interfaces.

Open source hardware and DIY (Do-It-Yourself) electronics allows developers to conceive alternative, customized solutions for end users [Mulfari et al. 2015]. Researchers and activists have identified the possibilities of these developments for AT, however the potential does not seem to be fully explored. In [Hamidi et al. 2015] the authors discuss the creation of TalkBox, which is an open-source, customizable Speech Generating Device. Regarding such a tool, two prototypes were developed. The first one made use of a Makey Makey board for input actions, whereas the second prototype used a more sophisticated system configuration by using capacitive touch sensors. Xiao et al. have developed an off-line navigation device that uses 3-D sounds to provide navigation instructions to a person who is blind [Xiao et al. 2013]. The proposed device relays directional information to the user through audio bone headphones, which use bone conduction technology. Sounds are recorded and can therefore be selected by the blind user, while navigation processing is handled by a Raspberry Pi board.

3. COMPUTER VISION SYSTEM OVERVIEW

A computer vision system evaluates data from an image source, typically a camera, and extracts information about captured images. In this Section, we present the design and the implementation of a CV system aimed at real time recognizing the content of a still captured from a wearable camera. The system consists of two separate pieces of hardware: a Technaxx Video Sport Sunglasses device and a Raspberry Pi 3 Model B Linux computer board. The former is an example of low cost vision sensor, i.e., a standard web camera, built-in on the user's glasses (Figure 1), while the Raspberry device has been used for the instantiation of our software application. In this way, we arranged a low cost, wearable system powered by a slim rechargeable external battery.

Figure 1. Hardware components of the proposed computer vision system: the Raspberry Pi 3 Model B board, the videoglasses with the camera, an earphone

Figure 2. A person wearing the CV system

From a software point of view, the Raspberry board allowed us to develop our software for the real time object recognition using the Python programming language running on a standard Linux environment based on the Raspbian operating system. Even if the Raspberry Pi 3 Model B board is, in essence, a low cost credit card sized Linux computer, there are a few things that distinguish it from a general purpose machine. One of the main differences is that the Raspberry Pi can be directly used in electronics projects because it includes GPIO pins right on the board. TensorFlow framework has been installed on the top of these software packages. Such a framework was originally developed by researchers and engineers working on the Google Brain Team within Google's Machine Intelligence research organization for the purposes of conducting machine learning and deep neural networks research, but the system is general enough to be applicable in a wide variety of other domains as well [Abadi et al. 2015].

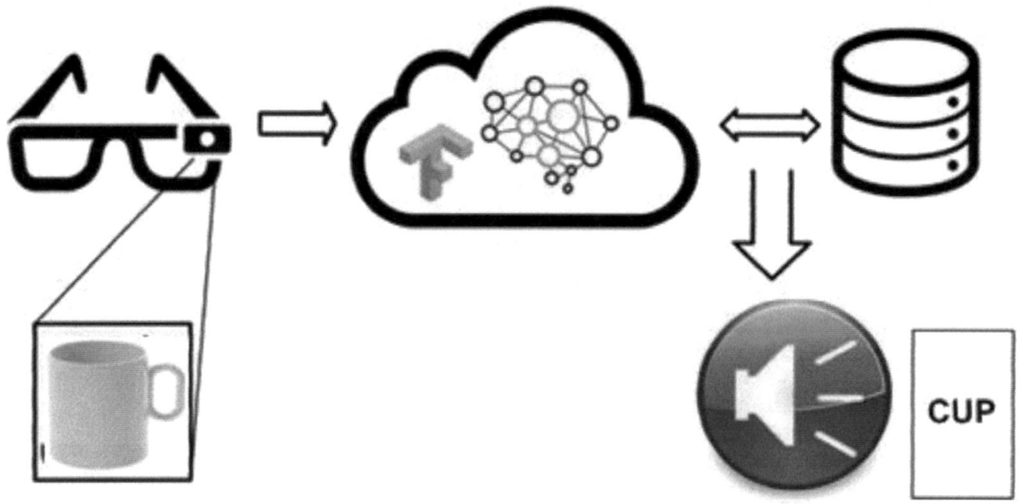

Figure 3. Object recognition process

By using dedicated Python TensorFlow API for the Raspberry devices, we have implemented specialized software for the real time image classification that takes input from the camera mounted on the user's glasses. Figure 3 shows the object recognition process based on Google TensorFlow. This task leverages the Inception V3 pre trained model, based on a dedicated Convolutional Neural Network (CNN) built by Google. At time of writing, such a model is able to classify visual data into 1000 classes, each class is associated with the name, i.e., a label, of the detected objects, such as car, digital clock, desktop, printer, and so on. Tensorflow's classification image procedure returns also a score index for each class, which represents the confidence level related to the entire recognition task. Our software computes this value, and after processing, vocalizes the names by running an off line text to speech application. In this way, the user gets an audio description of the objects in front of him via a traditional earphone or by using bone conduction headphones, which employ the conduction of sound to the inner ear through the bones of the skull. Moreover our assistive solution supports an infrared remote control that allows us to start (and stop) the image recognition and to manage the TTS interface. The entire process is an off line application, so it requires no Internet connection to work. Additionally, we have arranged our software according a simple server client model based on TCP / IP connections. The server side is responsible for image classification using the TensorFlow API, while the client side mainly manages the web camera, the infrared hardware interface and the text-to-speech software application. Therefore our software may run on the same single board computer (local host mode) or may be deployed across multiple devices.

4. CASE STUDY

In this Section, we investigate how the proposed CV system recognizes real world objects within images captured by our vision sensor. Each picture contains just only a single element within the Inception V3 model classes. An example is given in Figure 4.

Figure 4. Example of a recognized object: a digital clock

The image recognition software runs on a Raspberry Pi 3 Model B Board, it computes each visual data and, after processing, gives us a data structure containing ten textual descriptions of the considered pictures In other words, TensorFlow computes the name of the dominant entity within a single photo, this string is linked to a score confidence level between 0 and 100. In our analysis, results have been sorted by this index and we considered n. 248 pictures, each one containing a different real world object (such as a chair, a car, a desktop, a computer, and so on). The following graph summarizes our results.

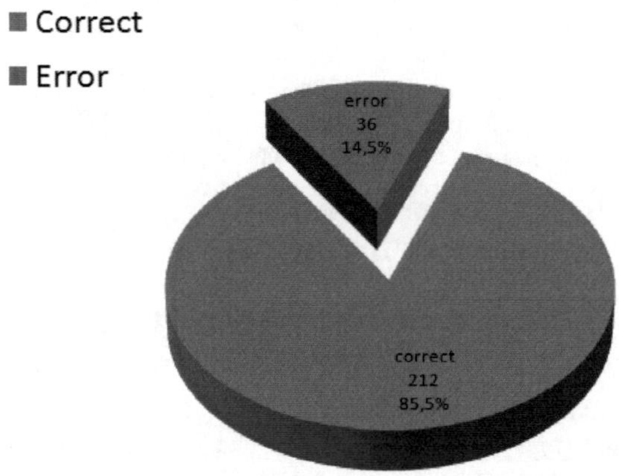

Figure 5. Results with no threshold on the score interval

The embedded CV system is able to recognize correctly 212 objects over 248 pictures (85.5%) and in this case the correct still's description was detected at the head of TensorFlow resultset, without applying any filter, i.e., a threshold, on the confidence level score. However, our main objective is to minimize the error rate, so we analyze the data error distribution on the following plot.

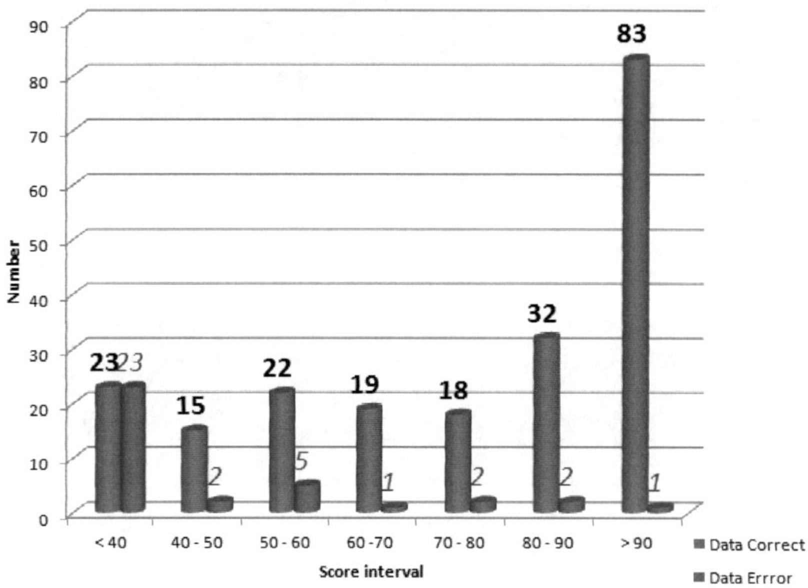

Figure 6. Data distribution with score interval

Figure 6 shows a bar graph in order to evaluate the TensorFlow's response by considering the detected confidence level interval on the x-axis. To minimize many data errors (25), we set a 50 threshold on the confidence level score within our TensorFlow resultset: so the software rejects the image classification process if its score is less than 50. The graph in Figure 7 highlights such an event; the overall number of missing responses increases (63) while the number of data errors decreases (11). In our opinion, this may be a promising result, because the computer vision system does not provide its user with wrong information.

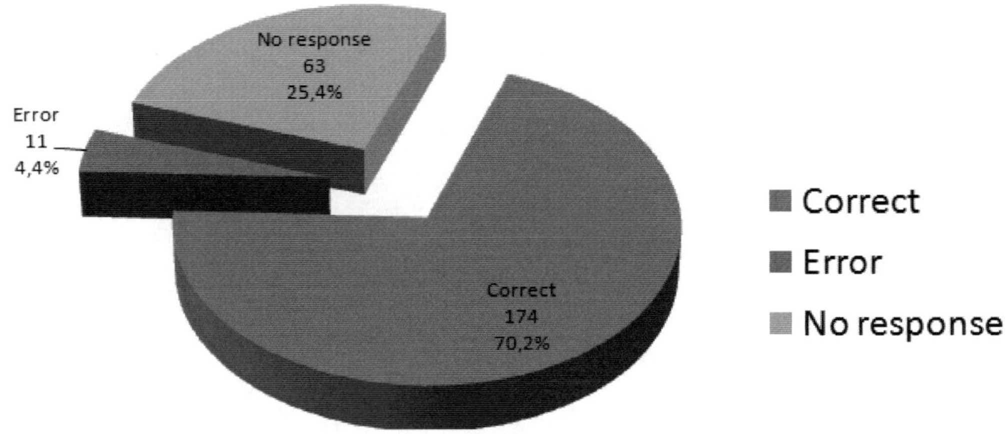

Figure 7. Results after applying a 50 threshold on the score interval

5. CONCLUSION

A CV system for users with visual impairments has been presented in this paper. The tool uses a web camera mounted on the user's glasses and a Raspberry embedded Linux computer in order to real time classify the captured stills and to recognize objects within the images. The image recognition system is the key component of the proposed solution and it exploits Google TensorFlow, a deep learning framework for pattern recognition solutions. Our implementation currently leverages specialized convolutional neural networks and a pre trained model, called Inception V3. At the present, the image classification process is able to detect visual data into 1000 classes. We are working in order to retrain deep neural network to add new classes with the aim of adjusting such a model to a particular user's environment. Furthermore, in future work we plan to design the discussed AT solution on a single wearable computer device that includes camera, bone conduction transducer and on board processing capabilities.

REFERENCES

Abadi, M., Agarwal, A., Barham, P., Brevdo, E., Chen, Z., Citro, C., ... & Ghemawat, S. (2016). Tensorflow: Large-scale machine learning on heterogeneous distributed systems. *arXiv preprint arXiv:1603.04467*.

Abadi, M., Barham, P., Chen, J., Chen, Z., Davis, A., Dean, J., ... & Kudlur, M. (2016, November). TensorFlow: A system for large-scale machine learning. In *Proceedings of the 12th USENIX Symposium on Operating Systems Design and Implementation (OSDI). Savannah, Georgia, USA.*

Fanucci, L., Roncella, R., Iacopetti, F., Donati, M., Calabro, A., Leporini, B., & Santoro, C. (2011). Improving mobility of Pedestrian visually-impaired users. *Assistive Technol. Res. Ser*, *29*, 595-603.

Hamidi, F., Baljko, M., Kunic, T., & Feraday, R. (2015). TalkBox: a DIY communication board case study. *Journal of Assistive Technologies*, *9*(4), 187-198.

Mulfari, D., Celesti, A., Fazio, M., Villari, M., & Puliafito, A. (2015). Embedded systems for supporting computer accessibility. *Studies in health technology and informatics*, *217*, 378.

Poggi, M., & Mattoccia, S. (2016, June). A wearable mobility aid for the visually impaired based on embedded 3D vision and deep learning. In *Computers and Communication (ISCC), 2016 IEEE Symposium on* (pp. 208-213). IEEE.

Poole, A., & Ball, L. J. (2006). Eye tracking in HCI and usability research. *Encyclopedia of human computer interaction*, *1*, 211-219.

Xiao, J., Ramdath, K., Losilevish, M., Sigh, D., & Tsakas, A. (2013, June). A low cost outdoor assistive navigation system for blind people. In *Industrial Electronics and Applications (ICIEA), 2013 8th IEEE Conference on* (pp. 828-833). IEEE.

REGULARIZED BOOTSTRAP FILTER FOR IMAGE RESTORATION

Bassel Marhaba and Mourad Zribi
Université du Littoral Côte d'Opale, Maison de la recherche Blaise Pascal, Laboratoire d'Informatique Signal et Image de la Côte d'Opale (LISIC- EA 4491), 50 Rue Ferdinand Buisson BP 719, 62228 Calais Cedex France

ABSTRACT

The bootstrap filter is a method for nonlinear Bayesian filtering that uses stochastic sampling for an approximation of probability density functions. It is wide spread and perhaps the most implemented method in particle filters. It can be considered as the repetition of the sampling importance resampling over time. In this paper, we propose an image restoration method based on bootstrap filter using multivariate kernel density estimation. The multivariate Kernel density estimation of posterior density is used in the resampling step. This estimation technique makes it possible to regularize the bootstrap filter, which gives the name of the regularized bootstrap filter. Experimental results are shown to demonstrate the performance and effectiveness of our method in restoring images.

KEYWORDS

Bootstrap Filter, Probability density function, Multivariate kernel density estimation, Particle filters, Image restoration

1. INTRODUCTION

In recent years, restoration of digital images has become a very active field in computer applications and research (Marhaba et al., 2016) (Vijendran et al., 2013) (Hymagayathri et al., 2014). Restoration is a process that attempts to reconstruct or recover the original image after being degraded by using a previous knowledge of the degradation process. A number of different techniques have been proposed for digital image restoration, utilizing a number of different models and assumptions. The kalman filter is one of these techniques and is wide applied in the field of image and signal processing (Koch et al., 1993) (Nagayasu et al., 2011). It is a powerful recursive filter for estimating the internal state of a linear dynamic system from the series of noisy measurements. In recent works, adopting the particle filter (Arulampalam et al., 2002) to recursively restore degraded image has attracted interest due to its promising applicability to nonlinear and non-Gaussian problems (Vijendran and Lukose, 2012) (Lukose and Vijendran, 2014) (Kesharwani, 2016). Based on an autoregressive (AR) model of the prior statistical knowledge of a given image, the particle filter recursively provides optimal estimations of the original image asymptotically in the number of particles. The bootstrap filter (Gordon, 1995) method is based upon two methods: Bayesian state estimation, and Monte Carlo method. The bootstrap filter has a great advantage in handling any functional, non-linear system and/or measurement noise of any distribution. In this paper, we propose a method for image restoration based on Bootstrap filter and multivariate kernel density estimation (Wand and Jones, 1993). The image restoration issue can be considered as a recursive Bayesian estimation problem. Resampling steps need to be used in Bootstrap filter method to solve degradation problem. But the discrete sampling with no measurement in resampling steps can easily introduce errors (Gordon, 1995) (Arulampalam et al., 2002). To overcome this problem, we use the regularized bootstrap filter (RBF). In RBF the particles will be sampled from regularized continuous distribution in the resampling step. The multivariate Kernel density estimation of posterior density is used in the resampling step.

We organize our paper as follows. Section 2 presents image and blur model. In the third section, we will describe the regularized bootstrap filtering algorithm for image restoration. Experimental results are presented to demonstrate the accuracy of the proposed algorithm in section 4. Finally, the conclusion is made in section 5.

2. IMAGE AND BLUR MODEL

We can pose the issue of restoring an image to its original as an issue of dynamic state-estimation. In order for us to describe the RBF, we model the discrete original image $s(m, n)$ by a 2-D auto-regressive (AR) process

$$s(m,n) = \sum_{(k,l)\in\Gamma} c_{k,l} s(m-k, n-l) + w(m,n) \quad (1)$$

where $c_{k,l}$ are the image model coefficients, Γ the support of the image model, which is not necessarily causal, and $w(m, n)$ is a zero-mean homogeneous Gaussian distributed process with covariance $\sigma_w^2(m,n)$.

The observed image $y(m, n)$ is modeled as the output of a 2-D linear space-invariant system, which is characterized by its point-spread function (PSF). The observation noise $v(m, n)$ is assumed to be an additive zero-mean homogeneous Gaussian distributed process with covariance $\sigma_v^2(m,n)$. Then, the noisy blurred image is given by

$$y(m,n) = \sum_{k,l\in\Psi} g(k,l) s(m-k, n-l) + v(m,n) \quad (2)$$

where Ψ is the support of the PSF $g(k, l)$.

3. REGULARIZED BOOTSTRAP FILTER FOR RESTORATION

Our major problem in image restoration is the determining of an appropriate estimation for the original image s, given the observations y for all image pixels. Our approach to this solution is to propose RBF. To implement the RBF, we must incorporate this model into a state dynamical model. The image model, which describes the evolution of the state space, is represented in the form of

$$\begin{aligned} x(m,n) &= f(x(m-1,n), w(m,n)) \\ &= Cx(m,n-1) - Eu(m,n) + Dw(m,n) \end{aligned} \quad (3)$$

where $x(m,n) = [s(m,n), s(m,n-1), s(m-1,n+1), s(m-1,n)]^T$ is the state vector at spatial pixel location (m, n), $u(m, n)$ denotes a deterministic input, and C, D and E are system matrices.

The measurement model relating the degraded image intensity to its corresponding state vector can be written as

$$y(m,n) = g(x(m,n)) + v(m,n)) = Gx(m,n) + v(m,n) \quad (4)$$

where $y(m, n)$ is the known measurement at location (m, n) and G is system matrix.

3.1 Multivariate Kernel Density Estimation

In statistical filters, the estimation of probability density functions is very important step. To estimate the probability density function (PDF), nonparametric estimation methods can be used (Wand and Jones, 1993) (Scott, 2015). In our work, we choose the kernel density estimation technique. It is considered as a histogram density estimation generality that has statistical properties improvements. In this section, we recall the multivariate kernel density estimation.

Let $X=(X_1, X_2, \ldots, X_d)^T$ denotes a d-dimensional random vector with density $f(x)$ defined on $\mathbb{R}^d$, and let $\{x_1, x_2, \ldots, x_n\}$ be an independent random sample drawn from a common distribution described by the density function $f(x)$. The kernel density estimate (Wand and Jones, 1993) is defined to be

$$\hat{f}_H(x) = \frac{1}{n}\sum_{i=1}^{n} K_H(x - x_i) \quad (5)$$

where H is the bandwidth $d \times d$ matrix which is symmetric and positive definite and K is the kernel function which is a symmetric multivariate density;

$$K_H(x) = |H|^2 K(H^{-1/2}x) \tag{6}$$

Here, we use the standard multivariate normal kernel given by

$$K_H(x) = (2\pi)^{-d/2} |H|^{-1/2} e^{-\frac{1}{2}x^T H^{-1} x} \tag{7}$$

where H plays the role of the covariance matrix.

The bandwidth matrix H can be restricted to a class of positive definite diagonal matrices, then the corresponding kernel function will be known as a product kernel. When the data are observed from the multivariate normal density and the diagonal bandwidth matrix, denoted by H=diagonal (h_1, $h_2, \cdots$, h_d), is considered, as the optimal bandwidth (Wand and Jones, 1993) can be approximated by

$$h_i = \sigma_i \left[\frac{4}{(d+2)n} \right]^{1/(d+4)} \tag{8}$$

for i=1, 2,. … ., d, where σ_i is the standard deviation of the ith variate, and can be replaced by its sample estimator in practical implementations.

3.2 Regularized Bootstrap Filter

In our work, we will implement the RBF in the image restoration field based on Bootstrap filter and nonparametric techniques for PDF estimation. RBF is an algorithm for propagating and updating the random samples from the PDF of the state. In the following, we recall the BF (Gordon, 1995).

Let $Y_{m,n} = \{y(i,n)\}_{i=1}^{m}$ be the set of measurements up to time m. Suppose we have a set of random samples $\{x_i(m-1,n) : i = 1,\ldots,N_b\}$ from the PDF $p(x(m-1,n)/Y(m-1,n))$, where N_b is the number of bootstrap samples. To obtain a set of samples distributed as $p(x(m,n)/Y(m,n))$, we do the following:

1) Prediction step: Each one sample from PDF $p(x(m-1,n)/Y(m-1,n))$ will go through the system model to obtain samples from the prior at time step m

$$\overset{*}{x_i}(m,n) = f(x_i(m-1,n), w_i(m-1,n)) \tag{9}$$

where $w_i(m-1,n)$ is a sample drawn from the PDF of the system noise $p_w(w(m,n))$.

2) Update step: When obtaining the measurement $y(m,n)$, calculate the likelihood of each prior sample, then obtain a normalized weight q_i for each sample

$$q_i = \frac{p(y(m,n)/\overset{*}{x_i}(m,n))}{\sum_{j=1}^{N} p(y(m,n)/\overset{*}{x_j}(m,n))} \tag{10}$$

Thus define a discrete distribution over $\{\overset{*}{x_i}(m,n) : i = 1,\ldots,N_b\}$, with probability mass q_i associated with element i. Now resampling N_b times from the discrete distribution to generate samples $\{x_i(m,n) : i = 1,\ldots,N_b\}$, so that for any j, $\Pr\{x_j(m,n) = \overset{*}{x_i}(m,n)\} = q_i$.

Prediction and update steps stated above will form one iteration of the recursive algorithm. To initiate the algorithm, N_b samples $x_i^*(m,n)$ will be obtained from the known prior $p(x(1,n)/Y_{0,n}) = p(x(1,n))$. These samples will be fed directly into the update stage of the filter. We contend that the samples $x_i(m,n)$ are approximately distributed as the required PDF $p(x(m,n)/Y_{m,n})$. The resampling update stage is performed by drawing a random sample u_i from the uniform distribution over (0, 1]. The value $x_J^*(m,n)$ corresponding to

$$\sum_{j=0}^{J-1} q_j < u_i \leq \sum_{j=0}^{J} q_j \quad (11)$$

where q_0=0, is selected as a sample for the posterior.

In update step of BF, the resampling from the discrete distribution was suggested as a method to reduce the degeneracy problem, which is prevalent in BF. On the other hand, the resampling procedure was noticed to produce other problems, particularly, the problem of losing diversity among the particles (Scott, 2015). To resolve this problem, we suggest to regularize the BF. This regularization is established at the level of the resampling stage, where the samples are drawn from a continuous distribution rather than a discrete one, hence the name of RBF algorithm. By using a multivariate kernel density estimation, samples are drawn from the approximation

$$p(x(m,n)/Y_{m,n}) = \sum_{i=1}^{N_b} q_i K_H(x(m,n)-x_i(m,n)) \quad (12)$$

where K_H is given by (7).

4. EXPERIMENT RESULTS

For the implementation of the RBF, we have described the notations in equations (3) and (4) by the following expressions

$$C = \begin{bmatrix} a_1 & 0 & a_2 & a_3 \\ 1 & 0 & 0 & 0 \\ 0 & 0 & 0 & 0 \\ 0 & 0 & 1 & 0 \end{bmatrix}, \quad E = \begin{bmatrix} 0 \\ 0 \\ 1 \\ 0 \end{bmatrix}, \quad D = \begin{bmatrix} 1 & 0 \\ 0 & 0 \\ 0 & 1 \\ 0 & 0 \end{bmatrix} \text{ and } G = \begin{bmatrix} 1 & 0 & 0 & 0 \end{bmatrix}.$$

The input term $u(m, n)$ is introduced as the recent estimate of pixel $s(m-1, n+1)$. The image model parameters a_1, a_2, and a_3 are identified using the Least Squares method (Arulampalam et al., 2002). In this section, we will use the "Bateau" and "Columns" gray images of size 256×256 pixels shown in Fig. 1.a and Fig. 2.a respectively to evaluate the performance of the RBF algorithm with respect to the extended kalman filter (EKF) (Gustafsson and Hendeby, 2012). In the implementation process of the RBF, we have chosen the values of the parameters N_b, a_1, a_2, and a_3 given in Table 1.

Table 1. Values of parameters

Image	N_b	a_1	a_2	a_3
Bateau	100	0.8075	0.5063	- 0.3152
Columns	100	0.7415	0.7327	- 0.4728

The evaluation of the performance of the restoration methods will be made based on the following metrics: *ISNR* and PSNR are given respectively by

$$ISNR = 10\log_{10}\left[\sum_{m,n}[s(m,n)-y(m,n)]^2 / \sum_{m,n}[s(m,n)-\hat{s}(m,n)]^2\right] \quad (13)$$

$$PSNR = 10\log_{10}\left[\frac{255\times 255}{MSE}\right] \quad (14)$$

where MSE is the Mean Square Error defined by

$$MSE = \frac{\sum|s(i,j)-\hat{s}(i,j)|^2}{rows\times col} \quad (15)$$

and s, y, $\hat{s}$, and $rows\times col$ represent original image, degraded image, restored image, size of the image respectively.

In Figure 1(a), Figure 1(b), Figure 1(c) and Figure 1(d), we show the original Bateau image, the degraded image, the image restored by EKF and the restored image by RBF respectively. In Figure 2(a), Figure 2(b), Figure 2(c) and Figure 2(d), we show the original Columns image, the degraded image, the image restored by EKF and the image restored by RBF respectively.

In Table 2, we present the metric results obtained from the restoration process for Bateau and Columns images using RBF compared to the results obtained from restoring same Bateau and Columns images using the EKF.

The results shown in Figure 1(d) and Figure 2 (d), and the improved PSNR, and ISNR measurements from Table II, obtained by the RBF restoration, emphasizes the enormous visual quality and the high performance of the RBF.

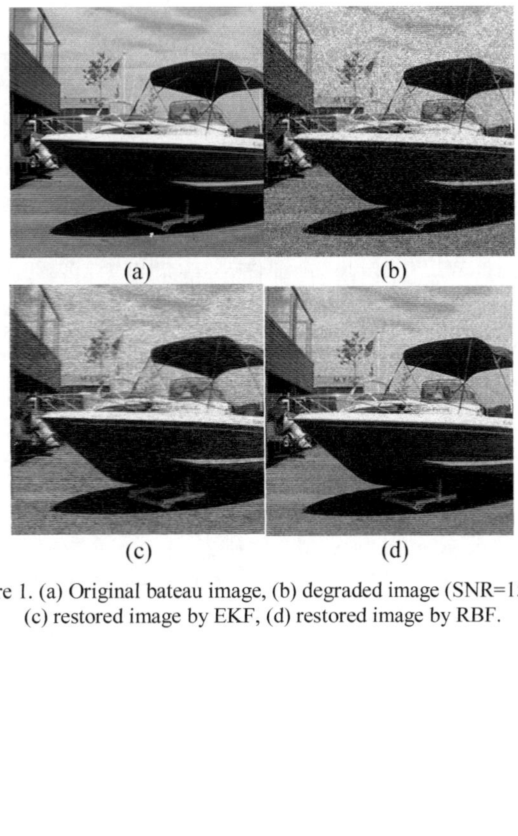

Figure 1. (a) Original bateau image, (b) degraded image (SNR=15 dB), (c) restored image by EKF, (d) restored image by RBF.

(a) (b)

(c) (d)

Figure 2. (a) Original Columns image, (b) degraded image (SNR=15 dB), (c) restored image by EKF, (d) restored image by RBF.

Table 2. Metrics results

Image	PSNR (dB)		ISNR (dB)	
	EKF	RBF	EKF	RBF
Bateau	23.287	27.063	1.586	3.521
Columns	21.792	26.322	0.954	3.264

5. CONCLUSION

Image restoration has been an active area in image processing. In this paper, we have introduced the RBF for image restoration. In RBF, we used the multivariate kernel technique for estimating the posterior distribution in the resampling stage. The obtained experimental results show that the proposed RBF gives better performance in both, noise reduction and detail preservation, as well the overall visual results are more clearly compared with the EKF.

REFERENCES

Arulampalam, et al, 2002. A tutorial on particle filters for online nonlinear/non-Gaussian Bayesian tracking. *In IEEE Transactions and Signal Processing,* Vol. 50, No 2, 174–188.

Gordon, N., 1995. A hybrid bootstrap filter for target tracking in clutter. *In IEEE Transactions on Aerospace and Electronic Systems.* Vol. 33, No. 1, pp. 628–632.

Hymagayathri, M., Prakash, A.J., Madhusudhana Rao, T.V., 2014. An Efficient Adaptive Linear Filtering Algorithm for Image Restoration Using Inverse Filter. *International Journal of Advanced Research in Electrical, Electronics and Instrumentation Engineering*, 12858–12863.

Kesharwani, E., 2016. Image Denoising Based on Particle Filtering: A Literature Review. *Indian Journal of Computer Science and Engineering.* Vol. 7, No. 6, pp 223–229

Koch, S., Kaufman, H., Biemond, J., 1993. Restoration of spatially varying images using multiple model extended Kalman filters, in: Decision and Control, 1993. *Proceedings of the 32nd IEEE Conference on. IEEE*. San Antonio, Texas pp. 1216–1221.

Lukose, B., Vijendran, A., 2014. Image Noise Removal Using Rao-Blackwellized Particle Filter with Maximum Likelihood Estimation. *International review on computers and software*. Vol. 9, No. 5, pp 784–792.

Marhaba, B., Zribi, M., Khoder, W., 2016. Image Restoration Using a Combination of Blind and Non-Blind Deconvolution Techniques. *International Journal of Engineering Research & Science*, Vol. 2, No. 5 pp 225–239.

Nagayasu, et al, 2011. Restoration method for degraded images using two-dimensional block Kalman filter with colored driving source, *in: Digital Signal Processing Workshop and IEEE Signal Processing Education Workshop (DSP/SPE)*, pp 151–156.

Scott, D.W., 2015. *Multivariate density estimation: theory, practice, and visualization*. John Wiley & Sons, New Jersey USA.

Vijendran, A., Lukose, B., 2012. Image Restoration Using Particle Filters By Improving The Scale of Texture With MRF. *International Journal of Image Processing*. Vol 6, No 5, pp 306–316.

Vijendran, A.S., Lukose, B., Head, D., 2013. Fast and Efficient Method for Image Denoising. *International Journal of Engineering and Innovative Technology*, Vol. 3, No 1,pp 200–207.

Wand, M.P., Jones, M.C., 1993. Comparison of Smoothing Parameterizations in Bivariate Kernel Density Estimation. *Journal of the American Statistical Association*. Vol. 88, No. 422, pp 520-528.

AN AUTOMATED OVARIAN TISSUE DETECTION APPROACH USING TYPE P63 COUNTER STAINED IMAGES TO MINIMIZE PATHOLOGY EXPERTS OBSERVATION VARIABILITY

T M Shahriar Sazzad[1], Leisa Armstrong[1] and Amiya Kumar Tripathy[1, 2]

[1]*Edith Cowan University, WA, Australia*

[2]*Don Bosco Institute of Technology, Mumbai, India*

ABSTRACT

Pathology experts are more interested to work and analyze microscopic digitized color images in compare to other available image processing modalities especially electronic ultrasound scanners. Ultrasound has the capability to identify larger sized and more mature sized tissues in compare to smaller ones. Ovarian reproductive tissues are smaller in size in compare to other available tissues in the ovary for which it is hard for ultrasound scanners to analyze ovarian reproductive tissues. Microscopic digitized color images are more viable for which at present most appropriate approach to analyze ovarian reproductive tissues remains microscopic analysis process. Manual analysis process is costly, extensive analysis time requires with observation variations between experts. To improve accuracy and reduce processing time computer based approaches have become popular for the last two decades but mostly to analyze cancer cells. To analyze small ovarian reproductive tissues accurately type P63 counter stained images with 3 different magnifications a fully automated approach is presented in this paper. The study's experimental results have higher accuracy rate in compare to manual analysis and electronic scanners.

KEYWORDS

Histopathology, Color Digitized Microscopic Image, Image Artifacts, Mean Shift; Region Fusion, Cluster; Ovarian Reproductive Tissues

1. INTRODUCTION

To conceive a child ovarian reproductive tissues play important role. Women who face conceiving complications require expert consultation. As part of consultation process it is important for experts to study and analyze the situation of ovarian reproductive tissues. To perform this task there are several analysis process among which computerized imaging modalities especially ultrasound imaging is popular (Kiruthika & Ramya, 2014). This is due to the fact that ultrasound is comparatively cheap and easy to analyze (Kiruthika & Ramya, 2014). A major limitation of ultrasound is it is more suitable to process mainly large and mature tissues (Skodras et al., 2009). To minimize the issues with ultrasound scanner microscopic slide analysis is measured as most reliable general clinical choice for smaller tissue analysis by experts in the laboratory (Skodras et al., 2009).

Microscopic analysis approach is useful for both larger and smaller sized tissue or cell analysis but analysis time is long and laborious (Muskhelishvili, Freeman, Latendresse, & Bucci, 2002). To minimize the issues with microscopic analysis approach; computer based approaches using digitized images from biopsy slides are more suitable as a fact that computer based approaches requires a reduced amount of processing time and cost efficient (Lamprecht, Sabatini, & Carpenter, 2007; Muskhelishvili, Wingard, & Latendresse, 2005).

Study of (T. Sazzad, Armstrong, & Tripathy, 2015) stated that there are different types of biopsy slides are used by experts for pathology microscopic analysis. Study of (Magee et al., 2009) indicates how ovarian tissue biopsy slides are prepared in the laboratory using dyes or colored organic substances. Most popular biopsy stain is H&E (Picut et al., 2008).

Expert analysis study by (Muskhelishvili et al., 2005) mentioned that type H&E has similar issues like ultrasound for which digitized images of type H&E may not be an appropriate choice for computerized analysis. A more suitable option could be to use type PCNA (Picut et al., 2008). Another study by (Kelsey, Caserta, Castillo, Wallace, & Gonzálvez, 2010) worked with type PCNA and suggested type P63 as a more viable option.

Research work of (T. Sazzad, Armstrong, & Tripathy, 2016a) indicated that there are two types of P63 biopsy stains. Experts use various magnifications if they cannot validate the results from one specific magnification image. Three different magnifications (40x, 100x and 200x) for type P63 counter stained images are shown in Figure 1.

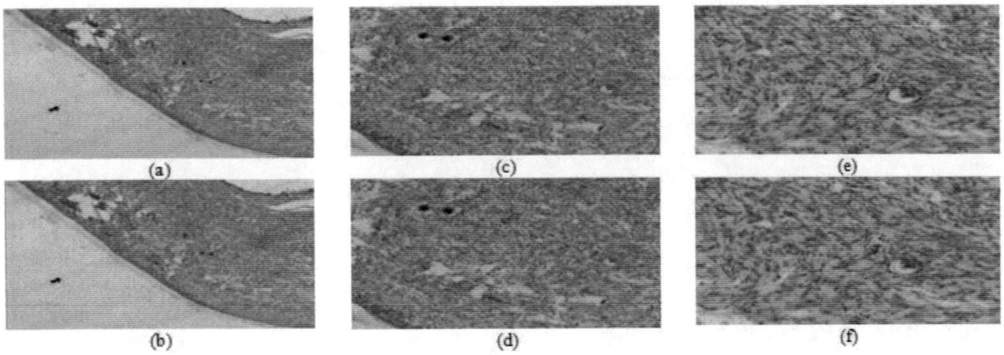

Figure 1. (a) type P63 counter stained (40x), (b) annotated image for (a), (c) type P63 counter stained image (100x), (d) annotated image for (b), (e) P63 counter stained image (200x), (f) annotated image of (e). Red marked regions are confirmed nucleus identified by 2 experts and blue marked regions by at-least 1 expert

2. RELATED WORK

Study of (Sertel, Catalyurek, Shimada, & Guican, 2009) mentioned that existing related research works are mainly based on cancer tissue, blood vessel and lymphatic vessel analysis. A few related research works were carried out by (Picut et al., 2008; Skodras et al., 2009; Soucek & Gut, 1992) using animal tissues (ovine and rats) of type PCNA which are semi-automated. Automated analysis using human ovarian tissue was carried out by (Kelsey et al., 2010) where type PCNA was used. Study of (T. Sazzad et al., 2015, 2016a; T. Sazzad, Armstrong, & Tripathy, 2016c, 2016d, 2016h, 2016i) worked with type P63 human ovarian tissues. Other automated existing approaches are also available which are mainly for cancer cell or tumor cell detection.

Among all available automated approaches for ovarian reproductive tissue analysis work of (Kelsey et al., 2010) is not fully automated where type PCNA images were incorporated. This is due to the fact that calibrations of the processing parameters are essential for each new batch of images. Research works of (T. Sazzad et al., 2015, 2016a, 2016c, 2016d, 2016h, 2016i) using type P63 images are proposed as automated approaches as new batch of images do not require any human intervention.

3. PROPOSED WORK

This research study automated processing flowchart is shown in Figure 2. This research study proposed method is similar to existing works of (T. Sazzad et al., 2015, 2016a; T. Sazzad, Armstrong, & Tripathy, 2016b; T. Sazzad et al., 2016c, 2016d; T. Sazzad, Armstrong, & Tripathy, 2016e, 2016f, 2016g; T. Sazzad et al., 2016h, 2016i) which include correcting image artifacts issues, noise filter operation, segmentation of regions, cluster operation and finally identification of ovarian reproductive tissue regions followed by classification approach to increase the accuracy rate.

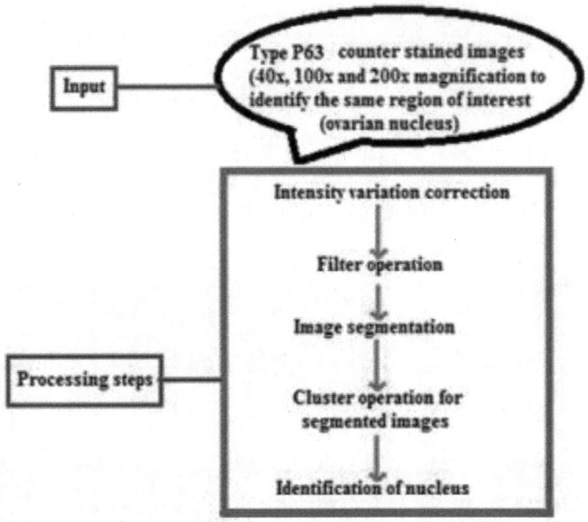

Figure 2. Block Diagram for Automated Identification Process

3.1 Correcting Image Artifacts

Use of color chemical during biopsy slide preparation causes intensity variations due to the fact that different tissues consume color chemical differently (Magee et al., 2009). There are several approaches available to correct artifact or intensity variation issues but study of (T. Sazzad et al., 2015) mentioned and proposed that morphological operation performs better results among all existing approaches. Study of (T. Sazzad et al., 2016a, 2016c) proposed modified morphological operation of (T. Sazzad et al., 2015). Further modification is carried out in this research study as a fact that microscopic eye lid magnification, magnification of the image while captured by a digital camera, Full Width Half Maximum (FWHM) and cell diameter provided by experts were considered to compute the disk radius for morphological operation. HSV color model was incorporated (T. S. Sazzad & Islam; T. S. Sazzad, Islam, Mamun, & Hasan, 2013). Basic algorithm of this proposed method is shown in Figure 3. Figure 4 indicates the test results for this study proposed method.

Algorithm for mathematical morphological operation
Input: a RGB image, CellDiameter(D), EyePieceMagnification(L1), LensMagnification(L2),FWHM,
Output: Corrected Image (intensity variation minimized)

1. *Convert the RGB image to HSV format*
2. *Compute disk_radious (d) using FWHM, D, L1 and L2*
3. *Compute SE (structuring element) based on step 2*
4. *Compute morphological operation on V channel*
5. *Calculate final V by subtracting value of step 4 and initial V*
6. *Convert the HSV image to RGB image*

Figure 3. Basic Algorithm for Mathematical Morphological Operation Proposed by This Research Study

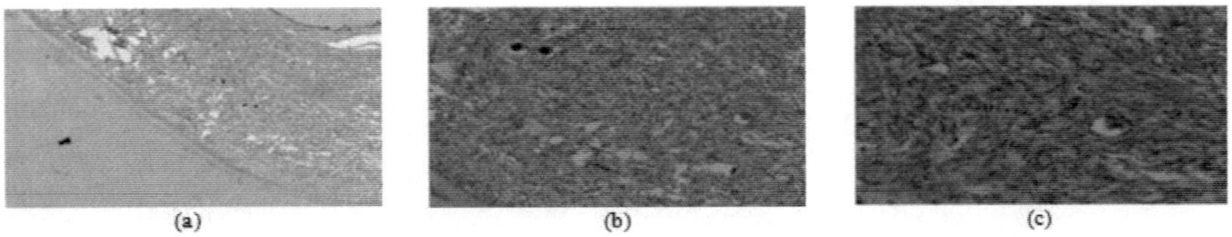

Figure 4. (a) 40x magnification, (b) 100x magnification and (c) 200x magnification indicates corrected images using this study proposed modified approach

3.2 Filter Operation

There are various types of existing filter approaches available and among all existing ovarian tissue analysis approaches proposed mean-shift pixel based filter approach by (T. Sazzad et al., 2015) provided acceptable results for type P63 images. Research work of (Kelsey et al., 2010) used median filter which did not provide satisfactory result. This research study followed the approach of (T. Sazzad et al., 2015) but instead of using a single point pixel based operation this study has proposed a modified new approach which is described below. At first all the regions will be clustered based on the intensity. These cluster number will be used for filter operation. For each iteration cluster number will be changed and this number will be used as of starting points for filter operation. Other steps are same as proposed in (T. Sazzad et al., 2015). This approach is faster than the approach of (T. Sazzad et al., 2015) and provides similar results. The results are shown in Figure 5. Table 1 indicates the comparative processing time between of this study proposed approach and the approach of (T. Sazzad et al., 2015).

Table 1. Comparative Results of Different Existing Approaches

Proposed approach	Image type (P63 counter stained)	Time required (seconds)
Existing approach of (T. Sazzad et al., 2015)	40x	5.20
	100x	7.54
	200x	9.52
Proposed approach	40x	4.12
	100x	5.02
	200x	7.36

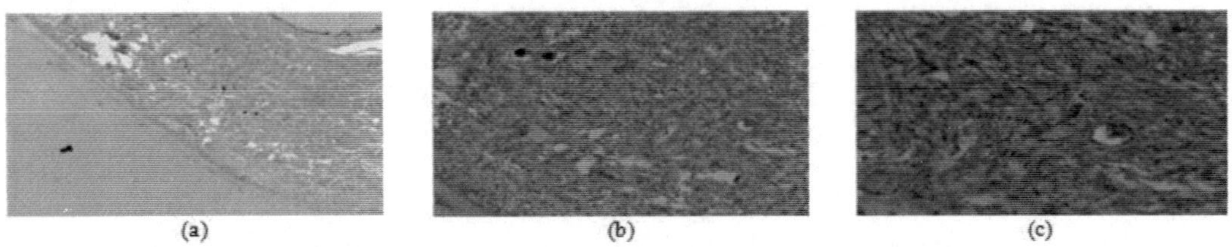

Figure 5. (a), (b) and (c) indicates filtered image using this study proposed approach

3.3 Color Segmentation

Threshold and watershed based segmentation approaches are mainly used for gray-scale image processing rather than for color images. This study tested threshold based method (OSTU threshold method) used by (Kelsey et al., 2010) but the results were not reasonable. Study of (T. Sazzad et al., 2015) proposed a modified region fusion approach which has shown to provide satisfactory results. Study of (T. Sazzad et al., 2016c) applied modified approach of (T. Sazzad et al., 2015) to improve the segmentation results. Further modification has been carried in this research study.

Instead of using RGB image proposed by (T. Sazzad et al., 2016c), this study divided RGB image in-to 3 channels (R,G,B). Secondly, region indexing was performed for all 3 channels. Thirdly, equation (1) from (T. Sazzad et al., 2015) was used to minimize the standard deviation error. Finally, segmentation operation carried out using region merging test shown Figure 6.

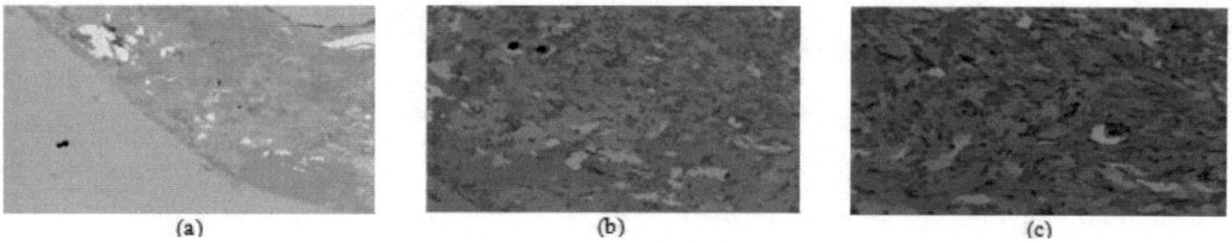

Figure 6. (a), (b) and (c) are segmented images using this study proposed approach

3.4 Cluster Approach

Modified mean-shift cluster based approach was proposed by (T. Sazzad et al., 2015) to provide satisfactory result which does not require any predefined parameters like k-means (most popular) or density based clustering approaches. Like other existing research studies (T. Sazzad et al., 2016a, 2016c) cluster approach proposed by (T. Sazzad et al., 2015) was used in this study.

3.5 Identify Ovarian Nucleus

Study of (Kelsey et al., 2010; T. Sazzad et al., 2015, 2016a, 2016c) incorporated experts provided features which include intensity, region area, major axis length, minor axis length and circularity for type PCNA and type P63 counter and non-counter stained images to identify the regions of interest. This research study incorporated same features to identify the ovarian nucleus regions. In addition, border touching regions were eliminated as study of (T. Sazzad et al., 2015) mentioned that experts ignores border touching regions. Identified results for this research study proposed approach is shown in Figure 7.

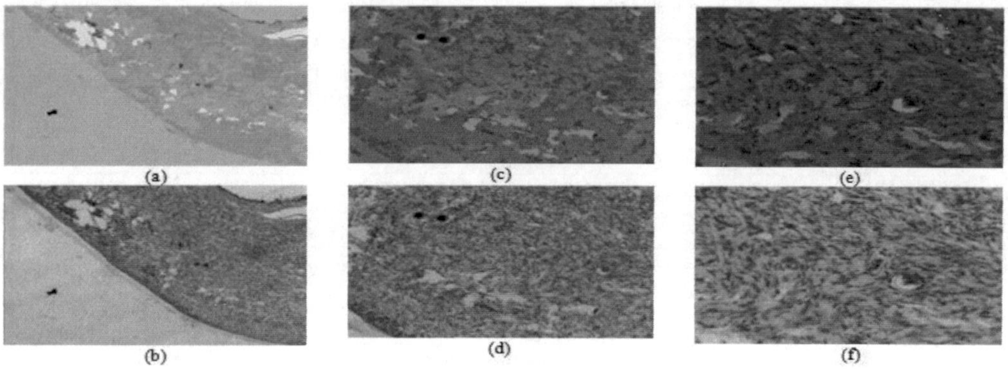

Figure 7. (a) identified regions for P63 (40x) image using this study proposed approach, (b) annotated results from experts. (c) identified regions for P63 (100x) images using this study proposed approach, (d) annoted result from experts. (e) identified regions for P63 (200X) images using this study proposed approach, (f) annotated result from experts. 1 region was missed by at-least one expert for 100x magnification but validates as NGF for both 40x and 200x magnification. This study results found that all the regions correctly without any identifying any false regions

4. EXPERIMENTAL RESULTS

From Table 2 it is clear that the new proposed method identified ovarian reproductive tissues (nucleus) with a remarkable accuracy rate of over 90% for all 3 magnifications. According to (Kelsey et al., 2010) Table 2 also indicates that proposed modified approach maintain the "gold standard" criteria.

Conventional threshold based approach proposed by (Kelsey et al., 2010) did not provide satisfactory result as a fact that under 80% accuracy been achieved shown in Table 2. Table 2 also indicates that the proposed method needs a reduced amount of processing time in comparison to other existing approaches.

Table 2. Comparative Results for Accuracy and Processing Time

Number of test images (P63 counter) 40x (403), 100x (493), 200x (475)	Image Type	avg. processing time (sec)	Precision	Recall
Proposed method	40x	18.25	0.91	0.91
	100x	20.05	0.975	0.985
	200x	21.04	0.995	0.995
Automated approach (T. Sazzad et al.)	40x	20.02	0.89	0.90
	100x	21.40	0.955	0.965
	200x	22.30	0.995	0.995
Automated approach (T. Sazzad et al., 2015)	40x	20.41	0.90	0.89
	100x	21.43	0.955	0.95
	200x	22.41	0.995	0.995
Automated approach (Kelsey et al., 2010)	40x	23.37	0.79	0.74
	100x	24.12	0.75	0.73
	200x	26.43	0.79	0.80
Automated approach (T. Sazzad et al., 2016c)	40x	20.45	0.875	0.91
	100x	21.53	0.955	0.955
	200x	22.49	0.995	0.995

5. DISCUSSION AND CONCLUSION

All existing ovarian tissue analysis automated computerized approaches were reviewed in this research study. As cancer cells are different from ovarian reproductive tissues therefore; this study only focused on existing ovarian tissue analysis approaches.

This study is novel as a fact that this is the first available study for type P63 counter images where three different magnifications were incorporated to analyze and identify the ovarian tissues accurately while minimizing the error rate in compare to manual approach. In Figure 9 for 40x magnification both experts identified 1 region, in 100x magnification that region was missed and in 200x magnification both regions were marked as confirmed nucleus. It is to mention that expert generally use 100 magnification images for analysis. This study proposed approach was able to identify all the regions correctly for 40x, 100x and 200x. For 500 slides (as for example) if the accuracy rate increased to 1% then it is possible to identify at least 100 tissues correctly as one identified tissue is enough for a medical expert to prescribe a proper treatment. The study proposed approach was able to improve the accuracy rate. This study analyzed a considerable amount of type P63 (counter) stained images and comparison has been carried out with other exiting approaches. For analysis purpose 21 different image batches were used in this research study. Human involvement is not required for this proposed approach. Only parameter required is to change the magnification for the test image as a processing parameter.

It may be possible to increase the accuracy rate if expert can correctly identify the regions without any observation variability.

ACKNOWLEDGEMENT AND FUTURE WORK

The authors would like to thank the domain expert Dr. S. Islam Talukder for providing the test images, annotated images and necessary feature information. In future different magnification will be considered as a review for type P63 digitized color images.

REFERENCES

Kelsey, T. W., Caserta, B., Castillo, L., Wallace, W. H. B., & Gonzálvez, F. C. (2010). Proliferating cell nuclear antigen (PCNA) allows the automatic identification of follicles in microscopic images of human ovarian tissue. *arXiv preprint arXiv:1008.3798*.

Kiruthika, V., & Ramya, M. (2014). *Automatic Segmentation of Ovarian Follicle Using K-Means Clustering.* Paper presented at the Signal and Image Processing (ICSIP), 2014 Fifth International Conference on.

Lamprecht, M. R., Sabatini, D. M., & Carpenter, A. E. (2007). CellProfiler™: free, versatile software for automated biological image analysis. *Biotechniques, 42*(1), 71.

Magee, D., Treanor, D., Crellin, D., Shires, M., Smith, K., Mohee, K., & Quirke, P. (2009). Colour normalisation in digital histopathology images.

Muskhelishvili, L., Freeman, L. D., Latendresse, J. R., & Bucci, T. J. (2002). An immunohistochemical label to facilitate counting of ovarian follicles. *Toxicologic pathology, 30*(3), 400-402.

Muskhelishvili, L., Wingard, S. K., & Latendresse, J. R. (2005). Proliferating cell nuclear antigen—a marker for ovarian follicle counts. *Toxicologic pathology, 33*(3), 365-368.

Picut, C. A., Swanson, C. L., Scully, K. L., Roseman, V. C., Parker, R. F., & Remick, A. K. (2008). Ovarian follicle counts using proliferating cell nuclear antigen (PCNA) and semi-automated image analysis in rats. *Toxicologic pathology, 36*(5), 674-679.

Sazzad, T., Armstrong, L., & Tripathy, A. (2015). *An Automated Detection Process to Detect Ovarian Tissues Using Type P63 Digitized Color Images.* Paper presented at the Tools with Artificial Intelligence (ICTAI), 2015 IEEE 27th International Conference on, Italy.

Sazzad, T., Armstrong, L., & Tripathy, A. (2016a). *An Automated Approach to Detect Human Ovarian Tissues Using Type P63 Counter stained Histopathology Digitized Color Images* Paper presented at the IEEE-EMBS International Conference on Biomedical and Health Informatics (BHI).

Sazzad, T., Armstrong, L., & Tripathy, A. (2016b). *An Automated Ovarian Tissue Detection Approach Using Type P63 Non-Counter Stained Images to Minimize Pathology Experts Observation Variability* Paper presented at the IEEE-IECBES 2016, Malaysia.

Sazzad, T., Armstrong, L., & Tripathy, A. (2016c). *A Comparative Study of Computerized Approaches for Type P63 Ovarian Tissues Using Histopathology Digitized Color Images.* Paper presented at the 10th International Conference on Computer Graphics, Visualization, Computer Vision and Image Processing (CGVCVIP 2016), Portugal.

Sazzad, T., Armstrong, L., & Tripathy, A. (2016d). *A Comprehensive Analysis and Review: Automated Ovarian Tissue Detection Using Type P63 Pathology Color Images.* Paper presented at the The 13'th IEEE International Joint Conference on Computer Science and Software Engineering (JCSSE2016), Thailand.

Sazzad, T., Armstrong, L., & Tripathy, A. (2016e). *A Comprehensive Analysis: Automated Ovarian Tissue Detection Using Type P63 Pathology Color Images.* Paper presented at the 12th International Conference on Machine Learning and Data Mining MLDM 2016, New York, USA.

Sazzad, T., Armstrong, L., & Tripathy, A. (2016f). *P63 Digitized Color Images Performs Better Identification for Ovarian Reproductive Tissue Analysis.* Paper presented at the IEEE Second International Image Processing, Applications and Systems Conference, Tunisia.

Sazzad, T., Armstrong, L., & Tripathy, A. (2016g). *Type P63 Digitized Color Images Performs Better Identification for Ovarian Tissue Analysis.* Paper presented at the 11th International Conference on Mass Data Analysis of Images and Signals, New York, USA.

Sazzad, T., Armstrong, L., & Tripathy, A. (2016h). *Type P63 Digitized Color Images Performs Better Identification than Other Stains for Ovarian Tissue Analysis.* Paper presented at the Conference on Articulated Motion and Deformable Objects, Spain.

Sazzad, T., Armstrong, L., & Tripathy, A. (2016i, 19 - 22 July 2016). *Type P63 Non-Counter Stained Digitized Color Images Performs Better Identification than Other Stains for Ovarian Tissue Analysis.* Paper presented at the 20th IEEE International Conference on Information Visualisation, Portugal.

Sazzad, T. S., & Islam, S. (2013). Use of gamma encoder on HSL color model improves human visualization in the field of image processing. *Issues, 1*(1), 177-182.

Sazzad, T. S., Islam, S., Mamun, M. M. R. K., & Hasan, M. Z. (2013). Establishment of an efficient color model from existing models for better gamma encoding in image processing. *International Journal of Image Processing (IJIP), 7*(1), 90.

Sertel, O., Catalyurek, U. V., Shimada, H., & Guican, M. (2009). *Computer-aided prognosis of neuroblastoma: Detection of mitosis and karyorrhexis cells in digitized histological images.* Paper presented at the Engineering in Medicine and Biology Society, 2009. EMBC 2009. Annual International Conference of the IEEE.

Skodras, A., Giannarou, S., Fenwick, M., Franks, S., Stark, J., & Hardy, K. (2009). *Object recognition in the ovary: quantification of oocytes from microscopic images.* Paper presented at the Digital Signal Processing, 2009 16th International Conference on.

Soucek, P., & Gut, I. (1992). Cytochromes P-450 in rats: structures, functions, properties and relevant human forms. *Xenobiotica, 22*(1), 83-103.

A FEATURE SIMILARITY INDEX BASED ON THE OPPONENT WEIGHTING FUNCTION FOR IMAGE QUALITY ASSESSMENT

Chengho Hsin, Zheng Chiu Chen and Shaw-Jyh Shin
Department of Communications Engineering, Feng Chia University, Taichung, Taiwan

ABSTRACT

Automatic image quality assessment (IQA) plays a vital role in various image and video processing applications. The most successful approach is based on the concept of structural similarity. In this paper, a high-performance full reference IQA model based on this approach is proposed that utilizes joint feature similarity and opponent weighted pooling. Three types of features including gradient magnitude, high-pass filtered component, and luminance mean are used altogether to establish a joint similarity map, which can account for most of the distortions encountered in real applications. By considering the shortcomings of the commonly used weighted pooling, a novel opponent weighting function is devised to assign larger weights to the distorted structures, smaller weights to those distortion-free structures. The experimental results on three image databases show that the proposed index provides comparable or better predictions than the competing state-of-the-art IQA metrics in the literature, it is effective and reliable.

KEYWORDS

Image quality assessment, gradient similarity, weighted pooling, full reference

1. INTRODUCTION

Images may suffer from various types and degrees of distortions in numerous image and video applications (Wang, 2011), such as image acquisition, compression, transmission, restoration, enhancement, and multimedia communication. Hence, image quality assessment (IQA) plays an important role in these applications. Since the ultimate receivers in these applications are the human vision, it is natural to resort to the subjective evaluation of image quality. However, the subjective IQA methods cannot be readily and routinely incorporated into real applications. It has been becoming a vital issue to develop objective IQA algorithms to automatically measure image quality. The objective evaluation results must be statistically consistent with those of the human observers. The objective IQA models can be classified as full-reference (FR), reduced reference, and no reference, as it depends on whether the reference image is available, the partial information of the reference image is available, and the reference image is unavailable, respectively.

This paper focuses on FR-IQA models, where the reference image means the original distortion-free image. The FR-IQA is also referred to image fidelity. The most commonly used FR-IQA metrics are the peak signal-to-noise ratio (PSNR) and the mean-squired error (MSE). They do not correlate well with the subjective ratings. Many IQA models have been proposed to improve the limitations of PSNR and MSE by using the characteristics of the human visual system (HVS). One approach based on a bottom-up framework simulates the hierarchical processing stages in the HVS. Various visual psychophysical properties, such as contrast sensitivity, just noticeable difference, and masking effect, have been incorporated into this type of IQA models. The noise quality measure (NQM) (Damera-Venkata, 2000) and the visual SNR (VSNR) (Chandler and Hemami, 2007) are two representatives. Another approach based on information-fidelity quantifies image quality using a distortion channel as well as an HVS model. Sheikh *et al.* (2005) proposed the information fidelity criterion (IFC) for IQA. The model measures the amount of information about the reference image that could be extracted from the distorted image. The IFC model was expanded to the visual information fidelity (VIF) (Sheikh and Bovik, 2006) metric by using an additional HVS channel model. The most successful approach in the literature is based on structure similarity between the reference and the distorted images. It assumes that the HVS is adapted to perceive the local structures in an image when evaluating its quality. The structure similarity (SSIM) index (Wang et al, 2004) and its variants are representatives of this approach.

The IQA models based on structure similarity share a common two-step framework. Firstly, a pair of local structure images is computed from the reference and the distorted images, respectively. A local similarity (local quality) map is established by locally comparing the two structure images with each other through a pre-defined similarity function. Then, convert the values of the local similarity map to a single overall quality score via a *pooling* strategy. The classical SSIM metric uses local luminance mean, standard deviation, and covariance to build a similarity map and then uses average pooling to compute the final similarity score. The multiscale extension of SSIM, called MS-SSIM (Wang et al, 2003) improves the performance of the original metric. Different features are adopted to establish the similarity maps. The most popular feature chosen for computing the similar map is gradient magnitude, for example, Chen et al. (2006), feature similarity index (FSIM) (Zhang et al, 2011), Liu *et al.* (2012), visual saliency-induced index (VSI) (Zhang et al, 2014), gradient magnitude similarity deviation (GMSD) (Xue et al, 2014), and Mean deviation similarity index (MDSI) (Nafchi et al, 2016), etc. The FSIM metric also uses phase congruency features to build up the similarity map. Sampat et al. (2006) use complex wavelet coefficients for calculation of the similarity map. As mentioned earlier, a pooling strategy is followed after computing the similarity map. The state-of-the-art pooling strategies for IQA models are based on the weighted average and Minkowski summation. Examples of IQA models using the weighted average pooling are Wang and Li (2011), FSIM, and Liu *et al.* (2012). GMSD uses standard deviation pooling and MDSI uses mean deviation pooling, which are two examples of Minkowski summation.

Designing a highly effective IQA model needs to consider two important factors: features that establish the similarity and the pooling strategy. In this paper, we propose an IQA model called the *opponent* weighting similarity (OWSIM) index that shows high performance. The proposed index uses gradient magnitude to measure structural distortions, use the high-pass filtered feature to measure phase-sensitive structure distortions, and use luminance mean to measure brightness distortion. These three similarity maps are then multiplied together to form a single similarity map. We then propose a novel opponent weighting pooling strategy and use it to calculate the final quality score. Unlike previous weighting pooling methods, our new opponent weighting function gives larger weights to the distortion structures than those to the distortion-free structure, which is more likely to follow the HVS. This statement is supported by visual examples and experimental results.

The remainder of the paper is organized as follows. Section 2 presents in detail the computation of the proposed OWSIM index. Section 3 reports the experimental results. Finally, Section 4 concludes the paper.

2. THE PROPOSED FEATURE SIMILARITY INDEX

The proposed image quality index is designed for grayscale images or the luminance components of color images. Denote an image as $f(\mathbf{x})$, where $\mathbf{x}$ represents the pixel coordinates of the image. Color to luminance conversion is computed by $f(\mathbf{x}) = 0.299R(\mathbf{x}) + 0.587G(\mathbf{x}) + 0.114B(\mathbf{x})$, where R, G, and B indicate the red, green, and blue components, respectively. The computation of the proposed image quality index consists of two stages. In the first stage, the local feature similarity maps are computed, and then in the second stage, these similarity maps are weighted and pooled into a single similarity score. In the following discussion, we adopt the subscripts r and d to denote the quantities of the reference and distorted images, respectively. For instance, $f_r(\mathbf{x})$ represents a reference image and $f_d(\mathbf{x})$ refers to a distorted image. Figure 1(a) and (b) show an example of a pair of reference and distorted images, respectively. The local block-wise distortions of different intensities are shown in the distorted image.

2.1 Feature Similarity Maps

Three types of low-level features including gradient magnitude, high-pass filtered component, and luminance mean are used to compute the corresponding similarity maps. These features can characterize most of the distortions encountered in real applications.

2.1.1 Gradient Similarity

The image gradient represented by the first-order partial derivatives along two orthogonal directions is approximated by convolving an image with two orthogonal gradient operators. The horizontal $G_x(\mathbf{x})$ and vertical $G_y(\mathbf{x})$ derivatives of an image $f(\mathbf{x})$ using Scharr gradient (Jähne et al, 1999) operators are given by

$$G_x(\mathbf{x}) = \frac{1}{16}\begin{bmatrix} 3 & 0 & -3 \\ 10 & 0 & -10 \\ 3 & 0 & -3 \end{bmatrix} * f(\mathbf{x}), \quad G_y(\mathbf{x}) = \frac{1}{16}\begin{bmatrix} 3 & 10 & 3 \\ 0 & 0 & 0 \\ -3 & -10 & -3 \end{bmatrix} * f(\mathbf{x}) \quad (1)$$

where $*$ indicates convolution. The gradient magnitude defined as $G(\mathbf{x}) = \sqrt{G_x^2(\mathbf{x}) + G_y^2(\mathbf{x})}$ is used to construct the gradient similarity map. Denote $G_r(\mathbf{x})$ and $G_d(\mathbf{x})$ as the gradient magnitudes of the reference $f_r(\mathbf{x})$ and the distorted $f_d(\mathbf{x})$ images, respectively. From which, the gradient similarity map is computed as follows:

$$S_G(\mathbf{x}) = \frac{2G_r(\mathbf{x})\, G_d(\mathbf{x}) + C_1}{G_r^2(\mathbf{x}) + G_d^2(\mathbf{x}) + C_1} \quad (2)$$

where C_1 is a positive constant to increase the stability of $S_G(\mathbf{x})$. An example of the gradient magnitude images $G_r(\mathbf{x})$ and $G_d(\mathbf{x})$ is shown in Figure 1(c) and (d), respectively. The structure information of an image is clearly preserved in its corresponding gradient magnitude image. The gradient similarity map $S_G(\mathbf{x})$ shown in Figure 1(g) accurately delineates the distortion structure, where the pixels with darker color indicate the more dissimilarity between the reference and the distorted images.

2.1.2 High-Pass Filtered Similarity

If the corresponding edge pairs in the reference and distorted images have exactly the same amplitude but with the opposite gradient directions, then the gradient magnitudes are blind to this type of distortion. We adopt a high-pass filtered image to solve this issue, which is obtained by the difference between the input image and its low-pass filtered image. Let $H(\mathbf{x})$ denote a high-pass filtered image which is defined by

$$H(\mathbf{x}) = f(\mathbf{x}) - f(\mathbf{x}) * g(\mathbf{x}; \sigma_H) \quad (3)$$

where $g(\cdot)$ represents the Gaussian function with the standard deviation σ_H. Similarly, the high-pass filtered images $H_r(\mathbf{x})$ and $H_d(\mathbf{x})$ from $f_r(\mathbf{x})$ and $f_d(\mathbf{x})$, respectively, are compared, and the similarity measure is defined as follows:

$$S_H(\mathbf{x}) = \frac{2H_r(\mathbf{x})\, H_d(\mathbf{x}) + C_2}{H_r^2(\mathbf{x}) + H_d^2(\mathbf{x}) + C_2} \quad (4)$$

where C_2 is a positive constant determined by the dynamic range of $H(\mathbf{x})$ and to control numerical stability. An example of the high-pass filtered images $H_r(\mathbf{x})$ and $H_d(\mathbf{x})$ is shown respectively in Figure 1(e) and (f). Figure 1(h) shows the high-pass filtered similarity map $S_H(\mathbf{x})$. The lower similarity values in the map are represented by the darker gray areas and they obviously indicate the distortion parts occurred in the distorted image.

2.1.3 Luminance Mean Similarity

Both the gradient magnitudes and the high-pass filtered images are incapable of detecting the difference of luminance mean between the reference and the distorted image. Hence, the luminance mean similarity is defined as follows:

$$S_M = \frac{2\mu_r \mu_d + C_3}{\mu_r^2 + \mu_d^2 + C_3} \quad (5)$$

where μ_r and μ_d represent the global means of the reference and distorted images, respectively, and C_3 is a positive constant to control numerical stability. Note that S_M is a scalar.

The three feature similarity maps are combined to obtain the complete similarity $S(\mathbf{x})$ between $f_r(\mathbf{x})$ and $f_d(\mathbf{x})$. Through a multiplication scheme, we define $S(\mathbf{x})$ as follows:

$$S(\mathbf{x}) = S_G(\mathbf{x})\, S_H(\mathbf{x})\, [S_M]^{\gamma} \tag{6}$$

where the parameter γ is used to adjust the relative importance of the luminance mean similarity.

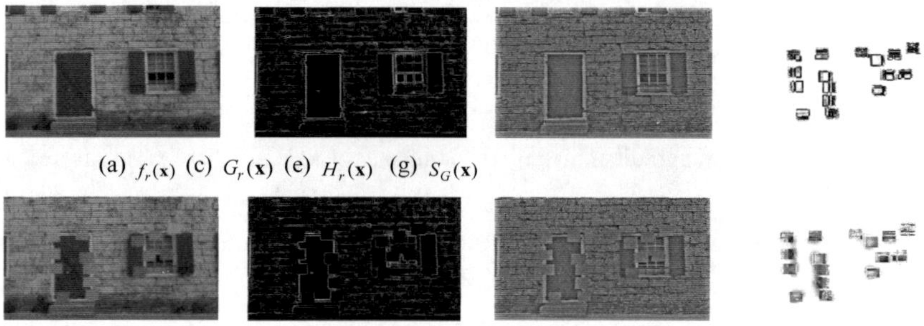

(a) $f_r(\mathbf{x})$ (c) $G_r(\mathbf{x})$ (e) $H_r(\mathbf{x})$ (g) $S_G(\mathbf{x})$

(b) $f_d(\mathbf{x})$ (d) $G_d(\mathbf{x})$ (f) $H_d(\mathbf{x})$ (h) $S_H(\mathbf{x})$

Figure 1. Illustration of images (a) and (b), gradient magnitudes (c) and (d), high-passed filtered features (e) and (f), and similarity maps (g) and (h) (The subscripts r and d refer to respectively reference and distortion, and the subscripts G and H indicate gradient and high-pass filtered, respectively.)

2.2 Pooling by an Opponent Weighting Function

The similarity map $S(\mathbf{x})$ must be pooled to generate a single score indicating the image quality. We adopt a weighted pooling approach. An appropriate weighting function is provided with two properties. Firstly, it can extract the salient features which are highly perceptible to the human vision. Secondly, it gives larger weights to the distorted salient features than those to the non-distorted features. To derive the desired weighting function, we introduce the absolute local variation of an image, denoted by $a(\mathbf{x})$, which is defined as follows:

$$a(\mathbf{x}) = \sum_{\mathbf{x}' \in N(\mathbf{x})} |\, \ell(\mathbf{x}) - f(\mathbf{x}')\, |\, g(\mathbf{x}' - \mathbf{x}; \sigma_a) \tag{7}$$

where $\ell(\mathbf{x})$ is the low-pass filtered image defined by $f(\mathbf{x}) * g(\mathbf{x}; \sigma_a)$, σ_a determines the size of the Gaussian mask, and $N(\mathbf{x})$ represents a local neighborhood of $\mathbf{x}$ specified by the Gaussian mask. Figure 2(a) and (b) shows respectively, $a_r(\mathbf{x})$ and $a_d(\mathbf{x})$, the maps of the absolute local variation of the reference and the distorted images. The weighting function defined by $a_m(\mathbf{x}) = \max(a_r(\mathbf{x}), a_d(\mathbf{x}))$ is used commonly. It considers the saliency altogether in $f_r(\mathbf{x})$ and $f_d(\mathbf{x})$. Figure 2(c) displays this commonly used weighting function $a_m(\mathbf{x})$. Obviously, this type of weighting function is unable to give larger weights to the distorted saliency, smaller weights to the non-distorted saliency. We propose a division approach to facilitate the unequal weights to the distorted and the normal salient parts in the similarity map. The two maps $a_r(\mathbf{x})$ and $a_d(\mathbf{x})$ are divided each other, which we obtain

$$W_d(\mathbf{x}) = \frac{a_d(\mathbf{x})}{a_r(\mathbf{x}) + k}, \quad W_r(\mathbf{x}) = \frac{a_r(\mathbf{x})}{a_d(\mathbf{x}) + k} \tag{8}$$

where k is a positive constant to control numerical stability and also to play as a soft threshold. The final weighting function is given by

$$W(\mathbf{x}) = \max(W_r(\mathbf{x}), W_d(\mathbf{x})) \tag{9}$$

Since the above weighting function implies the opponency of $a_r(\mathbf{x})$ and $a_d(\mathbf{x})$, it is named as the opponent weighting function. Figure 2(d) shows an example of the opponent weighting function, and it clearly indicates that the distorted salient parts receive the predominantly large weights.

The overall quality prediction score of a distorted image, where the reference image is available, is computed by taking the weighted average of the similarity map. The proposed IQA model with the similarity map $S(\mathbf{x})$ and the opponent weighting function $W(\mathbf{x})$ defined in the above, we name it as the opponent weighting similarity (OWSIM) index and it is defined as follows:

$$\mathrm{OWSIM} = \frac{\sum_{x \in Z} W(\mathbf{x})\, S(\mathbf{x})}{\sum_{x \in Z} W(\mathbf{x})} \tag{10}$$

where Z represents the whole image spatial domain.

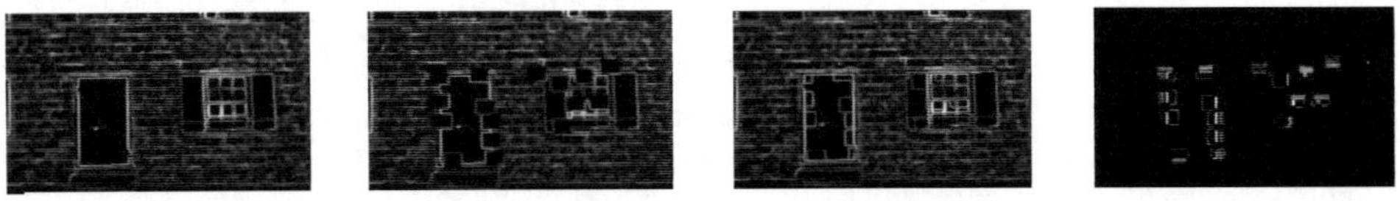

(a) $a_r(\mathbf{x})$ (b) $a_d(\mathbf{x})$ (c) $a_m(\mathbf{x})$ (d) $W(\mathbf{x})$

Figure 2. Illustration of the absolute local variation (a) and (b), the weighting function formed in a common manner (c), and the opponent weighting function (d) (The subscripts r and d refer to respectively reference and distortion, and the subscript m indicates the max operation.)

3. EXPERIMENTAL RESULTS

3.1 Databases and Methods for Comparison

Three large scale and publicly available IQA databases: TID2008 (Ponomarenko et al, 2009), CSIQ (Larson et al, 2009), and LIVE (Sheikh et al, 2014) will be used here for model validation and comparison. The characteristics of these three databases are summarized in Table 1. Either the MOS (mean opinion scores) or the DMOS (differential mean opinion scores) subjective ratings of the distorted image quality are provided from each database. To evaluate how well the metric values correlate with the provided subjective scores, three commonly used evaluation criteria are employed to access the competing IQA metrics. The Spearman rank-order correlation coefficient (SRC) measures the degree of monotonicity between the IQA objective metric scores and the subjective ratings. It relies only on the rank of the data points and disregards the relative distance between data points. To compute the Pearson linear correlation coefficient (PLC) along with the root-mean-squared error (RMSE), we need to apply a regression analysis to find a nonlinear mapping between the objective scores and the subjective ratings. The logistic mapping is employed for the nonlinear regression, which is defined by

$$P(m) = \beta_1 \left(\frac{1}{2} - \frac{1}{1 + e^{\beta_2 (m - \beta_3)}} \right) + \beta_4 m + \beta_5 \tag{11}$$

where m is the IQA model scores, $P(m)$ is the *predicted* subjective ratings, and β_i, i = 1, 2, …, 5, are the parameters to be found for the data-fitting. After the regression, the PLC and the RMSE between the *true* and the *predicted* subjective ratings can be calculated to predict the accuracy of the IQA model scores. The higher values of the SRC and the PLC along with the smaller values of the RMSE indicate the better performance of the IQA models.

3.2 Determination of Parameters

We tuned the parameters of the proposed OWSIM by following the same procedure of the FSIM method. As a result, the parameters required in the proposed method were set as: $C_1 = 160$, $C_2 = 256$, $C_3 = 0$, $\sigma_a = 1$, $\sigma_H = 3.8$, $\gamma = 0.2$, and $k = [0.03 \times \text{dynamic range}]^2$, assuming that the maximum gray-level is 255. In our experiments, all the parameters were fixed to all image databases.

3.3 Analysis of the Performance of the Proposed OWSIM Index

The proposed method OWSIM is composed of the three similarity maps and an opponent weighting function. We decomposed the OWSIM into four different combinations and analyzed their performances on the largest database TID2008. In case 1, the performance of the gradient similarity $S_G(\mathbf{x})$ pooled by the non-opponent weighting function $a_m(\mathbf{x})$ was evaluated. In contrast, the case 2 assessed the performance of $S_G(\mathbf{x})$ averaged by the opponent weighting function $W(\mathbf{x})$. In case 3, the performance of the similarity map $S_G(\mathbf{x}) \cdot S_H(\mathbf{x})$ pooled by $W(\mathbf{x})$ was evaluated. Finally, the performance of the OWSIM itself was computed in case 4. The results are shown in Table 2. The increased performance from case 1 to case 2 is remarkable by employing the opponent weighting function. The performance is improved slightly when the additional similarity maps are adopted.

Table 1. Benchmark IQA databases

Database	Source Images	Distorted Images	Distortion Types	Image Types	Observers
TID2008	25	1700	17	color	838
CSIQ	30	866	6	color	35
LIVE	29	779	5	color	161

Table 2. Analysis of the performance of the proposed OWSIM index

		CASE 1	**CASE 2**	**CASE 3**	**CASE 4**
TID2008	**SRC**	**0.8626**	**0.8990**	**0.9018**	**0.9044**
	PLC	**0.8602**	**0.8824**	**0.8898**	**0.8912**
	RMSE	**0.6844**	**0.6315**	**0.6123**	**0.6087**

4. PERFORMANCE COMPARISON

To demonstrate the effectiveness of the proposed OWSIM, we compared it with 8 representative IQA models, including 7 state-of-the-art metrics (FSIM, MS-SSIM, VIF, SSIM, IFC, VSNR, and NQM) and the classical PSNR. We mainly focus on the models based on the grayscale images and weighted summation. We have not included GMSD, VSI, and MDSI for comparison although the proposed metric performs better than or comparable to these models. Table 3 lists the overall performance described by the SRC, the PLC and the RMSE of nine IQA models on TID2008, CSIQ, and LIVE databases. For each performance measure and database, the top three IQA models are highlighted in boldface. It can be seen that the proposed OWSIM has the best results on almost all the databases, except for LIVE database. Even on this database, our method achieves nearly the same performance as the best results. In addition, we examined the performance of the IQA models on individual distortion type. The aim of this experiment is to understand the performance of the competing IQA models when the distortion type is known beforehand. We used the SRC as the evaluation measure and the experimental results are summarized in Table 4. The top three IQA models producing the highest SRC values are highlighted in boldface. Except for the PSNR metric, the proposed method and other IQA models do not perform well on impulse noise distortion. The performance of our method on blur distortion is slightly inferior to the best results. However, the proposed OWSIM achieves the most leading and stable performance across all the distortion types, while the FSIM and the VIF have comparable performance.

Table 3. Performance comparison of IQA metrics on three benchmark databases

		OWSIM	FSIM	MS-SSIM	VIF	SSIM	IFC	VSNR	NQM	PSNR
TID 2008	SRC	0.9044	0.8805	0.8528	0.7496	0.7749	0.5692	0.7046	0.6243	0.5245
	PLC	0.8912	0.8738	0.8425	0.8090	0.7790	0.7359	0.6820	0.6135	0.5309
	RMSE	0.6087	0.62525	0.7299	0.7888	0.8511	0.9086	0.9815	1.0598	0.1372
CSIQ	SRC	0.9468	0.9242	0.9138	0.9193	0.8756	0.7482	0.8106	0.7402	0.8057
	PLC	0.9308	0.9120	0.8998	0.9277	0.8613	0.8381	0.8002	0.7433	0.1575
	RMSE	0.0905	0.1077	0.1145	0.0980	0.1334	0.1432	0.1575	0.1756	0.8001
LIVE	SRC	0.9600	0.9634	0.9445	0.9631	0.9479	0.9234	0.9274	0.9086	0.8755
	PLC	0.9568	0.9597	0.9430	0.9598	0.9449	0.9248	0.9231	0.9122	0.8721
	RMSE	7.9448	7.6780	9.0956	7.6734	8.9455	10.392	10.506	13.511	13.368

Table 4. SRC values of IQA metrics for each distortion type

		OWSIM	FSIM	MS-SSIM	VIF	SSIM	IFC	VSNR	NQM	PSNR
TID 2008	Awgn	**0.8922**	0.8566	0.8094	**0.8799**	0.8107	0.5817	0.7728	0.7679	**0.9114**
	Awgn-color	**0.8808**	0.8527	0.8064	**0.8785**	0.8029	0.5528	0.7793	0.7490	**0.9068**
	spatialcorr-noise	**0.9031**	0.8483	0.8195	**0.8703**	0.8144	0.5984	0.7665	0.7720	**0.9229**
	masked noise	**0.8203**	0.8021	0.8155	**0.8698**	0.7795	0.7326	0.7295	0.7067	**0.8487**
	high-fre-noise	**0.9123**	**0.9093**	0.8685	0.9075	0.8729	0.7361	0.8811	0.9015	**0.9323**
	impulse noise	0.7236	0.7452	0.6868	**0.8331**	0.6732	0.5334	0.6471	**0.7616**	**0.9177**
	quantization noise	**0.8853**	**0.8564**	0.8537	0.7956	0.8531	0.5911	0.8270	0.8209	**0.8699**
	blur	0.9288	0.9472	**0.9607**	**0.9546**	**0.9544**	0.8766	0.9330	0.8846	0.8682
	denoising	**0.9704**	**0.9603**	**0.9571**	0.9189	0.9530	0.8002	0.9286	0.9450	0.9381
	jpg-comp	**0.9525**	**0.9279**	**0.9348**	0.9170	0.9252	0.8181	0.9174	0.9075	0.9011
	jpg2k-comp	**0.9815**	**0.9773**	**0.9736**	0.9713	0.9625	0.9445	0.9515	0.9532	0.8300
	jpg-trans-error	**0.8855**	**0.8708**	**0.8736**	0.8582	0.8678	0.7966	0.8056	0.7373	0.7665
	jpg2k-trans-error	**0.8922**	**0.8544**	0.8525	0.8510	**0.8577**	0.7303	0.7909	0.7262	0.7765
	pattern-noise	**0.7882**	0.7491	0.7336	**0.7608**	0.7107	**0.8410**	0.5716	0.6800	0.5931
	block-distortion	**0.8448**	**0.8492**	0.7617	0.8320	**0.8462**	0.6767	0.1926	0.2348	0.5852
	mean shift	**0.7208**	0.6720	**0.7374**	0.5132	**0.7231**	0.4375	0.3715	0.5245	0.6974
	contrast	**0.6489**	**0.6481**	0.6400	**0.8190**	0.5246	0.2748	0.4239	0.6191	0.6126
CSIQ	awgn	**0.9675**	0.9262	**0.9471**	**0.9571**	0.8974	0.8460	0.9241	0.9384	0.9363
	jpg-comp	0.9539	**0.9654**	**0.9622**	**0.9705**	0.9546	0.9395	0.9036	0.9527	0.8882
	jpg2k-comp	**0.9720**	**0.9685**	**0.9691**	0.9672	0.9606	0.9262	0.9480	0.9631	0.9363
	1/f noise	**0.9538**	0.9234	0.9330	**0.9509**	0.8922	0.8279	0.9084	0.9119	**0.9338**
	blur	0.9683	**0.9726**	**0.9720**	**0.9747**	0.9609	0.9593	0.9446	0.9587	0.9289
	contrast	**0.9445**	0.9420	**0.9521**	0.9361	0.7922	0.5416	0.8700	**0.9479**	0.8622
LIVE	jpg-comp	**0.9804**	**0.9717**	0.9654	**0.9683**	0.9614	0.9100	0.9551	0.9435	0.8954
	jpg2k-comp	0.9695	**0.9834**	**0.9793**	**0.9842**	0.9764	0.9440	0.9657	0.9647	0.8809
	awgn	0.9831	0.9652	0.9731	**0.9845**	0.9694	0.9377	0.9785	**0.9863**	**0.9854**
	blur	0.9596	**0.9708**	0.9584	**0.9722**	0.9517	**0.9647**	0.9413	0.8379	0.7823
	jpg2k-trans-error	0.9525	0.9499	0.9321	**0.9652**	**0.9556**	**0.9644**	0.9027	0.8147	0.8907

5. CONCLUSION

We have proposed an effective and reliable FR-IQA model, namely OWSIM index, which is based on a joint feature similarity map and a new opponent weighting function. The features adopted in the proposed model are able to capture the salient low-level features perceived by the HVS. The opponent weighting function devised by the absolute local variation and the novel division principle demonstrate its effectiveness in pooling the similarity map. Extensive experimental results on benchmark databases prove that the proposed index performs better in terms of both accuracy and consistency compared with the state-of-art FR-IQA metrics.

ACKNOWLEDGEMENT

This work has been supported by the Ministry of Science and Technology under Grant No. MOST 104-2221-E-035-054.

REFERENCES

Chen G.-H. et al, 2006. Gradient-based Structural Similarity for Image Quality Assessment. *Proc. IEEE Int. Conf. Image Process.* pp. 2929-2932.

Chandler D. M. and Hemami S. S., 2007. VSNR: A Wavelet-based Visual Signal-to-Noise Ratio for Natural Images, *IEEE Trans. Image Process.* Vol. 16, no. 9, pp. 2284–2298.

Damera-Venkata N. et al, 2000. Image Quality Assessment Based on a Degradation Model. *IEEE Trans. Image Process.* Vol. 9, No. 4, pp. 636–650.

Jähne B. et al, 1999. *Handbook of Computer Vision and Applications*. Academic, New York.

Liu A. et al, 2012. Image Quality Assessment Based on Gradient Similarity. *IEEE Trans. Image Process.* Vol. 21, No. 4, pp. 1500-1512.

Larson E. C. et al, 2009. Categorical Image Quality (CSIQ) Database [Online]. Available: http://vision.okstate.edu/csiq

Nafchi H. Z. et al, 2016. Mean Deviation Similarity Index: Efficient and Reliable Full-Reference Image Quality Evaluator. *IEEE Access.* Vol. 4, pp.5579-5590.

Ponomarenko N. et al, 2009. TID2008 - A Database for Evaluation of Full-Reference Visual Quality Assessment Metrics. *Adv. Modern Radio Electron.* Vol. 10, No. 4, pp. 30-45.

Sampat M. P. et al, 2009. Complex Wavelet Structural Similarity: A New Image Similarity Index. *IEEE Trans. Image Process.* Vol. 18, No. 11, pp. 2385-2401.

Sheikh H. R. et al, 2005. An Information Fidelity Criterion for Image Quality Assessment Using Natural Scene Statistics. *IEEE Trans. Image Process.* Vol. 14, No. 12, pp. 2117–2128.

Sheikh H. R. and Bovik A. C., 2006. Image Information and Visual Quality, *IEEE Trans. Image Process.* Vol. 15, No. 2, pp. 430–444.

Sheikh H. et al, 2014. *Live Image Quality Assessment Database Release 2*. [Online]. Available: http://live.ece.utexas.edu/research/quality

Wang Z. et al, 2003. Multiscale Structural Similarity for Image Quality Assessment. *Proc. 7th Asilomar Conf. Signals, Syst. Comput.* Vol. 2, pp. 1398-1402.

Wang Z. et al, 2004. Image Quality Assessment: From Error Visibility to Structural Similarity. *IEEE Trans. Image Process.* Vol. 13, No. 4, pp. 600-612.

Wang Z., 2011. Applications of Objective Image Quality Assessment Methods. *IEEE Signal Process. Mag.* Vol. 28, No. 6, pp. 137-142.

Wang Z. and Li Q., 2011. Information Content Weighting for Perceptual Image Quality Assessment. *IEEE Trans. Image Process.* Vol. 20, No. 5, pp. 1185-1198.

Xue W. et al, 2014. Gradient Magnitude Similarity Deviation: A Highly Efficient Perceptual Image Quality Index. *IEEE Trans. Image Process.* Vol. 23, No. 2, pp. 684-695.

Zhang L. et al, 2011. FSIM: A Feature Similarity Index for Image Quality Assessment. *IEEE Trans. Image Process.* Vol. 20, No. 8, pp. 2378-2386.

Zhang L. et al, 2014. VSI: A Visual Saliency-Induced Index for Perceptual Image Quality Assessment. *IEEE Trans. Image Process.* Vol. 23, No. 10, pp. 4270-4281.

IN SITU VISUALIZATION INFRASTRUCTURE FOR LARGE SCALE SIMULATIONS WITH STRUCTURED MESHES

Yi Cao, Zeyao Mo, Zhiwei Ai, Aiqing Zhang, Li Xiao and Huawei Wang
High Performance Computing Center, Institute of Applied Physics and Computational Mathematics
CAEP Software Center for High Performance Numerical Simulation, Beijing, China

ABSTRACT

To resolve complex multiscale, multiphysics problems at high resolution, modern large-scale parallel scientific and engineering simulations with structured meshes have exceeded the scale of tens of billions mesh elements. In situ visualization play an important role in avoiding the slowest component of post-processing workflow on exasale architectures: accessing the file system twice with input/output bottlenecks. Tightly coupling in situ visualization with simulations requires minimum modification to existing code. Most previous in situ work has focused on achieving in situ visualization with individual simulation code with less regard to the promising parallel programming frameworks that can guarantee quick adaptation to a batch of simulation applications. In this paper, we present an in situ visualization infrastructure based on the parallel programming framework, J Adaptive Structured Meshes applications Infrastructure (JASMIN), which supports large-scale simulations with structured meshes. We describe an approach that opens up new applications for in situ visualization, the key technologies on which it depends, and our experiences of integrating our infrastructure into two domain-specific simulations.

KEYWORDS

In situ visualization, exascle computing, large-scale simulation, SAMR simulation

1. INTRODUCTION

Many important science and engineering simulation problems involve the rapid formation, propagation, and disintegration of fine-scale features combined with multiple physical models. Frequently, such problems are modeled using coupled systems of partial differential equations (PDEs) (Bateman, 1932). Therefore, a broad range of applied PDE problems exhibit multiscale and multiphysics behavior (Lethbridge, 2004). To overcome the numerical problems related to these physical phenomena, structured adaptive mesh refinement (SAMR) is an effective technique for focusing computational resources in numerical simulations of PDEs (Berger et al, 1984). However, SAMR presents complications for massively parallel computing that are absent in uniform mesh calculations (Colella et al, 2007). The parallel programming framework hides some of the parallelism within libraries and application-specific frameworks, so that application programmers do not use the message passing interface (MPI) interface directly (Dubey et al, 2014). These software layers will continue to be important on exascale machines and may help to ease the transition to systems that require resilience, memory hierarchies, and so on.

To resolve complex multiscale, multiphysics problems at high resolution, modern large-scale parallel scientific and engineering simulations with structured meshes have exceeded the scale of tens of billions of mesh elements. The size of writing the results of these numerical simulations to disk files reaches terabytes, petabytes, or even larger. The visualization performance of such large-scale datasets on current and next-generation architectures of HPC systems is essential. As simulations reach extreme scales, domain scientists can no longer depend on the traditional method of simply saving raw data occasionally and then performing visualization in a post-process (Childs et al, 2010). A promising approach that can able to overcome the bottleneck of a post-process related to the extreme-scale data problem is in situ visualization technology (Ma et al, 2009).

However, there has always been the challenge of the deep and adaptable integration of the visualization code into the simulation, which allows transparent and conflict-free sharing of data (Ma et al, 2007). Most previous work has focused on the in situ coupling of the individual parallel simulation programs (Buffat et al, 2015; Tu et al, 2006; Woodring et al, 2016; Yu et al, 2010) with less regard to the promising parallel programming frameworks that can guarantee quick adaptation to a batch of simulation applications, whereas we focus on the latter concern. We present an in situ visualization infrastructure for large-scale simulations to accomplish the following:

1. an in situ visualization infrastructure based on J Adaptive Structured Meshes applications Infrastructure (JASMIN), a parallel programming framework that uses structured meshes, to provide an adaptable tightly coupled approach that can use the same supercomputer that is running the simulation for visualization;
2. a batch in situ rendering pipeline for the common use cases on modern HPC architectures; and
3. a customizable engine interface to enable flexible coupling in a simulation with low code integration cost.

The infrastructure introduced in this paper provides a user-friendly and general-purpose in situ scheme that can guarantee quick adaptation to a batch of simulation applications, developed based on the JASMIN framework, with a low instrumentation cost. This infrastructure has been evaluated and successively applied to two simulations, the complex electromagnetic environment code (JEMS-TD, 2017) and the reactor analysis code (JSNT, 2017), with representative visualization results.

2. BACKGROUND

2.1 Parallel Programming Frameworks

A parallel programming framework can help scientists to write efficient and portable applications. The framework approach is feasible because most parallel applications exhibit the same parallel structure that exploits the same paradigms of parallelism, such as data parallel, task farming, and pipeline (Kung et al, 1989). Domain scientists can then use the high- level language independently from any specific architecture and concentrate on domain-specific algorithms rather than their low-level parallel implementation.

2.2 JASMIN

JASMIN (Mo et al, 2010; JASMIN, 2017) is a parallel software infrastructure for scientific computing developed by the Institute of Applied Physics and Computational Mathematics (IAPCM) in China. It is a general SAMR framework because it supplies full functionality for solving equation sets containing hyperbolic, parabolic, and elliptic equations, and facilitates the development of code for simulating a wide variety of applications. The main objective of JASMIN is to accelerate the development of parallel programs for large-scale simulations of complex applications on supercomputers.

In the JASMIN framework, data are organized by level; thus the description of the hierarchy is fundamentally defined by the union of blocks at each level. Within the JASMIN code, the fundamental data structure is the “grid patch.” The patch level consists of a series of patches. A patch hierarchy is used to manage SAMR meshes that consist of many patch levels that are defined at different mesh resolutions. By contrast, individual patches are composed of a number of physical fields, which are defined as patch data. The data structures of JASMIN are closely related to the efficient management of SAMR meshes for the cache-based memory hierarchy of modern computers. The application domains covered by JASMIN code include high-energy physics, material science, inertial confinement fusion, electromagnetic environment, climate science, computational fluid dynamics flow, turbulence, and fission/fusion energy.

2.3 Requirements of Exascale Simulation

Simulation code has become more complex, uses more resources, produces ever-larger data sets, and many tasks are performed during post-processing (for example analyzing and visualizing the simulation results).

The exascale applications suffer heavily in post-processing workflows because they access the file system twice: the first access is introduced by the simulation writing to disk and the other by the post-processing application reading from it. A promising approach to overcome such bottleneck issue is through in situ visualization. The tightly-coupling in situ method (Kuhlen et al, 2011; Fabian et al, 2011) is desirable for our work because it does not lead to significant data movement in the workflow. The data processing directly accesses the memory of the simulation code and visualization algorithms run on the same nodes of the HPC systems as the simulation. This approach does not require massive data movement in the workflow.

Most in situ works have been conduced for the individual parallel simulation programs. The application domains include eddy simulation in climate science (Woodring et al, 2016), earthquake simulation in seismogeology (Tu et al, 2006), turbulent combustion simulation in energy and combustion science (Yu et al, 2010), and turbulent flow analysis in computational fluid dynamics (CFD) (Buffat et al, 2015). However, complex domain-specific applications usually have different data structures with varying degrees of complexity in data management. Therefore, in situ processing requires the reworking of the code of the in-memory data adapter for individual applications so that the simulation data can be passed to the visualization pipeline. Although the implementation is relatively noninvasive to existing code bases, the one-on-one approach is obviously not desirable for a batch of simulations. Thus, a new in situ strategy that can perform quick adaptation to a batch of simulation applications with low instrumentation cost is required.

3. SYSTEM DESIGN

The infrastructure introduced in this paper is middleware that provides the functionality of batch in situ visualization and analysis to domain scientists. Batch processing is a common use case for modern HPC architectures, and is defined as the execution of a simulation program on a computer without manual intervention (non-interactive). Although the in situ visualization using batch processing mode does not involve user interaction, it provides greater flexibility and usability of simulations on exascale architectures. In the following sections, we describe the system architecture and how the system is designed to addresses the requirements of large-scale simulations with structured meshes.

3.1 Architecture Overview

Figure 1 illustrates the layout of our proposed software infrastructure. The system infrastructure partially extends previous work called TeraVAP (Xiao et al, 2014; TeraVAp, 2017), a distributed post-processing visualization system. The result is a more flexible and powerful system; in situ visualization engine, which permits in situ processing with distributed simulation, supporting on-demand data analysis; and interactive exploration with the current instance of simulation data. Figure 1 shows how the in situ visualization engine interfaces with the JASMIN framework and provides in situ visualization capabilities for high-level domain-specific applications. Starting from the top, domain-specific applications are developed based on the JASMIN framework, and then the hierarchy simulation mesh data are stored by means of the key data structure of JASMIN. The patch-based hierarchy raw data are described and converted using the in-memory data adapter within the in situ component of JASMIN, and passed into the in situ visualization engine through the in situ component.

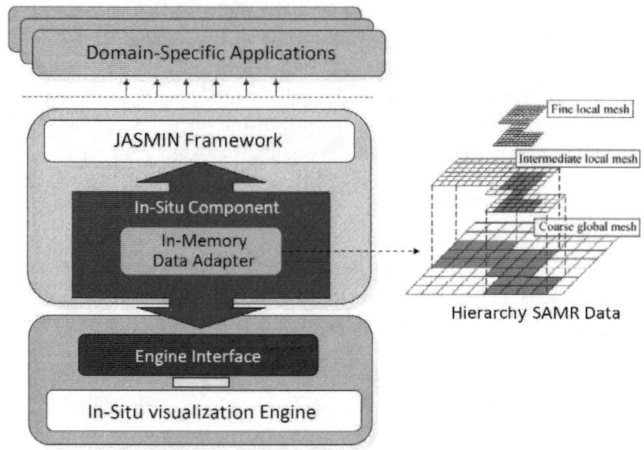

Figure 1. System Infrastructure

The in situ component is a bridge between simulation and visualization. The component model is a concept that specifies how interfaces should be defined and the elements that should be included in an interface definition, where a component is a software element that conforms to a component model and can be independently deployed and composed without modification according to a composition standard. The in situ component mainly plays two roles in the JASMIN framework: the customization and distribution of the behavioral actions for visualization, and the startup and scheduling of the in situ visualization engine. The in situ component specifically provides the customizable capability of the in situ pipeline for the domain scientists. The desired in situ actions are described by the component and passed into engine interface. The in situ visualization engine provides the fundamental functionality of the data visualization and analysis through the engine interface.

3.2 Batch in situ Rendering Pipeline

Considering the in situ rendering pipeline as an example (Fig. 2), we illustrate the data and communication flow within our system. A user requests batch processing of a large-scale simulation from the job scheduler in HPC systems via the remote terminal using a batch environment. Batch processing is performed after checking the multiple nodes, CPU cores, and memory of the values specified using the options of the job. Each MPI task executes a simulation code within a CPU core and simultaneously couples an in situ visualization engine during runtime. Each in situ engine that is invoked and executed within a simulation process can access the raw simulation data locally over an in-memory data adapter. As soon as the requested data is described and passed to the in situ engine via the in situ component, a rendering pipeline is constructed using the action descriptions customized by the high-level simulations. At present, our engine receives and processes the input data based on the visualization toolkit (VTK) format (Will et al, 2004).

When the input hierarchy SAMR data described by the in situ component is ready, the in situ visualization pipeline invokes filters and a rendering infrastructure within the in situ engine to render the subsets of the data owned by each MPI task. The pipeline infrastructure follows the data flow paradigm of the VTK model (Schroeder et al, 1996). The in situ visualization engine provides various functional algorithms implemented at the top VTK pipeline level to generate geometry or image. They all support sort-last parallel rendering, including mesh, surface, and volume rendering techniques, in a distributed memory parallel environment. For example, when adding a volume rendering plot in the pipeline to support high-quality data visualization, the subsets of image data are rendered by each MPI task. Then parallel image compositing is used for compositing these renders across MPI tasks to create and output time-varying final images on the supercomputer side. Additionally, to achieve the desired rendering results, it is also necessary to define the parameters that describe the domain-specific details of the rendering scene in the input file.

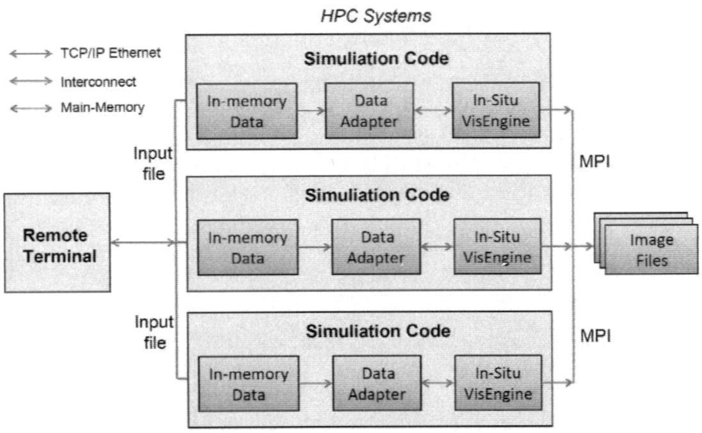

Figure 2. Communication and data flow during in situ rendering

3.3 Customizable Engine Interface

The in situ visualization engine consists of many function API calls. According to the functional classification, the engine interfaces are divided into the initialization, startup, scheduling, and cleanup for the engine (Fig. 3). The in situ engine is first initialized with a few parameters, including MPI communicator, MPI rank, and MPI size for the settings of the parallel running case. Second, the metadata and data structures for structured meshes are described and converted into the VTK data model using the instances of the patch-based hierarchy data structure defined in the JASMIN framework. After data description and conversion, the mesh data are set as the input to the engine via the engine interface. In this case, the sources object in the VTK model has been assigned. Next, the set of desired in situ actions are specified using the in situ component in JASMIN and passed to the in situ engine via Execute. The several important action interfaces supported by our system are listed in fig. 3. Specifically, the user can customize the rendering pipeline by adding a number of filters and plots according to the requirements of data analysis. These actions are then translated and built into an in situ rendering pipeline and executed as described in Section 3.2. At present, our system can support a hybrid rendering pipeline that includes multi-filters and multi-plots.

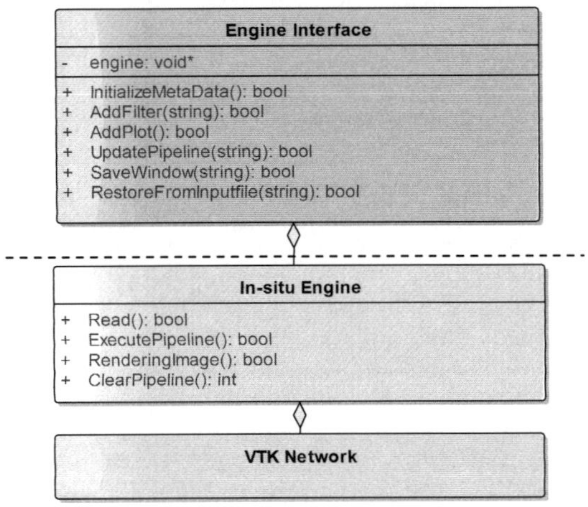

Figure 3. Engine interface and call sequences during in situ rendering

4. RESULTS

To test in situ integration with a batch of simulations based on the JASMIN framework, we selected two large-scale multiphysics simulations: JEMS-TD and JSNT. JEMS-TD is written in C++ and uses a Maxwell's electromagnetic wave approach on a three-dimensional (3D) structured mesh to simulate an electromagnetic environment. JSNT is written in C++ and uses a deterministic discrete ordinate solver on a 3D structured mesh to simulate particle transport. Fig. 4 and 5 show images produced from the in situ integrations for each simulation.

4.1 Code Integration

To evaluate the instrumentation cost of code integration, we present the lines of code required to integrate our in situ infrastructure into each simulation to produce the most common visualization result, such as subset, pseudocolor and ray-casting volume rendering (RCVR). As mentioned in Section 3.1, three steps are required to integrate our in situ infrastructure into a simulation code, which includes the description of the patch-based hierarchy simulation data, description of the actions defined in the in situ component within JASMIN, and construction of the in situ rendering pipeline by calling the in situ engine API. The sample integrated codes of the three steps for JEMS-TD are shown below.

```
simulation_data sim;
sim->rawData          = (tbox::Pointer<hier::PatchHierarchy<DIM> >) src_hierarchy;
sim->max_levels       = src_hierarchy->getFinestLevelNumber();
sim->refinement_ratio = 4;
sim->cycle            = time_step_number;
sim->time             = simulation_time;
sim->savingFiles      = 1;
```

Listing 1. Description of the patch-based hierarchy simulation data

```
Engine_interface engine_proxy;
engine_proxy->AddPlots("plane.stl", "Subset",      "STL_mesh",    plotID[0], width, height);
engine_proxy->AddFilter("Clip",  plotID[1] );
engine_proxy->AddPlots(NULL,     "Pseudocolor", "E_Field_Mag", plotID[1], width, height);
engine_proxy->AddFilter("Clip",  plotID[2] );
engine_proxy->AddPlots(NULL,     "Volume",      "E_Field_Mag", plotID[2], width, height);
engine_proxy->SaveWindow(filename, width, height, PNG)
```

Listing 2. Description of the actions defined in the in situ component within JASMIN

```
InSitu_Engine engine;
engine->Read();
engine->ExecutePipeline(pipelineID);
engine->RenderingImage(filename)
engine->ClearPipeline(pipelineID);
```

Listing 3. The construction of the in situ rendering pipeline by calling the in-situ engine API

Listing 1 presents how patch-based hierarchy simulation data is described in the in situ component. PatchHierarchy is the key data structure defined in JASMIN, which is used to manage the SAMR meshes that consist of many patch-based meshes in different mesh resolutions. For framework-based applications, the interpretation of patch-based hierarchy data can be applied to most applications when it is defined in the in situ component, without further modification. In the case of JSNT, the data description code is almost identical. Listings 2 and 3 present how the visualization actions are defined, translated and built into an in situ rendering pipeline and then executed as described in Section 3.2. Using the engine interface, three in situ rendering pipelines that are associated with different plots are defined, including subset, pseudocolor, and volume plot. In particular, the latter two plots are also coupling the Clip filter. After the rendering pipeline is defined, the in situ engine translates the actions, and builds and executes the pipeline immediately. The result of the execution is the rendered image file. In the case of JSNT, the only differences are the mesh type and name of the physical variable that is used in the description of the actions. Based on these sample codes, it can be seen that both the complexity and cost of code integration using our infrastructure is low.

4.2 Performance

To evaluate the performance of our in situ infrastructure, we selected an electromagnetic pulse simulation against aircraft for shielding protection using the JEMS-TD code with mesh sizes of 64 million units, which has a larger application size than the JSNT application. We ran the JEMS-TD simulations using the batch in situ mode on 16 CPU cores within a single node of Inspur's high-performance server (Inspur, 2017). The description of the actions defined in the in situ component is shown in Listing 2. Table 1 shows the average computational time per time step of both simulation and visualization when rendering an image in 1024×1024 pixels.

Table 1. Computational time of the proposed simulation and visualization

Vis-Actions	Simulation (sec)	Visualization (sec)
Subset + Pseudocolor	4.04	8.38
Subset + Pseudocolor + RCVI	4.06	17.52

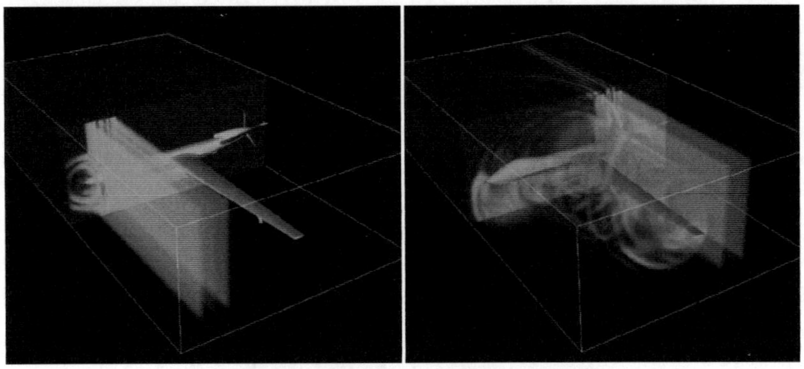

Figure 4. Time-varying in situ rendering results from the electromagnetic pulse simulation using JEMS-TD code

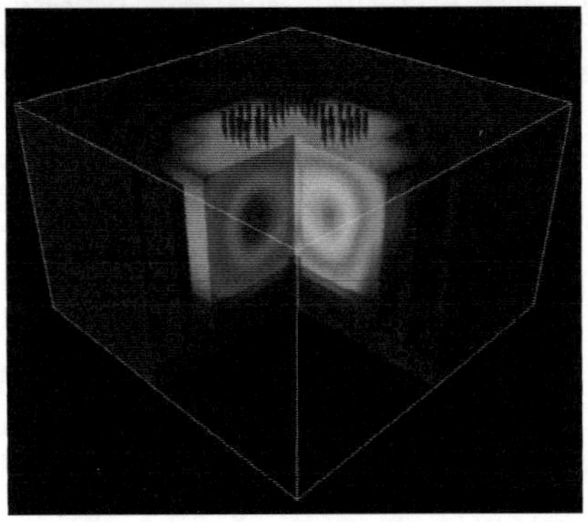

Figure 5. In situ rendering of the radiation shielding simulation of reactor pressure vessel using the JSNT code

5. CONCLUSION

In this paper we introduced an in situ visualization infrastructure based on the parallel programming framework, JASMIN. We described how our framework-based in situ approach can enable domain scientists to explore an HPC system that meets their requirements: user-friendly interface, minimal cost of in situ code integration, and adaptation to the modern HPC architecture. Previous work on in situ approaches has largely focused on coupling individual parallel simulation programs, with less regard for the parallel programming frameworks. Our results were promising, especially in terms of the code integration approach using our infrastructure. As future work, we plan to evaluate our in situ infrastructure more extensively on a massive supercomputer.

ACKNOWLEDGEMENT

This work was supported by the Key Program of Science and Technology Funds of China Academy of Engineering Physics (CAEP) under Grant No. 2014A0403019, the Defense Industrial Technology Development Program of China (Grant No. C1520110002), and the Science and Technology Founds of CAEP under Grant No. 2015B0403093.

REFERENCES

Bateman H., 1932. *Partial Differential Equations of Mathematical Physics*. Cambridge University Press, Cambridge, UK.

Berger M.J. et al, 1984. Adaptive mesh refinement for hyperbolic partial differential equations. *Journal of computational Physics*, 53(3): 484-512.

Buffat M. et al, 2015. In situ analysis and visualization of massively parallel computations. *International Journal of High Performance Computing Applications*, 1094342015597081.

Childs H. et al, 2010. Extreme scaling of production visualization software on diverse architectures. *IEEE Computer Graphics and Applications*, 30(3): 22-31.

Colella P. et al, 2007. Performance and scaling of locally-structured grid methods for partial differential equations. *Journal of Physics: Conference Series*. IOP Publishing, 78(1): 012013.

Dubey A. et al, 2014. A survey of high level frameworks in block-structured adaptive mesh refinement packages. *Journal of Parallel and Distributed Computing*, 74(12): 3217-3227.

Fabian N. et al, 2011. The paraview coprocessing library: A scalable, general purpose in situ visualization library. *Large Data Analysis and Visualization (LD*AV), 2011 IEEE Symposium. IEEE, pp 89-96.

Inspur, 2017. http://en.inspur.com/inspur/494735/index.html

JASMIN, 2017. http://www.caep-scns.ac.cn/JASMIN.php

JEMS-TD, 2017. http://www.caep-scns.ac.cn/JEMS-TD.php

JSNT, 2017. http://www.caep-scns.ac.cn/JSNT.php

Kuhlen T. et al, 2011. Parallel in situ coupling of simulation with a fully featured visualization system. *In Eurographics Symposium on Parallel Graphics and Visualization*. Eurographics Association , pp 101–109.

Kung H.T., 1989. *Scientific applications on multiprocessor, chapter Computational models for parallel computers*. Prentice Hall, Upper Saddle River, NJ, USA.

Lethbridge P., 2004. Multiphysics Analysis. *Industrial Physicist*, 10(6): 26-29.

Ma K.-L., 2009. In situ visualization at extreme scale: Challenges and opportunities. *IEEE Computer Graphics and Applications*, 29(6): 14-19.

Ma K.-L. et al, 2007. In-situ processing and visualization for ultrascale simulations. *Journal of Physics: Conference Series*. IOP Publishing, 78(1): 012043.

Mo Z. et al, 2010. JASMIN: a parallel software infrastructure for scientific computing. *Frontiers of Computer Science in China*, 4(4): 480-488.

Schroeder W. J. et al, 1996. The design and implementation of an object-oriented toolkit for 3D graphics and visualization. *Proceedings of the 7th conference on Visualization'96*. San Francisco, California, USA, pp. 93-ff.

TeraVAP, 2017. http://www.caep-scns.ac.cn/TeraVAP.php

Tu T. et al, 2006. From mesh generation to scientific visualization: An end-to-end approach to parallel supercomputing. *Proceedings of the 2006 ACM/IEEE conference on Supercomputing*, Tampa, USA, 91.

Will S. et al, 2004. *The Visualization Toolkit: An Object Oriented Approach to 3D Graphics*, Kitware Inc.

Woodring J. et al, 2016. In situ eddy analysis in a high-resolution ocean climate model. *IEEE transactions on visualization and computer graphics*, 22(1): 857-866.

Xiao L. et al, 2014. Large-scale data visual analysis for numerical simulation of laser fusion. *Chinese Journal of Computer-Aided Design and Computer Graphics*, 26(5): 675-686.

Yu H. et al, 2010. In situ visualization for large-scale combustion simulations. *IEEE computer graphics and applications*, 30(3): 45-57.

A VISUALIZATION PIPELINE FOR COMPUTABLE GEOMETRIC MODEL DATA

Huawei Wang [1, 2, 3], Li Xiao [2, 3], Zhiwei Ai [2, 3] and Yi Cao [2, 3]
[1]*Laboratory of Computational Physics, 6 Huayuan Road, Haidian, Beijing 100088, China*
[2]*Institute of Applied Physics and Computational Mathematics, 2 Fenghao East Road, Haidian, Beijing 100094, China*
[3]*CAEP Software Center for High Performance Numerical Simulation, 6 Huayuan Road, Haidian, Beijing 100088, China*

ABSTRACT

A visualization pipeline is proposed in this paper to realize visual interaction of computable geometric models. It is an extension of the VTK pipeline, which processes mesh data in general. To achieve this, a new data structure is designed to encapsulate the computable geometric model and connect a pre-processing engine to parse the model in real time. And then, the VTK pipeline is adapted for the data structure at several aspects, including data filtering, data rendering, data picking and so on. Based on the data structure, effective algorithms for filtering and picking are also proposed so as to reduce runtime intermediate data as much as possible. As a result, the seamless docking of the pre-processing engine to the visual analysis engine is achieved. This work strongly supports the development of integrated application software of pre-processing, numerical simulation and post-processing visual analysis.

KEYWORDS

Visualization pipeline, computable geometric model, data structure, data filtering, data picking

1. INTRODUCTION

With the development of supercomputers and numerical simulations, more and more three-dimensional (3D) simulations are conducted in applied science fields such as numerical reactor and engineering mechanics. A development policy of application software comes into being accordingly in our organization. In the policy, the mid-ware are developed based on the commonness, from which application software are developed based on the individuality. Here, the mid-ware include parallel software infrastructure (Mo et al. 2010), pre-processing engine (Zheng et al. 2017) and post-processing visual analysis engine, and application software are made up of simulation program and pre-/post- processing graphics user interface (GUI) and running over the mid-ware. In a whole simulation, the pre-processing engine takes charge in geometric modeling, physical attributes assignment and mesh generation, and then the simulation program conducts simulation computing and output physical field data, which are finally handed to the visual analysis engine for post-processing.

So far, the pre-processing engine and the visual analysis engine have their own user interfaces; the former is responsible for visual interaction of geometric models, and the latter for visual analysis of physical variables in a data field. They do not support each other's data files, and moreover their processes, visual effects and interaction styles are different, thus it is difficult to directly integrate them in application software.

One may convert geometric models into unstructured meshes and write them to disk files, which can then be interactively displayed in the visual analysis engine. However, the way to write files does not adapt to the need of online interaction. In integrated software, static display is not enough, and it is necessary to dynamically edit the models and set physical-attributes/boundary-conditions to the models according to users' needs. Such model for numerical simulation is called the computable geometric model (CGM).

To solve the problems as above, a solution is that the visual analysis engine couples the pre-processing engine and completes online display and interaction of CGM data based on real-time parsing of the pre-processing engine, and on the other hand it provides a set of visual analysis functions for GUI's calling. In this way, the consistency requirement in visualizing geometric models and field data can be met. The docking relationship between the two engines and GUI is shown in Figure 1.

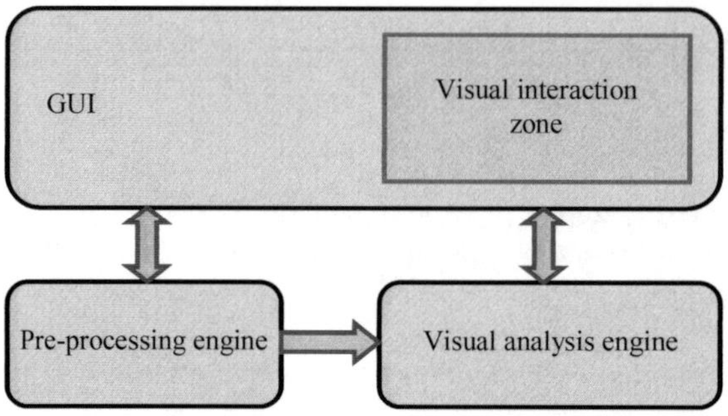

Figure 1. Interfaces between pre-processing engine, visual analysis engine and GUI

We thereout propose a visualization pipeline coupling the pre-processing engine to deal with CGM data. The differences between the proposed pipeline and the VTK visualization pipeline (Kitware 2006) or other visualization pipelines (Childs et al. 2005, Moreland 2013) exist at three aspects: (1) Our pipeline deals with CGM data, which come from computer-aided design (CAD) software like UG (Shao et al. 2014) and are saved in CAD file formats; (2) The CGM data are not fully expanded in the pipeline but real-time parsed by a coupling pre-processing engine when necessary; (3) Some efficient algorithms are proposed specially to deal with CGM data.

Based on work divide, three teams including us in our organization are developing the pre-processing engine, the visual analysis engine and GUI, respectively, under a set of prescribed interfaces. That is, the three teams are both cooperative and dividual. Thus, in this work, we will not involve or improve any techniques in the pre-processing engine. We can only develop the proposed pipeline based on its interfaces for parsing CGM data.

2. VISUALIZATION PIPELINE FOR CGM

The VTK visualization pipeline (Kitware 2006) is actually a pipeline of data, from a source of information to an image rendered on the screen. Generally speaking, the pipeline includes a data source, n data filters ($n \geq 0$) and a data sink. The data source provides initial data input from a file or a generation function. There are basically two types of sources: readers and independent sources. The data filters receive data, modify the data and then deliver the modified data as output. The filters modify the data in some way, such as conversion, reduction, interpolation, merging, etc. The other components related to data rendering, including mappers, actors, renderers and windows, are roughly regarded as a data sink in this paper. Mappers convert data into tangible objects, actors adjust the visible properties, and renderers and windows represent the end of the VTK pipeline, which users actually see on the screen. Data query can also be regarded as a data sink; Here, we mainly pick up geometric entities and deliver them to GUI.

We will extend the VTK's visualization pipeline to deal with CGM data, which belongs to the function expansion in the visual analysis engine. On the one hand, the extended functions will be provided to GUI's calling so as to realize display and interaction of CGM data in the user interface of the integrated software. On the other hand, these functions rely on the pre-processing engine, which parses CGM data via the function interfaces, such as all entities and their geometry. The software architecture and the positioning of the proposed pipeline are shown in Figure 2.

The pre-processing engine mainly resolves 3D entities in CGM as the boundary representation format, which is significantly different from the data formats in the visual analysis engine. Therefore, in the visual analysis engine, we first need to extend a new data structure to enclose a CGM and connect the pre-processing engine, and at the same time we also need to expand all aspects of the visualization pipeline, including data filtering, data rendering and data picking. As a result, we can achieve seamless docking of the pre-processing engine to the visual analysis engine.

In detail, we derive a new CGM data structure from the unified data structure of the visual analysis engine, including the description of a CGM and processing functions, so as to maintain the consistency of the data interfaces in the whole pipeline. Then, based on the plug-in technology, we develop a CGM data read module, where the pre-processing engine is started to read a data file and then a CGM data object is built. In data filtering, we need to extend typical filtering modules, including threshold selection, spatial box selection, slicing and clipping. In data rendering, according to the characteristics of CGMs, we use the subset structure plot to show CGM data. In order to meet the need of online interaction of CGMs in the integrated software, we need to extend the data picking module to support CGM data, and thus realize interactive pick-up of the geometric entities including points, lines, faces and bodies.

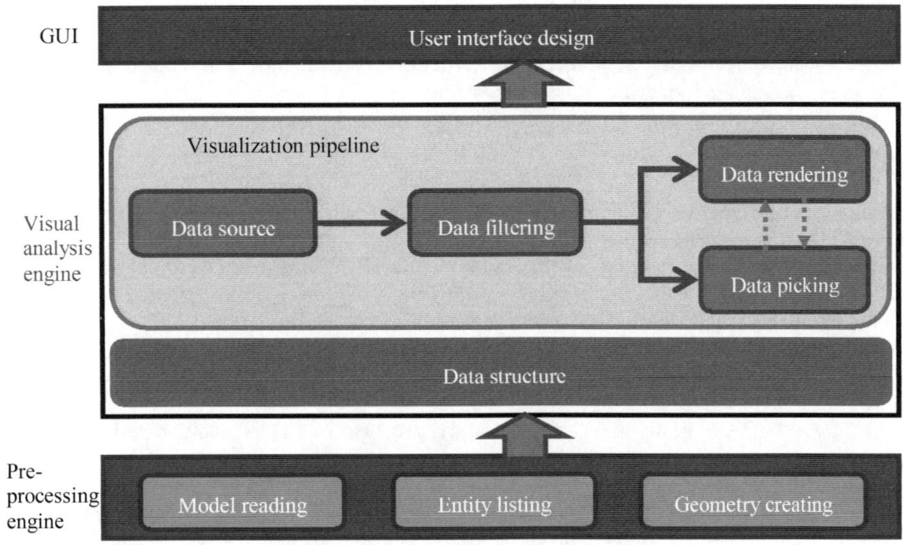

Figure 2. Software architecture of CGM visualization pipeline

Figure 2 also shows the relationship between data rendering and data picking. On the one hand, according to the rendering result, we will select an entity on the screen with mouse click for online interaction, that is, the rendering result helps the picking action in proving the position parameter. On the other hand, picked geometric entities like points, lines, faces or bodies should be highlighted in the original model, that is, the picking result will feed back to data rendering.

3. IMPLEMENTATION TECHNIQUES FOR CGM VISUALIZATION PIPELINE

Here, we explain some concepts in the pre-processing engine (Zheng et al. 2017). Geometric entities refer to basic geometric elements in a CGM, which can be of various dimensions, including points, lines, faces, bodies, etc. In general, an entity of dimension m has son entities of dimension m-1. For a complex model, 3D geometric entities are the basic components of its structure, which correspond to mesh cells in a usual VTK dataset. Thus, we take an independent 3D entity as entity cell for CGM data, which is also the basic unit in later processing.

In order to support CGM data, we design a new data structure and accordingly expand the functions of each link in the visualization pipeline. In the following, we will introduce the main function modules.

3.1 Data Structure

A new data structure is designed based on the VTK's data structure so as to enclose CGM datasets. It connects the pre-processing engine, obtaining the basic information of a CGM including metadata and moreover parsing the model to provide necessary data in all stages of the visualization pipeline according to the needs of visual analysis. On the other hand, it records marker information and intermediate results in the execution of the visualization pipeline, reducing the generation of intermediate data as much as possible and maintaining high efficiency of the pipeline execution.

The CGM data structure contains: (1) metadata information, including interval trees, the bounding box, variables and subset structures; (2) cell information, including pointer to entity object, valid status of cell, pointer to changed geometry; and (3) some functions, including entity access interface and selection functions based on interval tree. In detail, there are three members corresponding to cell sequence, namely cellEntity[], validStatus[] and changedGeometry[]. The array cellEntity[] records object pointers of entity cells in the pre-processing engine. The array validStatus[] indicates whether the cells persist after data filtering. If the shape of a cell changes after data filtering, changedGeometry[] will record the pointer to its current geometry object. Based on the data structure, we expand entity cells only when necessary, thus intermediate data are reduced as much as possible.

3.2 Data Filtering

According to the interaction requirements of CGMs, four typical data filtering functions are extended to support CGM data objects, which are threshold selection, spatial box selection, slicing and clipping. Threshold selection is used to extract entity cells from a CGM whose variable values fall into a specified range. One may use this function when searching for cells with certain values. Spatial box selection is used to select entity cells of a CGM within a volume defined by an axis-aligned box. It does not cut the entity cells across the box boundaries. In slicing, a plane, whose normal can be arbitrary, is used to cut open a 3D CGM to show the structure of the model on the plane. By clipping, one can use any plane to cut a CGM and remove the part of the model above the plane.

In the algorithm, we firstly select the possibly processed cells coarsely based on the interval tree, and then, when processing the remaining cells, we actually cut only the cells intersecting with the cutting plane and save the results accordingly while only modify the marked tags for all other cells according to their filtering statuses. Aiming at solid cells of boundary representation, we implement a triangulation algorithm for the cross section in order to maintain the closed form of 3D geometric shape. As an example, Figure 3 shows the diagram of our clipping algorithm, which is a representative one of data filtering in the proposed visualization pipeline.

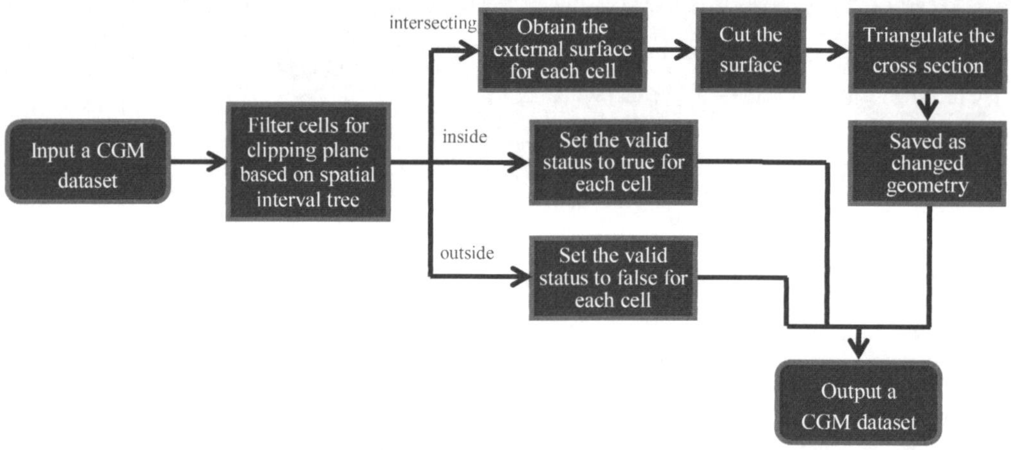

Figure 3. Algorithm diagram for clipping

3.3 Data Rendering

We realize the rendering of the subset structure plot for CGM data, which supports the modes including surface filling rendering, wireframe rendering and transparent rendering. The geometric cells can be classified into some subsets according to a CGM's data characteristics, such as the branch/nesting structure, the name of geometric component, the material attribute, etc. In the rendering, for valid geometric cells, we firstly obtain the triangular meshes of their external surfaces from the pre-processing engine and remove internal sides in the case of the wireframe mode, then we calculate the normals of the vertices and set the color for each subset according to the subset classification, and finally we render the CGM using OpenGL.

If some geometric entities are picked up, we need to highlight them in the plot of a CGM. For body/face entities, we will render them in a specific color instead. For a line entity, we will assign to it the appropriate "thickness", so the straight line is explained as the cylindrical surface and the curve can be drawn using the canal surface (Durix et al. 2015). In this way, a line entity can be viewed clearly from a CGM. Similarly, for a point entity, we can use a small sphere to highlight its drawing.

3.4 Data Picking

We realize interactive pickup of geometric entities of various dimensions, such as points, lines, faces and bodies. Based on the spatial interval tree of a CGM, we continue recursive intersection judgment between the picking ray and the bounding box of a node of the tree from the root. If the ray intersects with a node, we will proceed with the children of the node; otherwise halt. If we have gone to a leaf node, we will perform actual intersection calculation of the ray and the corresponding geometric entity (for point/line/face/body picking), or further find the point/line entity within the given tolerance in distance (for point/line picking). At the same time, by comparison, we find out the closest entity to the point of view, which is the final result of picking. The picking algorithm can be described as the diagram shown in Figure 4.

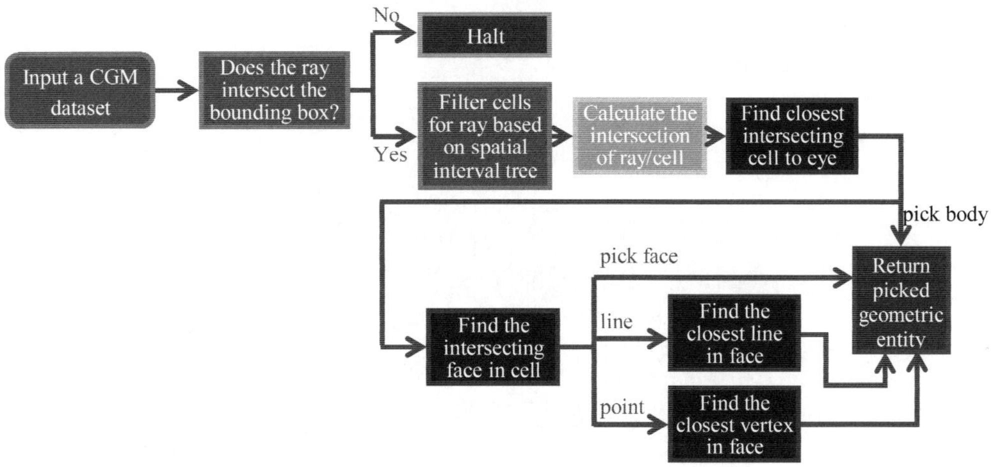

Figure 4. Algorithm diagram for picking

4. EXPERIMENTAL RESULTS

Figure 5 is a GDML model for test. Based on the structure of the GDML hierarchy tree, we classify all entity cells into several subsets and set them in different colors. As shown in the figure, we can choose different drawing modes, such as surface filling, wireframe, transparent map, and the rendering effect is different. Surface filling is the usual way to show the geometric structure, the wireframe can show the skeleton of a model, and the transparent map can show the internal geometry.

We can process a CGM using the four filtering functions: threshold selection, spatial box selection, slicing and clipping. We can apply one or more operations on a CGM at a time. We take the clipping operation as an example to show the effect of CGM data filtering, as shown in Figure 6. On the left side is the original model, which is obtained from a SATA file. We use an arbitrary plane to cut off a part of the model. Since the model is given in the form of boundary representation, we seal off the surface for each cell after clipping, as shown in the middle. On the right side, the clipped model is shown in the wireframe mode.

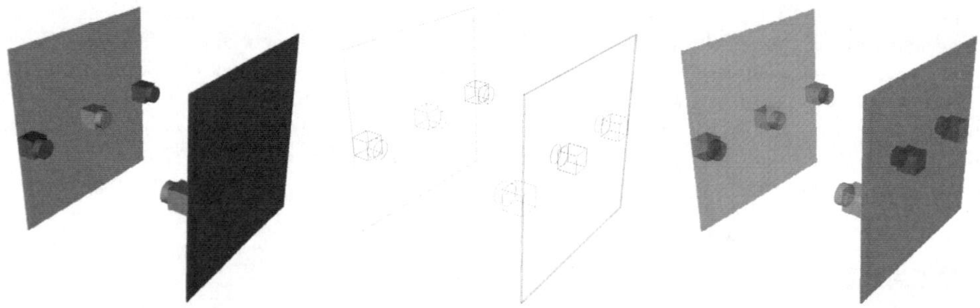

Figure 5. Three drawing modes: surface filling, wireframe and transparency

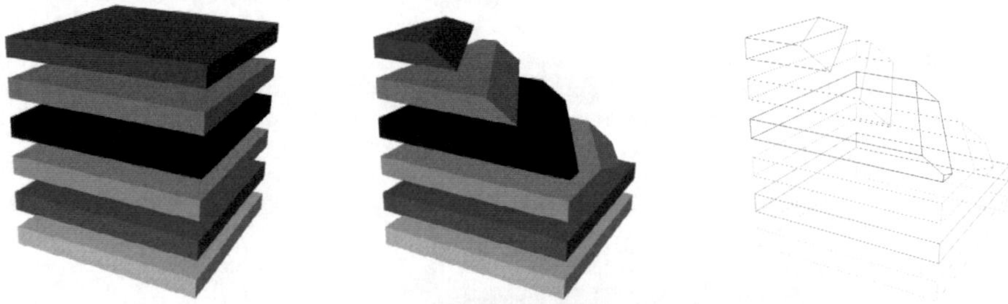

Figure 6. A geometric model before and after clipping

Figure 7. Picked entities of dimension 0~3 highlighted in green

In our pipeline, we can pick geometric entities of four dimensions, including point, line, face and body. For example, in Figure 7, we highlight picked entities of dimension 0~3 in green. In detail, three 0D points are represented by small green spheres, two 1D lines by green cylinders, and two 2D faces and one 3D body painted green instead. In Figure 8, a curve is picked up, so we generate a canal surface to express it. The enlarged plot on the right shows the smoothing effect of the canal surface. Obviously, if one uses independent cylinders corresponding to the discretized broken line to show the curve, the gaps will be inevitable.

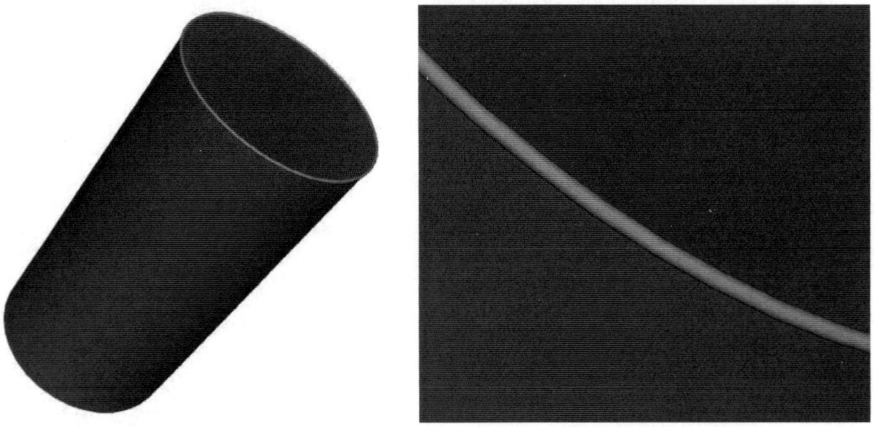

Figure 8. Highlighted rendering of a picked curve entity and its local magnification

For CGM visualization functions, we have established the interfaces in the visual analysis engine, which are now available to the GUI team. Based on these interfaces, the GUI team have custom-designed the JSNT software for particle transport and the HASEM software for energetic material. Figure 9 shows a CGM processed and rendered by the visual analysis engine, namely the 1/4 Venus model. The original model is shown on the left. In order to clearly observe an internal region of interest, we have applied spatial box selection and clipping at the same time, and the final result is shown on the right.

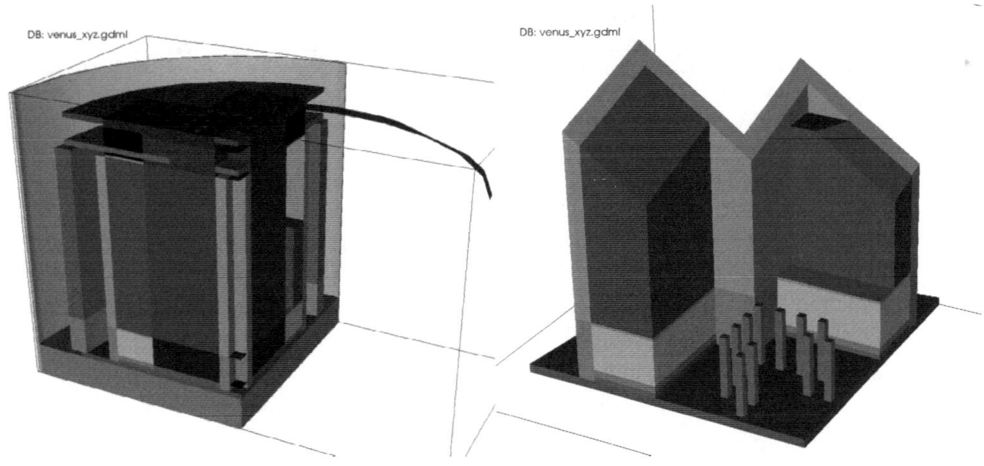

Figure 9. The 1/4 Venus model and the result after spatial box selection and clipping

5. CONCLUSION

This work extends the VTK visualization pipeline to deal with computable geometric model data. We design and implement a new data structure and accordingly adapt the visualization pipeline at several aspects for the data structure, thus a seamless docking of the visual analysis engine with the pre-processing engine is achieved. In the pipeline, we also propose effective filtering and picking algorithms, which can reduce the generation of intermediate data. This work strongly supports the development of application software integrated pre-processing, numerical simulation and post-processing.

ACKNOWLEDGEMENT

The authors wish to thank the anonymous reviewers for their comments. This work is supported by Foundation of Laboratory of Computational Physics, Science and Technology Funds of Chinese Academy of Engineering Physics under grant No. 2015B0403093 and Key Program of Science and Technology Funds of CAEP under grant No. 2014A0403019.

REFERENCES

Childs, H. et al., 2005. A contract based system for large data visualization. *Proceedings of IEEE Visualization '2005*, Minneapolis, MN USA, pp. 191-198.

Durix, B. et al., 2015. Towards Skeleton based Reconstruction: From Projective Skeletonization to Canal Surface Estimation. *Proceedings of International Conference on 3D Vision (3DV 2015)*, Lyon, France, pp. 545-553.

Kitware, Inc., 2006. *The Visualization Toolkit User's Guide*.

Mo, Z. et al., 2010. JASMIN: a parallel software infrastructure for scientific computing. *Front. Comput. Sci. China*, 4(4), pp. 480-488. See also the JASMIN's homepage: http://www.caep-scns.ac.cn/JASMIN.php.

Moreland, K., 2013. A Survey of Visualization Pipelines. *IEEE Transactions on Visualization & Computer Graphics*, 19(3), pp. 367-378, DOI:10.1109/TVCG.2012.133.

Shao, W. et al., 2014. A digital management system of part processing parameter based on UG. *Proceedings of 2014 IEEE International Conference on Mechatronics and Automation (ICMA)*, DOI: 10.1109/ICMA.2014.6886020.

Zheng, P. et al., 2017. Parallel AFT Tetrahedral Mesh Generation for JAUMIN [J/OL, In Chinese]. *Journal of Frontiers of Computer Science and Technology*, http://kns.cnki.net/kcms/detail/11.5602.TP.20170103.1036.006.html. See also the SuperMesh's homepage: http://www.caep-scns.ac.cn/SuperMesh.php.

TIGHTLY COUPLED IN SITU VISUALIZATION WITH SIMULATIONS ON THOUSANDS OF CPU CORES

Zhiwei Ai, Yi Cao, Li Xiao, Huawei Wang and Aiqing Zhang
High Performance Computational Center in Institute of Applied Physics and Computational Mathematics, Beijing 100094, China
CAEP Software Center for High Performance Numerical Simulation, Beijing 100088, China

ABSTRACT

Scientific visualization is an effective way to analyze the complex datasets generated from numerical simulations. Current supercomputer I/O performance struggles to match the rapidly improving computing performance. Therefore, there is in urgent need for in situ visualization to reduce the amount of data output during large-scale scientific simulations. This paper presents an in situ component technique that enables a general purpose visualization tool to be flexibly coupled with the simulations based on JASMIN, a parallel programming framework for large-scale numerical simulations. Using the presented technique, the data analysis and visualization tasks are shifted to run in situ, that is, closer to the simulation via resource sharing. It is beneficial to avoid storing large-scale datasets for post-processing. Subsequently, a tightly coupled in situ visualization mode is proposed, in which visualization code can be deployed into application code with low code-integration cost. This code can then run on the same supercomputer resources as the simulation code. The JASMIN-based in situ component provides a bridge between a batch of parallel simulation applications and existing visualization packages. The implemented component allows applications to integrate the rich functionality of existing visualization tools with a unified data-management interface. It also enables efficient use of supercomputer resources through a batch processing mechanism. In situ visualization of the electromagnetic interference surrounding an aircraft is simulated using a model that comprises 8.5 billion grid cells on the TianHe-2 supercomputer.

KEYWORDS

In situ visualization, extrascale simulation, JASMIN infrastructure, common component architecture

1. INTRODUCTION

Supercomputers' massive processing power drives scientific discovery in many areas, and their computing power and storage capacity grow rapidly every year. As scientists gain access to more powerful machines, they attempt to solve larger and more complex problems. A common strategy during the simulation run is to output as much raw data as storage capacity allows. Subsequent data analysis and visualization occurs offline. This traditional offline post-processing visualization can involve reducing petabytes of simulation-generated data to a more manageable size. Errors or gaps in the information due to this reduction of data will affect subsequent analysis and accuracy of the numerical simulation results (Yu et al. 2010).

High-efficiency and high-confidence simulation programs continue to improve, and the required computing resources have reached tens of thousands of CPU cores. The number of grid cells has exceeded billions of cells and the data output has increased to hundreds of terabytes. Supercomputer I/O performance is struggling to keep up with the rapidly accelerating CPU performance. To access effectively and extract scientific knowledge from large-scale datasets (often in the order of gigabytes or terabytes), appropriate tools and techniques are needed. The conventional post-processing approach will be further challenged by petascale computing to realize ultra-large-scale data visualization analysis.

Real-time, efficient scientific computing visualization and analysis is needed. To meet this need, in situ visualization can be used to solve the problem of mismatch between data I/O performance and post-processing visualization. In situ visualization utilizes the same computing resources that run the simulation computing on high-performance computer systems. It couples the numerical simulation and the visualization, thereby reducing data transmission and I/O operating overhead. This helps it to provide efficient visual analysis of ultra-large-scale numerical simulation results. In situ visualization libraries enable the user to connect directly to a running simulation, examine the data, do numerical queries and create graphical output while the simulation executes. It addresses the need of extreme scale simulation, avoiding the need to write the data to disk. This paper presents an in situ component technique that enables a general purpose visualization tool to be flexibly coupled with simulations based on JASMIN, a parallel programming framework for large-scale numerical simulations. The tightly coupled in situ visualization mode, through the in situ component, provides a bridge between a batch of parallel simulation applications and existing visualization packages. This visualization code can be deployed into the application code with low code-integration cost. The implemented in situ component allows applications to integrate the rich functionality of existing visualization tools with a unified data-management interface. It also enables efficient use of supercomputer resources through a batch processing mechanism.

2. RELATED WORK

SCIRun (Parker and Johnson 1995, Johnson et al. 1999) was one of the first general purpose frameworks with a visual programming environment to assist users in assembling data flow networks. SCIRun was designed from the ground up to enable computational steering, by constructing re-usable components for modeling, computation and visualization. Ellsworth (Ellsworth et al. 2006) copied simulation data to a shared memory segment on a different set of compute nodes to isolate mission-critical computations from other components. Esnard and Coulaud (2006) emphasize data redistribution with parallel data transfer from M compute nodes to N (N << M) visualization nodes, using CORBA to implement the communication protocol.

Kageyama et al. (2013) proposed a method for the interactive analysis of in situ visualization images produced by a batch simulation job. The user could change the viewing angle, the visualization method, and the parameters interactively by retrieving an appropriate sequence of images from the movie dataset. Rivi et al. (2012) investigated techniques and frameworks supporting in situ visualization, and tested two techniques. They exploited different visualization tools on both techniques using a ParaView (Henderson 2005) plug-in, ICARUS, and a library, VisIt. Larsen et al. (2015) presented Strawman, a system designed to explore the in situ visualization and analysis needs of simulation code teams planning for multi-physics calculations on exascale architectures. Malakar et al. (2013) presented an adaptive framework for loosely coupled visualization, in which data was sent over a network to a remote visualization cluster at a frequency that was dynamically adjusted depending on resource availability. Other studies have incorporated domain knowledge and tasks into simulations (Ma et al. 2007, Whitlock et al. 2011, Lorendeau et al. 2013).

To allow direct access to data and sharing of compute resources, we provide a tightly coupled in situ visualization technique in which visualization code is collocated with the simulation code and run on the same supercomputer resources as the simulation code. We accomplish this using an in situ component developed in JASMIN (Mo and Zhang 2008). JASMIN is a parallel programming framework for large scale numerical simulations, and is designed based on the component-based software engineering technology. The Common Component Architecture (CCA) provides a means for software developers to manage the complexity of large-scale scientific simulations. Thanks to the plug-and-play feature of the component, domain scientists can easily build their own codes for high-performance (Benjamin et al. 2006). Our in situ component provides a bridge between the parallel simulation applications and existing visualization packages. Units of software functionality are encapsulated as components which interact with each other only through well-defined interfaces. In the implementing of tightly coupled in situ visualization, the actual implementation is opaque to other components, and application integration is achieved through providing and using these interfaces.

3. ARCHITECTURE

We present an in situ framework designed to explore the visualization needs for large-scale numerical simulation on exascale architectures. This design incorporated several key requirements, including lightweight usage of shared resources, batch processing, ability to leverage modern architectures, and ease of software integration.

3.1 Design Overview

Tightly coupled in situ visualization refers to numerical simulation and visualization using common computing resources and sharing the memory in compute nodes. This method establishes data access channels for simulation computing and visualization, and realizes online real-time and efficient visualization of large-scale numerical simulation data results, while avoiding the overhead introduced by massive data I/O operations.

As shown in Figure 1, the key components of our system include an in situ component inside the JASMIN framework, an in situ visualization engine, and the engine programming interface. The in situ visualization engine is a lightweight engine that provides universal visualization functions for large-scale datasets. The in situ component is implemented following the programming specification of the JASMIN framework, to achieve uniform access to the hierarchical data structure defined in JASMIN. The engine programming interface is a bridge between the in situ component and the in situ visualization engine. The in situ visualization engine can couple with JASMIN-based applications to establish and execute a visualization pipeline, including data loading, data processing and rendering.

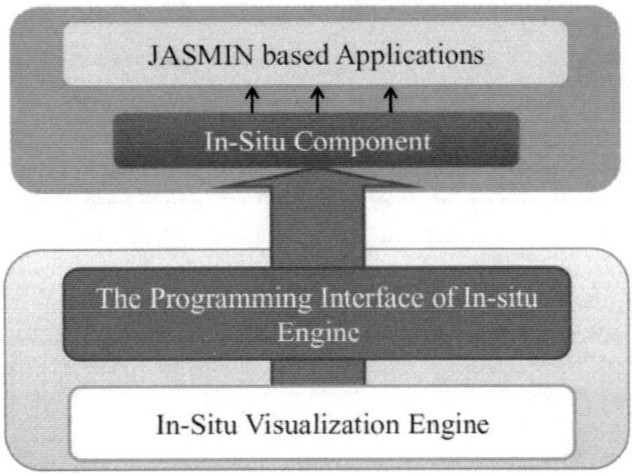

Figure 1. Architecture of our in situ visualization system

3.2 In Situ Component

Numerical algorithms typically involve time iterations with given initial conditions, such as a time integration algorithm. Complex algorithms can be broken down into smaller, more manageable parts. These parts are arranged to be executed adhering to some rules. Figure 2 shows the flow of a general time integration algorithm in a numerical simulation. Generally the algorithm involves three key modules—initialization, iteration and termination—which are organized in a loop; the user provides parameters to control the termination of the loop. All modules should be implemented according to concrete computational components (Liao et al. 2014). Parallel numerical applications have been developed by assembling these configured components in their code when using the JASMIN framework. Each component in JASMIN corresponds to a special computational task that is operated on the local data patch.

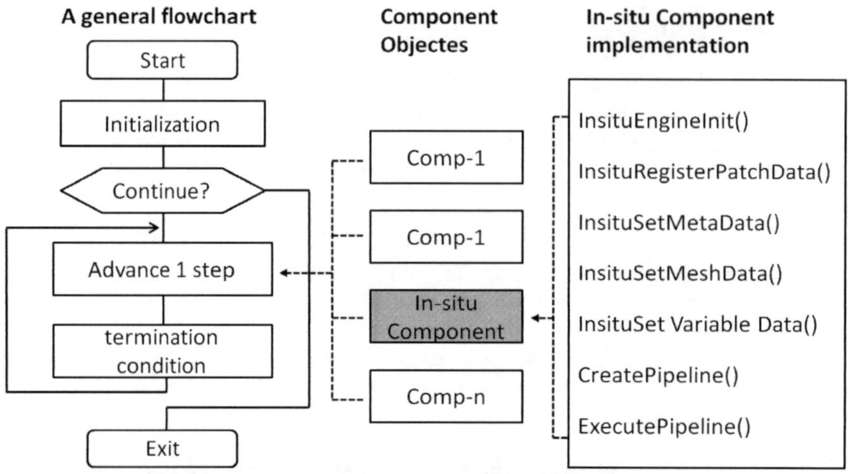

Figure 2. Architecture of JASMIN based application and the invoking model

The in situ component is responsible for the four parts of the task: accessing to the grid and physical data stored in the hierarchical data structure of JASMIN; scheduling the in situ visualization engine; performing a customizable visualization task; and outputting the image file. The internal call relationship of the in situ component includes three parts: configuration of the visualization pipeline by using the engine programming interface; scheduling of the visualization engine and launching of the visualization pipeline; and executing the in situ visualization task. Consequently, the in situ component provides two software interfaces. The first interface is for configuring the detailed parameters of visualization pipeline. It is responsible for setting the three main processes of the visualization pipeline and for gathering the configuration information, including the input datasets, the data filter methods, and the rendering method. The second interface is for performing the configured visualization pipeline. It dispatches and runs the in situ visualization engine, sets the output image resolution and other detailed runtime parameters, performs the visualization tasks, and finally outputs the rendered image files.

3.3 Data Management

JASMIN is a general parallel programming framework for numerical simulation. It provides large-granularity software reuse in scientific high-performance computing. Data parallelism is the main form of parallelization in computing. In this kind of parallelism, as shown in Figure 3, the region is decomposed into many domains during the process of the computation. Each domain is extended with ghost zones to satisfy the needs of the numerical scheme. The data in the white area is the true calculation data area of the numerical simulation program. The ghost zone data is the boundary data of the data of the adjacent domain, and is used to ensure the correctness of the region decomposition calculation. The red area data is the boundary ghost data, and it does not participate in the data communication between the data blocks. The blue area data is the internal ghost data, and the data communication is needed in the numerical simulation process.

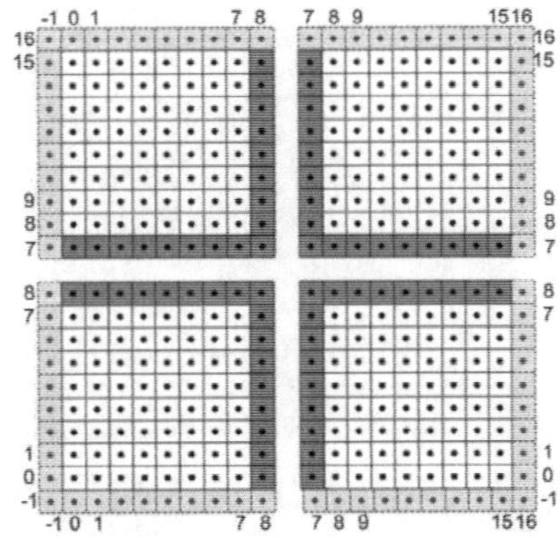

Figure 3. Domain decomposition for data parallelism

As a data adapter, the in situ component plays the role of data management of the numerical simulation domain, realizing an efficient data interface between the JASMIN-based parallel applications and the in situ visualization engine. An appropriate data organization and management strategy is used to reduce the in situ processing time and to optimize resource utilization. The data management module within the in situ component takes the hierarchical data structure as the input, and converts the raw datasets into visualization data objects. These objects include metadata, mesh data, and variable data objects. Metadata objects include the basic information of raw datasets such as data type, dimensions and spatial extents. Mesh data objects include descriptive information about the computing grid, such as mesh types and spatial coordinates of the grid. Variable data objects include the descriptive information, such as variable types and values. The data management module shares or converts the raw datasets in memory.

3.4 Batch Processing Mechanism

To adapt the batch job environment for supercomputers, batch-style in situ visualization is required. During batch processing, once the job is running, it is no longer subject to user intervention. Users often batch-deliver multiple jobs to share the use of supercomputer resources. Batch in situ visualization allows numerical iteration computation of simulation programs that is not affected by the user except for loading of user-defined visual analysis pattern files at the initial stage. In the batch processing mode, the application can proactively trigger actions such as configuration of the visualization pipeline, startup of the in situ visualization engine, and image saving. The visualization engine will then automatically complete the specified visualization tasks and obtain the visualization results at each simulation time-step. To avoid mutual interference between the in situ parallel visualization and the parallel numerical simulation, the in situ component creates a duplicate of the communicator for parallel visualization.

4. RESULTS AND DISCUSSION

The in situ visualization tests were performed for the electromagnetic interference characteristics of an aircraft, based on the JEMS-TD (Li et al. 2014) simulation code developed at the Institute of Applied Physics and Computational Mathematics. In electromagnetic interference applications, the focus is usually on near-field coupling and far-field scattering of strong electromagnetic pulses under the Gaussian pulse plane wave excitation. We used the subset plot to describe the geometric model of the aircraft, with pseudo-color and volume plots to illustrate the electromagnetic field distribution surrounding the aircraft. The obtained high-confidence visualization images are shown in Figure 4, the image resolution is 1024 × 1024. All tests were simulated on the TianHe-2 supercomputer at the National Supercomputer Center, Sun Yat-sen University.

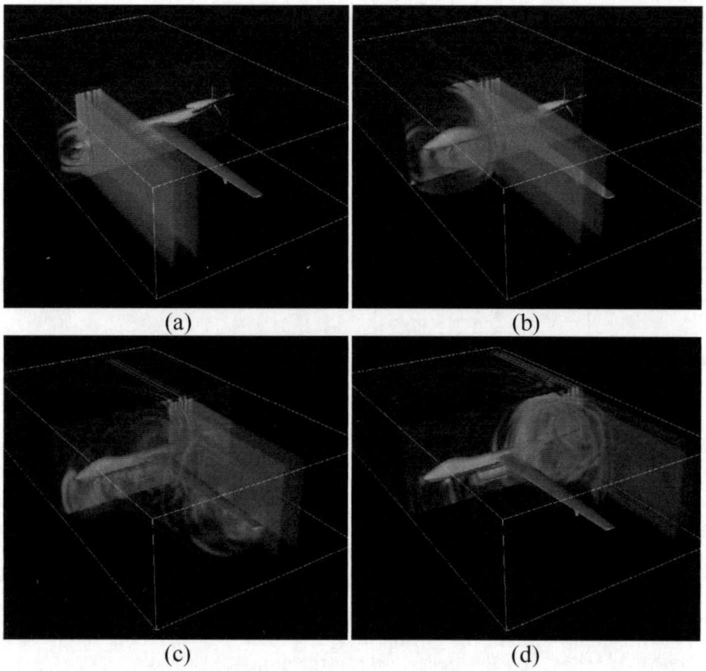

Figure 4. In situ visualization results of the electromagnetic interference simulation of an aircraft using JEMS-TD code at a 3000 cycles, b 7000 cycles, c 11,000 cycles and d 15,000 cycles

TianHe-2 has 32,000 Intel Xeon E5-2692 2.2-GHz processors, and 48,000 Xeon Phi 31S1P Co-processors.

We examined in situ visualizations for JEMS-TD applications of a fixed problem size (fixed number of cells). The grid resolution was 1024 × 1024 × 1024 (approximately one billion grid cells) and a single time-step dataset reached approximately 17 GB. The performance statistics of this test are shown in Table 1. The simulation is obviously burdened with the visualization when using 2048 CPU cores. All images were rendered at 1024 × 1024 pixels. After every 50 iterations, the numerical simulation performs in situ visualization or an I/O action. As the number of CPU cores was increased from 256 to 2048, the required computing time decreased. There was increased competition for memory resources and network, resulting in a slight increase in I/O time overhead. In particular, the in situ visualization time increased significantly, from 11% to 46.55% of the total program execution time. As a result, the in situ visualization time dominates the required execution time because of the lower parallel efficiency.

Table 1. Timing statistician for simulation, I/O, and visualization

CPU cores	Simulation Time (sec)	I/O Time (sec)	In Situ Visualization Time (sec)	Total Time(sec)
256	148.79	4.53	18.94(11.00%)*	172.26
512	85.89	4.77	19.79(17.92%)	110.45
1024	55.22	5.69	25.16(29.23%)	86.07
2048	39.912	7.09	40.94(46.55%)	87.94

**Percentages represent the ratio of visualization time to total simulation time*

Table 2 shows the performance of in situ visualization rendering of the images shown in Figure 4. The scalability analysis of the in situ visualization includes the data processing time of subset plot and pseudo-color plot, image compositing time, and volume rendering time. All images were generated at a resolution of 1024 × 1024. Because the task on each CPU core responsible for dealing with roughly the same amount of geometric data, the data processing time changes slightly as the number of CPU cores increases. Owing to load balancing, the electric field data is also evenly distributed between the processing tasks running on each CPU core. As the number of CPU cores increases, the amount of data processed by each CPU core is reduced. Thus, the processing time of the pseudo-color plot decreases linearly. In this rendering scene, the geometric rendering time includes the rendering time of both the subset plot and the pseudo-color plot. However, the image composition stage during geometric rendering requires global communication of the partial images, including RGB color and depth values. Because of the required communication, the geometric rendering time is increased with the increase in the number of CPU cores. Similarly, the volume rendering method involves global communication of sampling point data, so the rendering time increases substantially as the number of CPU cores increases. When using 256 CPU cores, the rendering time, including geometric rendering and volume rendering, is almost 50% of the in situ visualization time. When using 2048 CPU cores, the ratio of rendering time to the in situ visualization time is further increased to 91%. Thus, both geometric rendering and volume rendering have poor scalability.

Table 2. Performance of in situ visualization

CPU cores	Data Processing for Subset Plot (sec)	Data Processing for Pseudo-color plot (sec)	Geometric Rendering (sec)	Volume Rendering (sec)	In Situ Visualization (sec)
256	1.69	5.66	5.99 (31.61%)*	3.16(16.67%)*	18.94
512	1.51	2.92	8.09 (40.85%)	4.85(24.52%)	19.79
1024	1.52	1.53	9.33 (37.08%)	11.59(46.04%)	25.16
2048	1.57	0.92	14.35(35.05%)	23.03(56.26%)	40.94

**Percentages represent the ratio of opaque rendering time or volume rendering time to in situ visualization total time*

We also evaluated the performance of in situ visualization with a larger problem of application on increased computational resources. The grid resolution of the large-scale simulation was 2048 × 2048 × 2048 (approximately 8.5 billion cells), and the in situ visualization test used up to 8192 CPU cores. As shown in Figure 5, the computing time and the data I/O time fluctuate slightly with increasing number of CPU cores, and there is an upward trend. The increase in in situ rendering time is much greater than that of computing time and data I/O time. In situ rendering time is about 5.6 times I/O time when using 1024 CPU cores. For 8192 CPU cores, the ratio between the I/O time and in situ rendering time increases to 16.55 times. For 8192 CPU cores, in situ time rendering accounts for 80.56% of the total in situ visualization time. In future we intend to conduct further analysis and optimization of the scalability of the parallel visualization algorithm.

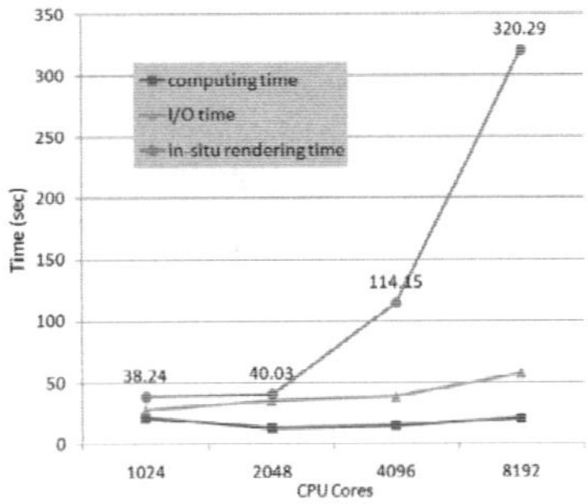

Figure 5. Performance of in situ visualization with large-scale JEMS-TD simulation

5. CONCLUSION

In situ visualization is a promising potential method for tackling challenges in exascale simulations. The slower rate at which I/O performance increases, compared with that of computational capabilities, necessitates new approaches for gaining insights from large-scale simulations. Tightly coupled in situ visualization appears to be a viable approach to reduce the pressure on I/O and file systems. Therefore, we propose a tightly coupled in situ visualization technique, in which the visualization code is collocated with the simulation code and run on the same supercomputer resources. We accomplish this through in situ component technology that provides a user-friendly in situ visualization approach to JASMIN-based parallel simulation with a low code-integration cost. We tested our approach using JEMS-TD code and applied it to an electromagnetic interference simulation of an aircraft on the TianHe-2 supercomputer. In future work we intend to conduct further analysis and optimization of the performance and scalability of the parallel visualization algorithms within the in situ component.

ACKNOWLEDGEMENT

This work was supported by the Key Program of Science and Technology Funds of China Academy of Engineering Physics (CAEP) under Grant No. 2014A0403019, the Defense Industrial Technology Development Program of China (Grant No. C1520110002), and the Science and Technology Founds of CAEP under Grant No. 2015B0403093.

REFERENCES

Aurelien Esnard N. R., Coulaud O. *A steering environment for online parallel visualization of legacy parallel simulations*. In Proceedings of the 10th International Symposium on Distributed Simulations and Real-Time Applications (DS-RT2006) (2006).

Benjamin A. A., Robert A.,David E. B.,etc. 2006. *A component architecture for high-performance scientific computing*. The International Journal of High Performance Computing Applications,20(2):162-202

Ellsworth D., Henze C., Green B., Moranp.2006. *SANDSTROM T: Concurrent visualization in a production supercomputer environment*. IEEE Transactions on Visualization and Computer Graphics (Proceedings Visualization 2006) (2006), pp997–1004.

H Yu, C Wang, RW Grout, JH Chen, KL Ma. 2010. *In Situ Visualization for LargeScale Combustion Simulations*. IEEE Computer Graphics & Applications,30(3):45-57

Henderson, *ParaView Guide, A Parallel Visualization Application*. Kitware Inc., 2005. Web site: http://www.paraview.org

Johnson, C. R., Parker, S. G., Hansen, C., Kindlmann, G. L., and Livnat, Y.1999. *Interactive simulation and visualization*. IEEE Computer 32, 12 (1999), 59–65.

K. Moreland, U. Ayachit, B. Geveci, and K.-L. Ma. 2011. *Dax Toolkit: A Proposed Framework for Data Analysis and Visualization at Extreme Scale*. In Proceedings of the IEEE Symposium on Large-Scale Data Analysis and Visualization, pp97-104, Oct 2011.

Kageyama, Akira, Yamada, Tomoki. 2013. *An approach to exascale visualization: Interactive viewing of in-situ visualization*. Computer Physics Communications, 185(1):79-85

L Li, J Cuiping, W Wei, Z Aiqing. 2014. HiPro-CodeGen automatic programming for parallel numerical simulations. International Conference on Software Engineering & Applications, 2014:125-131

Li Hanyu, Zhou Haijing, Liu Yang, et al. 2014. *Massively parallel FDTD program JEMS-FDTD and its applications in platform simulation*. IEEE International Symposium on Electromagnetic Compatibility. pp.229-233.

Lorendeau, Y. Fournier, and A. Ribes. 2013. *In-situ visualization in fluid mechanics using catalyst: A case study for code saturne. In Large-Scale Data Analysis and Visualization* (LDAV), 2013 IEEE Symposium on,pages 53-57. IEEE.

M Dorier, R Sisneros, T Peterka, G Antoniu. 2013. *Damaris/Viz: A nonintrusive, adaptable and user-friendly in situ visualization framework*. Large-scale Data Analysis & Visualization, 2013:67-75

M Larsen, E Brugger, H Childs, J Eliot, K Griffin etc. 2015. *Strawman: A Batch In Situ Visualization and Analysis Infrastructure for Multi-Physics Simulation Codes*. Workshop on in Situ Infrastructures for Enabling Extreme-scale Analysis & Visualizaiton, 2015:30-35

M Rivi, L Calori, G Muscianisi, V Slavnic. 2012. *In-situ Visualization: State-of-the-art and Some Use Cases*. Prace White Paper

Ma K-L, Wang C, Yu H, et al.2007. *In-situ processing and visualization for ultrascale simulations* [J]. Journal of Physics: Conference Series (S1742-6588), 2007, 78:012043

Mo Z Y, Zhang A Q. 2008. *User manual for JASMIN (in Chinese). IAPCM Technical Report* T09-JMJL-01. 29-38

Parker, S. G., and Johnson, C. R.1995. *SCIRun: A scientific programming environment for computational steering*. In Proceedings of ACM/IEEE Supercomputing 1995 Conference (1995).

VisIt Users Manual, https://wci.llnl.gov/codes/visit/1.5/VisItUsersManual1.5.pdf. https://wci.llnl.gov/codes/visit/

Whitlock B, Favre J M, Meredith J S.2011. *Parallel In Situ Coupling of Simulation with a Fully Featured Visualization System* [C]// Eurographics Symposium on Parallel Graphics and Visualization, 2011. Llandudno, UK: Eurographics Association, pp101-109

EXPLOITING SPATIO-TEMPORAL COHERENCY IN TIME-VARYING VISUALIZATION OVER NETWORK ENVIRONMENTS

Lazaro Campoalegre, Tom Noonan and John Dingliana
Graphics Vision and Visualization Group , Trinity College Dublin, Ireland

ABSTRACT

We propose an efficient client-server interaction system for multi-user visualization of real-time time-varying volumetric simulations. The approach is designed to reduce data transfer over network environments, while enabling users to interact independently with the visualization. Exploiting spatio-temporal coherence and parallel processing on Graphical Processing Units (GPU's) on both server and client, a predictive mechanism on the server evaluates, on the fly, whether blocks of data can be extrapolated with sufficient accuracy based on previous frames of simulation. If so, a simple instruction is sent to the client to extrapolate the block, in lieu of transmitting actual volume data of the block. A comparative analysis indicates that we can achieve visualization performance, for time-varying datasets, on par with previous techniques whilst considerably reducing the size of data sent through the network. Perceptual evaluations using an established metric indicate that the visual quality is not noticeably reduced.

KEYWORDS

Time-varying data, Volume Rendering

1. INTRODUCTION

Effective collaborative research is a major challenge in scientific visualization. Scientists in various fields often want to analyze, discuss and evaluate data interactively at their own locations, but real-time interaction, in particular, has always been difficult in distributed visualization environments. Remotely accessing large modern-day datasets requires provision of robust systems that guarantee acceptable image quality and low latency. Despite continual advances in computing power, the use of high performance graphics workstations is still considerably restricted due to the cost of the most modern hardware. Widespread deployment of high-speed wireless networks have increased interest in remote rendering, which offers some evident advantages. It provides the potential for rich rendering experiences to thin clients such as mobile devices with limited computing resources, shared by multiple clients and is a simple but effective solution. However the minimization of interaction latency still remains a challenge. Exploiting spatial and temporal coherence is a potential means of avoiding increasing computational cost and reducing display time. Decreasing the time required to transfer a sequence of volumes to the rendering engine is still a considerable challenge. Any such improvements must be achieved without removing fine visual details, which could be relevant to the task being supported by the visualization.

Our main contribution is a novel approach for multi-user remote rendering of time-varying volumetric data. We propose a robust, perceptually-based predictive mechanism that exploits spatiotemporal coherency to reduce the bandwidth of data transferred over the network during real-time visualization of volume data, with minimal loss of visual quality. Our scheme is buffer-based, allowing us to deal with time-varying datasets with an arbitrary number of timesteps. We exploit the parallel computing capabilities of modern Graphics Processing Units (GPUs) to support a GPU-GPU client-server framework, which allows several users to simultaneously and independently interact with visualizations of complex real-time volumetric simulations.

2. PREVIOUS WORK

Remote visualization has become a topic of significant interest in recent years. Various client-server approaches have been proposed to compensate for limitations in low performance devices or to reduce costs. We discuss, here, the previous works most relevant to our solution and, for more extensive reviews, we refer the reader to the recently published surveys on interactive remote rendering systems by Shi & Hsu (2015), and compressed GPU based volume compression techniques by Balsa & Vázquez (2012).

Several commercial applications have already been developed for remote visualization of volume data. For instance, Vizserver (Ohazama, 1999), is a system that allows OpenGL programs to run in a client-server environment without modification and almost no restrictions on the visualization. However the number of users that are allowed to visualize and interact independently with a dataset simultaneously under the same graphics pipeline is limited. GLX (Kilgard, 1996) is an OpenGL extension for the X server system that employs command streaming to allow 3D graphics rendering applications to display on a remote X server.

Bethel et al. (2000) proposed a system for large-volume scientific data visualization, where a server performs the rendering and transmits resultant images to clients. Similarly, in the remote visualization framework proposed by Engel et al. (2000), a subset of volume data output from a local slicing tool is transferred to a high-end server, where it is rendered off-screen and transmitted back as compressed images to the client for display. Qi & Tyler (2005) proposed a 3D medical visualization system that progressively transmits losslessly encoded data, which is reconstructed on-the-fly in the rendering client.

Sharp et al. (2010) claim to be the first to present a system for multi-client volume rendering that leverages a server GPU environment. They achieve efficient remote rendering of medical volume data, using a transfer function-aware, GPU-based, empty space-skipping algorithm. In the COVRA system, proposed by Gobbetti et al. (2012), a block-based multiresolution compression domain is employed that allows very large volume datasets to be compressed offline and decompressed on-demand in real-time. They achieve a high compression ratio while maintaining good visual results. Bajaj et al. (2002) proposed a parallel volume rendering system, which uses the GPU of the client to edit the transfer functions (TF) and color maps, while the server comprises a multi-PC framework for rendering high quality images on demand.

A popular strategy is to exploit temporal coherence in improving the efficiency of processing time-varying datasets. For instance Shen et al. (1999) propose a data structure called the Time-Space Partitioning tree to capture spatial and temporal coherence to improve rendering speed for large-scale out-of-core rendering of time-varying fluid dynamics simulation. Gao et al. (2005) extended upon this by employing adaptive retrieval of regions based on visibility for distributed collaborative visualization. More recently Jang et al. (2012) used a functional representation of animated volumes to develop an efficient encoding technique that takes into account the temporal similarity between timesteps. Akiba et al. (2006) designed a technique that uses time histograms for simultaneous classification of time-varying data. Younesy et al. (2005) exploit temporal coherence using a Differential Time-Histogram Table that stores voxels which change between timesteps or during transfer function updates, while Fang et al. (2007) employ a Time Activity Curve to identify temporal patterns. Janicke et al. (2007) implemented a technique that detects important regions based on local statistical complexity. After applying conditional entropy, Wang et al. (2008) compute importance curves that are used to evaluate the temporal behavior of blocks. Noonan et al. (2015) exploited block-wise temporal coherence to improve streaming time-varying volume data from CPU to GPU on a single workstation.

Although interesting practical solutions have been proposed in recent years, there remain a number of open problems that merit further investigation. Transmitting the whole volume model to the client device ensures the best interaction capabilities but is still a challenging problem. Some previous works have achieved promising results but typically restrict size of models or are prone to network latency, limiting interaction capabilities. Compression is a good solution for volume models whose size exceeds current hardware capabilities but performance during decompression is an area in need of improvement. A recent trend is to move decompression to the final stages of the graphics pipeline and potential on the GPU, resulting in better exploitation of available bandwidth.

In this paper, we address some of the open problems of previous approaches to deliver a simultaneous multi-user visualization of time-varying volume data by taking advantage of the spatio-temporal coherence of consecutive timesteps in volumetric animation to reduce the network load. Our scheme involves the GPUs of both server and client in a synchronized framework where the server simulates the client's pre-rendering functions, allowing the extrapolation of local datasets on the client side, reducing the explicit transfer of data.

3. OVERVIEW

The framework discussed in this paper is extended from an approach we previously proposed (Noonan et al. 2015) for improving performance in the streaming of time-varying volume datasets from CPU to GPU on a single workstation. That is, we exploit a similar strategy of data reduction through prediction, but extend upon it to support a wholly different use-case, namely that of a networked client-server mechanism capable of facilitating simultaneous multi-user interactions with time-varying volume simulations. In particular, we support real-time interaction, which we define as the ability to process the data on-the-fly with no requirement for preprocessing the entire dataset. We provide a number of novel improvements to the core of the previous approach including added consideration for spatial coherency that results in improved visualization quality. We also exploit the GPU on both server and client, specifically we employ the NVIDIA CUDA platform[1], which provides gains in terms of scalability, performance and the allowable size of datasets that can be handled. Unlike our previous approach, which requires all simulation timesteps to be preloaded into memory, our new mechanism is buffer-based and reads, sequentially, a subset of timesteps on the fly, thus it is not limited to dealing with datasets that can wholly fit in CPU memory. Finally, we provide an added mechanism for dealing with null blocks to further improve data reduction.

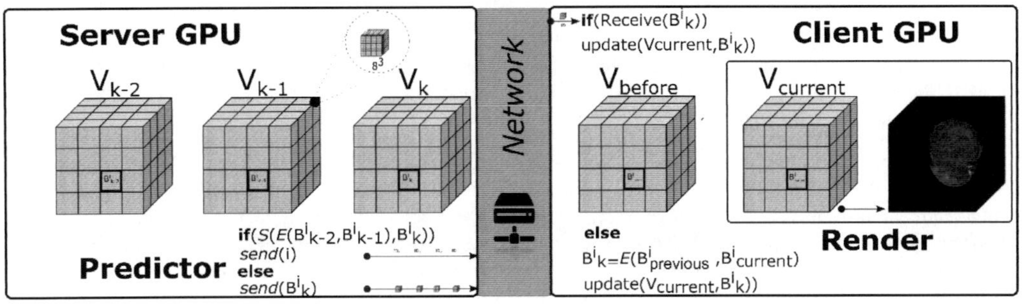

Figure 1. Overview of the proposed approach: volumes are transmitted in a block-wise manner from server to client. Data transmission is reduced when it is determined that the client can approximate, using a predictor function (E), a given block with sufficient accuracy, determined by a similarity function (S)

Figure 1 provides an overview of our framework, which comprises a synchronized mechanism that involves both server and client GPUs. Our scheme reads, from disk, subsequent timesteps, V_k, of a time-varying volume dataset composed of n timesteps, where $k \in [1, n]$. We start by sending the first two volumes corresponding to the first two timesteps V_0 and V_1 to the server-GPU, subdivided into blocks B^i of $8 \times 8 \times 8$ voxels, and then subsequent volumes are transferred, in a block-wise manner, to the client.

On the server-GPU, we employ a CUDA-based *prediction mechanism* that computes, in parallel, linearly extrapolated blocks, B^i_{new}, for each timestep k, based on the two previous timesteps. Then, a *similarity function* evaluates whether the extrapolation result is a sufficiently accurate approximation of the actual data of the timestep B^i_k. If the extrapolation result is not sufficiently similar to the actual data, a full block is transmitted to the client, which performs an update of the timestep volumes on the client-GPU's memory with the newly received data. Otherwise, an instruction is sent to the client to approximate the block B^i_{new} in lieu of transmitting the actual data. In this case, the client executes an identical extrapolation scheme to the server, before the timestep volume is updated and rendered.

In Section 4 and 5, we describe in detail the *prediction mechanism* and *similarity function* respectively. Section 6 discusses our networking framework for visualization on multiple clients.

---

[1] NVIDIA CUDA webpage: http://www.nvidia.com/object/cuda_home_new.html

4. GPU-BASED PREDICTIVE DATA REDUCTION

At run-time, the server is responsible for instructing the client whether to receive new volume blocks or to extrapolate blocks, B^i_{new}, where it has determined that such an extrapolation can accurately approximate the local behavior of the simulation. In this manner, we exploit computational resources to make significant savings on data transfer. As a key improvement over the approach presented in our previous work (Noonan et al. 2015), we exploit parallel computing capabilities of GPUs on both the server and client. Importantly, this enables real-time processing of large time-varying volume datasets, which in turn allows us to support a networked client-server framework facilitating remote collaborative visualization.

Assuming some degree of spatio-temporal coherence between subsequent timesteps, our approach tries to approximate the behavior of scientific simulations as linear within short periods of time. We apply a linear extrapolation to each voxel inside each block, by forcing the second derivatives (Laplacian) to be 0, as follows: $d_k = 2 \cdot d_{k-1} - d_{k-2}$, where d_{k-2}, d_{k-1} and d_k are consecutive values of the voxel d in corresponding timestep volumes V_{k-2}, $V_{k-1}$and V_k respectively.

The predictive mechanism starts at timestep $k = 2$, where blocks B^i_{new} are calculated in the server GPU by extrapolating from the two consecutive co-spatial blocks $B^i_{current}$ and $B^i_{previous}$. After this, a *similarity function*, S (detailed in the next section), evaluates whether the extrapolation result, B^i_{new}, is a sufficiently accurate approximation of the actual data of the next timestep, B^i_k. If so, the server sends a signal with the block identifier, i, to the client-GPU. Otherwise the actual block B^i_k is transmitted to the client. Then we update the two consecutive volume timesteps held in the server's GPU memory.

The manner in which we manage data transmission between server and client is a key ingredient of the networked visualization approach. On the client, we compute $B^i_{new} = 2 \cdot B^i_{current} - B^i_{previous}$, at each step following initial setup and update $B^i_{previous} \leftarrow B^i_{current}$. Then we update $B^i_{current} \leftarrow B^i_{new}$ if a block identifier (i) is received from the server, or $B^i_{current} \leftarrow B^i_k$ if a block (B^i_k) is received. Performing the extrapolation on a block-wise basis allows us to reduce storage on the client-GPU to just two full frame volumes, which allows us to support a buffer based mechanism that works regardless of the number of timesteps in the dataset.

We further improve performance by avoiding extrapolation of null regions in the volume datasets by evaluating whether all the voxels in B^i_k are empty. If so, the algorithm proceeds by assigning a *null* identifier, transmitted using only 1 byte, to avoid the redundant transmission or extrapolation of the block on the client GPU. When a block with a null identifier is received by the client, the algorithm examines the $null$ identifier of the preceding co-spatial block. If this is also $null$, no update of $B^i_{current}$ is performed. Otherwise we assign 0 to each voxel in $B^i_{current}$, thus substituting the extrapolation function by a more efficient assignment function.

5. SPATIO-TEMPORAL SIMILARITY FUNCTION

In previous work (Noonan et al. 2015), we proposed a *similarity function* that evaluates temporal coherency of blocks, determining whether they should be extrapolated or transmitted from server to client. This is done by computing the Root Averaged Squared difference between consecutive co-spatial voxels and comparing it to an empirical threshold value, ε. Whilst the temporal coherency component accounts for how a voxel changes from one frame to the next, if the value in the voxel moves within the block, the overall block may not be significantly changed. Thus, we improve upon this by additionally accounting for spatial similarity within blocks by using a weighting factor, W^i_k (denoted for convenience as W), in the *similarity function*, S (see Equations (1) and (2)).

$$S = \begin{cases} true & if \sqrt{\frac{1}{m} \cdot \sum_{v=0}^{m} W \cdot (x_v - x'_v)^2} < \varepsilon \\ false & otherwise \end{cases} \quad \text{(Erro! Marcador não definido.)}$$

$$W = b \cdot Max[(x_v - x_u)^2] + 1 \quad (2)$$

In these equations, x_v and x_v' are co-spatial voxels corresponding to the two consecutive timesteps; m is the block size in voxels (typically $8 \times 8 \times 8$); and $x_u$is one of six neighbors of the voxel x_v in the same timestep.

The parameter b, which we call the *spatial parameter*, assigns a weight that captures the influence of the spatial distribution of voxels at each block during the simulation. The ε variable is analogous to a compression factor and adjusting it leads to varying degrees of accuracy in the final result. In practice, the value can be subjectively chosen for a given dataset or use-case but the ideal value of ε varies across different datasets and transfer functions. Our CUDA implementation on both server and client allows us to evaluate both temporal and spatial behavior of blocks without decreasing the performance in the simulation. A study of the influence of W on the visual result and the extrapolation behavior is presented in Section 7.

6. DATA TRANSMISSION FOR NETWORKED MULTI-USER VISUALIZATION

As previously discussed, our objective is to facilitate a networked multi-user system where the server transmits, to the client, only non-null blocks that cannot be extrapolated in the client-GPU. These are sent as part of packets that are classified as either *initialization* packages, *empty* or packages containing only *data*. An initialization packet contains the required information for setting up a 3D texture as well as managing the volume animation on the client side, that is, the resolution, number of timesteps, timestep identifier and bytes per voxel. Packets that contain data include the block ID and the voxel information. An empty packet serves as an identifier for null blocks.

On the client, a receiving function collects the information to generate the blocks of data within a 3D texture corresponding to the current timestep of the volumetric simulation. The block update within the current texture is performed directly within the client-GPU memory, each time a new block is fully received or extrapolated on the client side.

We use TCP (Transmission Control Protocol), which offers error detection ensuring the correct delivery of our blocks of data in the transmitted packages. TCP also includes a flow control that determines when data needs to be re-sent, and stops the flow of data until previous packets are successfully transferred. The result is a robust client-server scheme that guarantees interactive rendering in both server and multiple clients and allows unrestricted, independent simultaneous interaction of a large number of users with large scale datasets.

7. RESULTS AND DISCUSSION

For generality of results, we tested our approach using different types of data, namely:

- A *Supernova* simulation dataset made available by Dr. John Blondin at the North Carolina State University through US Department of Energy's SciDAC Institute for Ultrascale Visualization, Figure 2 (left), with a resolution of $432 \times 432 \times 432$ voxels and 60 times steps.
- A *Smoke Simulation*, Fig. 2 (middle), which is simulated based on the method presented by Fedkiw et al. (2001) with a resolution of $100 \times 100 \times 100$ voxels and 500 timesteps.
- A *4D MRI lung* dataset, Fig. 2 (right) (von Siebenthal, 2008) that contains dynamic sagittal image slices of free breathing. The model is composed of 200 timesteps with $50 \times 224 \times 224$ resolution.

All images in this section were rendered at a resolution of 817×534, using our own implementation of a GPU volume ray-caster based on the approach by Hadwiger et al. (2006).

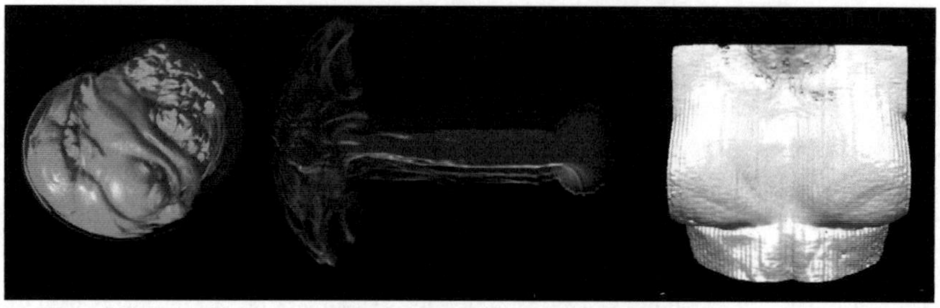

Figure 2. Volumetric datasets used in our experiments

Multi-user interaction: Figure 3 shows images from simultaneous multi-user interactions with the *Super Nova*, where users on four remote clients independently view synchronized data streamed from a server, running the simulation. Each client employs a different transfer function that can be manipulated independently along with other viewing parameters, such as rotation, zooming. The transfer functions represent different density ranges and were chosen to study the extrapolation behavior across a variety of functions.

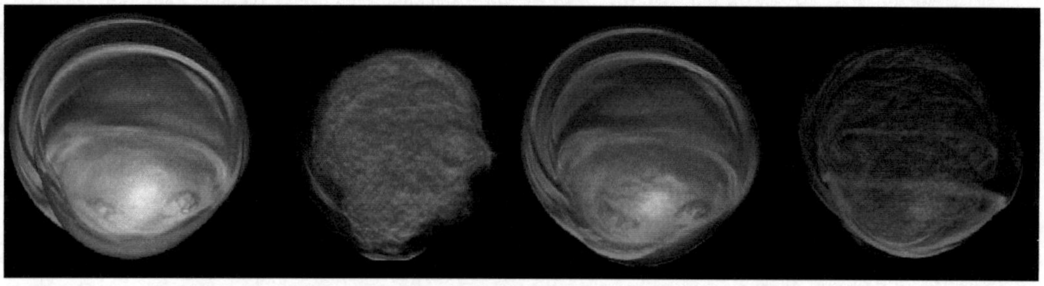

Figure 3. Multi-user visualizations of the Supernova using different transfer functions

Reduction in Data Transmission: We characterize the performance of our scheme by the extrapolation ratio, E_r, where $0 \leq E_r \leq 1$. This is defined, for any particular simulation, as the ratio of the total number of extrapolated volume blocks across all the simulation frames to the total number of rendered blocks.

In general, our approach achieves similar results to those reported by Noonan et al. (2015), which is generally around 50% reduction of data transmission for typical viewing conditions, when compared to the full volume data. However, since, many volume datasets consist of a significant subset of empty blocks (null regions) which might simply be skipped, we report, E_r as the reduction achieved purely in the non-null regions.

The graph in Figure 4(a) shows a study of the visual quality and extrapolation behavior of the three simulations mentioned previously across discrete values of the *spatial parameter*, b. Quality scores, Q, are calculated using the High Dynamic Range Visual Difference Predictor (HDR-VDP2) (Mantiuk et al. 2011), which is an established metric for perceptual similarity.

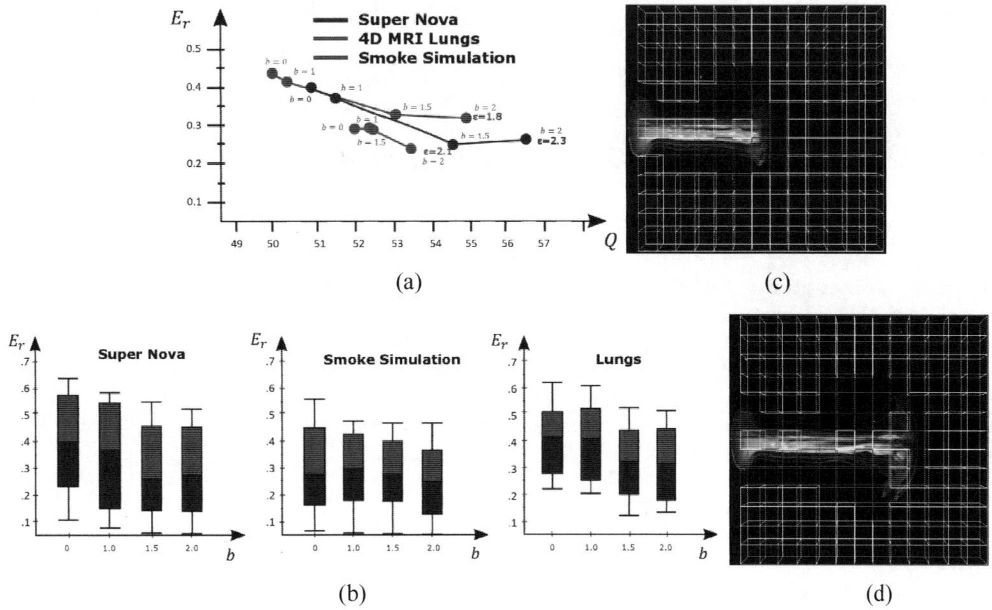

Figure 4. (a) Study of visual quality and extrapolation ratio (Er) for test datasets using different values of the spatial parameter b; (b) Study of achieved by our technique for the three datasets (c) Cross-section of the smoke simulation at timesteps 76; blocks marked in white are either extrapolated or empty (d) similar visualization of timestep 122

As previously mentioned, the ideal value of ε varies across different datasets. In order to assure acceptable visual quality, we empirically chose an ε value for each simulation, so that the visual quality of 99% of the timesteps of the simulation were at least $Q = 50$, which was taken as an indicator of good visual similarity. Note that for each simulation there is a significant influence of the parameter, b, on the visualization, that is, when other parameters are constant, incrementing b leads to considerable improvement in visual quality, Q, across the simulation.

The quartiles in Figure 4(b) show the mean E_r (in non-null regions) across all frames of the Super Nova, Smoke Simulation and MRI Lungs for four empirically tested values of the *spatial parameter*, b. Although the mean E_r values generally fall under 0.50, the extent of the upper half of the box plots indicate that a considerable amount of blocks are extrapolated in a high percentage of the timesteps at each studied simulation. The ε used here are as in Figure 4(a). Note also that there is generally a decrease of E_r when increasing b.

The images in Figure 4(c) and (d) show cross-sections of the rendering of the smoke simulation to distinguish the $8 \times 8 \times 8$ blocks extrapolated in timesteps 76 and 122 respectively. Blocks outlined in red are transmitted to the client, while the white blocks are either extrapolated or recorded as null blocks of the volume. Note that a considerable amount of blocks in the non-*null* region are also extrapolated.

Figures 5 and 6 show the rendering of the Smoke Simulation and Supernova respectively, in order to visually demonstrate the influence of the *spatial parameter*, b, on the visual quality of the images as described in Figure 4(a). In both cases, we selected a fixed ε value whilst increasing the parameter b. Note that the visual quality Q is considerably better in the cases where $b = 2.0$ (see figures 5(left) and 6(left)).

Table 1 shows how average frame processing times are affected by the spatial parameter, b, when applied to a number of time-varying datasets. Timings include network transfer time over local wifi and were captured on a server equipped with 16GB RAM and an Nvidia GeForce GT 750M with 2GB RAM, and a single local client with identical specifications. Note that there exists a clear increase of the frame processing time when b is increased.

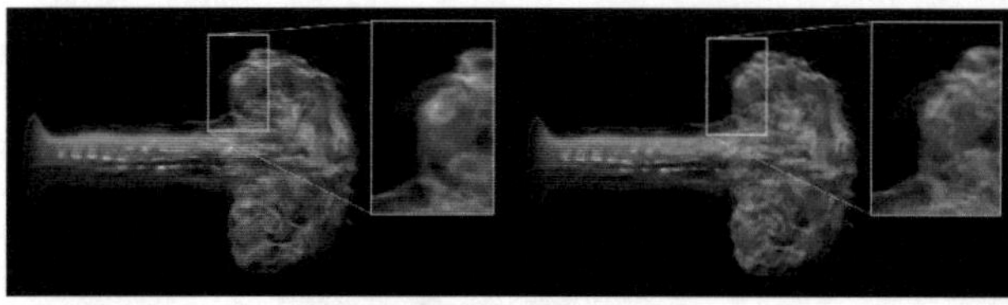

Figure 5. Influence of the spatial parameter, b, on image quality for the smoke simulation: b=2.0, Q=55.62 (left); and b=0.5, Q=50.20 (right). In both cases ε =1.5

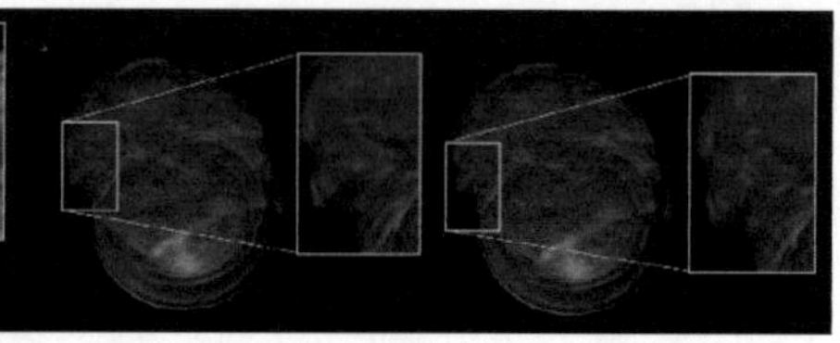

Figure 6. Influence of b for Supernova: b=2.0, Q=58.38 (left); and b=0.5, Q=53.18 (right). In both cases ε =1.8

Comparative Analysis: Table 2 presents a feature comparison between our technique and popular approaches in the literature for network-based visualization of volume datasets. The rows of the table indicate, respectively, the size of datasets used in the comparison; suitability for multi-user visualization; whether the approach is real-time, in other words whether it can visualize data on-the-fly without pre-processing the full frame sequence; support for time varying volume data; and whether the volume data resides on the client side. In addition, performance indicators are provided in terms of average *frames per seconds* (FPS) and the effective compression ratio (equivalent of E_r).

Table 1. Influence of *b* on performance

b	**Rendering Time (ms)**		
	Smoke Simulation	Supernova	4DMRI Lungs
0	19.5	24	20.14
0.5	23.21	27.36	24.75
1	25.18	34.73	30.46
1.5	28.11	37.19	31.8
2	34.5	39.08	35.22

Table 2. Feature comparison with other published techniques

Approach	Gobetti et. al. (2012)	Sharp et. al. (2010)	Bajaj et. al. (2002)	This Paper
Dataset	Supernova (432^3)	512^3	512^3	Supernova (432^3)
Multi-user	✗	✓	✗	✓
Real-time	✗	✓	✓	✓
Time-variant data	✓	✗	✗	✓
Volume-on-client	✓	✗	✗	✓
FPS	10	15	10-12	6-11
Compression ratio	0.98	-	0.9977	0.5

Note that Gobetti et al. (2012) achieve interactive frame rates for very large datasets, is suitable for volume animations and considerably reduces traffic over the network. Their limitations lie in the time needed for pre-processing and lack of support for simultaneous users independently interacting with the visualization. Support for a wide range of users interacting in real-time is provided by Sharp et al. (2010) with a transfer-function aware medical image application. However, since the rendering is performed on the server, their approach requires a very complex server-side mechanism composed of multiple GPUs for simultaneously rendering images on-demand from several different users. The approach also involves the CPU in the task of managing the transfer functions received from each user simultaneously. Thus the reduction in data transmission is dependent on the selected transfer function at each client. The thin-client proposed by Bajaj et al. (2002) achieves interactive exploration of volume data, but is not suitable for multi-user systems and has not been designed for time-varying volume data. The compression ratio in the related column in Table 2 is approximated based on the ratio of the transmitted image size versus the volume data and the FPS (frames per second) figures for our approach are based on a simulation with 8 simultaneous users interacting independently with the supernova visualization over the network.

Our approach overcomes a number of limitations of these previous techniques. We guarantee simultaneous interactive visualization of large scale datasets, while considerably reducing the data sent over the network. Although we do not achieve ratios as high as Gobetti et al. (2012), we have the advantage of not requiring a pre-processing stage. In the case of the supernova dataset ($432^3 \times 60$, float 18 GB), the average size of a frame transmitted to the client GPU was $\sim$158 MB.

As stated, our system mainly extends upon the technique proposed by Noonan et al. (2015) but in contrast to this previous approach, we exploit GPUs on the client, which facilitates the system to run in real-time for time-varying data of arbitrary timesteps; in other words our buffer-based approach is not limited to data that fits into GPU memory. In fact our approach is well suited for in-situ visualization with multiple clients, where a stream of volume data may be rendered on the fly as it is simulated or acquired.

8. CONCLUSIONS

We presented a novel framework for time-varying-volume data visualization designed for bandwidth-constrained network environments. In our block-wise scheme, a server-GPU simulates client-GPU pre-rendering functions characterizing the local behavior of the volume dataset, exploiting this to avoid transmission of complete per-frame volumes to the client-GPU. Results indicate that we are able to considerably reduce the transfer bandwidth, exploiting both temporal and spatial coherency.

The technique requires no pre-processing and allows multiple users, over the network, to have simultaneous, personalized independent interactions with the simulation data. Analysis of the output using an established perceptual metric suggest that the visual quality is not noticeably reduced. The resulting frame rates provide evidence of the viability of our technique compared to popular approaches described in the literature. In our framework, the 3D data reside in both server and client GPUs, allowing each client to independently change viewing parameters as well as the transfer function.

Due to the linear extrapolation component, the technique is ideally suited for large scale models where a first order approximation can be made of the dynamic behavior of a significant proportion of the dataset. The proposed method assumes that multiple users will access the data in a sequential manner, in other words, it does not particularly aid volume data visualization if users want to look at random frames, and the server side cost will increase if users access different timesteps simultaneously. However, the system would be well suited for instance for in-situ visualization where the data is being viewed *on-the-fly* as it is generated by a simulation or acquired using some sensor technology. We also assume that the rendering client will be equipped with a GPU, however mobile devices are becoming increasingly equipped with graphical computing capabilities, and although our current implementation is implemented in CUDA, we believe it can be ported to other parallel computing platforms such as OpenCL.

The results presented in the paper are based on a block size of 8^3 voxels. We also tested the system with 16^3 blocks but found negligible difference in performance as the gains seemed to be counter-balanced by overhead costs of processing larger blocks. In future work we plan to investigate the use of adapted block sizes corresponding to the temporal volume behavior. We plan to replace the Linear Extrapolation function with a more complex scheme based on the use of localized filters as predictive functions. Using our approach alone, the size of individual frame of volume data needs to be within the maximal size allowed by the available GPU RAM but we believe our solution could be coupled with other strategies for downsampling or adaptively accessing only parts of the volume that are visible within the viewport at a particular time. We plan to integrate and test our system with such approaches in the future. We also plan to conduct perceptual evaluations based on user tests to further study the quality of the results. With increasing adoption of mobile technologies, we would like to test the effectiveness of our technique on such devices and adapt our algorithms to run optimally on clients with reduced hardware capabilities.

ACKNOWLEDGEMENT

This research has been conducted with the financial support of Science Foundation Ireland (SFI) under Grant Number 13/IA/1895.

REFERENCES

Akiba, H., Fout, N., & Ma, K.-L. (2006). Simultaneous Classification of Time-varying Volume Data Based on the Time Histogram. *Proceedings of the Eighth Joint Eurographics / IEEE VGTC Conference on Visualization* (pp. 171-178). Eurographics Association.

Bajaj, C., Park, S., & Thane, A. (2002). Parallel multi-PC volume rendering system. *CS \& ICES Technical Report, University of Texas at Austin, 2.*

Balsa, M., & Vázquez, P. (2012). Practical Volume Rendering in Mobile Devices. In *Advances in Visual Computing* (pp. 708-718). Springer.

Bethel, W., Tierney, B., Lee, J., Gunter, D., & Lau, S. (2000). Using high-speed WANs and network data caches to enable remote and distributed visualization. *Supercomputing, ACM/IEEE 2000 Conference*, (pp. 28-28).

Engel, K., Ertl, T., Hastreiter, P., Tomandl, B., & Eberhardt, K. (2000). Combining local and remote visualization techniques for interactive volume rendering in medical applications. *Proceedings of the conference on Visualization'00*, (pp. 449-452).

Fang, Z., Möller, T., Hamarneh, G., & Celler, A. (2007). Visualization and Exploration of Time-varying Medical Image Data Sets. *Proceedings of Graphics Interface 2007* (pp. 281-288). ACM.

Fedkiw, R., Stam, J., & Jensen, H. W. (2001). Visual simulation of smoke. *Proceedings of the 28th annual conference on Computer graphics and interactive techniques*, (pp. 15-22).

Gao, J., Huang, J., Johnson, C. R., & Atchley, S. (2005, Oct). Distributed data management for large volume visualization. *VIS 05. IEEE Visualization, 2005.*, (pp. 183-189). doi:10.1109/VISUAL.2005.1532794

Gobbetti, E., Guitián, I. a., & Marton, F. (2012). COVRA: A compression-domain output-sensitive volume rendering architecture based on a sparse representation of voxel blocks. *Computer Graphics Forum*, *31*, pp. 1315-1324.

Hadwiger, M., Kniss, J. M., Rezk-salama, C., Weiskopf, D., & Engel, K. (2006). *Real-time Volume Graphics.* Natick, MA, USA: A. K. Peters, Ltd.

Jang, Y., Ebert, D. S., & Gaither, K. (2012). Time-varying data visualization using functional representations. *Visualization and Computer Graphics, IEEE Transactions on, 18*, 421-433.

Janicke, H., Wiebel, A., Scheuermann, G., & Kollmann, W. (2007). Multifield Visualization Using Local Statistical Complexity. *IEEE Transactions onVisualization and Computer Graphics, 13*, 1384-1391.

Kilgard, M. J. (1996). *OpenGL programming for the X Window System.* Addison Wesley Longman Publishing Co., Inc.

Mantiuk, R., Kim, K. J., Rempel, A. G., & Heidrich, W. (2011). HDR-VDP-2: A Calibrated Visual Metric for Visibility and Quality Predictions in All Luminance Conditions. *ACM Trans. Graph., 30*, 40:1--40:14.

Noonan, T., Campoalegre, L., & Dingliana, J. (2015). Temporal Coherence Predictor for Time Varying Volume Data Based on Perceptual Functions. In D. Bommes, T. Ritschel, & T. Schultz (Ed.), *Vision, Modeling \& Visualization.* The Eurographics Association.

Ohazama, C. (1999). OpenGL Vizserver. *White Paper, Silicon Graphics Inc.*

Qi, X., & Tyler, J. M. (2005). A progressive transmission capable diagnostically lossless compression scheme for 3D medical image sets. *Information Sciences, 175*, 217-243.

Sharp, T., Robertson, D., & Criminisi, A. (2010). *Volume Rendering on Server GPUs for Enterprise-Scale Medical Applications.* Tech. rep. 72, Microsoft Research, Cambridge, UK, Microsoft Research, Cambridge, UK.

Shen, H. W., Chiang, L. J., & Ma, K. L. (1999, Oct). A fast volume rendering algorithm for time-varying fields using a time-space partitioning (TSP) tree. *Visualization '99. Proceedings*, (pp. 371-545).

Shi, S., & Hsu, C.-H. (2015). A Survey of Interactive Remote Rendering Systems. *ACM Computing Surveys, 47*, 57.

von Siebenthal, M. (2008). *Analysis and modelling of respiratory liver motion using 4DMRI.* Ph.D. dissertation, Citeseer.

Wang, C., Yu, H., & Ma, K.-L. (2008). Importance-driven time-varying data visualization. *IEEE Transactions on Visualization and Computer Graphics , 14*, 1547-1554.

Younesy, J., Moller, T., & Carr, H. (2005). Visualization of time-varying volumetric data using differential time-histogram table. *Volume Graphics, 2005. Fourth International Workshop on*, (pp. 21-224).

VISUAL ANALYSIS OF DEFECT CLUSTERING IN ATOMISTIC SIMULATION OF THE IRRADIATION PROCESS

Guoqing Wu[1] and Deye Lin[2]

[1]*Institute of Applied Physics and Computational Mathematics, Beijing, Fenghao East Road No.2, Haidian District, Beijing, China*

[2]*CAEP Software Center for High Performance Numerical Simulation, Huayuan Road No.6, Haidian District, Beijing, China*

ABSTRACT

Large-scale time-varying 3D positional atomistic data are rich in information and attractive in interactive visual analysis. In this paper, we demonstrate an effective-efficient scheme to support visualization of the atom-position datasets generated in molecular dynamics simulations of the irradiation process. In this scheme, we analyze the atomic positions in the crystal, identify all vacancy and interstitial defects, obtain insight into the defect clustering and visualize them. We evaluate the scheme with high energy irradiation damage simulation data of metal Zr. The result is a better understanding of material structure and properties which is difficult to get using conventional visualization toolkits. The proposed method has potential applications in a wide range of simulated or experimental particle data.

KEYWORDS

Visual analysis, molecular dynamics, Voronoi tessellation, defect identification, cluster analysis

1. INTRODUCTION

Atomistic simulation methods such as molecular dynamics (MD) are well known to be used to study irradiation processes of nuclear materials on an atomistic level. These MD simulations involve time-varying complex structures with millions of atoms, posing many challenges for visualization and analysis. For example, crystal defect or defect clusters play an important role in materials behavior, and their visual analysis in the datasets is essential for the interpretation of simulation results and understanding of materials properties. For this purpose, we need to assign a structural type to each atom based on a computational analysis of its local environment and color different structural type atoms for feature tracking purposes. This information can also be used to filter the simulation data to reduce hardware burden by visualizing only the interesting atoms.

In the equilibrium state, all metal atoms are configured in a perfect crystal lattice and disturbed slightly. Defects are defined as a significant deviation from the arrangement of atoms. An atom is considered being displaced if it leaves the sphere centered at its initial lattice position with a cutoff radius parameter. If atoms are displaced and atomic environment is found to be different from the ideal crystal lattice, vacancy and interstitial defects are detected. A "vacancy" can be considered an in homogeneous region containing no atom. On the contrary, an "interstitial" is an in homogeneous region containing more than one atom. In many cases atoms that are displaced from their original positions will lead to the formation, recombination and aggregation of defect clusters by the irradiation damage impact. Domain scientists are very interested in the number, location, size and evolution of these clusters which are critical for investigating the nature of irradiation.

In this paper, we present an application for the exploration and visualization of MD simulations of irradiation damage process. Our visualization integrates defect feature detection and quantification into a pipeline to improve the effectiveness of atomistic visualization. We also describe temporal parallel acceleration techniques for exploring large-scale time-varying atomistic simulation data with excellent strong scalability.

In the following section, we present some related work. We discuss Wigner-Seitz defect analysis based on Voronoi tessellation in section 3. Then in section 4 we present a defect clustering algorithm based on neighbor propagation. Section 5 describes temporal parallel acceleration techniques. In section 6, experiments are conducted to show the applicability and effectiveness of our method in generating visual analysis results in the irradiation damage process.

2. RELATED WORK

This paper builds on previous research on atomistic data visualization and analysis.

Atomistic visualization: In recent years, visualization of atomistic simulation data has been intensively employed. Widanagamaachchi et al (2015) presented a simulation-visualization pipeline that uses the LAMMPS molecular dynamics simulator and the VTK to create a visualization and analysis environment for atomistic simulations of plasma-surface interactions. Reda et al (2013) presented an application for the interactive visualization and exploration of large-scale atomistic simulations in ultra-resolution immersive environments. Bhattarai et al (2006) developed an interactive atomistic visualization system integrating complex analyses with visualization. It is used to present the data on a space time multiresolution basis facilitating information extraction and understanding. Li (2005, p.1051) surveyed the state of the art in atomistic visualization and tools.

Atomistic data analysis: feature quantification and extraction of atomistic simulation data has received much recent attention also. Stukowski (2012) and Lummen and Kraska (2007) discussed existing and new computational analysis techniques to match a local structure to an idealized one (such as BCC, FCC or HCP) in large-scale atomistic computer simulations of crystalline solids. Stukowski et al (2012) presented a dislocation extraction algorithm for identifying and indexing dislocations in lattices and crystal interfaces. Medvedev (2002) studied a Voronoi based approach to study both local order of atoms and extended structure correlations of atoms. Keys et al (2010) introduced a shape matching framework to characterize complex particle morphologies. Peterka et al (2011) investigated a parallel particle tracing algorithm to analyze GB scale Atomistic data. Agrawal et al (2011) developed a software package for the calculation of atom density and radical distribution function.

In contrast to these, our goal here is to couple atomistic structure analysis and visualization, to get additional insights into the large scale atomistic simulations of irradiation damage process compared to traditional atomistic visualization.

3. DEFECT IDENTIFICATION

Voronoi definition used in our work is reviewed below followed by presentation of the defect identification approach.

3.1 Voronoi Tessellation

Given an input point data set, the Voronoi tessellation is a decomposition of the simulation domain into a set of convex polyhedron called Voronoi cells. For a point s_i, Voronoi cell V_i is the convex polyhedron that corresponds to a segment of a domain, all points of which are closer to s_i than to any other point s_j. s_i is defined as the site of Voronoi cell V_i. Formally,

$$V_i = \{x \in R^3 \mid d(x, s_i) \le d(x, s_j), \forall j\} \quad (1)$$

where $d(x,s_i)$ is the distance between a location x and the point s_i (Peterka et al, 2014). The faces of the Voronoi cell are equidistant from the neighbor points s_i and s_j. Figure 1 (left) demonstrates the Voronoi tessellation used throughout this paper. Compared with other decomposition (such as sphere), the Voronoi tessellation is space-filling and perfectly partitions the domain. It can serve as a geometric method for mapping the discrete 3D point cloud atomic data to a continuous field while minimizing the loss in structural information. It is an extremely helpful tool for characterizing the structure in "micro" and "macro" levels and has applications in many scientific disciplines (Okabe et al, 2000; Felfer et al, 2015). For example, the characteristic arrangement of near neighbors and spatial distribution of atoms in molecular dynamics simulations can be reflected by the geometric shape of the Voronoi polyhedron (Stukowski, 2012). Also the statistics of Voronoi polyhedron, i.e. the distribution of different types of polyhedron, can be used to find relations between the statistics and physical properties (Zhang et al, 2011). Several software libraries exist for Voronoi decomposition such as Qhull (www.qhull.org), CGAL (www.cgal.org), and VORO++ (Rycroft, 2009). In our implementation we use the VORO++ code library to construct Voronoi tessellations. In comparison, VORO++ is an open source software library and has been designed specifically for handling large-scale 3D tessellation. It has a modern C++ interface and is well-documented.

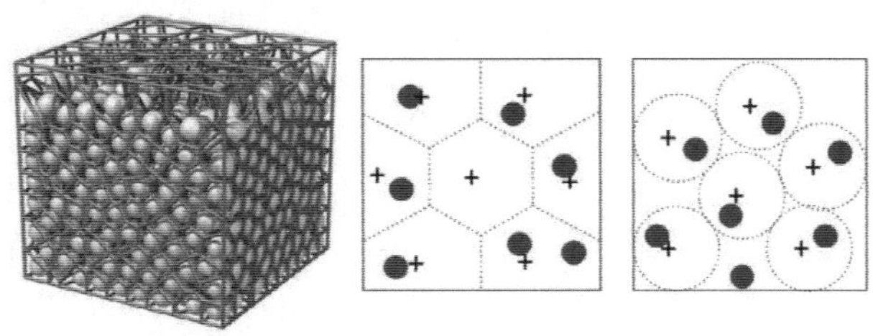

Figure 1. (left) Dense packing of spherical atoms and its 3D Voronoi tessellation. (middle) and (right) illustrate the schematic comparison of two different defect detection methods based on Voronoi and spherical tessellations, respectively. The black crosses represent the site atoms in the reference timestep, while the red balls indicate atoms in the current timestep that to be analyzed. Notice that the bottom atom in (right) locates outside of spherical tessellations and can not to be correctly detected because the spherical decomposition is not space-filling

3.2 Wigner-Seitz Method

An ideal defects identification algorithm should provide robustness and accuracy features. A small Voronoi volume is usually an indication of an interstitial-type defect and large ones suggest vacancies. The criterion for judging defect type does not meet the general considerations. To implement an automated vacancy and interstitial identification, we use Wigner-Seitz method which requires two different input time step datasets: the current time step containing the defects and a reference time step. The current time step is the data set to be analyzed, while the reference defines the defect-free state of the atomistic system. In most simulation cases, the initial state of the crystal lattice has been initialized defect free. So, we assume the first time step dataset to be the reference configuration and build Voronoi tessellations with it. Wigner-Seitz method firstly maps each input atom from the current time step dataset to the closest Voronoi cell in the reference time step (Laakkonen and Nieminen, 1988). Secondly, it counts the number of atoms located within the Voronoi cell of each reference site. The number is called site's occupancy number (Figure 1). Voronoi cells with no atoms were labeled vacancies, two or more atoms interstitials, and one atom normals. Then, each atom is assigned a defect type property (e.g., *enum(vacancy=0, normal=1, interstitial=2)*) and the positional data of atoms is converted to vectors of four elements *(x, y, z, type)*.

4. CLUSTER ANALYSIS OF DEFECTS

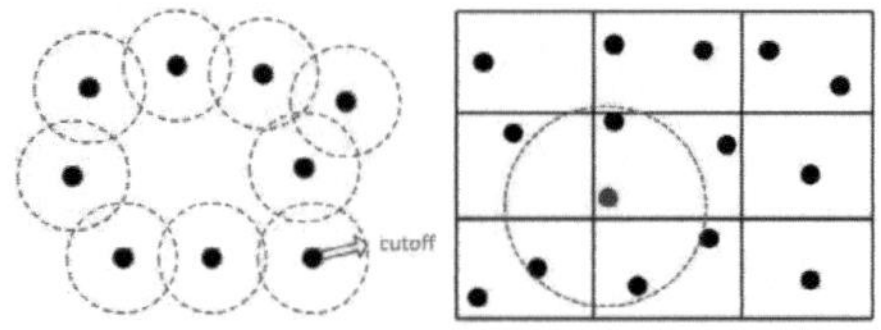

Figure 2. (left) Atom clustering based on neighbor propagation with specified cutoff distance (right) Cell neighbor list construction of the red atom

In the process of irradiation damage, single defects will composite, annihilation and aggregation in a diffusion way which induces the formation or growth of defect clusters. These defect clusters may in fact serve as nuclei for amorphization and affect the performance of materials. Therefore, the analysis of irradiation-induced defect clustering is another interesting issue after the defect identification procedure.

Defect cluster is defined as the set of defect atoms that are neighbors. Defect atom i and j belong to a cluster, if and only if the coordination distance is less than a threshold. Defect cluster analysis can be done by calculating the distance from each defect to all other defects. For commonly used cluster algorithms such as k-means, the cluster number needs to be specified which is often uncertain. Here, we present an algorithm based on neighbor propagation which is robust to test for spatial distribution of defects as well as extract the clusters. We adopt the following convention: For a group of extracted defect atoms, we traverse through from one atom to the another such that distance between any two atoms on the path are within the specified cutoff distance which is usually chosen to be lattice constant, then we determine that they are related in some fashion to be the same defect cluster. The procedure is similar with the maze runner. When all atoms are traversed, the clustering is implemented.

The above cluster algorithm needs to calculate the inter-atomic distances between all atom pairs. For N atoms, this procedure needs $O(N^2)$ number of loops and usually costs most of CPU time. Obviously it is unacceptable to conduct such a evaluation when there are more than a million atoms in the system, and a improved version is strongly needed to reduce the redundant computation. To improve the performance, we utilize a cell neighbor list method which is used routinely in large scale molecular dynamics simulations. The whole simulation space is divided into small cells. All atoms are assigned to cells according to their positions. The distances are calculated between atoms that are either in the same cell or in immediately adjacent cells and a linked list of the neighbor atom is created for every atom in the system (Figure 3). More details of the cell neighbor list method have been given by (Cui et al, 2009; Matin et al, 2003). Once the neighbor list is built, the algorithm 1 is more efficient because there are only few of neighbors for each atom, i.e., in the sphere of cutoff as the radius, need to be calculated the inter-atomic distances, and time complexity of the algorithm 1 is cut down to $O(N \times N_{neighbor})$, in which $N_{neighbor}$ is the average number of neighbors.

In this work, the pseudo code of overall procedure for defect clustering is shown in Algorithm 1.

Algorithm 1 cluster algorithm based on neighbor propagation

Initialization: *x,y,z* coordinates of each defect atom;

clusterNum = 0; *clusterID* = 0;

NeighborList Construction;

Output: *clusterID* of each defect atom;

1: for (all defect atoms in system) {

```
    if (clusterID >0)
        continue;
    else
        clusterID = clusterNum ++;
    insert the current atom into deque Q ;
    while (deque Q is not empty) {
        pop an atom p from deque Q ;
        for (all neighbors of the atom p) {
            if (clusterID = 0) {
                clusterID = clusterNum;
                insert neighbor atom into deque Q ;
            }
        }
    }
}
```

After cluster analysis, each defect atom is additionally assigned a *clusterID* property and associated with a vector of five elements *(x, y, z, type, clusterID)*. In most atomistic simulations, the number of atoms in the system is more than a million and exceeds the resolution of display screens. The interested defects are flooded by normal atoms. For targeted atomic visualization purpose, the type and *clusterID* property can be used as simple indicators to decide whether an atom is of interest to the domain scientists and filter out normal atoms by a threshold criterion.

5. TEMPORAL PARALLEL SCHEME

As the computing power grows rapidly, the ever-increasing data size of high resolution simulations poses another great challenge to atomistic visual analysis. In order to extend our work to large scale MD data, we applied an MPI based parallel technique to speed up the visual analysis. Firstly, we partition the entire time-varying datasets into a number of independent slices and each slice may contain a number of time step datasets. Then, the analysis of each slice is executed by processes separately. Figure 4 illustrates the basic idea of temporal parallel scheme. The first time step dataset is read in by all processes simultaneously and initialized as reference configuration. Defect identification and cluster analysis can be performed in parallel for the time steps 1~4. As there is no communication and synchronization between slices, the scheme has excellent strong scalability and can use multiple CPU cores which are the same number with time steps.

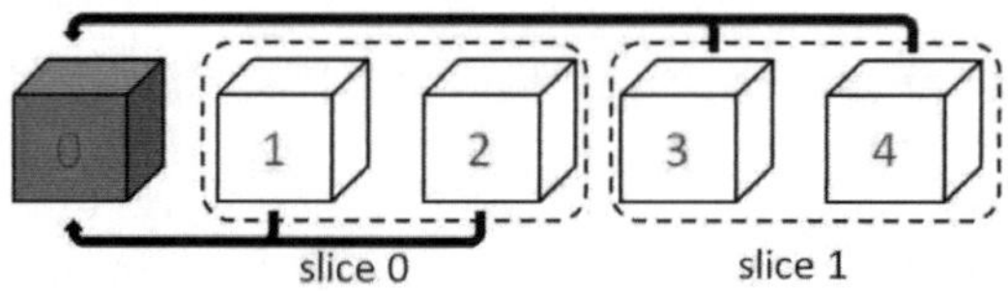

Figure 3. Temporal Parallel Analysis of Time-Varying Datasets

6. EXPERIMENT RESULTS

The data used in this paper are derived from a molecular dynamics simulation of neutron-irradiated Zr at 600 *K*. As Figure 4 shows, a system contains 1,485,000 atoms arranged in a hexagonal closed packed lattice replicated by 330×330×330 along all three dimensions is used. To prepare the test data with point defects, a displacement cascade is initiated by a 20 *keV* primary knocked atom. The simulation is conducted totally with 5720 time steps under NVT ensemble with periodic boundary conditions and output data every 10 time steps. A time interval of 0.5 *fs* and Embedded-Atom-Method potential is applied to describe interatomic interactions between atoms.

A sequence of snapshots of applying our visual analysis scheme to defect identification at different time steps is shown in Figure 5, showing how irradiated induced point defects develop with annealing. For simplicity, we have combined defect type property with thresholds to filter out normal atoms and only vacancies and interstitials are visualized. As Figure 5 shows, the number of displaced atoms shortly increases with time at the early stage of damage cascade, and arrives at the displacement spike after about 2000 time steps. Then the number of point defects is quickly annihilated by recombination between interstitials and vacancies, and parts of them tend to aggregate and form clusters. At the end of this defect clustering stage, after about 3000 steps equilibrated, the number of point defects seems to be stable and we can see these expressive clusters in Figure 6. The full process is called as primary radiation damage. In addition to visualization, obtaining statistics information about the defect cluster is also of interest to domain scientists, such as size, volume and shape. For example, Figure 7 illustrates the distribution of cluster size. The largest vacancy cluster contains 22 atoms and interstitial cluster 11 atoms. With the visual analysis results discussed here, we provide some very different kinds of analyses than traditional atomistic visualization and enable domain scientists to understand the evolution details of defects. Figure 8 shows that the proposed temporal parallel scheme obtains linear speedup and has excellent scalability to deal with big scientific data.

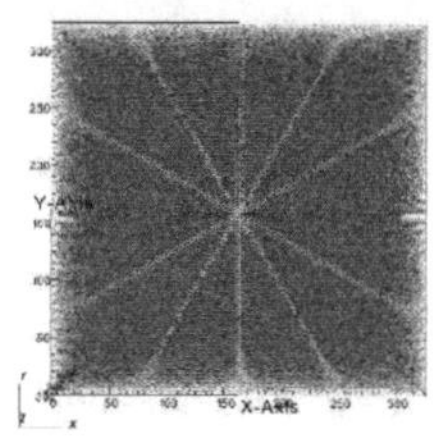

Figure 4. 3D Visualization of Atoms in the Simulation Cell

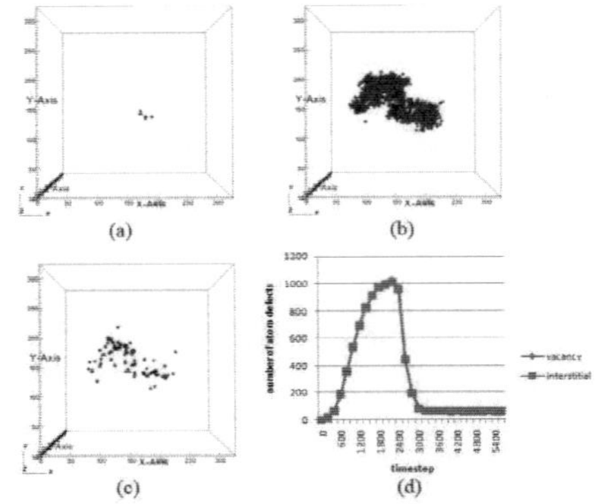

Figure 5. Snapshots of the positions of defects in the system. (a) timestep 100, (b) timestep 2000, (c) timestep 5000. The red indicates the vacancy atom and the blue interstitials. (d) temporal evolution of the number of defects

Figure 6. defect clusters in the system at timestep 5000. (left)vacancy clusters.(right) interstitial clusters

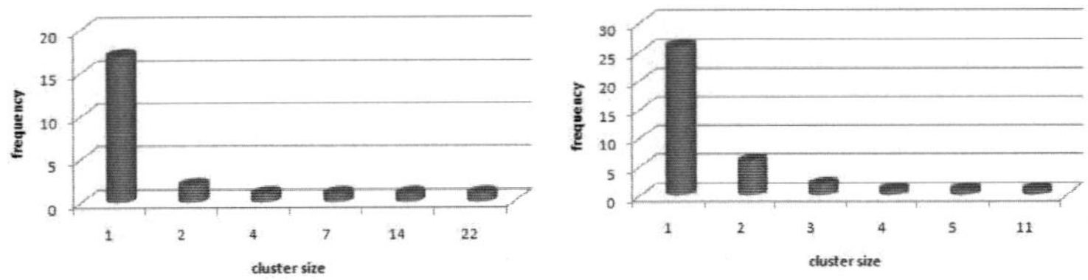

Figure 7. Distribution of cluster size of timestep 5000. (left) vacancy cluster size. (left) interstitial cluster size

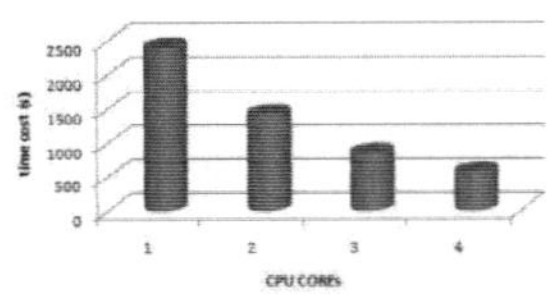

Figure 8. Performance of temporal parallel scheme

7. CONCLUSION

In this paper, we present an efficient visual analysis scheme for large-scale atomistic simulations of irradiation damage process. The proposed pipeline combines a set of algorithms to identify and label feature atoms, extract defect clusters, provide quantitative statistic and draw them in an expressive manner. We also present a temporal parallel strategy to accelerate the process. The results of our implementation, as demonstrated, are capable of providing insights into the evolution details of irradiation damage process and assisting domain scientists to investigate physical disciplines. In the future, we'll utilize graph-based representations and techniques to explore more details of defect evolution, such as cluster tracking, volume packing efficiency and lifetime measurement.

ACKNOWLEDGEMENT

This work was supported by National Natural Science Foundation of China (No.61403036), Science Challenge Project (No.TZ2016004) and National Key Research and Development Program of China (No.2016YFB0201200).

REFERENCES

Widanagamaachchi W. et al, 2015. Visualization and analysis of large-scale atomistic simulations of plasmasurface interactions. *Eurographics Conference on Visualization*. Cagliari, Sardinia，Italy. pp. 7-11.

Reda K. et al, 2013. Visualizing large-scale atomistic simulations in ultra-resolution immersive environments. *IEEE Symposium on Large Data Analysis and Visualization.* Atlanta, Georgia, USA, pp. 59–65.

Bhattarai D., Karki B. B., Stixrude L, 2006. Space-time multiresolution approach to atomistic visualization of mgo and $mgsio_3$ liquid data. *Visual Geosciences*, Vol. 11, No. 1, pp. 1–11.

Li J., 2005. *Atomistic visualization.* ed. S. Yip, Springer.

Stukowski A., 2012. Structure identification methods for atomistic simulations of crystalline materials. *Modelling and Simulation in Materials Science and Engineering*. Vol. 20, 045021.

Lummen N., Kraska T., 2007. Common neighbour analysis for binary atomic systems. *Modelling and Simulation in Materials Science and Engineering*, Vol. 15, pp. 319–334.

Stukowski A. et al, 2012. Automated identification and indexing of dislocations in crystal interfaces. *Modelling and Simulation in Materials Science and Engineering*, Vol. 20, 085007.

Medvedev N., 2002, Approach for the structure analysis of complex molecular systems at computer simulation. *Physica A: Statistical Mechanics and its Applications*, Vol. 314, pp. 678–685.

Keys A. S. et al, 2010. Charactering complex particle morphologies through shape matching: descriptors, applications, and algorithms. *Journal of Computational Physics*, Vol. 230, pp. 6438–6463.

Peterka T. et al, 2011. A study of parallel particle tracing for steady-state and time-varying flow fields. *IEEE International Conference on Parallel and Distributed Processing Symposium.* Anchorage, USA. pp. 580–591.

Agrawal N. M. et al, 2011. Mdanalysis: a toolkit for the analysis of molecular dynamics simulations. *Journal of Computational Chemistry*, Vol. 30, No. 10, pp. 2319–2327.

Peterka T. et al, 2014. High-performance computation of distributed-memory parallel 3d voronoi and Delaunay tessellation. *SC'14*. New Orleans, USA, pp. 16–21.

Okabe A. A. et al, 2000. *Spatial tessellations: concepts and applications of Voronoi diagrams*. John Wiley and Sons, Inc., New York.

Felfer P. et al, 2015. Detecting and extracting clusters in atom probe data: A simple, automated method using voronoi cells. *Ultramicroscopy*, Vol. 150, pp. 30–36.

Zhang S. L. et al, 2011. Voronoi structural evolution of bulk silicon upon melting. *Chinese Physical Letter*, Vol. 28, No. 6, pp. 067104.

Rycroft C. H., 2009. Voro++: A three-dimensional voronoi cell library in c++. *Chaos*, Vol. 19, No. 4, 041111.

Laakkonen J., Nieminen R. M., 1988. Computer simulation and identification of vacancies and interstitials in amorphous solids. *Journal of Physics C: Solid State Physics*, Vol. 21, pp. 3663–3685.

Cui Z. W. et al, 2009. The neighbor list algorithm for a parallelepiped box in molecular dynamics simulations. *Chinese Science Bulletin*, Vol. 54, No. 9, pp. 1463–1469.

Matin M. L. et al, 2003. Cell neighbor list method for planar elongational flow: rheology of a diatomic fluid. *Computer Physics Communication*, Vol. 151, No. 1, pp. 35–46.

CIRCUMPLEX SORT: A TWO-PHASE METHOD FOR REVEALING CIRCUMPLEX DATA PATTERNS IN REORDERABLE MATRICES

Miguel Mechi Naves Rocha, Pedro Kretikouski Roque Jr. and Celmar Guimarães da Silva
Software Engineering and Information Systems Laboratory, School of Technology, University of Campinas
R. Paschoal Marmo, 1888, Jd. Nova Itália, Limeira, SP, Brazil

ABSTRACT

Reorderable matrices are the basis of heatmaps and other tabular displays in which row and column permutations are possible. Matrix reordering algorithms try to provide a permuted version of these matrices, such that hidden patterns become visible for users. However, most of them fail on revealing Circumplex pattern, due to high execution time or to low quality of output matrix. In order to overcome this difficulty, we present a matrix reordering method (Circumplex Sort), whose goal is to permute a matrix in order to reveal a Circumplex pattern. In a first phase, our method reorders input matrix rows according to the index-weighted means of the values of each column. After that, the method creates and concatenates two stacks of rows based on a same initial row; for each row obtained according to the row order of the first phase, the method pushes this row at the stack whose top is most similar to it. Circumplex Sort runs the same two phases for columns. Our experiments with synthetic matrices revealed that our approach produces high-quality results (in terms of evaluation functions and runtime) when this pattern is hidden in data matrix. Besides, we present a real world dataset that exemplifies the use of Circumplex Sort for revealing Circumplex pattern.

KEYWORDS

Reorderable matrices, Circumplex data pattern, seriation, reordering algorithms, heatmap

1. INTRODUCTION

Information Visualization techniques help users to comprehend datasets in many ways, such as uncovering data patterns that are hidden due to inappropriate layout or data displacement. We may represent a dataset organized in rows (tuples) and columns (variables) as a heatmap by defining a background color for their cells according to their values. These colors may help users to understand a dataset, but is also necessary to consider if the current order of variables and tuples are useful for observing patterns that are present in the table, or if other orders could be more valuable for a visual analysis.

In this context, Bertin (2010) defined a reorderable matrix as a matrix that supports row and column permutations, such as a data table or a heatmap. One should pursue the goal of finding good permutations of a reorderable matrix, but the definition of what is a “good permutation” is also an open question. The works of Wilkinson (2005) and Behrisch et al. (2016) point out a set of data patterns that could be considered as goals for matrix reordering algorithms.

Another relevant issue is how to discover if some of these patterns are present at some appropriate permutation of a matrix. Using brute force is inconvenient due to the factorial nature of the problem space. Therefore, there are many alternative approaches based on heuristics, optimization, clustering, evolutionary computation, graph-theoretical techniques etc. that aim to provide good solutions (Behrisch et al., 2016)

In this paper, we deal with the task of uncovering a single pattern called Circumplex (Wilkinson, 2005). We propose an easy-to-implement algorithm for revealing this data pattern in matrices. It works in two phases: a first, global ordering, and a second, local similarity ordering that uses the previous ordering as input. We obtained an interesting cost-benefit algorithm in terms of time execution and quality of output matrix.

We organized the paper as follows. In Section 2, we detail Circumplex pattern and describe appropriate measures regarding the quality of permuted matrices. Section 3 summarizes related works on matrix reordering algorithms and highlights information about how they deal with Circumplex pattern. Section 4 presents our two-phase method. In Section 5, we discuss results of applying our method for reordering synthetic and real world matrices that have Circumplex patterns in some permutation. Section 6 concludes our paper and present future research directions.

2. THEORETICAL BACKGROUND

This section defines Circumplex pattern and presents some available measures for defining the quality of a matrix. We may present the Circumplex data pattern as a kind of "circular band" or a "band of a torus". If a Circumplex pattern is present, we may consider the list of rows (or columns) of a matrix as a circular list. The bigger the minor path between two rows (or columns) in this list, the bigger the difference of these rows (or columns). This implies that a distance-preserving bidimensional projection of these rows (or columns) assumes a circular format (Wilkinson, 2005). More formally, a Circumplex data pattern is a n × p matrix $X=\{x_{ij}\}$, where $x_{ij} = e^{-t^2}+u_{ij}$, $t=cos(\pi(s_j-r_i))$, $s_j=j/p$, $r_i=i/n$, and u_{ij} is a random error variable (Wilkinson et al., 2016). As Silva et al. (2016) does, we may consider u_{ij} as a salt-and-pepper noise. Figure 1 represents matrices that have Circumplex data pattern (Circumplex matrices) with distinct noise levels. We call *pre-Circumplex* a matrix to which at least one of its permutations reveals its Circumplex nature.

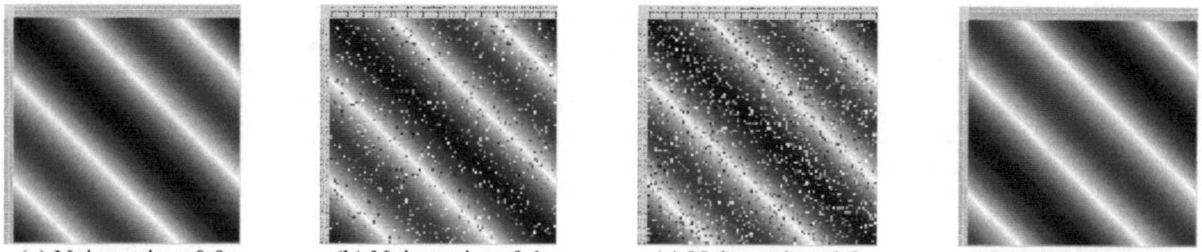

(a) Noise ratio = 0.0 (b) Noise ratio = 0.1 (c) Noise ratio = 0.2 (d) Noise ratio = 0.0

Figure 1. (a-c) 100x100 Circumplex matrices with noise ratios 0, 0.1 and 0.2. (d) The same matrix of (a), but flipped

In order to evaluate the quality of matrix permutations, one must use an evaluation function. This function analyzes the data matrix itself or its proximity data, *i.e.*, the row- and column-distance matrices. Anti-Robinson loss function (Wu et al., 2008) measures how many cells of a distance matrix disobey a monotonic decreasing of values from main diagonal to the matrix borders. Minimal Span loss function (Wu et al., 2008) is the sum of distances (*e.g.* Euclidean Distance) of pairs of adjacent rows (columns). Von Neumann and Moore stress functions (Niermann, 2005) consider the similarity of each matrix cell with its 4 or 8 neighbors, respectively. Given an input matrix *I* and a matrix *O* that a reordering algorithm returned as result, Wilkinson (2005) uses Spearman correlation to analyze if the row (or column) order of *O* is similar to the correspondent order in *I*. We could not found specific guidelines about which function is able to evaluate specifically the quality of a pre-Circumplex matrix, i.e., how close to a Circumplex matrix it is.

3. RELATED RESEARCH

This section briefly present matrix reordering approaches that we chose to use in this work due to empirical evidences that they could generate good quality outputs when reordering pre-Circumplex matrices. Readers interested on other reordering algorithms may read the survey of Belrisch et al. (2016) which is a relevant source of information about this.

One may map the problem of reordering the rows of a matrix to a Traveler Salesman Problem (TSP), if it maps rows to cities, and a measure of dissimilarity between rows as the distance between cities. The same is valid for columns. This is the approach of methods such as OREO (DiMaggio et al., 2008), TSPCluster (Climer and Zhang, 2004) and EM-ordering (Djuric and Vucetic, 2013). The last one uses a specific TSP solver to find permutations that minimize entropy in the matrix.

One may also apply classical clustering approaches to the reordering problem. Average linkage clustering constructs two dendrograms, one for rows and other for columns, according to its hierarchical agglomerative procedure. The resulting order of the dendrogram leaves defines the order of rows and columns at the output matrix. Silva et al. (2016) used it in comparisons with other matrix reordering methods. Bar Joseph et al. (2001) improves the ordering of dendrogram leaves, aiming to reach a better result.

Chen's work (Chen, 2002) presented some algorithms regarding the concept of elliptical seriation. We focus here at the "hierarchical divisive clustering tree with rank one splitting rule". He states that recursively calculating correlation matrices of previously calculated correlation matrices of a data matrix leads to a final correlation matrix (R^{∞}) with only values -1 and 1. R^{∞} enable the splitting of rows (or columns) of the data matrix in two groups. Chen defines that one may use this division for doing a hierarchical divisive clustering of matrix rows (or columns). As in previous clustering approach, the order of leaves in the created dendrograms are the order of rows and columns at the resulting matrix.

In the classification of Silva et al. (2016), the previous methods are proximity matrix reordering algorithms, given that work with distance matrices of rows and columns. It is also worth to cite a data matrix reordering algorithm (*i.e.*, one that does not use such matrices) called 2D-Sort (Mäkinen and Siirtola, 2000). It groups cells of higher values at the corners of the main diagonal of a matrix. It iteratively sorts rows of a matrix according to a row index-based weight mean of its cell values, and then sorts columns in a similar way. Its stop condition is to make an iteration in which initial and final matrix ordering are the same. We noted that 2D-Sort is not able to uncover Circumplex pattern, but its output inspired the first part of the approach we present at this paper.

4. CIRCUMPLEX SORT

We propose an algorithm called *Circumplex Sort*, which aims to permute pre-Circumplex matrices for revealing its Circumplex nature. It runs in two phases. In Phase 1, the algorithm permutes rows and columns of the input matrix, in order to group cells with higher values at the top left and bottom right corners of the matrix, and cells with lower values at the remaining corners. In pre-Circumplex matrices, this behavior creates at the same time a band of higher values parallel to the main diagonal, and a band of lower values parallel to the secondary diagonal (Figure 2, "Phase 1 Output"). The algorithm for doing this process is identical to one iteration of 2D-Sort. However, 2D-Sort runs many iterations until reach convergence, and we empirically observed that running only two iterations are sufficient for our goal with pre-Circumplex matrices.

Note that the resulting matrix of this phase seems to alternate two groups of similar rows. When we isolated both groups, we observed that their order was equal to the order they should have in a Circumplex pattern. Note this behavior in the first and second group of rows at Figure 2, in which the labels are in sequence. Therefore, we defined that the Phase 2 of our algorithm should split the rows in two groups according to similarity, and should obey the order of those rows inside their groups. After that, this phase should concatenate both groups (one flip is necessary in one group before this process). After doing the same steps also for columns, the output matrix should reveal a Circumplex pattern (bottom-right matrix of Figure 2). Our hypothesis is that when 2D-Sort finds a 1-dimensional order for the 2-dimensional circular structure, it flattens this circle. As a result, the nodes that compose this circle become interleaved, which justifies why we have to split them into two groups. Indeed, we recompose the circular order based on a starting node.

We define our complete algorithm as follow:

Circumplex Sort
Input: reorderable matrix M.
Step 1. M' = Phase_1 (Phase_1 (M));
Step 2. M''= Phase_2 (M');
Output: M''.

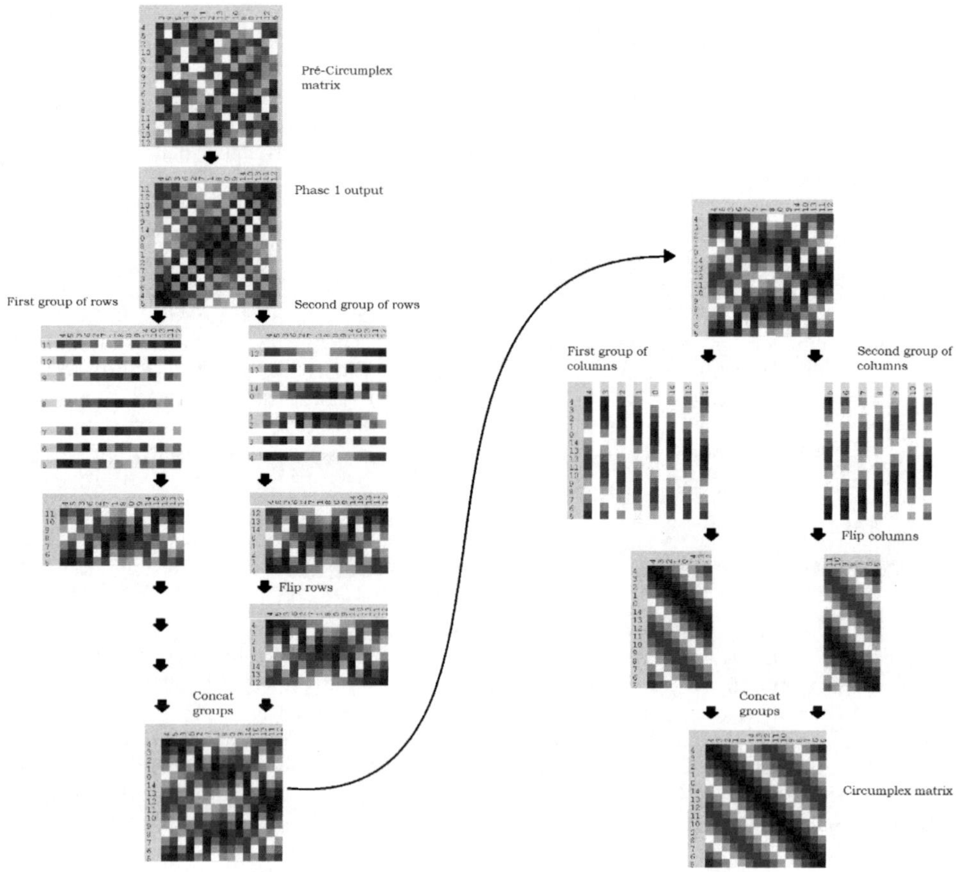

Figure 2. Steps of Circumplex Sort

Phase_1
Input: reorderable matrix M.
Step 1. Reorder the rows of M according to the index-weighted mean of the cell values of each row;
Step 2. Reorder the columns of M according to the index-weighted mean of the cell values of each column;
Output: M.

Phase_2
Input: reorderable matrix M.
Step 1. Define: M' = M,
row[] as the permutation vector of M',
row[0]=0 , *// the first row of M' is the same of M*
top1index = top2index = 0; *// indexes of tops of 2 stacks, one for each group of rows*
Step 2. For each row *r* of M (except row 0):
If *r* is more similar to the row at the *top of stack 1* than to the one at *top of stack 2*
top1index ++ ; row[top1index]=*r*; *// push r into stack 1*
else
top2index --; row[top1index]=*r*; *// push r into stack 2*
Step 3. Do the same for columns;
Output: M', ordered according to the calculated permutation vectors.

Observe that we defined our concatenation of groups in this algorithm as two stacks concatenated by a common initial node, each one representing a group of similar rows (or columns). Also, note that row and column vectors are circular vectors.

Figure 3 presents the results of reordering scrambled artificial-data pre-Circumplex matrices of distinct noise ratios with Circumplex Sort. Observe that the pattern is uncovered in most of them, sometimes with horizontal or vertical rotations.

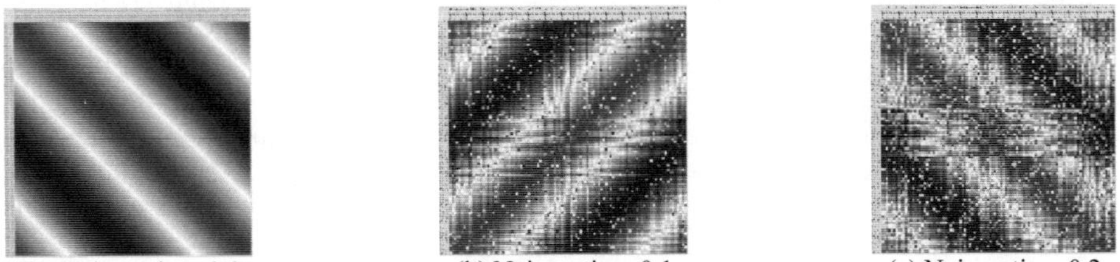

(a) Noise ratio = 0.0 (b) Noise ratio = 0.1 (c) Noise ratio = 0.2

Figure 3. Result of Circumplex Sort for reordering scrambled versions of Figure 1's matrices (a), (b) and (c)

5. RESULTS AND DISCUSSION

This section aims to compare Circumplex Sort against other reordering methods. First, we present a brief complexity analysis of the algorithm. After that, we discuss the results of an experiment for comparing output quality and execution time of a set of methods able to uncover Circumplex pattern, including Circumplex Sort. Finally yet importantly, we show the results of Circumplex Sort for reordering real-world data.

We opted for comparing four reordering methods to Circumplex Sort: EM-Ordering, Elliptical Seriation (more specifically, the hierarchical divisive clustering tree with rank one splitting rule), a TSP-based ordering method, and Average Linkage Clustering. Hereafter we will refer to them as EM, ES, TSP, and AVC for short, respectively. We chose those methods based on empirical observation of the results of a set of reordering algorithms implemented in a recent version of Matrix Reordering Analyzer (MRA) tool (Silva et al., 2014).

5.1 Complexity Analysis

In this section, we analyze the complexity of Circumplex Sort and some of its concurrent methods. This complexity analysis considers an $n \times n$ matrix as input for each method, without loss of generality.

The row-related part of Circumplex Sort Phase 1 calculates two times the weighted means of each row's cells ($O(n^2)$) and then sorts the rows according to these means ($O(n \log n)$). It does the same for columns. Therefore, Phase 1 is $O(n^2)$.

Phase 2 defines a new position for each of the n rows; this definition includes calculating the dissimilarity of two pairs of rows by iteration. We use Euclidean distance as dissimilarity function, whose calculation is $O(n)$. Therefore, Phase 2 is also $O(n^2)$. We conclude that the entire method is $O(n^2)$.

We observe the following aspects of time complexity of the other considered methods: (a) EM is $O(n \log n)$ (Djuric and Vucetic, 2013); (b) MRA implementation of AVC is $O(n^3)$ (Silva et al., 2016); (c) Chen (2002) does not define the time complexity of ES. ES is a recursive algorithm that splits a problem in two instances in the recursive case. However, Chen does not guarantee that the size of these instances is balanced. Therefore, in the worst case, we calculate ES time complexity as $O(n^4 t)$, where t represents the unknown behavior of ES iterative process of finding a convergence in one of its steps. (d) The documentation of Gurobi software, which we used for running TSP algorithm, does not specify the time complexity of TSP. Therefore, EM is faster than Circumplex Sort in the worst cases. The following section will show their behavior in distinct situations.

5.2 Experiment Definition

We designed an experiment for assessing the performance of Circumplex Sort and for comparing it to other reordering algorithms in terms of execution time and output quality. We analyzed the performance of reordering algorithms when applied to pre-Circumplex matrices. Our experiment is similar to that by Silva et al. (2014) and Silva et al. (2016), and we executed it through the MRA tool, in which we implemented Circumplex Sort. Our independent variables were as follows: (a) *Matrix size*. We used matrices of sizes 50×50, 100×100 and 200×200. We estimate that our results are extensible to matrices with intermediary sizes. (b) *Noise ratio*. We used 0.05, 0.1, 0.2 and 0.3 as noise ratios. We suppose that intermediary values would provide similar results.

Defining a quality measure directly related to uncovering Circumplex pattern was an interesting problem. First, similarity matrices of rows or columns of a Circumplex (not scrambled) matrix is also a Circumplex matrix. Therefore, we could use neither anti-Robinson nor minimal span loss functions in this case. Moore and von Neumann stress functions are also inappropriate because we discovered that a Circumplex matrix has a stress value higher than other possible pre-Circumplex versions of the same matrix.

We also observed that Wilkinson (2005) used as quality measure the mean of Spearman correlation between rows (and columns) indexes and their respective ranks in the output matrix. However, it is not sufficient for Circumplex matrices due to its circular/toroidal nature, *i.e.*, a row order vector [0,1,2,3,4,5] is an answer so good as [2,3,4,5,0,1] or [5,0,1,2,3,4]. Indeed, we need to consider row (and column) order vectors as circular vectors.

We overcome this situation by calculating Spearman correlation, as presented before, but for all possible order vectors extracted for the circular order vector. E.g., if the circular order vector is [2,3,0,1], we calculate Spearman correlation between the original indexes [0,1,2,3] and each vector of the set {[2,3,0,1],[3,0,1,2],[0,1,2,3],[1,2,3,0]}. After that, we return as result the maximum unsigned correlation value that we calculated. In other words, this measure, which we called *circular correlation*, indicates the best possible correlation between the rows (or columns) of an input matrix and their respective ranks in all possible shifted versions of rows (or columns) in the output matrix.

Our experiment also uses shuffling and noising procedures, in the same way as Silva et al. (2016) do.

The experiment procedure for each configuration tuple {matrix size, noise ratio, algorithm set} follows.

1. Create k matrices $\{M_1, \ldots, M_k\}$ with the pattern Circumplex, and with the defined matrix size and noise ratio.
2. Shuffle the rows and columns of these matrices.
3. For each matrix M_i, $1 \leq i \leq k$, do:
    a. Reorder M_i with each reordering algorithm from the algorithm set, and measure time spent by each of them.
    b. Measure circular correlation values of the columns and rows of reordered matrices.
4. Calculate mean circular correlation values for the results of the previous step for each algorithm, matrix size and noise ratio.
5. Calculate mean execution time for each algorithm.

We set k=50.

5.3 Experiment Results

Figure 4 presents Circular Correlation and execution time values for the analyzed matrices. We present only column correlations, but the results are similar for rows. We observe that TSP provides the best correlation for 50×50 and 100×100 matrices, followed by CS and EM. In addition, CS wins TSP in most situations of 200×200 matrices.

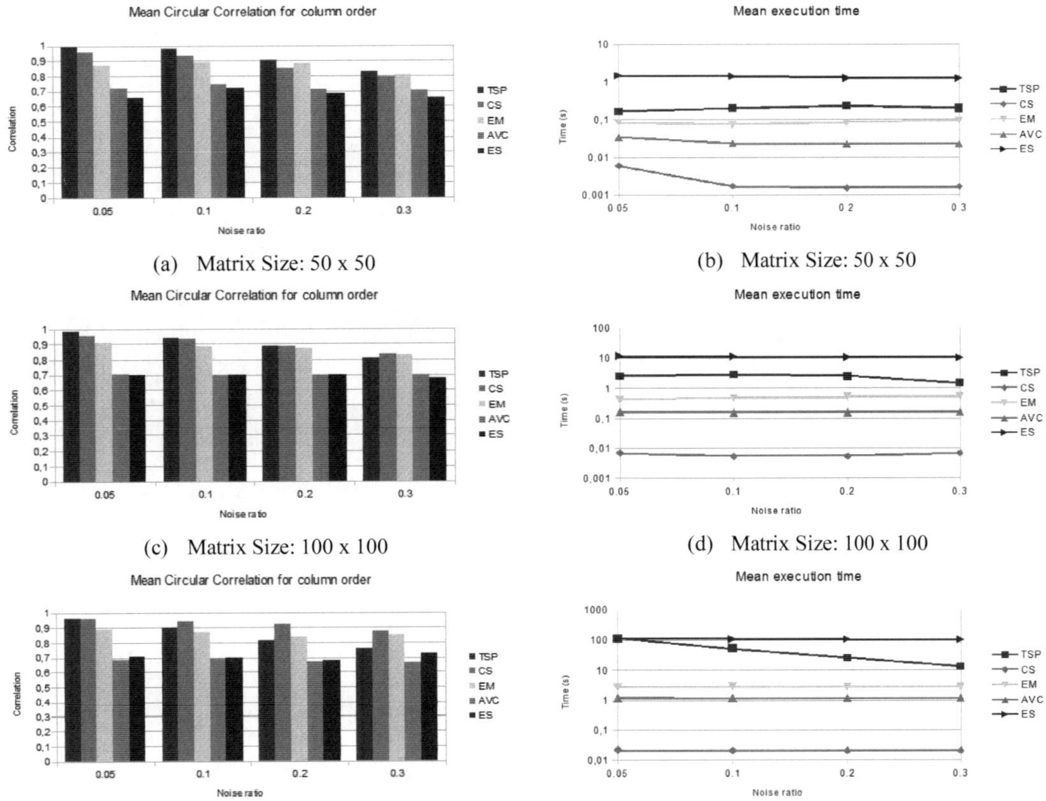

(a) Matrix Size: 50 x 50

(b) Matrix Size: 50 x 50

(c) Matrix Size: 100 x 100

(d) Matrix Size: 100 x 100

(e) Matrix Size: 200 x 200

(f) Matrix Size: 200 x 200

Figure 4. (a,c,e) Mean Circular Correlation for column order; (b,d,f) mean execution time

Execution time is the weakness of TSP: its mean execution time was around 1 s for 50 × 50 matrices, 10 s for 100 × 100 matrices, and varies between 10 and 100 s for 200 × 200 matrices. CS outperforms TSP (and all other tested methods) in all tested situations, with a mean execution time lower than 0.1 s (and in some situations lower than 0.01 s).

5.4 Real-world Example

We present, as a real world example, a Circumplex correlation matrix about mood. It correlates twelve items of a mood questionnaire administered to 472 persons (Browne, 1992). Figure 5 presents how Circumplex Sort ordered a scrambled version of it. It reveals, e.g., that relaxed, calm and placid status are very similar, but very different of gloomy, distress and nervous. Note that the Figure 5(c) differs from Figure 5(a) just because of rotations of the first row and the first column of the original matrix.

6. CONCLUSION

We presented our Circumplex Sort method as a fast ($O(n^2)$) method for reordering matrices without calculating distance matrices. It was able to reveal Circumplex patterns on pre-Circumplex matrices even with a noise level of 30%, and it was executed in much less time than other matrix reordering algorithms. Besides, we illustrated its use in a real-world example. Therefore, it is a competitive algorithm for cases when we know a priori that we have a pre-Circumplex matrix.

It is important to note that this algorithm is part of a set of algorithms under development in our research laboratory, which try to reveal a pattern that we already know that it is present (but not evident) in the dataset. We are also working on algorithms that are able to infer which pattern a data matrix hides, and we expect to use them in order to choose appropriate reordering algorithms for each input situation.

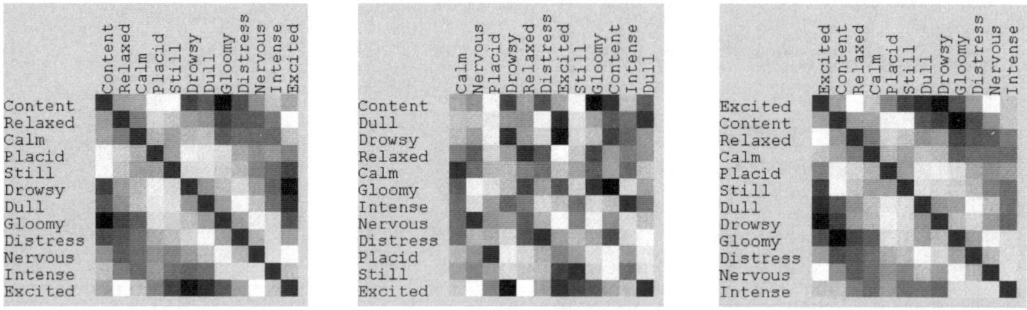

(a) (b) (c)

Figure 5. Correlation of a mood questionnaire: (a) original data; (b) scrambled version of (a); (c) version of (b) after Circumplex Sort

ACKNOWLEDGEMENTS

This work was supported by São Paulo Research Foundation (FAPESP) (grant number #2015/14854-7).

REFERENCES

Bar-Joseph, Z. et al., 2001. Fast optimal leaf ordering for hierarchical clustering. *Bioinform 17* ,Suppl 1: pp. S22–29.

Behrisch, B.B. et al., 2016. Matrix Reordering Methods for Table and Network Visualization. *Computer Graphics Forum 35*(3), pp. 693-716.

Bertin, J., 2010. *Semiology of graphics: Diagrams, networks, maps*. USA: Esri Press.

Browne, M.W., 1992. Circumplex Models for Correlation Matrices. *Psychometrika 57*(4), pp. 469-497.

Chen, C.H., 2002. Generalized association plots: Information visualization via iteratively generated correlation matrices. *Stat Sin 12*, pp. 7–29.

Climer, S. and Zhang, W, 2004. Take a walk and cluster genes: A TSP-based approach to optimal rearrangement clustering. In: *Proceedings of the 21th Int. Conf. on Machine Learning*, Banff, Alberta, Canada, pp.363–394.

DiMaggio, P.A. Jr. et al., 2008. Biclustering via optimal re-ordering of data matrices in systems biology: Rigorous methods and comparative studies. *BMC Bioinform*. 9: 458

Djuric, N. and Vucetic, S., 2013. Efficient visualization of largescale data tables through reordering and entropy minimization. In: *Proceedings of IEEE 13th Int. Conf. on Data Mining*, Dallas, Texas, pp.121–130.

Mäkinen, E. and Siirtola, H. Reordering the reorderable matrix as an algorithmic problem. In: Anderson, M. et al. (eds.), 2000. *Theory and application of diagrams*. New York, NY: Springer, pp.453–468.

Niermann, S., 2005. Optimizing the ordering of tables with evolutionary computation. *Am. Stat. 59*(1), pp. 41–46.

Silva. C.G. et al., 2014. PQR sort: using PQR trees for binary matrix reorganization. *Journal of the Brazilian Computer Society* 20:3, Springer.

Silva C.G. et al., 2016. A fast feature vector approach for revealing simplex and equi-correlation data patterns in reorderable matrices. *Information Visualization*, SAGE. (Pre-print online publication)

Wilkinson, L., 2005. *The Grammar of Graphics*. New York, NY: Springer Science & Business Media.

Wu, H.M. et al., 2008. Matrix visualization. In: Chen, C. et al. (eds.), *Handbook of data visualization*. New York, NY: Springer, pp. 681–708.

MUGDAD: MULTILEVEL GRAPH DRAWING ALGORITHM IN A DISTRIBUTED ARCHITECTURE

Antoine Hinge, Gaëlle Richer and David Auber
LaBRI, Université de Bordeaux, France

ABSTRACT

This paper presents a multiparadigm force-directed graph drawing algorithm with horizontal scalability on distributed storage clusters. Adaptations of the classical force-directed scheme that function on a distributed environment are presented. This distributed force-directed scheme is associated with a distributed-compatible multilevel approach for a more efficient graph drawing algorithm. MuGDAD is compared in terms of layout quality and speed with other algorithms.

KEYWORDS

Computational geometry, Graph drawing, Distributed computing, Apache Spark, Big Data

1. INTRODUCTION

The Internet provides massive datasets. In the case of social networks or maps, these data are stored on clusters in a distributed manner. Visualization is necessary to help analyze this newly available large amount of data and graphs are the tool of choice to represent networks. Very large graph drawing is needed in community management, for example, to help build a community or fight against harassment. It can also be used in cybersecurity to secure a network. In Big Data visualization, data stored on clusters must be processed there to avoid data transfer from the cluster to a dedicated computer or cluster. Such a transfer is impossible because of the data volume. Thus distributed graph drawing algorithm are needed.

This is the basis of recent graph drawing papers like Arleo (2015) or Hinge (2015). Both papers present an adaptation of force-directed algorithms on a distributed cluster, using Giraph (Avery 2011) and Apache Spark (Zaharia 2010) respectively. These approaches have refined with a multilevel scheme by Arleo et al. (2016). By using Giraph, a multilevel scheme is computed and the force-directed algorithm developed in 2015 is used at each level. This algorithm demonstrate the limitations of a purely force-directed approach, as a multilevel approach performs better with a reduced computation time. Following this approach, MuGDAD propose a distributed multilevel algorithm using Spark and the centroid-directed graph drawing algorithm developed by Hinge and Auber.

Force-directed graph drawing algorithms are a class of graph drawing algorithms based on a physical analogy to describe the interactions between nodes. The idea behind the physical model is to find its energy minimum which gives the position of each node in the graph layout (Eades 1984, Fruchterman 1991, Quinn 1979). Two forces are usually used to model the physical system: attractive forces between connected nodes and repulsive forces between all nodes. Force-directed graph drawing algorithms give aesthetically pleasing layouts but at the cost of high computational complexity. In Fruchterman and Reingold, for graph G=(V,E), the all-pair repulsive forces has $O(|V|^2)$ complexity. Force-directed algorithms usually run $O(|V|)$

iterations to converge to an acceptable layout. Stress minimization algorithms (Kamada 1989) define an energy function to minimize and use general optimization methods to find the energy minimum, which corresponds to the final layout.

Due to complexity, force-directed graph drawing algorithms do not scale well when used with a global repulsive force. Quigley and Eades (2001) and Hu (2005) chose to limit the repulsive force computation complexity by using quadtrees. Neighbouring vertices in the layout are stored recursively in a tree by dividing the layout space into equal parts and assigning nodes to the corresponding branches. The tree is then used to compute subtree-node repulsive forces, reducing complexity from $O(|V|^2)$ to $O(|V| \log |V|)$, the time needed to build the quadtree. Hachul and Jünger (2005) and Godiyal *et al.* (2009) limit the repulsive force computation complexity by using the Fast Multipole method. This method also divides the space into equal parts but the contribution of far-away nodes is computed with a multipole expansion. Using the potential field generated by nodes in their quadrants, an approximation of their effect can be computed for the other quadrants with an arbitrary precision. This also reduces complexity to $O(|V| \log |V|)$.

Many papers proposed techniques to reduce repulsive forces complexity but the $O(|V|)$ iterations needed to converge still remain too high for large graphs. To reduce algorithmic complexity, force-directed graph drawing algorithms can be associated with a multilevel scheme (Gajer 2001, Hachul 2005, Hu 2005). This technique creates a vertex filtration, selecting decreasing subsets of nodes. From this filtration, increasingly simple graphs are built and laid out successively using the layout obtained at the previous level as initial positions. This process reduces iterations needed to converge: the initial layout is already close to the energy minimum. It can be associated with an intelligent node placement (Gajer 2001) to further improve performances, placing missing nodes at a position close to their final position in the layout. Using this method, FM^3 (Hachul 2005) only computes a fixed number of iterations at each level instead of the $O(|V|)$ iterations usually needed. Thus the global complexity is $O(|V| \log |V| + |E|)$.

Parallel force-directed algorithms have also been developed to harness the power of the Graphical Processing Unit (GPU), which gives access to many parallel cores. Force-directed algorithms (Auber 2007, Sharma 2011, Yunis 2012) and multilevel force-directed algorithms (Frishman 2007, Godiyal 2009) have been developed, transforming how force-directed algorithms are usually processed. With the access to parallel cores, the computation times can be improved up to a thousand times on the GPU compared to performances on the CPU only (for example see results of Auber 2007). GPU force-directed algorithms, with their fast running time, contribute to the scalability of graph drawing. More recently, Mi et al. (2016) proposed a multilevel algorithm on the GPU using a clustering approach to draw graphs.

MuGDAD is a new multilevel distributed algorithm with an emphasis on distributed compatibility. It has horizontal scalability for distributed architectures. While scalable, the number of iterations needed to converge with algorithms like Arleo *et al.* or Hinge and Auber was too high. Multilevel algorithms were developed to limit the number of iterations, using an optimized initial layout for each level. With MuGDAD, we present a way to compute and use a multilevel decomposition in a distributed environment. This scheme is also compatible with the approximate repulsive forces described in Hinge (2015). Results from both our distributed and non-distributed versions are presented.

2. MUGDAD: DISTRIBUTED MULTILEVEL DRAWING

$G_0 = (V_0,E_0) \leftarrow$ Initial graph; $i \leftarrow 0$;	**Initialization**	
While($\lvert V_i\rvert > 3$)	**Filtration phase**	
$V_{i+1} \leftarrow$ Filtration(V_i)	*Maximal independent set*	*2.1.1*
$i \leftarrow i+1$		
Create graph $G_i = (V_i,E_i)$	*Edge & node collapse*	*2.1.2*
EndWhile		
For(j **from** i **to** 0)	**Layout phase**	
Compute layout of graph G_j (with few iterations)	*Centroid graph drawing*	*2.2*
Place nodes in G_{j-1} according to the layout of G_j	*Layout propagation*	*2.1.3*
EndFor		

Algorithm 1. General structure of the MuGDAD algorithm

Multilevel force-directed algorithms use recursive simplifications of the input graph and a force-directed approach to draw each graph. This is done in two steps: a filtration step to recursively simplify the input graph and a layout step where graphs are drawn iteratively with a force-directed algorithm. Starting with the smallest graph, layouts are computed until convergence. The final layout is used as the initial layout for the next step, adding missing nodes. Thus, initial layouts are close to the energy minimum and only a few iterations of the force-directed algorithm are needed to converge. This is summarized in Algorithm 1. In this section, the distributed multilevel filtration of MuGDAD is presented. Then, the force-directed model is described.

2.1 Distributed Multilevel Decomposition

In MuGDAD, the multilevel decomposition is done by computing a Maximal Independent Set (MIS). The neighbourhood of nodes selected this way is clustered and positions of nodes are propagated using an intelligent placement after the graph drawing algorithm has been applied. Thus, the decomposition is similar to FM^3 (Hachul 2005) but clusters are only formed at distance one around sun nodes.

2.1.1 Distributed Maximal Independent Set

In FM^3 (Hachul 2005), computing the multilevel decomposition is done using a sequential algorithm returning a MIS with a distance of at least three between sun nodes. Nodes are then clustered into solar systems with no overlap. Parallel algorithms of MIS filtration exist and can be directly transposed in a distributed paradigm.

Luby (1985) describes several parallel algorithms to find a MIS. Instead of choosing one vertex at a time from the set of remaining vertices, it uses a global ranking scheme (a permutation of the nodes) and select locally minimal vertices in regards to this ranking. This process is repeated until each node is either selected or is a neighbour to a selected node. Of the several variants presented in the paper (Luby 1985), MuGDAD implements the version with the lowest expected complexity of O(log |V|). This version generates more random numbers on average which is not a problem in our situation.

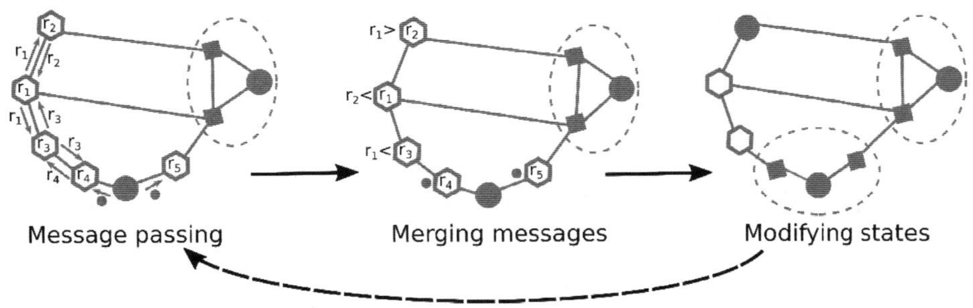

Figure 1. Pregel implementation of MIS and clustering algorithm. (*Left*) Messages are exchanged between unselected nodes. (*Right*) Messages received are merged. (*Bottom*) Nodes states are modified according to messages received

In MuGDAD, a Bulk Synchronous Parallel (BSP) model is used. This model defines supersteps during which tasks are executed for each node in the graph in parallel. Tasks include sending messages that will be read at the next superstep to another node, reading messages received from the previous superstep, as well as changing current node state.

To create clusters similar to the solar systems of FM^3, nodes track their state (unassigned, selected or clustered with a selected node) and the id of their cluster's sun node. In the message passing step, messages are exchanged between unselected nodes, containing the rank in the permutation of their neighbours. Selected nodes also send messages to their unselected neighbours. In the merging state, two cases are considered. Either the node has a selected neighbour and only this message is kept or it does not and the minimal rank of the unselected neighbours is computed. When modifying the node states, three cases can be considered. If a message has been received from a selected node and the node becomes clustered with a selected node. If not, if the reduced message rank is greater than its own rank it becomes selected. In the last case (message rank is lesser), the node does not change state. Then, new ranks are drawn and a new superstep begins.

2.1.2 Edge and Node Collapse Step

Clusters found in the previous step are collapsed into meta-nodes. New meta-edges are created between adjacent clusters. Weights of the meta-edges are computed. MuGDAD uses these weights in the layout phase as optimal edge length even though they do not reflect accurately the graph distance between nodes. These weights are also used to place yet unplaced nodes in the propagation phase, as described in next section.

In FM^3 (Hachul 2005), the weight of meta-edges is computed in two steps. First, the sum of weights of the shortest paths connecting solar systems is computed. Then, results are aggregated using a mean function. This proved to be inefficient in MuGDAD: the edge weight growth between levels is multiplied at each level by the mean graph distance between neighbour solar systems, due to the first step of the aggregation. In MuGDAD, this exponential growth is problematic because more levels are computed when computing a layout. Indeed, the MIS is done at distance two in MuGDAD instead of three in FM^3 which results in more levels being computed.

To avoid this exponential growth, the maximal edge weight of edges in the shortest path is taken. For the contribution of the other edges, a random value is drawn following a uniform law between one and the current level number. This heuristic ensures both a continuity of edge weight between levels (strictly increasing) and avoids the effect of an exponential growth.

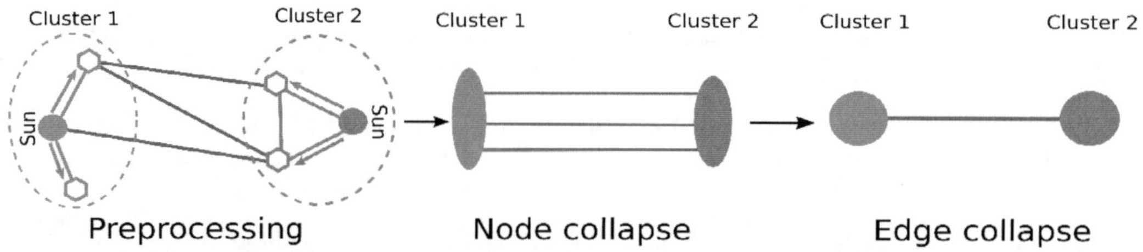

Figure 2. Edge collapse for two MuGDAD clusters. (*Left*) Pregel iteration: transmitting edge weights to set up map operation. (*Middle*) Map operation: creating meta-edges between clusters with total weight computation. (*Right*) Reduce operation: computing the mean weight of meta-edges between clusters

For our distributed implementation, we proceeded in three steps, see Figure 2. Let $G_i = (V_i,E_i)$ be the graph generated by our filtration at level i.

In the preprocessing step, the edge weight computation is set up. Information required to compute the edge weight is transmitted to planet nodes of clusters by sun nodes. Messages are sent along edges connecting sun and planet nodes of the clusters and contain the edge weight. These data are necessary to compute the weight of paths connecting clusters in the next step. This step is done using the Pregel functions implemented in GraphX. Up to $|E_i|$ messages are transmitted at level i of the filtration and that equality holds when there are no edges between clusters of the filtration.

The second step of this process is a map operation. This operation outputs meta-edges with endpoints set to the sun nodes of their respective cluster. Meta-edges are created by mapping edges connecting different clusters. There is up to $0.5\ |E_i|$ edges between clusters at level i and that equality holds when edges between clusters only connect planet and sun nodes in different clusters and no edges connect planet nodes inside the clusters. This can be proved by noticing that meta-edges connecting planet nodes represent three edges and that meta-edges connecting sun and planet nodes only represent two. This map operation is divided over several mappers, each processing part of the edges. Thus, total complexity of this step is divided by the number of mappers.

The last step is a reduce operation. Meta-edges duplicated between clusters are reduced into one with a mean function. The reduce operation is applied on the $O(|E_i|)$ meta-edges obtained at level i in the previous map operations. The mean total weight is computed in a distributed manner using the mean design pattern, as seen in Miner and Shook (2012) for example. This step is also distributed over several reducers.

2.1.3 Propagating the Layout

Once the layout of G_i is computed, positions of its nodes can be propagated to G_{i-1}. First, the position of sun nodes is propagated. Then, nodes not positioned (i.e. nodes in $V_{i-1} \backslash V_i$) are placed at the barycenter of placed nodes with desired edge length used as weight. If unplaced nodes are on several of these paths, their final position is at the barycenter of all computed positions. This process is explained with more details in FM^3 (Hachul 2005).

Nodes unplaced after this step are placed in a circle around their respective sun nodes. Indeed, these leftover nodes are not in the paths between solar systems and are not sun nodes.

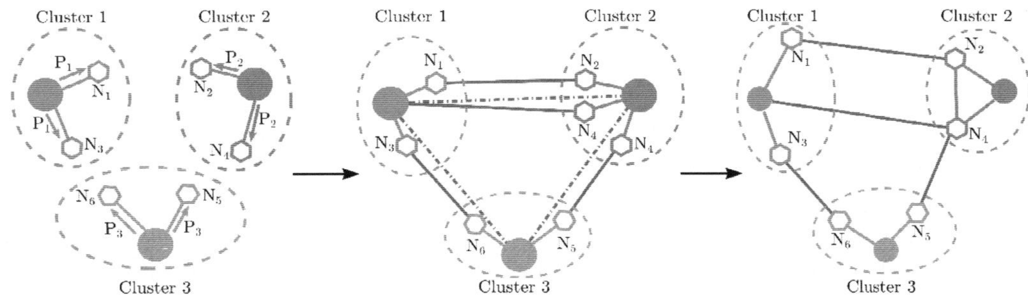

Figure 3. Propagating the layout for three MuGDAD clusters. *(Left)* Pregel iteration: transmitting sun node positions to set up map operation. *(Middle)* Map operation: positioning nodes on the segment connecting clusters. *(Right)* Reduce operation: computing the mean position of nodes

In distributed, propagating positions of sun nodes from graph G_i to graph G_{i-1} is done using a distributed join operation to match node positions between levels. Then, planet nodes are placed in three steps, see Figure 3. The three steps (preprocessing, map and reduce step) necessary to compute the initial placement of planet nodes are very similar to the ones necessary to compute meta-edges and their weight in the edge collapse step described in section 2.1.2. In the preprocessing step, messages are sent along edges connecting sun and planet nodes of the clusters to set up node positioning. They contain the edge weight connecting the two nodes as well as the position of the sun node. The map operation outputs nodes' positions for planet nodes. Nodes placed this way are created by mapping edges connecting two different clusters. Nodes' positions are computed using sun nodes' positions and the weight of the edges. With the reduce step, duplicated positions for planet nodes are reduced into one with a mean function, using a mean design pattern, see Miner and Shook (2012).

For nodes still unplaced, a single Pregel iteration is applied to send unplaced nodes the position of their respective sun node. Then, an angle is drawn at random for each of these nodes and they are placed at a constant radius around their sun node using this angle.

2.2 Distributed Force-Directed Graph Drawing

The initial layout is obtained by combining the layout of previous levels and the intelligent placement. Then, at each level of our graph filtration, a force-directed algorithm is applied to optimize the layout. In Fruchterman and Reingold (1991), two kind of forces are applied iteratively on each node to compute their displacement: attractive forces and repulsive forces.

Attractive forces, between adjacent nodes, can be computed directly in a distributed paradigm using edges of the graph, as shown in Hinge and Auber (2015) and Arleo *et al.* (2015). Regarding repulsive forces, Arleo *et al.* (2015) chose to limit their computation to nodes at graph distance k or less. This approach stems from the observation that in the final layout, nodes close to each other in the graph should also be close in the drawing. Hinge and Auber strike a compromise between locally optimal and globally optimal graph layout using centroids. Using node positions in the layout, clusters are formed and used to compute approximate repulsive forces. Far away nodes contribute as a cluster of nodes instead of contributing individually, generating $O(|V|)$ repulsive forces, instead of $O(|V|^2)$ for the all-pair repulsive forces computations.

For MuGDAD, we chose to implement centroid graph drawing. Our choice is motivated by the fact that this approach is compatible with the multilevel scheme, as explained in this section.

2.2.1 Centroid Graph Drawing and Multilevel Scheme

In Hinge and Auber, node clusters are computed using a process similar to k-means. K clusters are represented by centroids, whose positions are at the weighted position of all nodes in the cluster. Clusters are assigned every node closest to their centroid than any other centroid. Once nodes are assigned to a given cluster, the position of centroids are updated. Centroids are then used to compute approximate repulsive forces and the position of nodes is updated. This process is repeated each time the repulsive forces are computed. The advantage of using centroid graph drawing with a multilevel scheme is twofold.

First, centroid graph drawing is more efficient when the clusters are well defined. In their paper, Hinge and Auber start from a random layout to converge to the final layout. Clusters in the first steps of the force-directed method are not well defined which means that approximate repulsive forces are less accurate. In MuGDAD, the multilevel approach is combined with an intelligent placement and layouts at every level are already close to the final layout which improves the accuracy of centroid-repulsive forces greatly.

Secondly, centroids can be kept between levels to optimize repulsive forces. The clustering process of centroid graph drawing, which is similar to k-means, converges to a better solution with a good set of initial centroids. Algorithms like scalable k-means++ (Bahmani 2012) have shown that with a proper initialization the k-means algorithm converges to a better solution. Keeping centroids between levels ensures a good initialization to the k-means problem. Thus, resulting centroid-repulsive forces are more accurate.

2.2.2 Multi-Paradigm Graph Drawing

Computation in a distributed environment gives worst performances than a sequential algorithm when data is too small: the communication and synchronization overhead is way costlier than the gain obtained from the computation distribution and parallelism. Using a multilevel algorithm, the massive graph drawing problem is simplified until it can be processed on a single machine. At this point, computation is switched to this machine using the sequential algorithm.

MuGDAD is a good candidate as it functions similarly in a distributed and in a sequential environment. Using centroid graph drawing as our force-directed scheme in the two paradigms allows us to keep centroids between levels: when the computation is done in the sequential approach, the layout and clusters are transmitted to the distributed cluster that resumes computation where the sequential paradigm left it.

2.2.3 Adaptations to Centroid Graph Drawing

Minor changes are done to centroid graph drawing (Hinge 2015) to reflect edge weights. Edge weights represent theoretic distances between nodes in a multilevel scheme. Attractive forces are proportional to $d_{att} - d_0$ with d_{att} the distance between nodes and d_0 a nominal distance parameter set to the edge weight. Repulsive forces are multiplied by the average edge length in the level. This way, repulsive forces have as much impact as attractive forces.

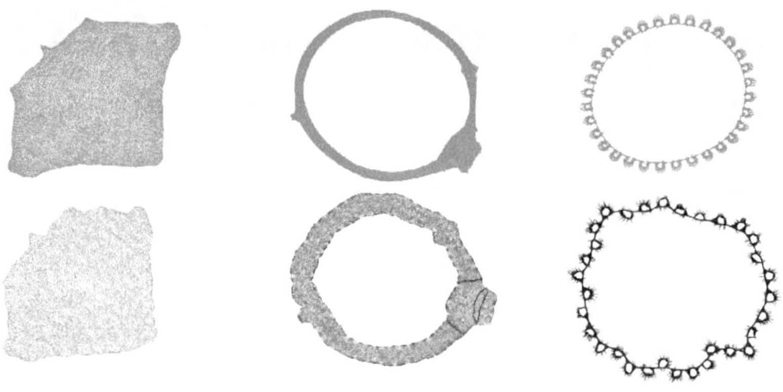

Figure 4. Layouts of crack (Left), fe_pwt (Middle) and finan512 (Right). (Top) Layouts obtained with FM3. (Bottom) Layouts obtained with MuGDAD

3. EXPERIMENTAL RESULTS

Table 1. Computation times (expressed in seconds)

Dataset	V	E	FM^3	MuGDAD	MuGDAD (Dist.)	MultiGila
crack	10,240	30,380	4.54	1.19	23.3	-
fe_pwt	36,463	144,794	15.69	2.77	54.2	-
finan512	74,752	261,120	36.97	12.93	133	-
Amazon0302	262,111	899,792	-	-	538	1577
ASIC_320	321,523	515,300	-	-	1124	1102
Com-DBLP	317,080	1,049,666	-	-	-	2366
Com-Amazon	334,863	925,872	-	-	4332	2242
Roadnet-PA	1,087,562	1,541,514	-	-	1129	2241

3.1 Implementation

MuGDAD has been implemented in two different versions: one developed to run sequentially in C++ and the other developed using Spark (Zaharia 2010). In Spark (Zaharia 2010), and more precisely in the graph library called GraphX (Xin 2013), an implementation of Pregel (Malewicz 2010) is available.

Furthermore, as described in section 2.2.2, the Spark implementation of MuGDAD relies on the C++ implementation to draw graphs too small to benefit from distribution. To do this, the Spark implementation relies on the Java Native Interface (JNI), allowing to run a native program through a Java interface.

3.2 Results

In Figure 4, layouts for FM^3 and MuGDAD are compared for three datasets (crack, fe_pwt and finan512). For crack and fe_pwt, MuGDAD layouts are comparable to the ones obtained with FM^3. Both the global structure and the lattice pattern are present. For finan512, the general structure is present in MuGDAD but the finer details of the structures are not clearly visible. More generally, the centroid repulsive force does not seem to be able to manage details at very fine scales.

Table 1 contains computation times for layouts shown in Figure 3. For the smaller graphs (upper part of Table 1), the CPU implementation of MuGDAD runs more quickly than FM^3, as can be expected since centroid graph drawing has a complexity of $O(|V|)$. The distributed version of MuGDAD performs relatively quickly considering that this data is too small to benefit from data distribution. This is due to the JNI implementation that computes the layout on a single machine.

For the larger graphs (lower part of Table 1), our implementation performs better than MultiGila for a series of graphs and significantly worse for some others. In the case of Com-DBLP, MuGDAD was stopped after 12h of computation. MultiGila uses a distributed clustering similar to the one in FM^3, a Maximal Independent Set at distance three. As a result, in some cases, our multilevel implementation takes many more levels than the one implemented in MultiGila. This is reflected on the computation times.

Algorithm comparison was conducted with a Core i7-4710HQ for the CPU algorithms. The implementation used for FM^3 is the OGDF implementation. Times from the MultiGila algorithm are taken from Arleo (2016). They are obtained on a cluster comparable to the one used for our results. Our distributed infrastructure is composed of 16 computers (non virtualized) with 64GB of RAM, 2x6 hyperthreaded cores at 2.1GHz and 2 hard drives of 1 TB each. Computers are linked by a 1Gb/sec network infrastructure.

4. CONCLUSION

MuGDAD is a distributed graph drawing algorithm that combines centroid repulsive forces with a multilevel scheme to draw distributed graphs efficiently. The scalability is proved in a distributed environment. Experimental results show that layouts are obtained quickly compared with methods like FM^3 but fewer details can be seen, due to the use of a distributed-compatible approximate repulsive force.

ACKNOWLEDGEMENT

This work has been carried out as part of "REQUEST" project supported by the French "Investissement d'Avenir" Program (Big Data - Cloud Computing topic - PIA O18062-645401).

REFERENCES

Arleo A. et al, 2015. A million edge drawing for a fistful of dollars. *In Graph Drawing and Network Visualization*, pp 44-51.

Arleo, A. et al., 2016. A Distributed Multilevel Force-Directed Algorithm. *International Symposium on Graph Drawing and Network Visualization,* pp 3-17.

Auber D. and Chriricota Y., 2007. Improved efficiency of spring embedders: Taking advantage of gpu programming. *In Visualization, Imaging, and Image Processing*, Vol. 2007, pp 169-175.

Avery C., 2011. Giraph: Large-scale graph processing infrastructure on hadoop. *Proceedings of the Hadoop Summit.*

Bahmani B. et al., 2012. Scalable k-means++. *Proceedings of the VLDB Endowment*, Vol. 5, No 7, pp 622-633.

Peter Eades, 1984. A heuristic for graph drawing. *Congressus numerantium*, Vol. 42, pp 146-160.

Frishman Y. and Tal A., 2007. Multi-level graph layout on the GPU. *Visualization and Computer Graphics, IEEE Transactions on*, Vol. 13, No.6, pp 1310-1319.

Fruchterman T. and Reingold M, 1991. Graph drawing by force-directed placement. *Softw., Pract. Exper.*, Vol. 21, No. 11, pp 1129-1164.

Gajer P. and Kobourov S., 2001. Grip: Graph drawing with intelligent placement. *In Graph Drawing*, pp 222-228. Springer.

Godiyal A. et al., 2009. Rapid multipole graph drawing on the GPU. *In Graph Drawing* , pp 90-101. Springer.

Hachul S. and Jünger M., 2005. Drawing large graphs with a potential-field-based multilevel algorithm. *In Graph Drawing*, pp 285-295. Springer.

Hinge A. and Auber D., 2015. Distributed graph layout with Spark. *In Information Visualisation (iV), 2015 19th International Conference on*, pages 271-276.

Hu Y., 2005. Efficient, high-quality force-directed graph drawing. *Mathematica Journal*, Vol. 10, No.1, pp 37-71.

Kamada T. and Kawai S., 1989. An algorithm for drawing general undirected graphs. *Information processing letters*, Vol. 31, No 1, pp 7-15.

Luby M., 1985. A simple parallel algorithm for the maximal independent set problem. *In Proceedings of the seventeenth annual ACM symposium on Theory of computing*, pp 1-10. ACM.

Malewicz G. et al., 2010. Pregel: a system for large-scale graph processing. I*n Proceedings of the 2010 ACM SIGMOD International Conference on Management of data*, pp 135-146. ACM.

Mi, P. et al., 2016. Interactive Graph Layout of a Million Nodes. *Informatics*, Vol. 3, No. 4, p 23.

Miner, D. and Shook, A, 2012. MapReduce Design Patterns: Building Effective Algorithms and Analytics for Hadoop and Other Systems. O'Reilly Media, Inc.

Quigley A. and Eades P, 2001. Fade: Graph drawing, clustering, and visual abstraction. *In Graph Drawing*, pp 197-210. Springer.

Quinn N. et al., 1979. A forced directed component placement procedure for printed circuit boards. *Circuits and Systems, IEEE Transactions on*, Vol. 26, No. 6, pp 377-388.

Sharma P. et al., 2011. Speeding up network layout and centrality measures for social computing goals. *In Social Computing, Behavioral-Cultural Modeling and Prediction*, pp 244-251. Springer.

Xin R. et al., 2013. Graphx: A resilient distributed graph system on spark. *In First International Workshop on Graph Data Management Experiences and Systems* , page 2. ACM.

Yunis E. et al., 2012. Scalable force directed graph layout algorithms using fast multipole methods. *In Parallel and Distributed Computing (ISPDC), 2012 11th International Symposium on*, pp 180-187. IEEE.

Zaharia M. et al., 2010. Spark: cluster computing with working sets. *In Proceedings of the 2nd USENIX conference on Hot topics in cloud computing*, Vol 10, p 10.

AN EFFICIENT SURFACE CLIPPING MODEL FOR VOLUMETRIC DATA

Fukun Wu[1,2], Zeyao Mo[2] and Xianfeng Bao[1,2]
[1]*Institute Of Applied Physics and Computational Mathematics, Beijing, China*
[2]*Software Center for High Performance Numerical Simulation, China Academy Of Engineering Physics, Beijing, China*

ABSTRACT

To address the realistic problem of visualizing the surface field of objects with complex geometry in volumetric datasets, we present and implement an efficient surface clipping method for visualizing significant field data on arbitrary object surface. This method first applies the surface-volume intersection equation to clip the volumetric data and transforms volume cells of the dataset to 2D plane. Then, a clipping algorithm for concave and convex polygons with several optimizations is specifically designed to accurately solve intersection polygon and its corresponding field value. Finally, this method is integrated into a visualization software to enhance the visualizing capability. The experimental results demonstrate that our method can efficiently and accurately achieve the surface clipping operation of complex geometry from volumetric datasets.

KEYWORDS

Surface clipping method, surface-volume intersection, polygon clipping

1. INTRODUCTION

In visualization, operators such as slicing, decimation and subdivision are main visualizing technologies, which enhance our deeper understanding of the underlying massive data. However, to acquire the full-surface characteristics of a given geometry, while ensuring the accuracy and performance as much as possible, is a challenging but significant technique. Existing visualization tools such as VTK, VisIt (VisIt 2005), ParaView (Squillacote 2007), and VisTrails (Bavoil et al. 2005) do not provide appropriate solutions for the accurate clipping based on the surface of complex geometry from volumetric data. For instance, VisIt applies the underlying VTK implicit function to perform surface extraction operation of regular objects such as planes, spheres, cones and cylinders, but lacks the ability to extract surface information based on irregular or more complex geometry such as aircraft from volumetric data.

The key of the surface clipping operation involves the polygon clipping which reconstructs the new data structure with the corresponding field variables by clipping the volumetric dataset. The polygon clipping is also a fundamental problem in computational geometry and computer graphics, and two representative clipping methods have been proposed (Sutherland and Hodgeman 1974, Liang and Barsky 1984). However, Sutherland and Hodgeman's algorithm (Sutherland and Hodgeman 1974} was limited to convex polygons, and Liang and Barsky (Liang and Barsky 1984) required that the clip polygon be rectangular. Some general algorithms are designed for the general case of arbitrary polygons. These clipping algorithms require an appropriate data structure to store the intersection points. For instance, Weiler (Weiler and Atherton 1977) combined the input polygons into a single graph structure. Greiner (Greiner and Hormann 1998) represented all polygons as doubly linked lists where each intersection point would be inserted into two-way linked lists of subject polygon and clipping polygon. Compared with Weiler's method, it reduces the complexity of data structure. As an extension, Liu et al. (Liu et al. 2003) adopted a single linked list to represent all polygons to further improve efficiency. However, these methods cannot be directly applied to clip large-scale volumetric data.

This paper presents an efficient surface clipping algorithm to accurately clip volumetric data based on the complex geometry structure. The algorithm firstly transforms volume cells into 2D plane domain according to the plane-volume intersection equations, then constructs an intersection method based on line clipping for general polygons, and specifically optimizes the calculation of intersection polygon where inefficient polygons are directly deleted. Here, the clipped polygons are associated with original variable properties of volumetric dataset in order to achieve high-precision extraction operation of field data. Finally, it is integrated into a visual analysis software for large-scale and time-varying datasets to demonstrate the efficiency and accuracy of the proposed method.

2. SURFACE CLIPPING MODEL

2.1 Plane-Volume Intersection

In the proposed clipping model, we assume that the clipping geometry is composed of linear polygon cells where the curved sides are ignored, and 3D data field is composed of linear volume cells such as voxel, tetrahedron and hexahedron. Take cube volume cells as example as shown in Figure 1, where a plane arbitrarily selected from the clipping geometry is used for cutting cubes to gain a complete 2D plane field.

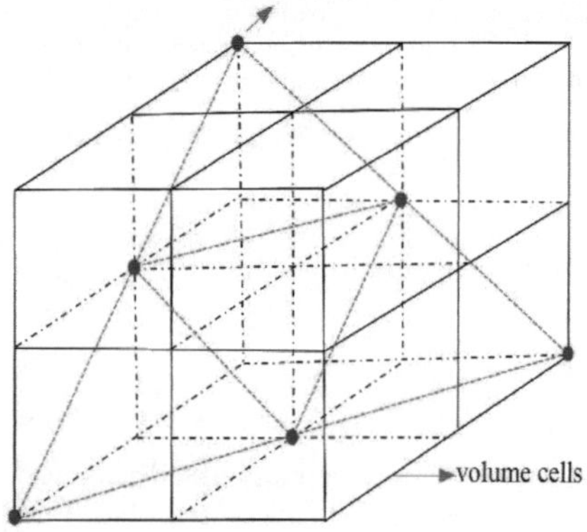

Figure 1. Intersection modeling of clipping plane and volume cells where red points denote the intersection points of clipping plane and sides of volume cells

Here, it is necessary to iteratively compute the intersection points of each edge of cube and the clipping plane in order to generate a new clipped polygon denoted by red points. Consider a straight line L, given by

$$x = a + n_1 * t$$
$$y = b + n_2 * t \qquad (1)$$
$$z = c + n_3 * t$$

where the point (a,b,c) is on the straight line L, the vector (n_1,n_2,n_3) denotes the direction of L and t is a parameter.

The clipping plane is represented by

$$A(x-x_i)+B(y-y_i)+C(z-z_i)=0 \qquad (2)$$

where (A,B,C) denotes the normal of the clipping plane and the point (x_i,y_i,z_i) is some point on the plane.

Substituting Equation (1) into Equation (2), we can gain the parameter t, written as

$$t=((x_i-a)*A+(y_i-b)*B+(z_i-c)*C)/(A*n_1+B*n_2+C*n_3) \qquad (3)$$

where $(A*n_1+B*n_2+C*n_3)!=0$ means that the edge L will intersect with the clipping plane. The rest of the intersection points of edges and clipping plane can be similarly calculated. However, there is a special case where a side of cube is inside the clipping plane. For this case, the points of intersection are considered to be the two end points of the side, and if the number of all intersection points of cube and clipping plane is less than 3, these points are ignored. For a large scale volume dataset, we can iterate the calculation of the plane-volume equations to generate all intersection polygons.

2.2 Polygon Clipping

By applying plane-volume intersection equations, the surface clipping operation for 3D field can be transformed to 2D polygon clipping operation. Figure 2 shows the intersection relationship between polygon $Poly_{\text{plane}}$ cutted from volume cells and clipping polygon $Poly_{\text{clipping}}$. Our goal is to accurately compute all plane polygons intersecting with $Poly_{\text{clipping}}$ and construct new polygon dataset whose values are determined by original data field.

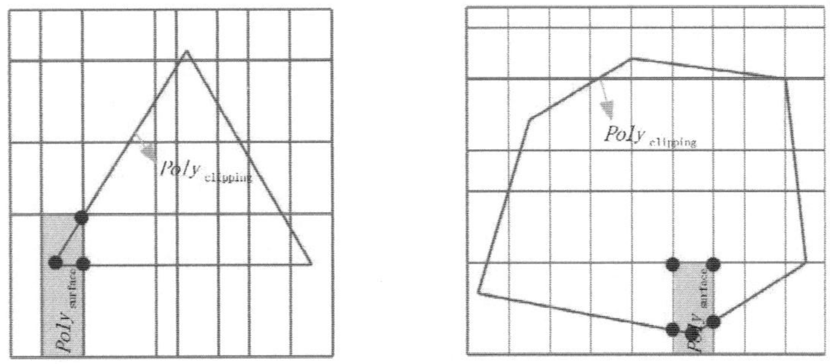

Figure 2. Intersection modeling of clipping polygon Polyclipping and plane polygon Polyplane

2.2.1 Pruning Strategy

It is necessary to generate new intersection polygons denoted by red points in Figure 2. However, because of the large number of polygons in the planar field, it takes a lot of time to accurately calculate the clipped polygons. It can be observed from Figure 2 that there are only three kinds of relations between the plane polygon $Poly_{\text{plane}}$ and the clipping polygon $Poly_{\text{clipping}}$, which are either intersected, included or far away.

In this paper, we first adopt the pruning strategy to return polygons included in clipping polygon according to the inclusion criteria of points in polygon. Given a point *P* and a polygon *S*, and ray casting method is applied to determine whether the point *P* is in the polygon. Since the polygon is bounded, one end of the ray L must be outside the polygon. Here, we trace ray from point *P* and compute its intersection points with the polygon. For general cases, if the number of points of intersection is odd, the point *P* is inside the polygon.

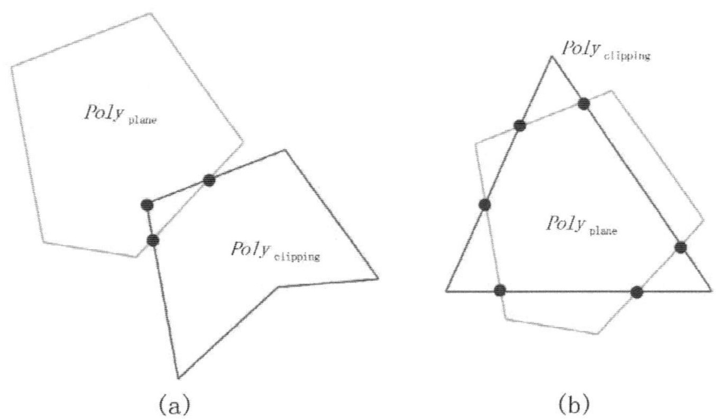

Figure 3. Two special cases of pruning strategy for the intersection determination of $Poly_{\text{plane}}$ and $Poly_{\text{clipping}}$

However, there is a special case to deal with as shown in Figure 3 where all vertices of the polygon $Poly_{\text{plane}}$ are outside the polygon $Poly_{\text{clipping}}$, but $Poly_{\text{plane}}$ actually intersects with $Poly_{\text{clipping}}$. For Figure 3(a), we only need check whether each vertex in $Poly_{\text{clipping}}$ is inside $Poly_{\text{plane}}$ to determine the intersection. For Figure 3(b), our pruning strategy is inefficient. If there actually exists this case, we set the metric as the maximum diameter of two polygons. If the distance between vertices of $Poly_{\text{plane}}$ and $Poly_{\text{clipping}}$ is larger than the metric, they will not intersect with each other.

2.2.2 Polygon Intersection

For the polygon $Poly_{\mathrm{plane}}$ that intersects with the clipping polygon $Poly_{\mathrm{clipping}}$, this paper proposes an efficient method based on line clipping to calculate the intersection polygon. As is known that the polygon is composed of line segments, the key of calculating intersection polygon is to judge and calculate the intersection of line segments. The general practice is to gain the points of intersection by solving linear equations and determining whether the point is on the line segment. However, it takes more time to directly solving linear equations. Because it has calculated the equations before it can determine whether the intersection point of two line segments is valid. If the calculated point is invalid, the whole calculation process is also invalid. It is a general practice to first determine whether there exists a valid intersection point, and then calculate it.

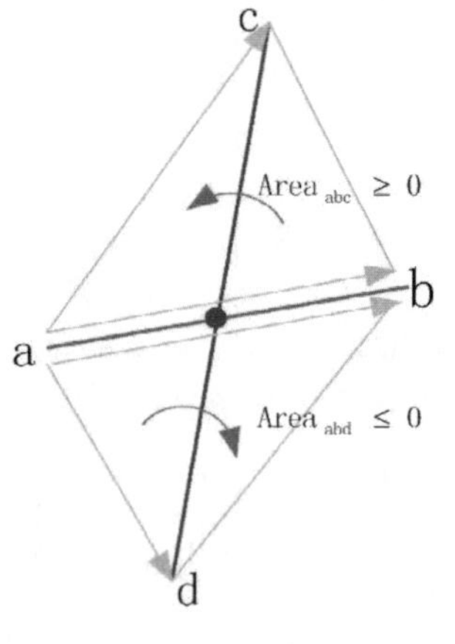

Figure 4. The intersection determination of line segments by signed areas of triangles

Given two line segments ab and cd as illustrated in Figure 4. If the two endpoints of each line segment are on both sides of the other line segment, they will intersect. Here, we determine the relationship between points and line segments by triangle area Equation 4.

$$\begin{aligned} Area_{\mathrm{abc}} &= \frac{1}{2}((b.x-a.x)*(c.y-a.y)-(b.y-a.y)*(c.x-a.x)) \\ Area_{\mathrm{abd}} &= \frac{1}{2}((b.x-a.x)*(d.y-a.y)-(b.y-a.y)*(d.x-a.x)) \end{aligned} \tag{4}$$

where $Area_{\mathrm{abc}}$ and $Area_{\mathrm{abd}}$ are the determinants that give the signed areas of triangles. For the triangle abc, three points are a counter-clockwise turn if $Area_{\mathrm{abc}}$, clockwise if $Area_{\mathrm{abc}}$, and collinear if $Area_{\mathrm{abc}}$. This is the same for the triangle abd.

So we can only judge the positive and negative signs of the areas. For example, if the signs of two triangle areas are opposite, point c and point d are located on both sides of line segment ab. Similarly we determine the signs of triangle cda and triangle cdb. Only if (sign(abc) $\cdot$ sign(abd) ≤ 0) and (sign(cda) $\cdot$ sign(cdb) ≤ 0) can two line segments intersect. After it is determined that two line segments intersect, the intersection point can be solved by the plane geometry method or the point oblique equation. However, it is cumbersome to solve the special case that the slope is 0 for the point oblique equation. Therefore, the first one is used to solve the intersection.

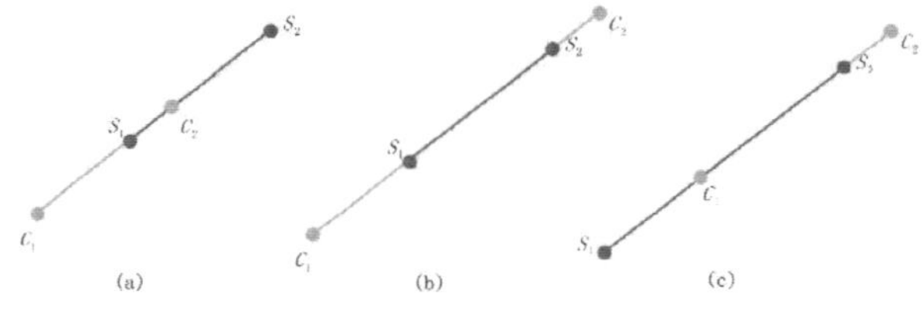

Figure 5. Geometric modeling of two line segments being collinear

Figure 5 shows some special cases of two line segments being collinear. The intersection points are set to S_1C_2, S_1S_2 and C_1S_2. At the same time, it is necessary to exchange the clipping polygon with the plane polygon to determine the rest of the common set of line segments in the same way. All the common line segments are sorted to construct the clipped polygon where the second point of the previous line segment points to the first point of the following line segment.

3. SIMULATION

We implemented our surface extraction model by creating a new operation plugin in our visualization system Teravap (Teravap 2015). We also demonstrated its validity by applying our method to two representative datasets for visualizing the surface field of objects with regular and irregular geometry. All of the images in this work were produced on a Dell T7600 workstation with a 2.40 GHz Intel Xeon CPU E5-2609.

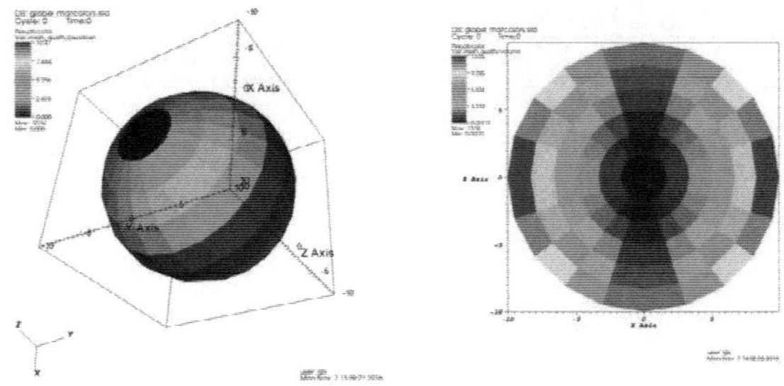

Figure 7. Visualization results of volume dataset clipped by a plane

We apply the cone with 7 faces, sphere with 56 faces, cylinder with 8 faces and cube of 6 faces to clip of interest field values from volume data corresponding to Figure 7(a) as illustrated in Figure 8. Referring to the results, although the inner values of volume data are completely hidden, our clipped results can still be demonstrated to be accurate by comparing with each other.

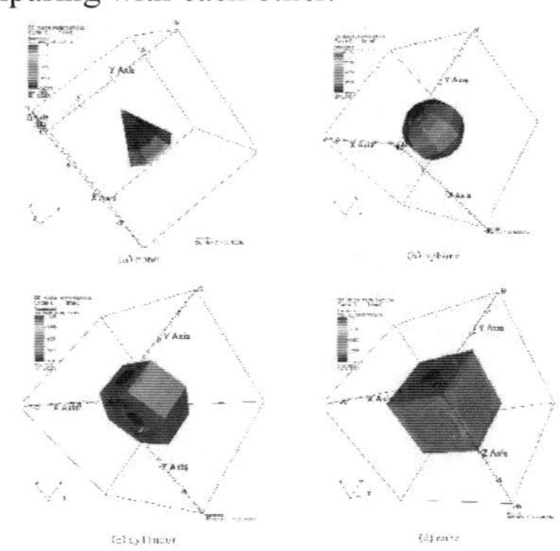

Figure 8. Clipped results of volume dataset using cone, sphere, cylinder and cube respectively

However, the above clipping models are very simple. In practical engineering field, it is very significant to generate insightful visualization results by extracting the full-surface characteristics of aircraft. For example, in electromagnetism field, the visualization results can help engineers to better understand environmental effects.

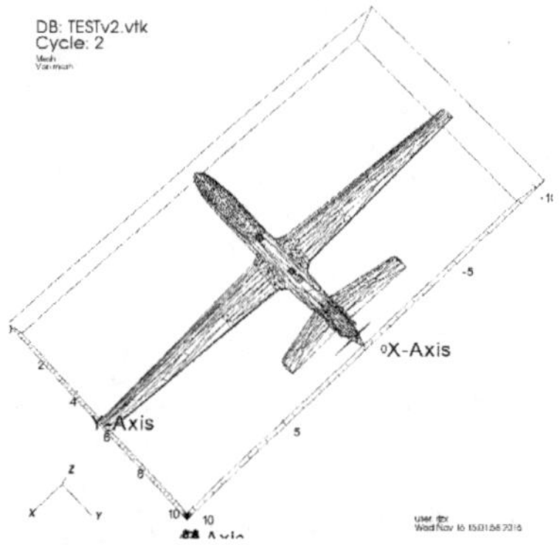

Figure 9. Geometry of aircraft used for clipping operation

Figure 9 shows a representative aircraft model that consists of 1917 points and 3737 polygons where the body part of interest has more levels of subdivision.

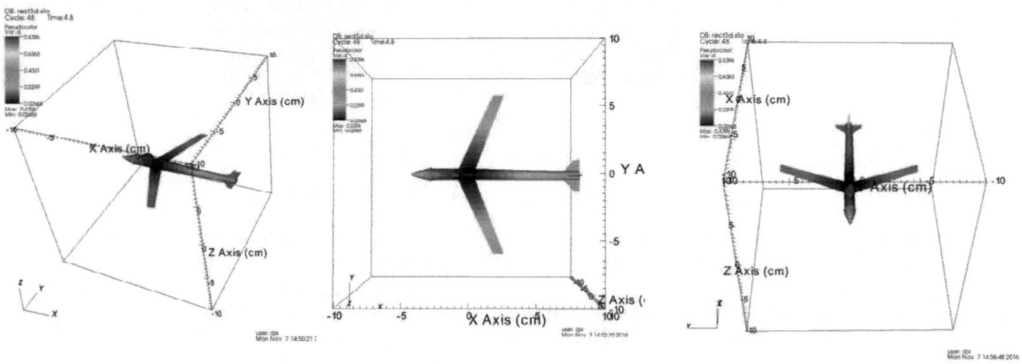

Figure 10. Visualization results of extracting field values using aircraft geometry under different viewpoints

Figure 10 shows the clipped results of aircraft under different viewpoints using the surface clipping model presented in this paper where field values of volume dataset are accurately maintained. In addition, the proposed extraction model supports the remote operation, i.e., the massive computing required for the clipping is performed on a remote server node, and users are able to analyze the results interactively on the local client node under MB-scale datasets.

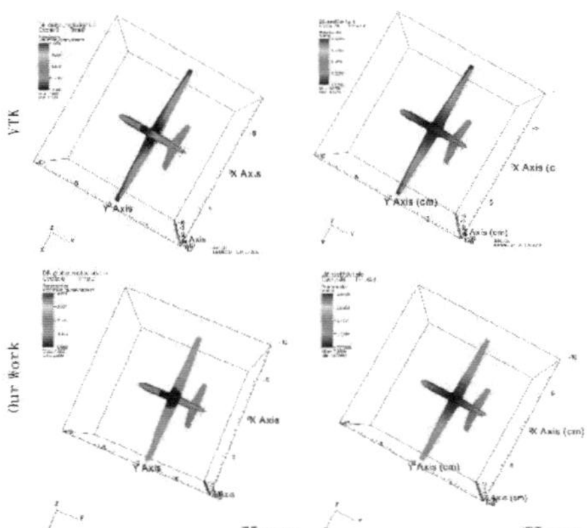

Figure 11. Comparison of clipping volumetric data using VTK (top row) and ours (bottom row)

Figure 11 shows comparisons of clipped results using VTK and our method. VTK samples data values by vtkProbeFilter that computes point attributes (e.g., scalars, vectors, etc.) at specified point positions. Because the point attributes are computed at the point positions of geometry by interpolating into the volumetric data, VTK's probing function cannot achieve accurate clipping operation of complex geometry where the relative structures of volume cells are abandoned. As showed in Figure 11, our method is demonstrated to maintain the original relative structures of volume cells and gain accurate field values by directly cutting volume cells.

4. CONCLUSION

In this paper, an efficient surface clipping method for regular and irregular geometry is constructed. This method applies the plane-volume equation to transform volume dataset to plane field. Then an efficient clipping algorithm for convex and concave polygons is proposed to calculate intersected polygons where common line segments are selected. Compared with the existing visualization toolkits such as VisIt and VTK, our model can accurately extract surface field values of geometry, not subjected to appearance of geometry and size of data set.

In the following work, we focus on improving the clipping performance by means of load-balancing strategies for rendering. In addition, considering the complexity of our extraction model, the level-of-detail method can be applied to substantially simplify the clipping operation by constructing multi-resolution surface geometry.

REFERENCES

Bao et al., 2013. Research on the Polygon Intersection Algorithm Based on Line Operation. *Bulletin of Surveying and Mapping*, Vol. 5,pp. 35-37.

Bavoil L. et al, 2005. VisTrails: enabling interactive multiple view visualizations. *Proceedings of IEEE visualization*, pp. 135-142.

Cyrus M. and Beck J., 1978. Generalized two- and three-dimensional clipping. *Computers and Graphics*, Vol. 3, No. 1,pp.23-28.

Greiner G. and Hormann K., 1988, Efficient clipping of arbirary polygons. *ACM Transactions on Graphics*, Vol. 17, No. 2,pp. 71-83.

Liang Y.D. and Barsky B.A., 1984. A new concept and method for line clipping. *ACM Transactions on Graphics*, Vol. 3, No. 1,pp. 1-22.

Liu et al., 2003. An efficient algorithm for polygon clipping. *Journal of Software*, Vol. 14, No. 4,pp. 845-856.

Squillacote A.H., 2007. *The ParaView guide: a parallel visualization application*. Kitware Inc.

Sutherland I.E. and Hodgeman G.W., 1974. Reentrant polygon clipping. *Communications of the ACM,* Vol. 17, No.1, pp.32-42.

Teravap, 2015. *http://www.caep-scns.ac.cn/TeraVAP.php,* Software Center for High Performance Numerical Simulation, China Academy Of Engineering Physics.

Vatti B.R., 1992. A generic solution to polygon clipping. ACM Transactions on Graphics, Vol. 35, No. 1,pp. 56-63.

VisIt, 2005. *VisIt User's Manual*. Technical Report UCRL-SM-220449, Lawrence Livermore National Laboratory.

Weiler K. and Atherton P., 1977. Hidden surface removal using polygon area sorting. *Proceedings of the 4th annual conference on Computer graphics and interactive techniques.* Vol. 11, No.2, pp. 214-222.

A QOS AWARE AD HOC MULTICAST BY COMBINING TDMA AND IEEE 802.11 DCF

Jing Lin, Ryo Yamamoto, Satoshi Ohzahata and Toshihiko Kato
University of Electro-Communications, 1-5-1, Chofugaoka, Chofu, Tokyo 182-8585, Japan

ABSTRACT

In this paper, we propose a QoS (Quality of Service) supporting method for ad hoc multicast by combining TDMA (Time Division Multiple Access) and IEEE 802.11 DCF (Distributed Coordination Function). In the proposed method, the time frame is composed of two different periods, specifically a TDMA period and a DCF period. A TDMA period provides contention free transmission for QoS multicast flows, and a DCF period provides contention-based access for best effort or low priority flows. Our proposal enhances MOLSR (Multicast Optimized Link State Routing) so that time slots are assigned and the admission of a QoS multicast flow is checked during the multicast tree construction. We evaluate the proposed method for an environment where QoS multicast flows and TCP flows coexist using the QualNet simulator. Simulation results show that our proposal is an efficient solution for QoS control in ad hoc multicast communication.

KEYWORDS

Ad Hoc Network, Multicast, QoS, TDMA, DCF

1. INTRODUCTION

An ad hoc network is a self-organizing infrastructure-less wireless network, which does not have any centralized control units. It is studied widely as a rescue service network in environmental disasters, a sensor network and so on. One of important research topics in ad hoc networks is the QoS (Quality of Service) support over a wireless multi-hop environment. As for this topic, there have been many protocols focusing on unicast communication. They are classified into four categories; an admission control based scheme, a contention-based MAC (Media Access Control) prioritization scheme, a TDMA (Time division Multiple Access) based scheme, and a hybrid scheme combining TDMA and CSMA/CA (Carrier Sense Multiple Access with Collision Avoidance).

In the QoS ad hoc communication such as voice and video conferences, multicast communication is also important. As for this research topic, several multicast routing protocols are proposed, but they focus only on construction multicast tree, and do not consider QoS aware multicast. In order to support multicast communication such as multi-party voice conference and real time video distribution, some QoS aware ad hoc multicast mechanisms are proposed. They are classified into two categories. One is a prioritization based mechanism, which assumes a current contention based MAC mechanism and provides an admission control and prioritization function in the MAC or network level. The other is a TDMA based mechanism, which introduces time slot based MAC function and transfers multicast packets on top of it. The former does not support a strict QoS, and so suffers from packet losses and delays in the multi-hop environment. In contrast, the latter supports a strict QoS, but it has a problem that it does not support best effort traffic effectively.

Our former paper [Lin, J., et al., 2017] proposed a hybrid type QoS ad hoc method, which has the following features. (1) Time frame is divided into TDMA periods and DCF (Distributed Coordination Function) periods, and QoS unicast traffic and best effort traffic are assigned to TDMA periods and DCF periods, respectively. (2) When a new QoS flow starts, the time slot assignment at individual links is performed dynamically. If a time slot cannot be assigned at some link, this QoS flow is not admitted. (3) Nodes in an ad hoc network know their locations, and based on the distance between nodes and the radio interference range, time slots are assigned effectively. In our former pater, the simulation based evaluation concludes that our method provides better performance on delay and packet delivery than the IEEE 802.11 based prioritization method (802.11e method) and the pure TDMA method.

In this paper, we propose a new method for QoS aware ad hoc multicast scheme, which extends our hybrid QoS ad hoc method combining TDMA and DCF. It provides dynamic and efficient TDMA time slots assignment for QoS multicast flows with rejecting flows when time slots are not assigned, and transmits best effort flow packets during DCF time periods. The rest of paper consists of the following section. Section 2 shows related work on QoS ad hoc protocol, ad hoc multicast, and QoS ad hoc multicast. Section 3 proposes our method. Section 4 gives the results of performance evaluation, and section 5 concludes this paper.

2. RELATED WORK

There are a lot of proposals on QoS aware unicast over ad hoc networks. They are classified into several schemes. The first is a scheme based on the routing and admission control. [Yang, Y. and Kravets, R., 2005] and [Su, S., et al., 2007] keep track of available bandwidth of individual links and select a route with enough bandwidth for an incoming QoS flow. If there are no such a route, the QoS flow is rejected. They reserve required bandwidth, but strict QoS for packet transmission is not guaranteed. The second one is the MAC level prioritization scheme. [Xiao, Y. and Li, H., 2004] proposes a method extending the IEEE 802.11e EDCA (Enhanced Distributed Channel Access) [LAN/MAN Standards Committee, 2005] to multi-hop communication. It maps local traffic loads into MAC back off parameters dynamically. [Lakrami, F., et al., 2015] proposes a similar algorithm by modifying transmission parameters according to channel error rate. However, these proposals provide only relative priority for QoS flows, and do not take account of admission control. The third one is a TDMA based scheme, where time slots are assigned to individual flows based on the clock synchronization among nodes. [Kas, M., et al., 2009] proposes OA-TDMA (OLSR-Aware TDMA), a TDMA based cross-layer channel access scheduling method, which uses the information collected by the OLSR (Optimized Link State Routing) protocol [Clausen, T. and Jacquet, P. Ed., 2003]. [Kanzaki, A., et al., 2009] proposes an adaptive time slot assignment with slot migration, which dynamically changes the frame length according to traffic load. Although those proposals provide efficient transmission for QoS flows, they use TDMA time slots for best effort flows and this provides poor throughput for them. The last one is a hybrid approach which uses a TDMA based contention free access and a CSMA based contention access. [Shrestha, B., et al., 2014] proposes a time slot based hybrid method, where a time frame between two beacons are divided into time slots and a QoS flow is handled according to a TDMA based scheme and a best effort flow is handled according to CSMA based assignment scheme. But, this uses a centralized control node and is limited to one hop communication. [Rhee, J, et al., 2008] is another example of hybrid approach called Z-MAC, where CSMA is used as a main access mode and TDMA is used in case of a lot of contentions over a link. That is, there are no differentiations for QoS flows and best effort flows. Our former proposal [Lin, J., et al., 2017] is a hybrid approach, where a QoS flow is transmitted in a TDMA scheme and a best effort flow is transmitted in a DCF scheme. It introduces a dynamic and efficient time slot assignment with admission control, and prioritization for QoS flow by using TDMA exclusively.

As for the ad hoc multicast, there are several proposals on a multicast routing protocol. [Royer, M. and Perkins, C., 1999] proposes MAODV (Multicast Ad-hoc On-Demand Distance Vector), which is an extension of AODV routing protocol [Perkins, C., et al., 2003]. AODV is a reactive routing protocol exchanging RREQ (route request) and RREP (route reply) packets. MAODV uses RREQ and RREP packets for a tree construction and the join to an existing tree. It newly introduces an MACT (multicast activation) packet used to add new branches into an existing tree. [Lee, S., et al., 2002] proposes ODMPR (On-Demand Multicast Routing Protocol), which uses a mesh of nodes called a forwarding group instead of a multicast tree. A source periodically floods a Join Query packet piggybacked in a multicast data. A receiver floods a Join Reply packet and this constructs a forwarding group. Multicast data packets are transferred over the group, which increases the reliability of dissemination and releases the overhead of tree maintenance. [Laouiti, A., et al., 2003] proposes MOLSR (Multicast OLSR), which is an extension to OLSR. A source floods a SOURCE_CLAIM packet using MPRs (multipoint relays) selected by OLSR. A receiver replies it by sending a CONFIRM_PARENT packet to its parents.

As described above, QoS aware ad hoc multicast mechanisms are classified into a prioritization based scheme and a TDMA based scheme. The followings are examples of the first category. [Lashkari, V. and Dehghan, M., 2007] proposes QoS-MAODV, which is an extension of MAODV. The control packets such as RREQ, RREP and MACT include the bandwidth information used in a multicast communication, and nodes maintain the link bandwidth with neighbors and the multicast consumed bandwidth. [Sihai, Z., et al., 2012] proposes QMMRP (QoS-based multicast MANET routing protocol), which uses the entropy of nodes, indicating how node positions are stable, and the bandwidth reservation to find a stable link with enough bandwidth. [Do, V. et al., 2015] proposes QMCOM (QoS Multipoint relay Connectionless Multicast). It is built on top of OLSR and uses the DiffServ architecture to prioritize QoS packets. All of those proposals, however, rely on the network level prioritization and resource reservation. So, QoS frames may interfere with each other during multi-hop frame transfer or congestion.

Among examples of TDMA based scheme, [Xu, Z., 2010] proposes a QoS multicast routing using the TDMA principle, but it uses IP addresses of multicast data receivers not multicast IP addresses. [Wang, N., and Lee, C., 2010] proposes MQMR (multi-path QoS multicast routing). It is based on TDMA principle and uses either a uni-path or a multi-path as a route so that the aggregate bandwidth can meet the bandwidth requirement of a QoS request. [Helmle, S., et al., 2013] discusses on how to realize QoS multicast over TDMA based mobile tactical networks with narrow bandwidths such as 25 kHz. In order to minimize packet collisions, it utilizes auxiliary nodes that forward reservation information to hidden nodes, and proposes how to select those auxiliary nodes. As mentioned above, although those TDMA based proposals provide strict QoS for QoS packet transmission, they do not consider the coexistence of QoS flows and best effort flows.

3. PROPOSAL

3.1 Design Principles

We have adopted the following design principles to realize our method.

- All nodes in an ad hoc network keep the clock synchronization and maintain the identical time period structure. The clock synchronization is realized by some mechanisms such as GPS, but its detail is out of scope. Nodes know their positions, and its information is flooded by the OSLR routing protocol.
- The time is organized into a two level structure; a frame cycle and a frame. A frame cycle contains one or more frames. Each frame is divided into two parts; a TDMA period (contention-free access) and a DCF period (contention-based access). In a TDMA period, transmission time slots are assigned to QoS flows using a TDMA-based approach. In a DCF period, IEEE 802.11 DCF based frame transmission is performed for best effort flows.
- Time slots in a TDMA period are allocated according to the demands of QoS flows. That is, the length of a TDMA period changes dynamically. In order to improve the channel utilization, the same time slots may be assigned over multiple links if they do not interfere with each other.
- The time slot assignment is performed together with the multicast tree construction. Since our former method uses OLSR, the proposed method in this paper uses MOLSR as a basis. When a multicast source tries to construct a QoS multicast tree, the source, receivers and forwarding members collaborate together to select time slots used by branches in the tree. After the time slots are determined, the results are flooded throughout the ad hoc network to allow all nodes in the network to maintain the up-to-date usage of time slots. This flooding method of time slot information is the same as our former proposal, which makes it possible to maintain the coexistence of QoS unicast and multicast communications.
- The admission control is performed at the time slot assignment. If any branch cannot reuse the already assigned time slots, a new time slot is allocated with the limit of the length of one frame. If a new time slot cannot be allocated, the part of this branch in a multicast tree is not established.

3.2 Time Frame Structure

Figure 1 shows an example of time frame structure. A frame cycle which contains N frames is repeated. The identical frames are repeated in every frame cycle. That is, N defines the lowest QoS communication rate.

Every frame has the same length, but different frames in a frame cycle may contain a different time slot structure. For one QoS communication, one time slot may be allocated in every frame at maximum. That is, the length of one frame defines the highest QoS communication rate.

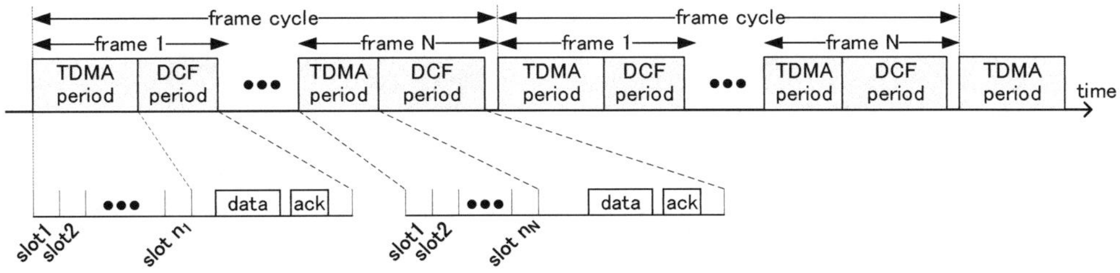

Figure 1. Time frame structure

3.3 Principle of Time Slot Selection

As described before, the proposed method tries to assign the same time slots over different links if they do not interfere with each other. Figure 2 shows an idea how to check the reusability of time slots. Here, we suppose that node *Ns* is going to send a QoS packet to node *Nr* with time slot t_a. Figure 2 (a) shows the check for node *Ns*. It checks the node status in the radio interference range, a range where a receiver detects the radio signal of a sender whether it can decode information correctly or not, and looks for the node which receives a packet using time slot t_a. If another node in the interference range receives a packet in the same time slot, the receiving node interfere with the data sent by *Ns* (case (s1)). On the other hand, even if another node in the interference range is a sending node, time slot t_a does not interfere with *Ns* in the case the receiving node is outside of the interference range (case (s2). So, for *Ns*, it needs to be checked whether any node in the interference range is a receiving node for a particular time slot. If not, *Ns* can select this time slot as a candidate for itself. On the other hand, in the check for *Nr*, it needs to be tested whether any node in the interference range is a sending node for a time slot or not (see Figure 2 (b)). If there are no sending nodes within the interference range, *Nr* can use the time slot for itself.

3.4 Control Packets for Time Slot Assignment

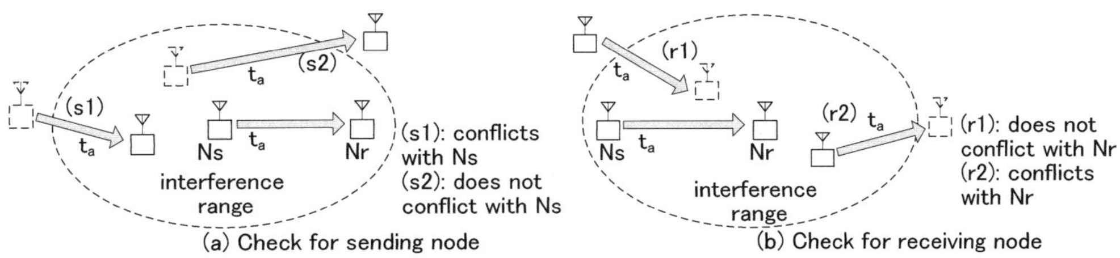

Figure 2. How to reuse time slots

The network assigns time slots over individual links consisting of a multicast tree when it is constructed according to MOLSR. This algorithm uses the following control packets.

- **SOURCE_CLAIM**: a multicast source floods this packet in order to invoke a multicast tree construction. Besides its original parameters, i.e., the multicast source address and the multicast group address, the required bandwidth is newly introduced in the proposed method.
- **CONFIRM_PARENT**: when a receiver receives a SOURCE_CLAIM packet, it sends this packet to its parent node (a neighbor node toward the source), and the parent node relays it to the further parent. This packet contains the original parameters such as the parent address, the multicast group address and the multicast source address, and the possible time slot list is added as a new parameter

in the proposed method. That is, a downstream node selects time slot candidates for a link to the parent and inform the parent of the possible time slots.

- **LEAVE**: a control packet used when a receiver requests to leave a multicast tree. The original parameters are used in the proposed method.
- **ASSIGN_TIMESLOT**: a newly introduced control packet. When a parent node in a multicast tree receives CONFIRM_PARENT packets from its downstream nodes, it determines the time slot used between itself and the downstream nodes, and inform them of the time slot by this message. The parameters are the multicast group address, the multicast source address and the selected time slot.
- **QSYN**: a control packet used to disseminate the usage of time slots throughout the network. This is also used in our unicast method. The parameters contained are the list of the time slot, the sending node position and the receiving node position. This packet is flooded using MPRs selected by OLSR.

3.5 Procedure for Multicast Tree Construction and Time Slot Assignment

This subsection describes the detailed procedure for the multicast tree construction and time slot assignment. Figure 4 shows an example ad hoc network comprising nine nodes, three of which are MPRs, connected by wireless links represented by solid lines. In this case, we assume that only the nodes connected by solid lines are in the radio interference range. That is, the radio interference range equals to the radio communication range. In this figure, three QoS unicast flows (from *d* to *e*, *f* to *g*, and *j* to *g*) have been started using three time slots, *t1*, *t2*, and *t3*, respectively. In this configuration, node *a* (multicast source) tries to establish a QoS multicast flow for which nodes *c* and *i* are multicast receivers. Figure 3 shows the sequence of control packet exchanges and Figure 5 shows the resultant time slot assignment. The detailed steps are as follows. For simplicity, we assume that a frame cycle has only one frame.

Step1: As described in Figure 3 (a), node *a* broadcast a SOURCE_CLAIM packet including the group address and the bandwidth requirement (one time slot in a frame in this case). Nodes (MPRs) *b* and *e* receive and rebroadcast it. The rebroadcasted packet is flooded by node *f*, and all nodes in the network receive this SOURCE_CLAIM packet.

Step 2: In this example, nodes *c* and *i* are receivers, and so they send CONFIRM_PARENT packets to individual parents (see Figure 3 (b)). Those packets include available time slots. Node *c* can use time slots *t1* and *t3* in receiving, according to the principle described above, and node *c* sends a CONFIRM_PARENT packet including *t1* and *t3* in the possible time slot list. Similarly, node *i* receives packets in *t1*, and a CONFIRM_PARENT node *i* sends includes *t2* and *t3* in the possible time slot list.

Step 3: After that, nodes *b* and *e* send CONFIRM_PARENT packets to node *a*. Since node *b* hears only packets in *t2*, a CONFIRM_PARENT node *b* sends includes *t1* and *t3* in the possible time slot list. Similarly, node *e* hears time slots *t1* and *t2*, a CONFIRM_PARENT node *e* sends includes *t3*.

Step 4: After COFIRM_PARENT packets reach the multicast source, ASSIGN_TIMESLOT packets are to be returned. Node *a* (multicast source) receives two CONFIRM_PARENT packets; one includes *t1* and *t3*, and the other includes *t3* in the possible time slot list. Node *a* also confirms that sending packet in time slot *t3* does not conflict with neighbors. As a result, node *a* selects time slot *t3* for sending QoS packets over the multicast tree. Node *a* sends ASSIGN_TIMESLOT packets to nodes *b* and *e*, as shown in Figure 3 (c).

Step 5: When node *b* receives an ASSIGN_TIMESLOT packet which tells the sender of this message has selected time slot *t3*, it selects *t1* (the remaining one) from the possible time slot list sent by node *c*, and it confirms that sending in *t1* does not conflict with neighbors. Then, node *b* sends an ASSIGN_TIMESLOT packet containing *t1* to node *c*. Similarly, node *e* selects *t2* and tells node *i* that *e* is going to use *t2* to transmit QoS packets over the QoS multicast tree.

Step 6: QSYN packets are exchanged among MRPs and then to their MPR selectors.

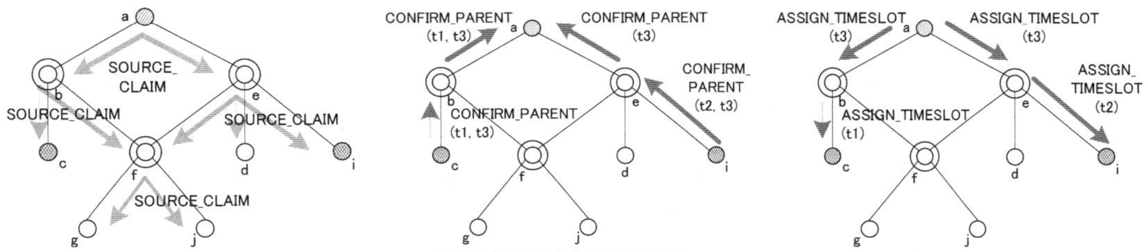

(a) SOURCE_CLAIN (b) CONFIRM_PARENT (c) ASSIGN_TIMESLOT

Figure 3. Exchanges of control packets

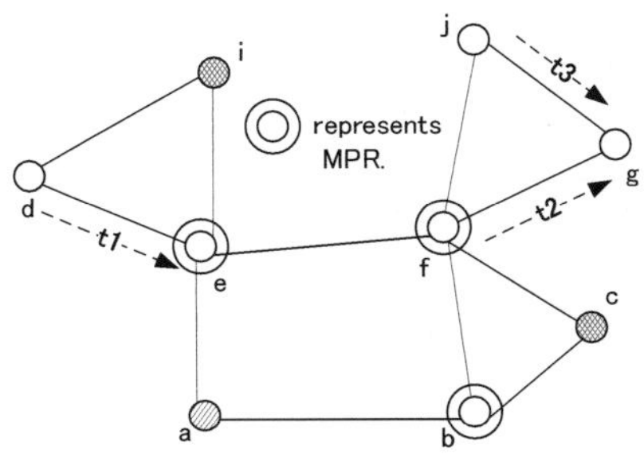

Figure 4. An example network

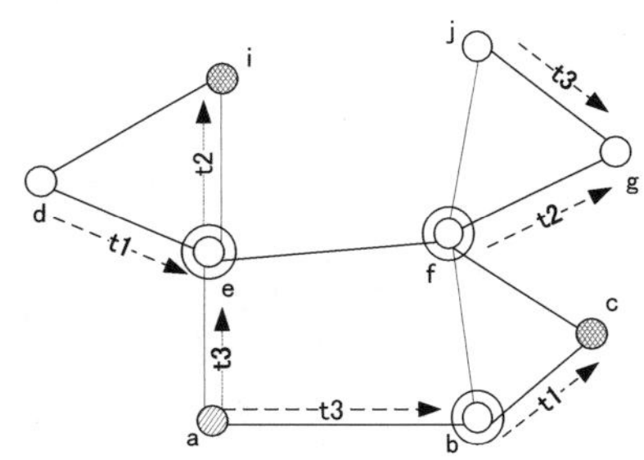

Figure 5. Result of time slot assignment

4. PERFORMANCE EVALUATION

This section describes the results of performance evaluation using QualNet 6.1 [Scalable Network Technologies, 2017]. Figure 6 shows the simulation environment. In a square area of 200 meter × 200 meter, 26 nodes are uniformly deployed. The simulation conditions are given table 1. The MAC data rate was fixed to 54 Mbps, which is the highest rate of IEEE 802.11g. The radio interference range is a circle whose radius is 540 meter. This is used to reuse time slots as shown in Figure 2. Since data rate is fixed to 54 Mbps, the radius of the radio communication range is 70 meter. A QoS multicast flow uses multicast constant bit rate (MCBR) data packets with fixed length (512 bytes). The time required to transmit one

MCBR data packet is less than 200 μsec including PHY header, MAC header, IP header and frame check sequence. So, the time slot size is set to 200 μsec for the TDMA period. We introduce a restriction that the maximum transmission rate of MCBR data packet is 1048 Kbps, and so the length of one frame time is set to 4 msec ($^{512 \times 8}/_{1048 \times 10^3}$), including 1 μsec inter-frame time. In this simulation, the length of frame cycle is set to 4 frames. This means that the minimum transmission rate of MCBR data packet is actually 256 Kbps. When an MCBR data packet is transmitted in lower rate, there is a wasted time portion in a time slot.

In the simulation, the proposed method and an IEEE 802.11e based method are evaluated. The latter corresponds to a prioritization based scheme. In simulation runs, both best effort flows (TCP flows) and QoS multicast flows (MCBR flows) start transmission from the beginning. All receivers of an MCBR flow have already joined to the multicast group when a simulation run starts. All TCP flows continue transmission until the end of a simulation run. All MCBR flows stop transmitting at 55 seconds. Hops of a flow are set to between one hop and five hops. In order to obtain one simulation result, we repeated 24 simulation runs by selecting different nodes joining communication, and calculated an average and a 95% confidence interval.

Figures 7, 8, and 9 give the results. Figure 7 gives the results when the transmission rate of MCBR flows is changed. Here, the number of MCBR flows is 3, the number of receivers in each MCBR flow is 3, and the number of TCP flows is 3. Figure 8 gives the results when the number of MCBR flows is changed. In this experiment, the MCBR transmission rate is set to 512 Kbps, the number of receivers in each MCBR flow is 3, and the number of TCP flows is 3. Lastly, Figure 9 gives the results when the number of TCP flows is changed. Here, the MCBR transmission rate is set to 512 Kbps, the number of MCBR flows is 3, and the number of receivers in each MCBR flow is 3. In all experiments, the delivery ratio and the end-to-end delay in MCBR flows and the TCP flow throughput are evaluated.

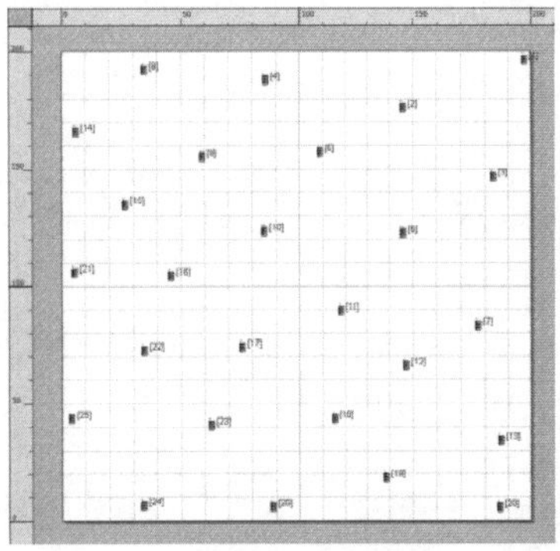

Figure 6. Simulation environment

Table 1. Simulation conditions

Simulation time	60 seconds
PHY	IEEE 802.11g
Data rate	54 Mbps (fixed)
Interference range	540 meter
Communication range	70 meter
Application traffic	QoS: Multicast CBR (packet size: 512 bytes, max. rate: 1024 Kbps), Best effort: TCP
Time slot	200 μ sec
Frame time	4 msec
Frame cycle	4 frames

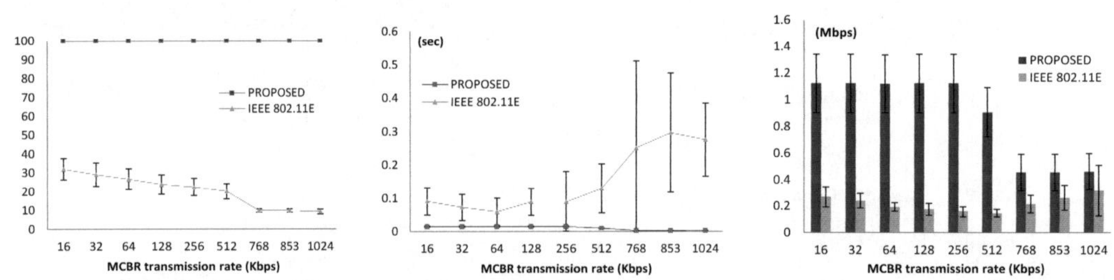

(a) MCBR delivery ratio (b) MCBR delay (c) TCP throughput

Figure 7. Results by changing MCBR flow transmission rate

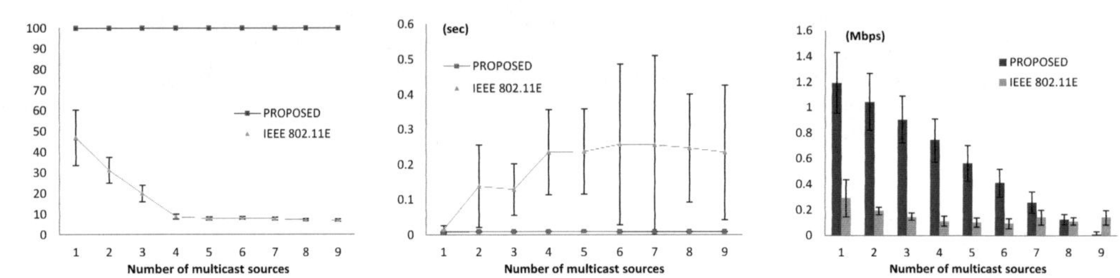

(a) MCBR delivery ratio (b) MCBR delay (c) TCP throughput

Figure 8. Results by changing number of MCBR flows

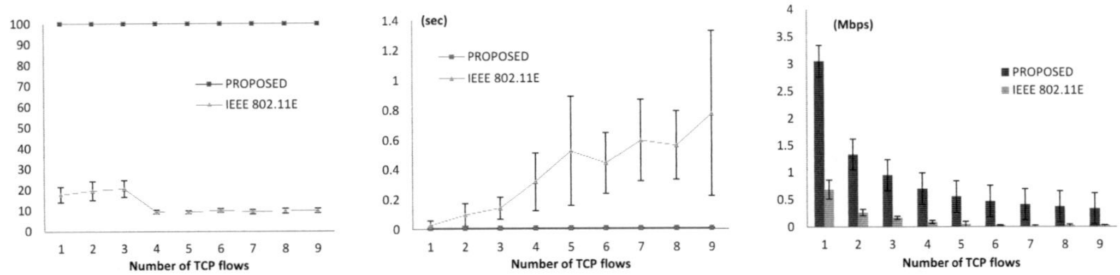

(a) MCBR delivery ratio (b) MCBR delay (c) TCP throughput

Figure 9. Results by changing number of TCP flows

In all results, the proposed method provides 100% MCBR data packet delivery ratio, which is in contrast with the IEEE 802.11e based method providing at most 40% delivery ratio. Similarly, as for the end-to-end delay in MCBR flows, the proposed method accomplishes a very low value while the 802.11e based method suffers from several hundred millisecond delay. As for the throughput of TCP flows, the proposed method provides much higher results than the other.

5. CONCLUSIONS

In this paper, we presented a QoS aware ad hoc multicast method by combining TDMA and IEEE 802.11 DCF. In the proposed method, the channel time is composed of two different periods, namely TDMA periods and DCF periods. The TDMA period provides contention free transmission for QoS multicast flows, and the DCF period provides contention-based access for best effort or low priority flows. The proposed method enhances MOLSR so that time slots are assigned and the admission of a QoS multicast flow is checked during the multicast tree construction. We evaluate the proposed method and the IEEE 802.11e based method for various numbers of TCP flows and different QoS multicast flows using the QualNet simulator. Simulation results show that the proposed method is able to provide a high delivery ratio and a low end-to-delay for QoS multicast flows and to accomplish high throughput for TCP flows.

REFERENCES

Clausen, T. and Jacquet, P. Ed., 2003. *Optimized Link State Routing Protocol (OLSR)*. IETF RFC 3626.

Do, V. et al., 2015. QoS Connectionless Multicast Routing for Mobile Ad Hoc Networks. Proc. European Wireless 2015, pp. 473-480.

Helmle, S., et al., 2013. A Simplified Node Selection Algorithm for Multicast Resource Reservation in TDMA-based Narrowband Mobile Ad-hoc Networks. Proc. 2013 IFIP Wireless Days (WD), pp. 1-7.

Kanzaki, A., et al., 2009. On a TDMA Slot Assignment Considering the Amount of Traffic in Wireless Sensor Networks. *Proc. 2009 International Conference on Advanced Information Networking and Applications Workshops*, pp. 984-989.

Kas, M., et al., 2009. OLSR-Aware Distributed Channel Access Scheduling for Wireless Mesh Networks. *Proc. WCNC 2009*, pp.1-6.

Lakrami, F., et al., 2015. An enforced QoS scheme for high mobile adhoc networks. *Proc. IEEE Wireless Networks and Mobile Communications*, pp.1-8.

LAN/MAN Standards Committee, 2005. *IEEE Standard for Information technology--Local and metropolitan area networks--Specific requirements--Part 11: Wireless LAN Medium Access Control (MAC) and Physical Layer (PHY) Specifications - Amendment 8: Medium Access Control (MAC) Quality of Service Enhancements*. IEEE.

Laouiti, A., et al., 2003. Multicast Optimized Lind State Routing. *[Research Report] RR-4721*, INRIA, <inria-00071865>.

Lashkari, V. and Dehghan, M., 2007. QoS-aware Multicast Ad hoc On-Demand Distance Vector Routing. Proc. World Congress on Engineering 2007, Vol. II, pp. 1506-1511.

Lee, S., et al., 2002. On-Demand Multicast Routing Protocol in Multihop Wireless Mobile Networks. *Journal Mobile Networks and Applications*, Vol. 7, Issue 6, pp. 441-453.

Lin, J., et al., 2017. A TDMA/DCF Hybrid QoS Scheme for Ad Hoc Networks. *IEICE Transactions on Communications*, Vol. E100-B, No. 1, pp. 42-53.

Perkins, C., et al., 2003. *Ad hoc On-Demand Distance Vector (AODV) Routing.* IETF RFC 3561.

Rhee, J., et al., 2008. Z-MAC: A Hybrid MAC for Wireless Sensor Networks. *IEEE/ACM Transactions on Networking*, Vol.16, pp.511-524.

Royer, M. and Perkins, C., 1999. Multicast Operation of the Ad-hoc On-Demand Distance Vector Routing Protocol. Proc. MobiCom '99, pp. 207-218.

Scalable Network Technologies, 2017. *QualNet.* http://web.scalable-networks.com/content/qualnet, accessed at Mar. 2017.

Shrestha, B., et al., 2014. Distributed and Centralized Hybrid CSMA/CA-TDMA Schemes for Single-Hop Wireless Networks. *IEEE Transactions on Wireless Communications*, Vol. 13, pp. 4050-4056.

Sihai, Z., et al., 2012. QoS-based Multicast Routing Protocol in MANET. Proc. 2012 International Conference on Industrial Control and Electronics Engineering, pp. 261-265.

Su, S., et al., 2007. A Novel QoS Admission Control for Ad Hoc Networks. *Proc. IEEE WCNC 2007*, pp. 4196-4200.

Wang, N., and Lee, C., 2010. A Time Slot Assignment Scheme for Multi-Path QoS Multicast Routing in Mobile Ad Hoc Networks. Proc. 2010 International Computer Symposium (ICS), pp. 529-534.

Xiao, Y. and Li, H., 2004. Local Data Control and Admission Control for QoS Support in Wireless Ad Hoc Networks. *IEEE Transaction on Vehicular Technology*, Vol. 53, No. 5, pp. 1558-1572.

Xu, Z., 2010. Bandwidth-Satisfied QoS Multicast Routing in TDMA-based Mobile Ad Hoc Networks. *Proc. International Conference on Advanced Intelligence and Awareness Internet (AIAI 2010)*, pp. 1-5.

Yang, Y. and Kravets, R., 2005. Contention-aware admission control for ad hoc networks. *IEEE Transaction on Mobile Computing*, Vol. 4, No. 4, pp. 363-377.

A CLOUD-BASED DATA ANALYTICAL FRAMEWORK FOR MEDIUM SCALE SCIENTIFIC APPLICATIONS

Reena Bharathi[1], Shailaja Shirwaikar[1], Vilas Kharat[1] and Gajanan Aher[2]
[1]*Department of Computer Science, Savitribai Phule Pune University, Pune, India*
[2]*Department of Physics, Nowrosjee Wadia College, Pune, India*

ABSTRACT

Data intensive science focuses on extracting, exploring and mining knowledge from a huge ever growing data that is obtained from various instruments and simulations. Scientific applications earlier were using High Performance Computers, then focus was on cluster computing and then towards grid computing. As the technologies in the networking domain improved, distributed networking and cloud computing have become prevalent.
Scientific applications using cloud computing paradigm, faces several challenges such as data transportation cost, computing costs, data privacy and data security. A small dedicated cluster, with a cloud like interface, designed from low cost commodity machines, is often affordable by a group or an individual researcher, and is reasonably cost-effective.
In this paper, the authors demonstrate how a low cost inexpensive cluster setup can be designed and customized as a cloud based data analytical services framework, to provide data storage and analytical capabilities, for exploratory needs of a small or medium scale scientific application.

KEYWORDS

Cloud computing, big data analytics, Hadoop, MapReduce, Workflow

1. INTRODUCTION

Big Data refers to huge volumes of data, both structured and unstructured, produced by high-performance applications falling in a wide and heterogeneous group of application scenarios from scientific computing to social networks, from e-governance to medical information systems. A major shift in technologies applied for data collection, processing, visualization, and archiving, has resulted in the birth of a 4th research paradigm, the Data-Intensive science. It focuses on extracting, exploring and disseminating knowledge from huge continuously growing data, coming from instruments, sensors and simulations.

Scientific applications can be categorized as data intensive applications, or compute intensive applications, or a combination of both (Gannon, Fay, Green, & Yi, 2014). Data analytics is the science of examining a raw data set with the purpose of drawing some meaningful information from it which can be used to support high level decisions. Big data Analytics refers to the tools and techniques used to acquire, store, analyze and generate intelligence from big data (Ekanayake, Pallikara, & Fox, 2008), within tolerable elapsed times (Talia, 2013). Various clouds, commercial and science, like Amazon Ec2, Nebula, OSDC etc provide the necessary infrastructure for data analytics in scientific domain (Padhy, 2013). However, to be able to execute the scientific applications on the cloud, the application must be migrated to frameworks that can successfully exploit the cloud resources, like the MapReduce framework (Vavilapalli, V.K et al., 2013).

For most small to medium scale scientific experiments, small clusters can be designed and customized to provide a data analytics portal, as per the user need. The concept of a distributed file system is used at the backend, for big data storage, exhibiting reliability and fault tolerance (Gannon et al., 2014). A big data value chain comprising of data pre-processing, analytics, and post-processing can be provided, as part of customization of the cluster. The absolute cost of such clusters is often small enough than going in for any scientific cloud computing environments. One of the main advantages of these clusters is that they will provide a simpler User interface, and dedicated resources as per the application need, compared to generic clouds. Figure 1 provides a view of the existing solution versus the proposed solution to overcome these challenges

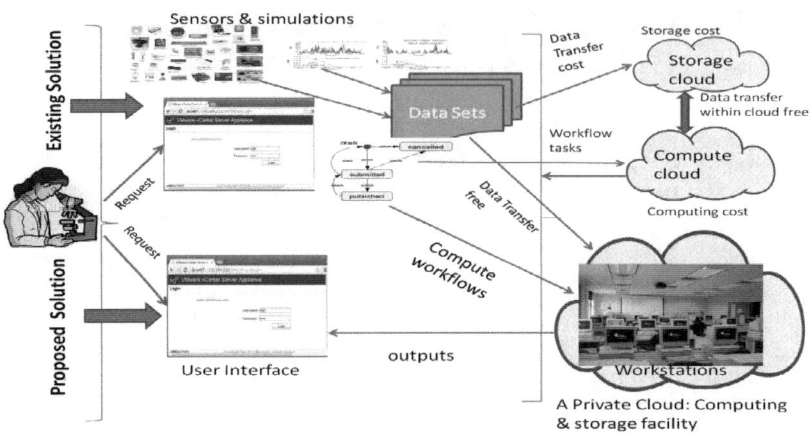

Figure 1. Existing Solution Vs Proposed Solution

In this paper, the authors demonstrate how a low cost inexpensive cluster setup with cloud like interface, can be designed with data storage and analytical capabilities, to support big data analytics in the scientific applications domain. In the next section background and existing work related to big data analytics in scientific environment is presented. Section 3 describes design and implementation while Section 4 presents the usage of the low-cost cluster setup. The paper ends with conclusion and presents some future directions.

2. BACKGROUND & RELATED WORK

Technological advancements in computing and communication have led to a flood of data from different scientific domains like healthcare, biomedicine, atmospheric physics, astronomy etc. Scientific computing requires an ever-increasing number of resources to provide results to growing problem sizes in a reasonable time frame. Based on the funding capacity of the scientific research projects, these needs were addressed using high-performance computing solutions and installed facilities such as HPCs, Cluster of commodity machines, & Grids. Some of the most representative examples of scientific grid computing are the TeraGRID and the Open science grid (Juve & Deelman, 2010). Cloud computing provided a cheaper option in this case the resources aren't hosted using the researcher's computational facilities, but leased from data centres, based on demand. Grids support for resource sharing across organizations, but the cloud provide resources to the application on demand, giving the impression of a single dedicated resource.

The emergence of cloud computing made large-scale computational infrastructures available for a broad spectrum of scientific applications (Srirama, Jakovits, & Vainikko, 2012).The analytical requirements of applications from the scientific domain are often different from their enterprise counterparts. Scientific applications are often composed of many interdependent tasks and consume and produce huge volumes of data. They also contain parallel components, which are generally handled using MPI(Message Passing Interface) to support message passing between processors. Clouds use the concept of virtualization, to provide a set of physical resources to a broader range of users, which in turn affects the performance factor of scientific applications (Juve & Deelman, 2010). This resulted in the emergence of clouds in the academia, providing limited computational resources on demand.

Various science clouds have been developed in academia, providing features and services that match the specific requirements of a scientific application and a limited number of computational platforms on demand: Cumulus (Wang, L et al., 2008), Eucalyptus (Nurmi, D et al., 2009), Nimbus (Tudoran, Costan, Antoniu, & Bouge, 2012), Azure (Grossman, R et al., 2010), OpenNebula (Milojicic, Llorente, & Montero, 2011), and OSDC (Grossman, R et al., 2010). Earlier clouds provided infrastructure as a service, primarily meant for data storage and providing computing power. Infrastructure as a service science clouds like Amazon EC2 (Hazelhurst, 2008), Azure etc, can provide access similar to the ones found in HPC systems, and also parallel storage systems. Platform as a service science clouds such as Magellan (Ramakrishnan, L. et al., 2011) &

OSDC are similar to science portals that provide tools to develop and deploy applications using domain-specific APIs and frameworks. These science clouds thus provide a platform to the researchers to test out their ideas and codes, before investing money and resources in potentially large-scale infrastructures.

The distributed software framework of Apache Hadoop (Vavilapalli, V.K et al., 2013), with the MapReduce parallel programming model (Ekanayake et al., 2008) and various tools like Hive (Thusoo, A. et al., 2009), Pig (Olston, Reed, Srivastava, Kumar, & Tomkins, 2008), Flume, Storm, Sqoop, Mahout (Owen & Robin, 2011) etc. present a rich ecosystem for big data analytics in commercial as well as scientific domain.

3. ARCHITECTURAL FRAMEWORK FOR DATA ANALYTICS

Scientific application, based on how data intensive and compute intensive it is, can be categorized as large scale, medium scale, or small scale application. Medium scale applications are not compute intensive, but generate big data sets and need analytics that's primarily statistical analysis, descriptive analysis and some predictive analysis. As far as computing power is concerned, they are not like large scale applications; but storage requirements are not like small scale applications, that they can be performed on a single machine.

There are several challenges such as managing, analyzing, transporting and archiving the large data sets and the cloud computing paradigm was introduced to overcome them.

3.1 Challenges of Medium Scale Applications

Cloud-based outsourcing of computing may be attractive to science applications because it can potentially lower the costs of purchasing, operating, maintaining, and periodically upgrading a local computing infrastructure. Despite these advantages, there are a few challenges that are faced by the researchers, in using the cloud computing paradigm for their data analytics.

a) Need for wide-area high performance networks for transporting large data sets to the cloud (Grossman, R et al., 2010).
b) Public cloud computing infrastructures are loaded with different types of services, thus making it more complex for a medium scale researcher to understand, assimilate and use only the needed services.
c) Public clouds work on the principle of pay-on-use model. Private clouds are proprietary clouds.
d) Several unresolved security threats like data privacy, data staging, data centre hacking etc exist in cloud computing. (Grossman, R et al., 2010; Hashem, I et al., 2015)

3.2 Proposed Solution Architecture

The above challenges can be overcome, by defining a small community cluster setup, from cheap commodity machines/workstations that exhibit the properties of resource provisioning, reliability and scalability. This section describes about an experimental setup that supports data analytics in the domain of medium scale scientific applications, which have been implemented using the Hadoop and MapReduce framework.

3.2.1 Hardware Setup

With the objective of having an experimental setup for analytical needs of a scientific application, the authors have set up a dynamically configurable cluster, of 5 nodes using low cost computers, LAN and wired internet connection. The cluster is composed of one master and 4 slave nodes and can be configured to extend to more nodes. Each node has a configuration of 2GB RAM. The HDFS, for the cluster, has a configured capacity of 250GB. The cluster is developed using the most popular Hadoop distributed computing framework (Lam, 2010). Further to provide analytics support, the MapReduce parallel programming model is used over the Hadoop distributed framework (Lee, K.H et al., 2012).

This cluster setup stands out from the traditional cluster/grid computing paradigms, due to the following reasons:

a) Provides scalability, with respect to the use of resources, which is an inbuilt characteristic of Hadoop framework.
b) Reliability against node failures, through data replication.
c) The machines that form the cluster are workstations, as against dedicated machines in a traditional grid/cluster
d) Parallelization of computing logic, handled by Hadoop with MapReduce parallel programming model makes the application / computing code much lighter.

The above reasons thus provide the researcher the freedom to concentrate on the migration of the computing logic into a MapReduce model, rather than being burdened with embedding the parallelization logic into the application code.

3.2.2 Analytical Functionalities Setup

Supervised learning algorithms work using a training dataset, to classify a data member to its appropriate class with a great accuracy. Unsupervised learning algorithms, on the other hand, characterize the entire data set, due to which the size of the data set affects the scalability factor of the algorithms (Leskovec, Rajaraman, & Ullman, 2014). Here there is a need for providing additional support to adapt the algorithms for big data.

Advanced clustering algorithms like fuzzy c-means, tend to involve complex computations that need time and memory, thus there is a need of parallelization of these algorithms. MapReduce is a programming model for designing distributed computations on massive data sets and an execution framework for massive data processing on a bunch of commodity servers (Gannon, D et al., 2014).

This section provides a description of the various analytical algorithms implemented and provided as services on the cluster setup. The algorithms have been broadly categorized based on the passes made on the data set (Ekanayake et al., 2008).

a. One pass Algorithms: These algorithms traverse through the data set only once, and can be adapted as a single execution of MapReduce model. These include zero level statistical analysis like finding the min/max/average, variance, and correlation analysis between a set of attributes. A summary of the algorithms developed as one pass algorithms is given in table 1.

Table 1. One-Pass Algorithms Implemented

	Algorithm types	Scope
1.	Basic Statistical Functions	Max / Min / Average / Standard Deviation
2	Data Sorting Algorithm	Sorting based on a single key & on multiple keys.
3	Correlation Analysis	Pearson's Coefficient analysis
4	Matrix Operations for Big matrices	Addition, Multiplication, Transpose, Max / Min /Average / Count

The Map phase iterates over the data set and generates partial output. The Reduce phase collects the partial outputs, and applies final aggregation / summarization, to generate the final value.

b. Iterative / Multi pass Algorithms: Iterative algorithms are algorithms that can be defined as an aggregation of multiple subtasks. The performance of the algorithm is measured based on some criteria. These algorithms traverse through the data set multiple times, equivalent to the number of iterations. Descriptive Algorithms such as K-Means, Fuzzy C-means etc belong to this class.

3.3 Performance Validation of the Cluster Setup

a. One-pass Algorithms: The cluster was validated for performance and scalability, with respect to one-pass algorithms, like basic statistical algorithms and matrix operations. A sample output of the validation process, for different matrix operations is given in Table 2, which shows a considerable improvement in turn-around time, in executing various matrix operations on a single node and on multiple nodes as a parallel task. Another point to note is that the turn-around time decreases as parallelization across multiple nodes increase.

Table 2. Cluster Performance for Matrix Operations

Number of Nodes	Time required for Data Summarization	Time Required for Executing different Matrix based operations						
		Multiplication	Addition	Transpose	Average Row/Columnwise	Average whole Matrix	Min/Max whole matrix	Min/Max & their Count Whole Matrix
ne	25.79 sec	25.63 sec	24.17 sec	23.67 sec	25.59 sec	24.65 sec	24.82 sec	24.90 sec
Three	15.37 sec	22.29 sec	17.28 sec	12.44 sec	14.34 sec	14.44 sec	12.33 sec	14.23 sec
Five nodes	5.04 sec	13.63sec	7.04 sec	5.13 sec	6.50 sec	5.32 sec	4.08 sec	5.13 sec

b. Iterative/multipass algorithms: The cluster setup was validated for performance and scalability with respect to iterative algorithms. As seen from Table 3, there is a considerable improvement in algorithm execution timing, as the number of nodes is increased in the cluster.

Table 3. Cluster Performance for K-Means Algorithm

Number of Nodes	Time Required for Data Pre-processing	Time Required for Executing K- means	
		On pre-processed Data	On raw data
Pseudo node	2 min 53 sec	8 min 7 sec	9 min 14 sec
Two Nodes	2 min	6 min 29 sec	8 min 17 sec
Three nodes	1 min 23 sec	6 min 27 sec	8 min 16 sec

3.4 Algorithm Validations

Clustering is a descriptive data mining algorithm of grouping a collection of objects into "clusters" according to some distance measure. The most popular clustering algorithms, Kmeans and the Fuzzy C-means were designed and integrated into the setup. This section describes the various validations that were embedded into these two clustering algorithms.

a. Determining the value of K, the number of clusters, in Kmeans algorithm:

The correct choice of K often depends on the shape and scale of the distribution of data points and the desired clustering resolution by the user. If an appropriate value of K is not apparent from prior knowledge of the properties of the data set, it can be chosen using the elbow test, which calculates the percentage of variance given as a function of the number of clusters.

As an example, the Kmeans algorithm was run for different values of k: 2, 3, 4, 5, 6, 7 & 8, on the air trajectories data set. As per the values and graphs given in table 4, the final number of clusters was set to 5, since the elbow bent / steep fall occurs at this point (Bharathi, Shirwaikar, & Kharat, 2016).

Table 4. Elbow Test Values & Corresponding Graphs

Height	**No. of cluster s: 2**	**No. of clusters: 3**	**No. of clusters: 4**	**No. of clusters: 5**	**No. of Clusters:6**	**No. of Clusters: 7**	**No. of clusters: 8**
Height 1	2.890	2.587	2.195	1.9064	0.4551	0.4301	0.357
Height 2	7.345	3.660	3.463	3.176	1.017	0.1221	0.190
Height 3	1.274	0.9353	0.862	0.846	0.3207	0.2984	0.2917

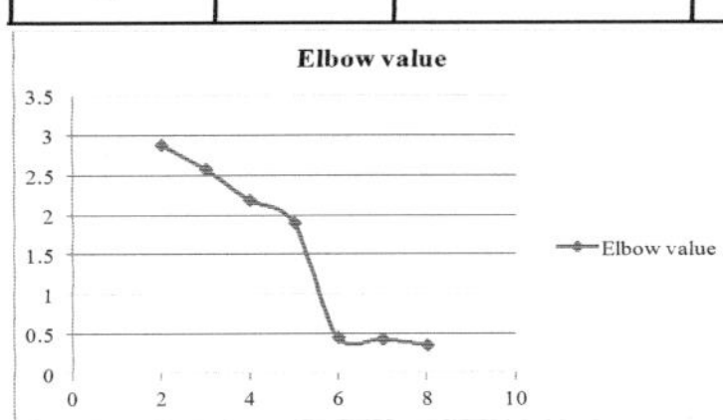

Height 1 graph

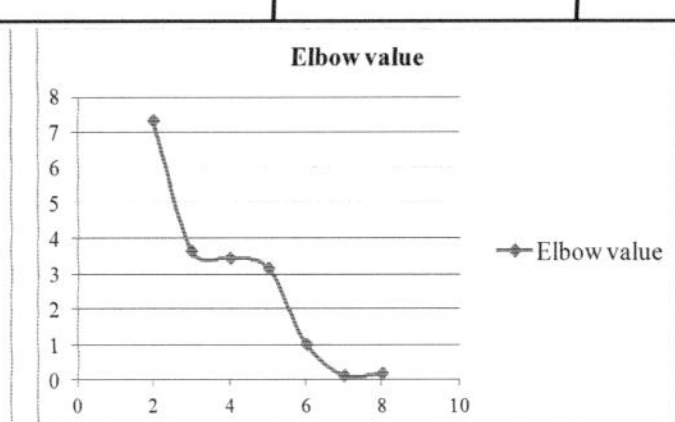

Height 2 graph

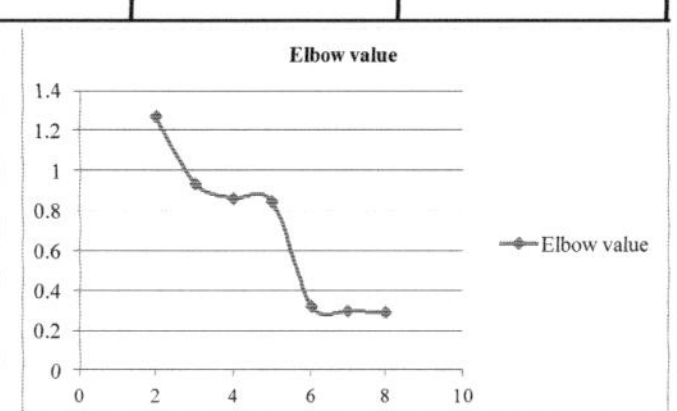

Height 3 graph

b. Validations embedded into Fuzzy C-means algorithm:

i. For determining the optimal value for k, the number of clusters, there are different methods in literature defined generally as a function of the membership values, the centroid coordinates and the data set. One of the methods, that is implemented, is based on minimizing the objective function.

$$J_m = \sum_{i=1}^{N}\sum_{j=1}^{C} u_{ij}^{m} \left\| x_i - c_j \right\|^2 , \quad 1 \leq m < \infty$$

As an example, the fuzzy c-means algorithm was executed for different values of k, on a sample data set , and the run that gave the smallest final value of the objective function, was chosen for final analysis (Ross, 2009). Table 5 gives the value of J_m for different values of k (Bharathi, Shirwaikar, & Kharat, 2016).The objective function value is minimum at k = 2, as seen in the graph in table 5 and hence its optimal to split the data set into two clusters.

Table 5. Value of Objective Function (J_m)

k : No. of clusters	Value of J_m
2	2.9256
3	3.0503
4	3.1271
5	3.1708
6	3.1973
7	3.2140

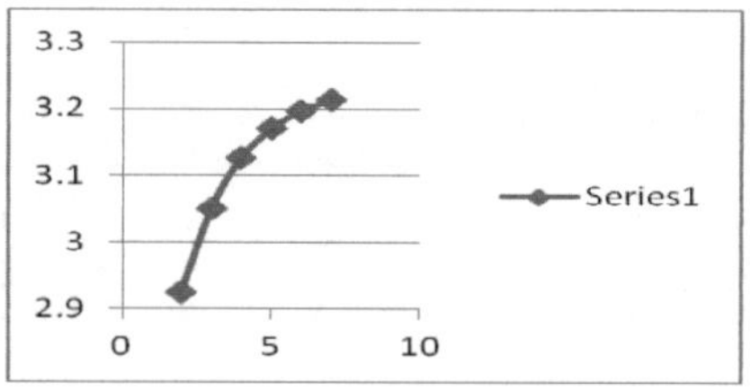

The second method used to determine the value of k, is using the minimum centroid distance concept (Li & Lewis, 2016). The cluster validity is based on the identifying the value of k, that gives the minimum distance between its set of centroids. Table 6 provides the minimum centroid distance for different values of k. As seen in graph in table 6, there is a sharp decay in the centroid distance at k = 2 (Bharathi, Shirwaikar, & Kharat, 2016).

Table 6. Minimum Centroid Distance Method

K : No. of cluster centroids	**Minimum centroid distance**
2	2.7323
3	1.2826
4	0,8408
5	0.6087
6	0.4673
7	0.3733

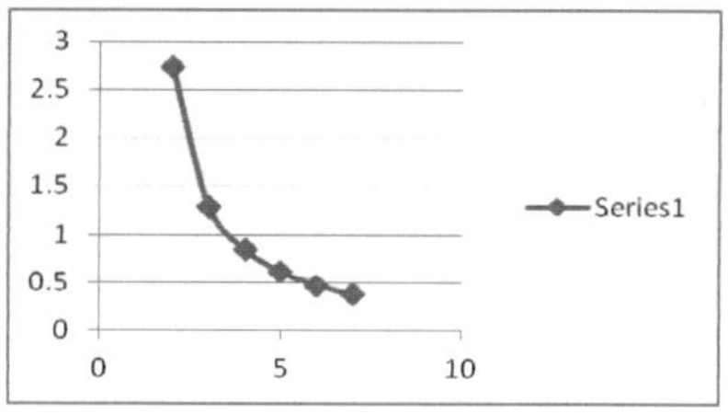

ii. Performance analysis by tuning the threshold parameter in the fuzzy c-Means algorithm:

The threshold value defines the maximum error that can be allowed in fuzzification of the clusters. The difference between the old and the new membership value, gives the error. This error value is compared with the threshold for the convergence of the algorithm. The value of the threshold is given between 0 and 1.

As an example, the algorithm implementation was tested, using a sample data set, for different values of termination threshold, while keeping m, the fuzzifier, fixed at 2 and the data set size i.e N, fixed. The number of cluster centers, k, was fixed to 4. The table 7 lists the actual error values obtained, for different termination threshold values (Bharathi, Shirwaikar, & Kharat, 2016). From the values and the graph in table 7, it is seen that the optimum value for the threshold (epsilon) is at 0.03, since at this value, the actual error value is constant at 0.004.

Table 7. Error values for Different Thresholds

Epsilon / No. of iterations	1	2	3	4	5	6	7	8	9
0.8	0.99	0.83	0.9	0.84	0.15				
0.5	0.99	0.83	0.9	0.84	0.15				
0.3	0.99	0.83	0.9	0.84	0.15				
0.08	0.99	0.83	0.9	0.84	0.15	0.19	0.11	0.03	
0.05	0.99	0.83	0.9	0.84	0.15	0.19	0.11	0.03	
0.03	0.99	0.83	0.9	0.84	0.15	0.19	0.11	0.03	0.004
0.02	0.99	0.83	0.9	0.84	0.15	0.19	0.11	0.03	0.004

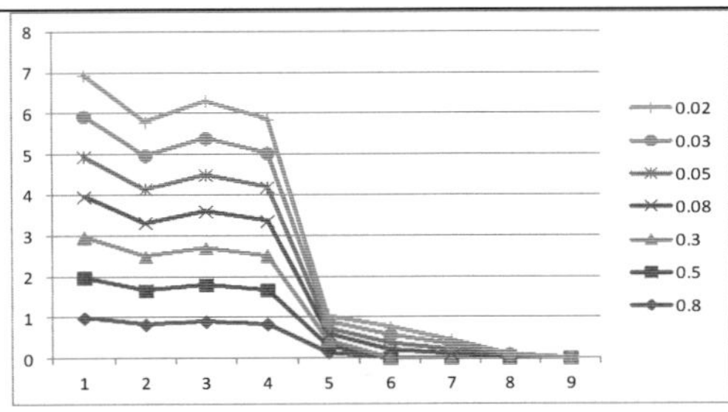

c. Scalability measure related to increasing data size and increasing number of nodes in the cluster setup:

The performance timing of the algorithm (with m=2 & epsilon = 0.03) was analyzed to test scalability, across different sized cluster setup, for different sized data sets. Table 8 presents the execution time taken with respect to varying data sizes and varying number of nodes in the cluster, along with the graph.

Table 8. Scalability Measure (Data size Vs Number of Nodes)

Data Size / No. of nodes	Time Taken in Seconds			
	1	2	3	4
1.66Mb	41.99	53.61	39.98	45.05
2.25MB	53.68	52.16	52.35	58.06
4.66Mb	80.11	80.37	80.26	79.95
6.55MB	109.54	113.43	112.44	112.55

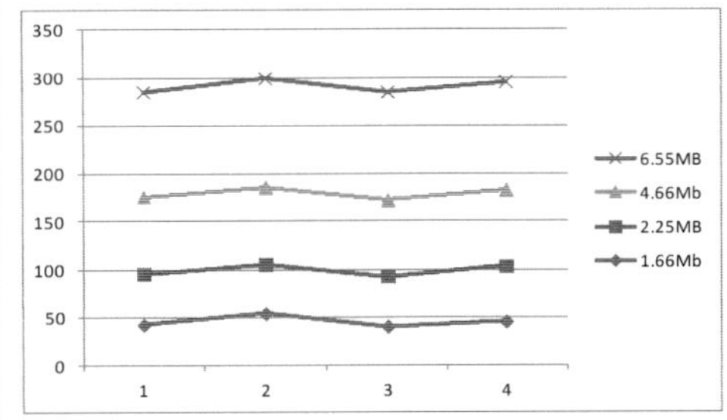

4. USING THE EXPERIMENTAL CLUSTER SETUP

The steps to be pursued for using the cluster set up, for data analytics, are as given below:

4.1 Connecting to the Cluster

Secure Shell (SSH) is a cryptographic network protocol for operating network services securely over an unsecured network. It is generally used for remote login to computer systems by users. The Hadoop cluster users will use the SSH protocol either directly or through Putty software, and connect to the Hadoop Master node. Once connected, the users can issue commands to start the cluster, upload data into the HDFS using FTP, and run analytical algorithms on it.

4.2 Loading Data Sets into the HDFS

Once a user connects to the cluster master node, the next step is to load the data set onto the HDFS. The following steps are done to load the data set onto the HDFS:

a. Creation of directories to store the input data sets and the outputs, using the Hadoop fs –mkdir command.

b. Copy the data sets into the directory. The command to copy the data depends on the location of the data file, as given in table 9:

Table 9. Commands to copy data set to HDFS

	Location of the data set	Command
1	On the local file system, of the master node	hadoop fs -copyFromLocal source_location destination_location.
2	On a remote machine	Using http / ftp and the Hadoop 'wget' command.

4.3 Choosing a Service

After the data sets are loaded into the HDFS, the next step is to perform analytics on it. The cluster set up provides a set of services that can be invoked through the command line interface for data analytics. Table 10 provides a list of supported services for data analytics, along with their argument requirements.

Table 10. List of Services

Sr. No	Name of Service	Purpose	Arguments to the service
1	Data_Sort	Sort a data set, based on one or more attributes.	Input_data_file_path, Output_file_path,Key_attribute_col/s
2.	Max_Min_Avg	Maximum, Minimum and Average, of each attribute	Input_data_file_path, Output_file_path, Key_attribute_col
3.	Freq_Distribution	The frequency distribution, for a set of values, in a attribute coloumn	Input_data_file_path, Output_file_path, Attribute_col
4.	AvgStdDeviation	To find the standard deviation for a attribute	Input_data_file_path,Output_file_path, Attribute_col/s
5.	Pearson_Correlation	Correlation between a set of attributes (X & Y)	Input_data_file_path, Output_file_path, AttributeX_Col, AttributeY_Col
6.	KmeansClustering	To cluster a set of values, using the Kmeans algorithm	Input_data_file_Path,Output_file_path Initial_centers_file_path, K (No. of clusters required)
7.	FuzzyCmeansClustering	To cluster a set of values, using the Fuzzy C-means algorithm	Input_data_file_Path, Output_file_path, Initial_centers_file_path, K (No. of clusters required)
8.	Matrix Library Services:	Multiplication, Addition, Transpose, Max/Min/Average on matrices. Input data conversion into matrix form	Input_data_file_path, Output_file_path
9	Data_Clean	Input Data cleaning, and combine them to form a single large file.(Sequential format)	Input_data_file_path,Output_file_path Number_of_lines_to_skip

The above services can be invoked, through command line interface, using the following command:

```
bin/hadoop jar service_name.jar Classname [Arguments]
```

4.4 Download the Outputs

The outputs generated after execution of a service, is stored in the output directory that is specified during the service invocation. The following command can be used to access the output file through command line, where the $$$$ is replaced by the file number.

```
bin/hadoop dfs -cat /user/output/part-r-$$$$
```

Figure 2 shows a sample output of accessing through command line. Figure 3 shows the HDFS browser. The Utilities option can be used to download the output files onto a local area.

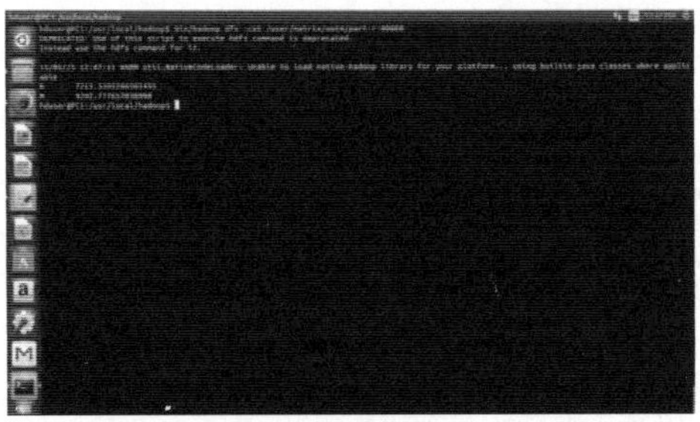

Figure 2. Accessing output through command line interface

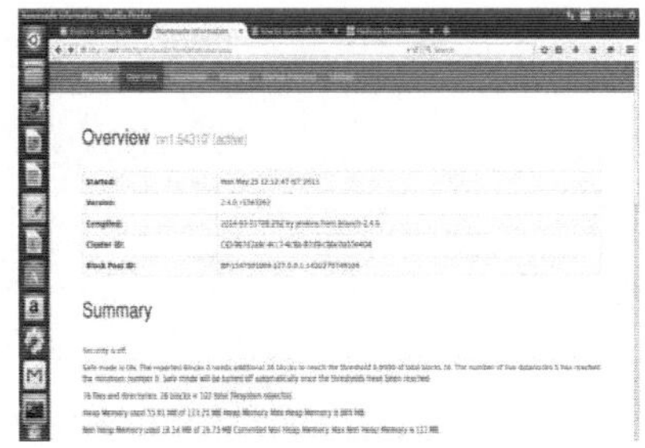

Figure 3. Accessing output through HDFS browser

4.5 Visualization of the Outputs

Visualization helps in providing a better inference of the outputs. After successful execution of the analytical algorithms, the outputs can be obtained or downloaded from the output directory. Figure 4, depicts some of the outputs that were visualized as graphs, obtained by applying statistical analysis to Weather data sets, in the domain of Atmospheric Physics (Bharathi, Shirwaikar, & Kharat, 2016).

The Cluster Setup was also used for clustering Air trajectories data set, from the domain of atmospheric physics. K-means clustering algorithm was applied to the trajectories data set, and output clusters were visualized using the 'Origin' software. Figure 4 depicts the visualization of the clusters: (Bharathi, Shirwaikar, & Kharat, 2016)

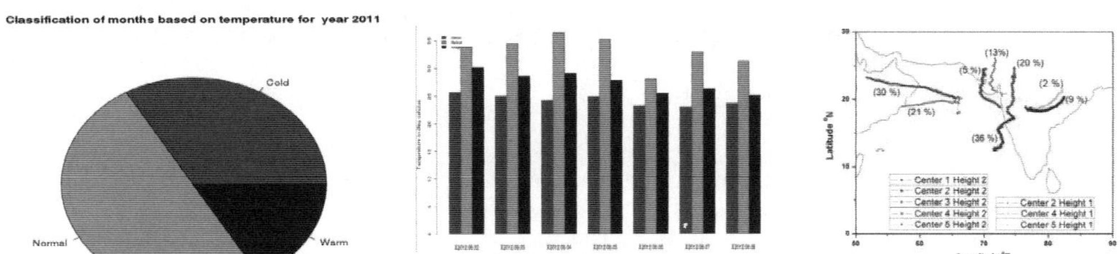

Daily temperature analysis

. Cluster plot superimposed on the map of India

Figure 4. Visualization using MS-Excel & Origin

5. CONCLUSION AND FUTURE DIRECTIONS

Medium scale scientific applications surpass processing limits of a single machine but need not be exposed to bear the complexity of a cloud computing environment for its analytics. In this paper, the authors have described the design, implementation and usage details of a cluster setup with cloud like interface, for big data analytics. A variety of algorithms were parallelized using Hadoop and Map Reduce framework and has been exposed as services to be used by the scientific community. A low cost experimental setup, as defined above, can be used by a realistic medium scale scientific application for its data analytics, thus eliminating the need for any specialized, high cost computing environment requiring dedicated and high speed networks.

In future, the focus would be on customization and parallelization of predictive analytics algorithms, and provide them as services on the cluster. Also, extensions to existing algorithm and new algorithms will be designed and integrated into the setup, as per future requirements of scientific applications.

REFERENCES

Bharathi, R., Shirwaikar, S., & Kharat, V. (2016). A distributed, scalable computing facility for Big data analytics in Atmospheric Physics. In *Proceedings of ICACDS 2016* (pp. 162), Ghaziabad, India.

Bharathi, R., Shirwaikar, S., & Kharat, V. (2016). A distributed, scalable parallelization of Fuzzy c-Means Algorithm. In *Proceedings of IEEE Bombay Symposium (IBSS)* 978-1-5090-2730-9/16/$31.00 ©2016. IEEE.

Dean, J., & Ghemawat, S. (2010). MapReduce: a flexible data processing tool. *Communications of the ACM*, *53*(1), 72-77.

Ekanayake, J., Pallickara, S., & Fox, G. (2008, December). Mapreduce for data intensive scientific analyses. In *eScience, 2008. eScience'08. IEEE Fourth International Conference on* (pp. 277-284). IEEE.

Gannon, D., Fay, D., Green, D., Takeda, K., & Yi, W. (2014, June). Science in the cloud: lessons from three years of research projects on microsoft azure. In *Proceedings of the 5th ACM workshop on Scientific cloud computing* (pp. 1-8). ACM.

Grossman, R. L., Gu, Y., Mambretti, J., Sabala, M., Szalay, A., & White, K. (2010, June). An overview of the open science data cloud. In *Proceedings of the 19th ACM International Symposium on High Performance Distributed Computing* (pp. 377-384). ACM.

Hashem, I. A. T., Yaqoob, I., Anuar, N. B., Mokhtar, S., Gani, A., & Khan, S. U. (2015). The rise of "big data" on cloud computing: Review and open research issues. *Information Systems*, *47*, 98-115.

Hazelhurst, S. (2008, October). Scientific computing using virtual high-performance computing: a case study using the Amazon elastic computing cloud. In *Proceedings of the 2008 annual research conference of the South African Institute of Computer Scientists and Information Technologists on IT research in developing countries: riding the wave of technology* (pp. 94-103). ACM.

Juve, G., & Deelman, E. (2010). Scientific workflows and clouds. *Crossroads*, *16*(3), 14-18.

Lam, C. (2010). *Hadoop in action*. Manning Publications Co..

Lee, K. H., Lee, Y. J., Choi, H., Chung, Y. D., & Moon, B. (2012). Parallel data processing with MapReduce: a survey. *AcM sIGMoD Record*, *40*(4), 11-20.

Leskovec, J., Rajaraman, A., & Ullman, J. D. (2014). *Mining of massive datasets*. Cambridge University Press.

Li, J., & Lewis, H. W. (2016, November). Fuzzy Clustering Algorithms—Review of the Applications. In *Smart Cloud (SmartCloud), IEEE International Conference on* (pp. 282-288). IEEE.

Milojičić, D., Llorente, I. M., & Montero, R. S. (2011). Opennebula: A cloud management tool. *IEEE Internet Computing*, *15*(2), 11-14.

Nurmi, D., Wolski, R., Grzegorczyk, C., Obertelli, G., Soman, S., Youseff, L., & Zagorodnov, D. (2009, May). The eucalyptus open-source cloud-computing system. In *Proceedings of the 2009 9th IEEE/ACM International Symposium on Cluster Computing and the Grid* (pp. 124-131). IEEE Computer Society.

Olston, C., Reed, B., Srivastava, U., Kumar, R., & Tomkins, A. (2008, June). Pig latin: a not-so-foreign language for data processing. In *Proceedings of the 2008 ACM SIGMOD international conference on Management of data* (pp. 1099-1110). ACM.

Owen, S., & Robin, A. (2011). Ellen, Friedman: Mahout in Action. *Manning Publications*, *1*, 570-570.

Padhy, R. P. (2013). Big data processing with Hadoop-MapReduce in cloud systems. *International Journal of Cloud Computing and Services Science*, *2*(1), 16.

Ramakrishnan, L., Zbiegel, P. T., Campbell, S., Bradshaw, R., Canon, R. S., Coghlan, S., ... & Liu, A. (2011, June). Magellan: experiences from a science cloud. In *Proceedings of the 2nd international workshop on Scientific cloud computing* (pp. 49-58). ACM.

Ross, T. J. (2009). *Fuzzy logic with engineering applications*. John Wiley & Sons.

Srirama, S. N., Jakovits, P., & Vainikko, E. (2012). Adapting scientific computing problems to clouds using MapReduce. *Future Generation Computer Systems*, *28*(1), 184-192.

Talia, D. (2013). Toward cloud-based big-data analytics. *IEEE Computer Science*, 98-101

Thusoo, A., Sarma, J. S., Jain, N., Shao, Z., Chakka, P., Anthony, S., & Murthy, R. (2009). Hive: a warehousing solution over a map-reduce framework. *Proceedings of the VLDB Endowment*, *2*(2), 1626-1629.

Tudoran, R., Costan, A., Antoniu, G., & Bougé, L. (2012, April). A performance evaluation of Azure and Nimbus clouds for scientific applications. In *Proceedings of the 2nd International Workshop on Cloud Computing Platforms* (p. 4). ACM.

Vavilapalli, V. K., Murthy, A. C., Douglas, C., Agarwal, S., Konar, M., Evans, R., ... & Saha, B. (2013, October). Apache hadoop yarn: Yet another resource negotiator. In *Proceedings of the 4th annual Symposium on Cloud Computing* (p. 5). ACM.

Wang, L., Tao, J., Kunze, M., Castellanos, A. C., Kramer, D., & Karl, W. (2008, September). Scientific cloud computing: Early definition and experience. In *High Performance Computing and Communications, 2008. HPCC'08. 10th IEEE International Conference on* (pp. 825-830). IEEE.

CULTURAL MACHINE TRANSLATION USING MRF GIBBS MODEL & BAYESIAN LEARNING

Fernand Cohen and Zheng Zhong
Electrical & Computer Engineering Department, Drexel University, Philadelphia, PA 19104, USA

ABSTRACT

In this paper, we introduce a novel Gibbs language model constructed on a multi-layered dependency semantic graph to lexically disambiguate words, phrases, and sentences that lend themselves to different possible meaning and interpretations for use in machine translation (MT). The model looks at semantic cliques of words (key words) and assigns Gibbs potentials and conditional probabilities in proportion to the importance and degree of interactions between a given word and its neighbors within the semantic clique. Efficient estimates (maximum likelihood estimators (MLE)) for the Gibbs clique parameters are obtained using bilingual parallel corpora. Our method also naturally factors in the beliefs of expert translators, maps them into expert Gibbs parameters, and updates the MLE to maximum a posterior probability (MAP) estimates. Experimental results using our model and method are reported on testbeds in the medical and literary fiction domains and our results fare more than favorably when compared to the state-of-the-art long short-term memory (LSTM) Neural Network (NN) approach.

KEYWORDS

Cultural translation; MRF; Gibbs model; MLE; MAP; Iterative relaxation

1. INTRODUCTION

Translation is not the mere act of literal conversion of a word from one language to another, but rather an intricate process of unravelling the cultural nuances that exist in the original text and of finding ways to faithfully express it through the host language (Bassnett, 2013). As such translation can shape the identity of the translated as it gets perceived by the translator and the reader 'other'. Translational literature transcends the technical aspects of linguistic transfer and dwells into cultural translatability (or untranslatability), discourse of difference, and the construction of cultural identities (Hassan, 2006). If the space between translators and translated is not grounded in a good understanding of the culture of the translated, the translation becomes an act of politics of reception where the translated becomes more shaped in the host culture than the cultural dynamics of the originating one, creating in the process an alternative canon that reinforces preexisting stereotypes and misconceptions (Tam and Chan, 2012).

A successful machine translation (MT) needs to factor the various layers that exist within the original language both culturally and linguistically to faithfully capture the meaning (semantic) of the translated. One of the main challenges in translating text or speech from one language to another is the ability to correctly understand the cultural nuances of what is written or said. This dictates setting a multi-layered foundation that pays very close attention to cultural semantic, with the intricate interdependency of a word on its cultural context within its immediate and removed neighboring words and sentences properly captured.

In this paper, we introduce a probabilistic language model (Markov Random Field (MRF) Gibbs model (Cohen, 1986; Li, 2009)) that is built on this multi-layered dependency semantic structure foundation within a text to help lexically disambiguate words, phrases, and sentences that lend themselves to different possible meaning and interpretations. The model looks at semantic cliques of words (key words) and assigns Gibbs potentials and conditional probabilities in proportion to the importance and degree of interactions between a given word and its neighbors within the clique. The joint probability of words in a sentence, paragraph, or whole text, is expressed in terms of the product of these Gibbs conditional probabilities of a word taking a particular meaning given the state (meaning) of its neighbors within the clique. Within that semantic graph, the conditional probability of a word x given all words in a text is only dependent on n key words in contrast to the dependency on the n closest neighbors of x in an n-gram approach (Marcu and Wong, 2002; Koehn et al., 2003; Och and Ney, 2004). Efficient MLE for the Gibbs potentials are obtained using bilingual parallel corpora and can be augmented using MAP estimators that naturally factor in the beliefs of expert translators with intimate knowledge of the cultural semantic of the word within its clique. We map the expert's belief (the likelihood of given word taken a certain meaning) after translating it into expert Gibbs parameters (potentials). This allows a machine translator to combine data and expert driven learning, with the dominance of one kind (corpus versus expert translators) of learning over the other depending on the degree of belief (variance of the Gibbs potential parameters) derived from the corpus versus the cultural expert translator. This collective learning lays the foundation for a culturally meaningful and faithful MT framework that goes well beyond the current literal state of MT. This paper also obtains the most likely translation (highest probability) of a given text (one sentence, paragraph(s), a whole chapter, etc.) using a computationally efficient iterative relaxation algorithm that changes the possible meaning of ambiguous words as long as the joint likelihood (probability) of the text to be translated increases. The relaxation algorithm uses the MLE or MAP estimates (when expert translator opinion is available) for the Gibbs clique parameters. Experimental results using our model and method are reported on testbeds in the medical domain as well as in the literary and fiction domains, and our results are compared to the state-of-the-art LSTM Neural Network (NN) (Sutskever et al., 2014; Cho et al., 2014) approach with Glove word-vector (Cho et al., 2014) to solve words' disambiguation, where both methods are run on the same dataset for comparison. We observe a 13% on average improvement of our method (accuracy range 95%-98%) over the LSTM NN method (accuracy range 75%-91%) for the medical data (Medical Subject Headings) MSH; and for the literary (Center for Chinese Linguistics) CCL data set we observe a 6% mean accuracy improvement using MLE, and 28% accuracy improvement using MAP over the LSTM NN method, respectively.

The paper is organized as follows. In section 2 we introduce a brief survey on work done in MT. In section 3 our approach and method are introduced. Experimental results are shown in section 4. Finally, conclusions are drawn in section 5.

2. RELATED WORK

Present works of MT have shown great success on literal translation. They are quite adequate for handling simple texts (e.g., texts of weather report, menus, scientific papers, etc.), but when it comes to fiction and other literary works where authors' intentions must be clarified, a machine translation task is far from straightforward. When translating source text with lexical ambiguity (more than one intended meaning) due to cultural nuances, slang, dialect, etc., a MT system based on literal translation often fails to deliver the correct meaning. For example, the literal meaning of *lover* in Chinese has a single meaning of *husband* or *wife*, so when given a literal translation of the sentence "*Her husband found a love letter from her lover*," a literal Chinese translation of *lover* would result into *husband* instead of the correct translation *paramour*.

Work on MT falls into Statistical Machine Translation (SMT) and Neural Machine Translation (NMT). State-of-the-art SMT system *Pharaoh* (Marcu and Wong, 2002; Koehn et al., 2003; Och and Ney, 2004) uses a phrase-based n-gram model to address translation. It rests on the assumption that words appearing in closer proximities are likely to be more dependent on each other (Bengio et al., 2003), and that a sequence of words can be represented by the product of the conditional probability of the next word given the previous n words. Our Gibbs model shares common points with the n-gram model but it also has major differences with it. Both models rest upon exploiting the dependence of a word on neighboring words, with the n-gram model defining 'neighbors' in terms of spatial proximity (vicinity graph), whereas our Gibbs model extends the concept of 'neighbors' to cultural semantic proximity (semantic graph). Within that semantic graph, the conditional probability of a word x given all words in a text is only dependent on n key words in contrast to the dependency on the n closest neighbors of x for the n-gram approach. The following example illustrates that point succinctly. Consider the following sentence (originally in Arabic), "*It was a sizzling hot afternoon in Cairo's summer. The wife left the house to talk to her neighbor, while her man jumped on the opportunity to wear the jellabiya locking the door of the bedroom behind him.*" The word *jellabiya* in Arabic either means a woman dress or traditional attire that men in the Middle East wear at home or for going out. We see that in the absence of a cultural semantic dependency graph, the translation of *jellabiya* into a 'woman dress', which will most likely be the translation of choice for an n-gram approach, would completely and totally alter the meaning of the sentence with insinuation of the husband being a cross dresser, something that was definitely not intended in the Arabic text. In contrast a culturally semantic graph would recognize key words such as *Cairo*, the *sizzling hot* and *afternoon* to easily recognize that *jellabiya* here is the traditional equivalent of men's pajamas in the west and that the husband was merely jumping on the opportunity to take a nap while his wife was out of the house talking to her neighbor.

For NMT work, an encoder-decoder model (Sutskever et al., 2014; Cho et al., 2014) is widely used. For an encoder, it computes the representation code for source text. Based on the output from the encoder, a decoder is applied to generate the text of the target language. Cho et al. (2014b) have shown that this model fails to compress all the information from the source text especially when dealing with long text. To deal with that problem, the structure of Neural Network needs to be enlarged, which in turn would require large data set for training the NMT system (Valiant, 1984). This constitutes the biggest drawback associated the NMT approach and in the absence of large data sets for training machine translation accuracy suffers. For a successful machine lexical disambiguation large sized training sets are needed. These data sets are by and large manually extracted from existing corpora such as WordNet (Mihalcea and Moldovan, 2001), which makes the data acquisition for training a very time consuming task. This is compounded by the fact that online dictionaries provide semantic information in a mostly unstructured way (Navigli and Velardi, 2005).

3. SEMANTIC GRAPH PROBABILITIC MODELS TO LEXICALLY DISAMBIGUATE WORDS IN MT

3.1 MRF Gibbs Language Model and Semantic Cliques

As indicated in the introduction section the MRF Gibbs language model builds on the multi-layered dependency structure foundation within a text to help lexically disambiguate word, phrases, and sentences that lend themselves to different possible meaning and interpretations. The model looks at cliques defined on a graph of semantic interdependencies between words (i.e., dependence of a word on key words) and assigns Gibbs potentials and conditional probabilities in proportion to the importance and degree of interactions between a given word and its neighbors within the clique. Within that semantic graph, the conditional probability of a word x given all words in a text is only dependent on n key words that might be close or far removed in proximity to the word x. For clique of order 2, the disambiguation of a word is dependent on the meaning of its neighbor in the semantic clique. Similarly, a clique of order 3, the disambiguation of a word is dependent on the joint occurrence of the word with two of its neighbors that now form a triplet.

3.2 MRF Gibbs Model Structure

Let $\{x_r\}$ denote a random field, with x_r the field at word r, $X = (x_1, x_2, \ldots x_m)$ a vector represents the field of the whole given m length sentence, and $X_{(r)}$ be the entire sentence not including the word r. By $\{x_r\}$ a MRF, it presents a family of random variables with joint probability density function on the set of all possible realizations X of the given sentence which satisfies the following:

$$p(X) > 0 \; for \; all \; X \tag{1}$$

$$p(x_r|X_{(r)}) = p(x_r|x_v, v \in D_p) \tag{2}$$

where D_p is the clique neighborhood of r and $p(x_r|X_{(r)})$ denotes the conditional likelihood of x_r given $X_{(r)}$. v is the neighborhood word which belongs to D_p. Pairwise cliques are the sets $\{(x_r, x_i) : x_i \in X \,\&\, x_i \neq x_r\}$, whereas tripleton cliques are the sets $\{(x_r, x_i, x_j): x_i, x_j \in X \,\&\, x_i \neq x_j \neq x_r\}$, etc. If we limit ourselves to cliques of order 3, then according to the Hammersley-Clifford theorem (Cohen, 1986; Li, 2009) $p(x_r|X_{(r)})$ takes the form

$$p(x_r|X_{(r)}) = \frac{\exp\{\sum_{v \in Dp} G_{k,v} + \sum_{v,w \in Dp} G_{k,v,w}\}}{Z} \tag{3}$$

$$Z = \sum_{k=1}^{K} \exp\{\sum_{v \in Dp} G_{k,v} + \sum_{v,w \in Dp} G_{k,v,w}\} \tag{4}$$

Here x_r has totally K meanings, $G_{k,v}$, & $G_{k,v,w}$ are the clique energy functions set here to be

$$G_{k,v} = \delta(x_r - k)\theta_{k,v}, ; G_{k,v,w} = \delta(x_r - k)\theta_{k,v,w} \quad (5)$$

where $\theta_{k,v}$, & $\theta_{k,v,w}$ are the clique parameters. $p(x_r|X_{(r)}) = p(x_r|X_{(r)}, \theta)$ is a parametric distribution parametrized by the clique vector parameters $\theta = \{\theta_{k,v}, \& \ \theta_{k,v,w}, k = 1,..K, \& \ v, w \in D_p\}$. The parameter vector θ is estimated given training sets obtained from bilingual parallel corpora. In the next section we show how to obtain efficient estimators (achieving the Cramer Rao bound) for the clique parameters. This is of great significance especially when the training set is somewhat limited. Finally note that the joint likelihood $p(X|\theta)$ is expressed as the product of conditional probability densities $p(x_r|X_{(r)}, \theta)$ and hence is completely determined by the conditional probability densities (Cohen, 1986; Li, 2009).

3.3 Efficient Estimates for the Clique Parameters: MLE

As the Gibbs distribution is a canonical d −parameter exponential family with the parameter space of θ being an open subset $\Re^d$, and since the score function is linear in θ, an efficient estimator exists and is the maximum likelihood estimator (Zacks, 1981). Given bilingual parallel corpora, let $n_{x,v}$ be the number of times x occurred simultaneously with $x_v, v \in clique\ of\ order\ 2$, with $n_{x,v} = \sum_{k=1}^{K} n_{k,v}$; and let $n_{x,v,w}$ be the number of times x occurred simultaneously with x_v, x_w, with $v, w \in clique\ of\ order\ 3$, with $n_{x,v,w} = \sum_{k=1}^{K} n_{k,v,w}$. Then MLE for $\theta_{k,v}$, & $\theta_{k,v,w}$ are given by

$$\theta^*_{k,v} = \ln\{\frac{n_{k,v}}{n_{x,v}}\} = \ln\{\beta^*_{k,v}\};\ \theta^*_{k,v,w} = \ln\left\{\frac{n_{k,v,w}}{n_{x,v,w}}\right\} = \ln\{\beta^*_{k,v,w}\}, k = 1,2,..,K. \quad (6)$$

Based on the MLE θ^* the classification of a given x is in accordance with the Bayes decision rule

$$\max_{1 \le k \le K} p(x = k|\theta^*) \quad (7)$$

3.4 Ranking the Neighbors in a Semantic Graph Neighborhood

There are two distinct ways to determine what the key neighboring words are in the Gibbs MRF semantic graph. The first would be a decision rendered by expert translator(s) on what the key words for the word x (with more than one possible meaning) should be. The expert translator can also rank the key words in terms of their importance, for the disambiguation of the word x given the neighbors, hence allowing an ordering of the neighbors in the clique. For example, suppose x takes one of two meanings (1 or 2) and suppose we are considering pairwise interaction between x with all the other words (Y) in the text. If an expert determines that the key words when $x = 1$ is the set $y_1 = (y_{11}, y_{12}, .., y_{1p})$ and for $x = 2$ is the set $y_2 = (y_{21}, y_{22}, .., y_{2p})$, then in that case $p(x|Y) = p(x|y, y \in D_p) = p(x|y_1, y_2)$, i.e., the dependencies are not on the whole text but on only the subset y_1 & y_2, hence the Markovinity property. If in addition the key words are ranked in accordance with their importance to the disambiguation of x, we can then associate specific order for the neighboring points in the Gibbs distribution. For a first order $p(x|Y) = p(x|y_{11}, y_{21})$, whereas a second order $p(x|Y) = p(x|y_{11}, y_{21}, y_{12}, y_{22})$, and so on until the pth order.

We can also determine the keys words from bilingual corpora by estimating the pairwise potential of $x = 1$ & $x = 2$ with all the y words in the text using MLE as in section 3.3, then rank the potentials from larger to smaller and keep $y_1 = (y_{11}, y_{12}, .., y_{1p})$ (for $x = 1$) and $y_2 = (y_{21}, y_{22}, .., y_{2p})$ for ($x = 2$) with the biggest p potential values each. We can also determine the largest p potential value by eliminating the ranked potentials that fall below a given threshold.

3.5 Incorporating Cultural Expert(s)' Opinion for Updating the Clique Parameters: MAP Estimates

With the availability of cultural expert translators, the clique vectors parameters can be augmented using MAP estimators through naturally factoring in the beliefs of expert translator(s) (with intimate knowledge of the cultural semantic of the words within its clique). We map the expert's belief (the likelihood of given word taken a certain meaning) to clique vectors parameters as shown in next section 3.5.1. Since $p(X|\theta)$ can be expressed as (using a 2nd order Taylor series expansion of ln $\{p(X|\theta\}$ around $\theta*$ (Zacks, 1981)

$$p(X|\theta) \cong p(X|\theta^*)\exp[-\frac{1}{2}(\theta - \theta^*)^t[J(\theta^*)](\theta - \theta^*)] \quad (8)$$

where $[J(\theta^*)] = [J_{m,n}(\theta^*)] = [-\frac{\partial^2 \ln\{p(X|\theta^*)\}}{\partial\theta_m \partial\theta_n}], m, n = 1, 2, \ldots, d$ is the inverse covariance matrix of the MLE θ^*, and under a Gaussian assumption on the expert prior for the Gibbs clique parameters, i.e., taking $p(\theta) \sim N(\mu_0, [\Sigma_0])$, where μ_0 & $[\Sigma_0]$ are computed based on expert beliefs probabilities as explained in section 2.4. Then the posteriori probability $p(\theta|X)\ ) \sim N(\mu_{\mathrm{MAP}}, [\Sigma_{\mathrm{MAP}}])$ (Duda et al., 2001) where

$$\mu_{\mathrm{MAP}} = ([J(\theta^*)]^{-1} + [\Sigma_0])^{-1}[\Sigma_0]\,\theta^* + ([J(\theta^*)]^{-1} + [\Sigma_0])^{-1}[J(\theta^*)]^{-1}\mu_0 \tag{9}$$

$$[\Sigma_{\mathrm{MAP}}]^{-1} = [J(\theta^*)] + [\Sigma_0]^{-1} \tag{10}$$

The MAP estimation is then given as $\theta_{\mathrm{MAP}} = \max_\theta \ln\{\{p(\theta|X)\} = \mu_{\mathrm{MAP}}$, where μ_{MAP} is given above. Based on $\theta_{MAP}$the classification of a given x is in accordance with the Bayes decision rule

$$\max_{1\le k\le K} p(x = k|\theta_{\mathrm{MAP}}) \leftrightarrow \max_{1\le k\le K} \mu_{\mathrm{MAP},k} \tag{11}$$

3.5.1 Mapping Cultural Expert Prior Beliefs into Prior Clique Parameters Probabilities

Given M experts translators, let $\beta^m_{k,v} = p_{m,x}(x = k|v)$ be the degree of belief given that expert m gives for x taking the value k based on the simultaneous appearance of the x and v words together; and finally let $\beta^m_{k,v,w} = p_{m,x}(x = k|v, w)$ be the degree of belief given that expert m gives for x taking the value k based on the simultaneous appearance of the x, v, and w words together. Similar to the MLE for θ, the m expert values for θ are assigned in accordance with

$$\theta^m_{k,v,0} = \ln\left\{\beta^m_{k,v}\right\};\ \theta^m_{k,v,w,0} = \ln\{\beta^m_{k,v,w}\}, k = 1,2,.., K. \tag{12}$$

Thus μ_0 and $[\Sigma_0]$ are given by:

$$\mu_0 = \frac{1}{M}\sum_{m=1}^{M} \theta_{0,m}\,; [\Sigma_0] = \frac{1}{M}\sum_{m=1}^{M}(\theta_{0,m} - \mu_0)(\theta_{0,m} - \mu_0)^t \tag{13}$$

with $\theta_{0,m} = \{\theta^m_{k,0}, \theta^m_{k,v,0}, \theta^m_{k,v,w,0}, k = 1,..K, \&\ v, w \in D_p\}$. When there is only one expert translator, the expert needs not only supply values for $\beta_{k,v}$ and $\beta_{k,v,w}$values but also a degree of confidence in these $\beta_{k,v}$ and $\beta_{k,v,w}$ values. $[\Sigma_0]$ is computed from the degree of confidence intervals.

3.6 Iterative Relaxation

In this section, we show how we can obtain the most likely translation (highest probability) of a given text (one sentence, paragraph(s), a whole chapter, etc.) using a computationally efficient iterative relaxation algorithm that changes the possible meaning of ambiguous words as long as the joint likelihood (probability) of the text to be translated increases. Note that the relaxation algorithm assumes that the Gibbs clique parameters are known or have been estimated using the MLE or MAP estimates (when expert translator opinion is available) prior to the start of the iterative relaxation. Let X be the sentence to be translated, with $X = (x_1, x_2, \ldots, x_M) = (X_{\mathrm{amb}}, X_{\overline{\mathrm{amb}}})$ with X_{amb} being the set of words in X with ambiguous meaning & $X_{\overline{\mathrm{amb}}}$ being the set of words in X with one possible meaning (translation), hence there is of no need to be disambiguated, and let Y_{amb} be the set of key words for the set X_{amb}, where elements of Y_{amb} could have elements in X or be X itself in the absence of key words. The most likely translation of the ambiguous word set X_{amb} is the one that maximizes the joint likelihood function $p(X_{\mathrm{amb}}|Y_{\mathrm{amb}})$. To achieve that maximum we use an iterative procedure where an initial assignment for all ambiguous words is made, then we visit each ambiguous word (one at a time) and check if a change in meaning for that point given that everything else remains constant (i.e., in accordance with the initial assignment) will increase $p(X_{\mathrm{amb}}|Y_{\mathrm{amb}})$. This is equivalent to saying we make the change from $x_{\mathrm{amb},n}$ to $x_{\mathrm{amb},n+1}$ only if $p(x_{\mathrm{amb},n+1}|Y_{\mathrm{amb},n-1}) > p(x_{\mathrm{amb},n}|Y_{\mathrm{amb},n-1})$ where n stands for the nth iteration in the relaxation. We reach the end of the relaxation when there are no further changes in the state of any of the ambiguous words. We show an example of the relaxation in the experiment section with the initial assignment for the ambiguous words made in accordance with the frequency of occurrence of the ambiguous words in the bilingual corpora, which in most cases will be close to pure random assignment.

4. EXPERIMENT RESULTS

4.1 Experiment 1 - Medical Data Set

We test the effectiveness of the 2nd order clique model and up to 3rd clique model on a medical data set (the MSH WSD Data Set) (Jimeno-Yepes et al., 2011). This set consists of tagged texts with ambiguous abbreviations extracted from citations from the MEDLINE journal. For each text, one labeled ambiguous abbreviation is included. For each of the abbreviation around 100 texts (where a text here can consist of 1 to 4 sentences) where the abbreviation appears are chosen. These are processed by removing common words (e.g., I, am, is, are etc.). Out of the 100 texts, a set of 99 texts are used for training and a set of 1 is used for testing, and we resample using a leave one out approach, where a different text sample (out of the 100 texts) is used for testing and the rest 99 texts used for training. This brings the size of the testbed to 100 cases. Note that key neighboring words are automatically extracted as explained in section 3.4 using the MLE method in section 3.3 in estimating the clique parameters. We also implement the state-of-the-art LSTM Neural Network (Sundermeyer et al., 2015) approach with Glove word-vector (Pennington et al, 2014) on the same set of data for comparison. Mean accuracy performance based on the 100-sized testbed is reported in Table 1, where mean value accuracy (with perfect accuracy taking the value 1 and worse accuracy taking the value 0). The results fare very favorably compared to NN results with a mean accuracy (average over the 6 words) of 0.96 and standard deviation (std) of 0.01) for 2nd order clique and 0.97 (std of 0.01) for the up to a 3rd order clique as compared to 0.84 (std of 0.06) for the NN.

Table 1. MSH accuracy

Ambiguous word	Second order clique	Up to 3rd order clique	NMT
BSE	0.96	0.97	0.85
ADH	0.98	0.98	0.91
ALS	0.96	0.97	0.90
BSA	0.96	0.97	0.85
AA	0.97	0.98	0.78
BAT	0.95	0.95	0.75
mean/std	0.96/0.01	0.97/0.01	0.84/0.06

4.2 Experiment 2 - Literary Fiction Data Set

We also test our model on CLL bilingual corpus (Bai, X et al., 2002) which consists of text from literary fiction. For each of the word around 100 texts (consisting of 1 to 3 sentences each) where the ambiguous word appears are chosen. Mean accuracy based on the 100-sized testbed is reported in Table 2.

Table 2. CLL accuracy

Ambiguous word	Up to 3rd order clique model	MAP model	NMT
address	0.82	0.91	0.72
appreciate	0.58	0.90	0.52
column	0.84	0.86	0.74
cover	0.52	0.85	0.50
bond	0.70	0.94	0.68
perspective	0.80	1.00	0.70
rest	0.69	1.00	0.65
beat	0.68	1.00	0.70
provision	0.75	0.92	0.72
figure	0.71	0.95	0.62
Mean/std	0.71/0.10	0.93/0.06	0.65/0.08

We follow the exact leave-one-out method followed in section 4.1 to bring the size of the testbed to 100 cases. Key neighboring words are automatically extracted using our method in section 3.4 employing the MLE (for up to 3rd order clique) and MAP methods in section 3.5 for estimating the clique parameters based on 20 fluent English and Chinese speakers. Our method is compared to the state-of-the-art LSTM Neural Network (Sundermeyer et al., 2015) approach with Glove word-vector (Pennington et al, 2014) on the same data set. The results fare very favorably compared to NN results for both MLE and MAP (especially for the MAP), with a mean accuracy (average over the 10 ambiguous words) of 0.71 (std of 0.10) based on the MLE for up to a 3rd order clique, and 0.93 (std of 0.06) based on MAP compared to 0.65 (std of 0.08) for the NN.

4.3 Experiment 3 - A Relaxation Example

The relaxation method on sentences with more than one ambiguous word is shown on the following example sentence "***Provisions*** ***address*** *children's education to prevent the dropout problem.*" Bolded words are ambiguous and need to be translated, whereas the underlined words are found to be key words selected using our key words selection method in section 3.4 using the MLE method in section 3.3 based on the bilingual corpora. *Provisions* can either be *supplies* or *rules* while *address* can take two different meanings *location* or *deal with* which means that $X_{\mathrm{amb}} = \{x_{\mathrm{amb1}} = provision,\ x_{\mathrm{amb2}} = address\}$, & $Y_{\mathrm{amb}} = \{provisions, address, education, problem\}$. Let $Y_{\mathrm{amb1},n} = \{\boldsymbol{address}, education, problem\}$ and $Y_{\mathrm{amb2},n} = \{\boldsymbol{provisions}, education, problem\}$ at iteration n, where the bolding the current state of the ambiguous word at the nth iteration. Using a random assignment for the initial states of the ambiguous words resulted into having $x_{\mathrm{amb1,0}} = supplies$, $x_{\mathrm{amb2,0}} = location$. Note that the second suffix stands for the iteration number (0 here) in the relaxation. The first iteration starts by examining whether the state of the word *provisions* should remain as is (i.e., $x_{\mathrm{amb,1,0}} = supplies$) or should be changedto $x_{\mathrm{amb,1,1}} = rule$. Since from Table 3, $p(x_{\mathrm{amb1,1}} = rules|Y_{\mathrm{amb1,0}}) < p(x_{\mathrm{amb1,1}} = supplies|Y_{\mathrm{amb1,0}})$, this means that the word *provisions* remains in its initial state *supplies*, and $Y_{\mathrm{amb2,1}} = \{provisions = supplies, education, problem\}$. Next we visit the word *location* and examine whether or not its state should be changed or remained the same. From Table 3 $p(x_{\mathrm{amb2,1}} = deal\ with|Y_{\mathrm{amb2,1}}) > p(x_{\mathrm{amb2,1}} = location|Y_{\mathrm{amb2,1}})$, hence a change for $x_{\mathrm{amb2,1}} = deal\ with$ and an update for $Y_{\mathrm{amb1,1}} = \{address = location, education, problem\}$. Next we revisit word *provisions* and check whether its state should be changed now that $Y_{\mathrm{amb1,1}}$ has changed. Since $p(x_{\mathrm{amb1,2}} = rules|Y_{\mathrm{amb1,1}}) > p(x_{\mathrm{amb1,2}} = supplies|Y_{\mathrm{amb1,1}})$ (see Table 3). This leads to a change in *provisions* to *rules* and a subsequent update of $Y_{\mathrm{amb2,2}} = \{provisions = rules, education, problem\}$. This is repeated until there are no change in the states of both ambiguous words. The states of the ambiguous words are shown in Table 3 with the conditional probabilities of the ambiguous words at stage n given the state of their respective key words at stage $n-1$ (given in % between brackets) at every iteration. At the end of the relaxation, the sentence translation is based on the following sentence semantic "*Rules deal with children's education to prevent the dropout problem.*"

Table 3. Iterative relaxation

Iteration	Provisions	Address
Initial	Supplies (50%)	Location (50%)
1st	*Supplies* (66%)	*location*
2nd	*supplies*	*deal with* (83%)
3rd	*rules* (80%)	*deal with*
4th	*rules*	*deal with* (87.5%)

5. CONCLUSIONS

We presented a novel Gibbs model that exploits the dependence of a word on its neighboring words with the concept of 'neighbors' extending to cultural semantic proximity (semantic graph). The model allows for the determination of what the keys words are from bilingual corpora as well as from expert translators' feedback to unravel the cultural nuances that exist in the original text and of finding ways to faithfully express it through the host language. The efficient MLE Gibbs model parameters are obtained from bilingual corpora data and when expert translators' feedback is available the MLE's are replaced by MAP estimates that combine both sources of knowledge. The model and approach allows for optimal statistical decision as to the best disambiguation of a word to be translated. For a text with multiple ambiguous words, the most likely translation (highest probability) of the given text (one sentence, paragraph(s), a whole chapter, etc.) is attained using a computationally efficient iterative relaxation algorithm that changes the possible meaning of ambiguous words as long as the joint likelihood (probability) of the text to be translated increases. Finally, we show using common testbed data how our approach more than favorably compares to the state-of-the-art LSTM Neural Network (NN) approach.

REFERENCES

Bai, X. et al., 2002. The construction of a large-scale Chinese-English parallel corpus. In Recent Development in Machine Translation Studies-Proceedings of the National Conference on Machine Translation , pp. 124-131.

Bassnett, S., 2013. *Translation studies*. Routledge, New York, USA.

Bengio, Y. et al., 2003. A neural probabilistic language model. Journal of machine learning research, 3(Feb), pp. 1137-1155.

Cho, K. et al., 2014. Learning phrase representations using RNN encoder-decoder for statistical machine translation. *arXiv preprint arXiv:1406.1078*.

Cho, K. et al., 2014, On the properties of neural machine translation: Encoder-decoder approaches. *arXiv preprint arXiv:1409.1259*.

Cohen, F., 1986. Markov Random Fields for Image Modelling & Analysis. In: U. Desai, ed., *Modelling and application of stochastic processes*, 1st ed. pp. 243-278.

Duda, R. et al., 2001. *Pattern classification*. John Wiley & Sons, New York, USA.

Hassan, W., 2006. Agency and Translational Literature: Ahdaf Soueif's The Map of Love. *PMLA*, 121(3), pp. 753-768.

Jimeno-Yepes, et al., 2001. Exploiting MeSH indexing in MEDLINE to generate a data set for word sense disambiguation. *BMC Bioinformatics*, 12(1), pp. 223.

Koehn, P. et al., 2003. Statistical phrase-based translation. In *Proceedings of the 2003 Conference of the North American Chapter of the Association for Computational Linguistics on Human Language Technology*, Volume 1, pp. 48-54. Association for Computational Linguistics.

Li, S., 2009. *Markov Random Fields for image modeling in image analysis*. Springer Science & Business Media, London, UK.

Marcu, D. and Wong, W., 2002. A phrase-based, joint probability model for statistical machine translation. In *Proceedings of the ACL-02 conference on Empirical methods in natural language processing*, Volume 10, pp. 133-139.

Mihalcea, R. and Moldovan, D., 2001. A Highly Accurate Bootstrapping Algorithm for Word Sense Disambiguation. *International Journal on Artificial Intelligence Tools*, 10(01n02), pp. 5-21.

Navigli, R. and Velardi, P., 2005. Structural semantic interconnections: a knowledge-based approach to word sense disambiguation. *IEEE Transactions on Pattern Analysis and Machine Intelligence*, 27(7), pp. 1075-1086.

Och, F. and Ney, H., 2004. The Alignment Template Approach to Statistical Machine Translation. *Computational Linguistics*, 30(4), pp. 417-449.

Pennington, J. et al., 2014. Glove: Global Vectors for Word Representation. In *EMNLP* Vol. 14, pp. 1532-1543.

Sutskever, I. et al., 2014. Sequence to sequence learning with neural networks. In *Advances in neural information processing systems*, pp. 3104-3112.

Sundermeyer, M. et al., 2015. From Feedforward to Recurrent LSTM Neural Networks for Language Modeling. *IEEE/ACM Transactions on Audio, Speech, and Language Processing*, 23(3), pp. 517-529.

Tam, K. and Chan, K., 2012. *Culture in translation*. Open University of Hong Kong Press, Kowloon, Hong Kong.

Valiant, L., 1984. A theory of the learnable. *Communications of the ACM*, 27(11), pp. 1134-1142.

Zacks, S., 2014. *Parametric Statistical Inference: Basic Theory and Modern Approaches* (Vol. 4). Elsevier, New York, USA.

PRIOR ART CANDIDATE SEARCH ON BASE OF STATISTICAL AND SEMANTIC PATENT ANALYSIS

Dmitriy M. Korobkin, Sergey S. Fomenkov, Alla G. Kravets and Sergey. G. Kolesnikov
Volgograd State Technical University, Volgograd, Lenin av., 28, Russia

ABSTRACT

In paper authors proposed a methodology to solve problem of prior art patent search, consists of statistical and semantic analysis of patent documents, and calculation of semantic similarity between application and patents on base of Subject-Action-Object (SAO) triples. The paper considers a description of statistical analysis based on LDA method and MapReduce paradigm. On the step of semantic analysis authors applied a new method for building semantic representation of SAO on base of Meaning-Text Theory. On the step of semantic similarity calculation we compare the SAOs from application and patent claims. We developed an software for the patent examination task, which is designed to reduce the time that an expert spends for the prior-art candidate search. This research was financially supported by the Russian Fund of Basic Research (grants No. 15-07-09142 A, No. 15-07-06254 A, No. 16-07-00534 A).

KEYWORDS

Prior-art patent search, patent examination, LDA, semantic analysis, natural language processing, SAO, big data

1. INTRODUCTION

From year to year the number of patent applications is increasing. Around 2.9 million patent applications were filed worldwide in 2015, up 7.8% from 2014. The escalating applications flow and more than 20 million World set of granted patents (from 1980 to 2015) increase the time that patent examiners have to spend to examine all incoming applications. Sometimes examiner has to make hundreds of search queries and to process thousands of existing patents manually during the examination procedure to make a decision: to approve the application or to reject it. The increasing workload of patent office's led to need for developing of new approaches for patents prior-art retrieval on base of statistical and semantic methods of natural language processing.

Many scientists tried to solve patent prior-art search task. Magdy used an approach based on unigrams and bigrams (Magdy, 2010), Verma's approach is based on keyphrase and citations extraction (Verma, 2011), Mahdabi used method based on a time-aware random walk on a weighted network of patent citations (Mahdabi, 2014), Xue's approach considers an actual query as the basic unit and thus captures important query-level dependencies between words and phrases (Xue, 2013), D'hondt tried to compare flat classification with a two-step hierarchical system which models the IPC hierarchy (D'hondt, 2017), Bouadjenek used query with a full patent description in conjunction with generic query reduction methods (Bouadjenek, 2015), Kim proposed the method to suggest diverse queries that can cover multiple aspects of the query (patent) (kim, 2014), Ferraro's approach consist in segmenting the patent claim, using a rule-based approach, and a conditional random field is trained to segment the components into clauses (Ferraro, 2014), Andersson used the techniques by addressing three different relation extraction applications: acronym extraction, hyponymy extraction and factoid entity relation extraction (Andersson, 2017), Park uses SAO (subject-action-object) for identifying patent infringement (Park, 2012), Yufeng combines the SAO structure with the VSM module to calculate the patent similarity (Yufeng, 2016), Choi uses SAO-based text mining approach to building a technology tree (Choi, 2012), authors this paper proposed the method of technical function discovery in patent databases (Korobkin, 2016).

In this paper we propose a novel approach, in which we tried to combine both statistical and semantic features to increase the accuracy of prior-art search.

2. STATISTICAL ANALYSIS

The basic idea of LDA (Blei, 2003) - patents are represented as random mixtures of latent topics, where each topic is characterized by a distribution according to the words from documents array. Based on the LDA model can be used a patent database statistical analysis and distribution of patents by the unnamed topics.

The first stage of the statistical analysis is the tokenization of the patent text. In this case the tokens will be individual words or N-grams from the patent text. After tokenization is necessary to make the lemmatization, i.e. converting the extracted words to their base form for the most accurate building of term-document matrix. The Big data processing framework Apache Spark and MLlib library for machine learning allows to get a dictionary of all words from the documents set and build a term-document matrix.

The statistic analysis software (Korobkin, 2016) produces a patent search by different methods and evaluates the efficiency of patent search. On base of statistical analysis testing results can be concluded: the most effective method for vectors storage is storing in HDFS, comparing the distribution vectors of patents by topics on base Cosine similarity, patent tokenization with replacing synonyms. Tokenization with replacing synonyms includes the removal of stop-words, but beyond that, all words-synonyms are present to one word (base alias). This approach allows us to build the most accurate term-document matrix and the LDA model but slow down compared to the usual tokenization.

3. SEMANTIC ANALYSIS

On this step we perform a dependency trees construction for application and patent claims (Kravets, 2015). The text of patent claims has one feature that makes the effective use of existing solutions for building dependency trees is difficult. This feature is that the patent claims are written in one sentence, which sometimes includes hundreds of words. To solve this problem has been developed algorithm of complex sentences segmentation (Korobkin, 2015). Sentences are segmented on base of transitional phrases of claims and special "marker" phrases such as ", wherein", ", said"; ", and"; "; and"; ", thereby"; "thereby"; "such that"; "so that"; "wherein"; "whereby"; "where"; "when"; "wile"; etc. For remove numbering like "A.", "a.", "1." or "1)" we used the regular expression: «^(\d{1,4}|[a-zA-Z]{1,2})(\.|\))\s», for remove the references like «4. The device according to claim 3...» we used the regular expression: «^.+(of|in|to) claim \d+(,)?». The sentences are separate by punctuation, such as: «:», «;», «.», «!», «?», with used the regular expression «(\.|!|\?|:|;)\s?».

Then, we perform a morphological analysis of the patent text with TreeTagger (Toutanova, 2000) for Russian and English language. After that we used MaltParser (Hall, 2006) to perform semantic parsing (building a dependency tree).

Now let us consider the semantic analysis of the sentence: "The second end electrode and the center electrode of the first tubular body are electrically connected to the center electrode and the first end electrode, respectively, of the second tubular body".

Table 1. Example of dependence tree in Conll'09 format

index word in sentence	word form itself	word's lemma or stem	POS	index of syntactic parent	Stanford typed dependencies
1	the	The	DT	4	Det
2	second	Second	JJ	4	Amod
3	end	End	NN	4	Nn
4	electrode	Electrode	NN	16	Nsubj
5	and	And	CC	4	Cc
6	the	The	DT	8	Det
7	center	Center	NN	8	Nn
8	electrode	Electrode	NN	4	Conj
9	of	Of	IN	8	Prep
10	the	The	DT	13	Det
11	first	First	JJ	13	Amod
12	tubular	Tubular	JJ	13	Amod
13	body	Body	NN	9	Pobj
14	are	Be	VBP	16	Cop
15	electrically	Electrically	RB	16	Advmod
16	connected	Connect	VVN	0	Null

Part-of-speech (POS) tags (Haverinin, 2010) are assigned to a single word according to its role in the sentence: the verb (base form (VV), past participle (VVN), verb "be", present, non-3rd person (VBP)), the noun (NN), adjective (JJ), preposition (IN), determiner (DT), adverb (RB), coordinating conjunction (CC), etc.

The Stanford typed dependencies (de Marneffe, 2016) representation was designed to provide a simple description of the grammatical relationships in a sentence: "amod" - adjectival modifier, "det" – determiner, "pobj" - object of a preposition, "nsubj" - nominal subject, "cop" - copula, "cc" - coordination, "conj" - conjunct, "nn" - noun compound modifier, "advmod" - adverb modifier, "prep" - prepositional modifier, "punct" - punctuation).

In the collapsed representation, dependencies involving prepositions, conjuncts, as well as information about the referent of relative clauses are collapsed to get direct dependencies between content words. We removed from dependence trees the grammatical relations such as "punct", "det", "prep", "cc", etc. The parent of removed node is transferred to the child node, фnd the indexes of words in the sentence are renumbered:

nsubj(connected-16, electrode-4)
cc(electrode-4, and-5)
det(electrode-8, the-6)
nn(electrode-8, center-7)
conj(electrode-4, electrode-8)

become

nsubj(connected-10, electrode-3)
nsubj(connected-10, electrode-8)

Authors used an approach based on the MTT (Meaning-Text Theory) (Mel'cuk, 1988). According to MMT collapsed Stanford Dependencies (SD) merge into the set of Deep Syntactic relations (Table 2).

Table 2. Transformation from Stanford Dependencies to Deep Syntactic Relations

Collapsed Stanford Dependencies	Deep Syntactic Structure
amod(electrode-3, second-1)	ATTR(electrode-3, second-1)
nn(electrode-3, end-2)	ATTR(electrode-3, end-2)
nsubj(connected-10, electrode-3)	I(connected-10, electrode-3)
nn(electrode-5, center-4)	ATTR(electrode-5, center-4)
nsubj(connected-10, electrode-5)	I(connected-10, electrode-5)
amod(body-8, first-6)	ATTR(body-8, first-6)
amod(body-8, tubular-7)	ATTR(body-8, tubular-7)
pobj(electrode-5, body-8)	II(electrode-5, body-8)
advmod(connected-10, electrically-9)	ATTR(connected-10, electrically-9)
root (ROOT-0, connected-10)	root (ROOT-0, connected-10)
nn(electrode-12, center-11)	ATTR(electrode-12, center-11)
pobj(connected-10, electrode-12)	II(connected-10, electrode-12)
amod(electrode-15, first-13)	ATTR(electrode-15, first-13)
nn(electrode-15, end-14)	ATTR(electrode-15, end-14)
pobj(connected-10, electrode-15)	II(connected-10, electrode-15)
advmod(connected-10, respectively-16)	ATTR(connected-10, respectively-16)
amod(body-19, second-17)	ATTR(body-19, second-17)
amod(body-19, tubular-18)	ATTR(body-19, tubular-18)
pobj(connected-10, body-19)	II(connected-10, body-19)

According to MMT we transformed Stanford Dependencies (SD) into the Deep syntactic relations (DSyntRel):

- Actantial relations: the relation I – Subject and all its transform, nominal and agentive complement: "nsubj", "nsubjpass", "csubj", "csubjpass", etc; : the relation II – Direct Object, Oblique (Prepositional) Object, predicative complement, complement of an adjective, a preposition and a conjunction: "dobj", "iobj", "pobj", etc; the relation III uses with semantically trivalent transitive verb or it's a SD such as pobj_in, pobj_on, etc. (used together with prepositions).
- The attributives relations (ATTR) cover all types of modifiers, determines, quantifiers, relative clauses, circumstantials: "amod", "advmod", "nn", etc.

4. SAO SIMILARITY CALCULATION BETWEEN PATENT APPLICATION AND PATENTS

On this step, we compare SAO (which are represented as semantic trees) for application claims with trees from selected subset received on the step of statistical analysis. We re-rank relevant patents from selected subset according to similarities between semantic trees.

In accordance with MTT trees at Deep syntactic representation level show dependency relations between terms (words) and look as networks with arrows running from predicate nodes ("action" of SAO) to argument nodes ("subject" and "object"). For example, SAO of patent application (from sentence "The second end electrode and the center electrode of the first tubular body are electrically connected to the center electrode and the first end electrode, respectively, of the second tubular body") and SAO of patent (from sentence "The center electrode is connected to the terminal through an internal wire") have views presented on Figure 1. At the null level of a SAO representation are the ROOTs ("actions"), at the first level are the actantial relations I, II ("subject" and "object" respectively), at the second level are the attributive relations.

After the stage of SAO constructing the patent application is compared with each patent in the database. A comparison of the application with the *i-th* patent occurs by comparing each of the *j-th* SAO of the application with each *k-th* SAO of the *i-th* patent.

4.1 The First Stage of SAO Comparison

According to a SAO structure the tree's root (ROOT) is the verb ("action"). If the ROOTs of the application and the patent do not match, further comparison of the SAOs is not performed and comparison is made for the next SAO of the patent application.

If the ROOTs of the application and the patent match, then the attributive (ATTR) structures associated with the ROOTs ("action") are compared.

If any terms (words) are not matched, then term from application is checked for significance. Testing the significance is based on a predetermined table that contains IDF (Salton, 1988) - inverse document frequency of terms in documents of patent databases. If the term's IDF is above a limit value then the term is not significant and is not taken into account of the similarity coefficient calculation.

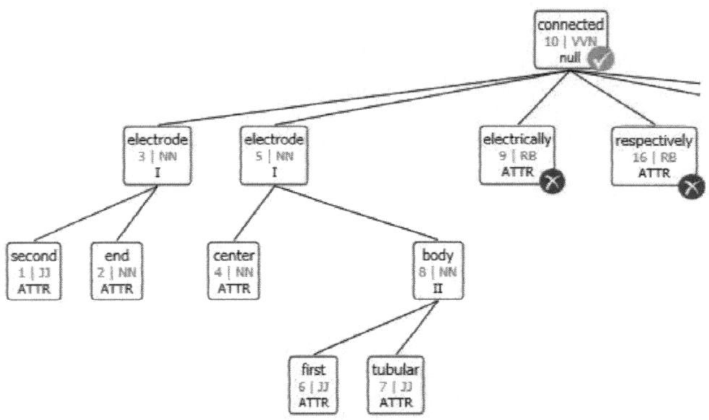

Figure 1. First stage of SAO comparison for application (left view) and of patent (right view)

We introduce the similarity coefficient of the ATTR structures, associated with the ROOTs ("action"):

$$K^{A}_{ATTR}(TA_k, TA_l) = \frac{\sum_{i=1}^{N_l} S(t_1, t_2)}{\max_{ATTR}(TA_k, TA_l)}, \quad (1)$$

where TA_k, TA_l are the semantic sub-trees (attributive (ATTR) structures, associated with the ROOTs) of k-sentence and l-sentence of an application claim and patent claim accordingly;

$max_{ATTR}(TA_k, TA_l)$ – maximum number of ATTR structures for application claim and patent claim with verification of term's significance;

$S(t_1,t_2)$ - MATCH function that determines a similarity of $t1$ and $t2$ terms of the compared semantic trees;

N_i – number of terms for semantic tree TA_k of application claim.

If the ROOTs of the application and the patent match, the similarity coefficient by "action" is:

$$K^A = 1 + K^A_{ATTR}(TA_k,\ TA_l),\ (2)$$

In application there are 2 such ATTR structures, in patent - 0 ATTR, the maximum is 2. Similar ATTR structures - 0. Without verification of term's significance, the similarity coefficient by "action" is equal to 1 (ROOTs are match) + 0/2. With verification of term's significance (IDF of term "respectively" more than limit value, then we assume that in the application only 1 ATTR structure) the similarity coefficient by "action" is equal to 1 (ROOTs are match) + 0/1.

4.2 The Second stage of SAO Comparison

At this stage, the I actantial relations and the attributive ATTR structures, associated with them, are compared. An example of comparison of application and patent is shown on Figure 2 (sentence from patent: "the center electrode and the terminal electrode are electrically connected to each other via the glass seal").

If the I actantial relations ("subject") of the application and the patent do not match, the coefficient of similarity by "subject" is equal 0 and comparison is made for the next I "nodes" of the patent application.

If the I actantial relations ("subject") of the application and the patent match, then the attributive (ATTR) structures associated with the I "nodes" are compared.

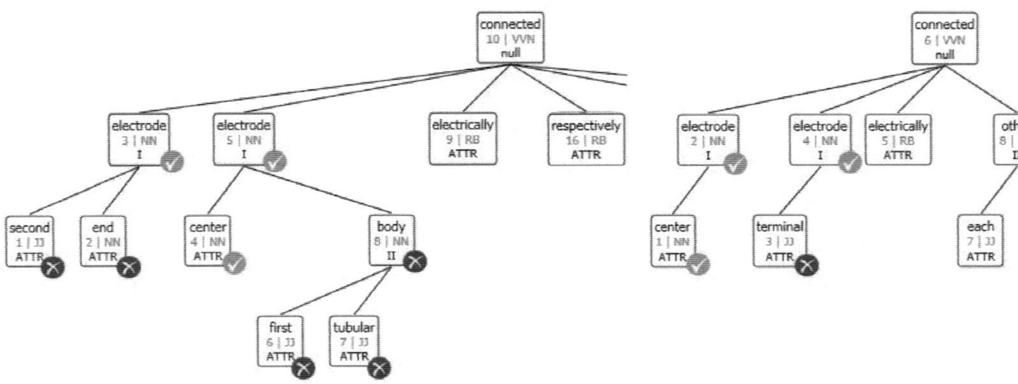

Figure 2. Second stage of SAO comparison for application (left view) and of patent (right view)

We introduce the similarity coefficient of the attributive (ATTR) structures, associated with the I actantial relation ("subject"):

$$K^I_{ATTR}(TI_k,\ TI_l) = \frac{\sum_{i=1}^{N_i} S(t_1,\ t_2)}{\max_{ATTR}(TI_k,\ TI_l)},\ (3)$$

where TI_k, TI_l are the semantic sub-trees (attributive (ATTR) structures, associated with the I actant) of k-sentence and l-sentence of an application claim and patent claim accordingly;

$max_{ATTR}(TI_k, TI_l)$ – maximum number of ATTR structures for application claim and patent claim with verification of term's significance;

N_i – number of terms for semantic tree TI_k of application claim.

We introduce the coefficient of similarity by "subject":

$$K^S = \frac{\sum_{i=1}^{N_1=|I_k|}(K^I_{M_i} + K^I_{ATTR_i})}{\max(I_k, I_l)}, (4)$$

where $K^I_{M_i}$ - similarity coefficient of the *i-th* I actantial relation, $K^I_{M_i} = 1$ if match, not match - $K^I_{M_i} = 0$,

$K^I_{ATTR_i}$ - similarity coefficient of the ATTR structures, associated with the *i-th* I actantial relation,

max (I_k, I_l) – maximum number of the *i-th* I actantial relations for application claim and patent claim.

In application there are 2 such ATTR structures, associated with I actantial relations, in patent - 2 ATTR, the maximum is 2. IDF for all term more then limit value. The maximum coefficient (1.25) is given by a pair "electrode (ATTR) center, body, first, tubular" → "electrode (ATTR) center". Accordingly, the second pair is "electrode (ATTR) second, end" → "electrode (ATTR) terminal" with coefficient similarity is equal 1. Similarity coefficient by "subject" is equal (1.25+1)/2=1.125.

4.3 The Third Stage of SAO Comparison

At this stage, the II actantial relations ("object") and the attributive ATTR structures, associated with them, are compared. It occurs by an algorithm similar to the algorithm used in the second stage.

We introduce the similarity coefficient of the attributive (ATTR) structures, associated with the II actantial relation ("object"):

$$K^{II}_{ATTR}(TII_k, TII_l) = \frac{\sum_{i=1}^{N_i} S(t_1, t_2)}{\max_{ATTR}(TII_k, TII_l)}, (5)$$

where TII_k, TII_l are the semantic sub-trees (attributive (ATTR) structures, associated with the II actant) of *k*-sentence and *l*-sentence of an application claim and patent claim accordingly;

$max_{ATTR}(TII_k, TII_l)$ – maximum number of ATTR structures for application claim and patent claim with verification of term's significance;

N_i – number of terms for semantic tree TII_k of application claim.

We introduce the coefficient of similarity by "object":

$$K^O = \frac{\sum_{i=1}^{N_1=|II_k|}(K^{II}_{M_i} + K^{II}_{ATTR_i})}{\max(II_k, II_l)}, (6)$$

where $K^{II}_{M_i}$ -similarity coefficient of the *i-th* II actantial relation, $K^{II}_{M_i} = 1$ if match, not match - $K^{II}_{M_i} = 0$,

$K^{II}_{ATTR_i}$ - similarity coefficient of the ATTR structures, associated with the *i-th* II actantial relation,

max (II_k, II_l) – maximum number of the *i-th* II actantial relations for application claim and patent claim.

The similarity coefficient of SAO is summarized for each level and the total coefficient of the application and patent similarity is the sum of trees similarity coefficients:

$$K_{SAO} = \frac{K^A + K^S + K^O}{6}, (7)$$

5. EXPERIMENTS AND RESULTS

The experiments are performed using a multiprocessor computer system with distributed memory (cluster) of the Volgograd State Technical University. The cluster entered the 22nd edition of the Top-50 rating of the Russian supercomputers.

The software was installed on the nodes of the cluster:

- Apache Spark - open-source cluster-computing framework, engine for large-scale data processing;
- Library for software implementation of the LDA method – Apache Spark MLlib;
- PostgreSQL.

Statistical and semantic portraits were formed for 990,000 Russian- and English-language patents and stored in the Document Storage on the basis of the HDFS file system.

The patent examination is implemented as MapReduce task (Figure 3). Initially, the input data stored in the "/input" folder, which contains files with SAO which extracted from patents. The file name is the patent number. All SAO from patent are stored in one file. The first stage – "only map" task divides each document into pairs (patent number, SAO), the result is stored in a temporary folder "/output". This folder serves as input data for the second stage. Mapper (Compare) receives as input a cached file with the SAOs from patent application and compares each of SAOs with the SAO from patent (folder "/output". As a result we get pairs (patent number, coefficient of similarity), a result is stored to "/output1" folder, from there it is read by the standard hdfs-command and sorted by the avrg (k) value.

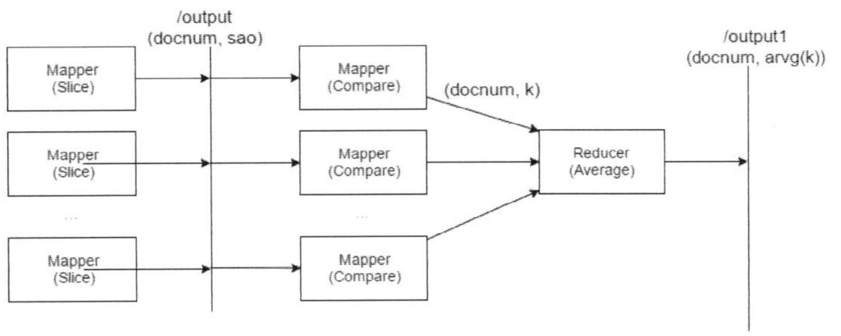

Figure 3. MapReduce task of patent examination.

For the test set we specified the root folder "/sample". It contains the folders: "/claims", "/morph", "/semantic", "/sao", for a patent application, morphological portrait of patent application, semantic portrait and extracted SAO, respectively. At the root of the folder "/sample" is stored a file with meta-data of all patents.

We chose the coefficient "Recall" for sets of the top 5, 25, 100 most relevant patents retrieved as a criterion of the semantic analysis effectiveness. The tables indicate the average Recall value for 10 tests (Table 3). For software test we perform an imitation of the expert's work. From 10 random patents we extract the citation lists, for the cited patents we also extract their citation lists and so on up to the fourth nesting level. As a result, we obtain a test set of approximately 1,000 patents. For each of the 10 selected patents the patents from the this citation list will be considered as relevant.

Table 3. Semantic analysis w/ & w/o verification of term's significance

Feature	Recall@5	Recall@25	Recall@100
with verification of term's significance	82	84	92
without verification of term's significance	78	80	86

Verification the term significance increases the Recall. This is due to a more accurate ranking of the SAOs similarity, since insignificant, commonly used words do not affect the patents ranking.

6. CONCLUSION

We developed software for patent examination on base of extracted triples "subject-action-object" (SAO) from patent texts. On the step of semantic analysis we applied a new method for building semantic network on base of Stanford Dependencies and Meaning-Text Theory. On the step of semantic similarity calculation we compare the SAOs for application and patent claims. Developed software prototype for the patent examination task significantly reduced search time and increased such criteria of search effectiveness as "Recall".

REFERENCES

Andersson, L., Hanbury, A., Rauber, A. (2017). The Portability of three type of Text Mining Techniques into the patent text genre. *Lupu, M., Mayer, K., Tait, J., Trippe, A. J. (eds.) Current Challenges in Patent Information Retrieval*

Blei, D. M. (2003). Latent Dirichlet allocation. *Journal of Machine Learning Research.* 3(4–5), pp. 993-1022

Bouadjenek, M., Sanner, S., Ferraro, G. (2015. A Study of Query Reformulation of Patent Prior Art Search with Partial Patent Applications. *15th International Conference on Artificial Intelligence and Law (ICAIL)*, pp. 1-11.

Choi, S., Park, H., Kang, D., Lee J.Y., Kim, K. (2012). An SAO-based text mining approach to building a technology tree for technology planning. *Expert Systems with Application*, 39, pp. 11443–11455

D'hondt, E., Verberne, S., Oostdijk, N., Boves, L. (2017). Patent Classification on Subgroup Level Using Balanced Winnow. *Current Challenges in Patent Information Retrieval*, pp.299-324

de Marneffe, M.-C., Manning, C.D. (2016). Stanford typed dependencies manual.

Ferraro, G., Suominen, H., Nualart, J. (2014). Segmentation of patent claims for improving their readability. *3rd Workshop on Predicting and Improving Text Readability for Target Reader Populations (PITR)*, pp. 66-73.

Hall, J. (2006). MaltParser – An Architecture for Inductive Labeled Dependency Parsing. University of Colorado

Haverinen, K., Viljanen, T., Laippala, V., Kohonen, S., Ginter, F., Salakoski, T. (2010). Treebanking Finnish. *Proceedings of the Ninth International Workshop on Treebanks and Linguistic Theories.* University of Tartu, Estonia

Kim, Y., Croft, W.B. (2014). Diversifying Query Suggestions based on Query Documents. *Proc. of SIGIR'14*, pp. 891-894. Queensland, Australia

Korobkin, D., Fomenkov, S., Kravets, A., Kolesnikov, S., Dykov, M. (2015). Three-Steps Methodology for Patents Prior-Art Retrieval and Structured Physical Knowledge Extracting. *CIT&DS*, pp. 124-136. doi: 10.1007/978-3-319-23766-4_10

Korobkin, D. M., Fomenkov, S. A., Kolesnikov, S. G. (2016). A function-based patent analysis for support of technical solutions synthesis. ICIEAM. – [Publisher: IEEE]. doi: 10.1109/ICIEAM.2016.7911581

Korobkin, D. M., Fomenkov, S. A., Kravets, A. G., Golovanchikov, A. B. (2016). Patent data analysis system for information extraction tasks. *13th International Conference on Applied Computing (AC)*, pp. 215-219

Kravets, A.G., Korobkin, D. M., Dykov, M.A. (2015). E-patent examiner: Two-steps approach for patents prior-art retrieval. *IISA 2015 Conference Proceeding / Ionian University, Institute of Electrical and Electronics Engineers (IEEE)* [Piscataway, USA]. doi: 10.1109/IISA.2015.7388074

Magdy W., Jones, G. J. F. (2010). Applying the KISS Principle for the CLEF-IP 2010 Prior Art Candidate Patent Search Task. *Workshop of the Cross-Language Evaluation Forum.* Padua, Italy

Mahdabi, P., Crestani, F. (2014). Query-Driven Mining of Citation Networks for Patent Citation Retrieval and Recommendation. *ACM International Conference on Information and Knowledge Management.* doi: 10.1145/2661829.2661899

Mel'čuk, I.A. (1988). Dependency Syntax: Theory and Practice. *SUNY Publ.*, NY

Park, H., Yoon, J., Kim, K. (2012). Identifying patent infringement using SAO based semantic technological similarities. *Scientometrics*, 90, p. 515. doi:10.1007/s11192-011-0522-7

Salton, G., Buckley, C. (1988). Term-weighting approaches in automatic text retrieval. *Information Processing & Management*, 24 (5), pp. 513–523

Toutanova, K., Manning, C.D. (2000). Enriching the Knowledge Sources Used in a Maximum Entropy Part-of-Speech Tagger. *EMNLP '00*, pp. 63-70

Verma, M., Varma, V. (2011). Exploring Keyphrase Extraction and IPC Classification Vectors for Prior Art Search. *CLEF Notebook Papers/Labs/Workshop.* Amsterdam, Netherlands

Xue, X., Croft W.B. (2013). Modeling reformulation using query distributions. *Journal ACM Transactions on Information Systems.* ACM New York, NY, USA. doi:10.1145/2457465.2457466

Yufeng, D.U., Duo, J.I., Lixue, J., et al. (2016). Patent Similarity Measure Based on SAO Structure[J]. *Chinese Sentence and Clause for Text Information Processing*, 30(1), pp. 30-36

FULL MODEL SELECTION IN HUGE DATASETS UNDER THE MAPREDUCE PARADIGM

Angel Díaz-Pacheco, Jesús A. Gonzalez-Bernal, Carlos Alberto Reyes-García
and Hugo Jair Escalante-Balderas
Instituto Nacional de Astrofísica, Óptica y Electrónica (INAOE), Computer Science Department
Luis Enrique Erro No.1, Santa María Tonantzintla, Puebla, 72840, Mexico

ABSTRACT

The analysis of large amounts of data has become an important task in science and business that led to the emergence of the Big Data paradigm. This paradigm owes its name to data objects too large to be processed by standard hardware and algorithms. Many data analysis tasks involve the use of machine learning techniques during the model creation step. The goal of predictive models consists on achieving the highest possible accuracy to predict new samples, and for this reason there is high interest in selecting the most suitable algorithm for a specific dataset. This trend is known as model selection and it has been widely studied in datasets of common size, but poorly explored in the Big Data context. As an effort to explore in this direction this work propose an algorithm for model selection in very large datasets.

KEYWORDS

Big Data, Model Selection, Machine learning

1. INTRODUCTION

In many fields of human activity there is a growing interest in storing and analyzing information. This information is quickly generated and in large amounts. This is the case of airline reservation systems or in the CERN Large Hadron Collider (LHC). The quantity and variety of information has grown to unprecedented scales. It is estimated that in 2014, 2.5 quintillions of Bytes of information were daily created (Wu et al., 2014). Big Data became popular due to this phenomenon. A widespread definition of Big Data describes this concept in terms of three characteristics of information in this field: **Volume, Velocity** and **Variety**, subsequently other V's have been added: **Veracity** and **Value** (Tlili & Hamdani, 2014). **Value** refers to the capacity to turn the data into valuable assets through its analysis. In this regard, many predictive data analysis tasks are carried out through machine learning techniques. Choosing a classification algorithm is not a trivial task. This process requires finding the combination of algorithms together with their hyper-parameters to achieve the lowest misclassification rate in a wide search space (Thornton et al., 2013). Other factors that have a major impact in the generalization capacities of a classification algorithm are: feature selection and data-preparation. These factors, in combination with the selection of a classification algorithm integrate the full model selection paradigm (Escalante, Montes & Sucar, 2009). Full model selection has been addressed as an optimization problem varying the search technique employed. As an example, Kaneko & Funatsu (2015) proposed a hybrid method based on grid search and the theoretic hyper-parameter decision technique (ThD) of Cherkassy and Ma for the algorithm SVR (Support Vector Regression). Referring to bio-inspired methods, Escalante et al. (2009) tackled and defined the full model selection problem with the use of a particle swarm optimization algorithm (PSO), meanwhile Bansal & Sahoo (2015) proposed the use of the bat algorithm for solving FMS. In the case of evolutionary algorithms, Chatelain et al. (2010) presented a method for model selection based on a multi-objective genetic algorithm where the evaluation function takes into account sensitivity as well as specificity. On the other hand, Rosales-Perez et al. (2014) also tackled the search phase with a multi-objective genetic algorithm. They take into account the misclassification rate and the complexity of the models. In 2015 Rosales-Pérez et al. proposed the inclusion of surrogate functions in order to decrease the use of expensive fitness functions. All of the previous approaches for the model selection problem work with datasets that can be loaded in main memory, but if the amount of data is larger than a conventional personal computer can store, the trials of the combinations in the dataset cannot be performed and therefore, the model exhibiting the lowest error will not be found. This paper has the following organization. In section 2 we present background on Big Data. Section 3 describes our proposed algorithm. Section 4 shows the experiments performed. Finally, section 5 presents conclusions and future work.

2. BIG DATA AND THE MAPREDUCE PARADIGM

In this section we present some antecedents about the MapReduce programming model. MapReduce (Dean & Ghemawat, 2004) enables the parallelization and distribution of big scale computation required to analyze large datasets. This programming model was designed to work over computing clusters and it works under the master-slave communication model. The design of MapReduce considers the following fundamental principles: 1) Low-Cost Unreliable Commodity Hardware. The MapReduce framework is designed to run on large clusters of commodity hardware. 2) Extremely Scalable Cluster. The nodes can be taken out of service with almost no impact to keep the MapReduce jobs running. 3) Fault tolerant. The MapReduce framework applies straightforward mechanisms to replicate data and keep processes running in case of failures. In MapReduce a computing task is specified as a sequence of stages: map, shuffle and reduce that works on a dataset $X = \{x_1, x_2, \ldots, x_n\}$. The map step applies a function μ, to each value x_i to produce a finite set of key-value pairs (k,v). To allow for parallel execution, the computation of function $\mu(x_i)$, must depend only on x_i. The shuffle step collects all the key-value pairs produced in the previous map step, and produces a set of lists, $L_k = (k; v_1, v_2, \ldots, v_n)$ where each of such lists consists of all values v_i such that $k_i = k$ for a key k assigned in the map step. The reduce stage applies a function ρ to each list $L_k = (k; v_1, v_2, \ldots, v_n)$, created during the shuffle step, to produce a set of values $y_1, y_2, \ldots, y_n$. The reduce function ρ is defined to work sequentially on L_k but should be independent of other lists $L_{k'}$, where $k' \neq k$ (Goodrich, Sitchinava & Zhang, 2011). Despite being an extended definition, the 5 V's of Big Data are little ambiguous and do not provides rules to identify a huge dataset. Therefore in this work we propose an alternative definition but related to the model selection problem. For our definition we propose that a huge dataset for the model selection problem must accomplish two rules: 1) The dataset size is big enough that at least one of the considered classification algorithms in their sequential version cannot process it. 2) The dataset size is defined by their file size considering the number of instances (I) and features (F) as long as I ≫ F.

3. FULL MODEL SELECTION THROUGH A GENETIC ALGORITHM BASED ON MAPREDUCE

This section describes our proposed model selection algorithm for Big Data. This algorithm was developed under Apache Spark 1.6.0, a framework based on the MapReduce programming model. We selected this framework because of its enhanced capacity to deal with iterative algorithms and the possibility to perform data processing in main memory (if memory capacity allows it). Full model selection is the combination of several factors in order to obtain the lowest classification error for a given dataset. An attempt of a formal definition is given in **Eq. 1.** Given a set of learning algorithms *A,* data preparation techniques *P,* and feature selection algorithms *F,* the goal of the FMS is to determine the combination of algorithms: $a^*_{wA} \in A$ (a machine learning algorithm with an specific configuration in its hyper-parameters values), $p^* \in P$ and $f^* \in F$ with the lowest misclassification rate, which is estimated over the dataset *D* and this dataset is splited in two disjoint partitions ($D^{(i)}_{train}$ and $D^{(i)}_{validation}$ for $i = 1,2,\ldots,k$). Misclassification rate is calculated with the loss function $L(a^{(j)}_{wA}, p^j, f^j, D^{(i)}_{train}, D^{(i)}_{validation})$, training the algorithm a_{wA} in the partition $D^{(i)}_{train}$, and evaluated in the partition $D^{(i)}_{validation}$. The data partitions are previously transformed by *p* and *f.*

$$a^{*}_{wA}, p^{*}, f^{*} \in \arg\min L(a^{(j)}_{wA}, p^{j}, f^{j}, D^{(i)}_{train}, D^{(i)}_{validation})$$
$$a^{(i)} \in A, p^{(i)} \in P, f^{(i)} \in F, w_A \in W_A \quad (1)$$

In order to perform the FMS, we developed a genetic algorithm (GA) to explore the large search space of **Eq. 1**. It was designed as a blend of some aspects of the approach known as CHC (Cross-generational elitist selection, Heterogeneous recombination, Cataclysmic mutation) (Eshelman, 1991) and Eclectic (Kuri & Quezada, 1998). From CHC we take the crossover operator HUX (Half Uniform Crossover), adapted to real codification, meanwhile from the Eclectic approach, the selection model known as Vasconcelos Model (VM) (Kuri & Quezada, 1998) was taken. The traditional mutation operator was preserved as well as the cataclysmic mutation operator; the last one was used as a way to avoid the stagnation in the algorithm.

3.1 Representation

Every individual encoded in the GA represents a potential solution (or model) to the full model selection problem. Therefore, under this approach, each model is represented by a 16-dimensional vector of real codification $x^i = [x_1^i, x_2^i, ..., x_{16}^i]$. The information encoded by the vector that represents an individual can be summarized as follows: In position 1 the fitness of the potential model is stored. Position 2 allows determining which operation will be done first: data-preparation or feature selection. Position 3 indicates if the data-preparation step will be done. Positions 4 to 6 are parameters for the data-preparation step (method identifier, parameter 1 and parameter 2). Position 7 determines if the feature selection step will be done. Positions 8 and 9 are for the feature selection step. Positions 10 to 16 are for the machine learning algorithm construction. For each individual, it is necessary to apply certain transformation to the dataset; these transformations will lead to a new dataset that will serve to train/test the classification algorithm encoded in such individual. The range of values that every element in the vector can take is as follows: [0-100],[0-1],[0-1],[1-30],[1-Number of features],[1-50].[0-1],[1-5],[1-Number of features],[1-6],[1-2],[1-4],[1-100],[1-60],[1-400],[-20,20].

3.2 Crossover and Mutation Operators

HUX operator produces offspring's that are maximally different from their parents because exactly half of the alleles that are different in both parents are changed. In order to maximize the genetic diversity, the selection model known as Vasconcelos Model (VM) was employed. In this strategy the best individual is mated with the worst in the population, in other words, the "*k*" individuals in the population are ranked by their fitness. Subsequently VM will select individuals as follows: *(1,k),(2,k-1)...(k/2,k/2+1)*. Concerning to mutation, we maintain both approaches. We observed that using just the cataclysmic mutation operator slows the convergence of the algorithm but if instead it is used in conjunction with the traditional operator we prevent stagnation. We measure the stagnation as the number of generations in that the best individual found so far is the same or there is little change in their fitness. The use of real codification in this work makes it necessary to use ad hoc crossover and mutation operators adapted from (Haupt & Haupt, 2004).

3.2.1 Crossover Operator

$$off_i = \beta P_{mn} + (1-\beta) P_{fn} \quad (2)$$

In **Eq. 2**, the i-th offspring (off_i) is obtained multiplying the n-th allele of parent 1 (P_{mn}) by a random number in the range [0,1] (β) added to the multiplication of the n-th allele of parent 2 (P_{fn}) by 1- β.

3.2.2 Mutation Operator

$$off_i^{'} = off_i + \sigma N_n(0,1) \quad (3)$$

In **Eq. 3**, the i-th mutated offspring ($off_i^{'}$) is obtained by adding the value of the i-th offspring (off_i) to a normally distributed number ($\sigma N_n(0,1)$) in the interval [0,1].

3.3 Model evaluation

The evaluation of every individual requires a series of data transformations and the construction of classifiers. In this work the framework Apache Spark is employed. This framework is an improvement over traditional MapReduce specially regarding to main memory use in order to reduce several reading/writing operations to disc. The cornerstone of this framework is the RDD or Resilient Distributed Dataset which is a collection of partitioned data elements that can be operated in parallel (Guller, 2015). In **Algorithm 1** a procedure to obtain an RDD from a plain text file is shown. An analysis of the advantages of Spark over traditional MapReduce is out of the scope of this work, but we refer to (Zaharia et al., 2016).

Algorithm 1. Get the RDD

```
procedure getRDD(PathDataset,numparts)
RowRDD = Load(PathDataset,numparts) //Obtains RDD[String]
RDDcol = RowRDD.map(row → row.split(","))//split function is applied to every row
RDDVect = RDDcol.map(row → Vector(row.map(ColInR→ ColInR.toDouble)))
/* Every column is transformed to Double type */
Return(RDDVect)
end procedure
```

Function **getRDD** is employed to obtain the training and test RDDs and are used as parameters for the proposed Genetic Algorithm, from now onward called **GAMRFMS** showed in **Algorithm 2**.

Algorithm 2. GAMRFMS

```
procedure GAMRFMS(TestSet,TrainSet,NG,ST)
Population = CreateInitialRandomPopulation() //Generate initial population
fitness = MRfitness(Population,TrainSet,labels)//evaluates the performance
GenCount = 0; StagnationThreshold = 0;
while(GenCount < NG) do
if(StagnationThreshold >= ST) then MuRate=0.35; StagnationThreshold=0;
else MuRate=0.1; //If stagnation exists then cataclysmic mutation
end if
Offspring = crossover(CrossoverIndex,Population) //Performs crossover
Offspring = Mutation(Offspring,MutRate)//Performs mutation
fitness = MRfitness(Offspring,TrainSet,labels)
Population = replacement(Population,Offspring) //Elitistic replacement
GenCount+ = 1
StagnationThreshold = updateST(fitness) //Updates the stagnation threshold
end while
finalMOdel = buildFM(Population) //Builds final model
finalFitness = evalFinalModel(finalModel,TestSet)//evaluates final model
end procedure
```

Algorithm 3. Fitness evaluation

```
procedure MRfitness(Population,TrainSet)
fitness = Array[Double](Population.length)
for(i = 0; i < Population:length; i++)do
individual = Population(i); precedence = individual(2);
if(precedence == 0) then
RDDPrep = DataPrep(TrainSet,individual) //Performs data preparation
RDDFS = FeatSelection(RDDPrep,individual) //Performs feature selection
fitness(i) = Classification(RDDFS,individual)// Performs classification
else
RDDFS = FeatSelection(TrainSet,individual) //Performs feature selection
RDDPrep = DataPrep(RDDFS,individual) //Performs data preparation
fitness(i) = Classification(RDDPrep,individual)/*Performs classification
end if
end for
Return(fitness)
end procedure
```

In our proposal, the mean error over the 2-fold cross validation is used in order to evaluate the performance of every potential model. Different number of folds were evaluated (2,...,10) without significant differences, but adding to the computing time factor, the 2-fold cross validation was the best choice. We also add a penalization term to the fitness of every individual. This term is an L2 norm over the hyper parameters of the classification algorithm. In other words, in the Random Forest algorithm we take the values of the number of trees, the maximum depth of the trees and the number of bins, the same way is for GBT algorithm. For the Decision Tree algorithm, we just took into account the depth of the tree and the number of bins. For SVM is the number of support vectors. Regarding to Logistic Regression, we penalize the number of features used by the algorithm and Naive Bayes is not penalized. The algorithms used in this work for data-preparation are: 1) Feature standardization, 2) Normalization, 3) Principal Component analysis, 4) Shift and scale and 5) Discretization. For feature selection, the algorithms are: 1) Joint Mutual Information, 2) Minimum Redundancy Maximum Relevance, 3) Interaction Capping, 4) Conditional Mutual Information Maximization and 5) Informative Fragments. Finally the classification algorithms are: 1) Support Vector Machine (SVM), 2) Logistic Regression (LR), 3) Naïve Bayes (NB), 4) Decision Tree (DT), 4) Random Forest (RF) and 5) Gradient-Boosted Trees (GBT).

4. EXPERIMENTS AND RESULTS

With the purpose to evaluate the proposed algorithm performance, we experimented with the datasets shown in **Table 2**. These datasets have been used in several classification research works for Big Data (del Rio et al., 2015). We also used two synthetic data sets generated with a tool for synthetic datasets generation in the context of ordinal regression: "*Synthetic Datasets Nspheres*" provided in (Sanchez-Monedero, 2013). The datasets and their characteristics are described in **Table 1**.

Table 1. Datasets used in the experiments

Dataset	Data points	Attributes	Samples by class	Type of variables	File size
Fars	50,164	52	(17,445;32,719)	Categorical	6.0 MB
Census-income	199,523	40	(187,141;12,382)	Categorical	18.0 MB
Covtype	495,141	54	(283,301;211,840)	Categorical	61.6 MB
RLCP	5,749,111	11	(5728197;20915)	Real	261.6 MB
KDD	4,856,150	41	(972780;3883369)	Categorical	653 MB
Synthetic 1	200,000,000	3	(100000000;100000000)	Real	5.5 GB
Higgs	11,000,000	28	(5170877;5829123)	Real	7.5 GB
Synthetic 2	49,000,002	30	(24500001;24500001)	Real	12.7 GB

The parameters of the genetic algorithm were determined experimentally by analyzing the classification performance on the following factor combinations: Population size = 30 and 50 individuals; and mutation rate = 0.05, 0.07, 0.1. With the purpose to tune the genetic algorithm parameters, we used the tenth part of the Covtype_2_vs_1 dataset. We made the model selection experiments with the termination criterion of performing 25 generations. The parameters combination that led to the best classification rate was Population = 30 individuals and Mutation rate = 0.1%. In order to obtain a statistical power of 90% 20 replications of each experiment for every dataset were performed. Each replication was performed with a particular random sample of the data points with different random samples among replications. For each experiment, the dataset was divided in two disjoint datasets with 60% of the data samples for the training set and 40% for the test set. In order to evaluate the performance of the proposed model, we need to choose the final model that will be put to test. Such choice could be slightly complex. As our proposed method has fully elitist policies, we take advantage of that fact and therefore the final model is a weighted-votation ensemble of all the individuals. We compared the performance of our algorithm against the Kernel "K" Nearest-Neighbor algorithm (**K-NN**) present in (Yu, Ji & Zhang, 2002) and the Apache Spark MLlib's tool for tuning machine learning algorithms (Apache org, Apr. 2017). This tool allows users to optimize hyper-parameters via Cross-Validation and employs a grid search mechanism. In order to make adequate comparisons, we set our algorithm to complete 47 generations as stopping criteria and therefore 1,410 models were evaluated during the search step.

Referring to the tool of the Apache Spark (**AST**) we set the number of models to be evaluated to 1,412. **Table 2** shows the obtained results.

Table 2. Mean classification error obtained in the test dataset by **GAMRFMS** and the obtained by **K-NN** (K=9,999) and **AST**, over 20 replications. The best results are in **bold**

Dataset	GAMRFMS	AST	K-NN
Fars	0.173± 0.028	**0.157± 0.042**	7.586± 0.154
Census-incom	**5.823± 0.130**	6.727± 1.018	6.408± 0.093
Covtype	**6.725± 0.188**	23.625± 0.090	42.791± 0.088
RLCP	0.009± 0.001	**0.001± 0.000**	0.500± 0.098
KDD	0.024± 0.005	**0.001± 0.000**	19.535± 0.261
Synthetic 1	**15.862± 0.003**	17.011± 0.120	50.088± 0.028
Higgs	**29.508± 0.127**	30.955± 0.228	46.916± 0.408
Synthetic 2	**6.683± 0.002**	22.152± 0.541	50.126± 0.115

Table 2 shows that **GAMRFMS** obtains the best performance in 5 of the 8 analyzed datasets. Next, we performed an ANOVA test with 95% of confidence and the Tukey test as a Post hoc test.

Table 3. F-statistic obtained from the ANOVA test and q-values from the Tukey HSD test for performing all possible pair wise comparisons among the proposed strategies for the final model construction. The critical values at the 95% confidence level for the ANOVA test are 3.16 (F(2,57)) for all datasets. The critical values at the 95 % confidence level for the Tukey HSD test are 3.44 (57 degrees of freedom). Cases that exceed the critical value are considered as a difference that is statistically significant at the fixed level and are marked with an asterisk (*)

Dataset	Anova F	GAMRFMS vs AST	GAMRFMS vs K-NN
Fars	**41758.60***	0.756	**353.56***
Census-income	**11.88***	**6.796***	**4.396***
Covtype	**381028.72***	**578.120***	**1233.700***
RLCP	**509.53***	0.628	**38.779***
KDD	**111462.85***	0.693	**577.920***
Synthetic 1	**1482574.07***	**71.957***	**2144***
Higgs	**23910.89***	**23.168***	**278.660***
Synthetic 2	**95220.24***	**216.77***	**608.800***

As it can be seen in **Table 3**, there is not statistically significant differences between **GAMRFMS** and **AST** in the Fars dataset. In the Census-income dataset, the lower error was achieved by **GAMRFMS**, the q-value of the Tukey HSD test shows that there are statistically significant differences. The same situation occurs regarding to Covtype dataset. In the datasets RLCP and KDD, AST obtained the lower error but the q-value shows that there are not statistically significant differences. In the datasets Synthetic 1, Higgs and Synthetic 2 the lower error was obtained by GAMRFMS and the q-values shows that there are significant differences. Even though our algorithm is not the best in 3 out of the 8 datasets, the statistical tests provides evidence that our algorithm has a good performance in all datasets even in those that our algorithm was not the best (Fars, RLCP and KDD). With the purpose to show the capacities of the proposed algorithm we compare it with other model selection algorithms present in the literature (Rosales-Pérez et al., 2013,2014) and (Escalante, Montes & Sucar, 2009) over non Big Data sets. In **Table 4** we show the results obtained with the **GAMRFMS** algorithm and those obtained with **PSMS**, **MOMTS-S2** and **SAMOMS** as reported in the literature.

Table 4. Average classification error obtained over 20 (In datasets: Image and Splice) or 100 (In datasets: Banana, Breast Cancer, Diabetes, Flare Solar, German, Heart, Ringnorm, Splice ,Thyroid, Titanic, Twonorm and Waveform) replications of the model selection algorithms: **PSMS**, **MOMTS-S2**, **SAMOMS** and **GAMRFMS**. The best results are in **bold**.

Dataset	PSMS	MOMTS-S2	SAMOMS	GAMRFMS
Banana	11.08±0.083	**10.48±0.046**	10.65±0.054	12.71±0.840
Breast Cancer	33.01±0.658	25.61±0.593	28.22±0.506	**25.32± 4.590**
Diabetes	27.06±0.658	23.08±0.174	24.46±0.212	**22.96±2.220**
Flare Solar	34.81±0.173	34.59±0.189	**33.04±0.236**	33.12±1.820
German	30.10±0.720	**23.67±0.224**	24.55±0.230	24.33±3.110
Heart	20.69±0.634	16.48±0.241	16.19±0.373	**15.30±2.950**
Image	2.90±0.112	**2.24±0.123**	3.73±0.117	2.26±0.760
Ringnorm	7.98±0.660	2.49±0.074	**1.81±0.035**	10.31±6.580
Splice	14.63±0.324	**4.84±0.156**	8.31±0.114	5.14±2.200
Thyroid	4.32±0.235	**4.00±0.194**	5.09±0.240	4.18±2.050
Titanic	24.18±0.193	22.08±0.085	23.19±0.217	**22.07±0.780**
Twonorm	3.09±0.127	3.73±0.179	**2.58±0.034**	2.88±0.730
Waveform	12.80±0.325	**9.93±0.043**	10.56±0.108	12.59±1.770

In the results shown in **Table 4**, it can be seen that the **MOMTS-S2** obtained the best performance in 6 of the 13 datasets and therefore it is the best of the model selection algorithms in the comparison. It is important to emphasize that **GARMFMS** obtained the best results in 4 of the datasets and consequently is the second best of the 4 compared algorithms, but also is the only one with the capability of analyze small and huge datasets.

5. CONCLUSION

In this work we described an approach to deal with the full model selection problem for very large datasets (Big Data). Our full model selection algorithm, based on a genetic algorithm, was implemented under the MapReduce programming paradigm. Experimental results showed that applying a model selection algorithm in order to analyze large and average size datasets is feasible. Our results show a significant predictive power improvement of the proposed algorithm compared with the base line algorithms (also designed for big data). Finally, our proposed algorithm obtained competitive results when compared with state-of-the-art algorithms, performing well on normal data sets, but with the advantage of being able to analyze larger datasets. It is worth noting that our algorithm design allows us to use a wide range of search methods and the MapReduce paradigm is capable to deal also with common size datasets. In our future work we will look for the reduction of calls to expensive fitness functions, decrease the variance of the error rate produced by our algorithm, and find alternative ways to control and penalize the complexity of the models obtained with this algorithm.

ACKNOWLEDGEMENT

The first author is grateful for the support from CONACyT scholarship no. 428581.

REFERENCES

Apacheorg (2017), 'Ml tuning: model selection and hyperparameter tuning', http://spark.apache.org/docs/latest/ml-tuning.html.

Bansal, B., Sahoo, A., Escalante, H. J., Montes, M. & Sucar, L. E. (2015), 'Full model selection using Bat algorithm', pp. 1–4.

Chatelain, C., Adam, S., Lecourtier, Y., Heutte, L. & Paquet, T. (2010), 'A multi-model selection framework for unknown and/or evolutive misclassifica-tion cost problems', Pattern Recognition 43(3), 815–823. URL: http://dx.doi.org/10.1016/j.patcog.2009.07.006

Dean, J. & Ghemawat, S. (2008), 'MapReduce', Communications of the ACM 51(1), 107–113. del Río, S., López, V., Benítez, J. M. & Herrera, F. (2014), 'On the use of mapreduce for imbalanced big data using random forest', Information Sciences 285, 112–137.

del Río, S., López, V., Benítez, J. M. & Herrera, F. (2015), 'A MapReduce Approach to Address Big Data Classification Problems Based on the Fusion of Linguistic Fuzzy Rules', International Journal of Computational Intelligence Systems 8(February), 422–437. URL: http://www.tandfonline.com/doi/abs/10.1080/18756891.2015.1017377

Escalante, H. J., Montes, M. & Sucar, L. E. (2009), 'Particle swarm model selection', Journal of Machine Learning Research 10(Feb), 405–440.

Eshelman, L. J. (1991), 'The chc adaptive search algorithm: How to have safe search when engaging', Foundations of Genetic Algorithms 1991 (FOGA 1) 1, 265.

Goodrich, M. T., Sitchinava, N. & Zhang, Q. (2011), Sorting, searching, and simulation in the mapreduce framework, in 'International Symposium on Algorithms and Computation', Springer, pp. 374–383.

Guller, M. (2015), 'Big data analytics with spark: A practitioners guide to using spark for large scale data analysis. apress', URL: http://www. apress.com/9781484209653.

Haupt, R. L. & Haupt, S. E. (2004), Practical genetic algorithms, John Wiley & Sons.

Kaneko, H. & Funatsu, K. (2015), 'Fast optimization of hyperparameters for support vector regression models with highly predictive ability', Chemometrics and Intelligent Laboratory Systems 142, 64–69. URL: http://linkinghub.elsevier.com/retrieve/pii/S0169743915000039

Kuri, M.A. & Quezada, C. V. (1998), A universal eclectic genetic algorithm for constrained optimization, in 'Proceedings of the 6th European congress on intelligent techniques and soft computing', Vol. 1, Citeseer, pp. 518–522.

Rosales-p, A. (2013), 'Surrogate-Assisted Multi-Objective Model Selection for Support Vector Machines'. Rosales-Pérez, A., Gonzalez, J. a., Coello Coello, C. a., Escalante, H. J. & Reyes-Garcia, C. a. (2014), ' Multi-objective model type selection', Neurocomputing 146, 83–94. URL: http://linkinghub.elsevier.com/retrieve/pii/S0925231214008789

Rosales-Pérez, A. (2014), Gonzalez, J. A., Coello, C. A. C., Escalante, H. J., & Reyes-Garcia, C. A. (2014). Multi-objective model type selection. Neurocomputing, 146, 83-94.

Sánchez-Monedero, J., Gutiérrez, P. A., Pérez-Ortiz, M. & Hervás-Martínez, C. (2013), An n-spheres based synthetic data generator for supervised classification, in 'International Work-Conference on Artificial Neural Networks',Springer,
pp. 613–621.

Thornton, C., Hutter, F., Hoos, H. H., Leyton-Brown, K. & Chris Thornton,Frank Hutter, Holger H. Hoos, K. L.-B. (2013), 'Auto-WEKA: Combined Selection and Hyperparameter Optimization of Classification Algorithms', Proceedings of the 19th ACM SIGKDD International Conference on Knowledge Discovery and Data Mining pp. 847–855.URL: http://dl.acm.org/citation.cfm?id=2487629

Wu, X., Zhu, X., Wu, G.-Q. & Ding, W. (2014), 'Data mining with big data', IEEE transactions on knowledge and data engineering 26(1), 97–107.

Yu, K., Ji, L. & Zhang, X. (2002), 'Kernel nearest-neighbor algorithm', Neural Processing Letters 15(2), 147–156.

Zaharia, M., Xin, R. S., Wendell, P., Das, T., Armbrust, M., Dave, A., Meng, X., Rosen, J., Venkataraman, S., Franklin, M. J. et al. (2016), 'Apache spark: a unified engine for big data processing', Communications of the ACM 59(11), 56–65.

ROBUST VERSIONS OF PRINCIPAL COMPONENT ANALYSIS

Boris Polyak and Mikhail Khlebnikov
Trapeznikov Institute of Control Sciences RAS, Profsoyuznaya 65, Moscow, Russia

ABSTRACT

The modern problems of optimization, estimation, signal processing, and image recognition deal with data of huge dimensions. It is important to develop effective methods and algorithms for such problems. An important idea is the construction of low-dimension approximations to large-scale data. One of the most popular methods for this purpose is the principal component analysis (PCA), which is, however, sensitive to outliers. There exist numerous robust versions of PCA, relying on sparsity ideas and ℓ_1 techniques. The present paper offers another approach to robust PCA exploiting Huber's functions and numerical implementation based on the Iterative Reweighted Least Squares (IRLS) method.

KEYWORDS

Principal component analysis, robustness, outliers, IRLS method, Huber's functions

1. INTRODUCTION

Big Data problems are central to modern data analysis. One of the core ideas in this context is design of low-dimensional approximations to large-dimensional data. Its implementations generated such techniques as sparse algorithms, LASSO-regression, compressed sensing, ℓ_1 approach, etc.; see (Bruckstein et al., 2009) and the references therein. The simplest problem of low-dimensional presentation of data is approximation of a cluster via affine manifold. In statistics, the solution is given in the framework of principal component analysis (PCA). PCA techniques is highly popular in wide class of applications - from data visualization and machine learning to sociology, bio-informatics, and risk-management. The idea of PCA goes back to the paper (Pearson, 1901). Pearson provided no statistical validation of the method, it was just the least square approximation of data by straight line or hyperplane. More general results related to statistical models where obtained later. At present, there exist dozens of monographs and hundreds of papers on PCA; e.g., see (Jolliffe, 2002). However the standard PCA is highly sensitive to outliers. This effect of nonrobustness is well known to statisticians; the word “robustness” was coined in (Box, 1953). The monograph “Robust statistics” (Huber, 1981), strongly influenced the development of modern statistics. Thus “robustification” of PCA is highly desirable. The attempts in this directions are numerous. Most often (Candès et al., 2011; Wright et al., 2009; Zhou et al., 2010), the ideas of sparsity and ℓ_1 techniques are exploited. The technique of *M*-estimates, relative to our approach, is developed in (Maronna et al., 2006; Maronna and Yohai, 1998; Croux and Haesbroeck, 2000); see also (Zhang and Lehrman, 2014), where numerous references can be found. In the present paper, robust PCA versions are based on Huber's approach.

We provide two statistical models of samples with contaminated Gaussian distribution and instead of Least Squares, we apply Huber's estimates. Thus we arrive to nonconvex optimization problems in the matrix space. The main feature of our techniques is application of numerical methods based on *Iteratively Reweighted Least Squares* (IRLS). Our problems are well suited for application of the IRLS. First, quadratic approximations in the current point can be easily calculated. Second, minimization of the quadratic approximation is equivalent to the standard PCA. The use of IRLS for robust PCA is the main contribution of the paper. Simulation confirms high efficiency of the approach. However some problems of statistical and numerical validation remain open.

2. BASIC COMPONENTS OF THE METHOD

Consider the *cluster* $\mathrm{C} = \{x_i \in \mathrm{R}^n,\ i = 1,\ldots,N\}$ in the space of dimension n ? 1. The goal is to approximate C (in the mean square sense) by a *low-dimensional* linear subspace $\Pi : \dim \Pi = n - m,$ defined by m linear equations $Cx = b,\ \ C \in \mathrm{R}^{m\times n},\ \ b \in \mathrm{R}^m$, where the rows $c_1,\ldots,c_m$, of the matrix C are pairwise orthogonal and normalized: $(c_i, c_j) = \delta_{ij}$; in other words, $CC^T = I$. In this case, we obtain the optimization problem

$$\min_{b,CC^T=I} \sum_{i=1}^{N} \|Cx_i - b\|^2 . \tag{1}$$

The next result is well known and represents the essentials of the PCA approach.

Lemma 1. Solution of (1) is given by $C^* = \begin{pmatrix} e_1 & e_2 & \cdots & e_m \end{pmatrix}^T$, $b^* = C^*\bar{x}$, where $\bar{x} = \frac{1}{N}\sum_{i=1}^{N} x_i$, $H = \frac{1}{N}\sum_{i=1}^{N}(x_i - \bar{x})(x_i - \bar{x})^T$, $He_i = \lambda_i e_i$, $\mathrm{P}e_i\mathrm{P}{=}1$, $i = 1,\ldots,n$, $0 \le \lambda_1 \le \lambda_2 \le \cdots \le \lambda_n$.

The vectors $e_1, e_2, \ldots, e_m$, span the subspace orthogonal to Π (and principal components $e_{m+1},\ldots,e_n$ span the Π itself). Note that in Lemma 1, we seek a matrix C subject to the *nonconvex* constraint $\operatorname{rank} C = m$; however the solution is available in closed form.

We recall the idea of Huber's robustification for the simplest problem of location estimation. Given a 1D cluster $\mathrm{C}_1 = \{x_i \in \mathrm{R},\ \ i = 1,\ldots,N\}$, find its "center." If the samples are i.i.d. Gaussian $x_i :\ \mathrm{N}(a,1)$, then "the best" estimate of a is provided by the least squares method

$$\bar{x} = \arg\min_x \sum_{i=1}^{N}(x_i - x)^2 = \sum_{i=1}^{N} x_i / N, \tag{2}$$

i.e., the arithmetic mean. However the estimate is highly sensitive to outliers. A more robust estimate is

$$\mathrm{Me}\, x = \arg\min_x \sum_{i=1}^{N} | x_i - x |, \tag{3}$$

i.e., the sample median provided by the least absolute values method. Indeed, for the points $x_{(1)} \le x_{(2)} \le \cdots \le x_{(N)}$, $N = 2\ell - 1$, we have $\mathrm{Me}\, x = x_{(\ell)}$, and the median does not depend on the extreme statistics $x_{(1)}$ and $x_{(N)}$.

A natural tradeoff between (2) and (3) can be obtained if one considers *contaminated Gaussian distribution* $x :\ (1-\varepsilon)\mathrm{N}(a,Q) + \varepsilon \mathrm{P}(a)$ (where P is an arbitrary symmetric distribution), which contains a small fraction of outliers $\varepsilon > 0$. Then (Huber, 1981), the best minimax estimate is $x^* = \arg\min_x \sum_{i=1}^{N} h(| x_i - x |)$. Here

$$h(t) = \begin{cases} t^2/2 & \text{if } |t| \le \Delta, \\ \Delta |t| - \Delta^2/2 & \text{if } |t| > \Delta \end{cases}$$

is a *Huber function*; the choice of the *threshold* Δ will be considered below. This estimate can be extended to the multidimensional case and regression problems (Huber, 1981; Shevlyakov and Vilchevski, 2002; Poljak and Tsypkin, 1980).

The idea of *iteratively reweighted least squares* (*IRLS*) is well known. Originally, the approach has been proposed in (Weitszfeld, 1937) for the Steiner-Weber problem, see (Plastria, 2009): $\min_x \sum_{i=1}^{N} \mathrm{P}a_i - x\mathrm{P}$, $x \in \mathrm{R}^n$, where $a_1,\ldots,a_N \in \mathrm{R}^n$ are given points. Let x^k be the result of the k th iteration; by approximating quadratically the function $\mathrm{P}x - a_i\mathrm{P}$ at the point x^k (the values of the true function and its derivative coincide with those for the approximation) we obtain $(\mathrm{P}x - a_i\mathrm{P}^2/\mathrm{P}t_{ik}\mathrm{P} + \mathrm{P}t_{ik}\mathrm{P})/2$, where $t_{ik} = x^k - a_i$ (provided $x^k \ne a_i$). As a result we arrive at the minimization problem $\min_x \sum_{i=1}^{N} w_{ik}\, \mathrm{P}a_i - x\mathrm{P}^2$, where $w_{ik} = \mathrm{P}x^k - a_i\mathrm{P}^{-1}$, with the solution $x^{k+1} = \sum_{i=1}^{N} w_{ik} a_i \Big/ \sum_{i=1}^{N} w_{ik}$. The objective function monotonically decrease for such iterations. Indeed, $f(x) = \sum_{i=1}^{N} \|a_i - x\|$, $f_k(x) = \sum_{i=1}^{N} w_{ik} \|a_i - x\|^2$, thus $f_k(x)$ is an *upper* approximation of $f(x)$: $f_k(x) \ge f(x)$ for all x, and hence $f(x^{k+1}) \le f_k(x^{k+1}) \le f_k(x^k) = f(x^k)$. Convexity of the objective function implies global convergence of the method (provided $x^k \ne a_i$ for all iterations).

3. STATISTICAL MODEL I

Until now all considerations for PCA were purely deterministic. However PCA admits a well-known statistical validation. We recall two statistical models for this purpose, and later provide their robust versions. The first model is based on the assumption that the points $z_1, \dots, z_N \in \mathbb{R}^n$ lie in the $(n-m)$-dimensional subspace Π: $Cz_i = b$, $C \in \mathbb{R}^{m\times n}$, $b \in \mathbb{R}^m$; while available are their measurements

$$x_i = z_i + \xi_i, \tag{4}$$

corrupted by the i.i.d. standard Gaussian noise $\xi \sim \mathrm{N}(0, I_n)$. The problem is to reconstruct Π from the measurements x_i; that is, to estimate the matrix C and the vector b. Hence, we consider model (4) with $CC^T = I$, $\operatorname{rank} C = m$. Then the *maximum likelihood method* leads to the optimization problem $\min_{b, CC^T = I} \sum_{i=1}^{N} \|Cx_i - b\|^2$, and the estimates for C and b are given by Lemma 1. The first m principal components are the largest semi-axes of the ellipsoid $\mathrm{E} = \{x \in \mathbb{R}^n : (x - \bar{x})^T H^{-1} (x - \bar{x}) \le 1\}$. This is the classical result in the PCA framework.

Assume now that the x_i s contain *outliers* - their distribution differs from the standard Gaussian, and the distances to $\bar{x}$ are large enough; they can strongly influence the result. Huber's approach leads to the replacement of the obtained above optimization problem with

$$\min_{b, CC^T = I} \sum_{i=1}^{N} h(\|Cx_i - b\|), \tag{5}$$

and its solution provides the desired robust estimates. Problem (5) is nonconvex with respect to the variables C and b (the objective function is convex, while the constraints are not). Moreover, the constraint $CC^T = I$ (or the analogous rank constraint $\operatorname{rank} C = m$) are hard to deal with from the optimization point of view; a standard way is to apply convex relaxations.

Luckily, problem (5) is well-suited for the application of IRLS. Indeed, fix m; that is, fix the dimensions $n-m$ of the required subspace Π. At the initial step we let $\bar{x}^0 = \frac{1}{N}\sum_{i=1}^{N} x_i$, $H^0 = \frac{1}{N}\sum_{i=1}^{N} (x_i - \bar{x}^0)(x_i - \bar{x}^0)^T$, find the eigenvalues and eigenvectors of the matrix H^0: $H^0 e_i = \lambda_i e_i$, $\|e_i\| = 1$, $0 \le \lambda_1 \le \lambda_2 \le \dots \le \lambda_n$, and form the quantities $C^1 = (e_1 \;\; e_2 \;\; \cdots \;\; e_m)^T$, $b^1 = C^1 \bar{x}^0$. At the k th iteration we set

$$w_{ik} = \min\left\{1, \frac{\Delta}{\|t_{ik}\|}\right\} = \begin{cases} 1, & \|t_{ik}\| \le \Delta, \\ \Delta / \|t_{ik}\|, & \|t_{ik}\| > \Delta, \end{cases} \tag{6}$$

where $t_{ik} = C^k \bar{x}_i^k - b^k$.

Indeed, at the linear part of the function $h(\|t_{ik}\|)$, the weights are chosen in compliance with the method of reweighted least squares, and at its quadratic part, the weights are equal to unity. Moreover, this method is well-defined at any x^k (in contrast to the Steiner-Weber problem, where approximations are not defined at the points a_i). Thus we have

$$\bar{x}^k = \sum_{i=1}^{N} w_{ik} x_i \Big/ \sum_{i=1}^{N} w_{ik}, \qquad H^k = \sum_{i=1}^{N} w_{ik} \left(x_i - \bar{x}^k\right)\left(x_i - \bar{x}^k\right)^T \Big/ \sum_{i=1}^{N} w_{ik} \tag{7}$$

and

$$C^{k+1} = \begin{pmatrix} e_1 & e_2 & \cdots & e_m \end{pmatrix}^T, \qquad b^{k+1} = C^{k+1}\bar{x}^k, \tag{8}$$

where $H^k e_i = \lambda_i e_i$, $\|e_i\| = 1$, $i = 1,\dots,n$, $0 \le \lambda_1 \le \lambda_2 \le \dots \le \lambda_n$. As above, the rows of C^k are generated by the eigenvectors $e_1, e_2, \dots, e_m$, of the matrix H^k associated with its m least eigenvalues; they span the subspace orthogonal to Π; while $e_{m+1},\dots,e_n$ span Π itself. Thus the iterations of IRLS are equivalent to standard PCA problems with varying weights.

We make several remarks.

1. The threshold Δ depends on the contamination level: larger contamination implies larger threshold. For $\Delta ? \ 1$, we arrive at the standard PCA associated with Least Squares and optimization problem (1). On the other hand, $\Delta = \ 1$ corresponds to the Least Absolute Value method.
2. The points x_i with small weights w_{ik} (and large residuals t_{ik}) are treated as outliers. However, the points lying in the subspace Π far off the main cluster are not treated as outliers.
3. The dimension of Π is often unknown *a priori*, and the solution can strongly depend on m. The important problem of adjustment of this value is beyond the scope of the present research.
4. The key question is the convergence of the algorithm and its convergence rate. It is easy to prove the monotonicity of the algorithm (similar to the Steiner-Weber problem above). However one can not guarantee global convergence; moreover, evaluating the rate of convergence remains an open problem. Practice of simulation exhibits fast global convergence in the majority of examples.
5. Computationally, solving the complete eigenvalue problem for the matrices H^k is the most time-consuming procedure. In Matlab it can be replaced with svd, which is more efficient if compared to eig.
6. PCA is sensitive to scaling of variables. The same is true for its robust version. Thus it is recommended to scale data as in the standard PCA.
7. Statistical properties of robust PCA also remain an open problem. Recall that Huber's approach to location estimation (see Section 2) has rigorous statistical validation. It is the subject for future research to provide similar results for the robust PCA.

4. STATISTICAL MODEL II

Assume the points $x_1,\dots,x_N \in \mathrm{R}^n$ have Gaussian distribution with mean a and covariance matrix R^{-1}. In order to estimate the values a and R, we use the maximum likelihood method for the Gaussian distribution. Since the probability density has the form $p(x) = \frac{\sqrt{\det R}}{(2\pi)^{n/2}} e^{-\frac{1}{2}\|R^{1/2}(x-a)\|^2}$, it is necessary to minimize the likelihood function $\varphi(R,a) = -\sum_{i=1}^{N} \ln p(x_i) = \frac{nN}{2}\log(2\pi) - \frac{N}{2}\log\det R + \frac{1}{2}\sum_{i=1}^{N}\left\|R^{1/2}(x_i - a)\right\|^2$ in accordance to the maximum likelihood estimation. We conclude that the value

$$\hat{a} = \arg\min_a \varphi(R,a) = \arg\min_a \sum_{i=1}^{N}\left\|R^{1/2}(x_i - a)\right\|^2 = \frac{1}{N}\sum_{i=1}^{N} x_i = \bar{x}$$

is an estimate for a, while the value

$$R = \arg\min_{R\succ 0} \varphi(R,\bar{x}) = \arg\min_{R\succ 0}\left(-\frac{N}{2}\log\det R + \frac{1}{2}\sum_{i=1}^{N}\left\|R^{1/2}(x_i - \bar{x})\right\|^2\right)$$

is an estimate for R.

Now, for the matrix $H = \sum_{i=1}^{N}(x_i - \bar{x})(x_i - \bar{x})^T / N$ we obtain the identity $\sum_{i=1}^{N}\left\|R^{1/2}(x_i - \bar{x})\right\|^2 / N = \langle R, H\rangle$, where $\langle\cdot,\cdot\rangle$ is a scalar product in the space of symmetric matrices with Frobenius norm. As a result, we arrive at the minimization problem $\arg\min_{R\succ 0}\left(-\log\det R+\langle R,H\rangle\right)$. The matrix function $-\log\det R$ is convex and differentiable in R, with $\nabla\left(-\log\det R+\langle R,H\rangle\right)=-R^{-1}+H$. Hence, the optimization problem admits the closed-form solution $R=H^{-1}$. The eigenvectors of the matrix R^{-1} which correspond to its largest eigenvalues, are the principal components.

Assume now that $x_1,\dots,x_N\in\mathrm{R}^n$ have contaminated Gaussian distribution with unknown center a and unknown covariance matrix R^{-1}. Similarly to the considerations above, we take the likelihood function as

$$\varphi(R,a)=-\sum_{i=1}^{N}\ln p(x_i)=\frac{nN}{2}\log(2\pi)-\frac{N}{2}\log\det R+\sum_{i=1}^{N}h(\|R^{1/2}(x_i-a)\|) \qquad (9)$$

(the rigorous validation of such a choice is an open problem). Hence, the problem is to minimize this function in the matrix variable $R\succ 0$ and the vector variable a. The problem is bi-convex; i.e., it is convex with respect to each variable separately, but nonconvex in their combination. We conclude that the arising optimization problem is hard enough - it contains matrix variables and it is nonconvex. However there is a way to overcome this obstacle by use of IRLS. Then each iteration requires solution of the standard PCA.

The difference between Model I and Model II is as follows: in Model I, the points should lie close to a subspace, and in Model II, close to an ellipsoid. In particular, in contrast to Model I (see Remark 2), the points lying far off the main cluster are treated as outliers in Model II.

In order to minimize the likelihood function (9), we use its quadratic approximations and obtain the following algorithm. At the initial step we form $\bar{x}^0=\sum_{i=1}^{N}x_i/N$, $H^0=\sum_{i=1}^{N}(x_i-\bar{x}^0)(x_i-\bar{x}^0)^T/N$ and let $a^1=\bar{x}^0$, $R^1=(H^0)^{-1}$. Then we proceed as in Section 3; however, here the argument of the Huber function is $\|R^{1/2}(x_i-a)\|$ instead of $\|Cx_i-b\|$. At the k th iteration we find the new weights

$$w_{ik}=\min\{1,\frac{\Delta}{\|t_{ik}\|}\}=\begin{cases}1, & \|t_{ik}\|\le\Delta,\\ \Delta/\|t_{ik}\|, & \|t_{ik}\|>\Delta\end{cases} \qquad (10)$$

where $t_{ik}=(R^k)^{1/2}(x_i-a^k)$. Then we have

$$a^{k+1}=\bar{x}^k,\qquad R^{k+1}=(H^k)^{-1}, \qquad (11)$$

where

$$\bar{x}^k=\sum_{i=1}^{N}w_{ik}x_i\Big/\sum_{i=1}^{N}w_{ik},\quad H^k=\sum_{i=1}^{N}w_{ik}(x_i-\bar{x}^k)(x_i-\bar{x}^k)^T\Big/\sum_{i=1}^{N}w_{ik}. \qquad (12)$$

Again, each iteration of the algorithm is equivalent to the standard PCA procedure.

Several comments are due at this point:

1. Since the optimization problem discussed above is bi-convex, the issue of global convergence of the proposed algorithm remains open.

2. The algorithm yields a high, possibly exponential rate of convergence of the iterative routine.

3. The main components are represented by the eigenvectors of the covariance matrix $(R^*)^{-1}$ associated with its largest eigenvalues.

4. As above, the proper choice of the value of Δ in Huber's function depends on the level of contamination of the distribution.

5. Instead of Huber's functions, other detectors can be used, such as Cauchy, German-Maclure, Welsch functions and others.

5. EXAMPLE

To test various robust methods, there exist numerous collections of data; e.g., see (MLR, 2016; DASL, 2016). We consider a part of the data base *Sleep In Mammals*, see (OzDASL, 2016), which contains values of the body weight, brain weight, gestation time, and maximum life span for 55 species of mammals, including Asian and African elephants and human being.

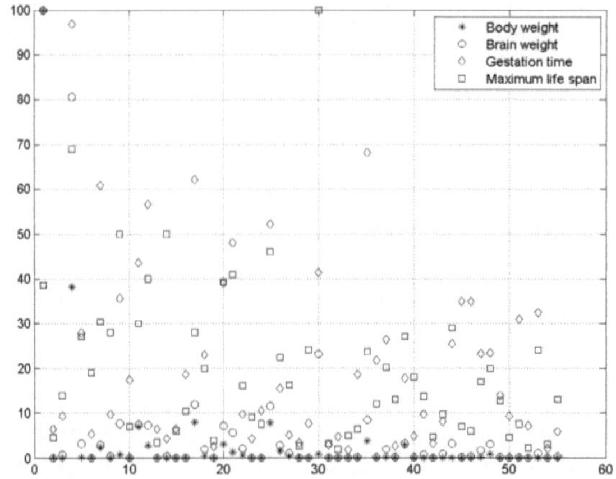

Figure 1. The standardized data set Sleep In Mammals

The standardised (after scaling to the common span $0 \div 100$) data set is given in Figure 1. In this case we have $N = 55$ and $n = 4$; the goal is to find the subspace Π of dimension $n - m = 2$. We consider both the classical PCA and two robust modifications of it discussed above. All the computations were performed in Matlab. We start with the robust Model I and algorithm (6)-(8). With $\Delta = 1$, the quantity $\sum_{i=1}^{N} h(\|t_{ik}\|)$ decreases fast enough, with its steady state value attained at $k \approx 15$. As a result, we obtain

$$C^* = \begin{pmatrix} 0,7925 & -0,6071 & 0,0118 & 0,0568 \\ -0,6066 & -0,7804 & 0,1169 & 0,0968 \end{pmatrix}, \quad b^* = \begin{pmatrix} 0,5287 \\ 1,7656 \end{pmatrix}.$$

To compare, we present here the values of the parameters of the desired plane found via the classical PCA:

$$C^{pca} = \begin{pmatrix} 0,7211 & -0,6764 & 0,0125 & 0,1494 \\ -0,3057 & -0,4110 & 0,7336 & -0,4466 \end{pmatrix}, \quad b^{pca} = \begin{pmatrix} 1,9594 \\ 4,5605 \end{pmatrix}.$$

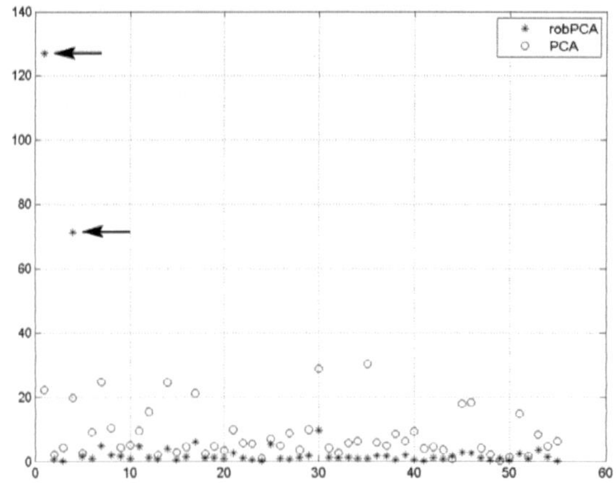

Figure 2. Norms of errors: Model I

In Figure 2, the final values $\|t_i\|$ of the norms of residuals $t_i = C^* x_i - b^*$ for $i = 1, \ldots, 55$ are marked by asterisks "$*$." By way of comparison, the corresponding values $C^{pca} x_i - b^{pca}$ obtained by using the standard PCA, are marked by the symbols "$\circ$." The robust version proposed here is seen to be capable of detecting the two obvious outliers associated with items 1 (African elephant) and 4 (Asian elephant). Approximations for the rest of the points are also much higher than those obtained with the standard PCA. This effect becomes more impressive when projecting the points x_i onto the subspace orthogonal to Π; see Figure 3.

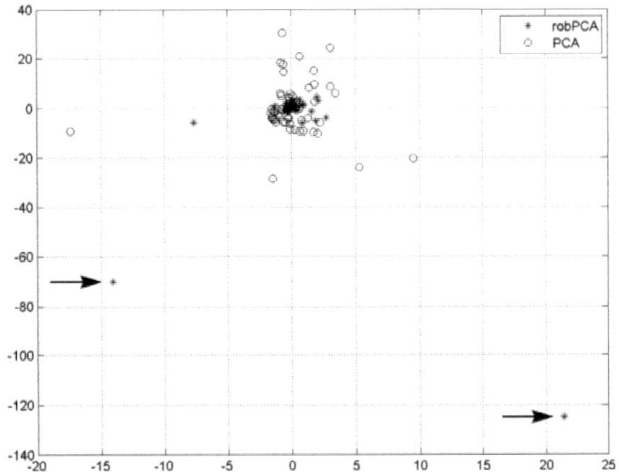

Figure 3. Projection on the orthogonal subspace: Model I

We now turn to the Model II and algorithm (12)-(14). For the same value $\Delta = 1$ of the threshold, the maximum likelihood function decreases exponentially, and we have

$$R^{*} = \begin{pmatrix} 0,6555 & -0,5129 & -0,0003 & 0,0533 \\ -0,5129 & 0,4845 & -0,0112 & -0,0509 \\ -0,0003 & -0,0112 & 0,0107 & -0,0063 \\ 0,0533 & -0,0509 & -0,0063 & 0,0195 \end{pmatrix}, \quad a^{*} = \begin{pmatrix} 0,5674 \\ 1,4348 \\ 15,1403 \\ 14,0260 \end{pmatrix}.$$

To compare, the values of the parameters of the distribution found by the classical PCA, are given by:

$$R^{pca} = \begin{pmatrix} 0,0582 & -0,0505 & -0,0009 & 0,0112 \\ -0,0505 & 0,0517 & -0,0033 & -0,0104 \\ -0,0009 & -0,0033 & 0,0052 & -0,0022 \\ 0,0112 & -0,0104 & -0,0022 & 0,0071 \end{pmatrix}, \quad a^{pca} = \begin{pmatrix} 3,3502 \\ 5,5499 \\ 22,9922 \\ 20,1527 \end{pmatrix}.$$

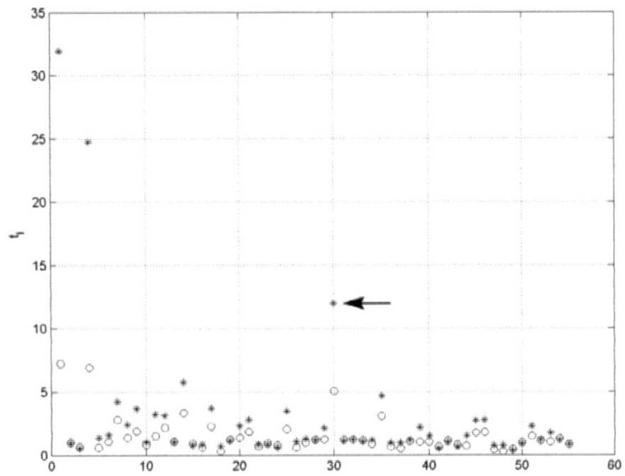

Figure 4. Norms of errors: Model II

Figure 4 depicts the final values of the norms of residuals $t_i = (R^{*})^{1/2}(x_i - a^{*})$ for $i = 1,\ldots,55$, obtained by our method (asterisks), together with those, $(R^{pca})^{1/2}(x_i - a^{pca})$ obtained by the standard PCA (marked by "$\circ$"). On top of the previously detected outliers (items 1 and 4), there is yet another one (item 30), associated with human being.Both robust versions exposed a much better approximation of the "main body" of the points (with discarded outliers) than the classical PCA. Needless to say, by no means can the example presented above be considered as a sound proof of the efficiency of the proposed robust PCA methods. Massive experiments with higher-dimensional data are required, and fine polishing the numerical details of the algorithms are needed.

6. CONCLUSION

We proposed two robust modifications of the principal component analysis method, based on the statistical approach by Huber. Both of them reduce to optimization problems with vector or matrix variables. To solve the problems numerically, we applied the iterative quadratic approximation method. Preliminary numerical examples demonstrate a fast convergence and obvious advantages of the new methods over the classical PCA. However numerous issues related to the statistical and numerical substantiation of the robust methods require a deeper analysis. Alternative numerical solution methods for the problems formulated in this paper are worth studying and comparing to the algorithm proposed in this paper.

ACKNOWLEDGEMENT

This work was supported by the Russian Science Foundation, project no. 16-11-10015.

REFERENCES

Box, G., 1953. Non-Normality and Tests on Variances. *In Biometrika*, Vol. 40, pp. 318-335.

Bruckstein, A., Donoho, D., and Elad, M., 2009. From Sparse Solutions of Systems of Equations to Sparse Modeling of Signals and Images. *In SIAM Rev.*, Vol. 51, No. 1, pp. 34-81.

Candès, E. et al, 2011. Robust Principal Component Analysis? *In J. Assoc. Comput. Math.*, Vol. 58, No. 3, Article 11.

Croux, C. and Haesbroeck, G., 2000. Principal Component Analysis Based on Robust Estimators of the Covariance or Correlation Matrix: Influence Functions and Efficiencies. *In Biometrika*, Vol. 87, No. 3, pp. 603-618.

DASL, 2016. The Data and Story Library, URL http://lib.stat.cmu.edu/DASL/DataArchive.html.

Huber, P., 1981. *Robust Statictics*. Wiley, New York, USA.

Jolliffe, I., 2002. *Principal Component Analysis*. Springer-Verlag, New York, USA.

Maronna, R. et al, 2006. *Robust Statictics*. Wiley, Chichester, England.

Maronna, R. and Yohai, V., 1998. Robust Estimation of Multivariate Location and Scatter. In *Encyclopedia of Statistical Sciences*, pp. 589-596. Wiley, New York, USA.

MLR, 2016. UC Irvine Machine Learning Repository, URL http://archive.ics.uci.edu/ml/.

OzDASL, 2016. Australasian Data and Story Library, URL http://www.statsci.org/data/general/sleep.html.

Pearson, K., 1901. On Lines and Planes of Closest Fit to Systems of Points in Space. *In Philosoph. Magazine*, Vol. 2, No. 6, pp. 559-572.

Plastria, F., 2009. Asymmetric Distances, Semidirected Networks and Majority in Fermat-Weber Problems. *In Ann. Oper. Res.*, Vol. 167, No. 1, Article 121.

Poljak, B. and Tsypkin, J., 1980. Robust Identification. *In Automatica*, Vol. 16. No. 1, pp. 53-63.

Shevlyakov, G. and Vilchevski, N., 2002. *Robustness in Data Analysis: Criteria and Methods*. VSP, Utrecht.

Weiszfeld, E., 1937. Sur le Point pour Lequel la Somme des Distances de *n* Points Donnés est Minimum. *In Tohoku Math. J.*, Vol. 43, pp. 355-386.

Wright, J. et al, 2009. Robust Principal Component Analysis: Exact Recovery of Corrupted Low-Rank Matrices by Convex Optimization. *Proceedings of 23 Ann. Conf. Neural Inform. Proc. Syst.* Vancouver, Canada, pp. 2080-2088.

Zhang, T. and Lehrman, G., 2014. A Novel *M*-Estimator for Robust PCA. *In J. Machine Learning Research*, Vol. 15, pp. 749-808.

Zhou, Z. et al, 2010. Stable Principal Component Pursuit. *Proceedings of IEEE Int. Symp. Inform. Theory*. Austin, Texas, pp. 1518-1522.

FAST RELEVANCE-REDUNDANCY DOMINANCE: FEATURE SELECTION FOR HIGH DIMENSIONAL DATA[1]

David Browne, Carlo Manna and Steven D. Prestwich
Insight Centre for Data Analytics, University College Cork, Ireland

ABSTRACT

Feature selection is used to select a subset of features for model construction. This reduces dimensionality which is important for simplification, efficiency and reducing overfitting. Filter-based methods are the most scalable, rating features by their relevance to the target variable via appropriate statistics. Browne, et al. proposed a filter feature selection method, called Relevance-Redundancy Dominance (RRD) with useful properties (no threshold setting, adaptability to any statistics etc.), but with a poor scalability. In this paper, we present a scalable version of RRD, called Fast Relevance-Redundancy Dominance which holds the same properties as RRD while improving scalability. To show the effectiveness of the proposed approach we have carried out extensive numerical experiments on high dimensional datasets (DNA microarray datasets) which shows that it outperforms state-of-the-art algorithms.

KEYWORDS

Feature-Selection, Filter-Based, High-Dimensional, Scalability, Microarray

1. INTRODUCTION

The task of feature selection is to select a subset of the original features present in a given dataset that provides most of the useful information. Hence, after selection has taken place, the dataset should still have most of the important information still present. The methods are usually categorized as filter, wrapper or embedded (Guyon, 2006). While filter methods rely on the general characteristics of the training data to select features, independently of any predictor, wrapper methods involve optimizing a predictor as part of the selection process; and embedded methods try to combine advantages of both. The advantage of filter methods over wrapper and embedded methods are that they are fast, independent of the classifier/predictor method, scalable and easy to interpret. For this reason they are particular suitable for large datasets.

Due to these advantages, many filter methods have been proposed in the past and recent years. The RELIEF algorithm (Kira & Rendell, 1992) estimates the quality of attributes according to how well their values distinguish between instances that are similar to each other, but was initially limited to two-class problems. An extension, ReliefF (Kononenko, 1994), not only deals with multiclass problems but is also more robust and capable of dealing with incomplete and noisy data. The main drawback of the Relief family methods is that they select features based only on relevance and do not remove redundant features.

Correlation-based Feature Selection (CFS) (Hall, 1998) is a simple filter algorithm that ranks feature subsets according to a correlation-based heuristic evaluation function. The bias of the evaluation function is toward subsets that contain features that are highly correlated with the class and uncorrelated with each other. However, redundant features are screened out as they are highly correlated with one or more of the remaining features. Moreover, there exists an improved CFS version called Fast Correlated-Based Filter (FCBF) method (Yu & Liu, 2003) based on symmetrical uncertainty (SU) (Press, et al., 1988). This version is designed for high-dimensionality data and has been shown to be effective in removing both irrelevant and redundant features, but on the other hand it fails to take into consideration interactions between features.

The INTERACT algorithm (Zhao & Liu, 2007) uses the same goodness measure as the FCBF filter (Press, et al., 1988) but also includes the consistency contribution (c-contribution). The c-contribution of a feature indicates how significantly the elimination of that feature would affect consistency. The algorithm

[1]This work was supported in part by Science Foundation Ireland (SFI) under Grant Number SFI/12/RC/2289.

consists of two major parts. In the first part, the features are ranked in descending order based on their SU values. In the second part, features are evaluated one by one starting from the end of the ranked feature list. If the c-contribution of a feature is less than a given threshold the feature is removed, otherwise it is selected.

Finally, Minimum Redundancy-Maximum Relevance (MRMR) (Peng, et al., 2005) is a heuristic framework which minimizes redundancy, using a series of measures of relevance and redundancy to select promising features for both continuous and discrete data sets.

In this paper we focus on filter-based methods, which are considered to be most scalable to high dimensional data. In (Browne, et al., 2016), the authors introduced a new filter-based feature selection method called Relevance-Redundancy Dominance (RRD) feature selection, with a simple feature elimination strategy based on relevance and redundancy. RRD has many advantages compared to state-of-the-art methods: (i) it can be applied to mixed data types, (ii) it can be used with a wide variety of statistics and (iii) it requires no threshold for choosing a feature subset. However, it shows poor scalability on high-dimensional data. In order to overcome this drawback, in this paper, we propose a fast version of RRD called Fast Relevance-Redundancy Dominance (FRRD) feature selection, with a simple feature elimination strategy also based on relevance and redundancy. The results of the proposed method, achieved on extensive numerical experiments using microarray data, are compared and contrasted with other methods in literature.

2. THE PROPOSED METHOD

Fast Relevance-Redundancy Dominance (FRRD) is an extension of the original *Relevance-Redundancy Dominance* (RRD) (Browne, at al., 2016), and although it uses the same principal idea of dominance, unlike RRD it is highly scalable. It should also be noted that RRD is step 2 in the FRRD algorithm, explained below. RRD was tested on high dimensional data, in particular the colon and leukaemia micro array datasets (Li, 2003), where experiments showed RRD retaining a lot more features than needed. For the colon dataset, RRD kept between 40-50 features, while, for the leukaemia dataset, between 80-100 features were retained. As a result of this, the computational time increased, along with the classification accuracy decreasing due to overfitting. FRRD was proposed, based on the same idea as RRD, to overcome the pitfalls of RRD.

Fast Relevance-Redundancy Dominance is a univariate filter-based feature selection method, which can use any suitable statistic to select a good (relevant and non-redundant) subset of features from a dataset. Before detailing the proposed approach, we first provide some definitions. Let f and f' denote features, t the target variable, and s the chosen statistic (which may be symmetric or asymmetric), then:

DEFINITION 2.1. f **dominates** f' if $s(f,t) > s(f',t)$ and $s(f,f') > s(f',t)$

DEFINITION 2.2. f' is **redundant** if it is dominated by some f that is not dominated by any other feature.

FRRD has 2 parameters, α, a reduction-rate and K, the number of features desired (K is user defined, and in this paper was set to $\log_2(N)$, N being the total number of features). FRRD is a two-step algorithm, the first comprises of the new scalable approach of the algorithm, while the second is the original RRD. Step one of FRRD selects all non-redundant features using the algorithm shown in Algorithm 1. Then, we calculate the number of features F which FRRD needs to retain to complete the feature selection. This is $\alpha N + 1$ which is then multiplied by the number of features desired. We initialize an empty set S. After this, in the while loop, we select the feature $\hat{f} \in F$ with greatest relevance x_{ft}, generate the set R of $f \in F$ that are the α most dominated by $\hat{f}$, remove $R \cup \{\hat{f}\}$ from F, and add $\hat{f}$ to S. The last four steps in the loop are repeated until the number of features desired K, is reached, then we return the set S of selected features.

Algorithm 1 FRRD Algorithm Step 1

given features F and target t
$\forall f \in F$
  $x_{ft} \leftarrow s(f,t)$
$F \leftarrow (\lceil \alpha N \rceil + 1)K$ most relevant features of F
$S \leftarrow \emptyset$
while $S < K$
  $\hat{f} \leftarrow \arg\max_{f \in F} x_{ft}$
  $R \leftarrow \lceil \alpha |F| \rceil$ features f with greatest $s(\hat{f}, f)$
  $F \leftarrow F \setminus (R \cup \{\hat{f}\})$
  $S \leftarrow S \cup \{\hat{f}\}$
return S

Algorithm 2 FRRD Algorithm Step 2

given remaining features F and target t
$\forall f \in F$
  $x_{ft} \leftarrow s(f,t)$ from part one
$S \leftarrow \emptyset$
while $F \neq \emptyset$
  $\hat{f} \leftarrow \arg\max_{f \in F} x_{ft}$
  $R \leftarrow \{f \mid f \in F \wedge s(\hat{f}, f) > x_{ft}\}$
  $F \leftarrow F \setminus (R \cup \{\hat{f}\})$
  $S \leftarrow S \cup \{\hat{f}\}$
return S

First we precompute the statistics $x_{ft} = s(f,t)$ between each feature f and the target variable t.

Once step 1 has selected the K features, named F in step 2, FRRD runs in order to select all non-redundant features using the procedure shown in Algorithm 2. We use the computed statistics of $x_{ft} = s(f,t)$ between each of the remaining features f and the target variable t. We initialise the set of selected features S to the empty set Ø. Then we select the feature $\hat{f} \in F$ with greatest relevance $x_{\hat{f}t}$, generate the set R such that $f \in F$ that are made redundant by $\hat{f}$, remove $R \cup \{\hat{f}\}$ from F, and add $\hat{f}$ to S. The last four steps in the loop are repeated until F is empty, then we return the set S of selected features. In theory at the end of step 2 the set K does not have to equal the set S, as it is possible that a feature in K may have been dominated by another feature in that set.

Note that FRRD typically does not compute all s-values between features (for example a full correlation matrix), nor does it sort a complete list of features. This is because after a feature has been removed from F no further computations on it need be performed. This means, the worst case time complexity is $O(\alpha NK^2M)$ for N, total number of features, K desired number of features and M samples. It is possible to construct datasets for which Algorithm 2 removes no features at all, or removes all but one, but in practice we find that it usually generates a small subset of features. Furthermore, FRRD is highly flexible in terms of the statistics it can use. In fact, the statistic can be symmetric ($s(f,f') \equiv s(f',f)$ (for example correlation or mutual information) or asymmetric (for example λ (Goodman & Kruskal, 1954)).

Finally, it should be pointed out that FRRD assumes that we can compute statistic $s(x,y')$ for all $x, y \in F \cup \{t\}$. Thus, before we can apply FRRD, if the target and/or features have mixed types (numerical, ordinal, nominal) they must first be pre-processed so that they are all of the same type. Discretization is used to transform continuous data to discrete form, which involves putting the continuous data put into 'bins', using well-known methods such as equal-width. This reduces and simplifies the data, improving the computational efficiency, and it has also been shown to increase the accuracy of filter algorithms (Bolon-Canedo, et al., 2010). Another advantage, showing the versatility of FRRD, is its ability to handle mixed data types by using any suitable statistic whether they are correlation criteria (such as Pearson's correlation coefficient) or information-based (such as mutual information) depending on the type of data being analysed.

3. EXPERIMENT DESIGN

The FRRD method has been evaluated from the perspective of classification performance, comparing it with state-of-the-art algorithms. Papers in the literature, using filter feature selection methods such as ReliefF, INTERACT, Information Gain, CFS and Consistency-based filter, use different cross-validation techniques in their analysis, i.e.: 5-fold, 10-fold and leave-one-out cross-validation, as well as different well-known classifiers, namely 3knn, 5knn, C4.5, Naive Bayes, IB1, SVM and Random Forest. In order to evaluate the effectiveness of the proposed method, this paper uses the same cross-validation and classifier techniques as the other methods in each comparison.

3.1 Datasets

Table 1. Microarray datasets: name of dataset, *N* is the number of features, *n* the number of samples, percentage of minimum *%min* and majority *%maj* classes, the imbalance ratio *IR* and the maximum Fisher's discriminant ratio *F1*

Dataset	N	n	(%min,%maj)	IR	F1
Alizadeh (DLBCL)	4026	47	(48.94,51.06)	1.04	120.35
Alon (Colon)	2000	62	(35.48,64.52)	1.82	22.45
Beer (Lung)	7129	96	(10.42,89.58)	8.6	484.02
Freije (Gli85 Brain)	22283	85	(30.59,69.41)	2.27	90.37
Gordon (Lung)	12533	181	(17.13,82.87)	0.21	187.37
Golub (Leukaemia)	7129	72	(34.72,65.28)	1.88	63.74
Petricoin (Ovarian)	15154	253	(35.97,64.03)	1.78	333.63
Pomeroy (CNS)	7129	60	(35,65)	1.86	16.92
Shipp (Lymph)	7129	77	(24.68,75.32)	3.05	103.32
Singh (Prostate)	12600	136	(43.38,56.62)	1.31	36.82
Spira (Lung)	19993	187	(48.13,51.87)	1.08	19.28
Veer (Breast)	24188	95	(46.32,53.68)	1.16	29.93
Pre-established training & test samples					
Singh (Prostate) Train	12600	102	(49.02,50.98)	1.04	66.46
Singh (Prostate) Test	12600	34	(26.47,73.53)	2.78	687.23
Veer (Breast) Train	24188	78	(43.59,56.41)	1.29	25.00
Veer (Breast) Test	24188	19	(36.84,63.16)	1.71	148.17

FRRD was evaluated on 12 microarray datasets, which are available on the Kent Ridge Biomedical Data Set Repository (Li, 2003) and Arizona State University (Arizona, 2016). Each dataset has a binary target variable. Table 1 provides an overview of the 12 datasets. The datasets chosen have a variety of characteristics: they are high dimensional, from 2000 up to 24188 features; from quite well balanced (with 1:1 being the ideal value) to fairly unbalanced (as shown by IR ratio); have a wide variety of complexity (as shown by F1 ratio), and finally like all microarray datasets, they are very challenging as all of them have very few samples (from 47 up to a maximum of 253). Furthermore, two of these datasets are pre-established training and testing samples which are detailed at the bottom of Table 1. The tables show the author's name (who originally used the dataset), along with the type of data being examined, the number of features (genes), and the number of samples. It also shows the percentages of the minimum and majority classes, as well as the imbalance between the classes. It can be seen that most of the datasets have an imbalance of between 1 and 2, which is reasonable. However, there are a few outside this range; the most notable are Beer and Gordon, both having one class more than 8 times larger than the other.

The F1 column shows the maximum Fisher's discriminant ratio of each dataset (Ho. & Basu, 2002). This shows the complexity of the datasets, which measures the overlapping within the dataset. The lower the F1 score, the more overlapping within the dataset, hence making it a greater challenge for classification. The two datasets with the lowest F1 values are Pomeroy and Spira. It will be shown in the results section, that these 2 datasets are harder to correctly classify, thus having poorer classification results when compared to the other datasets. Feature selection or Gene selection has been the subject of several papers (Bolon-Canedo, et al., 2011), (Mandal & Mukhopadhyay, 2013), (Navarro, 2009), making it an ideal test-bed for our method. Microarray data has a distinctive characteristic of high dimensionality (in our case 24188 genes) with a small sample size, which can be a very challenging problem for classification methods.

To compare our algorithm with others in the literature, we have run FRRD on each dataset, then we have compared our results with the results provided by other authors using the same model validation techniques and classifiers used in those papers.

3.2 Stability and Scalability

One of the challenges of feature selection is to select the smallest set of features which still classifies test data accurately. The stability of the filter algorithm is its ability to repeatedly select the same or similar subset of features in each k-fold. A variation of the formula used to calculate the Tanimoto distance between 2 sets, introduced by Kalousis (Kalousis, et al., 2007), is used to in this paper, and the results are compared to Bolon et al in Table 2 (Bolon-Canedo, et al., 2012). A greater Tanimoto distance indicates a better stability measure in the method. The results show that FRRD is more stable than the newly proposed method by Bolon et al, scoring higher than it in all eight datasets. FRRD and Information Gain (IG) both achieved the best stability result in three datasets each, while ReliefF scored best on the other 2 datasets.

Table 2. Comparison of FRRD's stability measure with the paper (Bolon-Canedo, V. et al., 2012) using 10-fold cross-validation

Dataset	FRRD	Ensemble	CFS	Cons	INT	IG	ReliefF
Alon (Colon)	0.512	0.511	0.319	0.138	0.264	0.529	**0.675**
Golub (Leukaemia)	0.59	0.396	0.213	0.17	0.246	**0.654**	0.396
Pomeroy (CNS)	**0.424**	0.266	0.208	0.151	0.182	0.252	0.307
Alizadeh (DLBCL)	0.576	0.38	0.274	0.47	0.232	0.488	**0.621**
Singh (Prostate)	**0.713**	0.363	0.34	0.077	0.207	0.322	0.395
Gordon (Lung)	0.704	0.287	0.247	0.126	0.221	**0.721**	0.605
Petricoin (Ovarian)	0.486	0.476	0.386	0.486	0.262	**0.875**	0.688
Veer (Breast)	**0.358**	0.229	0.194	0.061	0.178	0.212	0.301

Table 3. Comparison of FRRD time, using single thread core CPU, with the (Krawczuk & Lukaszuk, 2016), using leave-one-out cross-validation (in hours:minutes:seconds)

Dataset	FRRD	ReliefF	MRMR	SVM-RFE
Alon (Colon)	0:04:08	0:51:00	0:50:05	1:49:55
Golub (Leukaemia)	0:24:00	1:50:12	1:35:32	13:03:27
Pomeroy (CNS)	0:13:00	57:01:17	0:49:37	8:20:36
Singh (Prostate)	1:39:44	19:47:54	15:22:52	146:23:27
Gordon (Lung)	2:24:48	57:01:17	12:33:52	231:28:22
Veer (Breast)	2:36:49	18:45:00	10:31:17	250:50:00

Table 3 shows FRRD's computational time, which is compared to that of other well-known filter methods (Krawczuk & Lukaszuk, 2016). The experimental setup was on a single thread core, and it can be seen that FRRD requires much less computational time than the others. It should be noted that RRD's computational time for the colon dataset was slightly over an hour, showing it not to be a very scalable method. In the next section we will show that the classification accuracy of FRRD is also superior to well-known methods.

4. CLASSIFICATION RESULTS

FRRD results are compared with a number of different published methods, showing the robustness of the algorithm. We first run FRRD using 5-fold cross-validation to compare with the results of Bolon (Table 4) (Bolon-Canedo, et al., 2014). Out of the 18 experiments, FRRD was only beaten once, and that was by 0.09%, on the Ovarian dataset using the C4.5 classifier. On the other experiments, FRRD outperforms the seven well-known filter methods, including mRMR, CFS and FCBF. It should also be noted that FRRD also selected far fewer features than the other methods. Bolon conducted an analysis on pre-established training and testing samples, which, was also performed in this study using FRRD. The results show that using the same split in the datasets, FRRD still achieves better classification accuracy than the well-known methods.

Mandal (Table 5) introduced an improved version of mRMR, along with the results of 2 other versions of mRMR, which are compared with FRRD using 10-fold cross-validation (Mandal & Mukhopadhyay, 2013). On the two microarray datasets selected by Mandal, FRRD achieves 100% accuracy, equalling the improved mRMR on one dataset and being superior to the rest of the experiments on the paper.

Table 4. Comparison of FRRD with the paper (Bolon-Canedo, V. et al., 2014), using 5 fold and holdout cross-validation with C4.5, Naïve Bayes & SVM classifiers (Accuracy in percentage with number of features selected in brackets)

Dataset	FRRD	No FS	CFS	FCBF	INT	IG	ReliefF	SVM-RFE	mRMR
C4.5 Classifier									
Alizadeh (DLBCL)	98(12)	70	75(61)	73(35)	70(45)	75(10)	85(10)	82(50)	75(10)
Alon (Colon)	87(11)	74	79(24)	79(14)	79(14)	84(50)	82(50)	80(50)	82(10)
Freije (Gli85 Brain)	91(14)	75	79(141)	82(116)	78(117)	85(10)	85(10)	82(10)	75(50)
Petricoin (Ovarian)	99(8.4)	97	98(33)	99(26)	98(31)	96(10)	99(50)	98(10)	98(10)
Pomeroy (CNS)	78 (13)	58	62(44)	48(33)	55(33)	63(50)	53(50)	65(10)	58(50)
Spira (Lung)	74(14)	65	64(103)	61(51)	59(51)	65(50)	65(10)	65(50)	68(10)
Naïve Bayes Classifier									
Alizadeh (DLBCL)	100(12)	92	90(61)	90(35)	90(45)	94(10)	94(10)	92(10)	94(50)
Alon (Colon)	89(11)	55	85(24)	80(14)	77(14)	79(10)	84(50)	76(50)	80(10)
Freije (Gli85 Brain)	93(14)	84	82(141)	85(116)	82(117)	85(10)	89(50)	88(50)	85(10)
Petricoin (Ovarian)	100(8.4)	93	100(33)	99(26)	100(31)	98(50)	98(50)	99(10)	99(10)
Pomeroy (CNS)	80(13)	60	67(44)	70(33)	70(33)	63(10)	67(50)	70(50)	63(10)
Spira (Lung)	75(1)	63	65(103)	69(51)	64(51)	66(50)	67(10)	71(10)	67(10)
SVM Classifier									
Alizadeh (DLBCL)	100((12)	96	88(61)	81(35)	88(45)	94(10)	94(10)	88(50)	96(50)
Alon (Colon)	90(11)	77	81(24)	84(14)	81(14)	85(50)	85(50)	73(10)	84(50)
Freije (Gli85 Brain)	94(14)	92	88(141)	87(116)	88(117)	91(10)	89(50)	89(50)	89(10)
Petricoin (Ovarian)	100(8.4)	100	100(33)	100(26)	100(31)	100(50)	100(50)	100(10)	100(10)
Pomeroy (CNS)	80(13)	67	62(44)	65(33)	62(33)	67(50)	73(50)	73(10)	70(50)
Spira (Lung)	75(14)	72	64(103)	71(51)	66(51)	72(50)	69(10)	72(50)	68(10)
Pre-established training & test samples									
C4.5 Classifier									
Veer (Breast)	84(15)	74	68(130)	58(99)	79(102)	53(50)	58(10)	58(10)	74(50)
Singh (Prostate)	76(6)	26	26(89)	26(77)	26(73)	29(50)	29(50)	32(10)	41(10)
Naïve Bayes Classifier									
Veer (Breast)	89(15)	37	37(130)	37(99)	37(102)	37(10)	89(50)	68(10)	37(10)
Singh (Prostate)	85(6)	26	26(89)	26(77)	26(73)	26(10)	21(10)	26(50)	26(10)
SVM Classifier									
Veer (Breast)	89(15)	58	68(130)	58(99)	74(102)	79(50)	84(10)	68(10)	68(50)
Singh (Prostate)	100(6)	53	97(89)	97(77)	71(73)	97(10)	97(50)	79(10)	91 (50)

Table 5. Comparison of FRRD with the (Mandal & Mukhopadhyay, 2013), using 10 fold cross-validation (Accuracy in percentage with number of features selected in brackets)

Dataset	**FRRD**	**Improved mRMR**	**mRMR (MID)**	**mRMR (MIQ)**
Golub (Leukaemia)	100(8.7)	100(100)	97.22(100)	98.61(100)
Petricoin (Ovarian)	100(13)	99.8(100)	98.2(100)	98.6(100)

(Bontempi & Meyer, 2010) proposed a method called min-Interaction Max-Relevancy (mIMR) and have used 10-fold cross-validation (Table 6), and averaged the results of 5 classifiers 1knn, 3knn, 5knn, SVM-L and Random Forest, reasoning that the use of multiple classifiers would reduce the bias of the feature assessment based on a specific classification strategy. Also in this case is possible to see that our method outperforms mIMR along with the five state-of-the-art filters, used in the paper's experimental design.

Table 6. Comparison of FRRD with the paper (Bontempi & Meyer, 2010), using 10 fold cross-validation and averages 5 classifier results, 1knn, 3knn, 5knn, SVM-L & Random Forest (Accuracy in percentage)

Dataset	**FRRD**	**mIMR**	**mRMR**	**DISR**	**CMIM**	**MB**	**RANK**
Alon (Colon)	88.71	81.66	80.02	80.6	78.41	77.01	79.45
Golub (Leukaemia)	99.44	94.27	94.23	93.85	93.52	89.24	94.13
Alizadeh (DLBCL)	99.15	93.35	93.99	94.3	92.79	76	93.87
Beer (Lung)	100	96.25	96.3	97.12	92.6	98.7	97.25
Pomeroy (CNS)	80.33	50.88	50.18	50.05	52.01	44.22	49.34
Shipp (Lymph)	98.96	82.37	82.12	83.79	83.07	75.92	82.24

In (Krawczuk & Lukaszuk, 2016) (Table 7) the authors analysed 6 microarray datasets using leave-one-out cross-validation, with SVM as the classifier. FRRD was best in all 6 experiments, with far superior accuracy on the CNS dataset. This experiment shows that using another cross-validation technique, FRRD can still perform better than other commonly used filter methods such as mRMR, SVM-RFE and FeliefF.

Table 7. Comparison of FRRD with the paper (Krawczuk & Lukaszuk, 2016), using leave-one-out cross-validation and SVM classifier (Accuracy in percentage with number of features selected in brackets)

Dataset	FRRD	No FS	ReliefF	MRMR	SVM-RFE
Alon (Colon)	90.32(9.74)	83.87	85.48(33.29)	81.10(12.71)	85.48(9.98)
Golub (Leukaemia)	98.61(13)	98.61	66.67(57.97)	95.83(7.76)	94.44(6.68)
Pomeroy (CNS)	93.75(9.55)	66.67	63.33(18.62)	65.00(49.05)	58.33(14.87)
Singh (Prostate)	93.94(13.99)	91.91	72.06(87.17)	69.12(58.84)	88.24(87.37)
Gordon (Lung)	100(9.29)	99.45	97.24(97.06)	98.34(3.95)	98.90(5.69)
Veer (Breast)	75.79(14)	69.07	64.95(76.69)	70.10(31.65)	67.01(19.90)

Table 8. Comparison of FRRD with the paper (Bolon-Canedo, et al., 2012) using 10 fold cross- validation with C4.5, Naïve Bayes & IB1 classifiers (Accuracy in percentage with number of features selected in brackets)

Dataset	FRRD	Ensemble	No FS	CFS	Cons	INT	IG	ReliefF
C4.5 Classifier								
Alon (Colon)	88.71(11)	86.9	76.19	80.71	83.57	89.05	85.71	77.38
Golub (Leukaemia)	100(13)	88.04	76.96	83.75	85.18	83.75	87.5	88.75
Pomeroy (CNS)	83.33(8.2)	63.33	55	60	58.33	61.67	63.33	58.33
Alizadeh (DLBCL)	97.87(12)	79.5	77.5	73	85.5	76.5	75.5	75.5
Singh (Prostate)	93.38(14)	88.19	80.22	77.03	83.08	81.54	90.6	89.73
Gordon (Lung)	98.9(14)	97.25	93.92	93.92	92.78	93.33	98.89	98.33
Petricoin (Ovarian)	99.21(8.7)	98.8	95.66	97.2	98.43	97.23	98.02	97.65
Veer (Breast)	75.79(15)	63.78	61	61.67	60.22	59.89	66.67	58.89
Naïve Bayes Classifier								
Alon (Colon)	91.94(11)	83.81	52.14	81.9	80	80.71	77.14	85.48
Golub (Leukaemia)	100(13)	95.89	98.75	97.14	89.46	95.89	95.89	95.71
Pomeroy (CNS)	81.67(8.2)	70	63.33	61.67	53.33	63.33	58.33	66.67
Alizadeh (DLBCL)	100(12)	93.5	91.5	96	85.5	94	91.5	95
Singh (Prostate)	94.85(14)	58.13	55.22	63.3	60.99	69.07	57.2	59.73
Gordon (Lung)	100(14)	100	97.78	98.89	91.17	98.89	100	96.67
Petricoin (Ovarian)	100(8.7)	99.2	93.63	99.6	99.22	99.6	97.65	96.05
Veer (Breast)	80(15)	53.44	51.89	51.67	56.78	48.44	56.67	71.33
IB1 Classifier								
Alon (Colon)	88.71(11)	80.95	73.38	80.71	73.57	77.14	79.05	74.29
Golub (Leukaemia)	100(13)	94.46	90.54	94.46	90.54	95.89	93.39	93.04
Pomeroy (CNS)	81.67(8.2)	63.33	48.33	50	58.33	50	53.33	58.33
Alizadeh (DLBCL)	100(12)	96	76	93.5	81.5	91.5	93.5	93.5
Singh (Prostate)	94.12(14)	87.47	79.89	78.96	79.89	79.95	83.13	87.42
Gordon (Lung)	100(14)	98.89	95	99.44	92.78	99.44	98.89	97.81
Petricoin (Ovarian)	100(8.7)	100	94.46	100	99.6	99.2	97.26	98.82
Veer (Breast)	77.89(15)	71.89	60.22	63.78	61.67	67.78	71.89	69

The final set of results, again from (Bolon-Canedo, et al., 2012) (Table 8), uses 10-fold cross validation with C4.5, Naive Bayes and IB1 classifiers. In this experiment, FRRD is superior on all 24 experiments, except for 2, where it was equal best with 100% accuracy. FRRD scored 100% accuracy on 9 out of the 24 experiments, with both Naive Bayes and IB1 classifiers performing best, each of which achieving 100% accuracy on half of the datasets they analysed.

In summary, FRRD has been shown to out-perform all other filter methods mentioned in this paper, using a variety of different experimental set-ups, which we believe shows the robustness of FRRD. This is due to FRRD's ability to select the most dominant features, which are also the important features within the data. The stability of FRRD was examined and was quite competitive when compared to other filter techniques. Finally, the scalability of FRRD was explored, showing that FRRD is a very scalable method, with the potential to handle very high dimensional data.

5. CONCLUSION

We proposed a new filter-based feature selection algorithm called FRRD with several advantages over existing methods: it can use a wide variety of statistics, making it very flexible; it can handle combinations of nominal, ordinal and numerical data; it takes both relevance and redundancy into account; and it automatically decides how many features to select. In experiments on microarray data, FRRD outperforms the results of published methods, while being competitive with their stability scores and finally, has been shown to be a very scalable filter technique.

REFERENCES

Arizona, 2016. *Feature Selection Datasets at Arizona State University.* [Online] ,Available at: http://featureselection.asu.edu/datasets.php, [Accessed 12 7 2016].

Bolon-Canedo, V. et al., 2010. On the effectiveness of discretization on gene selection of. *The 2010 International Joint Conference on Neural Networks (IJCNN),* pp. 18-23.

Bolon-Canedo, V. et al., 2011. Toward an ensemble of filters for classification. *Proceeding of the 11th International Conference on Intelligent Systems Design and Applications*. Cordoba, Spain.

Bolon-Canedo, V. et al., 2012. An ensemble of filters and classifiers for microarray data classification.. *Pattern Recognition,* Vol. 45, No. 1, pp. 531-539.

Bolon-Canedo, V. et al., 2014. A review of microarray datasets and applied feature selection methods.. *Information Sciences,* Volume 282, pp. 111-135.

Bontempi, G. & Meyer, P., 2010. Causal filter selection in microarray data. *Proceedings of the ICML2010 conference.* Israel, pp. 95-102.

Browne, D., Manna, C. & Prestwich, S., 2016. *Relevance-Redundancy Dominance: a Threshold-Free Approach to Filter-Based Feature Selection.* Dublin, Irish Conference on Artificial Intelligence and Cognitive Science.

Goodman, L. & Kruskal, W., 1954. Measures of association for cross classifications. *Journal of the American Statistics Association,* pp. 732-764.

Guyon, I., 2006. *Feature extraction: foundations and applications.* vol. 207 ed. Heidelberg: Springer.

Hall, M., 1998. *Correlation-based feature selection for machine learning,* Hamilton, New Zealand: Waikato University.

Ho., T. & Basu, M., 2002. Complexity measures of supervised classification problems. *IEEE Trans. on Pattern Analysis and Machine Intelligence,* 24(3), pp. 289-300.

Kalousis, A. et al., 2007. Stability of feature selection algorithms: a study on high-dimensional spaces.. *Knowledge and Information Systems,* Vol. 12, No. 1, pp. 95-116.

Kira, K. & Rendell, L., 1992. A practical approach to feature selection. *Proceedings of the Ninth International Conference on Machine Learning,* pp. 249-256.

Kononenko, I., 1994. Estimating attributes: analysis and extensions of RELIEF. *Machine Learning: ECML-94,* pp. 171-182.

Krawczuk, J. & Lukaszuk, T., 2016. The feature selection bias problem in relation to high-dimensional gene data. *Artificial Intelligence in Medicine,* Volume 66, pp. 63-71.

Li, J., 2003. *Kent Ridge Bio-medical Dataset.* [Online], Available at: http://datam.i2r.a-star.edu.sg/datasets/krbd/, [Accessed 12 07 2016].

Mandal, M. & Mukhopadhyay, A., 2013. An improved minimum redundancy maximum relevance approach for feature selection in gene expression data. *Procedia Technol.,* Volume 10, pp. 20-27.

Navarro, F. & Muñoz, L., 2009. Gene subset selection in microarray data using entropic filtering for cancer classification. *Expert Systems,* 26(1), pp. 113-124.

Peng, H. et al., 2005. Feature selection based on mutual information: criteria of max-dependency, max-relevance, and min-redundancy. *IEEE Transactions on Pattern Analysis and Machine Intelligence,* 27(8), pp. 1226-1238.

Press, W. et al., 1988. *Numerical recipes in C.* Cambridge: Cambridge University Press.

Yu, L. & Liu, H., 2003. Feature selection for high-dimensional data: a fast correlation-based filter solution. *Proceedings of The Twentieth International Conference on Machine Learning,* pp. 1156-1161.

Zhao, Z. & Liu, H., 2007. Searching for interacting features. *IJCAI, Proceedings of International Joint Conference on Artificial Intelligence,* pp. 1156-1161.

MOBILE BIG DATA: THE SILVER BULLET FOR TELCOS? A CASE STUDY IN THE NORWEGIAN TELCOS MARKET

Dennis Y.C. Gan and Dumitru Roman
SINTEF, Oslo, Norway

ABSTRACT

The telecommunication industry has been undergoing tremendous changes in recent times. It is obvious that the industry is currently going through an identity crisis. Porter's Five Forces analysis is used in this paper to investigate the current state of the telecommunication industry in Norway today. The dwindling voice revenue of telcos necessitates the race to find the next revenue stream. This study explores the potential of mobile big data as a resource for telcos to gain competitive advantage with the VRIO Framework (Value-Rare-Imitability-Organization) from the Resources-based View (RBV) theory. Multiple case studies with embedded units that are explanatory and exploratory are applied to Norwegian telcos, following an inductive approach. This study finds that the outlook of the telecommunication industry is rather bleak and despite its promises, mobile big data can only provide temporary competitive advantage to the telcos. Mobile big data is valuable, rare and the telcos are organizing their other resources around it to exploit it, however mobile big data is imitable and not unique. The same data can be obtained by their peers in the industry. Instead, the interview data collected from qualitative research in this study has pointed to organizational culture as the resource that can provide sustained competitive advantage to the telcos. In a highly-competitive industry such as the telecommunication industry, telcos have to constantly rely on resources that can give them temporary competitive advantage; the ability to do this will ultimately be a resource itself that will give them sustained competitive advantage. Telcos have to constantly mix, match and reconfigure their different resources and capabilities to address a rapidly changing environment.

KEYWORDS

Big Data, Mobile Data, Telcos, Multiple Case Study, Resource-based View, Porter's Five Forces

1. INTRODUCTION

Voice revenue for telcos has been gradually leveling off since the turn of the century (Pradayrol and Cyrot, 2006). The landscape for the telco industry has become so competitive that subscribers pay a flat rate for all the calls and messages they make in a month (Taga, Cyrot et al., 2007). Naturally, this leads to the subsequent decrease of Average Revenue Per User (ARPU). Today, the monthly subscription fee depends mostly on the amount of data in the subscriber's data package. In addition, the once lucrative mobile roaming surcharges ended when the "Roam like Home" regulation came into effect 15th of June 2017 (EuropeanCommision, 2016).

The annual reports from Telenor (Telenor, 2016) and Telia (Telia, 2012), both publicly listed companies in Norway and Sweden, have disclosed financial performance of these companies which reflect this trend affecting telcos around the world. A very good indication of how the landscape for the telcos is changing is the ARPU. The ARPU for Telenor and Telia were 339 NOK and 342 NOK respectively in 2003 and declined to as low as 285 NOK and 248 NOK respectively in 2013. That constitutes a decline of 16% in ARPU for Telenor and 27% for Telia over the past decade.

According to (OECD, 2013), the use of data for the creation of new products is one of the five areas identified as drivers of innovation. (Otto, Jürjens et al., 2016) also advocates data to be treated as an economic asset and product, thus should be considered as a viable revenue stream to many businesses as well. As an example, in Norway, Eiendomsprofil AS provides a service called Nabolagsprofil Premium 2.0, a service, which combines free open data from the national statistics office with their own data to provide insights to potential house buyers on the neighborhood they are interested in.

Recent reports of use cases for mobile big data and analytics around the world published by MIT Technology Review (MIT, 2016) and in Norway by Telenor (DagensNæringsliv, 2016a; DagensNæringsliv,

2017c) suggested that such initiatives, whereby data can be used for the creation of new products (goods and services), is indeed a viable option in the telecommunication industry. This study aims to discover the forces affecting the telecommunication industry today and to explore the potential of mobile big data as a resource for telcos to gain competitive advantage.

The paper is organized as follows. Firstly, the definition of mobile big data is explained in Section 2. Section 3 introduces the research design and the rationale of using the proposed research method. In Section 4, the theoretical frameworks used in this paper are explained and analyzed from the interviews: (i) Porter's Five Forces to examine the different forces affecting the telecommunication industry; and (ii) VRIO Framework from Resource-based View theory to analyze the potential of mobile big data for telcos to gain competitive advantage. Finally, Section 5 concludes the paper and outlines avenues for further research.

2. MOBILE BIG DATA

(Loukides, 2010) defines big data as data for which "the size of the data itself becomes part of the problem" while (Beyer and Laney, 2012) defines big data as "high volume, high velocity, and/or high variety information assets that require new forms of processing to enable enhanced decision making, insight discovery and process optimization". According to McKinsey Global Institute (Manyika, Chui et al., 2011), big data refers to "datasets whose size is beyond the ability of typical database software tools to capture, store, manage and analyse".

Notwithstanding the different definitions of big data, size is clearly the first thing that comes to mind when people talk about big data. However, other characteristics of big data are gaining significance. (Laney, 2001) suggested that Volume, Variety and Velocity (or the Three V's) are the three dimensions of challenges in data management. Over time, the Three V's framework is becoming the more acceptable definition of big data. For example, Gartner, Inc. defines big data in similar terms: "Big data is high-volume, high-velocity and high- variety information assets that demand cost-effective, innovative forms of information processing for enhanced insight and decision making" (Gartner, 2017a).

In this paper, mobile big data refers, but not limited to telco's Call Detail Record (CDR), a type of data record produced by telephone exchange, subscriber data from Customer Relationship Management (CRM) system, movement data / mode of transport, installed apps on phones and payment history.

3. RESEARCH DESIGN

This is a case study organized around two or more cases. This study method is chosen based on the reasoning that a multiple case study provides a more robust conclusion than a single case study due to the fact that one will get a richer data from multiple sources (Yin, 2014). By doing a multiple case study, and collecting data from multiple sources, the reliability and internal validity of this study is improved. Triangulation (Yin, 2014), which is a method to collect data from multiple sources, is achieved by interviewing vendors to the telcos such as Nokia and Alpha Entrance.

The framework presented by (Eisenhardt, 1989), developing theories from case study, is used to conduct this study as this approach is very relevant to exploratory studies that research a new topic area.

3.1 Data Collection Method

The nature of this study encourages a combination of multiple data collection methods, through interviews, white papers and financial reports. However, inductive researchers are not confined to these methods. The rationales are the same as hypothesis-testing research, that triangulation is made possible by multiple data collection methods providing stronger substantiation of constructs and hypotheses (Eisenhardt, 1989).

Primary data collection. Semi-structured interviews with various actors in the telecommunication industry in Norway (see Table 1) was the primary method of data collection. In a semi-structured interview, the researcher has a list of questions for fairly specific topics to be covered, often referred to as interview guide, but the interviewee has a great deal of leeway in how to reply (Bryman and Bell, 2015). Seven interviews were conducted over a 3-month period, with a total of 4.5 hours of audio recordings and 52 pages of transcript. The data collected from interviews formed the bulk of the research.

Table 1. Interview Subjects

No.	Telco	Title
1.	Telenor	Lead Business Development Lead Developer Network Consultant
2.	Telenor	Senior Data Scientist
3.	Telia	Chief Data Officer (CDO)
4.	Telio	Project Management Office
5.	Ice.net	Project Management
6.	Alpha Entrance	Technical Manager
7.	Nokia	Customer Solution Manager

Secondary data collection. Financial reports for the major telcos in Norway and Sweden since early 2000 (Telia, 2012; Telenor, 2016) were gleaned to get the ARPUs over the period under investigation. Industry reports and white papers on telcos were examined as available. In addition, the social media channels for the telcos (LinkedIn and Twitter) were followed to get the latest news and announcements on the telcos.

4. FINDINGS & ANALYSIS BASED ON THEORETICAL FRAMEWORKS

The analysis of the interview data is conducted based on the qualitative (Creswell, 2014) and case study research (Yin, 2014) literature. To improve data reliability, the interview recordings were transcribed immediately while the memory of the interviews was still fresh in the mind (Yin, 2014). The interview data was later categorized by topics and frameworks for this study.

4.1 Findings and Analysis based on Porter's Five Forces Framework

Porter's Five Forces (Porter, 1979) is a framework to analyze the level of competition within an industry. Given the amount of changes taking place in the telecommunication industry, this framework draws upon the five forces that determine the competition, and hence the attractiveness of this industry:

(i) **Threat of substitute** – substitutes are defined as products and services that are not direct competitors, but can still fulfill a strategically equivalent role for the customers. The more potential the substitutes are, the closer they are in function to the firm's product or service, thus posing threat of substitution (Schilling, 2013).

According to the manager at Ice.net, *the traditional voice and SMS services which telcos offer are becoming more and more like commodities. If the users are using applications like Whatsapp, Skype or whatever, they are just going through those applications only, not in the voice anymore.* The data scientist at Telenor sums up very nicely, he stated that *during the last 10 years, there have been so many newcomers, Facetime, Skype, all these services deliver voice or even video. It's a better service than just using voice. Snapchat and all sort of instant messaging services, given that all the customers are really indeed different, the ones that are price sensitive will start hunting down and using the free services.* All these substitutes offer similar or superior services to existing services by the telcos, often times at no costs. From the interviews, it is clear telcos are facing tremendous threats of substitutes.

This is consistent with (Feng and Whalley, 2002), the traditional telecommunications value chain is deconstructing into a complex and rapidly changing value network. Within the value network a multitude of market entry points exist, where a variety of companies can enter the market through several possible routes.

(ii) **Threat of new entrants** – the attractiveness of an industry is determined by the entry of barriers of potential competitors. The higher the entry barrier, the more attractive an industry (Schilling, 2013). Gone are the days when a country only had one or two telcos monopolizing the market. The market is a crowded field. The manager at Ice.net rationalized that *one reason that the newcomers can enter the market is because all the prices for network and telecom equipment have decreased a lot since 2000. Most of the network he worked with recently, except the one in Norway, are all Huawei and ZTE. The price for building network has decreased dramatically over the past 5-10 years. Now it's very cheap. In addition, the new telcos can have the latest technology where the equipment is much cheaper and easier to maintain. They don't need that many people to maintain the network. They can do a lot of things that are application-based, where the subscribers are able to access and modify the subscription settings directly without the need to call customer service. The team to maintain the network is much smaller where new people enter the market, compared to those old companies who are there from before.* With cheaper network equipment coming from China, the entry barrier for telcos is significantly lower, thus allowing more players to come into the market.

(iii) **Rivalry among competitors** – the intensity of rivalry in an industry determines the attractiveness of an industry. If an industry is experiencing slow growth and has a lot of competitors which are homogenous in size and power, the rivalry in that industry will be very intense. This makes the industry less attractive (Peng, 2014).
The new telcos coming into the market naturally increase the rivalry among the competitors, these new telcos are aggressive and eager to gain market share. The manager at Ice.net reflected that in France, *they introduced Force Mobile Operators free. When the new one arrive, if you want to be successful, you have to be very, very disruptive and has to attack a lot on the prices. The incumbents who are in the market a long time ago suddenly realized they can't do charge high prices anymore.* In addition, telcos are under the pressure to offer new and innovative services too. Recently, one telco in Norway offered data-rollover service, which is a service that allows unused data package to be included in the following month's data package. Not long after, other telcos have no choice but to follow suit. This is confirmed by the senior data scientist at Telenor.

(iv) **Bargaining power of suppliers** – The number of suppliers in an industry can greatly influence the attractiveness of the industry. If there are a lot of suppliers in an industry and/or not very differentiated, a firm can be in the position to force the suppliers to bid against each other in order to get favorable pricing for their products or services (Schilling, 2013).
According to the manager at Ice.net, *in the early 1990s, the telecommunication equipment market was not that intense and the vendors were able to keep high prices. Then with the combination of internet bubble and the emergence of Chinese vendors such as Huawei and ZTE, the prices have been coming down. This resulted in the consolidation of the vendors, those with the smallest market share had to give up (Nortel) or was absorbed (Siemens), or merged with others (Alcatel, Lucent). Nokia later acquired Alcatel-Lucent in 2016.* In addition, *the products became more standardized, like commodities. No vendor today differentiates really based on products/features anymore.*
These two factors diluted the bargaining power of suppliers are consistent to (Peng, 2014). First, the supplier industry is no longer dominated by a few firms when the Chinese vendors came into the market. Second, when the suppliers' products ceased to be unique and cannot be differentiated from one another. The rivalry that happens in the subscriber market is happening in the vendor market as well, which is a good thing for the telcos.

(v) **Bargaining power of buyers** – If the firm's product is highly differentiated, buyers will typically experience less bargaining power, and if the firm's product is undifferentiated, buyers till typically experience greater bargaining power (Schilling, 2013).
The project manager at Telio adds, *more and more people are looking at prices and they compare. What I get here, what I get there, and as porting number is quite easy nowadays. When they (consumers) get a better offer, they will take the better offer.* The fact that consumers can keep (port) their numbers when they change providers does not help the telcos. When buyers do not face any switching cost, this increase their bargaining power. In addition, mobile services provided by telcos are undifferentiated, thus giving buyers greater bargaining power.

4.2 Findings and Analysis based on the VRIO Framework

The Resource-based View is used to probe the attractiveness of a resource within an organization. According to (Wade and Hulland, 2004), resources are defined as assets and capabilities that are available and useful in detecting and responding to market opportunities or threats. Normal applications of this are concerned with how access to specific difference resources will enable some firms to have a competitive advantage over those that lack such resources (Penrose, 1959; Wernerfelt, 1984; Barney, 1991; Peteraf, 1993).

The VRIO (Value-Rarity-Imitability-Organization) Framework provides one way to concretely analyze firm's resources (Barney, 1991). In this framework, a resource must possess four attributes in order to become a source of sustained competitive advantage. This framework can be thought of a series of steps to evaluate how effective a given resource's intrinsic values in providing competitive advantage to a firm.

The question of value. This is the most fundamental question to start in VRIO framework (Adner and Zemsky, 2006). This question asks if a resource adds value by enabling a firm to exploit opportunities or defend against threats. If the answer is yes, then a resource is considered valuable. The value of a resource has to be continually reviewed due to the constant changing internal or external conditions, which will render the value of this resource less valuable or useless.

Since the early days of the industry, telcos have been using the data generated within their network to optimize their mobile infrastructures, such as assessing the usage patterns of their subscribers to plan their next network equipment upgrade or fiber backbone upgrade. This type of data is vital in providing satisfying service to their subscribers and reducing churn-rate.

In recent years, mobile big data is inevitably coming into the play. The different type of analytics such as customer profiles, device / network data, customer usage patterns, location data and apps download data are very attractive to various businesses who want to get better analytics from to drive sales. The CDO at Telia *believes it's really valuable data. It is relatively unique in terms of seeing mobility. How people move around. Just as long as people bring the devices with them, all the time. We (the telcos) have the chance to understand a lot by how people actually move. We definitely believe there is a revenue potential.*

The mobile big data generated by mobile subscribers certainly add value to telcos, hence mobile big data can lead to competitive advantage for telcos.

The question of rarity. Resources that can only be acquired by one or very few firms are considered rare. If a resource is valuable and rare, then a temporary competitive advantage can be granted to that resource. When more than a few firms have the same valuable resources, this leads to competitive parity.

Although there are many types of data being generated in various industries, telcos are in a unique position with the type of data they are able to generate. Apart from the geolocations of their subscribers, telcos are also in the possession of demographics, network usage, device, application usage, preferences data of their subscribers. Telcos are starting to mine, model and aggregate these data sets to create powerful analytics that can add value to other type of verticals. For example, retailers are particularly interested in customer foot traffic analytics that can help them to decipher who is often around their retail stores.

The Business Development Executive at Telenor agrees that mobile big data is rare. The executive started to relate to a use case in Copenhagen where the public transport authority measure the passenger load in public transport to gauge the load capacity of public transport. *When they talk about the bus passengers that travel in the city. Of course, if you have 50 people that goes out in the morning in blue jackets and start questioning people. "Excuse me, where did you travel from this morning." You get some sort of insights. But you only do that as many days as you can afford these people in blue jackets in the morning. You can do it like, configure it once and do it every morning. So, I think it's rare.*

Hence, mobile big data are valuable and rare, providing temporary advantage to telcos.

The question of imitability. A resource is costly to imitate if other organizations that don't have it can't imitate it, buy or substitute it at reasonable price. Imitation can occur in two ways, by directly imitating (duplicating) the resource or providing the comparable product / service (substituting). A firm that has valuable, rare and costly to imitate resources can (but not necessary will) achieve sustained competitive advantage (Barney, 1991).

Although the richness of the mobile big data generated by telcos is valuable and rare compared to other type of data generated by other industries, they do however face competitions from the same type of data generated by their competitors in the same industry.

This is confirmed by both Telia and Telenor. According to the CDO at Telia, *since Telia is not the single player in the market, then it's copyable, to a large extent. So they think it is more in how you execute. They think it is possible to bring some extra value, but it's copyable, definitely. Telia does not think they have any different data than Telenor, there could be some differences in hardware and infrastructure which can give access to other type of data.* The executives at Telenor agree.

Hence, valuable and rare but imitable resources and capabilities may give telcos some temporary competitive advantage, leading to above-average performance for some period of time. However, such advantage is not likely to be sustainable. Only valuable, rare and hard- to-imitate resources / capabilities can provide a firm a sustained competitive advantage (Peng, 2014).

The question of being organized to capture value. To achieve sustained competitive advantage, a firm needs to organize itself around a resource in order to capture value from that resource. A firm must organize its management systems, processes, policies, organizational structure and culture to be able to fully realize the potential of its valuable, rare and costly to imitate resources or capabilities. Only then, a firm can achieve sustained competitive advantage.

According to the CDO at Telia, *about two years ago, Telia did not do anything in the big data area. Some in network and monitoring etc. But nothing to use it in a more forward looking way. Telia is going to increase this and as the Artificial Intelligence (AI) and Machine Learning (ML) becomes more and more mature. It's going to be easier to find good use cases for big data.*

Just as Telia, Telenor is investing a lot of resources to their big data initiative. According to the senior data scientist at Telenor, *organizations in Telenor Norway have been changed to reflect the need for a big data analytics group. That group is in charge of mobility analytics. They are setting up dedicated units to do the job. That is where they are really taking the bold steps in the right direction of changing the organization. You get an organization that is tailored made for the purpose.*

4.3 Summary of Results

Applying Porter's Five Forces analysis to the interviews of the telecommunication industry today paints a rather grim outlook for the telco industry. Apart from the bargaining power of the suppliers which favors the telcos, giving them great bargaining power, the other four factors are against the telcos.

Threat of substitutes. Although people still need mobile service from telcos, when it comes to the traditional SMS and voice services, there have never been more substitutes than today. With all the apps that run on smartphones, the border between mobile services and new apps coming into the local market of the telcos is becoming increasingly blurred. Services like Whatsapp, Skype and Facetime are competing head-on with the services provided directly by telcos and even replacing them, causing telcos to lose their revenues.

Threat of new entrants. Traditional telcos today are facing the threat of new emerging telcos in their home turf as well. The influx of telecommunication equipment makers from China such as Huawei and ZTE is lowering the barrier for new telcos to come into the market because the cost of setting up a mobile network is just a fraction of what it used to cost with these Chinese vendors. In addition, such new equipment has lower operational cost, thus requiring smaller teams to maintain and they require less customer service because the mobile subscribers are able to access and modify the subscription settings directly.

Rivalry among competitors. With the number of new telcos coming into the market today, it is only natural for the rivalry in the market to intensify. Apart from the monthly subscription fee which is coming under a heavy price war, telcos have to compete on new and innovative services as well. Recently when one of the telco in Norway started offering a data- rollover service; other telcos had no choice but to follow suit.

Bargaining power of suppliers. The same rivalry happens on the vendor side, which means the telcos have better negotiation power with their suppliers and get better deals for themselves. In addition to getting better pricing for pitching the suppliers against each other, the telcos get very favorable terms and conditions in procuring their network equipment as well.

Bargaining power of buyers. The intense rivalry among the competitors (telcos) and the lower entry barrier to become a telco only mean the buyers (subscribers) are spoilt for choice when it comes to choosing who they want as their telco providers. The low switching cost for buyers certainly does not help the telcos as well. With number portability, buyers can switch to a different telco provider without much hassle. Customer loyalty is rather low in the telco industry, buyers have no qualms switching to a different telcos if the subscription fee is lower. In addition, mobile connectivity which is the main service provided by telcos is highly undifferentiated, hence buyers have greater bargaining power.

The dwindling voice revenue of telcos necessitate the race to find the next revenue streams, in this case mobile big data is explored for opportunities. By applying the VRIO Framework on mobile big data as a resource, it can be concluded that mobile big data can only provide temporary competitive advantage to telcos.

On the question of **Value**, it is apparent that mobile big data is valuable to the telcos. The data generated by telcos is being used both internally, to do network planning; and externally, in gaining insights from the movement of people for different use cases such as crowd management during special events.

On the question of **Rarity**, the mobile big data generated by telcos is considered to be rare, when combined with other types of data that telcos already have, such as the demographics of their subscribers, telcos can gain interesting analytics and insights from their subscribers.

On the question of **Imitability**, since there is more than one telco in each country, the data collected is not unique, thus it is imitable. Telcos face competition from their peers when it comes to the data they manage to collect.

On the question of **Organizational**, all the telcos interviewed have very clear initiative to exploit the data generated in their network and are allocating resources around their mobile big data. Telenor and Telia both have data science lab and research divisions to exploit their mobile big data.

5. CONCLUSION AND OUTLOOK

In a highly competitive market such as the telecommunication industry that we know today, the fact that mobile big data can only provide temporary competitive advantage to telcos should not come as a complete surprise. (Day, 2014) even argued that increasingly there is no such thing as sustained competitive advantage. Highly competitive conditions ultimately result in all positions of competitive advantage being eroded by imitative or innovative competition. Hence, maintaining superior performance ultimately requires the continual renewal of competitive advantages through innovation and the development of new capabilities (Grant, 1996). Telcos have to constantly rely on resources that can give them temporary competitive advantage; the ability to do this will ultimately be a resource itself that will give them sustained competitive advantage. Telcos have to constantly mix, match and reconfigure their different resources and capabilities to address rapidly changing environments. Although this study started with exploring mobile big data as a resource for telco to gain sustained competitive advantage, the data collected from the interviews instead pointed towards organizational culture as the resource that can provide sustained competitive advantage, which is consistent with (Barney, 1986). As far as limitations of this study are concerned, one can argue about limited data from Telia: there were four employees from Telenor being interviewed in this study while there was only one from Telia. Quantitative research can be introduced into this study to allow for a broader study, involving a greater number of subjects, and enhancing the generalisation of the results (Yin, 2014).

Future research on this study can be conducted to determine the business model for monetizing mobile big data. Based on the interview data collected in this study, it is clear that the business model for telcos are undergoing seismic change, especially when it comes to monetizing the mobile big data. (Kijl, Bouwman et al., 2005; Osterwalder, Pigneur et al., 2005) research on business models can provide a very good basis to form a potential business model for mobile big data.

ACKNOWLEDGEMENT

This work is partly funded by the EC H2020 projects proDataMarket (Grant number: 644497), euBusinessGraph (Grant number: 732003), and EW-Shopp (Grant number: 732590). Thanks to Truls Erikson, the leader at Center of Entrepreneurship a University of Oslo and the managers at Telenor, Telia, Ice.net, Telio, Alpha Entrance and Nokia. Finally, Dennis Y.C. Gan would like to thank Till Lech and Bjørn Skjellaug for giving him the possibility to do his MSc thesis with SINTEF.

REFERENCES

Adner, R. and P. Zemsky 2006. "A demand- based perspective on sustainable competitive advantage." *Strategic Management Journal* 27(3): 215-239.

Barney, J. 1991. "Firm resources and sustained competitive advantage. (The Resource-Based Model of the Firm: Origins, Implications, and Prospects)." *Journal of Management* 17(1): 99.

Barney, J. B. 1986. "Organizational culture: Can it be a source of sustained advantage?" *Academy of Management Review* 11(3): 656.

Beyer, M. A. and D. Laney. 2012. "The Importance of "Big Data": A Definition."

Bryman, A. and E. Bell 2015. *Business Research Method*. Oxford, Oxford University Press.

Creswell, J. W. 2014. *Research design : qualitative, quantitative, and mixed methods approaches*. Los Angeles, Calif, SAGE.

DagensNæringsliv. 2016a. "Selger data - om mobilens bevegelser." Retrieved 8th May 2017, from http://bit.ly/2trtJsk.

DagensNæringsliv. 2017c. "Vil vite «alt» om deg." Retrieved 8th May 2017, from http://bit.ly/2stx1Xy.

Day, G. 2014. "An outside-in approach to resource-based theories." *Official Publication of the Academy of Marketing Science* 42(1): 27-28.

Eisenhardt, K. M. 1989. "Building theories from case study research. (Special Forum on Theory Building)." *Academy of Management Review* 14(4): 532.

EuropeanCommision. 2016. "Roaming." Retrieved 27th April 2017, from http://bit.ly/231ij7E.

Feng, L. and J. Whalley 2002. "Deconstruction of the telecommunications industry: From value chains to value networks." *Telecommunications Policy* 26(9 10): 451-472.

Gartner. 2017a. "Big Data." Retrieved 21st April 2017, from http://www.gartner.com/it-glossary/big-data.

Grant, R. M. 1996. "Prospering in Dynamically-Competitive Environments: Organizational Capability as Knowledge Integration." *Organization Science* 7(4): 375-387.

Kijl, B., H. Bouwman, T. Haaker and E. Faber 2005. *Developing a dynamic business model framework for emerging mobile services*. ITS 16th European Regional Conference.

Laney, D. 2001. "3D Data Management: Controlling Data Volume, Velocity, and Variety." http://gtnr.it/1bKflKH.

Loukides, M. 2010. "What is data science? The future belongs to the companies and people that turn data into products." Retrieved 8th Mar 2017, from http://radar.oreilly.com/2010/06/what-is-data-science.html.

Manyika, J., M. Chui, B. Brown, J. Bughin, R. Dobbs, C. Roxburgh and A. H. Byers 2011. Big data: The next frontier for innovation, competition and productivity.

MIT. 2016. "A Business Report On - Big Data Gets Personal." Retrieved 30th June 2017, from http://bit.ly/2uqzNOz.

OECD 2013. Exploring Data-Driven Innovation as a New Source of Growth: Mapping the Policy Issues Raised by "Big Data". OECD Digital Economy Papers No. 222. Paris, OECD Publishing.

Osterwalder, A., Y. Pigneur and C. L. Tucci 2005. "Clarifying business models: Origins, present, and future of the concept." *Communications of the association for Information Systems* 16(1): 1.

Otto, B., J. Jürjens, J. Schon, S. Auer, N. Menz, S. Wenzel and J. Cirullies 2016. Industrial Data Space, Digital Sovereignity Over Data. Germany, Fraunhofer-Gesellschaft zur Förderung.

Peng, M. W. 2014. *Global strategic management*. Australia, South-Western, Cengage learning.

Penrose, E. 1959. *The theory of the growth of the firm*. Oxford, Blackwell.

Peteraf, M. A. 1993. "The cornerstones of competitive advantage: a resource-based view." *Strategic Management Journal* 14(3): 179.

Porter, M. 1979. "How competitive forces shape strategy." *Harvard business review* 57: 137-145.

Pradayrol, A. and J.-L. Cyrot 2006. Facing off on convergence, Arthur D. Little, Exane BNP Paribas.

Schilling, M. A. 2013. *Strategic management of technological innovation*. New York, N.Y, McGraw-Hill/Irwin.

Taga, K., J.-L. Cyrot, B. Virag and C. Boehmer 2007. The world is becoming flat.... Overcoming infrastructure issues for mobile operators, Arthur D. Little.

Telenor. 2016. "Telenor Group Annual Report 2000-2016." Retrieved 12th May 2017, from http://bit.ly/2omNqeZ.

Telia. 2012. "Telia Sonera Annual Report 2012." Retrieved 30th June 2017, from http://bit.ly/2ur1Qxs.

Wade, M. and J. Hulland 2004. "Review: The Resource-Based View and Information Systems Research: Review, Extension, and Suggestions for Future Research." *MIS Quarterly* 28(1): 107-142.

Wernerfelt, B. 1984. "A Resource-Based View of the Firm." *Strategic Management Journal* 5(2): 171-180.

Yin, R. K. 2014. *Case study research : design and methods*. Los Angeles, Calif, SAGE.

Short Papers

SEMI-AUTOMATIC METHOD OF SEARCHING FOR THE CONTROL POINTS IN TWO FACIAL IMAGES

Olga Krutikova[1], Aleksandrs Sisojevs[2] and Mihails Kovalovs[1]
[1]*Riga Technical University, Setas street 1, Riga, LV-1048, Latvia*
[2]*Ventspils University Colleges, Inzhenieru street 101a, Ventspils, LV-3601, Latvia*

ABSTRACT

In this paper a method is proposed that is meant to solve one of the subtasks of facial recognition. One of the main problems in facial recognition is trying to recognize a face from different angles, with an insufficient training set. To solve this problem it is necessary to adapt an existing three-dimensional model of the head based on two facial images (full face and profile).

In this paper a semi-automatic method is proposed, that is based on modified Viola-Jones algorithm. The proposed method is used to process existing images of a person, extract the face region and main facial features from images (eyes, nose and mouth) and semi-automatically place control points on two facial images that will be later used in adapting an existing three-dimensional model of the face. The constructed model allows increasing the training set and acquiring additional information about the shape of the face.

KEYWORDS

Control points, facial images, face 3D model reconstruction

1. INTRODUCTION

Many papers are dedicated to the task of constructing a three-dimensional model of a face because it is currently in great demand for visualizing three-dimensional objects, in recognition systems and in controlling access. There are many algorithms that create a three-dimensional model of a face (Kakadiaris, 2007), (Park, 2006) etc. In these cases the task was to construct the polygonal model based on several images. However, many methods use control points that are manually placed on the image, in order to deform the polygonal mesh of the model. This approach significantly slows down the process of constructing a three-dimensional model of the head. There are also many methods of searching for control points on the images of faces (Pentland, Moghaddam, 1994), (Shi, Samal, 2006) etc. Unfortunately searching for control points depends on many factors, like face variability between individuals, but also due to extrinsic factors such as partial occlusion, illumination, expression, pose and camera resolution

The main goal of this paper is to create a semi-automatic algorithm of searching for control points that will be later used to adapting an existing three-dimensional model, where the operator can edit the placement of control points, if necessary. To find the control points it was necessary to locate the main facial features (eyes, nose and mouth) on two images. The proposed method consists of several steps and a different approach is used for each type of the image (full face, profile)

2. PROPOSED METHODS

The proposed methods allow selecting control points on the full face and profile images that will be later used to create a 3D model of the face. Due to the turn angle of the face being very different, two separate approaches are proposed for searching for the control points.

The images of the face are taken with a single camera from the same position, and then the images are aligned vertically and horizontally so that the main facial features would match on both images of full face and profile. After the images are aligned it is possible to start searching for the control points.

2.1 Searching for Control Points on the Full Face Images

1) Since digital images are exposed to different types of noise, it is necessary to remove noise on images with filtering, that contains a mask with a size of $m \times n$ pixels, and size of an image f is $M \times N$. The filtering process can be described with Formula 1.

$$g(x,y) = \sum_{s=-2}^{+2} \sum_{t=-2}^{+2} w(s,t) \cdot f(x+s, y+t) \tag{1}$$

where $w(s,t) = \frac{1}{9}\begin{pmatrix} 1 & 1 & 1 \\ 1 & 1 & 1 \\ 1 & 1 & 1 \end{pmatrix}$, is a convolution kernel with the size $m \times n$,

s,t - convolution kernel coordinates along the abscissa and ordinate.

2) The next step is contrast correction for each RGB channel. This is done with histogram normalization (González, Woods, 2007). Normalization is sometimes called contrast stretching or histogram stretching, that is necessary when the range of the histogram is smaller than needed and does not encompass all the gradations in the range from 0 to 255 (see Fig.1.1.). By normalizing the histogram, its range is extended (see Fig.1.2.) and the pixels with value less than a threshold T are discarded.

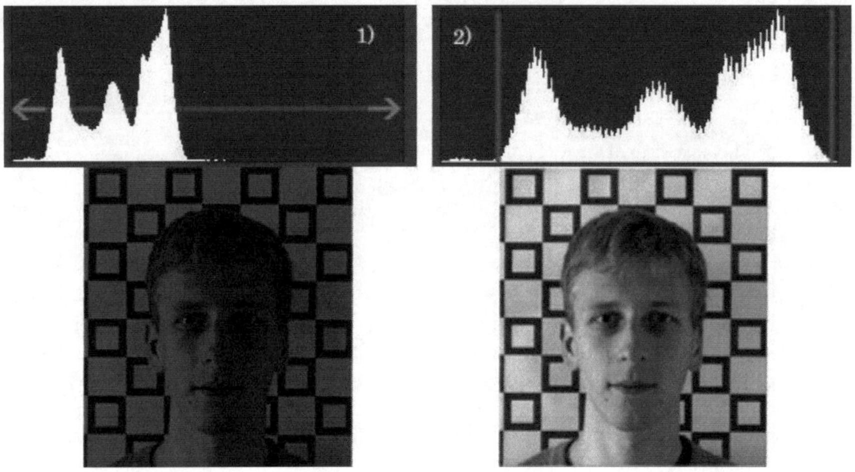

Figure 1. Histogram Normalization of Each Channel in the RGB Color Space

3) The Viola-Jones algorithm (Viola, 2001) is used to extract the face (and eyes, nose, mouth) from the image. The algorithm is implemented using the OpenCV library. The cascades are used to train the search for facial features. Then, based on the found regions, the control points are located on the image. The existing algorithm was edited to remove unnecessary located objects, and the rules were constructed for each region separately.

It is known that the eyes are located higher than the middle of the face, so the center point of the eyes region is $E_c < H/2$, where H is the height of the face region (see Fig.2.1.)

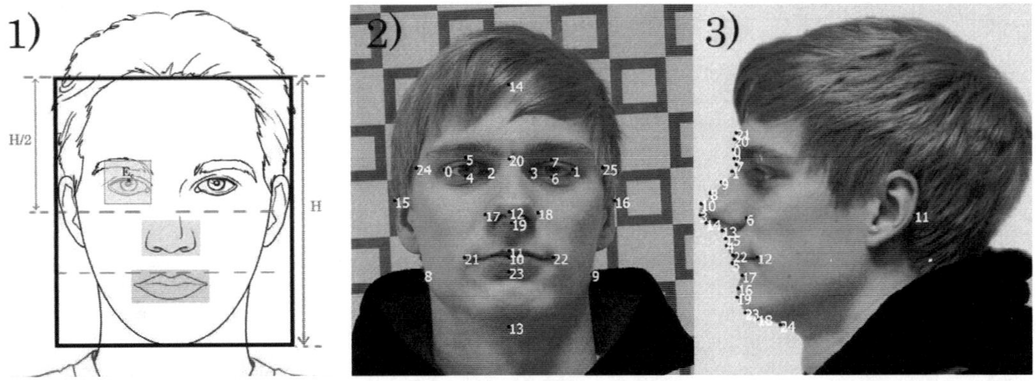

Figure 2. Region Extraction and Search for Control Points

After the eyes regions are extracted they are merged into a single region. It is also known that the mouth region is located in the bottom part of the face, below *H/4*. The nose is extracted from the area in between the eyes and mouth.

4) The transition from the RGB color space into the HSV space.

5) The region edges are extracted from the resulting image, using the Sobel operator (Hanno, 2007). The pixel intensity is calculated from the Value channel of the HSV color system.

6) The locations of control points are found in each extracted region. In the case of the eyes region, to locate the outer corners a vector moves along the x-axis until it finds a pixel with intensity greater than the predetermined threshold *T* (see Fig. 2.2.) Algorithm stops after all the extracted regions are processed.

2.2 Searching for Control Points on the Profile Images

The information acquired from processing the full face image (such as the region coordinates) can be also used to help process the profile image.

1) The first two steps of the algorithm are the same as with the full face algorithm and include the noise reduction and histogram normalization.

2) The next step contains the transition from the RGB color space into the HSV space. The Value channel in the HSV system is normalized to adjust the white color balance.

3) Then the pixels that belong to face are extracted using the following values (Sharif, Ayub, 2011):

$$\Theta_h = \bigcup_{i,j=1}^{m,n} (\alpha_{i,j} < \phi_{h\min} \cup \alpha_{i,j} > \phi_{h\max}) \tag{2}$$

where, $\alpha_{i,j}$, $\phi_{h\min}$, $\phi_{h\max}$ represent the hue value, minimum and maximum threshold value for hue respectively, and $\phi_{h\min} = 0.1$; $\phi_{h\max} = 0.5$.

$$\Theta_s = \bigcup_{i,j=1}^{m,n} (\beta_{i,j} < \phi_{s\min} \cap \beta_{i,j} > \phi_{s\max}) \tag{3}$$

where, $\beta_{i,j}$, $\phi_{s\min}$, $\phi_{s\max}$ represent the saturation value, minimum and maximum threshold value for saturation respectively, and $\phi_{s\min} = 0.15$; $\phi_{s\max} = 0.9$.

$$\Theta_{RGB} = \bigcup_{i,j=1}^{m,n} (\gamma_{i,j} < \phi_r \cup \gamma_{i,j} < \phi_g \cup \gamma_{i,j} < \phi_b) \tag{4}$$

where $\gamma_{i,j}, \phi_r, \phi_g, \phi_b$ represent threshold values for red, green and blue channels in RGB color space, and $\phi_r = 70$; $\phi_g = 60$; $\phi_b = 70$.

$$\Theta = \Theta_h \cap \Theta_s \cap \Theta_{RGB} \quad (5)$$

Where Θ gives the resultant detected skin region.

The color of the pixels that do not contain skin is set to white.

4) Then the face region is extracted. The location of the first skin pixel on the x-axis is defined as the tip of the nose (Fig. 2.3).

To extract the face in the profile image (the region of interest is between the tip of the nose and ears), a width of the face from the full face image is used (Fig. 2.2). The height of the region is set to be the same as in the full face image, where the y coordinates are already calculated.

5) The control points are calculated in the following step. Since region coordinates of the eyes, nose and mouth are already known on the full face image, the profile image can be scanned starting at the tip of the nose and move along the known y coordinates, until a pixel is found with intensity greater than threshold T.

In the future, the amount of control points could be increased to work with a more detailed model and to be able to more accurately calculate the relations between the control points and the polygonal mesh.

3. EXPERIMENTS

The proposed algorithm of searching for the control points was tested on 28 images of full face and profile that show 14 different people. The algorithm is intended to be used to adapt the three-dimensional models of faces that will be used in facial recognition tasks (Krutikova, Glazs, 2016).

The initial images were taken using a single Nikon D5200 camera, with a resolution of 1072x1200. The images were later manually aligned relative to each other in order to obtain the greatest possible correspondence between the points.

Further processing of the images and the search for control points were done automatically. The algorithms were tested on a Dell Inspiron 5720, processor Intel(R) Core(TM) i5-3210M, CPU 2.50Hz.

During the experiments, it was found that the amount of time required for the automatic processing of 28 images of full face and profile (total 14 persons) was 5.68 minutes (341.3 seconds), or in case of manual processing 17.5 minutes (1050 seconds). The automatic approach was 3 times faster than the manual approach and when a large amount of images needs to be processed it could significantly accelerate the process. In the case of semi-automatic approach, where the operator can edit the control point placement the time was 11.6 minutes (695.7 seconds), which is 1.5 times faster than the manual approach.

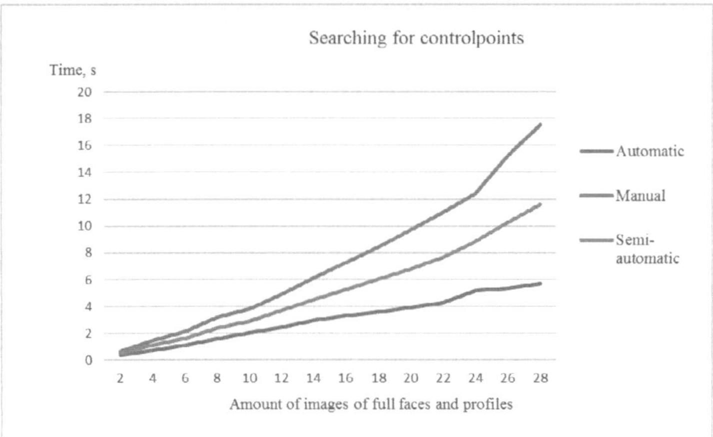

Figure 3. The Dependence of Algorithm Execution Time on the Amount of Images

During the experiments it was also found that control points were correctly places on the full face images in 71.4% of cases, and on profile images in 85% of cases. Therefore, it is preferable to use the semi-automatic mode of the algorithm, where the operator could adjust the position of the control points, if necessary.

The proposed method was further used to adapt and existing three-dimensional model of face. New coordinates were calculted for each vertex of the model, based on position of the control points that were placed on both images (see Figure 4,a,b). The model was divided into several regions that used different automatcally calculated scaling and translation coefficients.

A new texture was created for each adapted model (see Figure 4,c,d), based on the full face image (see Figure 4,b). The wireframe model (see Figure 4,g,h) is intended to be later used in facial recognition tasks.

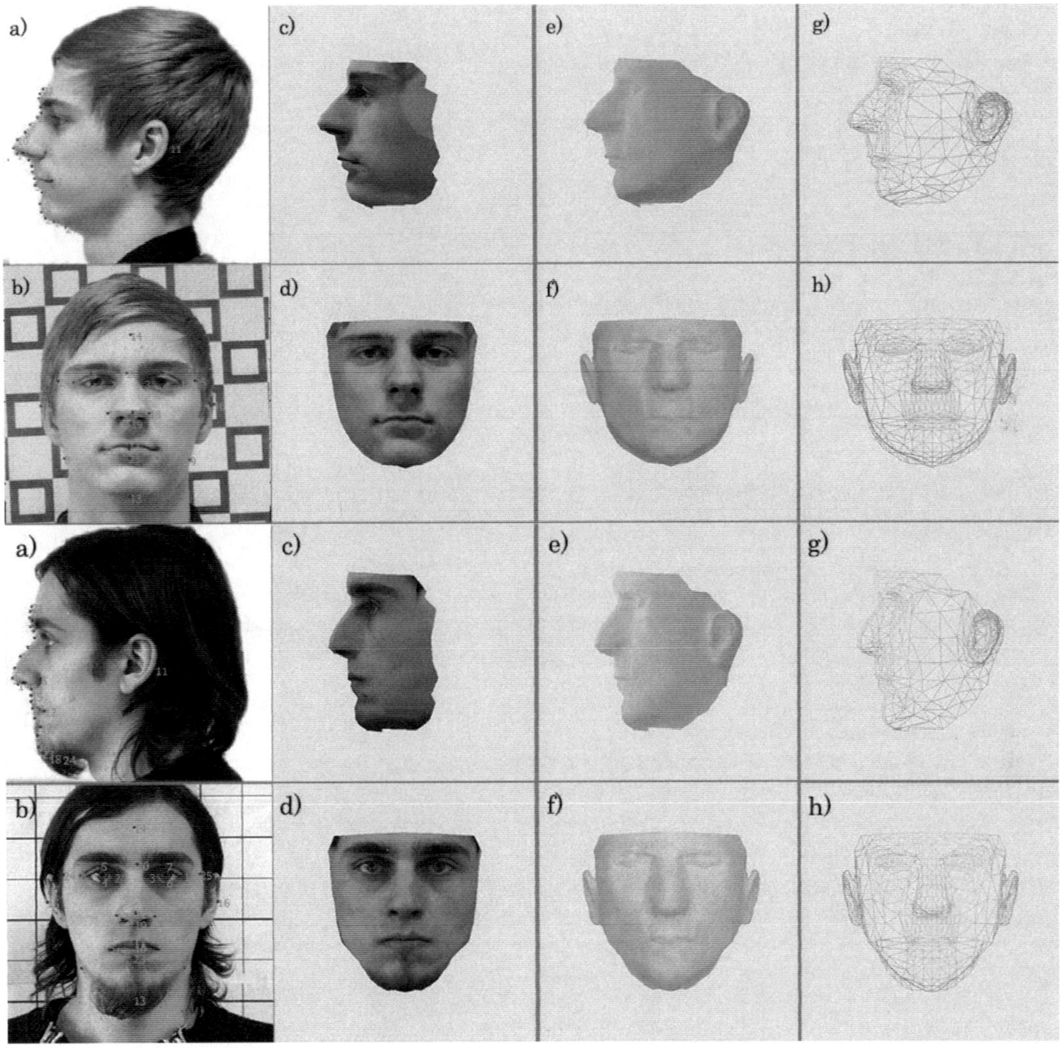

Figure 4. 3D Models of a Face Based that were Adapted, Based on Control Point Placement: A),B) Input Images, C),D) Adapted Textured Model of Face, E),F) Solid 3D Model, G),H) Wireframe of the 3D Models

4. CONCLUSION

In this paper a semi-automatic algorithm of searching for control points on images of full face and profile is proposed. During the experiments it was found that using the developed algorithm, image processing time is reduced by 3 times, compared to the manual approach. However, the accuracy of the algorithm for the full face images is 71.4%, and 85% for the profile images. Therefore, it is preferable to use the semi-automatic mode of the algorithm, where the operator could adjust the position of the control points, if necessary. The proposed algorithm could be used to adapt a three-dimensional model of a face that can be later used in tasks of face detection and recognition. Currently the proposed algorithm cannot be used for real time tasks, although it could be optimized in some cases, especially when processing profile images, where the Viola-Jones algorithm is not used.

ACKNOWLEDGEMENT

The research was supported by the National Research Program "The next generation of information and communication technologies" (NexIT, Project 2).

REFERENCES

González, R.C., Woods R. E., 2007. *Digital Image Processing.* Prentice Hall. pp. 85.

Hanno, S., 2007. Optimal second order derivative filter families for transparent motion estimation. *In 15th European Signal Processing Conference (EUSIPCO 2007)*, Poznan, Poland, September 3–7.

Kakadiaris, I., 2007, Three-Dimensional Face Recognition in the Presence of Facial Expressions: An Annotated Deformable Model Approach. *In IEEE Transactions on Pattern Analysis and Machine Intelligence*. V. 29, N 4., P. 640-649.

Krutikova, O., Glazs, A., 2016, Solving the task of face recognition in cases of insufficient training set. *In Proceedings of the 10th International Conference Computer Graphics, Visualization, Computer Vision and Image Processing*, Portugal, Funchal, Madeira, p. 303-308.

Park, U., Jain, AK., 2006, 3D face reconstruction from stereo images. *In Proceedings of Int. Workshop on Video Processing for Security*. Quebec City, Canada, p. 41.

Pentland, A., Moghaddam, B., Starner, T. 1994, View-based and Modular Eigenspaces for Face Recognition. *In Proceedings of IEEE Int. Conf. on Computer Vision and Pattern Recognition*. Seattle, Washington, pp. 84–91

Sharif, M., Ayub, K., Sattar, D., Raza, M., 2011. Real time face detection. *In Sindh University research journal (science series)*, V. 44(4), p. 598.

Shi, J., Samal, A., Marx, D., 2006, How effective are landmarks and their geometry for face recognition? *Comput. Vis. Image Understand.*, V. 102, pp. 117-133.

Viola, P., 2001, Rapid object detection using a boosted cascade of simple features. *In IEEE Conf. on Computer Vision and Pattern Recognition*, Kauai, Hawaii, USA, V. 1. pp. 511–518.

A NOVEL EDGE-PRESERVING FILTER FOR MEDICAL IMAGE ENHANCEMENT

Tzong-Jer Chen[1], Sixian Niu[1], Chengde Lin[1] and Ronghui Lu[2]
[1]*School of Information Engineering, Baise University, Baise, Guangxi, 533000 China*
[2]*Section of Laboratory Management Center, Wuyi University, Wuyishan, Fujian, 354300 China*

ABSTRACT

This paper presents a new approach for image enhancement. Traditional filters are usually employed to suppress the noise, but often lead to a blurred or enhanced edge that enforces noise. An edge-preserving algorithm for digital images based on spatial autocorrelation is proposed. The spatial statistical calculation is used as a threshold for adaptive filtering. Two synthetic images with various pixel values and Gaussian noise were produced for verification. The SNR of both noisy synthetic images are significantly raised. The PET images of various numbers of iterations using the proposed scheme are clearer than those using the non-adaptive average filter. The algorithm visual processing is good but more forward research is required.

KEYWORDS

Image enhancement, un-sharp masking, Moran statistics, adaptive filter, PET

1. INTRODUCTION

Digital image technology has grown significantly in a wide area of fields. It has led to rapid expansion in employment. In applications the input image quality affects its utilization [Javier S.B., 2011]. Digital images may be distorted by a variety of noise or blurring types during the acquisition, processing, transmission and reconstruction processes. The visual appearance of an image may be improved by emphasizing its high frequency parts to enhance the edge and detail information [Polesel A. et al., 2000].

High frequency content enhancement, such as edge and detail information may significantly improve the visual appearance of an image [Polesel A. et al., 2000]. The simplest algorithm, un-sharp masking (UM), is often employed for this purpose. The UM method is computationally and conceptually simple and works well in many applications producing a sharpening effect [Gui Z.G. et al., 2012]. However, the linear high-pass filter makes the system extremely sensitive to noise. In addition, it enhances high-contrast areas to a great degree but does not present a high dynamic image [Gui Z.G. et al., 2012, Polesel A. et al., 2000].

The local UM with adaptive un-sharp masking and nonlinear module was recently proposed [Fu S.J. et al., 2007, Gui Z.G. et al., 2012, Polesel A. et al., 2000]. These algorithms enhance images while effectively decreasing the noise. These methods can also be used to sharpen images with good noise reduction performance. The development of adaptive, nonlinear modules for image enhancement may be a good scheme.

Positron emission tomography (PET) was used to generate activity distribution images to extract patient's physiological information in medicine. The activity distribution projections obtained by the detector rings around the patient are reconstructed using various reconstruction algorithms. The filtered back-projection (FBP) algorithm is the most common image reconstruction method due to its accuracy, speed of computation and implementation simplicity [Kinahan et al., 2004]. However, due to the limited number of projection sets, the FBP algorithm introduces streak artifacts into the reconstructed images [Huesman R.H., 1977].

Most PET scanners employ maximum-likelihood expectation–maximization (MLEM) [Shepp L.A., Vardi Y., 1982] and ordered subsets expectation–maximization (OSEM) [Hudson M. and Larkin R.S., 1994] algorithms for iterative image reconstruction. The MLEM algorithm is an iterative method for computing maximum-likelihood estimates when the observations can be viewed as incomplete data.

In MLEM the low frequency image components appear first and then gradually the detailed parts are developed as the iterations progress. The quality of the reconstructed image improves steadily during the initial iterations. However, after a certain point the image quality becomes significantly noisier [Snyder D. L. and Miller M. T., 1985]. At higher iteration numbers, images produced by the MLEM algorithm become noisier even though the likelihood still increases. To yield a quality image, one can stop the algorithm before this deterioration phase develops or after a fixed number of iterations. Some researchers [Veklerov E. and Llacer J., 1987, Veklerov E., Llacer J. and Hoffman E. J., 1988, Kontaxakis G. and Tzanakos G., 1996, Bissantz et al., 2006] proposed a stopping rule to quit the iteration when the solution becomes so noisy that it is inconsistent with the data sets generated by the model. In practice, the MLEM iteration is stopped prematurely and a post-reconstruction low-pass filter is then applied [Hamill J. and Bruckbauer T., 2002]. Post-filtering can be easily optimized for specific tasks.

In clinical practice post-filtering is often performed using a Gaussian filter (GF) which is known for degrading contrast and spatial resolution. Although GF improved SNR in reconstructed PET images it was associated with a significant loss of quantitative information. The edge-preserving filter (EPF) was proposed for PET de-noising to replace GF [Mathieu H. et al., 2015]. They found that EPF provided significant SNR improvement and was more efficient at ensuring the quantitative image accuracy compared to GF.

A nonlinear module, Moran statistics, was suggested to measure the noise level in medical images [Chuang K.S. and Huang H.K., 1992]. Chen et al. and Shiao et al. proved the Moran statistics to be a good index for determining the image smoothness or sharpness [Chen T.J. et al., 2006, Shiao Y.H. et al., 2007]. A higher Moran Z value means that there is more structured information and less random noise in the image and vise versa. These statistics showed also that it had ability to distinguish image noise and edges [Chen T.J. et al., 2016].

This report proposes a new approach to image enhancement using a statistical method as apriority adaptation. Moran statistics are applied to determine if an area belongs to the edge or noise before filtering. The average filter is then applied to these noisy images. Two synthetic images with noises were made first to verify this method. After that, this scheme was then applied to PET simulation images. The SNR showed that this scheme is superior to the filtering method.

2. METHODS AND MATERIALS

2.1 The Moran Statistics

The Moran statistics are used to evaluate the randomness of mapped data by measuring the spatial autocorrelation [Cliff A.D .and Ord J.K.., 1981]. The Moran parameter measurement M in a window (a window is part of an image) was calculated as:

$$\mathrm{M} = \frac{N\sum_{j=1}^{mxn}\sum_{i=1}^{mxn}\delta_{ij}(x_i - \bar{x})(x_j - \bar{x})}{S_0\sum_{i=1}^{rxc}(x_i - \bar{x})^2} \tag{1}$$

where x_i is the gray level for pixel i, $\bar{x}$ is the mean gray level of the window, $S_0 = 2(2mn - m - n)$, m and n are the number of rows and columns in the window, N is the total number of pixels in the window, and $\delta_{ij} = 1$ if pixel i and j are adjacent and 0 otherwise. The numerator and denominator are measures of the covariance and variance among the pixels, respectively. When the size of N is large enough, the variable M approximately follows a normal distribution with the mean and variance given by

$$a = -1/(N-1) \tag{2}$$

and

$$\sigma^2 = \frac{N[(N^2-3N+3)S_1 - NS_2 + 3S_0^2] - K[N(N-1)S_1 - 2NS_2 + 6S_0^2]}{(N-1)(N-2)(N-3)S_0^2} - a^2 \tag{3}$$

where $K = N\sum(x_i - \bar{x})^4 / [\sum(x_i - \bar{x})^2]^2$, $S_1 = 2S_0$, and $S_2 = 8(8mn - 7m - 7n + 4)$. The standardized normal statistic,

$$Z = \frac{M - a}{\sigma} \quad (4)$$

, will show randomness in the image data. It can be used to determine noise, blurring and edge in an image.

2.2 Synthetic Images

Two synthetic images with various pixel levels were made in this study to verify the proposal. The image sizes are 512×512 and 12 bits in depth, as shown in Figure 1(a), (b). The outside background gray levels were 37 and inner 100. Sixteen different circles with gray levels from 300 (upper left) to 783 (bottom right), as in Figure 1 (a). The gray levels are from 1024 to 374 in white areas of stripe phantom, as in Figure 1 (b).

The Gaussian noise (μ=100, σ=20) is added to Figure 1 (a) and (μ=150, σ=100) is added to Figure 1 (b), respectively.

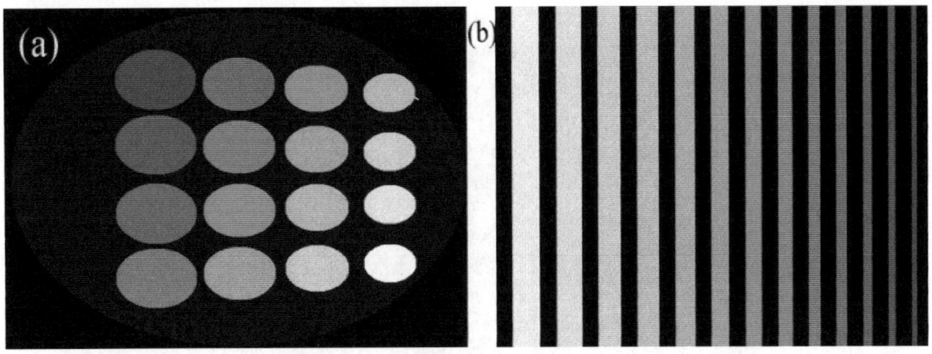

Figure 1. Synthetic images. (a) circle phantom, (b) stripe phantom.

2.3 Monte Carlo Simulation and PET Phantom

A 128×128 Hoffman phantom, as shown in Figure 2, was used for the simulations. The GATE (GEANT4 application for tomographic emission V3.1 x64) software was used in this report. This Monte Carlo simulation was based on the scanner ECAT 951/31 geometry (CTI, Knoxville, TN). The scanner has a radius of 300mm with 256 parallel detector tubes per angle and a total of 192 angles. The PET sinogram was produced when the simulation reached 900 Mega counts and without any post correction. PET images were obtained using the OSEM reconstruction algorithm in a division of four subsets. The 2, 4, 6, 8 numbers of image reconstruction iterations were chosen, as shown in Figure 4 (a, b, c, d).

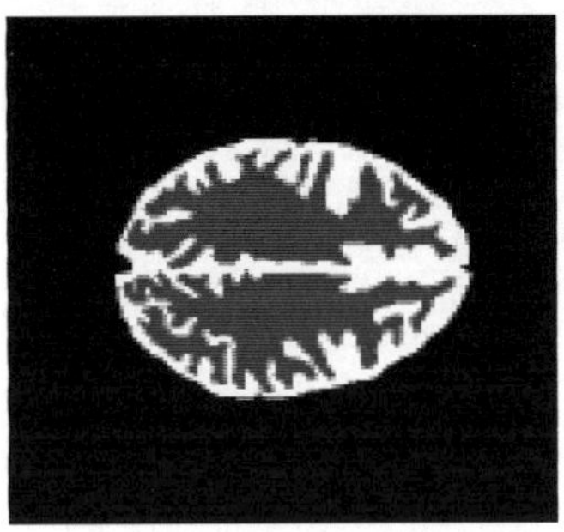

Figure 2. Original Hoffman Phantom

3. RESULTS

3.1 Synthetic Images

Both noisy synthetic images measured Moran Z values with a 5×5 window size first. The effectiveness of the proposed method was verified based on the fact that "A higher Moran Z value means that there is more structured information and less random noise in the image" [Chen T.J. et al., 2006, Shiao Y.H. et al., 2007]. The Moran Z values for the whole image can be binned as a Z histogram. After examining the histogram of Z values, image areas can be categorized as edge if Z >= 3.4. Moran Z values higher than 3.4 of two noisy synthetic images are shown in Figure 3. Only the edge is obviously shown in this figure.

These images were then subjected to a filtering process using an average filter with a 3×3 window. The filtering process depends on the Moran statistic calculations and skips those points if Moran Z values higher than 3.4. The noise was decreased and the edge was not excessively overshot. This new method accomplishes the dual objectives of successfully decreasing noise as well as not amplifying the detailed areas. The enhancement SNR using the adaptive method proposed in this paper and a traditional average filtering are shown in Table 1. The SNR of the average filter with Moran adaptation is obviously better than non-adaptive filtering for both the stripe and circle phantoms.

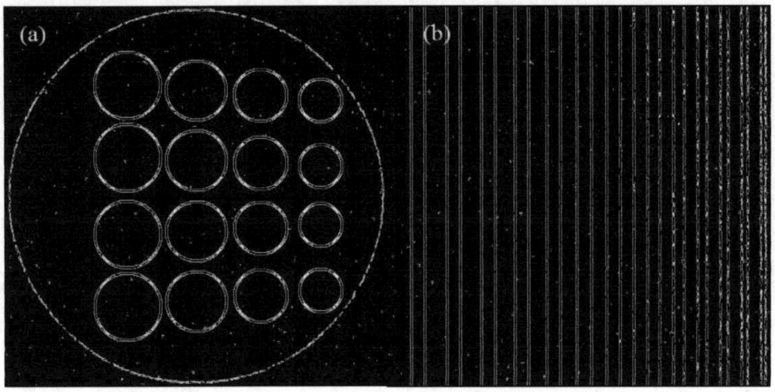

Figure 3. Images of Moran Z values higher than 3.4

Table 1. SNR of synthetic images

Image	Before Filtering	Average Filter (3×3)	Average Filter with Moran Adaptive
Stripe Phantom	15.21	11.38	17.87
Circle Phantom	12.37	12.04	12.72

3.2 PET Images

The PET images were processed using the same filtering as we used for synthetic images. PET images with different numbers of OSEM iterations are shown in Figure 4. The images in Figure 4 (a), (b), (c), (d) correspond to 2, 4, 6, 8 OSEM iterations. The (e), (f), (g), (h) images were processed using a 3×3 average filter. The proposed average filter results with Moran adaptation are shown in Figure 4. (i), (j), (k), (l). The SNR of PET images are shown in Table 2. The SNR of PET using the average filter with Moran adaptation are obviously closer to "before filtering" than those with non-adaptive filtering, as noted in Table 2. The processed images using the proposed scheme are clearer than the average filter.

4. CONCLUSION

A novel image enhancement method was presented. The proposed method uses spatial statistics named Moran Z as a threshold to adaptively proceed with filtering. The SNR of both noisy synthetic images were significantly improved. The PET images of various numbers of iterations using the proposed scheme are clearer than those using the non-adaptive average filter. The algorithm visual processing is good but more forward research is required. In the future, we should increase the SNR in this adaptive filtering process. A noise model such as the Poisson distribution will be considered to simulate medical imaging systems.

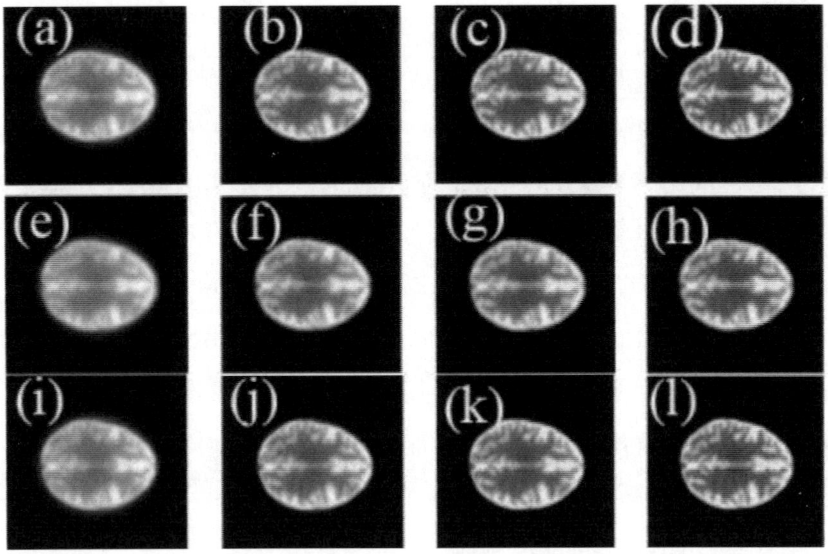

Figure 4. PET images with different numbers of OSEM iteration. non-processed (a)=2, (b)=4, (c)=6, (d)=8; average filtered (3×3)(e), (f), (g), (h); average filter with Moran adaptive (i), (j), (k), (l)

Table 2. SNR of PET images with different numbers of OSEM iterations

Numbers of Iteration (OSEM)	Before Filtering	Average Filter	Average Filter with Moran Adaptive
2(a)	11.89(a)	9.65(e)	11.86(i)
4(b)	36.80(b)	23.64(f)	36.36(j)
6(c)	62.58(c)	36.69(g)	61.15(k)
8(d)	82.02(d)	48.61(h)	79.03(l)

ACKNOWLEDGEMENT

This work was supported in part by a research grant from Guangxi, China. 2017 ability promotional project for young teacher in Guangxi, 2017KY0729.

REFERENCES

Bissantz N., Mair B.A, Munk A., 2006. Amulti-scale stopping criterion for MLEM reconstruction in PET. In: *IEEE medical imaging conference proceedings*.

Cliff A.D. and Ord J.K., 1981, *Spatial process: models and applications*. Pion, London, UK.

Chen T.J.et al., 2006. A blurring index for medical images. *J Digital Imaging*. 19: 118-125.

Chen T.J. et al., 2016. A pilot study on a new image enhancement method using spatial statistics. *Joint International Information Technology, Mechanical and Electronic Engineering Conference*. XiAn, China, pp. 33-38. (JIMEC 2016, Oct.4, 2016).

Chuang K.S., Huang H.K., 1992. Assessment of noise in a digital image using the join-count statistic and Moran test. *Phys. Med. Biol.* 37:357-369.

Fu S.J. et al., 2007. A feature dependent fuzzy bidirectional flow for adaptive image sharpening. *Neurocomputing.* 70: 883-895.

Gui Z.G. et al., 2012. An X-ray image sharpening algorithm using nonlinear module. *The Imaging Science Journal.*60: 3-8.

Hamill J. and Bruckbauer T., 2002. Iterative reconstruction methods for high-throughput PET tomographs. *Phys Med Biol.* 47: 2627–36.

Hudson M. and Larkin R.S., 1994. Accelerated image reconstruction using ordered subsets of projection data. *IEEE Trans Med Img*. 13: 601–9.

Huesman R.H., 1977. The effects of a finite number of projection angles and finite lateral sampling of projections on the propagation of statistical errors in transverse section reconstruction. *Phys Med Biol* .22(3):511–21.

Javier S.B., 2011. Structure similarity image quality reliability determining parameters and window size. *Signal Processing.* 91: 1012-1020.

Kinahan P.E., Defrise M., and Clackdoyle R., 2004. *Analytic image reconstruction methods*. in Wernick MN and Aarsvold JN ed. *Emission Tomography*. Elsevier Academic Press .

Kontaxakis G. and Tzanakos G., 1996. Stopping criterion for the iterative EM-MLE image reconstruction for PET. In: SPIE proceedings, vol. 2710. 133–44.

Mathieu H.et al, 2015. Comparison of edge-preserving filters for unbiased quantification in 18F-FDG PET imaging. *The J of Nuclear Medicine*. Vol. 56, No. supplement 3, 1828.

Polesel A., Ramponi G., and Mathews V.J. , Image Enhancement via Adaptive Unsharp Masking, IEEE Transactions on image processing 9 (2000) 505-510.

Shiao Y.H. et al., 2007. Quality of Compressed Medical Images. *J of Digital Imaging*. 20:149-159.

Shepp L.A. and Vardi Y., 1982. Maximum likelihood reconstruction for emission tomography. *IEEE Trans Med Img.* MI-1(2):113–21.

Snyder D. L. and Miller M. T.,1985. The use of sieves to stabilize images produced with the EM algorithm for emission tomography. IEEE Trans. Nucl. Sci. NS-32, 3864-3872.

Veklerov E., Llacer J.,1987. Stopping rule for the MLE algorithm based on statistical hypothesis testing. *IEEE Trans Med Img*. 6(4).

Veklerov E., Llacer J., Hoffman E. J., 1988. MLE reconstruction of a brain phantom using a Monte Carlo transition matrix and a statistical stopping rule. *IEEE Trans Nucl Sci.* 35(1).

A STEGANOGRAPHIC IMAGE-BASED APPROACH FOR PROTECTION OF PDF FILES

Valery N. Gorbachev, Lev A. Denisov, Elena M. Kainarova and Ivan K. Metelev
High School of Printing and Mediatechnologies St-Petersburg State University of Industrial Technology and Design, St. Petersburg, Russia

ABSTRACT

Digital images can be copied without an authorization and have to be protected. Two schemes for watermarking images in pdf document were considered. Both schemes include a converter to extract images from the pdf pages and return them back. Frequency and spatial domain embedding were used for hiding a message represented by a binary pattern. We considered visible and invisible watermarking and found that spatial domain LSB technique is more preferable than frequency embedding with the help of DWT.

KEYWORDS

Protection, watermarking, pdf, wavelet, least significant bit, Scalable Vector Graphics

1. INTRODUCTION

The wide spread PDF format has powerful cryptographic tools to protect information in pdf documents. However this is not the only method and there are a number of other viable solutions. The rich structure of PDF allows using steganographic techniques for embedding visible or invisible marks that can protect digital data. Numerous approaches consider varying the line or word, spacing, font characteristics also varying certain invisible characters as a cover to hide a secrete message. The White Space Coding technique is based on the fact that there are a lot of white-space characters separating syntactic constructs from one another (Wang and Tsai, 2008). Visually they are indistinguishable from one another or invisible and may be used as covers. This way a message bit can be encoded by two items as the normal and non-breaking space. White Space Coding may include a version of RSA encryption on quadratic residual (Lin et al., 2013). This modification is suitable for secrete communication via pdf files when a message is encoded by the between-word characters location. Also the operators such as a justified text operator TJ can be considered for hiding data (Zhong, Cheng and Chen, 2007). Indeed, we often make the text justified so that the right margin is not ragged. This edit format results in the position of each character being random. A stream of such positions generated by a TJ operator is a nice cover for hiding data by LSB (Least Significant Bit) embedding (Alizadeh-Fahimeh et al., 2012).

An example is a (t, n) secrete sharing scheme. It may be used to share a secret images (Thien and Lin, 2002) and to protect pdf files (Suiang-Shyan Lee, Shuo-Fang Hsu and Ja-Chen Lin, 2014). To protect a very important pdf file it is decomposed into n parts, each of them is embedded into its pdf cover. All stego covers look the same. This way the pdf file can be shared among n parties and any t parties can recover it if they cooperate. Indeed, for embedding, a standard option as Attach File, available in Adobe Acrobat Pro can be suitable (Suiang-Shyan Lee, Shuo-Fang Hsu and Ja-Chen Lin, 2014).

A digital watermark can be encoded by a self-inverting permutation: a permutation which cycles have length less or equal 2. With the use of a particular representation, named 1d and 2d, the permutation is embedded into a 1d and 2d array. This technique was developed for audio and image and generalized for pdf files (Chroni and Nikolopoulos, 2015). The key idea is that the self-inverting permutation allows to locate the watermarked area to recover the information instead of extracting the message directly. In the case of frequency domain watermarking this method is robust to JPEG lossy compression (Chroni, Fylakis and Nikolopoulos, 2013).

Numerous types of pdf files result in a large number of solutions. (Subhedara and Mankar, 2014). Indeed, now the Adobe Acrobat has an option to embed a visible watermark. It protects any important documents; the watermark printed on the background contains large gray digits or some inscription as "watermarked". This makes the content perception worse and the interested user can remove the watermark using a key for an additional fee. However Adobe Acrobat uses a simple technique and numerous suggestions how to delete the watermark data can be found on the Internet.

In our paper we focus on protection of images placed in pdf file and consider two steganographic schemes. The key idea is to extract the desired image and return it back in the file after embedding. We introduce a convertor that transforms PDF to SVG format and back [11]. SVG stores the image in PNG format and by this way a png cover is prepared. The aim of our paper is to investigate a spatial and frequency domain watermarking for images in pdf file. We consider LSB and DWT techniques for invisible and visible and removable watermarks. It was found that the embedding in spatial domain is more preferable. It introduces less degradation in the case of visible and invisible watermarking. For spatial watermarking we found nice quality of the image, retrieved after removing visible watermark, its degradation is less than for similar DWT technique developed in (Hu and Huang, 2006).

The paper is organized as follows. First we introduce the frequency and spatial embedding schemes then we present the found results on invisible and visible watermarking.

2. TWO SCHEMES

Contains text usual pdf document contains a text and images. The images we wish to protect can be extracted from the file, watermarked and returned back. The presented system includes a PDF-to-SVG convertor, embedding and detection algorithms.

Convertor. Instead of processing page by page of pdf file our convertor finds images and stores them in PNG format that is suitable for watermarking. Then the convertor restores the pdf file that contains the watermarked images. Convertor has to be reversible to not lose information of watermarks and we examined the next transformation

$$\text{PDF} \rightarrow \text{a.png} \rightarrow \text{PDF} \rightarrow \text{b.png}$$

where a.png is an image extracted from initial PDF file and b.png is supposedly the same image obtained after conversion. A large number of PDF convertors can be found on the Internet, however they are mainly irreversible. Indeed it was randomly chosen two convertors from the Internet[22]. In the case of grayscale images which pixels have brightness 0, 1, … , 255 the difference between the pixels of *a.png* and *b.png* was found to be up to 129/255=0.5059. For our convertor this difference is equal to zero, then the transformation can be considered as reversible within given pixel encoding.

With the help of the convertor, a cover work *C*, that is a png image, is prepared and watermarked by frequency and spatial techniques. We use watermark presented by a binary image *M*.

Frequency embedding scheme. Algorithm is based on one-level DWT and has the next steps.

- Transformation of the cover work C into four blocks of the DWT coefficients *cA*, *cH*, *cV* and *cD* known as approximation, coefficients of horizontal, vertical and diagonal details or *LL*, *LH*, *HL* and *HH* frequency blocks.
- Choose a block *Z* from *cA*, *cH*, *cV*, *cD* and replace a some of its coefficient with *M*.
- Inverse DWT to achieve the watermarked png image S.

For detection it needs inverse steps. Embedding algorithm replaces a part, *u*, of the block, *Z*, with *M*

$$uZ \rightarrow M/\alpha,$$

where $Z \in \{cA, cH, cV, cD\}$ and α is a scaling parameter. Assume $Z = cD$, $u = 0.9$ and $a = 2$, then 90% of *cD* coefficients will be replaced with *M* whose brightness is reduced two times.

The scaling parameter α is chosen experimentally and it plays an important role. The introduced changes depend on α and result in a visible or an invisible watermark. To get an invisible watermark it needs a large α.

---

[1] Available at http://pdf.welovehtml.ru.

[2] http://pdf-png-jpg.eu/, http://online2pdf.com/convertor-png-to-pdf.

This way any grayscale image can be embedded, however we focus on binary pattern to compare this method with spatial scheme.

Spatial embedding scheme. We use LSB technique to encode a binary image M. This method modifies a bit plane of the grayscale png cover, C, and has the next steps.

- Decompose cover into bit planes
  $C = B_1 2^0 + \ldots + B_V 2^{V-1} + \ldots$
  and chose a bit plane B_V, $V = 1,2,\ldots$ for embedding.
- Add M and B_V on modulo 2
  $B_{VM} = (B_V + M) \bmod 2$,
- Replace the bit plane B_V with B_{VM}
  $C \rightarrow S = C - B_V 2^{V-1} + B_{VM} 2^{V-1}$.
- Detection uses the relation
  $M = (B_V + B_{VM}) \bmod 2$.

This detection algorithm is not blind, it requires the bit plane B_V of the cover. Thanks to image redundancy the algorithm can be generalized in blind detection (Gorbachev, Denisov and Kaynarova, 2013) but it is not essential for our purpose. Note a secrete key, presented by a binary random pattern, K, can be introduced in the scheme by the way $B_{VM} = (B_V + M + K)$ mod2.

3. EXPERIMENT

The presented schemes have a large number of parameters such as type of wavelet, block of the DWT coefficients $Z \in \{cA, cH, cV, cD\}$, scaling factors u, α and others. A priori their role is unclear and they can be only be chosen experimentally. The main aims of our experiment are to find optimal parameters and to clarify which of the schemes is more preferable. The results are shown at Figure 1 - Two initial pdf documents are presented at Figure 1, they have grayscale and color images, that will be watermarked with the help of our techniques. These fragments were taken from the papers (Lai and Tsai, 2009) and (Chroni, Fylakis and Nikolopoulos, 2013). These images are extracted by our convertor that stores them as png covers. The watermark is a binary image shown at Figure 1 (a).

- Frequency and spatial embedding. We used DWT with wavelets of Daubechies family that have nice features such as smoothness. An example using db1, known as a wavelet of Haar, is presented at Figure 2. By varying the scaling parameters we can achieve visible watermarks, if $\alpha = 150$, $u = 0.7$, and invisible watermarks, if $\alpha = 150$, $u = 0.7$. For both cases it was chosen the diagonal block $Z = cD$, in which 70% of coefficients were replaced with binary watermark. For watermarking the color image, Figure 2 (c), the blue channel was used. For spatial embedding any biplanes can be watermarked. In the case of $V = 1,2,3$ the hidden watermark is invisible.
- **Measures of distortion.** To detect the embedded data, the pdf file was converted into SVG that has the watermarked images and the detection algorithms extract the data. Because all trans-formations are not reversible there are errors that we estimate by distortion measures. We calculated the Hamming distance $ham(M,M')$ between initial and extracted watermarks M and M'. In the case of two binary images the Hamming distance is relative number of positions in which pixels from M and M' are not equal. If $ham(M,M')=0.2$, then error is 20%. For binary images there is a simple relation with Euclidian distance, known also as RMSE (Root Mean Square Error), that is often used as distortion measure: $RMSE^2(M,M')=ham(M,M')$.
- For frequency embedding it was found that the degradation is depends weakly on scaling parameters and type of wavelets. For $\alpha = 150$ and $\alpha = 20$, in both cases $u = 0.3$, wavelet db6, the Hamming distance or error was 5.27% and 2.29% It tells about the high quality of extracted watermarks, that was in agreement with visual perception.
- The main reasons of the found degradation is accuracy loss due to averaging when image is stored in graphical format. We used PNG format with a standard 8-bit integer encoding 0, 1,…, 255. However after inverse DWT data have to be truncated to get the required items.
- For spatial embedding all calculations keep the initial encoding and the Hamming distance was zero because of our convertor is reversible. From this point of view the spatial scheme seems to be more preferable.

- **Visible and removal watermark.** The scaling parameters allow us to get visible watermarks that protect image and can be removed by a legitimate user. Here the main problem is to retrieve the initial cover image. We focus on our spatial scheme. If watermark is embedded into bit plane $V \geq 4, 5$, it becomes visible.
- At Figure 3 (a) it is shown a fragment of a pdf page with image: Fig. 1: Structure of a PDF file. This fragment was taken from Ref. (Meral et al. 2009). The watermark was embedded into the bit plane V = 7 of this image, it is visible and it makes the perception worse, But this watermark can be removed. The retrieved image and the fragment of pdf are shown at Figure 3 (c) and (b). They are visually indistinguishable from their originals.

To retrieve the cover work we used algorithm that produces a grayscale image with two equal bit planes (Gorbachev, Denisov and Kaynarova, 2013). This way we can get the cover image that has two bit planes, say $V = 7$, when one of the least significant planes, say $U = 2$, is replaced with $V = 7$. Then to retrieve the cover, the watermarked plane, $V = 7$, is replaced with $U = 7$. As result we get the original but without bit plane $U = 2$. The difference between the original C and the retrieved image CR may be visually indistinguishable. At Figure 3 (d) we calculate PSNR (Peak Signal Noise Ration) between C and $CU=C-B_U2^{U-1}$, where B_U is a bit plane removed from C. For our case $U=2$ and $PSNR = 43.3417dB$, that in agreement with the experiment.

Note, the more PSNR is, the retrieved image is closer to the original. For visible watermarking in the case of DWT technique PSNR is less: 37-40 dB (Hu and Huang, 2006). The authors of this technique deduced that most errors come from integer rounding operation when the wavelet coefficients are modified and the inverse DWT is applied. The watermarked image pixels must be rounded to integer values to form a digital image. This conclusions agree with our results.

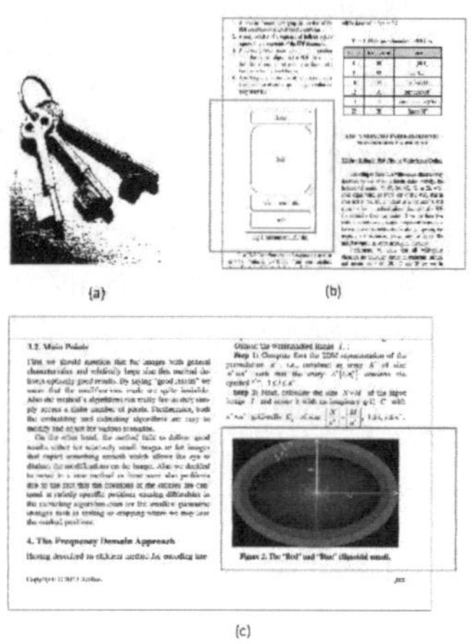

Figure 1. Watermark and the two fragments of pdf document with images. a) Binary watermark, b) a sample with a grayscale image: Fig. 1. Structure of a PDF file, c) a sample with color image: Figure 2. The "Red" and "Blue" ellipsoidal annuli

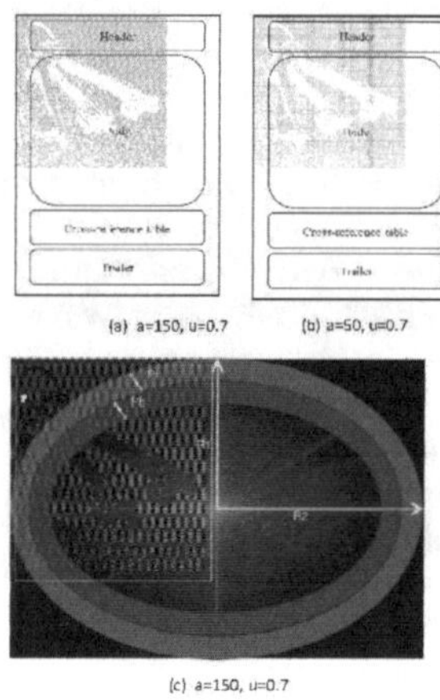

Figure 2. Frequency embedding with wavelet of Haar, visible and invisible watermarks

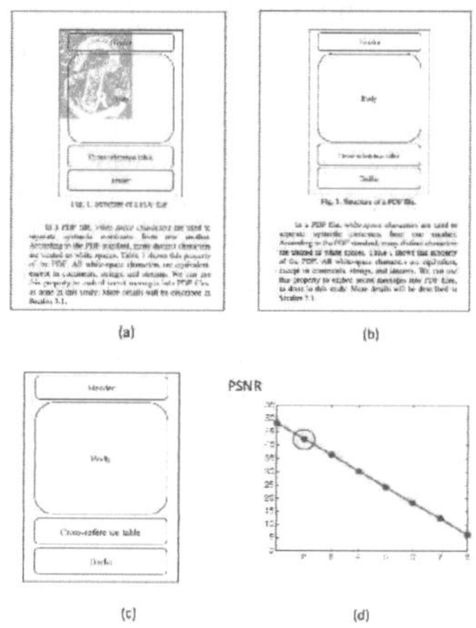

Figure 3. Visible and removable watermarking. a) Fragment of pdf page with watermarked image. b) the pdf page after removing watermark, c) the image after removing watermark, d) PSNR vs bit plane removed, for the presented case PSNR=43.3417 dB

4. CONCLUSIONS

Images in pdf document have to be protected against to unauthorized copying. This goal can be achieved by Image based watermarking with the help of a convertor that extracts the desired images from pdf pages and returns them back. For image watermarking standard techniques of frequency and spatial embedding can be used. In the case of the introduced PDF-to-SVG convertor the spatial LSB embedding is found to be more preferable than the frequency technique based on DWT. The considered schemes allow visible watermarking. The visible marks make the current perception worse and can be removed with high efficiency by the proposed algorithm.

REFERENCES

Alizadeh-Fahimeh, F. et al. (2012) Using Steganography to hide messages inside PDF files. SSN Project Report.

Chroni M., Fylakis A. and Nikolopoulos S. D. (2013) Watermarking Images in the Frequency Domain by Exploiting Self-Inverting Permutations. Journal of Information Security, 4, p. 80-91.

Chroni M. and Nikolopoulos S. D. (2015) Watermarking PDF Documents using Various Representations of Self-inverting Permutations. arXiv:1501.02686 [cs.MM].

Gorbachev V.N., Denisov L.A., Kaynarova E.M. (2013) Embedding of binary image into Gray planes. Russian Computer Optics, Russian Academy Science, v 37, p, 385.

Hu Y, S. K., J. Huang S.K. (2006) An algorithm for removable Visible Watermarking. IEEE. Transactions on circuits and systems video technology, v. 16, No 1, p.129-133.

Lin, H. F. et al. (2013) A copyright protection scheme based on PDF. Int J Innov Comput Inf Control, 9(1), 1-6.

Meral H.M. et al. (2009) Natural language watermarking via morphosyntactic alterations, Computer Speech & Language Journal, Volume 23, Issue 1, January. Pages 107-125.

Subhedara M. S. and Mankar V. H. (2014) Current status and key issues in image steganography: A survey. Computer Science Review, V. 13-14, p. 95-113.

Suiang-Shyan Lee, Shuo-Fang Hsu and Ja-Chen Lin (2014) Protection of PDF Files: a Sharing Approach. International Journal of u- and e- Service, Science and Technology Vol.7, No.2, pp.27-40.

Thien C.C. and Lin J.C. (2002) Secret image sharing. Computers and Graphics, vol. 26, no. 5, pp. 765-770.

Wang J. T. and Tsai W. H. (2008) Data hiding in PDF files and applications by imperceptible modifications of PDF object parameters. Proc. of 2008 Conf. on Computer Vision, Graphics & Image Proc., Yilan, Taiwan, Aug. 24-26.

Y-C Lai and W-H Tsai (2009) Covert communication via PDF files by new data hiding techniques, NSC project No, 97-2631-H-009-001.

Zhong S, Cheng X. and Chen T. (2007) Data hiding in a kind of pdf texts for secret communicationl. International Journal of Network Security, v. 4, p. 17–26.

AN ANDROID APPLICATION TO VISUALIZE POINT CLOUDS AND MESHES IN VR

Jules Morel

French Institute of Pondicherry, UMIFRE 21, India and LSIS, UMR 7296, Aix-Marseille University, France

ABSTRACT

This paper presents a review of well-known rendering techniques and their adaptation to the features of OpenGL ES 2.0 to develop an Android application dedicated to the visualization of surface meshes and point clouds in virtual reality.

KEYWORDS

Point clouds, surface meshes, Visualization, Virtual reality, Android application

1. INTRODUCTION

The increasing ease of use and popularity of 3D acquisition entails a wider use of digital representations. In order to visualize the point clouds acquired and their associated reconstructed surface, computer scientists and professionals rely on dedicated visualization tools using Oculus Rift or other similar virtual reality (VR) headsets. However, those devices are expensive and need to be powered by high end desktop PC. This paper presents an effective alternative to such costly virtual reality solutions: "LiDAR VR Viewer", an Android application, freely available on the Google Play Store, immersing the user into a virtual reality made of 3D point clouds and possibly reconstructed surfaces as mesh models. This paper builds upon well-known rendering techniques and describes how to adapt them to the features of OpenGL ES 2.0. This paper can also be seen as a literature review for scientists eager to implement a similar system.

2. DESIGN

The application has been developed following Android developer best practices proposed by Google. It is made of three different screens (called Activity among Android developers). After the splash screen, which proposes the download of a testing data-sets, the user sets up the parameters in the next activity, that is divided in sections. The *Display* section customizes the screen output and its behavior. It allows for instance to set up the rendering on the two sides of the screen in order to use the application with a head-mounted device for virtual reality purpose. Under the *Point cloud* section, one can set up the file containing the points and the parameters for their rendering such as their colors or sizes. Similarly, the colors and aspects of surface meshes are defined in the *Surface* section. The last section, *Lightning*, defines the shader used during the rendering. Once every settings have been chosen, one can proceed to the loading and rendering by clicking on the *Rendering* section. Actually the loading is done asynchronously and a format check on the file is performed.

3. FEATURES

The following sections give details on the main features we chose to implement in OpenGL shading language (Kessenich, 2004, Rost, 2009) to improve the visualization while keeping a flowing experience. Actually, this was the main challenge: to provide an immersive experience through devices with low computing power.

3.1 Immersive Mode

As shown on the Figure 1, the application proposes two rendering modes : 1a) a classic mode designed to be used without VR headset as a window on the world of the data, where the navigation is done by using the touchscreen, and 1b) an immersive mode dividing the screen in two parts, and designed to be used with a VR headset to reproduce the 3D effect with double-view stereo. In this mode, chromatic aberration and distortion induced by the lenses of the VR device are corrected.

Figure 1. Rendering in classic mode (a) and immersive mode (b) of an aerial LiDAR point cloud (2 million points)

3.2 Optimization of Buffers

The complexity of our scenes with millions of points and triangles on lightweight devices requires the use of vertex buffer objects. Instead of transferring vertex information from client memory at every frame, the information is transferred once and rendering is then performed directly from the graphics memory cache.

3.3 Points, Surfels and Surfaces Rendering

This section describes the methods implemented in the application to render points, surfaces and surfels.

3.3.1 Points Rendering

As the application has been designed to display heavy point clouds, such as the ones captured by 3D scanners, we focused on rendering efficiency. Indeed, provided the large size of handled point clouds and the double computation rendering for immersive mode (one for each eye), GPU cannot ran more than really simple shaders. With this in mind we kept the most simple vertex shader while allowing different processing in the fragment shader to propose the display of points, implemented as `GL_POINTS`, by squares, circles or spheres. By enabling point sprites, we get a special variable `glPointCoord` that can be read in the fragment shader and give the coordinates of the fragment in the square of the current point. To display a circle, we discard every fragment that falls outside of the in-scribed circle. To display spheres (illustrated in Figure 2), inspired by (Tarini, 2006), we draw them on the fly by relying on the concept of ray-traced impostors: we consider the square of the current point as a 2D frame always facing the user. We draw in that frame a virtual sphere which normal is assessed by relying on the symmetry of the sphere object.

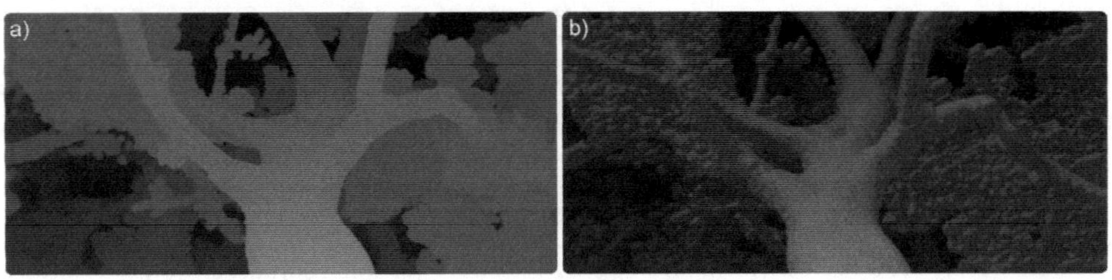

Figure 2. Terrestrial LiDAR point cloud rendered with points rendered as circles (a) and points rendered as spheres (b)

3.3.2 Surfaces Rendering

To improve the rendering of surfaces, we shade them according to a partial Phong reflection model (Phong, 1975). As specular reflection needs several computations in the fragment shader, only ambient and diffuse reflection were implemented to keep a flowing experience on highly detailed models. Inspired by Cook and Torrance (Cook and Torrance, 1982), we implemented another lightning model (see Figure 3). This model, known to be closer to the physical reality, simulates the specular reflectance of different materials. The model treats each surface as consisting of many micro-facets: Very small facets that reflect the incoming light. On rough surfaces, the slopes of these micro facets vary greatly, and on smooth surfaces the micro-facets are oriented in a similar direction (Torrance and Sparrow, 1967).

Finally, we propose a wire-frame view of the surfaces (see Figure 4) to improve visualization when transparency is required. Our procedure for wire-frame drawing is based on (Bærentzen, 2006). By providing the barycentric coordinates of the vertex to the fragment shader, we compute for each fragment the shortest distance to the edges of the polygon. Then, by setting a threshold on that distance and using alpha testing, triangles edges are drawn directly as a part of triangle rasterization, without resorting to line primitive, and so without any performance hit.

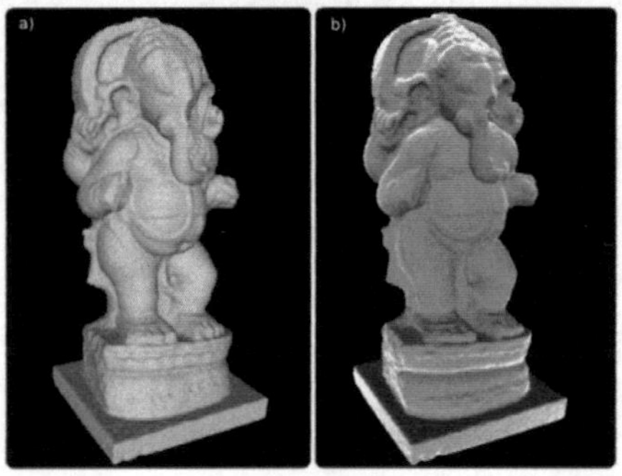

Figure 3. Surface model enlightened by (a) partial Phong reflection model and (b) Cook-Torrance modeL

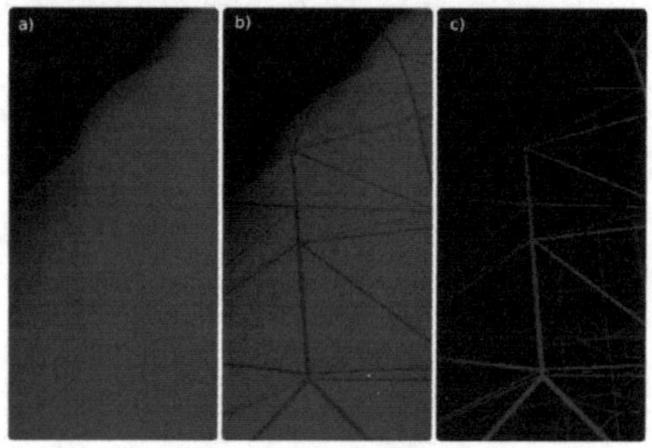

Figure 4. Close up on the rendering of mesh as smooth surface (a), as a surface with superimposed wireframe(b) and as a only (c).

3.3.3 Surfels Rendering

At the interface between point cloud and surface resides the concept of surface elements (surfels) (Merl, 1994): able to render complex geometric objects, surfels are point primitive without explicit connectivity, represented as small disks oriented with the local normals. While using surfel to render object geometries, we transfer two costly tasks as pre-processing: (i) the re-sampling of the point cloud to limit the redundancy of geometric information at a given resolution and (ii) the computation of the normals. Inspired by (Gross and Pfister, 2011), we parameterize the screen-space square over $[-r, r]^2$, where r is the surfel radius. For each of the pixel (x, y) in $[-r, r]^2$, a depth offset δ_z from the surfel center **p** is computed as a linear function depending on the surfel normal vector $\mathbf{n} = [n_x,n_y,n_z]^T$ expressed in the camera space:

$$\delta z = \frac{nx}{nz} \cdot x - \frac{ny}{nz} \cdot y$$

This depth offset is then used to compute the 3D distance from the surfel center: the pixel (x, y) corresponds to a point inside the surfel if $\|(x, y, \delta z)\| \leqslant r$. Otherwise,it is discarded. The quality of the model rendered rely on the expertise of the user and in the calibration of the pre-processing step: the point density and the surfels radius must match the expected output resolution of the image.

The upcoming developments on the surfel rendering will focus on the computation of the correct surfel radius. Currently, the splat-size is constant and set by the user. To estimate a correct radius dynamically, we propose to follow (Pajarola, 2003) approach in order to force the elliptical disks to cover the surface at all levels of details. That technique is related to a crucial improvement needing to be implemented: the optimization of the data to be loaded into the GPU according to the viewpoint, as presented by (Pauly, 2002).

4. PERFORMANCE

4.1 Points Rendering Performance

It is obvious that the smart-phones GPU can be strained when requested to display large point clouds. To detect potential bottlenecks in the rendering process, we relied on an average frame rate computation for point clouds loaded in the view frustum. Figure 5 shows an analysis of the performance on a Mali-T880 MP12 GPU with Exynos 8890 CPU system with a 1440 x 2560 pixels screen. It presents, for three point clouds of increasing size, the average frame-rate with respect to the size of the points displayed (variable `gl_PointSize` in the vertex shader). It highlights similar average frame rates for a given point cloud with a given point size for the three rendering modes of point primitives: squares, circles and spheres. This prove the efficiency of our fragment shader, whose extra computations do not induce frame-rate drop. Since the vertex shader has been kept the simplest possible for efficiency purpose, the bottleneck appears clearly in the data management on the CPU side: a level of detail approach is required to ease the GPU load on larger point cloud. The reader should note that the full point cloud is visible in the frustum view during this test. Moreover, the point size is kept as constant (`gl_PointSize = u_Size` in vertex shader). It is rarely the case in typical use: usually, only a portion of the point cloud is visible and the point size decreases with the depth (`gl_PointSize = u_Size/gl_Position.w` in vertex shader). In typical use, based on our experience and for the given hardware, users can explore point clouds with up to 2 million points while keeping a flowing experience.

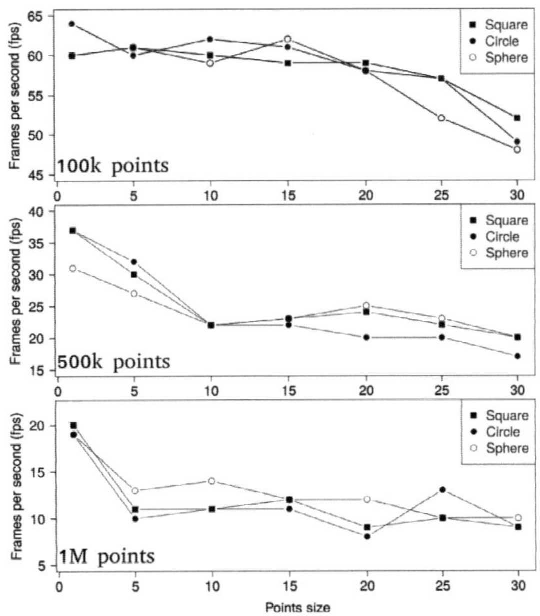

Figure 5. Evolution of the Average Frame per Second Ratio with the Points Size

4.2 Surfaces Rendering Performance

To analyze the impact of the shading effect on the surface rendering, we evaluated the average frame-rate for the display of meshes of increasing complexity. As shown in Figure 6, the application manages to render complex meshes of above one million of faces at a steady 20 frames per second, for both implemented shaders. This is more than satisfactory, given the screen resolution and pixel density of the targeted hardware.

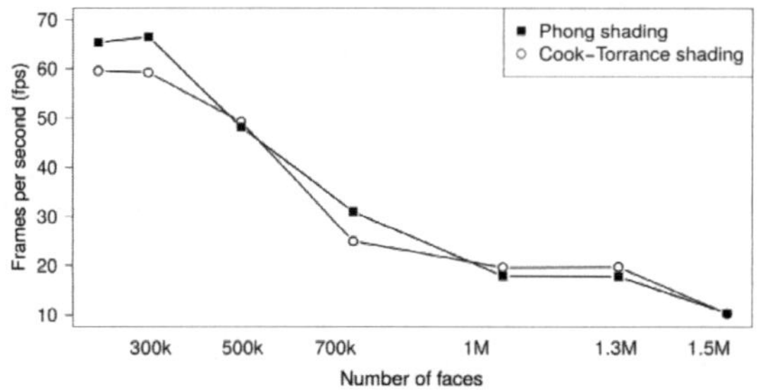

Figure 6. Evolution of the Average Frame per Second

5. CONCLUSION

The optimization of the OpenGL rendering allows our application to maintain a descent frame-rate for well detailed 3D data on lightweight devices. The new trends in development and the evolution of the technology will lead to much better performance in the near future. Indeed, the upcoming generations of smart phones with more powerful GPU promises enhancement of this virtual reality experience. The current developments focus on implementing a level of details (LOD) approach for the data management. By following an octree division of the point clouds as introduced by (Pauly, 2002) and loading on GPU only the relevant part, we expect a huge boost in performance.

REFERENCES

Andreas Bærentzen, Steen L Nielsen, Mikkel Gjøl, Bent D Larsen, and Niels Jørgen Christensen. Single-pass wireframe rendering. In ACM SIGGRAPH 2006 Sketches, page 149, 2006.

Robert L Cook and Kenneth E. Torrance. A reflectance model for computer graphics. ACM Transactions on Graphics (TOG), 1(1):7–24,1982.

Markus Gross and Hanspeter Pfister. Point-based graphics. Morgan Kaufmann, 2011.

John Kessenich, Dave Baldwin, and Randi Rost. The opengl shading language. Language version, 1, 2004.

Boston Merl. A survey and classification of real time rendering methods. 1994.

Renato Pajarola, Miguel Sainz, and Patrick Guidotti. Object-space blending and splatting of points. Information and Computer Science, University of California, Irvine, 2003.

Mark Pauly, Markus Gross, and Leif P Kobbelt. Efficient simplification of point-sampled surfaces.In Proceedings of the conference on Visualization'02, pages 163–170, IEEE Computer Society, 2002.

Bui Tuong Phong. Illumination for computer generated pictures. Communications of the ACM, 18(6):311–317,1975.

Randi J Rost, Bill Licea-Kane, Dan Ginsburg, John M Kessenich, Barthold Lichtenbelt, Hugh Malan, and Mike Weiblen. OpenGL shading language. Pearson Education, 2009.

Marco Tarini, Paolo Cignoni, and Claudio Montani. Ambient occlusion and edge cueing for enhancing real time molecular visualization. IEEE transactions on visualization and computer graphics, 12(5), 2006.

Kenneth E Torrance and Ephraim M Sparrow. Theory for off-specular reflection from roughened surfaces. JOSA, 57(9):1105–1112, 1967.

KEYPOINT-BASED OBJECT TRACKING AND LOCALIZATION USING NETWORKS OF LOW-POWER EMBEDDED SMART CAMERAS

Ibrahim Abdelkader[1], Yasser El-Sonbaty[1] and Mohamed El-Habrouk[2]
[1]*Dept. of Computer Science, Arab Academy for Science & Technology, Alexandria, Egypt*
[2]*Dept. of Electrical Engineering, Faculty of Engineering, Alexandria, Egypt*

ABSTRACT

Object tracking and localization is a complex task that typically requires processing power beyond the capabilities of low-power embedded cameras. This paper presents a new approach to real-time object tracking and localization using multi-view binary keypoints descriptor. The proposed approach offers a compromise between processing power, accuracy and networking bandwidth and has been tested using multiple distributed low-power smart cameras. Additionally, multiple optimization techniques are presented to improve the performance of the keypoints descriptor for low-power embedded systems.

KEYWORDS

WSNs, Object Tracking, ORB, Machine Vision, Distributed Cameras

1. INTRODUCTION

Object localization and tracking has been the subject of many research studies, with applications in military, surveillance, robotics and more. This paper introduces a new keypoints-based approach for object tracking and localization, which offers a compromise between processing power, detection rate and network bandwidth. Additionally, the paper presents optimization techniques to allow the keypoints descriptor to run on low-power smart cameras. The proposed approach uses a multi-view keypoints descriptor to track objects, created by fusing together multiple descriptors of the same object extracted from different views as shown in Figure 1. Each camera performs simple background subtraction, locally, via frame differencing to detect moving objects. The size and location of detected objects are used as the ROIs (Region of Interests) for keypoints extraction. Instead of sending full frames, each camera only sends the extracted keypoints to a server which performs the matching against the multi-view descriptor. Since the locations of the cameras are assumed to be fixed, object locations can be estimated as well.

Figure 1. Multi-view keypoints descriptor

2. RELATED WORK

Many different approaches with different end applications have been proposed for object tracking and localization, however a full survey of object tracking is beyond the scope of this paper, thus only the relevant work is reviewed in this section.

(Ercan et al, 2007) proposed a camera network to track a single object in the presence of static and moving occluders. Camera locations are assumed to be fixed. Additionally full knowledge about static occluders is required and some information about moving occluders are also assumed to be known. Simple background subtraction is performed on each node and the object is detected using features. The scene is then reduced to a single scan line which is sent to a cluster head for further processing.

(Yang et al, 2003) used a camera network to count people for the purposes of surveillance. Each camera performs local processing to extract foreground objects from the background, and sends bitmaps over the network for further processing. In contrast to our work, full bitmaps are sent over the network which increases network bandwidth and consumption.

(Shen et al, 2012) proposed an efficient background subtraction technique to implement an object tracking system using an embedded camera network. The background subtraction algorithm is shown to be as accurate as traditional systems yet faster, however the system can only track a single object and it is based on background subtraction which is affected by different lighting conditions.

(Nummiaro et al, 2003) described a multi-view color-based object tracking system for tracking faces using color histograms and particle filters. The system is robust against partial occlusions and transformations, however it depends on fixed lighting conditions.

(El-Sonbaty & Ismail, 2003) proposed a graph-based algorithm for matching partially occluded objects. The algorithm matches connected lines based on distance ratio. The algorithm is translation, rotation and scale invariant, however its complexity does not allow it to run on low-power, real-time systems, although the algorithm can be accelerated via parallelism (Nagy et al, 2006) or compression (El-Sonbaty et al, 2003).

(Rublee et al, 2011) created ORB (Oriented FAST and Rotated BRIEF), a fast binary feature descriptor. ORB is based on the BRIEF (Calonder et al, 2010) descriptor, designed to be a more efficient alternative to SIFT (Lowe, 2004) and SURF (Bay et al, 2006). The ORB descriptor is computed using simple binary tests between the pixels in the patch around a keypoint. To produce multi-scale keypoints, the FAST (Rosten & Drummond, 2006) corner detector is used on an image pyramid. The keypoints are sorted by Harris (Harris & Stephens, 1988) corner score and the top keypoints are selected. To achieve rotation-invariance, the orientation of each keypoint is determined using the *intensity centroid* (Rosin, 1999) and used to rotate (or steer) the binary sampling pattern.

The proposed approach uses FAST and ORB for feature extraction and description respectively. Using ORB makes the system inherently scale, rotation and lighting invariant and robust against partial occlusions. However, while ORB is much faster than alternatives (SURF or SIFT) improvements to the performance of the tracker were needed to allow it to run on a low-power embedded system. The following section presents ORB a few optimization techniques implemented in the tracking system.

3. OPTIMIZING ORB

To extract multi-scale descriptors, the FAST corner detector runs on all image pyramid levels. However, when matching this descriptor, the corner detector is only run on the first scale (full image). Since the descriptor contains keypoints from different scales, a detected keypoint will have a match in one of the scales. A similar approach is used in the work done by (Wagner et al, 2008) to optimize the SIFT descriptor for mobile phones. Additionally, the descriptor size is limited to 32-bytes, which performs almost as good as a 64-bytes descriptor as shown in Figure 2 from the experiments performed by (Calonder el al, 2010).

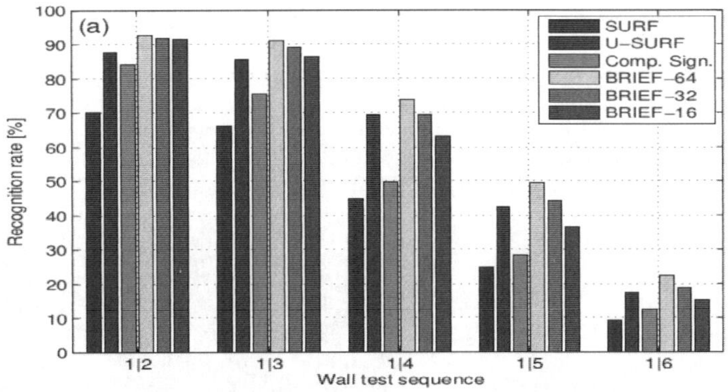

Figure 2. BRIF recognition rate using 16, 32 and 64 bytes

Furthermore, the keypoints descriptor is optimized by removing redundant keypoints detected at multiple octaves at the same position with the same or close angles of rotation. For example, keypoints which appear at multiple octaves at the same location and have the same (or slightly different) rotation angles, are merged into one keypoint in the final descriptor. Since ORB requires a Gaussian smoothing at every scale, a separable convolution (horizontal convolution followed by a vertical one) is used instead of a 2D convolution, to lower the number of operations required to perform the smoothing. Additionally, SIMD instructions are used in the inner loop of the separable onvolution to speed up the pixel level operations.

4. EXPERIMENTS AND RESULTS

The platform used for evaluation is a low-power machine vision camera developed by the author, called OpenMV shown in Figure 3-a. OpenMV is based on the STM32F7 ARM Cortex-M7 dual-issue MCU running at 216MHz. The MCU has 512KiBs SRAM, 2MiBs flash, a single precision FPU and DSP instructions. In addition, it includes a digital camera interface (DCMI), JPEG encoder and multiple serial peripheral interfaces. The camera can be extended with BLE (Bluetooth Low Energy) or WiFi modules, and consumes about 500mW on average when doing image processing.

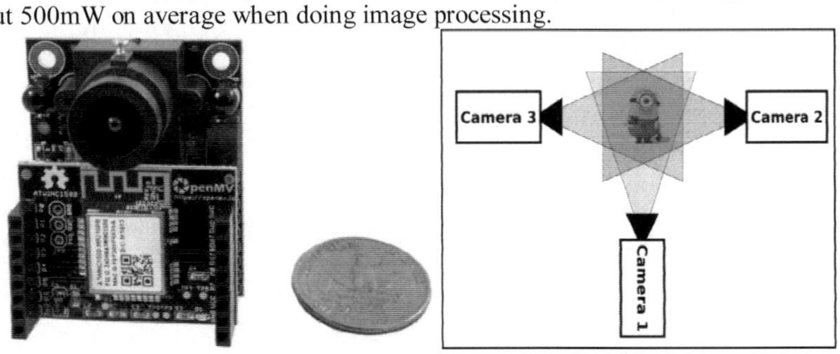

(a) (b)

Figure 3. (a) OpenMV camera with WiFi module. (b) An illustration of the Camera network setup

Multiple OpenMV cameras are placed in fixed locations to monitor a scene. Each camera is equipped with a battery for power supply and a 2.4GHz WiFi/802.11 extension module for communications. The cameras can use BLE for communications instead to reduce the power consumption further. Additionally BLE RSSI can be used to determine the distance between cameras without assuming prior knowledge of their locations. When a moving object is detected, the camera uses the object's location and size as the ROI passed to Fast/ORB to extract keypoints. The ROI and extracted keypoints descriptors are sent over the network to a sever for further processing. See Figure 3-b for an illustration of the setup used in this experiment.

A total of 38 bytes is sent for each keypoint (4 bytes for its location, 2 bytes for the angle of rotation and a 32 bytes descriptor). Limiting the maximum number of keypoints to 50 keypoints per frame, each camera sends a maximum of 1900 bytes (~1.8KiBs) for detection compared to sending a full frame (300KiBs at 640x480 grayscale). Figure 4 shows an example from the first camera, starting with frame differencing to detect moving objects followed by background subtraction, keypoints detection and keypoints optimization to further reduce the number of detected keypoints. The two other cameras produce similar results with different ROIs sizes depending on the distance of the object from each camera.

Figure 4. An overview of the approach. (a) The background image (b) moving object detection with frame difference (c) ROI used to detect keypoints (d) Keypoints reduction after optimization

The same scene is observed by two more cameras, which perform the same tasks and send their detection results to a server for further processing. The server performs object matching using the multi-view keypoints descriptor and localization using the ROI sizes. Figure 5 shows tracking results plotted compared to the ground truth.

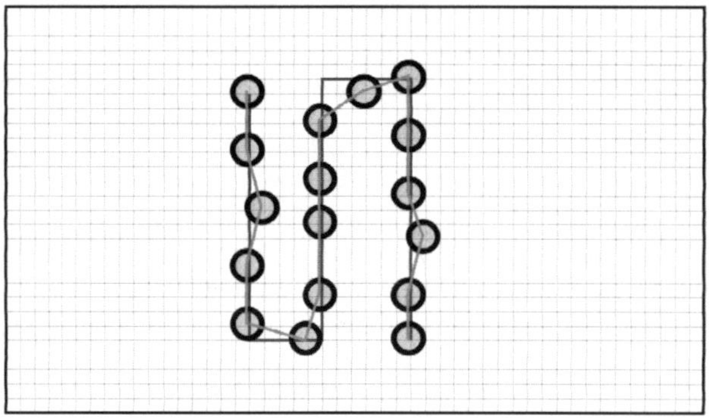

Figure 5. The tracking results. The circles represent detection locations connected with a green line. The ground truth is plotted in red

5. CONCLUSION

This paper presented a new approach for object tracking and localization. The proposed approach offers a compromise between processing power and networking bandwidth by sending keypoints instead of full frames, reducing the communications overhead significantly. Each camera sends only the location of the detected object and extracted keypoints to a server which performs the object matching using a multi-view keypoints descriptor. The size of the detected object as well as angles of rotations of matched keypoints allow the object location and orientation to be estimated as well. This paper also presented multiple optimization techniques to allow ORB to run on a low-power smart camera.

REFERENCES

Ercan, A. O. et al, 2007. Object tracking in the presence of occlusions via a camera network. In Proceedings of the 6th international conference on Information processing in sensor networks (pp. 509-518). ACM

Yang, D. B. et al, 2003. Counting People in Crowds with a Real-Time Network of Simple Image Sensors. In ICCV (pp. 122-129)

Shen, Y. et al, 2012. Efficient background subtraction for real-time tracking in embedded camera networks. In Proceedings of the 10th ACM Conference on Embedded Network Sensor Systems (pp. 295-308)

Nummiaro, K. et al, 2003. Color-based object tracking in multi-camera environments. In Joint Pattern Recognition Symposium (pp. 591-599). Springer Berlin Heidelberg

El-Sonbaty, Y. and Ismail, M., 2003. Matching occluded objects invariant to rotations, translations, reflections, and scale changes.. Image Analysis, 836-843

Nagy, Y. et al, 2006. VHDL-based Simulation of a Parallel Implementation of a Phase-based Algorithm for Optical Flow. In Video and Signal Based Surveillance, 2006. AVSS'06. IEEE International Conference on (pp. 27-27). IEEE.Chicago

El-Sonbaty, Y. et al, 2003. Compressing sets of similar medical images using multilevel centroid technique. In In Proceedings of Digital Image Computing: Techniques and Applications.Chicago

Rublee, E. et al, 2011. ORB: An efficient alternative to SIFT or SURF. International conference on computer vision (pp. 2564-2571). IEEE.

Calonder, M. et al, 2010. Brief: Binary robust independent elementary features. In European conference on computer vision (pp. 778-792). Springer Berlin Heidelberg.

Lowe, D. G., 2004. Distinctive image features from scale-invariant keypoints. International Journal of Computer Vision,60(2):91–110, 2004

Bay, H. et al, 2006. Surf: Speeded up robust features. In European conference on computer vision (pp. 404-417). Springer Berlin Heidelberg

Rosten, E. & Drummond, T., 2006. Machine learning for high-speed corner detection. In European conference on computer vision (pp. 430-443). Springer Berlin Heidelberg.

Harris, C. & Stephens, M., 1988. A combined corner and edge detector. In Alvey vision conference (Vol. 15, No. 50, pp. 10-5244)

Rosin, P. L., 1999. Measuring corner properties. Computer Vision and Image Understanding, 73(2), 291-307

Wagner, D. et al, 2008. Pose tracking from natural features on mobile phones. In Proceedings of the 7th IEEE/ACM International Symposium on Mixed and Augmented Reality (pp. 125-134). IEEE Computer Society

INTENSITY NORMALIZATION IN BRAIN MR IMAGES USING SPATIALLY VARYING DISTRIBUTION MATCHING

Evgin Goceri
Akdeniz University, Engineering Faculty, Computer Engineering Department , Dumlupinar Boulevard, 07058, Antalya, Turkey

ABSTRACT

Comparison of medical images is frequently needed for diagnosis or evaluation of a progressive disease. The comparison is performed by alignment and registration of images or warping them with a transformation function. It is possible to compare images of the same patient, which have been taken at different time periods to detect or quantify the changes that might have taken place in-between acquisitions. Also, a comparison can be performed using images from different subjects. In a Magnetic Resonance Image (MRI), intensity values do not only depend on the underlying tissue type. They also depend on developmental processes, scanner-related intensity artifacts and disease progression. Therefore, spatial normalization, which brings an image into the coordinate system of a template using a coordinate transformation to make meaningful comparisons of spatially varying data, is required. In this work, an intensity normalization method based on spatially varying distribution matching is proposed. The efficiency of the proposed method has been shown on brain MRIs.

KEYWORDS

Intensity normalization, bias field correction, intensity standardization, inhomogeneity correction, spatial transformation

1. INTRODUCTION

Diagnosis of a disease may not be accurate by looking at only one image modality. Therefore, different types of images can be acquired at the same time to get information from multimodal images. Combining (fusion) of these images or comparative analysis of them to make accurate interpretation and decision about the disease is a crucial task. Comparison of medical images is also needed for temporal evaluations during treatment of progressive diseases, such as multiple sclerosis, which requires a study on evaluation through time. A temporal series of examinations of a patient can be used to follow the evolution of the disease. To have similar properties, such as similar field of view, similar histograms, and image size, time series of images of a patient is obtained from the same imaging parameters with a definite protocol (Rey et al. 2002). Temporal evaluations and stages of a disease can be shown with time series analysis of images. Also, similar to inter-patient comparison, intra-patient comparisons by taking images from different subjects can be useful to make different interpretations about diseases. These operations are performed with registration or warping of images with a transformation function. To achieve these operations automatically is a challenging task because intensity values in a medical image do not only depend on the underlying tissue type. They also depend on developmental processes, scanner-related intensity artifacts and disease progression. Therefore, spatial intensity normalization, which brings an image into the coordinate system of a template using a coordinate transformation to make meaningful comparisons of spatially varying data, is required. In the literature, there are several normalization methods, which uses different techniques such as fuzzy c-means (Cai et al. 2007) and energy minimization (Li et al. 2014, Zosso et al. 2017, Chan and Vese 2001). In this work, the proposed intensity normalization method is based on spatially varying distribution matching. The efficiency of the proposed method has been shown on brain MRIs.

2. PROPOSED INTENSITY NORMALIZATION

The proposed normalization technique in this work has been implemented using brain MRIs and consists of subsequent steps (Figure 1). In the first step, three partitions, which have equal size and identified manually by a user, are taken from different regions in the foreground of a given reference image. In the second step, mean gray level values for each tissue component (i.e., for i) gray matter, ii) white matter, iii) cerebrospinal fluid) are computed from each partition. This process is achieved by fitting gray level values of a partition to Gaussian Mixture Model (GMM). In the third step, the average of the mean gray level values and the average of the mean gray level values of the 3 components in the observed image are calculated. In the next step, a transfer function is obtained by using those mean values. Finally, normalization of the intensity values in the observed image is performed according to the generated mapping function.

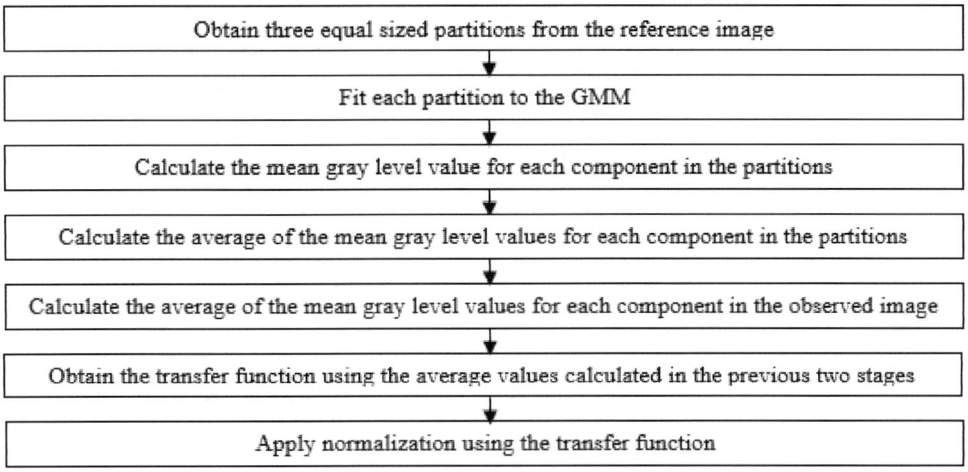

Figure 1. The steps applied in the proposed method

2.1 Identification of Partitions

In this work, the number of partitions is determined as 3 since the size of a brain image may not always be big enough to identify more regions in foreground area. Each partition has equal size and identified by a user manually on the regions where gray level values are in-homogenous as much as possible. Figure 2 shows example reference images and user defined partitions chosen from those images.

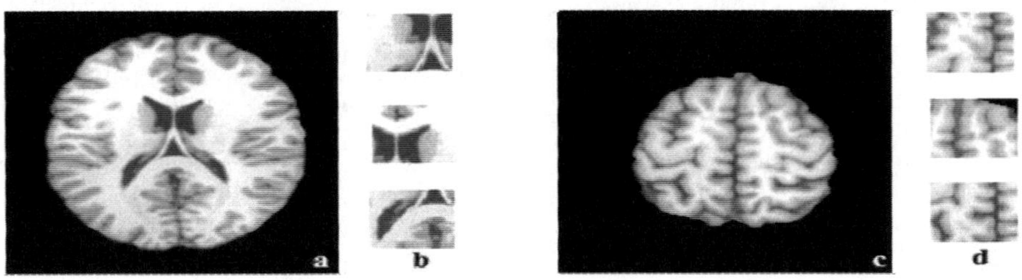

Figure 2. Example reference image (a) and user defined partitions (b); Example reference image (c) and user defined partitions (d)

2.2 GMM Fitting

A GMM (Bishop 2006) is a parametric probability density function, which is shown as a weighted sum of densities of Gaussian components. GMMs have been applied for various purposes in the literature (Costa

2012, Layer 2015, Jahromi et al. 2014, Somayajula et al. 2012, Han 2013, Chaddad 2015, Liu et al. 2012, Galimzianova et al. 2016). For instance, to measure heart rate variability (Costa 2012), PET image segmentation (Layer 2015), boundary segmentation from optical coherence tomography images (Jahromi et al. 2014), non-rigid registration of MRI/CT images (Somayajula et al. 2012), identification of diverse tumor microenvironments (Han 2013), feature extraction in brain tumor (Chaddad 2015), fiber tracking from diffusion tensor images (Liu et al. 2012), face identification (Cardinaux et al. 2006), and segmentation of white matter from brain images (Liu et al. 2012, Galimzianova et al. 2016). There are many works on segmentation of brain images using GMM. A recently published good review can be seen for GMM based segmentation method for brain MRIs in (Balafar 2014). In this work, mean value of gray levels for each component (i.e., gray matter, white matter, cerebrospinal fluid) in a partition is calculated by fitting gray level values to GMM, which mixtures three Gaussian models corresponding to the three components of the brain tissue. The parameters of the GMM are estimated iteratively using the Expectation Maximization (EM) approach (Dempster et al. 1977). To explain the estimation of the GMM parameters, let I is an image, which is a function that can be defined as $I: U \rightarrow [0.1]^c$, where $U = [\![0; n-1]\!] \times [\![0; m-1]\!]$ are pixels, n is the number of columns, m is the number of rows, and c corresponds to the number of color channels, which are usually $c \in \{1, 3\}$. In GMM, the image is modelled with the probability distribution that can be written using *I(i),* which is *i*th pixel value in the image *I*, as

$$P(I(i)) = \sum_{k=1}^{K} w_k N(I(i)|\mu_k, \sigma_k^2) \quad (1)$$

where K refers to the number of clusters, w_k is a positive weight value, $N(I(i)|\mu_k, \sigma_k^2)$ is the Gaussian function, μ_k and σ_k^2 are mean and variance values for cluster k. The computation in the EM algorithm is performed with the following three steps: 1) Initialization, 2) Expectation, 3) Maximization.

2.2.1 Initialization

All parameters (w_k,μ_k,σ_k^2) are initialized in this step for each cluster C_k. Initialization can be performed by randomly or assigning constant values. In our implementation, initial values were calculated automatically using K-means method, which is very popular and widely used (Amorim and Makarenkov 2016, Ayech and Ziou 2016, Sarrafzadeh and Dehnavi 2015, Frandsen et al. 2015). K-means is a deterministic and iterative clustering technique. The main idea is to find the best centers for K clusters. Each center should be placed properly since different locations of these centers cause different results. Therefore, to place centers far away from each other is the most appropriate choice. For this purpose, separation of data points into clusters is performed with minimization of an *objective function*, which is a squared error function and written as

$$J = \sum_{j=1}^{k} \sum_{i=1}^{U} \left\| x_i^{(j)} - c_j \right\|^2 \quad (1)$$

where $\left\| x_i^{(j)} - c_j \right\|^2$ is the metric for the distance between cluster center c_j, which is an indicator of the distance of n data points from their cluster centers, and a data $x_i^{(j)}$. Pseudo code of the K-means algorithm is:

1. Select k centers randomly (one center for each cluster)
2. Do assignment for every data point (assign points to the cluster that has the closest center)
3. After, assigning all data points to the clusters, calculate the center (mean of all points) in each cluster
4. Repeat the previous two steps (steps 2 and 3) until the clusters are stable (i.e.,centers no longer change).

2.2.2 Expectation

For each cluster C_k and pixel *I(i)*, conditional probability $P(C_k|I(i))$ is calculated with

$$P(C_k \mid I(i))^{(t)} = \frac{w_k^{(t)} N\left(I(i) \mid \mu_k^{(t)} \sigma_k^{2(t)}\right)}{\sum_{j=1}^{K} w_j^{(t)} N\left(I(i) \mid \mu_j^{(t)} \sigma_j^{2(t)}\right)} \quad (2)$$

where t is the number of iterations. This step can be interpreted as a construction of a local lower-bound to the posterior distribution. In the Maximization, the bound is optimized to improve the estimate for unknowns.

2.2.3 Maximization

In this stage, the parameters $w_k^{(t)}$, $\mu_k^{(t)}$, $\sigma_k^{2(t)}$ are maximized by using probabilities $P(C_k|I(i))$ from expectation stage with the following equations

$$\mu_k^{(t+1)} = \frac{\sum_i^U P(C_k \mid I(i))^{(t)} \cdot I(i)}{\sum_i^U P(C_k \mid I(i))^{(t)}}, \quad \sigma_k^{(t+1)} = \frac{\sum_i^U P(C_k \mid I(i))^{(t)} \cdot \left(I(i) - \mu_k^{(t+1)}\right)^2}{\sum_i^U P(C_k \mid I(i))^{(t)}}, \quad w_k^{(t+1)} = \frac{\sum_i^U P(C_k \mid I(i))^{(t)}}{U} \quad (3)$$

Expectation and Maximization stages are applied iteratively until all parameters converge. The convergence properties of the EM algorithm are discussed as detailed in (McLachlan and Krishnan 1996). The speed of convergence of the EM algorithm for GMM fitting depends on the amount of overlapping of the mixture components. If there is an overlapping among the mixture components, the convergence of EM algorithm becomes slower as the dynamic range among the mixing coefficients increases (Naim and Gildea 2012).

2.3 Obtaining a Transfer Function

In this step, the average of the mean gray level values of the partitions and the average of the mean gray level values of a given image, whose intensity values will be normalized, are calculated separately for each component. These average values are used to obtain a transfer (mapping) function. Gray level values of a given image are normalized according to the mapping function.

3. RESULTS AND CONCLUSION

Experimental results obtained by the proposed method are shown in Figure 3. The image in Figure 2.a has been used as the reference image (chosen partitions are presented in Figure 2.b) and the image given in Figure 3.a,d has been used as the image whose intensity values will be normalized. The transfer function generated with these images is shown in Figure 3.b,e, while the result of the normalization method is shown in Figure 3.c,f. The proposed intensity normalization technique is based on statistical features of images obtained by the EM optimization algorithm. The probabilistic normalization approach can be applied with other medical image modalities. The proposed method is a semi-automated normalization since the partitions (Figure 2.b,d) are defined by users manually. Different users may define different partitions, which can affect results. Therefore, the partitions will be defined automatically in the future work.

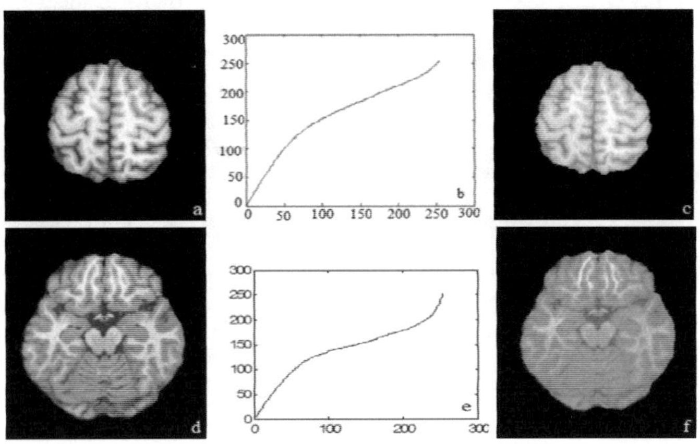

Figure 3. Original image (a,d); Transfer function (b,e) obtained with the partitions given in Figure 2.b; Image after the normalization method (c,f)

REFERENCES

Amorim RC. and Makarenkov V., 2016. Applying subclustering and Lp distance in weighted k-means with distributed centroids. *Neurocomputing*, Vol.173, No.3, pp. 700-707

Ayech MW. and Ziou D., 2016. Terahertz image segmentation using k-means clustering based on weighted feature learning and random pixel sampling. *Neuro.,* Vol.175, No.Part A, pp.243-264, ISSN 0925-2312

Balafar M.A., 2014. Gaussian mixture model based segmentation methods for brain MRI images. *Artificial Intelligence Review*, Vol.41, No.3, pp. 429–439

Bishop C.M., 2006. *Mixture models and EM*. Jordan M, Kleinberg J, Schölkopf B, editors. Pattern recognition and machine learning. Springer, New York, USA

Cai W., et al., 2007. Fast and robust fuzzy c-means algorithms incorporating local information for image segmentation. *Pattern Recognition,* Vol.40, No.1, pp.825-838

Cardinaux F., et al., 2006. User authentication via adapted statistical models of face images. *IEEE Transactions on Signal Processing*, Vol.54, No.1, pp.361–373.

Chaddad A., 2015. Automated feature extraction in brain tumor by magnetic resonance imaging using Gaussian mixture models. *International Journal of Biomedical Imaging*, Vol.2015, No.1, pp.868031.

Chan T.F. and Vese L.A., 2001. Active contours without edges. *IEEE Transactions on Image Processing,* Vol.10, No.1, pp.266–277

Costa T., 2012. Gaussian Mixture Model of Heart Rate Variability. *PLos One*, Vol. 7, No.5, pp.e37731

Dempster AP. et al., 1977. Maximum likelihood from incomplete data via the EM algorithm, *J. Roy. Statist. Soc. Series B (Methodological),* vol. 39, pp. 1–38

Frandsen PB., et al., 2015. Automatic selection of partitioning schemes for phylogenetic analyses using iterative k-means clustering of site rates. *BMC Evolutionary Biology*, vol.15, No.1, pp.13-39

Galimzianova A., et al., 2016. Stratified mixture modeling for segmentation of white-matter lesions in brain MR images. *Neuroimage*, Vo.124, No.Pt A, pp.1031-43

Han S.H., 2013. Gaussian mixture model-based classification of DCE-MRI data for identifying diverse tumor microenvironments: Preliminary results. *NMR Biomed.*, Vol.26, No.5, pp.519–532.

Jahromi M.K. et al., 2014. An automatic algorithm for segmentation of the boundaries of corneal layers in optical coherence tomography images using Gaussian mixture model. *Journal of Medical Signals Sensors*, Vol. 4, No.3, pp.171–180.

Layer T., 2015. PET image segmentation using a Gaussian mixture model and markov random fields. *EJNMMI Phys.*, Vol.2, No.9, pp.1-15.

Li C., et al., 2014. Multiplicative intrinsic component optimization (MICO) for MRI bias field estimation and tissue segmentation. *Magnetic Resonance Imaging,* Vol.32, No.1, pp.913-923

Liu M., et al., 2012. Unsupervised automatic white matter fiber clustering using a Gaussian mixture model. *Proc IEEE Int Symp Biomed Imaging*, Vol.2012, No.9, pp.522–525

McLachlan G. and Krishnan T. 1996. *The EM algorithm and extensions*. John Wiley & Sons, New York

Naim I. and Gildea D. 2012. Convergence of the EM algorithm for Gaussian mixtures with unbalanced mixing coefficients. *Proc. of the 29th Int. Conference on Machine Learning*, Edinburgh, Scotland, UK

Rey D. et al., 2002. Automatic detection and segmentation of evolving processes in 3D medical images: Application to multiple sclerosis. *Medical Image Analysis*, Vol.6, No.2, pp.163-179

Sarrafzadeh O. and Dehnavi AM., 2015. Nucleus and cytoplasm segmentation in microscopic images using K-means clustering and region growing. *J. of Advanced Biomedical Research*, Vol.4, No.1, pp.174-184

Somayajula S. et al., 2012. Non-rigid image registration using Gaussian mixture models. *Biomed Image Registration*, Vol.7359, No.1, pp.286–295

Zosso D., et al., 2017. Image segmentation with dynamic artifacts detection and bias correction. *AIMS Journal Inverse Problems and Imaging* (accepted)

DEEP LEARNING IN MEDICAL IMAGE ANALYSIS: RECENT ADVANCES AND FUTURE TRENDS

Evgin Goceri[1] and Numan Goceri[2]
[1]*Akdeniz University, Engineering Faculty, Computer Engineering Department*
Dumlupinar Boulevard, Antalya, 07058, Turkey
[2]*Evosoft GmbH, Business Function Information Technology Solutions*
Marienbergstr. 78-80, Nuremberg, 90411, Germany

ABSTRACT

Deep Learning (DL) methods are a set of algorithms in Machine Learning (ML), which provides an effective way to analysis medical images automatically for diagnosis/assessment of a disease. DL enables higher level of abstraction and provides better prediction from datasets. Therefore, DL has a great impact and become popular in recent years. In this work, we present advances and future researches on DL based medical image analysis.

KEYWORDS

Deep Learning, Medical Images, Image Analysis, Automated Segmentation, Machine Learning

1. INTRODUCTION

ML based approaches are very popular and forms the basis of several medical image analysis systems commercially available. Computerized methods decide the optimal decision boundaries in a high-dimensional feature space. The crucial step to develop such a computerized system is feature extraction, which is still done by manually, from images. The next step is ML, which lets computers learning the extracted features representing the data. This procedure is used in many DL algorithms, which models (i.e., networks) many layers to transform inputs to output data by learning higher level features. The term *deep* refers to the layered non-linearities in a learning system, which enables the model to represent a function by less parameters and increases efficiency in the learning (Bengio, 2009). In this survey, a comprehensive review has been performed on methods applied for medical image analysis with DL. It has been observed that most of the recent works in the literature for medical image analysis are based on DL, particularly in 2016 (Figure 1).

2. DL TECHNIQUES

The DL techniques applied with different medical images have been reviewed in this section. Activation of a neuron in a DL based architecture (mostly based on neural networks) is provided by inputs (x) and learned parameters (w,b) and an element-wise non-linearity σ(.):

$$a = \sigma\left(w^T x + b\right) \quad (1)$$

Neural networks are constructed by layers (*L*) of neurons, $\sigma\left(w_L^T \sigma\left(w_{L-1}^T \ldots\right) + b_L\right)$. A network with many layers is known as "Deep Neural Network (DNN)". Types of neural networks can be grouped as 1) AEs, 2) RBMs, 3) CNNs, 4) RNNs. AEs are trained to reconstruct an input x upon an output layer x_0 with a hidden layer (h). Two weight matrices ($W_{x,h}$ and $W_{h,x'}$) and biases ($b_{x,h}$ and $b_{h,x'}$) are used in AEs. This type of networks simply learns the identity function, when the hidden layer and the input has the same size.

However, there is an important feature, which is to apply a non-linear activation function ro calculate $h=\sigma\left(w_{x,h}x+b_{x,h}\right)$.

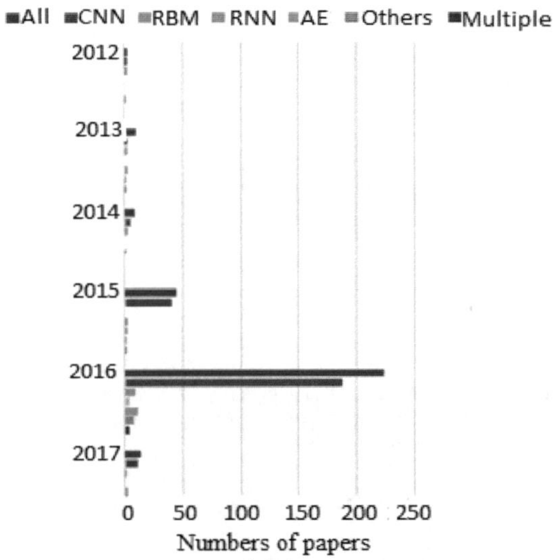

(a)

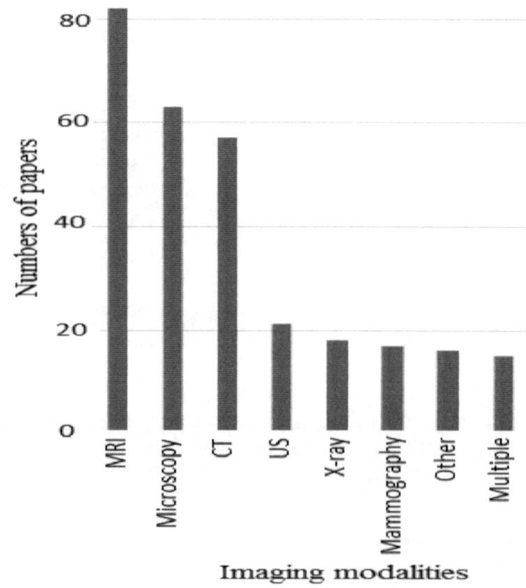

(b)

Figure 1. (a) The number of papers with DL in medical image analysis (CNN: Convolutional Neural Network, RBM: Restricted Boltzmann Machine, RNN: Recurrent Neural Network, AE: Auto Encoder); (b) Numbers of papers and imaging modalities used with deep learning based methods

Constraints on regularizations can be employed to obtain better structures. RBMs construct an input layer $x=(x_1,x_2,....x_N)$ and a hidden layer $h=(h_1,h_2,....,h_N)$, which representsries latent features (Hinton, 2010). The latent feature representation h can be obtained with a given input vector x. Also, an input vector can be obtained with a given latent feature. Therefore, the connection of nodes is bidirectional in this type of neural networks. In an RBMs, an energy function of input and hidden units can be defined as,

$$E(\mathrm{x},\mathrm{h})=h^T Wx-c^T x-b^T h \tag{2}$$

(where c and b are bias terms) for a particular state (x,h). Each layer in RBMs is trained as unsupervised. In CNNs, weight values can be shared so that they result in a convolution operation. The input image is convolved at every layer by using K kernels and biases are incorporated to generate a new feature map X_k. The set of features are used in a non-linear transformation with $\sigma(.)$ function and the operation is applied at each other layer. Therefore, the number of weights does not depend on the input images' size. Also, the amount of the parameters that need to be learned is reduced. In CNNs, convolutional layers are changed with pooling layers, where neighborhoods' pixel values are added with the mean or maximum operations. RNNs usually construct a hidden (or latent) state h at time t as,

$$P\left(Y=y\mid x_1,x_2,.....x_T;\Theta\right)=\mathrm{softmax}(h_T;W_{out},b_{out}) \tag{3}$$

3. DL IN MEDICAL IMAGE ANALYSIS

In image classification, multiple images or only one image is used as input and a single diagnostic variable (for instance, to show that a disease is present or not) is produced as output. Lesion, tumor or object classification refers to the classification of a tiny region in the image into two or more classes. However, both global and local information is required for an accurate classification of these structures and it is not possible in a generic DL architecture. To solve this main drawback, multi-stream architectures have been proposed (Shen et al. 2015, Kawahara and Hamarneh 2016). For instance, Shen et al. applied 3 CNNs. At a different scale, every CNN gets a nodule as an input (Shen et al. 2015). Then, a final vector is constructed with the result features obtained as outputs of these CNNs. An other multi-stream architecture was implemented in (Kawahara and Hamarneh 2016) to classify skin lessions by using each stream with different resolution of the image. In addition to local and global information, three dimensional (3D) infromation was used to increase accuracy of multi-stream CNNs in classification of an object/lesion (Setio et al. 2016, Nie et al. 2016b). RBMs (Zhang et al. 2016b, van Tulder and de Bruijne 2016), Convolutional Sparse AEs (CSAEs) (Kallenberg et al. 2016) and SAEs (Cheng et al. 2016) have also been applied to classify lesions/objects in medical images.

Among the works with DL in the literature, segmentation from medical images is the most common. Especially, RNNs have bacome important in this area. For instance, Xie et al. proposed to use a clockwork RNN with prior information, which was obtained by column and row predecessors of the current patch, for segmentation of pathological images (Xie et al. 2016). Andermatt et al. implemented an RNN (as 3D) with gated recurrent units for tissue segmentation from MR image slices (Andermatt et al. 2016). In addition to RNNs, U-net (Ronneberger et al. 2015), which takes into account the full context of an image and processesses the network in one forward pass, has been proposed. For instance, in (Cicek et al. 2016), the authors showed that an image segmentation task can be performed as fully 3D by feeding the network with only some 2D slices taken from the same dataset. In another paper (Drozdzal et al. 2016), both short and long skip connections have been used with a U-net. In (Milletari et al. 2016), the U-net architecture was applied with convolutional layers (3D) and the cost function that is based on Dice distance coefficients. Poudel et al. proposed to combine a gated recurrent unit with U-net architecture to achieve 3D segmentation (Poudel et al. 2016). Besides, fCNNs have been proposed for segmentation of vertebral body from MR image data sets (Korez et al. 2016), tissues from brain MR images, coronary arteries in cardiac CT angiography images and muscles in breast MR images (Moeskops et al. 2016b). To solve spurious response problem caused by voxel based classification, fCNN architectures have been combined with Conditional Random Fields (CRFs) (Christ et al. 2016, Gao et al. 2016, Fu et al. 2016, Dou et al. 2016b, Cai et al. 2016) and MRFs (Shakeri et al. 2016, Song et al. 2015). Also, patchtrained neural networks with a sliding window-based classification was applied in (Ciresan et al. 2012).

DL based methods proposed for object/lesion detection and organ segmentation have been combined for lesion segmentation. Both local and global information are required to achieve an accurate lesion segmentation. Therefore, a U-net based approach with a single skip connection was used for segmentation of white matter lesions in (Brosch et al. 2016). Also, non-uniformly sampled patches and multi-stream neural networks using different scales was proposed (Kamnitsas et al. 2017, Ghafoorian et al. 2016). In some works (Litjens et al. 2016, Pereira et al. 2016), authors focused on data imbalance (since, usually pixels are from the non-diseased class) in lesion segmentation and proposed to use augmented data to solve the balance problem.

4. APPLICATION AREAS

DL in medical image analysis have been applied with different images for different purposes. For instance, analysis of brain images with DL techniques have been performed for disorder classification (Suk et al. 2016, Suk and Shen 2016, Hosseini-Asl et al. 2016, Pinaya et al. 2016, Ortiz et al. 2016, Shi et al. 2017), lesion/tumor segmentation (Andermatt et al. 2016, Brosch et al. 2016, Chen et al. 2016a, Ghafoorian et al. 2016, Havaei et al. 2016, Kamnitsas et al. 2017, Moeskops et al. 2016a, Nie et al. 2016a, Pereira et al. 2016), lesion/tumor detection (Dou et al. 2016b, Ghafoorian et al. 2017) and also for enhancement or construction of brain images (Bahrami et al. 2016, Benou et al. 2016, Golkov et al. 2016, Hoffmann et al. 2016, Sevetlidis et al.2016).

Breast image analysis with DL is mostly performed for detection of lesions or mass-like structures and grading of breast cancer risk (Dalmis et al. 2016, Arevalo et al. 2016, Dubrovina et al. 2016, Fotin et al. 2016, Dhungel et al. 2016, Kallenberg et al. 2016, Samala et al. 2016, Zhang et al. 2016b, Wang et al. 2017, Kooi et al. 2017).

DL techniques have been applied to for segmentation of ventricles or cardiac structures from MR (Avendi et al. 2016, Poudel et al. 2016, Tran 2016, Zhang et al. 2016a, Ngo et al. 2017), CT (Zreik et al. 2016, Moradi et al. 2016b, Lessmann et al. 2016), or US (Chen et al. 2016b, Ghesu et al. 2016, Moradi et al. 2016a) cardiac images. Most of them use CNN architectures.

Segmentation of liver (Ben-Cohen et al. 2016, Dou et al. 2016a, Hu et al. 2016b, Lu et al. 2017), kidney (Thong et al. 2016), pancreas (Roth et al. 2016, Cai et al. 2016) and bladder (Cha et al. 2016) with DL based methods has been usually applied with CT images and CNNs. In the literature, there is only one work that proposes segmentation of multiple organs, which are spleen, kidney and liver, by using DL (Hu et al. 2016a).

5. CONCLUSIONS

It has been observed that DL based techniques are used effectively in medical image analysis especially in recent years. CNNs are successful models for image analysis. Therefore, mostly, CNN architectures have been prefered and integrated into other techniques such as, SVM and level sets. We expect that DL will become more popular for analysis of medical images and have great impact in this research area.

REFERENCES

Andermatt S. et al., 2016. Multi-dimensional Gated Recurrent Units for the Segmentation of Biomedical 3D-data. *DLMIA*. Vol.10008, pp.142–151.

Arevalo J. et al, 2016. Representation Learning for Mammographymass Lesion Classification with Convolutional Neural Networks. *Computer Methods and Programs in Biomedicine,* Vol. 127, pp.248–257.

Avendi M. et al, 2016. A Combined Deep Learning and Deformable-model Approach to Fully Automatic Segmentation of the Left Ventricle in Cardiac MRI. *Medical ImageAnalysis,* Vol.30, pp.108–119.

Bahrami K. et al, 2016. Convolutional Neural Network for Reconstruction of 7T-like Images from 3T MRI using Appearance and Anatomical Features. *DLMIA*. Vol. 10008, pp. 39–47.

Ben-Cohen A. et al, 2016. Dlmia. *Workshop on Large-Scale Annotation of Biomed. Data.* Vol. 10008, pp. 77–85.

Bengio Y., 2009. Learning Deep Architectures for ai. *Found.Trends Mach. Learning,* Vol. 2, pp.1–127

Benou A., 2016. De-noising of Contrast-enhanced MRI Sequences by an Ensemble of Expert Deep Neural Networks. *In: DLMIA*, Vol. 10008, pp. 95–110.

Brosch T., 2016. Deep 3D Convolutional Encoder Networks with Shortcuts for Multiscale Feature Integration Applied to Multiple Sclerosis Lesion Segmentation. *IEEE Transactions on Medical Imaging,* Vol.35, No.5, pp.1229–1239.

Cai J., et al, 2016. Pancreas Segmentation in MRI using Graph-based Decision Fusion on Convolutional Neural Networks. *Medical Image Computing and Computer-Assisted Intervention*, Vol. 9901, pp. 442–450.

Cha K.H., et al., 2016. Bladder Cancer Segmentation in CT for Treatment Response Assessment: Application of deep-learning convolution neural network-a pilot study. *Tomography,* Vol.2, pp.421–429.

Chen H. et al, 2016a. VoxResNet: Deep Voxel Wise Residual Networks for Volumetric Brain Segmentation. *arXiv*:1608.05895.

Chen H. et al, 2016b. Iterative Multi-domain Regularized Deep Learning for Anatomical Structure Detection and Segmentation from Ultrasound Images. *Med. Image Comp.and Computer-Assist. Intervention*, Vol.9901, pp. 487–495.

Cheng JZ. et al, 2016. Computer-Aided Diagnosis with Deep Learning Architecture: Applications to Breast Lesions in US Images and Pulmonary Nodules in CT Scans. *Nature Scientific Reports,* Vol.6, pp.24454.

Christ P.F. et al., 2016. Automatic Liver and Lesion Segmentation in CT using Cascaded fully Convolutional Neural Networks and 3Dconditional Random Fields. *Med. Image Comp.and Computer-Assist. Interv.* Vol. 9901, pp. 415–423.

Cicek O. et al, 2016. 3D U-Net: Learning Dense Volumetric Segmentation from Sparse Annotation. *In: Medical Image Computing and Computer-Assisted Intervention.* Vol. 9901 of LNCS. Springer, pp. 424–432.

Ciresan D. et al, 2012. Deep Neural Networks Segment Neuronal Membranes in Electronmicroscopy Images. *In: Advances in Neural Information Processing Systems*. pp. 2843–2851.

Dalmis M. et al, 2016. A Computer-aided Diagnosis System for Breast DCE-MRI at High Spatiotemporal Resolution. *Medical Physics,* Vol.43, No.1, 84–94.

Dhungel N. et al, 2016. The Automated Learning of Deep Features for Breast Mass Classification from Mammograms. Medical Image Computing and Computer-AssistedIntervention. Vol. 9901, LNCS, pp. 106–114.

Drozdzal M. et al, 2016. The Importance of Skip Connections in Biomedical Image Segmentation. *In: DLMIA,* Vol.10008, pp. 179–187.

Dou Q. et al, 2016a. 3D Deeply Supervised Network for Automatic Liver Segmentation from CT Volumes. *arXiv*:1607.00582

Dou Q. et al, 2016b. Automatic Detection of Cerebral Microbleeds from MR Images via 3D Convolutional Neural Networks. *IEEE Trans. on Med. Imaging,* Vol. 35, pp.1182–1195.

Dubrovina A. et al, 2016. Computational Mammography using Deep Neural Networks. *Computer Methods in Biomechanics and Biomedical Engineering: Imaging & Visualization,* Vol.0, No.0, pp.1–5.

Fotin S.V. et al, 2016. Detection of Soft Tissue Densities from Digital Breast Tomosynthesis: Comparison of Conventional and Deep Learning Approaches. *Medical Imaging.* Vol. 9785, pp. 97850X.

Fu H. et al, 2016. Deepvessel: Retinal Vessel Segmentation via Deep Learning and Conditional Random Field. *In: Medical Image Computation and Computer-Asst. Intervention,* Vol.9901, pp.132–139.

Gao M. et al, 2016. Segmentation Label Propagation using Deep Convolutional Neural Networks and Dense Conditional Random Field. *In: IEEE Int. Symposium on Bio. Imaging.* pp. 1265–1268.

Ghafoorian M. et al, 2016. Non-uniform Patch Sampling with Deep Convolutional Neural Networks for White Matter Hyperintensity Segmentation. In: IEEE International Symposium on Biomedical Imaging. pp. 1414–1417.

Ghafoorian M. et al, 2017. Deep Multi-scale Location Aware 3d Convolutional Neural Networks for Automated Detection of Lacunes of Presumed Vascular Origin. *NeuroImage: Clinical,* in press.

Ghesu FC. et al, 2016. Marginal Space Deep Learning: Efficient Architecture for Volumetric Image Parsing. *IEEE Trans. on Medical Imaging,* Vol.35, pp.1217–1228.

Golkov V. et al, 2016. q-Space Deep Learning: Twelve-fold Shorter and Model-free Diffusion MRI Scans. *IEEE Trans. on Med. Imaging,* Vol.35, pp.1344 – 1351.

Havaei M. et al, 2016. Brain Tumor Segmentation with Deep Neural Networks. *Med. Image Analysis,* Vol.35, pp.18–31.

Hinton G., 2010. A Practical Guide to Training Restricted Boltzmann Machines. *Momentum,* Vol.9, No.1, pp.926.

Hoffmann N. et al, 2016. Learning thermal process representations for intraoperative analysisof cortical perfusion during ischemic strokes. *In: DLMIA.* Vol.10008, pp. 152–160.

Hosseini-Asl, et al, 2016. Alzheimer's Disease Diagnostics by a Deeply Supervised Adaptable 3D Convolutional Network. *arXiv*:1607.00556.

Hu P. et al, 2016a. Automatic Abdominal Multi-organ Segmentation using Deep Convolutional Neural Network and Time-implicit Level Sets. *Int. J. of Computer Assisted Radiology and Surgery.*

Hu P. et al, 2016b. Automatic 3D Liver Segmentation Based on Deep Learning and Globally Optimized Durface Evolution. *Physics in Medicine and Biology,* Vol.61, pp.8676–8698.

Lu F. et al, 2017. Automatic 3D Liver Location and Segmentation via Convolutional Neural Network and Graph Cut. *International Journal of Computer Assisted Radiology and Surgery,* Vol.12, pp.171–182.

Kallenberg M. et al, 2016.Unsupervised Deep Learning Applied to Breast Density Segmentation and Mammographic Risk Scoring. *IEEE Transactions on Medical Imaging*, Vol.35, pp.1322–1331.

Kamnitsas K., et al, 2017. Efficient Multi-scale 3D CNN with Fully Connected CRF for Accurate Brain Lesion Segmentation. *Medical Image Analysis* 36, 61–78.

Kawahara J. and Hamarneh G., 2016. Multi-resolution-tract CNN with Hybrid Pretrained and Skin-lesion Trained Layers. *In: Machine Learning in Medical Imaging*, Vol. 10019, pp. 164–171.

Korez R. et al, 2016. Model-based Segmentation of Vertebral Bodies from MR Images with 3D CNNs.*In: Medical Image Computing and Computer-Assisted Intervention*, Vol. 9901, pp. 433–441.

Kooi T. et al, 2017. Discriminating solitary cysts from soft tissue lesions in mammographyusing a pretrained deep convolutional neural network. *Medical Physics.*

Lessmann N. et al, 2016. Deep Convolutional Neural Networks for Automatic Coronary Calcium Scoring in a Screening Study with Lowdose Chest CT. *Medical Imaging,* Vol. 9785, pp. 978511–1 – 978511–6.

Litjens G. et al, 2016. Deep Learning as a Tool for Increased Accuracy and Efficiency of Histopathological Diagnosis. *Nature Scientific Reports*, Vol. 6, pp.26286.

Milletari F. et al, 2016. V-Net: Fully Convolutional Neural Networks for Volumetric Medical Image Segmentation. *arXiv*:1606.04797.

Moeskops P. et al, 2016a. Automatic Segmentation of MR Brain Images with a Convolutional Neural Network. *IEEE Trans.on Med Imaging,* Vol.35, No.5, pp.1252–1262.

Moeskops P. et al, 2016b. Deep Learning Formulti-task Medical Image Segmentation in Multiple Modalities. *Medical Image Computing and Computer-Assisted Intervention,* Vol. 9901, pp. 478–486.

Moradi M. et al, 2016a. A Cross-modality Neural Network Transform for Semiautomatic Medical Image Annotation. *Medical Image Computing and Computer-Assisted Intervention,* Vol. 9901, pp. 300–307.

Moradi M. et al, 2016b. A Hybrid Learning Approach for Semantic Labeling of Cardiac CT Slices and Recognition of Body Position. *In: IEEE Int. Symposium on Biomedical Imaging.*

Nie D. et al, 2016a. Fully Convolutional Networks for Multi-modality Isointense Infant Brain Image Segmentation. *IEEE International Symposium on Biomedical Imaging*, pp. 1342–1345.

Nie D. et al, 2016b. 3D Deep Learning for Multi-modal Imaging-guided Survival Time Prediction of Brain Tumor Patients. *In: Medical Image Comp. and Computer-Assisted Intervention,* Vol. 9901, pp. 212–220

Ngo TA. et al, 2017. Combining Deep Learning and Level Set for the Automated Segmentation of the Left Ventricle of the Heart from Cardiac cine Magnetic Resonance. *Medical ImageAnalysis,* Vol.35, pp.159–171.

Ortiz A. et al, 2016. Ensembles of Deep Learning Architectures for the Early Diagnosis of the Alzheimer's Disease. *International Journal of Neural Systems,* Vol. 26, pp.1650025.

Pereira S. et al, 2016. Brain Tumor Segmentation using Convolutional Neural Networks in MRI Images. *IEEE Transactions on Medical Imaging*

Pinaya WHL. et al, 2016. Using Deep Belief Network Modelling to Characterize Differencesin Brain Morphometry in Schizophrenia. *Nature Scientific Reports,* Vol. 6, pp.38897.

Poudel RPK. et al, 2016. Recurrent Fully Convolutional Neural Networks for Multi-slice MRI Cardiac Segmentation. *arXiv*:1608.03974.

Ronneberger O. et al, 2015. U-net: Convolutional Networks for Biomedical Image Segmentation. *In: Medical Image Computing and Computer-Assisted Intervention,* Vol. 9351, pp. 234–241.

Roth HR. et al, 2016. Spatial Aggregation of Holistically-nested Networks for Automated Pancreas Segmentation. Medical Image Computing and Computer- Assisted Intervention. Vol. 9901, LNCS. pp. 451–459.

Samala RK. et al, 2016. Mass Detection in Digital Breast Tomosynthesis: Deep Convolutional Neural Network with Transfer Learning from Mammography. *Medical Physics,* Vol.43, No.12, pp.6654–6666.

Setio AAA. et al, 2016. Pulmonary Nodule Detection in CT Images: False Positive Reduction using Multi-view Convolutional Networks. *IEEE Transactions on Medical Imaging,* Vol.35, Np.5, pp.1160–1169.

Sevetlidis V. et al, 2016. Whole Image Synthesis using a Deep Encoder-decoder Network. *In: Simulation and Synthesis in Medical Imaging,* Vol. 9968, pp. 127–137.

Shakeri M., et al, 2016. Sub-cortical Brain Structure Segmentation using F-CNNs. *IEEE Symp.on Biomed. Imaging.* pp. 269–272.

Shen W. et al, 2015. Multi-scale Convolutional Neural Networks for Lung Nodule Classification. *Information Processing in Medical Imaging,* Vol. 9123, pp. 588–599.

Shi J. et al, 2017. Multimodal Neuroimaging Feature Learning with Multimodal Stacked Deep Polynomial Networks for Diagnosis of Alzheimer's Disease. *IEEE J. of Biomedical and Health Informatics*, in press

Song Y. et al, 2015. Accurate Segmentation of Cervical Cytoplasm and Nuclei Based on Multi Scale Convolutional Network and Graph Partitioning. *IEEE Trans. on Bio.Eng*., Vol.62, No.10, pp.2421–2433.

Suk HI. et al, 2016. State-space Model with Deep Learning for Functional Dynamics Estimation in Restingstate fMRI. *NeuroImage*, Vol. 129, pp.292–307.

Suk HI. and Shen D., 2016. Deep Ensemble Sparse Regression Network for Alzheimer's Disease Diagnosis. *In: Medical Image Computingand Computer-Assisted Intervention,* Vol. 10019, pp. 113–121.

Thong W. et al, 2016. Convolutional Networks for Kidney Segmentation in Contrast-enhanced CT Scans. *Computer Methods in Biomechanics and Biomedical Engineering: Imaging & Vis.,* pp.1–6.

Tran PV. 2016. A Fully Convolutional Neural Network for Cardiac Segmentation in Short-axis MRI. *arXiv*:1604.00494

van Tulder G. and de Bruijne M., 2016. Combining Generative and Discriminative Representation Learning for Lung CT Analysis with Convolutional Restricted Boltzmann Machines. *IEEE Trans. on Medical Imaging,* Vol.35, No.5, pp.1262–1272.

Wang J. et al, 2017. Detecting Cardiovascular Disease from Mammograms with Deep Learning. *IEEE Transactions on Medical Imaging,* Vol.36, No.5, pp.1172-1181.

Xie Y. et al, 2016. Spatial Clockwork Recurrent Neural Network for Muscle Perimysium Segmentation. *Conf. on Med. Image Comp. and Computer-Assisted Intervention,* Vol. 9901, pp. 185–193.

Zhang L. et al, 2016a. Automated Quality Assessmentof Cardiac MR Images using Convolutional Neural Networks. *SASHIMI,* Vol. 9968, pp.138–145.

Zhang Q. et al, 2016b. Deep Learning Based Classification of Breast Tumors with Shear-wave Elastography. *Ultrasonics,* Vol.72, pp.150–157.

SELECTION OF VULNERABLE FIREFIGHTING AREAS USING SPATIAL REGRESSION ANALYSIS MODEL

Yonghee Shin, Jiyoung Kim and Kiyun Yu
Dept. of Civil & Environmental Engineering, Seoul National Univ., Korea

ABSTRACT

In this study, fire incident damage data is considered as a dependent variable of a spatial regression model. First, we investigate previous fire case analysis studies and select the factors that affect firefighting activity. Next, the spatial regression model is estimated by performing spatial regression analysis with these factors as numerical values appropriate for target spatial unit. Finally, we use a spatial regression analysis model to select fire-vulnerable areas.

KEYWORDS

Spatial Regression Model, Spatial Data Mining, Spatial Autocorrelation, Quantification of Spatial Data

1. INTRODUCTION

Recently, when a large fire occurred in the Dongtan Metropolitan of Republic of Korea, the fire damage was increased because the manager of a welding project ceased the operation of the fire alarm, ventilation facilities, and sprinkler for the convenience of the welding work, despite the vulnerable work situation. Likewise, most people in the Republic of Korea do not have a sense of how exposed they are to the risk of fire; thus, insecurity is a prevalent issue. Even the officials in charge of managing and preventing fires have difficulty in efficiently recognizing and managing the risk of fire, because there is no indicator for comprehensively predicting fire risk.

Therefore, in this study, we investigate precedent fire safety index studies and select factors that can predict fire damage. Through these factors, a spatial regression analysis model that can predict fire damage is estimated. Lastly, we will use the estimated fire risk prediction model to select areas with a high fire risk.

2. RESEARCH METHODOLOGY

In this paper, we analyze precedent fire research for selecting the elements to be used in the spatial regression model and collect existing fire damage data as output of the spatial regression model. Next, we estimate the spatial regression model using these factors and damage data. Finally, we will use the estimated spatial regression model to select vulnerable areas.

2.1 Analysis of Precedent Research

According to the Development of Model for GIS-based Analysis and Management of Firefighting Vulnerable Areas(2015) in the next-generation core fire safety development project, which was ordered by the National Security Agency of Korea, a firefighting vulnerable area is defined as a spatial area where there is an environmental condition cannot perform firefighting activities or prevents the performance of firefighting activities; therefore, there is concern about large-scale human injury and property damage in such areas. These firefighting vulnerable areas are divided into four types: Mobility Kill Zone, which is an area in which there is a time lag between the dispatch and the arrival of fire-fighting forces; Operability Kill Zone, which is a space area where there are resource operation difficulties such as equipment division or the availability of fire water; Identified Hazardous Zone, which is a spatial area where hazardous substances exist; and Fire

Vulnerability Zone, which is a spatial area in which there are fire brigade districts and fire safety management objects.

Each firefighting vulnerable area has key factors that define its fire vulnerability. In the case of the Mobility Kill Zone, the key factors are the fire force to be mobilized by the local fire department and the time required for the fire force to travel to the fire area. The Operability Kill Zone's key factors are defined as the space required for firefighting work and firefighting water required for firefighting activities. In the Identified Hazardous Zone, the location and characteristics of identified hazardous substances, and the hazardous substance itself, are defined as key factors. Finally, in the Fire Vulnerability Zone, the location and type of fire control objects are defined as key factors. Each type of firefighting vulnerability is combined to obtain a comprehensive vulnerability assessment of the region.

Table 1. Explanation and Key Factors of each type of firefighting vulnerable areas

Type of vulnerability	Explanation	Key Factors
Mobility Kill Zone	a space area in which there is a time lag between the dispatch and the arrival of fire-fighting forces	Fire force, Arrival time
Operability Kill Zone	a space area where there are resource operation difficulties such as equipment division and the availability of fire water	Workspace, Fire water
Identified Hazardous Zone	a spatial area where hazardous substances exist	Location and Type of hazardous substances
Fire Vulnerability Zone	a spatial area in which there are fire brigade districts and fire safety management objects	Location and Type of , fire safety management objects

2.2 Estimate Spatial Regression Model

There are differences between this study and precedent studies, which collect the existing fire cases and visualize them by finding the areas with a high frequency of fire, or analyze the fire cases to visualize the fire risk according to the fire risk factors. The goal of this study is to estimate predictable fire risk indicators by existing fire cases and risk factors. This research uses the spatial regression analysis model to define the selected fire risk factors as a comprehensive indicator.

2.2.1 Fire Case Collection as Output Variable and Unit Setting of Regression Model

The output factors used to estimate the spatial regression model are obtained from the fire damage data provided by fire statistics of the National Security Agency. This data consists of the types of fire incidents and number of fire incidents that occurred in the administrative districts during a defined period. The factors that will be used as the output variables of the spatial regression model are human injury and property damage. In addition, since the property damage data is set in the specific administrative unit, the spatial range of the spatial regression analysis model will also be the administrative unit of Eup-myeon-dong.

2.2.2 Selection of Fire Risk Factors

The input factors used in the spatial regression analysis model are defined as factors that cause vulnerability of firefighting, and these factors come from a previous study, GIS-based Model Development Study for Vulnerable Area Analysis Management (2015). The factors can be obtained from the parameters that capture the key factors of the vulnerability types, respectively. These parameters include the fire force of the jurisdiction of the fire department, access area of the fire department, structural disorder due to the regional fire fighting force, inaccessible area of the local fire force, unconfirmed fire area of the firefighting area, location of the firefighting water, information on the characteristics of dangerous goods and pests, location information on fire control objects, and use of fire control objects.

In order to utilize the parameters as an input factor in the spatial regression analysis, it is necessary to perform numerical calculation in the administrative space unit of Eup-myeon-dong. In the case of the firefighting force of the fire station, it will be numerically counted as the manpower number and number of holding pump cars of the local fire department. Three parameters; The access area of the fire department, structural disturbance due to the dispatch of the fire brigade by region, and inaccessible area of the fire brigade will be quantified by the area ratio of the 5 Minutes arrival area, and the area ratio of the 8 Minutes arrival area which consider roads with a road width of 4 meters or less, roads with no turning radius. The lack of space for fire-fighting work space will be quantified as the ratio of the area where fire-fighting work space is insufficient during the fire in the administrative area of the town. The location of installed firefighting water will be calculated as the ratio of the space that is more than 150 m away from the nearest firefighting water location in the area. The location of the identified hazardous substances and the characteristics of the identified hazardous substances these two parameters will be quantified as the number of dangerous goods and pests in the administrative area. The location information of the fire control object and the use of the fire control object will be numerically expressed by the number of fire control objects managed in the area. In the existing fire case analysis, the time of the fire incidents will also be an important parameter for predicting the fire. Therefore, it is necessary to divide the seasons – March to May, June to August, September to November, and December to February –and collect output factors for each season.

2.2.3 Estimate Spatial Regression Model

The spatial regression model is estimated from the output values and input factors. To set the output as dependent variable in the spatial regression model, we weight the output factors collected in the previous process, such as human injury and property damage. Input factors are the numerical factors obtained in the previous process. Input factors analysis and multi-collinearity analysis will remove input factors that are considered to be meaningless in the spatial regression model. Next, we need to solve the spatial autocorrelation problem arising from the use of the spatial unit of the polygon space, the administrative unit of Eup-myeon-dong. A general method to solve this problem is to use the spatial error model, which is used to control spatial autocorrelation by the error term in the spatial regression model, or use the spatial lag model that utilizes spatial autocorrelation as one input variable. Alternatively, the two models can be combined. This study will use all three methods and select models with the highest accuracy. In order to evaluate the accuracy, the collected data will be divided into K groups, and K-1 groups will be used as training data to calculate the spatial regression model, except for one group. The remaining group is used as the validation data to evaluate the accuracy. In addition, we will perform K-Fold Cross-Validation, which evaluates the accuracy by averaging the errors obtained by repeating the process K times for different groups.

2.3 Selection of Vulnerable Firefighting Areas

If we estimate a sufficiently accurate spatial regression model in the previous process, and the input variables of the region are known by existing data, the risk of fire damage in the region can be predicted. In this case, even if there is no fire history data in a specific area, if the input variables are collected, the fire risk of the corresponding area can be predicted. The area with higher results than the fire risk can be defined as a new fire-vulnerable area.

3. CONCLUSION

In this study, the fire cases were collected and the fire damage was set as a dependent variable. Next, the fire risk factors were selected from the precedent studies and quantitated into the administrative space unit of Eup-Myeon-dong; these fire risk factors were input factors of the spatial regression model and were used to estimate the spatial regression model. The spatial regression model estimated through this study focuses on the prediction of future fire vulnerability rather than the existing case analysis by studying the risk of fires in specific fire incidents. Therefore, if there is a spatial regression model estimated from a large amount of data, the risk of fire in other areas without fire data can be predicted with input variables. However, in this study, the majority of input variables used to estimate fire risk are based on firefighting activity; therefore, the damage in case of fire can be predicted, but it is difficult to predict the area where the fire occurs frequently because the cause of the fire is not used as the input variable. Therefore, in the future, by using the causes of the fire as input variables, we can create a more practical and comprehensive fire prediction model.

ACKNOWLEDGEMENT

This research, 'Geospatial Big Data Management, Analysis and Service Platform Technology Development', was supported by the MOLIT (The Ministry of Land, Infrastructure and Transport), Korea, under the national spatial information research program supervised by the KAIA (Korea Agency for Infrastructure Technology Advancement) (17NSIP-B081023-04).

REFERENCES

E.M Jang and S.W Lee, 2015.*Development of Model for GIS-based Analysis and Management of Firefighting Vulnerable Areas*, National Security Agency of South Korea. Seoul, Republic of Korea

SeulJi Lee and Jiyeong Lee, 2011. Vulnerability Analysis on Fire Service Zone using Map Overlay Method in GIS. *Journal of the Korean Society of Surveying, Geodesy, Photogrammetry and Cartography*, Vol. 29, No. 1, pp 91-100.

Sung-Jae KIM. et al, 2015, Producing Firefighting Vulnerability Maps Using GIS- A Case Study of Dalseo-gu, Daegu, *Journal of the Korean Association of Geographic Information Studies*, Vol. 18, No. 3, pp 11-20

SeongGon Kim. et al, 2014, Discussion on Formulation Process and Configuration of Fire-Fighting Vulnerable Zone Model, *Journal of Korea Spatial Information Society*, Vol. 22, No. 3, pp 71-77

Chang-Seok Oh. et al, 2012, A Spatial Analysis about Arrival Delay and Dispatch Distribution of the 119 Rescue-Aid Service utilizing GIS - Gyeongsangbuk-Do Case Study, *JOURNAL OF THE KOREAN SOCIETY OF CIVIL ENGINEERS*, Vol. 32, o. 1D, pp 13-22

Hwang Bae and Kim Sigon, 2006, A Site Selection of Public Facility Based on An Accessibility Theory & GIS Spatial Analysis Technologies, *JOURNAL OF THE KOREAN SOCIETY OF CIVIL ENGINEERS*, Vol. 26, No. 3D, pp 385-391

ACADEMIC CONFERENCE CLASSIFICATION ACCORDING TO SUBJECTS USING TOPICAL KEYWORD EXTRACTION

Sue Kyoung Lee[1] and Kwanho Kim[2]
[1]*Dept. of Industrial and Management Engineering, Incheon National University*
[2]*Assistant Professor, Dept. of Industrial and Management Engineering, Incheon National University*
Academy-ro, Yeonsu-gu, Incheon, 22012, South Korea

ABSTRACT

The automatic classification of academic conference information according to research subjects enables researchers to search related academic conference efficiently. Information provided by most conference listing services is limited on title, date, location, and website URL. However, among these features, the only feature containing topical words is title, which causes information insufficient problem. Therefore, we propose methods that aim to resolve the lack of information by utilizing an web contents. Specifically, the proposed methods extract the main contents from a HTML document crawled through the website URL. Based on the similarity between the title of a conference and its main contents, the topical keywords are selected to enforce the important keywords among the main contents. Experiment results show that the use of important keywords based on websites by using the proposed method is successfully to improve the performances of classification for academic conference information.

KEYWORDS

Academic conference classification, Topical information extraction, Text mining, Text categorization, Web contents analysis

1. INTRODUCTION

Services that provide academic conference information are essential since researchers are required to search for academic conferences related to the subject of their research results. However, since most of the services depend on handcrafted categorization, it needs human expertise and takes a lot of time and costs. Moreover, as the classification system of academic field changes, it has to be classified again by hand and so becomes worse. Therefore, an automated classification is needed to minimize such inefficient processes. Automatic classification of academic conferences can save time and cost. And it is possible to construct massive classification system, so that it can provide faster and more accurate information.

The academic conference information provided by most related services is limited on title, date, location, and website URL. However, among these features, the only feature represented topic is title, which causes information insufficient problem(Li et al., 2017). For example, in a conference titled 'The predicted conference Dublin', only 'Predict' is a meaningful. So, it is difficult to grasp the exact academic field using just one word. In addition, in each of '2017 International academic conference on business' and '4th International HR conference 2017', it is a clue that only the 'Business' and 'HR' words could identify the subject of the conference.

In (Xia et al., 2010), the authors proposed academic conference classification method using CFP (Call for paper) and social tag. However, since the tag used is already extracted, it is impossible to classify a new conference without social tag. Therefore, there is a limit to apply to the actual environment. Therefore, we propose academic conference classification methods that resolve the lack of information by extracting the topical web contents from conference websites. The web contents are used as a good solution to the information insufficient problem. For example, in the above-mentioned 'The predict conference Dublin', if we know only two words 'Data' and 'Artificial intelligence' on the conference website, will be recognized that it is related to computer engineering. In other words, the use of web contents provides not only information expansion but also high quality information that can grasp the subject of the conference more clearly.

In this paper, we propose the following three methods to compare the effect of extracted main contents and topical keywords. The first T-classifier is composed of only conference titles, and acts as a baseline for evaluating the performance of others. The second TC-classifier uses the conference title and the main contents proposed in Section 2.1. Finally, TCK-classifier uses the conference title, the main content and the topical keywords selected in Section 2.2., and was used to evaluate the effect of topical keyword selection on model performance.

2. THE PROPOSED MEHTODS

2.1 Extraction of Main Contents

Since the conference web site mostly includes additional information that is not relevant to the subject of the conference such as a menu for using the web, a site link of related conference, various advertisements and images, it is necessary to extract the main content (Lee, 2009).

First, the tags related to text such as <div>, <p>, <span>, <table>, <h>, <ul> and <li> are extracted from the HTML documents collected from conference websites. Second, the extracted tag including words such as 'Footer' and 'Copyright' in Class and ID attributes is an unnecessary content causing noise. Therefore, 'Non-informative attribute list' in table 1 is selected, and tags included in the list are deleted. Finally, the extracted web content is defined as main contents.

Table 1. Non-informative attribute list.

Non-informative list
combx, comment, com-, contact, foot, footer, footnote, masthead, media, meta, outbrain, promo, related, scroll, shoutbox, sidebar, sponsor, shopping, tags, tool, widget, menu, fax, download, register, admin, copy.

2.2 Selection of Topical Keywords

Although the conference title is short information, it is used as reference information for identifying topical keywords from main contents. Because it is meaningful information that most directly expresses the subject of the conference. The keyword selection method uses the dice similarity method to calculate the semantic similarity of two words based on the frequency of co-occurrence of words in the existing document set (Meng, Gu & Zhou, 2013).

The similarity of the two words is calculated based on N documents consisting of M unique words as shown in figure 1. Specifically, the jth document is defined as d_j and the ith word is defined as w_i. Also, d_j consisting of only the conference title is represented by d_j^T, d_j of the main content is represented by d_j^S, and each document is represented by $d_j^T = \langle f_{1j}^T, \cdots, f_{Mj}^T \rangle$ and $d_j^S = \langle f_{1j}^S, \cdots, f_{Mj}^S \rangle$ since the document consists of the vector of frequency of each word. Here, f_{ij}^T and f_{ij}^S are the ith word frequencies of d_j^T and d_j^S respectively.

$\mathrm{sim}(w_t, w_s)$ is the level of the documents in which two words, w_t and w_s, co-occur, and is given by the equation (1). Where $\delta(\cdot)$ is a discriminant function that returns 0 if the given value is less than or equal to 0, and 1 otherwise.

$$\mathrm{sim}(w_t, w_s) = \frac{2\sum_{j=1}^{N} \delta(f_{tj}) \cdot \delta(f_{sj})}{\sum_{j=1}^{N} \delta(f_{tj}) + \sum_{j=1}^{N} \delta(f_{sj})}, t = 1, \cdots, M, s = 1, \cdots, M, t \neq s. \quad (1)$$

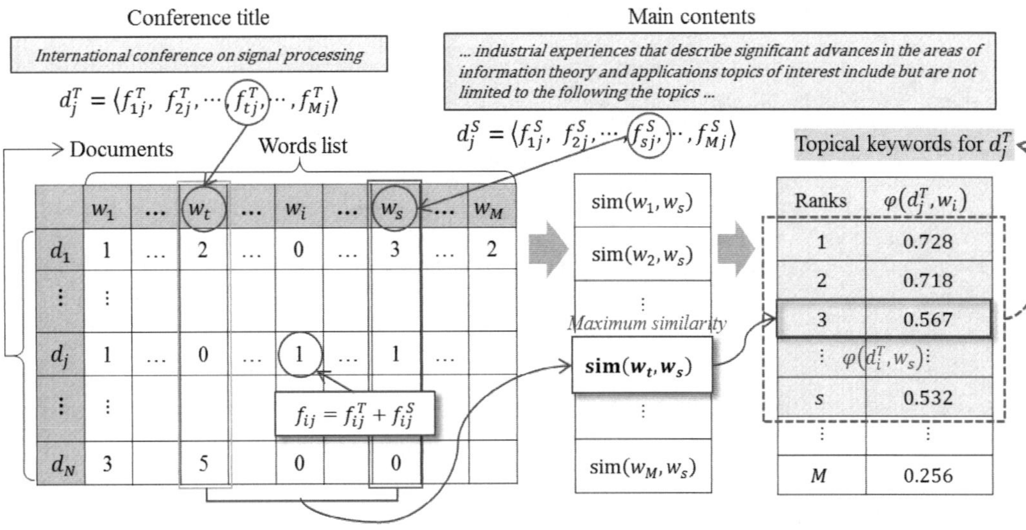

Figure 1. Topical keywords selection based on dice similarity

The final similarity score between d_j^T and w_s, $\varphi(d_j^T, w_s)$, is defined as

$$\varphi(d_j^T, w_s) = max_t\{sim(w_t, w_s) \cdot \delta(f_{tj}^T) \cdot \delta(f_{sj}^S)\}, j = 1, \cdots, N, t = 1, \cdots, M, s = 1, \cdots, M, t \neq s. \quad (2)$$

Then, among $w_i, i = 1, \cdots, M.$, the top keywords of d_j are selected based on $\varphi(d_j^T, w_i), i = 1, \cdots, M.$

Table 2. Examples of selected topical keywords

Conference title	Topical keywords
Annual Privacy Forum	secure, trust, mobile, data, service, network, internet, information, evaluate, digital
International Conference on Foundations Digital Games	technology, system, limit, design, science, industrial, technique, learning, social, human, education, tool, evaluate, community
Annual Drug Discovery Summit	protein, clinic, model, discovery, drug, medicine, network, tissu, learning, system
Partitional Clustering Algorithms Springer	classification, large, visual, data, pattern, graph, grid, analysis, statistic, computing
International Baltic Conference Cruise	engineering, science, management, education, knowledge, business, health, economics, policy, energy

Table 2 shows examples of topical keywords selected based on high similarity. As a result of the topical keywords, it shows that significant keywords are selected.

2.3 Classifier

In this study, we construct a classification model using linear SVM. It is known that input data has good results when it has many dimensions and is suitable for text classification (Joachims, 1998). Since this study classifies into L multiple classes, it is necessary to use linear SVMs. Therefore, the number of SVM classifiers is $L(L-1)/2$ for all pairs of L binary classes (Kreßel, 1999).

3. EVALUATION OF EXPERIMENT

In order to evaluate the proposed method, we collected 7,875 data according to the 9 categories of academic conferences provided by an academic conference service, called WikiCFP. We have randomly selected the same number of data for each category. The categories consist of mechanical engineering, computer science, electrical and electronic engineering, industrial engineering, civil and environmental engineering, medicine, education, nature science, and social science. Each document was pre-processed with a stemmed (Lee & Kim, 2009), and TFIDF-weighted word frequency vector (Sebastiani, 2002). A stop list of common words like "a, an, the, if, for" was used.

The performance evaluation measure of the proposed method was the F1 measure. We randomly partition the data set to Training Set (80% of the dataset) and Test Set (20% of dataset). The Training Set is used to build the representation of academic conference, while the Test Set is used to examine the proposed method.

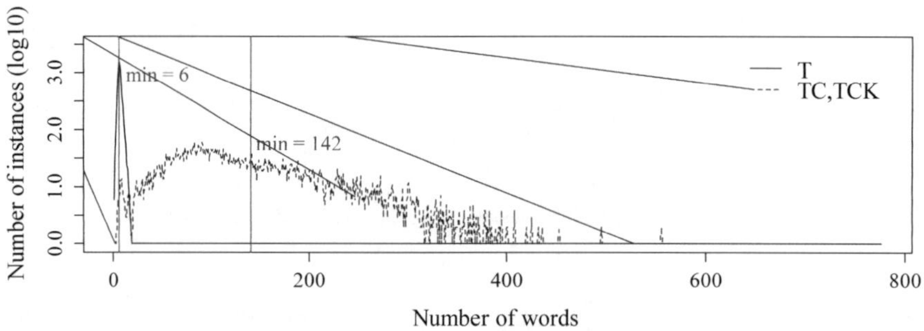

Figure 2. Document distribution according to the number of words

Figure 2 shows that the proposed method has been successfully performed with large information, which can be used to mitigate the insufficient problem. The horizontal axis of the graph indicates the number of unique words appearing in each document, and the vertical axis indicates the log value of the number of documents. T has an average of 6 words in 6,300 documents. On the other hand, TC and TCK documents contain an average of 142 words. Therefore, this result shows that main content is successfully to resolve the lack of information.

Table 3. Classification performances according to classifier

	SVM			Naïve Bayes			Decision Tree		
	F1	Recall	Precision	F1	Recall	Precision	F1	Recall	Precision
T	0.6405	0.6394	0.6416	0.5016	0.5103	0.4933	**0.6003**	**0.6015**	**0.5992**
TC	0.6570	0.6566	0.6574	0.4893	0.4975	0.4814	0.5033	0.5028	0.5039
TCK	**0.6937**	**0.6826**	**0.6941**	**0.5521**	**0.5409**	**0.5489**	0.5307	0.5503	0.5304

Table 3 shows classification performance according to classifiers in the order of f1-measure, recall, and precision. As a result of classification using the most commonly used machine learning classification algorithms, SVM (Support Vector Machine), Naive Bayes, and Decision Tree, SVM showed much higher performance. Also, T, TC, and TCK classifier showed the best F1 value of 0.6937, 0.6570, and 0.6405 using SVM, respectively. This indicates that the use of additional information and the selection of topical keywords has a positive impact on the classification tasks. Therefore, it has been shown that the proposed method not only solves the information shortage problem but also improves the classification performances.

4. CONCLUSION

We propose a method to extract the information related to the conference title from the web contents with complementary data for improving the performance of the classification. As a result of performance evaluation, TCK classifier shows the best performance. This means that the extraction of topical information has a positive effect on academic conference classification. Therefore, the proposed methods are expected to improve the classification quality of conference search services.

This paper contributed to technological innovation by developing a classification technique using information specialized in the field of academic conference. In addition, it provided the efficiency of the related research process according to the research subject.

ACKNOWLEDGEMENT

This research was supported by Research Program through the National Research Foundation of Korea(NRF) funded by the Ministry of Education(No. 2017R1D1A1B03035639), and X-mind Corps program of National Research Foundation of Korea(NRF) funded by the Ministry of Science, ICT & Future Planning.

REFERENCES

Joachims, T., 1998. Text Categorization with Support Vector Machines: Learning with Many Relevant Features. Proceedings of the 10th European Conference on Machine Learning, Chemnitz, Germany, Vol. 1398, pp. 137-142.

Kreßel, U., 1999. Advances in Kernel Methods Support Vector Learning, MIT Press Cambridge Publishers, MA, USA.

Lee, S., and Kim, H., 2009. Keyword Extraction from News Corpus using Modified TF-IDF. Journal of Society for e-Business Studies, Vol. 14, No. 4, pp. 59-73.

Lee, Y., 2009. A Study on Extracting News Contents from News Web Pages. Journal of the Korean Society for information Management, Vol. 26, No. 1, pp. 305-320.

Li, J., Cai, Y., Cai, Z., Leung, H., and Yang, K., 2017. Wikipedia Based Short Text Classification Method. International Conference on Database Systems for Advanced Applications. Suzhou, China, pp. 275-286.

Meng, L., Gu, J. and Zhou, Z., 2013. A Review of Semantic Similarity Measures in Wordnet. International Journal of Hybrid Information Technology, Vol. 6, No. 1, pp. 1-12.

Sebastiani, F., 2002. Machine Learning in Automated Text Categorization. ACM Computing Surveys, Vol. 34, No. 1, pp. 1-47.

Xia, J., Wen, K., Li, R. and Gu, X., 2010. Optimizing Academic Conference Classification Using Social Tags. 2010 13th IEEE International Conference on Computational Science and Engineering. Hong Kong, China, pp. 289-294.

THE ENERGY INDEX OF CHILLERS OF AIR-CONDITIONING SYSTEM USING DATA ENVELOPMENT ANALYSIS

Yung-Yu Wen and Wen-Shing Lee

Department of Energy and Refrigerating Air-Conditioning Engineering, National Taipei University of Technology
1, Section 3, Zhongxiao E. Road, Taipei, Taiwan, ROC

ABSTRACT

In this paper, we apply the data envelopment analysis to evaluate the operation strategy of chillers of air-conditioning by the innovated method which builds the performance index of chiller efficiency according to pure technology efficiency of data envelopment analysis with factors of chiller load capacity and outside air wet bulb temperature. The study will analyze the chiller operation based on the real case of high tech factory, and the result leads to the power consumption of chillers with high pure technology efficiency is less than it with the low pure technology efficiency. Furthermore, this paper proves the innovated index, pure technology efficiency, can use to present the energy efficiency of chillers.

KEYWORDS

Data Envelopment Analysis; Chiller; energy index

1. INTRODUCTION

Modern commercial buildings and high tech factory must use air conditioning systems to supply a necessary office and operation environments, so the study of the heart of air conditioning system and the most power consumed unit - chiller can't be overemphasized. Therefore, many experts have proposed to reduce the power consumption and improve the operating efficiency for chiller. In (Muzaffar Ali et al., 2013) introduced the optimized method of the design of the chiller system by dynamic simulation model and emulation procedure, to reduce the power consumption of building. In (X. Zhang et al., 2006) proposed a novel method for improving the energy efficiency of air-cooled water chiller operating on partial load conditions. In (Lu Lu et al.,2005) proposed a mathematical model for optimizing the Heating, Ventilation and Air-Conditioning (HVAC) systems of buildings by means of part characterization. The purpose of previous studies is mainly on how to achieve the optimal operation strategy and control method by arranging the system components. Nevertheless, some complicated computing skills and professional refrigeration knowledge are necessary to build the model. Practical speaking, it's not possible to support professional engineers to understand how to achieve the optimal operation efficiency. Therefore, many experts have proposed the DEA application, in (Yu and Chan., 2013) use DEA analysis to analysis the energy performance of air-conditioning and set the pure technology efficiency as the operation index, then the authors find the chiller system COP can be improved to 5.83 from 5.73 by water temperature adjustments.

For a more effective raising power management efficiency of air conditioning system, this paper uses the chillers of air-conditioning operation data of a high tech factory to be the case study, and applies pure technology efficiency of data envelopment analysis to be the performance index of chiller efficiency to discover the influenced factors of the chiller efficiency then issue the improvement actions of system operation.

This paper is organized by five sections as the following: The first section is introduction. The second section is method, data envelopment analysis. The third section is case study, a high technology fabrication in Taiwan. The fourth section is the results and discussion of energy index of chiller. The final section is conclusions.

2. METHODS

Data envelopment analysis (DEA), a "data-oriented" approach to evaluate the performance a set of peer entities, it is accords to the concept of Pareto optimal solution, and express with mathematics model of fractional programming to apply the optimal efficiency solution through linear aggregation with segmented transformation. There are two basic model for DEA: 1. CCR mode: issued by (Charnes, Cooper and Rhodes., 1978) under the constant returns to scale, to evaluate the productivity differences with multiple inputs and outputs. 2. BCC mode: issued by (Banker, Charnes and Cooper., 1984) revised the CCR model to be variable returns to scale and evaluate the relative efficiency of each DMU (Decision Making Unit). Since DEA evaluates each DMU by efficiency, so it's suitable to evaluate the performance of chillers. In this paper, the study of chiller power consumption is varied with the actual loading and to consider the scale return can't be fixed, so to apply DEA-BCC model is necessary.

In Fig. 1 CCR and BCC model presentation, there are 10 decision units, and the inputs and outputs show on each axis of X (Input) and Y (Output). The line connected by dots A, E, B, H, C, Q call BCC efficiency frontier line. Therefore, A, E, B, H, C, Q are recognized to be effective decision unit. That means, the pure technology efficiency is 1.

Compare with D and E, once the output scales are similar, only XE input for E can generate the same output with DMU D. On BCC theory basis, define the chiller loading requirement to be the output item, and the power consumption of chiller to be the input item, once the output items of loading requirement are the same but the input items of power consumption are different, it leads to there must be something can be improved. In other words, under the circumstance of the same scale efficiency, we can treat the loading difference to be scale efficiency and the operation management of chiller to be technology efficiency, then focus on the variance analysis of power consumption of DMU input items, to help power manager to find out system efficiency influence factors. Many studies before (Z. Zhang et al.,2011;K.P.Lee et al.,2012; Sen Huanga et al.,2017) keep illustrating the temperature change of outside air is the primary factor which influences the power consumption efficiency of chiller directly, so it has to be considered to be a parameter of the analysis. In Fig.2 shows consumption and output items of loading and outside air temperature. Let's describe by P1, P2 points. These two points present the different power consumption under the same scale conditions (loading and outside air) of two evaluations with input items of power consumption in points of P3 and P4. Under the same circumstance of same scale condition, the power consumption of point P1 is lowest and the pure technology efficiency is 100% and we treat point P2 to be evaluation unit then the P3P4 line means the possible power saving for P2. In other words, the higher the pure technology efficiency means the lower the system potential power saving. Therefore, the pure technology efficiency could be the index of power management under the same output scale.

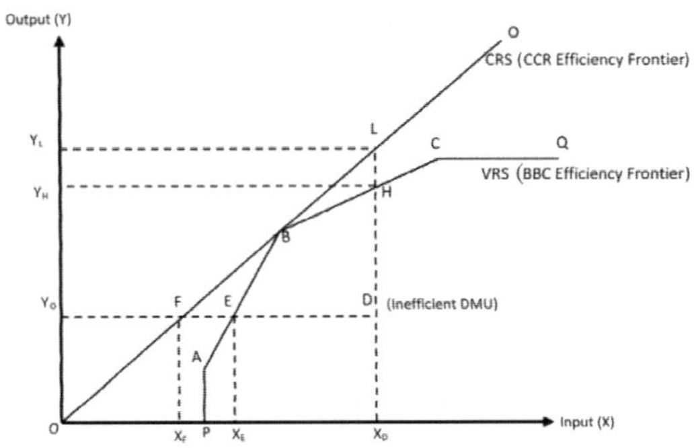

Figure 1. The relation between CCR and BBC Model [Kumar and Gulati, 2008]

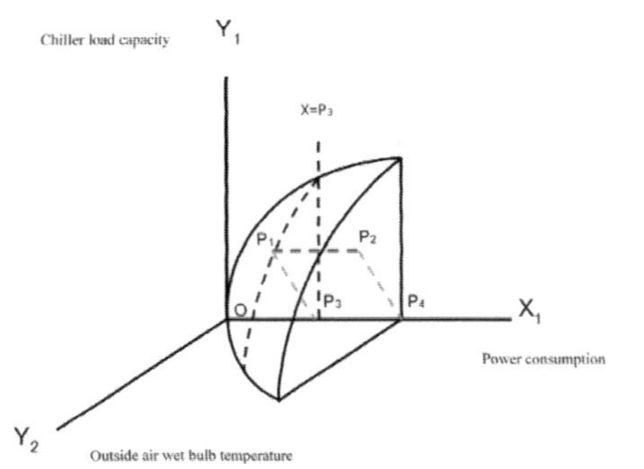

Figure 2. 3 dimensions diagram which is composited by input item of power consumption (X1) and output items of Chiller load capacity (Y1) and outside air wet bulb temperature (Y2)

3. CASE STUDY

In this paper, we analyze a high technology fabrication in Taiwan. The total chiller system as Fig 3 and capacity is list in Table 1 which is composited by 4 chillers, 4 chiller water pumps and 17 sets of cooling towers. The operation requires two concurrent sets chillers to sustain, and switch each set by schedule.

Table 1. Chiller capacity in the case study

For each Chiller	Chiller -1	Chiller -2	Chiller- 3	Chiller-4
Cooling Capacity (kW)	3516	3516	2051	2461

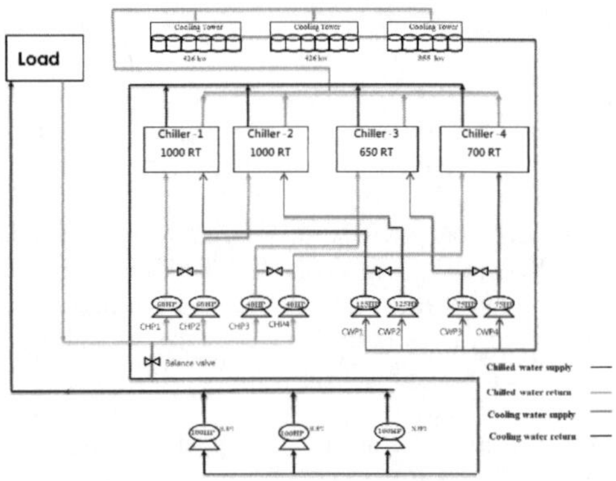

Figure 3. Chilled water system flow char

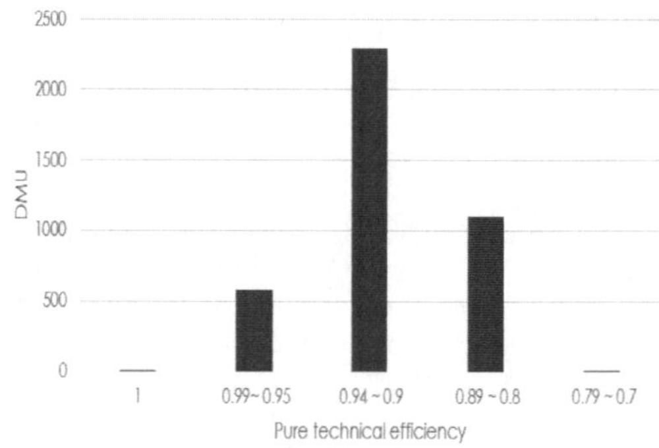

Figure 4. Pure technical efficiency chart

4. RESULTS AND DISCUSSION

In this study with data envelopment analysis with two output items (loading and outside air wet bulb temperature) and one input factor (power consumption), and the overall system efficiency which is equal to scale efficiency multiple pure technology efficiency will be influenced by the scale factor and management factor. Therefore, the management efficiency could be treated as pure technology efficiency and can be calculated by the same scale efficiency circumstance. Based on the data of chiller collected from October to March, and analyzed by DEAP computer program, the evaluated management index is generated as Fig 4. Obviously, according to the analysis result, 72.3% records in the fabrication which the chiller pure technology efficiency > 0.9. Though it illustrates the system runs in well operation most of time, but there is still room for power saving improvement. In addition, on evaluation of system management, it's too ideal to achieve in real operation to define the pure technology efficiency is 1. Therefore, we segregate the pure technology efficiency into 3 groups with > 0.95, in-between 0.95 and 0.9 and < 0.9 for analysis in order to find the method of potential power saving.

For understanding the influence of pure technology efficiency by different loading, in Table 2, the temperature of chiller returned water of group 1 (pure technology efficiency > 0.95) is lower 1.5%~ 1.8% than group 2. By Mollier Chart, the power consumption of chiller is in direct proportional to the water temperature of cooling water – the power consumption of chiller will reduce 2% ~ 3% for each 1% lower of cooling water temperature. According to the relationship, the power consumption of group 1 (pure technology efficiency > 0.95) should be lower than group 2 about 4.5 % ~ 5.4%, and it really shows by real data that the power consumption of group 1 (pure technology efficiency > 0.95) is lower than group 2 about 5.2% with actual data in Table 3. Therefore, based on the theory of refrigeration, it works indeed to find out the factor which impacts chiller efficiency by pure technology efficiency analysis.

The operation number control of cooling fans is based on the dew point of outside air in that fabrication. If we analyze the effectiveness of control by pure technology efficiency analysis of temperature variety of outside air, it's clear the condition of pure technology efficiency > 0.95 happened in November almost from

Table 3. In accordance of the average temperature of outside air dry bulb temperature is a little lower than other months, so the relative enthalpy is dropped in the condition of same dew point temperature, then it leads to a better effect of heat dissipation of cooling tower and the pure technology efficiency is better than other months, too. Based on the view point of pure technology efficiency analysis, though there is room to improve of the control model of cooling tower fans by temperature of outside air dew point, but it still can provide valuable information for power manager to evaluate how to improve the power saving.

Table 2. Comparison of different pure technical efficiency groups and chiller water system running data in 1000 ~ 1200RT

Group	1 (PTE>0.95)	2 (0.95 >PTE > 0.9)	3 (PTE < 0.9)
Outside temperature(°C)		20 - 20.5	
Loading range(RT)		1000 - 1200	
Average loading demand (RT)	1018.5	1040.1	1061.4
Average chillers power consumption(KW)	634.8	670.1	726.7
The average power consumption of chilled water pump	100.8	100.4	103.7
The average power consumption of cooling water pump	54.7	56.4	72.7
The average power consumption of cooling tower fan	79.3	68.2	71.1
Total power consumption of chiller water system	869.6	895.1	974.2
The average temperature of chiller supply water	7.0	7.0	6.9
The average temperature of chiller return water	10.3	10.4	10.4
The average temperature of cooling supply water	24.5	25.7	25.5
The average temperature of cooling return water	27.9	29.7	29.4

It's obvious to find out the pure technology efficiency is worse in the condition of any one chiller running with #1 cooling water equipment from the pure technology efficiency comparison table of equipment combination in Table 4; and the power consumption of #1 cooling water equipment is higher than others in many different loading requirements because of condenser scaling issue after system manager found the root cause with manufacturer. Condenser scaling issue is the most major factor of efficiency of cooling water equipment, and it shows the pure technology efficiency analysis can help to analyze the operation efficiency of cooling water equipment.

In addition, it helps system manager to analyze the management efficiency of chiller by pure technology efficiency analysis indeed. In this study, to switch chiller operation method in accordance to the pure technology efficiency, we can find the highest power saving rate is 9.6% with loading requirement of 1000 RT ~ 1200RT from the results of Table 5.

Table 3. Comparison of different pure technical efficiency groups and outside - dry bulb temperature in 1000 ~ 1200RT

Group	1(PTE >0.95)	2 (0.95 >PTE >0.9)	3 (PTE < 0.9)
Outside temperature (°C)		20 - 20.5	
Loading range (RT)		1000 - 1200	
October (number)	1	42	18
November (number)	24	3	0
Average dry bulb temperature in October (°C)	26.2	24.4	26.8
Average dry bulb temperature in November (°C)	23.7	24.8	N/A

Table 4. Comparison of pure technical efficiency and combination chiller operation data in 1000 ~1200RT

Group	1 (PTE >0.95)	2 (0.95 > PTE > 0.9)	3 (PTE < 0.9)
Outside temperature (°C)		20 - 20.5	
Loading range (RT)		1000 - 1200	
CH2 + CH4 (The number of combination running)	25	32	0
CH2 + CH4 average power consumption (kW)	635.1	668.5	0
CH2 + CH4 average loading (RT)	1018.5	1045	0
CH2 + CH3 (The number of combination running)	0	13	0
CH2 + CH3 average power consumption (kW)	0	674	0
CH2 + CH3 average loading (RT)	0	1027.9	0
CH1 + CH4 (The number of combination running)	0	0	18
CH1+ CH4 average power consumption (kW)	0	0	726.7
CH1 + CH4 average loading (RT)	0	0	1061.4

Table 5. Pure technical efficiency as operation combination of chillers index in 1000~1200RT

Loading range (RT)		1000-1200	
Outside temperature (℃)		20-20.5	
Pure technology efficiency	0.95 >PTE> 0.9		PTE < 0.9
The operation combination of chillers	CH-2+ CH4	CH-2+ CH3	CH-1 + CH4
Average chillers power consumption (KW)	668.5	674	726.7
The operation combination of chillers (Reference PTE> 95%)		CH-2+ CH4	
Average chillers power consumption (KW)	N/A	670.7	656.4
Energy saving rate	N/A	-1.6%	9.6%

5. CONCLUSIONS

To utilize the DEA, the average pure technology efficiency of chiller operation and management is 0.915, and it shows the system is under effective running most of time. But if we use pure technology efficiency analysis on chillers, we can really understand all the efficiencies of each chiller are different. It can help power manager to analyze further to find out the way to raise efficiency. For example, by changing chiller operation combination, the power saving rate is 9.6% with 1000RT ~ 1200RT.The results demonstrate the effectiveness of using pure technology efficiency analysis on power management.

This paper proves the effectiveness of applying data envelopment analysis which is utilized on economics to chiller power management with data analysis. In addition, without extra cost, professional complex technology and models, it helps power managers to manage well by judging pure technology efficiency only and enable the self-capability of best operation combination of chiller sets in advance. Finally, the propagation of the innovated index in this paper is able to apply to other industries' chiller systems widely.

REFERENCES

Banker, R., A. Charnes and W.W. Cooper, 1984. Some models for estimating technical and scale inefficiencies in data envelopment analysis, Management Science 30,pp 1078-1092.

Charnes, A., W.W. Cooper, and E. Rhodes, 1978. Measuring the efficiency of decision making units, European Journal of Operational Research 2,pp 429-444.

F.W Yu, K.T.Chan, 2013. Improved energy management of chiller systems with data envelopment analysis, Applied Thermal Engineering 50,pp 309-317.

K.P. Lee, T.A. Cheng, 2012. A simulation optimization approach for energy efficiency of chilled water system, Energy Build. 54,pp 290-296

Kumar and Gulati, 2008. An Examination of Technical, Pure Technical, and Scale Efficiencies in Indian Public Sector Banks using Data Envelopment Analysis, Eurasian Journal of Business and Economic.1(2),pp 33-69.

Lu Lu,Wenijian Cai ,Lihua Xie , Shujiang Li, Yeng Chai Soh, 2005. HVAC system optimization-in building section ,Applied Energy and Buildings 37.pp 11-22

Muzaffar Ali,Vladimir Vukovic,Mukhtar Hussain Sahir, Giuliano Fontanella, 2013. Energy analysis of chilled water system configuratins using simulation-based optimization, Applied Energy and Buildings 59,pp 111-122.

Sen Huanga, 1, Wangda Zuoa, Michael D. Sohn, 2017. Improved cooling tower control of legacy chiller plants by optimizing the condenser water set point. Building and Environment 111, pp 33-46.

X.Zhang, G.Xu, K.T.Chan, Y.Xia, 2006. A novel energy-saving method for air-cooled chiller plant by parallel connection, Applied Thermal Engineering 26,pp 2012-2019

Z. Zhang, H. Li, W.D. Turner, S. Deng, 2011. Optimization of the cooling tower condenser water leaving temperature using a component-based model, ASHRAE Trans. 117 (1), pp 934-944.

EFFICIENT LOG MANAGEMENT USING OOZIE, PARQUET AND HIVE

Gopi Krishnan Nambiar
Salesforce, 50 Fremont Center, 50 Fremont St, San Francisco, CA, USA

ABSTRACT

The software industry produces a large volume of data in the form of application logs. This data is useful since it can help debug issues in production, provide many hidden insights and is a treasure trove for data scientists and researchers. The volume of the data, however causes multiple issues with querying, storage and maintenance over a period of time. In this paper, we share the architecture and the steps we implemented for efficiently storing the application logs based on the data requirements from our partners and also discuss various optimization techniques adopted.

KEYWORDS

Data Management, Oozie, MapReduce, Parquet, Scalability

1. INTRODUCTION

In this paper, we describe an efficient method of data management for large volumes of application logs that a software company generates, with techniques on how to enable efficient querying and automatic management of the data without compromising on the query time and storage efficiency.

To illustrate the scale of the system at Salesforce, we provide some statistics for the same: in the year 2016, we processed more than 3 PB of data, which contained important information that needed to be analyzed and queried by our internal customers and data scientists.

This paper is organized as follows: in section 2 we explore related works in this domain and compare those with our implementation. Section 3 describes the key technologies we used and why they were chosen, In Section 4, we discuss architecture of our workflow. We describe some of the key optimizations we implemented in our system in Section 5. We propose some improvements to the system in Section 6 and conclude in Section 7.

2. RELATED WORK

As part of the research for this implementation, we looked into sample implementations where log records were analyzed and made available for consumers. Mavridis and Karatza (2015) discuss how logs can be efficiently processed using Hadoop and Spark, but their focus is mainly on comparing the two technologies and benchmarking their performance. In our work, we offer a fully automated solution with architecture and optimizations that can be replicated and deployed at any software company for the purpose of efficient log management, reduction of query times and disk space usage optimization being few of the benefits offered by our methodology. Beitzel et al (2004) in their paper discuss the methods they used for the analysis of a categorized web application logs. The techniques they used involved examining the logs over hourly periods and narrowing down the patterns over the course of a day. They examined the popularity trends and other statistics at an hourly rate, whereas in our work we examine the entire dataset and allow the users the flexibility to query for any period of time and discover the patterns in the logs. We also focus on automation and optimization more than the pattern recognition and popularity of topics in the various log lines and allow users to query and discover the patterns rather than surfacing them upfront.

3. KEY TECHNOLOGIES

We chose Apache Oozie as a workflow management system because of the multiple capabilities it offered in terms of scalability, scheduling and ease of use. Oozie is an open source workflow engine that is specialized in executing workflow jobs with actions that execute MapReduce, Pig, Hive and Java jobs. A key benefit with Oozie was the flexibility to wait for the input data sets. In case the data for a particular date was delayed or not available, the Oozie job would not run and produce incorrect or incomplete output. Instead it would wait for the input data to be available and execute the workflow only if that condition is successful. This coupled with an internal retry logic and the ability to parameterize the execution of jobs based on time stamps were the main reasons for choosing Oozie. In their research paper Islam M. et al (2012) discuss that the key features of Oozie in detail. Oozie also provided the flexibility to configure and launch jobs for a long period of time (a year) that execute as and when the input dataset becomes available on a day to day basis.

Parquet is a columnar format that provides multiple advantages over raw files. Parquet provides us the benefit of compression and encoding which leads to disk space usage savings and also reads only the necessary columns while querying the data which provides memory savings. This format also provides schema evolution which is crucial since we may get log lines in the following releases where the schema has changed and we would be able to handle this change seamlessly. As mentioned in the research from Bisoyi et al (2017), it is a tough choice between Optimized Row Columnar format (ORC) and Parquet considering performance but in our case the storage optimizations offered by Parquet were more valuable than the read optimizations offered by ORC format.

Apache Hive is a data warehouse that facilitates reading, writing and managing large datasets residing in distributed storage and queried using SQL syntax. Hive also provided us with the flexibility of easily loading data from Parquet by means of external tables. The only requirement was that the location of the external table partition had to be specified. Our log data was originally stored in the ORC format then later switched to Parquet format considering space and query optimizations.

4. ARCHITECTURE OF THE JOB

The job consists of on an Oozie workflow that contains 4 different Oozie actions. First is the decisionNode, where we decide whether to clean up the existing data present at an output location. If the job is determined to be a catchup job (which aims at collecting late arriving data) then we do not delete the existing output folder. Otherwise, we assume that the folder contains old or invalid data and delete the folder and its data contents.

The next step consists of a MapReduce action. This task takes the raw log as input data and a set of log record types which are needed by downstream consumers for analysis and returns Parquet files in the compressed format (GZIP compression) as output. We use GZIP instead of Snappy as the space savings for GZIP format were in the range of 65% in comparison to Snappy.

The mapper has access to a list of log record types which is interpreted from a property file that consists of a list of key log record types requested by our consumers. The map task reads only those log record types and emits a key value pair with the hostname as the key and the logline as the value. The reducer has access to release schema files which contain a standard format for each release. This aids in creating a uniform schema and we also take extra precautions to collect extra fields that are added by different upstream users in the spirit of data completeness. The reducer builds a pig tuple, based on the already existing information it obtained from the schema information and stores the extra fields as well. The fields are stored in the form of a bytearray to maintain easy interoperability. We maintain an internal mapping from the Parquet schema to the Hive schema in the code. The Hive schema is created based on this internal field mapping and data is entered from each field in the Parquet schema. The final output of the map reduce job is a set of Parquet files compressed in GZIP format.

The third step is a Hive action. The data created in the map reduce action needs to be recognized by Hive as a partition and to enable this we run an alter table command to add the new partitions generated as part of the map reduce action.

The final step is a validation action. Each job needs to be validated against the source on its correctness. The jobs may run into multiple issues, may lose data or contain corrupt records and we do not want our customers to have their jobs running on incomplete or incorrect data. The validation job serves this purpose. It validates the correctness of the produced data with the source and sends an email alert for notifying the team in case the validation does not pass. Figure 1 below illustrates all the actions in the form of a detailed architecture diagram

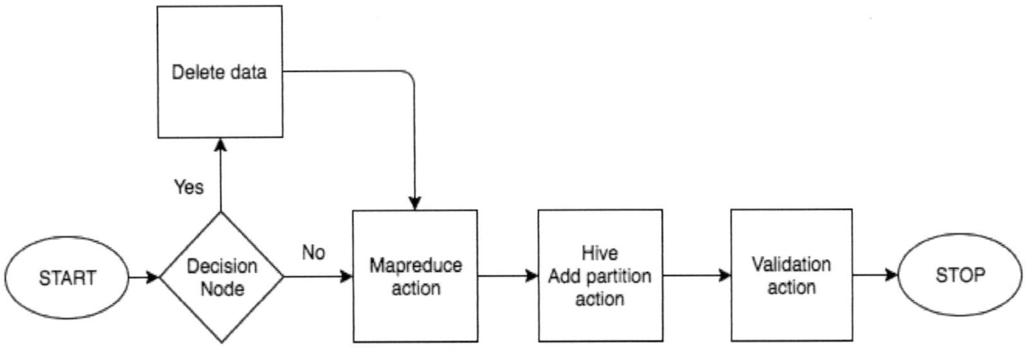

Figure 1. Architecture Diagram

5. OPTIMIZATIONS TO MAPREDUCE TASK

In the initial stages, the map reduce job used to take significant amount of time to complete for each datacenter, about 20 hours. This was problematic since it would cause a significant lag and impede efficient log processing for the organization. Hence, we conducted multiple experiments to optimize the job completion times. For MapReduce jobs, a key suspect for long running jobs are inefficiently distributed mapper keys and is termed as a data skew, which is explained by Kwon et al (2013). An important investigation in this case would be to modify the map keys so that they are evenly distributed and your reducers receive an even distribution of keys to process. This phenomenon can be detected by observing completion times for the reducers. If you observe some reducers completing in few minutes whereas others take multiple hours to complete, then it is a clear indication of data skewness. Once we modified the logic to achieve an even distribution of keys, the job run times were reduced to 2 hours.

Another important optimization is to tweak the memory allocated to mappers and reducers. Examining the counters and physical memory utilized by the Hadoop jobs can give valuable insights into the amount of memory needed. The parameters that you should look at are mapreduce.map.memory.mb, which is the upper limit that Hadoop allocates to its mappers and similarly mapreduce.reduce.memory.mb for the reducer. If you have simple mapper jobs and complex reducer jobs, the memory assignment should take this into account. Other properties that help in job optimizations are mapreduce.map.java.opts, and mapreduce.reduce.java.opts. These properties control the amount of maximum heap memory allocated to the Java process running inside the mapper and reducer respectively. We also tweaked the yarn.scheduler.minimum-allocation-mb, which controls the minimum amounts of RAM increments that the Resource Manager can allocate to containers so that the increments did not need to be in terms of the default 1024 MB and granted us more flexibility.

6. FUTURE WORK

The current data management technique is susceptible to schema changes as the current Parquet schema we use is fixed and a change in the log file format (addition of new log fields) would cause the system to ignore the updates. Though Parquet has the schema evolution feature available, due to limitations of our experiment and time constraints, this has not yet been incorporated. This is a beneficial and critical feature for this project to be future proof and compatible with later versions of log files. Currently, the job is constrained based on the schema and fields that are predefined, but if we build and utilize capability to incorporate a dynamic schema, then it would be easy to include new fields and consume metadata for logs and hence improve the runtime further. As per Mehmood et al in (2016), exploring alternate options like Impala in place of Hive also look promising due to the benefits it offers with the Parquet file format.

7. CONCLUSION

The data management technique illustrated in this paper has been beneficial to Salesforce for optimizing disk space consumption and improving query processing times while keeping the data available for partners and customers to query efficiently.

We have discussed the job architecture, optimizations and storage format for data management and also suggested areas in which the data management model could potentially improve.

REFERENCES

Beitzel, S. M., Jensen, E. C., Chowdhury, A., Grossman, D., & Frieder, O. (2004, July). Hourly analysis of a very large topically categorized web query log. In *Proceedings of the 27th annual international ACM SIGIR conference on Research and development in information retrieval* (pp. 321-328). ACM.

Bisoyi, S.S., Mishra, P. and Mishra, S.N., 2017. Relational Query Optimization Technique using Space Efficient File Formats of Hadoop for the Big Data Warehouse System. *Indian Journal of Science and Technology*, *8*(1).

Islam, M., Huang, A. K., Battisha, M., Chiang, M., Srinivasan, S., Peters, C., ... & Abdelnur, A. (2012, May). Oozie: towards a scalable workflow management system for hadoop. In *Proceedings of the 1st ACM SIGMOD Workshop on Scalable Workflow Execution Engines and Technologies* (p. 4). ACM.

Kwon, Y., Ren, K., Balazinska, M., Howe, B., & Rolia, J. (2013). Managing Skew in Hadoop. *IEEE Data Eng. Bull.*, *36*(1), 24-33.

Mavridis, I., & Karatza, E. (2015). Log file analysis in cloud with Apache Hadoop and Apache Spark

Mehmood, A., Iqbal, M., Khaleeq, M., & Khaliq, Y. (2016, August). Performance analysis of shared-nothing SQL-on-Hadoop frameworks based on columnar database systems. In *Innovative Computing Technology (INTECH), 2016 Sixth International Conference on* (pp. 128-133). IEEE.

ASSESSING MATCHING ERRORS IN PREDICTIVE MODELS

Krzysztof Dzieciolowski and Daniel Marinescu
John Molson School of Business, Concordia University, Canada

ABSTRACT

Acquisition of new customers and selling new products to them are essential conditions for business success. Predictive models, can greatly improve the effectiveness of this task. In a consumer setting, predictive models have been effectively used to acquire new donors for a charity or new subscribers for an insurance company. The success of a binary acquisition model can be defined as an event in which the prospect has become a firm's customer. To determine such an event, it is necessary to match the external prospects with the firm's internal customer base. Methods of fuzzy logic, based on the similarity distance between the strings, are often used for matching. However, two errors may occur in matching: false-positive, when the prospect is incorrectly classified as a firm's customer; and false-negative, when the customer is incorrectly classified as a prospect. These errors introduce bias in the design of the binary model universe. In an extreme case of complete misclassification, the predictive model would predict an event of interest as a nonevent. These errors and their consequences have so far not yet been considered in the modeling research and practice. In the paper, we assess how the classification errors affect performance of the models. The applications of our approach extend to other areas of binary classification such as network security, spam filtering or medical testing. We provide recommendations for model building strategies and illustrate the approach with actual data.

KEYWORDS

Predictive model, matching errors, model performance, confidence level

1. INTRODUCTION

Ability of matching disparate databases is essential to research and applications. For example, if a firm wants to acquire new prospects it must be able to identify if they are not on its customer database. Often, matching is conducted using customers' billing records such as names and addresses. We begin with a brief introduction to matching algorithms in section 2. Our approach to matching records is given in section 3. The design of modeling universe is provided in section 4. We simplify the presentation and extend the methodology of evaluating matching errors of Dzieciolowski et al (2017) in section 5.

2. MATCHING ALGORITHMS

Several algorithms exist to compare a pair of strings. An overview of matching algorithms can be found, for example, in Navarro (2001). The matching algorithms assign a similarity measure that reflects how close they are to each other. Here is a brief review of some matching functions.

- SPEDIS: This function calculates the number of character transformations required to transform one character string into another and assigns the cost, i.e., character swap cost 50, character replacement cost 100. The incremental costs are summed and normalized to generate a similarity measure.
- COMPGED: This function calculates an edit distance between two strings. This is a generalization of the Levenshtein's (1966) edit distance, which calculates the number of deletions, insertions and replacements of single characters that are required to convert one string into another. A match is declared at the confidence level c, if COMPGED < c.

- N-GRAM: An N-gram algorithm typically searches for a pattern of similarities between two strings by comparing adjacent character N-tuples between the two strings, often with N=2. DeShon (2016) have outlined a basic method to formulate an N-gram algorithm. Sloan et al (2016) reviewed fuzzy-matching algorithms and suggested using COMPGED along with character handling functions.

3. OUR MATCHING APPROACH

Our approach is based on matching records between two datasets based on recorded names and address fields. This is done through the following steps:

a) First, records intended for comparison are matched in the small geographical areas, which reduces the Cartesian product of records to be compared to a manageable size within realistic geographic proximity.
b) The records are compared according to numeric matches comprising of suite and building numbers in their respective address fields. This step acts as a filter to remove records with no number match.
c) The names and address fields are then decomposed into their individual terms, and paired. Pairs of words from the name fields are matched, and similarly, for the address fields. The matching process is done via a COMPGED procedure, with a pre-selected confidence level value c.
d) At this point, a single record from the source one dataset may have been matched with multiple records from the other target dataset which is then resolved with the N-gram algorithm.

4. THE UNIVERSE DESIGN

We investigate the effect of varying the matching confidence levels on performance of predictive models in the context of acquiring new customers. New customers must be identified as a new match between the records of the firm's internal database and an external list of prospects. Given the matching confidence levels $c_1<c_2$, we define the respective conservative and liberal-matched universes. The true-positives and false-positives of the conservative-matched universe are the subsets of the respective classification errors in the liberal-matched universe, and consequently: TP1 $\leq$ TP2, FP1 $\leq$ FP2. Similarly, TN1 $\geq$ TN2 and FN1 $\geq$ FN2, see Table 1. Of course, the number of actual positives, APi = TPi + FNi and actual negatives ANi = FPi + TNi (i=1,2), although unobservable, remains the same, hence AP1=AP2 and AN1=AN2. The total of the modeling universe, N= FP1+AN1= FP2+AN2, also remains constant. The nested structure of the two universes in Table 1 will be used to assess the models' performance.

Table 1. Actual (unobservable) and matched events for the conservative and liberal-matched universes

			Conservative Universe (c1)		Liberal Universe (c2)	
		Actual event:	**Yes**	**No**	**Yes**	**No**
		Universes:				
Matched event:	**Yes**	**overlap**	TP1	FP1	TP2	FP2
	No	**not overlap**	FN1	TN1	TP2	FP2
	No	**overlap**	FN1	TN1	FN2	TN1

5. MATCHING ERRORS IN PREDICTIVE MODELS

We assess model performance in the context of fuzzy matching using of two business-related datasets, internal and external, matched at two COMPGED confidence levels; conservative c_1 and liberal c_2, such $c_1 < c_2$. Two different logistic regression models were fit to the conservative and liberal-matched. To measure the model's performance, we define the model's lift as a ratio of the conditional probability of the event given the model's rank R (e.g. quantile), and the overall probability of the event, that is: lift(R) = Prob(EVENT | R) / Prob(EVENT). The lifts were calculated for each of the conservative and liberal models in their own- and alternate-matched universes, denoted as (A, B) and (C, D) respectively. To examine the effect of matching on models, we compare the lifts for the following pairs: AD, BC, AC and BD.

The effect of matching confidence levels can be shown in the difference of model performance as measured by lift. All lifts calculated here are cumulative. To measure the difference between two lift curves, we introduce pseudo t-statistic, t*. Let W denote the difference between the lifts in k ranks (k=20) and S_W its standard deviation. Then, t* is defined as:

$$t^* = \frac{\bar{W}}{S_W/\sqrt{k}}$$

To measure the difference between two lifts, we use log-worth value L* = -log(p), where p is a p-value of 2-sided t-test. Turning to the models' comparison, as shown in Figure 1, the conservative model (A) outperforms the liberal model (D) in its own-matched universes (A vs. D, thick curves), likely, due to fewer false-positive misclassifications. A substantial difference between the two lift curves is indicated by pseudo- value L*=3.39. Hence the own-universe assessment favors the conservative-matched model. Of course, we would want it to perform well in an alternate-matched universe too.

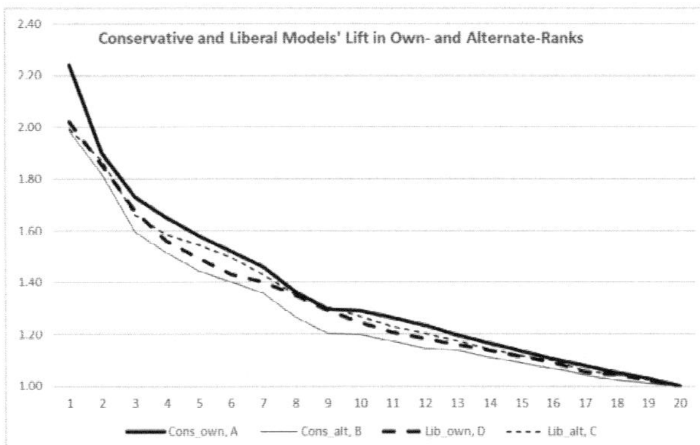

Figure 1. Conservative and liberal models in own- and alternate-matched universes

However, the liberal model (C) outperforms the conservative model (B) in the alternate-matched universes (C vs. B – thin curves). A plausible explanation for this is that the liberal-universe generated model is more robust than the conservative one since it is estimated in the less restrictive matching. As a result, the log-worth L*=5.99 is large and assessment in the alternate-universe favors a liberal-matched model.

As expected, the conservative model in its own-matched universe (A) outperforms itself in an alternate-universe (B) with high pseudo value L*=5.67. On the other hand, surprisingly, the lift of the liberal model in its own-matched universe is slightly lower than its lift in the conservative-matched universe, (D vs C) with L*=1.95.

To gain additional insight into the performance of the models based on conservative and liberal-matched universes we extend the approach of Dzieciolowski et al (2017) to focus on two subsets of the universe: 1) an overlapping subset of the conservative- and liberal-matched universes, where Positive and Negatives respectively coincide, that is P1=P2 and N1=N2; and 2) a non-overlapping universe where N1=P2 as shown in Table 1. The performance of both models in an overlapping subset 1), as shown in Figure 2, is largely the same (L*=0.51) except for the higher lift of the conservative model in the top semi-decile. However, interestingly, the performance of the liberal model in a non-overlapping subset 2) is, as shown in Figure 3, substantially better than that of a conservative model (L*=5.84), which suggests that a liberal matching is a safer choice for building a predictive model when the classifications disagree.

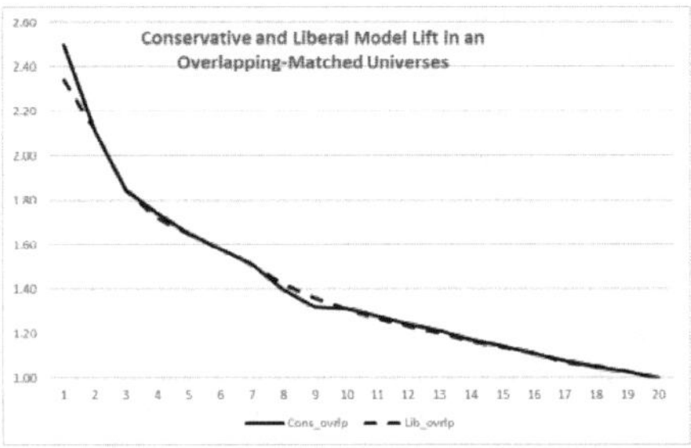

Figure 2. Models in an overlapping subset

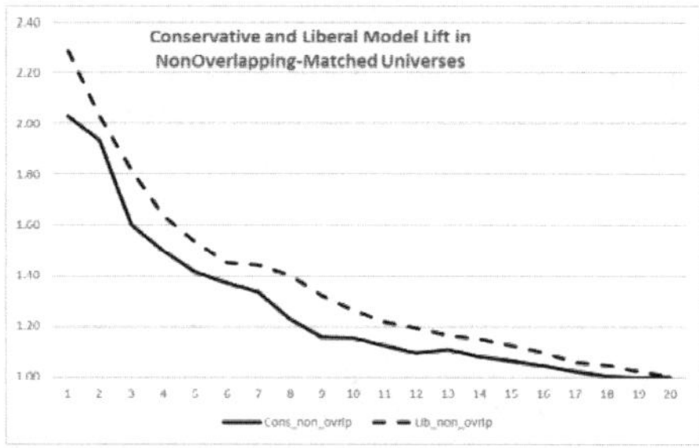

Figure 3. Models in non-overlapping subset

6. CONCLUSIONS

We note that, as expected, both conservative- and liberal-matched models perform in a consistent manner with higher lift in their own-matched universe than in an alternate one. There has been a noticeable effect of matching errors on a model's performance. As a result, the conservative model seems to perform better than the liberal model but only in its own-matched universe. On the other hand, the liberal model has shown to be more robust, and performs better than the conservative model in both alternate-matched universe and in its non-overlapping subset of the universes. It seems that a conservative approach would be a proper choice if we want the model to be highly accurate (lift), whereas the liberal approach is preferable when we value more model's robustness. From the broader perspective, it appears that the choice between the conservative and liberal matching is interrelated to the classical choice between accuracy and robustness, through a decomposition of the Expected Prediction Error, Hastie (2009). To make a rational choice between matching alternatives we suggest incorporating the analysis of matching errors in the model building strategy.

ACKNOWLEDGEMENTS

Authors would like to thank Concordia University Part-Time Faculty Association (CUPFA) for funding of this research.

REFERENCES

DeShon, J. (2016) "*Creating a Q-gram algorithm to determine the similarity of two character strings.*" BIV.

Doklady. 10 (8): 707–710.

Dzieciolowski, K., Marinescu, D. (2017). *"Fuzzy Matching and Predictive Models for Acquisition of New Customers".* SAS Global Forum, 881-2017. Orlando, Fl.

Hastie et al., (2009), *The Elements of Statistical Learning. Data Mining, Inference, and Prediction.* 2nd, Springer-Verlag.

Levenshtein, V. I. (1966). *"Binary codes capable of correcting deletions, insertions, and reversals"*. Soviet Physics

Navarro, G. (2001). *"A guided tour to approximate string matching"*. ACM Computing Surveys. 33 (1): 31–88.

Roesch, A. (2012). "*Matching Data Using Sounds-Like Operators and SAS® Compare Functions.*" ETS, SGF 122-2012

Sloan, S., Hoicowitz, D. (2016). "*Fuzzy Matching: Where Is It Appropriate and How Is It Done? SAS® Can Help.*" SAS Global Forum 2016, 7760-2016.

BIOCARIAN: A SEARCH ENGINE FOR PERFORMING EXPLORATORY SEARCHES OF BIOLOGICAL DATABASES

Nazar Zaki and Chandana Tennakoon
College of Information Technology, United Arab Emirates University, Al Ain, UAE

ABSTRACT

There are a large number of web-based biological databases publicly available for scientists. In addition, many private databases are generated in the course of research projects. Web standards have evolved in recent times, and semantic web technologies are now available to interconnect diverse and heterogeneous sources of data. Therefore, the integration and querying of biological databases can be facilitated by semantic web techniques. The key idea is to describe data in the Resource Description Format (RDF) and to query them using the SPARQL language. In this paper, we introduce "BioCarian" an efficient and user-friendly search engine that can be used to perform exploratory searches of biological databases. The search engine acts as an interface for running SPARQL queries in RDF databases. In addition, we also provide a graphical interface based on facets that can be used to create advanced SPARQL queries. The facet interface is more advanced and novel than conventional facets. It allows complex queries to be constructed and includes additional features such as allowing facet values to be ranked based on several criteria, visually indicating the relevance of a facet value, and presenting the most important facet values when a large number of choices are available. We have constructed a prototype database that combines public databases that have gene-level, protein-level, and disease-level information. The search engine can be accessed from *www.biocarian.com.*

KEYWORDS

Semantic Web, Search Engine, Biological Databases, SPARQL

1. INTRODUCTION

There is a large number of biological data available in the public domain, and this data has steadily increased in recent years. According to the latest Nucleic Acids Research database edition, there are more than 1600 listed databases (Rigden et al. 2016). However, this is an under-representation of the total number of databases because there are also many commercial and private archives available. The number and size of private databases are on the rise mainly due to the introduction of drafts of the human genome sequence and the development of high-throughput technologies that could be used to interrogate the wealth of data available in the human genome, transcriptome and other biological data.

One of the main issue is that these biological databases can be in standard formats such as flat files, VCF, XLS, GFF, BED, etc. or other user-defined formats. Furthermore, some databases are only accessible through an API or via a website (e.g., gene-cards.org). Generally, exploratory searches of these databases require customized solutions, especially when multiple databases are involved. This process is cumbersome for scientists who do not have a sufficient background in computer science and information technology (IT).

To find an answer to a query, a scientist may generally need to access several databases. For example, a query to find a mutation relevant to some disease using the result of Next-generation sequencing (NGS) experiment may entail searching several databases that contain information on genes, proteins, and diseases. This type of search may be a tedious task for a scientist who is not versatile in programming and IT. As such, they would find it very useful to have access to a search engine that can help them to perform intelligent exploratory searches across several databases. A search engine which is capable of automatically and efficiently finding links and relationships between biological knowledge.

Scientists have used semantic web technologies to develop methods of linking diverse sources of data. As such, these technologies can be used to create well-established methods of integrating different databases. Semantic web methods require databases to be in RDF format. Several popular databases are already in RDF format (e.g., Ensemble, UniProt, GWAS) and several projects actively convert popular databases into RDF format (e.g., Belleau et al. 2008; Momtchev et al. 2009). Nevertheless, there are many databases, such as those at the National Center for Biotechnology Information (NCBI), that are not accessible in RDF format. An SQL-like query language called SPARQL has been developed to query RDF data (Harris & Seaborne 2013).

In this paper, we present "BioCarian", a search engine that utilizes semantic web technology. We observe that the common file formats that are used to store information in databases can be converted into tabular form. We start by converting tabular data into RDF format. In the search engine, we provide an interface where SPARQL queries can be run on the converted RDF files. For those users who may not have a working understanding of the SPARQL language, we provide a faceted interface that they can use to explore the databases. Furthermore, we provide several ranking methods that help to identify the most relevant facet values which will narrow the search results and provide better focused knowledge. We also provide a graphical interface that can be used to create advanced SPARQL queries using facets.

2. METHODS

The databases are structured into tab-separated tables. Each database is assigned a name-space. A table can be thought of as a collection of objects in which each row is a subject, and the columns are predicates. With this abstraction, each entry in the table can be represented as a subject-predicate-object triplet. The ith row will be given the subject name $N: i$, where N is the name-space of the database. The ith column of the table will be given a descriptive predicate name, P_i. This approach makes it straightforward to form subject-predicate-object triplets in RDF format. The structure of the database is defined using RDFS (*https://www.w3.org/TR/rdf-schema/*). It describes the properties of each predicate (e.g., human-readable name, data type, and whether free-text search is possible and a facet should be generated). It also describes the dependence of facets, where relevant. Finally, a reverse-text index will be constructed for the databases using Apache Lucene (*https://lucene.apache.org/core/quickstart.html*). If the user inputs a free-text query, the text index created by Lucene will be searched for a match. This search result will be processed to get subjects containing the matches and the match scores. Only the best matches (default 100) that do not score below a percentage of the top score (default 25%) are retained. The subjects are sorted according to the match score. Next, all the entries for the subjects are extracted and displayed in tabs that correspond to different databases. The facets are generated by querying for the predicates of the subjects in the search results. If no free-text is specified, all the possible facets are displayed. Unlike classical faceted searching, advanced queries can be constructed that contain the conjunction and disjunction of different facets. The flow of the search engine is illustrated in Figure 1. Merely displaying a list of facet values is not very useful for the user. It is better if the user can get a sense of the importance of each facet value according to ranks. Let us assume that a database contains N distinct facet values for a given facet, labeled $n_1, \dots, n_N$, and there are $c_1, c_2, \dots c_N$ entries in each category, respectively. After a query, assume that there are $c_1', c_2', \dots, c'_N$ entries respectively in each category. In cases where the user might want to identify the property that has the highest or lowest representation, we should rank facet entries according to the descending order of the raw counts $c_1, c_2, \dots, c_N$. In cases where the user wants to know what categories appear with a probability higher/lower than we expect, we can use the following method:

Let us consider the facet value n_i. We would expect an entry in this category to be selected with a probability $p_i = \frac{n_i}{\sum_{j=1}^{N} n_j}$. We can calculate the probability of selecting n_i' elements from the category n_i using the formula $\alpha\_i \;= P(Bin(\sum_{j=1}^{N} n_j' \;, p_i))$. In this equation, *Bin* is the binomial distribution. A lower value of α_i indicates that the category n_i appears with a higher or lower probability than we expect. We can rank these categories by the ascending order of α_i. Similarly, we can rank facet values according to their "over" or "under" representation.

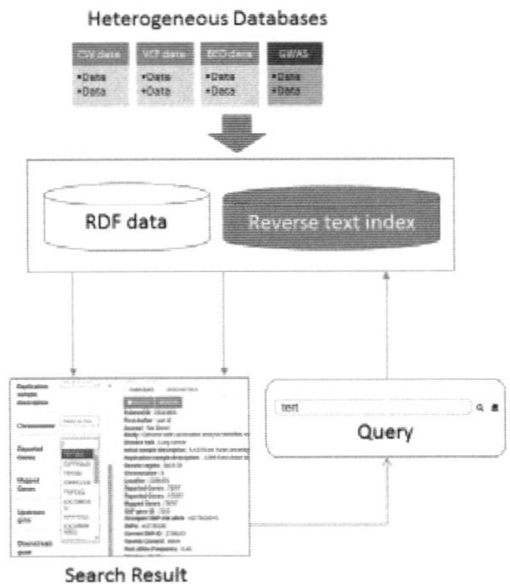

Figure 1. The schematic diagram of the BioCarian search engine

Facets with a large number of values are more likely to confuse a user than to help him or her out. In these cases, we provide options to retain only the "important" values in the facet. These options are based on the heuristic that exploratory searches focus mostly on facet values that deviate from, or are close to, the average. For facet values that are ranked according to their frequency, we select values that are within or outside a given multiple of the standard deviation from the median value in the respective cases. For facets that are ranked based on probability-based methods, we exclude the facets that have a probability higher or lower than ten (10) times the min/max probability. For example, in case of gene expression, the user is concerned with average, under, over or extreme cases of expression. When the user is presented with a large number of choices, we can use this observation to present a smaller set of choices. If the user is browsing a facet that is ordered by the frequency of facet values, the average values can be displayed by reporting the facet values having frequency in the interval $\mu \pm M\sigma$, where M is some positive number and μ is the mean and σ is the standard deviation of the facet value frequencies. By decreasing M, values that are closer to the average can be found. For finding values in the upper (lower) extremes, frequencies that are larger (lower) than $\mu + \overline{M}\sigma$ $(\mu - \overline{M}\sigma)$ can be filtered for some positive integer $\overline{M}$. When probabilities have been used to rank facet values we use a different approach to filter relevant results. If the top probability is P_M , we report only those facet values with the probability smaller than λP_M for some positive λ. This will reject all the facet values with probability exceeding the best facet value by λ times or more.

The search engine is implemented using Perl and JavaScript. We use the Apache Jena server to store the RDF data in N3 format and SPARQL queries. Our server is hosted on a 10 GB Linux virtual machine with 8 cores. In the future we plan to incorporate Bio2RDF databases to our search engine.

3. RESULTS

We used our framework to construct an example search engine that browses several selected public databases. The databases represent a sample collection of DNA-level data (dbSNP, GWAS, Ensembl), Protein data (UniProt), pathway data (KEGG, Reactome), and disease data (OMIM, DisGeNET) and contain more than 1.4 million 3-tuples. A private database has also been added that contains viral integration sites related to liver cancer patients identified (Sung et al. 2012). BioCarian in action is shown in Figure 2, Figure 3, and Figure 4.

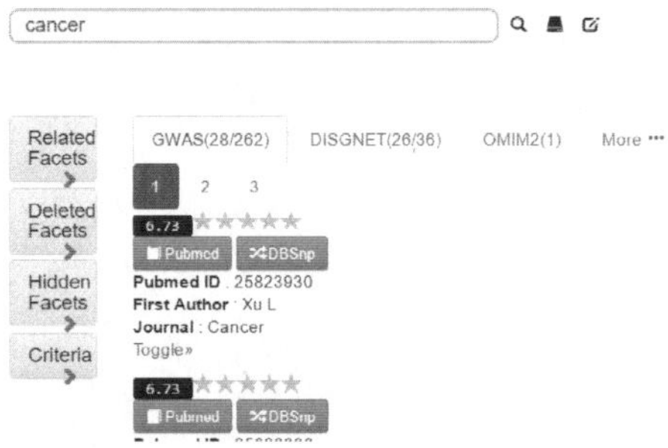

Figure 2. This figure shows the results of free-text searches for the term "cancer". The relevant hits are arranged by the databases in separate tabs. Each hit has an associated star rating and a score that shows the relevance of the hit

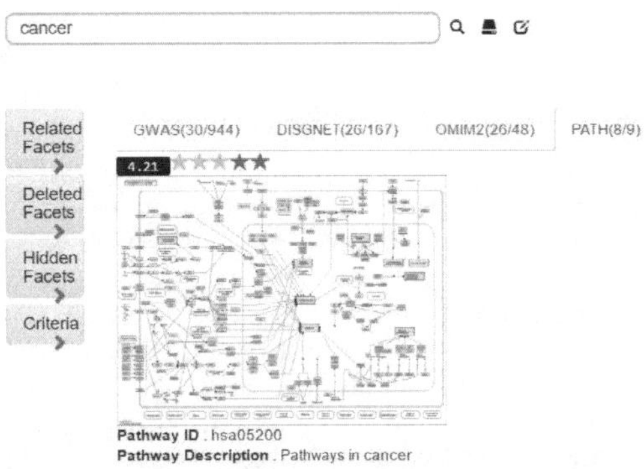

Figure 3. This figure shows pathways related to the search term "cancer". When the user clicks on the image, he/she will be directed to a resource that will show further details of the cancer pathways shown here

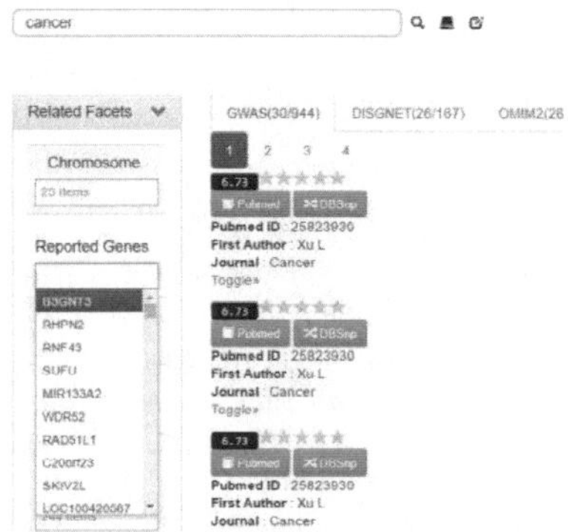

Figure 4. Without browsing the whole search result, users can get a quick overview of genes involved. They can choose genes of interest from the facets and filter out the hits that do not contain them. BioCarian also provides ways to manipulate facets like filtering extreme facet values and most significant facet values to the search

ACKNOWLEDGEMENT

The authors would like to acknowledge financial support received from the ICT Fund (Ref: ICT Fund/CEO/L/21/152) by Telecommunications Regulatory Authority, UAE.

REFERENCES

Belleau, F. et al., 2008. Bio2RDF: Towards a mashup to build bioinformatics knowledge systems. *Journal of Biomedical Informatics*, 41(5), pp.706–716.

Harris, S. & Seaborne, A., 2013. SPARQL 1.1 Query Language. *W3C* (http://www.w3.org/TR/sparql11-query/).

Momtchev, V. et al., 2009. Expanding the Pathway and Interaction Knowledge in Linked Life Data. *International Semantic Web Challenge*. Available at: http://challenge.semanticweb.org/.

Rigden, D.J., Fernandez-Suarez, X.M. & Galperin, M.Y., 2016. The 2016 database issue of Nucleic Acids Research and an updated molecular biology database collection. *Nucleic Acids Res.*, 44(D1), pp.D1-6

Sung, W.-K. et al., 2012. Genome-wide survey of recurrent HBV integration in hepatocellular carcinoma. *Nature genetics*, 44(7), pp.765–9.

Reflection Papers

AN ARCHITECTURE FOR A CONTINUOUS AND EXPLORATORY ANALYSIS ON SOCIAL MEDIA

Diogo Cunha, Nuno Guimarães and Álvaro Figueira
CRACS / INESC TEC & Universidade do Porto, Rua do Campo Alegre, 1021/1055, 4169-007 Porto, Portugal

ABSTRACT

Social networks as Facebook and Twitter gained a remarkable attention in the last decade. A huge amount of data is emerging and posted everyday by users that are becoming more interested in and relying on social network for information, news and opinions. Real time posting came to rise and turned easier to report news and events. However, due to its dimensions, in this work we focus on building a system architecture capable of detecting journalistic relevance of posts automatically on this 'haystack' full of data. More specifically, users will have the change to interact with a 'friendly user interface' which will provide several tools to analyze data.

KEYWORDS

Architecture, Relevancy Detection, Social Media, Analysis Tools, User Interface, Big Data, Data Mining

1. INTRODUCTION

Nowadays, Facebook and Twitter, two of the largest social networks in the world, already have more than 1 billion users and more than 340 million posts daily (Zephoria. 2017). Consequently, the amount of data available is growing every day. With the easiness of access (through mobile devices), users update their profile almost in real time. Therefore, there are many relevant events reported first through social networks post, and only then reported in journalistic media sources. Wherefore, it is necessary to detect this kind of information at early stages. This paper will address part of the work developed in (omitted) project, which main goal to develop a system that can detect journalistic relevance in public information available through Facebook and Twitter. This work focuses on the system design and workflow which has been built to provide users with an easy way analyze posts. The system does not only classify the posts with a relevance score but also provides complementary information that intends to enlighten the user regarding that post relevance classification. All modules can be manipulated by the user in order to obtain the result wanted. Finally, data visualization tools are used to allow the user to comprehend the reasons of each post classification.

2. COLLECTING DATA TO OBTAIN INTELLIGENCE

Twitter data has already been used to predict stock market (Bollen, Johan, Huina Mao, and Xiaojun Zeng 2011), and identify client's satisfaction with negative and positive sentiment (Alhojely, Suad 2016). Recently, several systems have been proposed to detect events in tweets (Alhojely, Suad 2016). Other authors, like Sakaki, Takeshi, Makoto Okazaki, and Yutaka Matsuo (2010) present a system that monitors, detects and predicts the trajectory of events in Twitter. They assume that the occurrence of an event may be detected by observing abrupt increases on the used keywords. Nevertheless, collecting data from Twitter has not been the only aim for researchers. Some authors have already talked about data extraction and analysis from Facebook (Rieder, Bernhard 2013). Manning et al. (2008) provide a generous literature review of technical contributions related to Facebook data retrieval and others offer a practical introduction on information retrieval in general (De Meo, Pasquale et al. 2014). The work in (Gjoka, Minas et al. 2008) presents a system of Facebook analytics. They compared the daily statistics provided by Adonomics (Adonomics. 2017) with the ones reported by Facebook on its application directory in order to test data reliability. However, there are some limitations related to the current state of the art. First, although event detection may include detection of earthquakes or car accidents (which are journalistic relevant) they might be limited when it comes to other types of news (such as gossip or sports news). Second, most of the studies use Twitter as their main data source. Finally, the majority of studies haven't implemented a system that provides user interface and a complete customization of the data to be retrieved. The current paper describes a system for retrieval and analysis of posts from two of the most used social networks.

3. SYSTEM WORKFLOW

Our system relies on three different modules: crawler, data cleaning + filtering and analysis engine. Through the web user interface, it is possible to change the crawling, filtering and analyzing options; The crawler is continuously collecting posts from both (Facebook and Twitter) APIs. A MongoDB database saves all the data (which is structured in JSONs) in collections, depending on the social network. The cleaning + filtering module is responsible for restraining the data to the user input parameters. Finally, the main component of the system is the Analysis Engine, which detects the relevance of each post based on sentiment analysis, entity detection and fact checking features. All this information is sent to the web based interface, where it is displays using more visual tools such as histograms and time series plots. Currently, the system is implemented using the R programming language and Shiny library (Chang, Winston et al. 2016). In addition, Bootstrap and Plotly libraries are used in the visualization module.

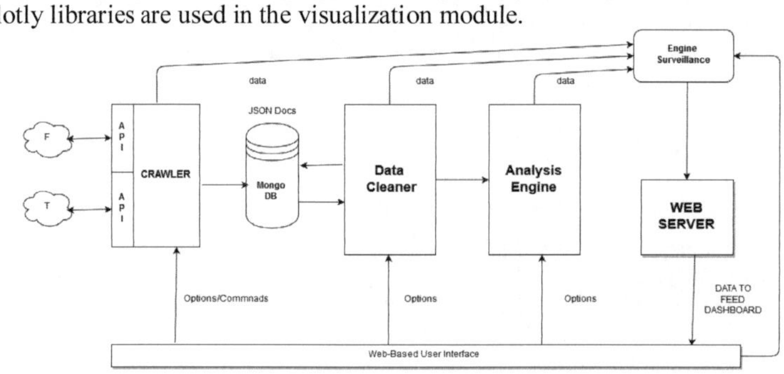

Figure 1. System Workflow

3.1 Crawler

The crawler is responsible to extract raw data from on Facebook and Twitter and is continuously running and searching posts from the social network APIs. Twitter's API is called by sending a single keyword to search through the latest tweets. Facebook does not allow keyword search. Therefore, the system requires from the user a set of Facebook pages to retrieve content from. Then, all the posts that do not contain the keywords mentioned are excluded. We use MongoDB architecture due to its flexibility on modelling many different entries in one single collection (Jackson, Joab. 2017). MongoDB excludes the notion of a formally defined schema by ignoring fields that are missing in each entry. For example, Facebook data is saved in one single collection. However, each entry has information that differs from post to post such as likes and comments. In addition, all the information retrieved from the APIs is stored in JSON format on our database (such as Figure 2). However, depending how many posts the user wants, we implement an "intelligent query". The implementation relies on the assumption that, if the database does not have in storage the necessary amount of data requested from the user, we use the social network API's to search for more. Simultaneously, between the system and the user, the server can detect when is collecting a significant amount of posts. Therefore, the feedback provided is the data available in our database (to be independently analyzed). In addition, the system sends a feedback message telling that the 'rest of the result is being collected' and may require some time, turning user-system relation more interactive.

3.2 Filtering

Filtering is a mandatory option that the system supplies in order to make the data more customized. Users can select individually all options for both social networks (presented in Figure 2). On Facebook, we provide tools for filtering data such as: number of likes, comments, and shares. All these criteria are defined in intervals, which means the user can create a domain of that particularly option selected. For example, users can choose to see only data with likes between 100 and 1000. In Twitter's API, user can select the interval of number of favourites and retweets.

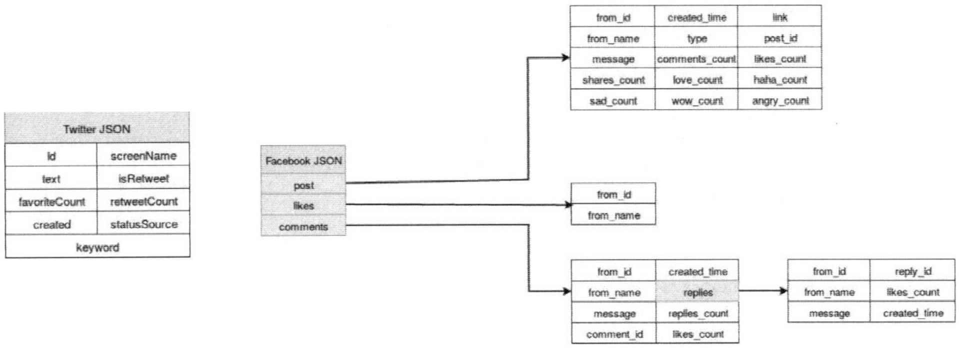

Figure 2. Facebook and Twitter's JSON retrieved from the APIs

In addition, the option of filtering retweets is given. Facebook has the following filters: shares, comments and likes. Regarding Twitter the options are: Favorite, Retweet and isRetweet. There are also filters common to both social networks: language and size of the post and time range regarding the publication.

3.3 Analysis Module

The last module allows the user to analyze several aspects of the data collected. First, the posts are classified regarding their relevance using supervised learning algorithms explored in previous works (Alvaro Figueira, Miguel Sandim, Paula Fortuna. 2016). Then, the indicators which led the system to classify the post with such label are shown to the user in a suitable interface. Since the features used in Twitter and Facebook differ, the supervised models are also specific to each social network. For example, whether in Twitter we use learning features (and therefore we can analyze) such as the sentiment score of the tweet, in Facebook not only the sentiment of the post is used, but also the sentiment of the comments and replies and how they evolve over time. The same applies to the number of likes and shares (Facebook) and favourites and retweets (Twitter). Other features such as the number of entities (locations, organizations and persons), length, capitalization percentage, types of punctuation, domain and number of pronouns are common to both social networks and therefore are used as features in both learning models.

3.4 Visualization Module

The visualization module runs on the client-side of the application and is filled with the data from the analysis module. The visualization is dynamic since that, if the user input changes, the surveillance engine is notified and the visualization data is updated. The interface was built using Bootstrap (Mark Otto. 2017) and Plotly (Plotly. 2016) libraries. The first allows a multi-device adaptation since it provides a scalable interface. The second is a library to create interactive and dynamic plots. In addition, JavaScript is used to restrain the user to input incorrect parameters (eg. characters instead of numbers, large quantities of text). The data can be shown to the user in any step. For example, after the crawling step is over users can visualize individual analysis retrieved in a table; or visualize the analysis such as the aggregation of sentiment of all data in a graphic.

4. CONCLUSION AND FUTURE WORK

This paper describes an architecture for a continuous and exploratory analysis on social media using a large set of user-defined parameters through a web-based interface. The system consists in four parts: Crawler (Module 1), Filtering (Module 2), Analysis (Module 3) and Visualization (Module 4). Module 1 is crawling data from Facebook and Twitter's API into our database. Then, filtering module provides the user with tools to extract information from the raw data. Finally, module 3 uses algorithms to quantify individually relevance of each post and module 4 wraps up the data to the web interface. Event detection systems for Twitter data have being an area of interest for researchers. However, fewer publications use Facebook with the same purpose. In addition, event detection and relevance detection can be seen as two separate topics. The main contribution of this paper is to provide a system with a 'friendly user interface' and good filtering and analysis tools, both on Facebook and Twitter. Simultaneously, we also implemented an intelligent server to afford a good and fast communication between our system and the users. Several further directions can be explored, including the usability of our interface, the display of results and its performance. In future work, we will focus on testing our interface with a set of users. The feedback received will provide improvements allowing the system to become more intuitive and easy to use.

ACKNOWLEDGMENTS

This work is supported by the ERDF – European Regional Development Fund through the COMPETE Programme (operational programme for competitiveness) and by National Funds through the FCT (Portuguese Foundation for Science and Technology) within project «Reminds/UTAP-ICDT/EEI-CTP/0022/2014»

REFERENCES

Alhojely, Suad. "Sentiment Analysis and Opinion Mining: A Survey". International Journal of Computer Applications 150.6 (2016): 22-25. Web.

"Adonomics.Com". Adonomics.com. N.p., 2017. Web. 8 May 2017.

Alvaro Figueira, Miguel Sandim, Paula Fortuna."An Approach to Relevancy Detection: Contributions to the Automatic Detection of Relevance in Social Networks". Advances in Information Systems and Technologies (2016). 8 May 2017.

Bollen, Johan, Huina Mao, and Xiaojun Zeng. "Twitter Mood Predicts The Stock Market". Journal of Computational Science 2.1 (2011): 1-8. Web. 8 May 2017.

"Cite A Website - Cite This For Me". Zephoria.com/top-15-valuable-facebook-statistics/. N.p., 2017. Web. 8 May 2017.

Chang, Winston et al. (2016). shiny: Web Application Framework for R. R package version 0.14.1.

De Meo, Pasquale et al. "On Facebook, Most Ties Are Weak". Communications of the ACM 57.11 (2014): 78-84. Web. 8 May 2017.

Gjoka, Minas et al. "Poking Facebook". Proceedings of the first workshop on Online social networks - WOSP '08 (2008): n. pag. Web. 8 May 2017.

Jackson, Joab. "Mongodb Competes On Speed And Flexibility". Computerworld. N.p., 2017. Web. 8 May 2017.

Manning, Christopher D, Prabhakar Raghavan, and Hinrich Schütze. Introduction To Information Retrieval. New York: Cambridge University Press, 2008. Print.

Mark Otto, and Bootstrap contributors. "Bootstrap · The World's Most Popular Mobile-First And Responsive Front-End Framework.". Getbootstrap.com. N.p., 2017. Web. 8 May 2017.

Rieder, Bernhard. "Studying Facebook Via Data Extraction". Proceedings of the 5th Annual ACM Web Science Conference on - WebSci '13 (2013): n. pag. Web. 8 May 2017.

Miguel Sandim, Paula Fortuna, Alvaro Figueira, Luciana Oliveira Studies. "Journalistic Relevance Classification in Social Network Messages: an Exploratory Approach". International Workshop on Complex Networks and their Applications (2016). Web. 8 May 2017.

Sakaki, Takeshi, Makoto Okazaki, and Yutaka Matsuo. "Earthquake Shakes Twitter Users". Proceedings of the 19th international conference on World wide web - WWW '10 (2010): n. pag. Web. 8 May 2017.

"Visualize Data, Together". plotly. N.p., 2017. Web. 8 May 2017.

ANALYSIS OF KEYWORD EXTRACTION METHOD IN UNSTRUCTURED DATA USING SOCIAL DISASTER INFORMATION

Janghyuk Yim[1], Jiyoung Kim[2] and Kiyun Yu[3]
[1]*Department of Civil and Environmental Engineering*
[2]*Institute of Construction and Environmental Engineering (ICEE)*
[3]*Professor, Department of Civil and Environmental Engineering*
Seoul National University, Seoul, Republic of Korea

ABSTRACT

In this paper, we extract keywords necessary for spatial analysis of social disaster using news and social media data, which are unstructured data composed of natural language. Documents are composed of unstructured data which contain a large number of words, and all words do not reflect the important contents of the document. Therefore, it is important to extract important words reflecting the contents of the document. Based on the extracted keywords, a user selects a sentence containing the desired information, and extracts a specific keyword using an algorithm that recognizes patterns involved in recognizing necessary information. As a result, keywords are classified into location, time, and disaster information according to their characteristics.

KEYWORDS

Unstructured data, keywords extraction, Machine learning, Social disaster

1. INTRODUCTION

Big data has been used in many fields for many years because it can analyze the current situation according to the use of the data and can predict the future. However big data also contains unstructured data, which makes it more difficult to obtain information than from structured data. If the necessary information can be quickly and accurately extracted from unstructured data, a more effective management system can be constructed and operated.

In natural language text documents, not all words in the document contain important or relevant content; nouns or verbs reflect the important content of the document. Prepositions, articles, conjunctions, and pronouns in English are not related to the contents of the sentence. These words are referred to as stop words, and words other than those can be keywords and reflect the contents of the document (G. Salton, 1988). There are similar words in Korean.

In order to analyze information from unstructured data, it is necessary to define the keywords to be extracted in accordance with a template and store them in a database. This template should be made appropriately according to the subject of the data. In this process, we analyze the patterns of keywords and surrounding stop words to analyze the information.

In this paper, we extract information about the Avian Flu situation based on social media and news. It is expected that if we expand the keyword to extract other information in the same way in the future, we will be able to use many text sources on the Internet more efficiently.

2. RELATED WORKS

Text-based index keyword extraction techniques have been in progress since the 1980s. A study on the TF-IDF technique, which is one of the most widely used methods, was proposed by Jones (S. Jones, 1972).

Using the TF-IDF technique, keywords can be extracted by assigning weighting values of IDF (Inverse Document Frequency) and TF (Term Frequency) to words included in each document. Then, the Bayesian Decision Theory or Hidden Markov Model is used based on the statistical classification technique (J.M. Conroy, 2001). Turney first presented a supervised learning-based keyword extraction technique (P.D. Turney, 2000). A method utilizing ANN (Artificial Neural Network) also emerged using not only TF and IDF but also input values corresponding to the presence or absence of T (Title), FS (First Sentence) and LS (Last Sentence) (Teaho Jo, 2006). In the case of Korean, it can define the network of patterns by using the combination between the main noun and postposition to extract the keywords (HJ Oh, 1998).

3. OVERVIEW OF THE METHOD

In this paper, we conduct experiments as follows:

- Data collection: Collect data from news and social media.
- Data preprocessing and natural language processing: After the data refining process, including cleaning and noise removal, the text contents are analyzed using morphological analysis through NLP.
- Keyword extraction: Extract keywords in a document using factors such as TF and IDF. It is necessary to create a reference database (DB) based on extracted keywords.
- Disaster information keyword classification: Classify keywords into location, time, and disaster information based on patterns of sentence elements matched with the keywords selected above.

3.1 Keywords Weighted Values

As with previous studies, we utilize TF and IDF. Moreover, in the news data, the main contents often appear in the title or the first sentence. Therefore, the inclusion of the first sentence (FS) and the title (T) should be considered. Most of the articles about incidents tend to report events in specific numbers. For example, there are dates, times, and disaster damage details. As important sentences are indicated by the inclusion of numbers as described above, we set a value NS (NN sentence, NN is numeral) for judging whether or not a number exists in a sentence. We then set the weights given above as input values and perform ANN to extract important keywords.

3.2 Information Keywords Classification

Based on the extracted keywords, we proceed in the following order. Once a location DB and a disaster damage history DB are built by using keywords based on key words and documents containing existing disaster details, the damage history DB is constructed based on past history. Keywords that are adjacent to a number can represent the detail of an accident; therefore, we divide the keywords according to whether they are adjacent to the number. Numbers and non-adjacent keywords are categorized by the <LOC> and <Dmg> keywords, in contrast to the database you have built. <LOC> keywords and <Dmg> keywords are location keywords and damage classification keywords respectively, and <unit> keywords include date, time, and damage details information. Flowchart is shown in Figure 1.

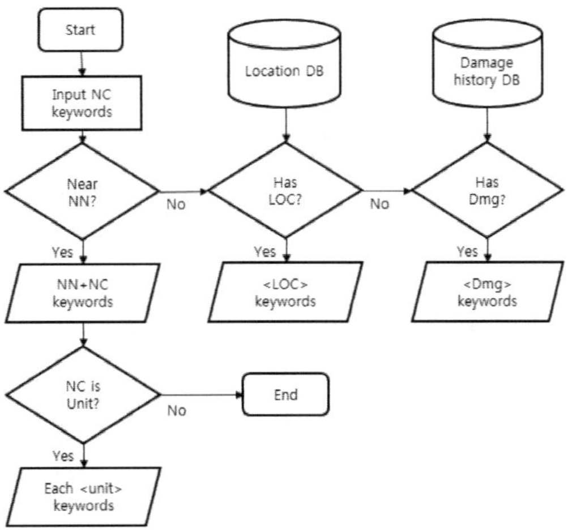

Figure 1. Flowchart of keyword classification

4. DATA AND ANALYSIS

We collected news articles from News Chosun from November 12, 2016 to January 22, 2017, which coincided with the outbreak of Avian Influenza in Korea. A total of 685 documents were collected and analyzed using the statistical open source program R.

First, using SVM for the document classification, we sorted out 51 documents that fit the subject. The SVM used a classification scheme based on the similarity of the document using the TF-IDF value of the document. After constructing a Term-Document Matrix, which constructs each keyword weight in the 51 documents, ANN is performed to extract the keywords from the information.

The extracted keywords are categorized and stored as information keywords in the order described above.

5. CONCLUSION

In this paper, only 51 proper documents were collected from 685 source documents. Therefore, the accuracy of keyword classification could not be validated. We collected additional data after January 22, 2017 onwards and have added about 700 documents. In addition, some errors were induced due to the incomplete Korean natural language processing package in R. These errors can be reduced by the development of additional packages or the use of other programs in the future. This process can also be applied to Twitter data or other social media data through additional DB accumulation. It is expected that more accurate extraction will be possible if the deep learning algorithm used in artificial intelligence is added.

ACKNOWLEDGEMENT

This research, 'Geospatial Big Data Management, Analysis and Service Platform Technology Development', was supported by the MOLIT (The Ministry of Land, Infrastructure and Transport), Korea, under the national spatial information research program supervised by the KAIA (Korea Agency for Infrastructure Technology Advancement) (17NSIP-B081023-04).

REFERENCES

Journal

G. Salton and C.Buckley, 1988, Term Weighting Approaches in Automatic Text Retrieval, *Information Processing and Management*, Vol 24 No 5, pp 513-523.

S. Jones, 1972, A statistical interpretation of term specificity and its application in retrieval. *Journal of Documentation*, Vol 28 No 1, pp 11–21.

P.D. Turney, 2000, Learning Algorithms for Keyphrase Extraction, *Information Retrieval*, Vol 2 Issue 4, pp 303–336.

Conference paper or contributed volume

J.M. Conroy and D,P, O'leary, 2001, Text summarization via hidden Markov models, *SIGIR '01 Proceedings of the 24th annual international ACM SIGIR conference on Research and development in information retrieval*, New Orleans, USA, pp 406-407.

T.H. Jo. et al, 2006, Keyword Extraction from Documents Using a Neural Network Model, *International Conference on Hybrid Information Technology*, Cheju Island, Korea, pp 194-197.

H.J Oh. Et al, 1998, An Information Extraction System Using Finite State Automata, *The 10th Annual Conference on Human and Cognitive Language Technology*, Seoul, Korea, pp 97-194.

J.H Yang. et al, 2016, A proposal for construction of a Floor Noise Map using Web Scraping, 2016 Conference Korean Society for GeoSpatial Information Science, Gunsan, Korea, pp 185-187.

Posters

PHYSICALLY-BASED LINEAR BLEND SKINNING

YoungBeom Kim[1] and JungHyun Han[2]
[1]*Korea Electronics Technology Institute, Seoul, Korea*
[2]*Department of Computer Science and Engineering, Korea University, Seoul, Korea*

ABSTRACT

This paper proposes an example-based linear blend skinning system that incorporates the torques applied to the skeletal joints. For this purpose, deformation gradient predictors are trained using a set of examples with the minimum torque and another set with the maximum torque. The run-time algorithm takes an animated skeleton and joint torques as input. It computes the deformation gradients from the predictors. They are then combined with torque-based blending functions. The functions are trained at the preprocessing stage using a set of skeleton-mesh-torque examples with the aid of statistical analysis. The experimental results show that the proposed system runs at real-time and produces quite realistic skinned meshes based on the input torques.

KEYWORDS

Computer animation, linear blend skinning, skeletal joints, torques

1. INTRODUCTION

Geometric skinning works with a polygonal mesh, a skeleton, and bone weights for every vertex of the mesh. Linear blend skinning (LBS) (Lewis et al. 2000) is the most pervasive geometric skinning technique used in real-time applications. It transforms each vertex with a linear blend of bone transforms. This paper extends the LBS with torques applied to the joints. Clearly explain the nature of the problem, previous work, purpose, and contribution of the paper.

2. RUNTIME SYSTEM

Torque-integrated skinning proposed in this paper uses two deformation gradient predictors. One is trained using the examples generated with the minimum torque. It is denoted by $Dmin(\mathbf{q})$. The other is trained using the examples with the maximum torque and is denoted by $Dmax(\mathbf{q})$.

Shown below is the run-time system built upon $Dmin(\mathbf{q})$ and $Dmax(\mathbf{q})$. The system takes animated skeleton $\mathbf{q}$ and joint torque τ as input. It computes the deformation gradients, $Dmin$ and $Dmax$, using $Dmin(\mathbf{q})$ and $Dmax(\mathbf{q})$, respectively. They are then blended. The result is the torque-based deformation gradient, which finally produces the deformed mesh $\mathbf{y}(\mathbf{q}, \tau)$.

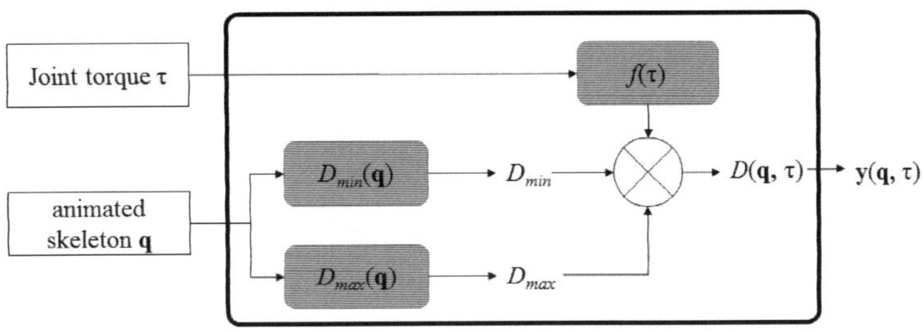

Figure 1. System overview

3. EXPERIMENTS AND DISCUSSION

As typically done for skinning, the joints affecting each vertex are designated at the authoring stage. In addition, the joints to which torques are applied are specified. When a dumbbell is lifted, for example, the elbow needs torque and affects the vertices of the upper arm and forearm. The following figure shows the surfaces deformed with varying torques. The character surfaces are reconstructed at real-time.

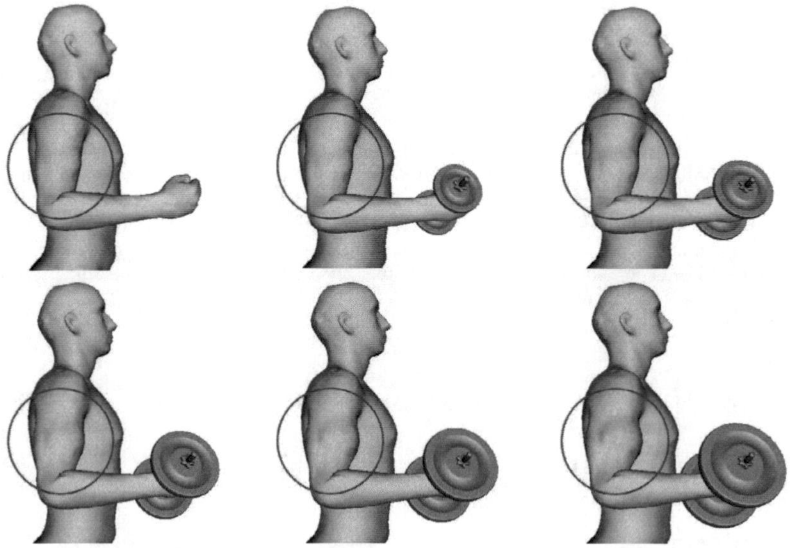

Figure 2. Reconstruction results

4. CONCLUSION

The torque-integrated example-based skinning has been tested on the single joints. In reality, however, torques are often exerted on multiple joints. We are currently investigating how the proposed system can be extended to cope with multi-joint torques. It can be also extended if the anatomic data of human is considered. The anatomy and physics based simulation methods (Lee et al. 2009, Si et al. 2014) can be used as skeleton-mesh-torque example generator.

ACKNOWLEDGEMENT

This work was supported by Institute for Information & communications Technology Promotion (IITP) grant funded by the Korea government (MSIP) (No.R0115-16-1011). J. Han is the corresponding author.

REFERENCES

Lee, S. et al, 2009. Comprehensive Biomechanical Modeling and Simulation of the Upper Body. In ACM Transactions on Graphics, Vol. 28, No. 4, pp. 99:1–99:17.

Lewis, J. et al, 2000. Pose Space Deformation: A Unified Approach to Shape Interpolation and Skeleton-driven Deformation. Proceedings of SIGGRAPH. New Orleans, USA, pp. 165–172.

Si, W. et al, 2014. Realistic Biomechanical Simulation and Control of Human Swimming. In ACM Transactions on Graphics, Vol. 34, No. 1, pp. 10:1–10:15.

TOWARDS SUB-PIXEL DISTANCE MEASURES FOR DISTANCE TRANSFORMATIONS

Ingemar Ragnemalm
Information Coding Group, Dept of EE, Linköping University, 581 83 LINKÖPING, Sweden

ABSTRACT

Distance Transformations are usually defined for binary images, and therefore subject to sampling noise. This paper presents a distance correction that can be applied to any existing distance transform algorithm to achieve sub-pixel accuracy, and evaluates the result. Measurements display a significant improvement in precision.

KEYWORDS

Distance function, Distance transform, Euclidean, sub-pixel

1. INTRODUCTION

A distance transformation (DT) is traditionally defined as a transformation taking a binary image as input, generating a distance map as output. This is an image where each non-object pixel holds the distance to the closest object pixel. This means that most DTs are defined as the distance to the center of an object pixel, which is really a rough approximation for the distance to the edge between object and background.

Errors of DTs have been thoroughly investigated. The original City Block transform by Rosenfeld & Pfalz (1966) has an error that is 29% of the distance. The original Euclidean Distance Transform (EDT) (Danielsson 1980) has a maximum error of 0.09 pixel distances. Finally, error-free EDT (Rutowitz 1989, Ragnemalm 1989, Paglieroni 1992, Fabbri et. al. 2008) are error-free in this context. However, that refers to the distance to the closest object pixel, not the edge.

In order to overcome this limitation, Satherly and Jones (2001) initialize their (in this case 3D) DT by assigning vectors to the actual surface. The calculation is made from data available before thresholding, with an approach based on splitting voxels into tetrahedra. Another approach is made by Gustavson and Strand (2011) who use the grayscale information of anti-aliased images to estimate the distance to the edge.

This paper covers yet another method for producing sub-pixel accuracy, namely correcting the error of the distance in binary images. In this paper, we will present methods to make estimates of the distance to the edges of binary images, that are applied to DT algorithms.

2. A SUB-PIXEL CORRECTION FOR DISTANCE TRANSFORMATIONS

In order to reduce the errors from sampling, we need some kind of sub-pixel edge information. Sub-pixel methods are common for other problems, but DTs have usually been working on pixel-bound edges.

Solving this problem working entirely from binary data has not, to our knowledge, been studied before. There are a few possible approaches. One would be to do an anti-aliasing post-processing (Jimenez et. al. 2011), which can then be processed by the algorithm by Gustavson and Strand (2011).

This, however, would be a multi-pass solution, taking the detour over grayscale coverage. We will here present a solution that immediately produces a sub-pixel distance correction. Two variants have been examined, one with a rough measure but simple computations, and one that is more complex but with a better estimate. We also test a global -0.5 offset. Object pixels are considered inside the object and therefore have distance 0. Then a distance estimate is made for background pixels along the border.

Method 1: Detecting 4- and 8-neighbor object pixels

With this method, two tests are made, for background pixels only. The first tests whether a pixel has any 4-neighbor object pixel. If so, the distance is 0.5. Otherwise, a test is made for diagonal neighbors, and if any such object pixel is found, the distance is 1.10. These values are made according to the geometry and measurements in Figure 1.

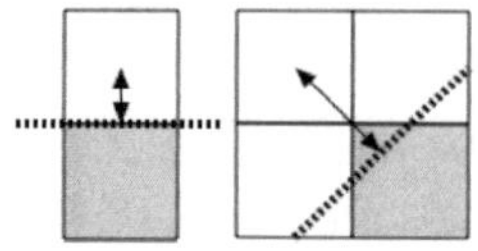

Figure 1. Corrected distance, method 1, with assumed edge marked. Left: axis aligned neighbor, distance 0.5. Right: diagonal neighbor, $1.10 \approx 3/(2*\text{sqrt}(2))$

These corrected distances are both made assuming a straight edge, which makes the edge marked in Figure 1 the only possible guess when inspecting single neighbors.

Method 2: Neighborhood table

In this method, a 3x3 neighborhood is used to produce a 256 entry table, partially shown in Figure 2.

1: 0.5	17: 0.5	33: 0.5	49: 0.5	65: 0.5	81: 0.5	97: 0.5	113: 0.39
2: 1.10	18: 0.5	34: 1.10	50: 0.75	66: 0.5	82: 0.5	98: 0.75	114: 0.39
3: 0.75	19: 0.5	35: 0.75	51: 0.75	67: 0.5	83: 0.5	99: 0.75	115: 0.39
4: 0.5	20: 0.5	36: 0.5	52: 0.5	68: 0.5	84: 0.5	100: 0.5	116: 0.39
5: 0.5	21: 0.5	37: 0.5	53: 0.5	69: 0.5	85: 0.5	101: 0.5	117: 0.39
6: 0.75	22: 0.5	38: 0.75	54: 0.75	70: 0.5	86: 0.5	102: 0.75	118: 0.39
7: 0.39	23: 0.39	39: 0.39	55: 0.39	71: 0.39	87: 0.39	103: 0.39	119: 0.39
8: 1.10	24: 0.75	40: 1.10	56: 0.49	72: 0.5	88: 0.5	104: 0.75	120: 0.15
9: 0.5	25: 0.5	41: 0.5	57: 0.49	73: 0.5	89: 0.5	105: 0.5	121: 0.15
10: 1.10	26: 0.75	42: 1.10	58: 0.49	74: 0.5	90: 0.5	106: 0.75	122: 0.15
11: 0.75	27: 0.75	43: 0.75	59: 0.49	75: 0.5	91: 0.5	107: 0.75	123: 0.15
12: 0.75	28: 0.39	44: 0.75	60: 0.15	76: 0.6	92: 0.39	108: 0.75	124: 0.15

Figure 2. A part of our look-up table for distances for all possible 3x3 neighborhoods

In order to produce this table, the following method was used. In the 3x3 neighborhood, lines were produced at varying angles, denoted α, and a varying distance to the center of the center pixel, denoted r. The angle as well as the distance were varied in constant steps, the angle from 0 to 2π and the distance from 0 to sqrt(2)*3/2, the maximum distance within the 3x3 neighborhood from center to the farthest corner of the pixels. This produces an arbitrary number of cases depending on resolution. We chose 10000 steps for each, with linear spacing, resulting in 10^8 cases. The geometry is illustrated in Figure 3.

For each case, the eight neighbors were inspected, in order to find which ones were on the far side of the line, which are considered object pixels. For every constellation of object pixels, the average of the distance r is calculated. This gives us a good estimate for the distance value, assuming that the edge is straight.

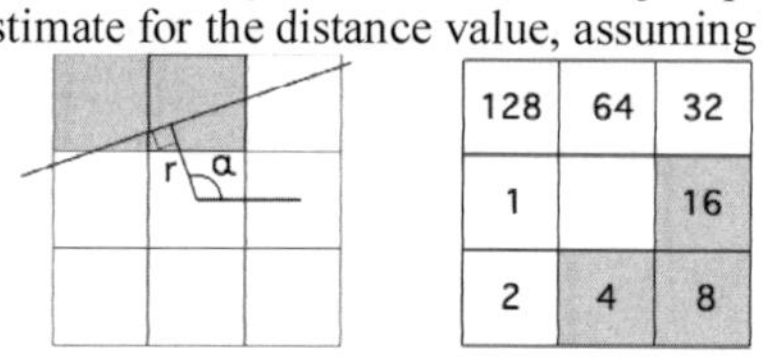

Figure 3. Left: Geometry for measuring edge distances for various arrangements of object pixels. Right: Encoding of neighbor pixels (shading illustrates the neighbor 28)

From this, we create a lookup table entries for all resulting object pixel constellations. This will not cover all 256 combinations of neighbors, only the ones that corresponds to a single straight edge. In order to get a reasonable measure for other cases, we have identified cases that can be constructed as combinations of edges and use a suitable distance for that (the one with the smallest distance). Together with the assumption that an isolated 4-neighbor has distance 0.5, this gives us the complete table.

3. EVALUATION

We evaluated the methods by comparing to a ground truth distance using images for which an exact ground truth can be easily calculated, in our case circles of varying dimensions.

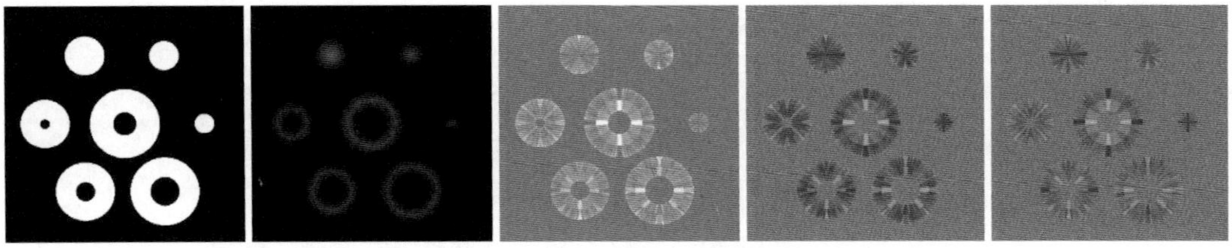

Figure 4. Test images and results. From left to right: "Circles" test image, ground truth, EDT difference, method 1 difference, method 2 difference

We performed a test according to Figure 4. The three difference images show the (emphasized) difference to the ground truth. The ideal result, no errors, would be a flat gray image. We ran other tests with similar results but must limit ourselves to this for publication reasons. The resulting precision is shown in Table 1.

Table 1. Error measurements vs ground truth

Algorithm	Max and min difference	RMS
Ground truth	0.00, 0.00	0.00
Method 1	0.5000, -0.5000	0.1149
Method 2	0.4900, -0.5100	0.0829
EDT	1.0000, 0.0000	0.1619
EDT - 0.5	0.5000, -0.5000	0.1439

As both the images and the table shows, Method 2 is significantly better than Method 1 as well as the 0.5 offset, and all are clearly superior to conventional EDT, which always over-estimates the distance.

4. CONCLUSION

We have presented a correction method for distance transformations of binary images, which makes the actual value refer to the edge of the objects rather than pixel centers, and demonstrate its effect, which is significantly better than both the original and more trivial corrections.

Future work includes testing with larger data sets and using larger neighborhoods, including 3D.

REFERENCES

Danielsson, P.E., 1980, "Euclidean Distance Mapping", Computer Graphics and Image Processing 14, pp 227-248.

Fabbri, R., Luciano Da F. Costa, Julio C. Torelli and Odemir M. Bruno, 2008, "2D Euclidean Distance Transform Algorithms: A Comparative Survey", ACM Computing Surveys, Vol 40, No 1, Article 2.

Gustavson, S., Strand, R., 2011, "Anti-aliased Euclidean distance transform", Pattern Recognition Letters 32, pp252-257.

Jimenez, J. et al. "Filtering approaches for real-time anti-aliasing." ACM SIGGRAPH Courses 2.3 (2011): 4.

Paglieroni, D., 1992, "A Unified Distance Transform Algorithm and Architecture", Machine Vision and Applications 5.

Ragnemalm, I., "Contour Processing Distance Transforms", 1989, Proc of the 5th Int Conf on Image Analysis and Proc.

Rosenfeld, A., Pfaltz, J.L., 1966. Sequential operations in digital picture processing. Journal of the ACM 13 (4), 471–494.

Rutowitz, D., "Efficient processing of 2-D images", 1989, Proc of the 5th Int Conf on Image Analysis and Processing.

Satherley, R., Jones, M.W., 2001, "Vector-city vector distance transform", Computer Vision and Image Understanding.

DETECTION OF SUBJECT-BASED KEY PLAYER USING SOCIAL NETWORK ANALYSIS

Minseon Kim[1], Jiyoung Kim[2] and Kiyun Yu[3]
[1] *Department of Civil and Environmental Engineering*
[2] *Institute of Construction and Environmental Engineering (ICEE)*
[3] *Professor, Department of Civil and Environmental Engineering*
Seoul National University, Seoul, Republic of Korea

ABSTRACT

In recent times, the growth in the use of Social Network Service (SNS) has caused an exponential growth in the generation of data among people. As social relations are established and communication becomes more active through SNS in the Big Data era, defining relationships among people becomes increasingly important. One way to define this relationship is through Social Network Analysis. This study applies categories from news articles (e.g. Culture, Politics and Economy etc.) to Twitter and extracts thematic keywords from Twitter. Those users who refer to the extracted keywords are selected, and WKC (Weight of Key Player Connectivity) is given to the relationships among the selected users to form a weighted network. Finally, we detect the key player using M-reach closeness centrality to the weighted network. In this study, the user ID "161" with the highest M-reach closeness centrality value (0.1213) points to the user who is the key player. It means that the ID "161" turns out to be a key player in the network who can communicate in the best manner with all the other users on the topic "culture." Finding a key player for each subject is advantageous because information on the subject can then be obtained on the SNS through the key player.

KEYWORDS

SNA (Social Network Analysis), Key player, SNS, M-reach closeness centrality

1. INTRODUCTION

As the number of people using SNS increases in the Big Data era, the relationship between users becomes more complicated. Therefore, defining relationships among people becomes increasingly important. Relationships can be defined using a method called Social Network Analysis (SNA). SNA contributes to forming a co-author network in the domain of literature as well. By applying SNA to the SNS field, it is possible to obtain the relationships between the SNS users for each keyword related to a topic. In addition, it is possible to search for the most influential key player. Here, 'key player' refers to the most important person or thing in a specific organization, event, or situation, in a dictionary sense. However, in this study, we define the key player as a Twitter user who can communicate with all the users in the network who are networking on a specific topic on Twitter. The purpose of this study is to detect the key player of each subject by applying SNA, which is used to analyze co-author networks, to Twitter.

2. RESEARCH METHODS

2.1 Data and Keyword Extraction

Categories of news articles were used to extract keywords. After crawling through articles in each category of news articles, we extracted keywords for each topic using TF-IDF (Term Frequency – Inverse Document Frequency). In this study, keywords were extracted from news articles for the category "Culture." The extracted keywords are shown in Table 1 below. The extracted keywords are applied to Twitter and SNS data, and the IDs referring to the keywords are selected. A matrix between the IDs is formed based on the frequency of simultaneous mentioning. The Twitter data used in the research was collected over a period of about seven months, from July 2015 to February 2016.

Table 1. Keywords in "Culture"

Keyword	TF-IDF
Performance	3.813
Book	3.544
Author	2.978
Professor	2.952
Composition	2.935
Picture	2.450
South Korea	2.272

2.2 WKC (Weight of Key Player Connectivity)

In this study, the weight of connectivity between users is given as follows:

$$WKC(A,B) = \frac{keywords(A,B)}{\sum_X keywords(B,X)} \times \frac{n(followers(A))}{n(followers(A+B))}$$

Here, $keywords(A,B)$ is the number of times the same keywords are referred to by users A and B, and $\sum_X keywords(B,X)$ is the sum of the number of times the same keyword is referred to between user B and other users. The factor obtained by dividing the number of times the same keyword is referred to by A and B, by the number of times the same keyword is mentioned between user B and other users represents the influence of A on the number of keyword references. Thus, WKC denotes the influence of A on the number of keyword references multiplied by the ratio of A and B followers.

2.3 Key Player Detection

We used M-reach closeness centrality to detect key players. The M-reach closeness centrality is the sum of the shortest path values that can be reached in the M-step at the reference node. The M-reach closeness centrality value of the WKC-assigned ID matrix is shown in Table 2.

Table 2. Top 5 IDs and M-reach closeness centrality (Topic: Culture)

No	ID	M-reach closeness centrality
1	161	0.12125
2	225	0.10479
3	111	0.09808
4	322	0.09161
5	187	0.07655

Here, ID "161" with the highest M-reach closeness centrality value points to the user who is the key player. Thus, the user with ID "161" turns out to be a key player in the network who can communicate in the best manner with all the other users on the topic "culture."

3. CONCLUSION

This study differs from previous studies in that it applies the co-author network principle, used in the domain of literature, to SNS data, which is Big Data. In addition, by finding key players for each subject, it is possible to obtain information on each subject on SNS through the key players. This study will be developed as a research to find key player of each region including user's location information in the future.

ACKNOWLEDGEMENT

This research, 'Geospatial Big Data Management, Analysis and Service Platform Technology Development', was supported by the MOLIT (The Ministry of Land, Infrastructure and Transport), Korea, under the national spatial information research program supervised by the KAIA (Korea Agency for Infrastructure Technology Advancement) (17NSIP-B081023-04).

REFERENCES

Borgatti, S. P. (2006). Identifying Sets of Key Players in a Social Network. *Computational & Mathematical Organization Theory*, Vol. 12, No. 1, pp 21-34.

Byung-Hak, L. (2012.3). An Effect of Co-authorship Network on Research Performance: Focusing on Co-authoring of Logos Management. *Logos Management Review*, Vol. 10, No. 1, pp 1-20.

Hae-Lan J. (2015). Generation of Collaboration Network and Analysis of Researcher's Role in National Cancer Center. *Journal of the Korea Contents Association*, Vol. 15, No. 10, pp 387-399.

Hangal, S. et al. (2010). All Friends are Not Equal: Using Weights in Social Graphs to Improve Search.

Jae Yun L. (2014). A Comparative Study on the Centrality Measures for Analyzing Research Collaboration Networks. *Journal of the Korean Society for Information Management*, Vol. 31, No. 3, pp 153-179.

Long, J. C. et al. (2013). Who are the key players in a new translational research network? *BMC Health Services Research*, Vol. 13, No. 1.

Opsahl, T., Agneessens, F., & Skvoretz, J. (2010). Node centrality in weighted networks: Generalizing degree and shortest paths. *Social networks*, Vol. 32, No. 3, pp 245-251.

USING INTERACTIVE VISUAL ANALYTICS TO ANALYZE INFLUENCES OF CLIMATE ON INDUSTRIAL PRODUCTION

Dieter Meiller
East Bavarian Technical University Amberg-Weiden, Kaiser-Wilhelm-Ring 23, 92224, Amberg, Germany

ABSTRACT

The paper discusses a solution to make methods of data analytics accessible to persons working in industry, who are not specialists in this domain. Small and medium enterprises should benefit from this approach.

KEYWORDS

Industry 4.0, swarm intelligence, information visualization, visual analytics, clustering

1. INTRODUCTION

A fundamental part of the project ISAC@OTH-AW (Gerlang 2017) is to cooperate with the local industry to generate innovations for the age of Industry 4.0. The project started at the end of 2015 and will last till the end of 2021. It is funded by the Ministry of Economics in Bavaria (Germany). Nowadays, in modern digital factories large amount of data are transmitted to interfaces for controlling and monitoring. Our industrial project partners appreciate that the next phase will be the analysis of data to get more insights in to the production process. There are several goals: improving product quality, saving energy, simplifying processes and more. Two partners are manufacturing plastic parts or parts made of foamed material and cardboard. They are collecting data from several sensors during the production process. The product quality is measured, too. They want to know whether atmospheric conditions would have any influence on the quality of their products. In our project, we designed new kinds of data logging devices. These devices are working independent form external power source for several months and are able to measure different climate variables every minute. At the time of writing this paper we are installing these devices inside and outside the factories. The goal is to collect data over a long time (one year). In combination with data form existing sensors and the measured product quality we will have enough data to find correlations of climate influences and product quality. The next problem is that often there is little knowledge about data analytics and machine learning in small or medium enterprises (Burns, 2015). Therefore, we want to provide a system that allows engineers to analyze data interactively without special knowledge. Though there are other interesting solutions (Liu et al. 2013), it is still not easy to make interactive visualizations of this huge amount of data, we implemented software that allows to resample data to different resolutions. It is possible to select the density and the time range.

2. INTERACTIVE CLUSTERING

Users are able to select parts of the whole resampled dataset with a range slider and get direct visual feedback (Figure 1). The visualization is divided in two parts: A plot of data below and a swarm-based visualization. Instead of using a flocking algorithm (Reynolds 1987) as proposed earlier (Meiller 2015) we decide to use a force-based algorithm (Battista et al. 1999). The similarity of two single data objects determines the strength of their attraction. Users are able to cluster data with an interactive k-modes algorithm (Meiller and Niewiera 2016). They are able to add and remove centroids interactively by touch or click complementary to the to the dynamic FClust approach (Saka, and Nasraoui 2010). The interactive way of selecting the amount of clusters should give more insight into the structure of data than other approaches where the number of clusters are generated automatically (Shafeeq and Hareesha 2012). In future, we want to use our approach in combination with other methods of data analytics and machine learning to get best results for industry and to evaluate our approach.

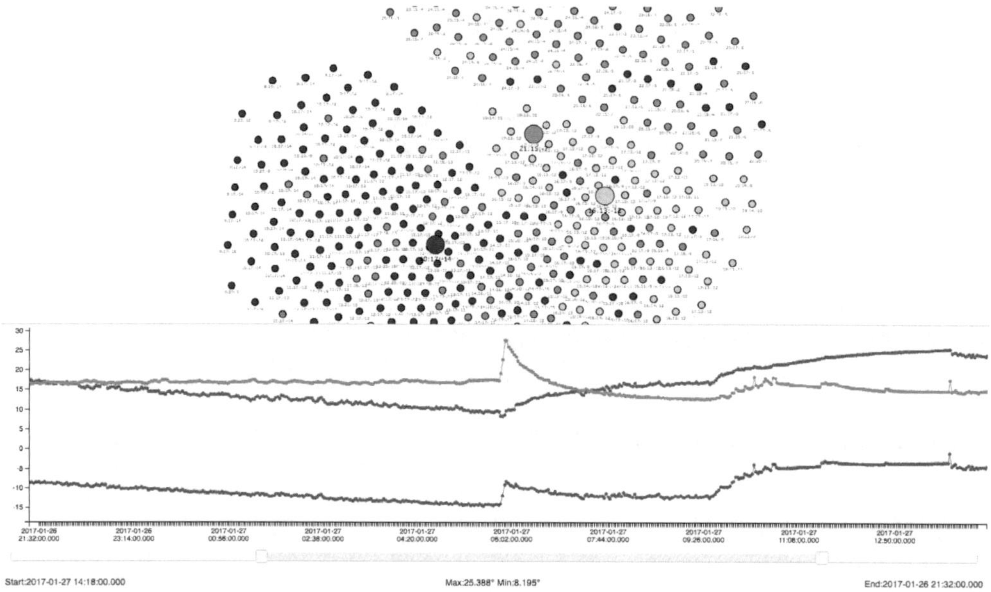

Figure 1. Screenshot of interactive clustering

ACKNOWLEDGEMENT

We thank Prof. Dr.- Ing. H.-P. Schmidt, Dirk Possardt Florian Schöler-Niewiera for their valuable suggestions.

REFERENCES

Battista, G. D. et al, 1999. *Graph drawing: algorithms for the visualization of graphs*.

Burns, E., 2015. Why haven't SMEs cashed in on big data benefits yet? *TechTarget,* [online] Available at: http://searchbusinessanalytics.techtarget.com/feature/Why-havent-SMEs-cashed-in-on-big-data-benefits-yet [Accessed 04 Apr. 2017].

Gerlang, B., 2017. ISAC@OTH-AW. *OTH-AW*, [online] Available at: http://www.isac-oth.de [Accessed 04 Apr. 2017].

Liu, Z. et al., 2013. imMens: Real-time Visual Querying of Big Data. *In Computer Graphics Forum*, Vol. 32, No. 3pt4, pp. 421-430.

Meiller, D., and Niewiera F., 2016. Data Visualization and Evaluation for Industry 4.0 using an interactive k-Means Algorithm. *In Conf. Proc. WSCG 2016 – 24nd International Conference in Central Europe on Computer Graphics, Visualization and Computer Vision,* pp. 33-37.

Meiller, D., 2015. Diving into the Data Ocean, *International Federation for Information Processing 2015, Interact 2015, Part IV*, LNCS 9299, pp. 465-468.

Reynolds, C. W., 1987. Flocks, Herds and Schools: A Distributed Behavioral Model. *In ACM SIGGRAPH computer graphics*, Vol 21, No.3, pp. 25-34.

Saka, E. and Nasraoui, O., 2010. On dynamic data clustering and visualization using swarm intelligence, *IEEE 26th International Conference on Data Engineering Workshops (ICDEW),* pp. 337-340.

Shafeeq, A., and Hareesha, K.S., 2012. Dynamic Clustering of Data with Modified k-Means Algorithm, *International Conference on Information and Computer Networks (CICIN 2012)*, Vol.27, pp. 221-225.

AUTHOR INDEX

International Association for Development of the Information Society (IADIS)
Rua Sao Sebastiao Da Pedreira
No. 100, 30, 1050-209
Lisbon, Portugal

ISBN 978-1-5108-6528-0

CURRAN ASSOCIATES INC.
proceedings.com